LITI(
ON **EXPERTS**

Strategies for Managing Expert Witnesses
from Retention through Trial

Wendy Gerwick Couture and Allyson W. Haynes, Editors

ABA
AMERICAN BAR ASSOCIATION
Section of Litigation

FIRST
CHAIR
·PRESS·

Cover design by ABA Publishing.

The materials contained herein represent the opinions of the authors and editors and should not be construed to be the views or opinions of the law firms or companies with whom such persons are in partnership with, associated with, or employed by, nor of the American Bar Association or the Section of Litigation, or First Chair Press, unless adopted pursuant to the bylaws of the Association.

Nothing contained in this book is to be considered as the rendering of legal advice for specific cases, and readers are responsible for obtaining such advice from their own legal counsel. This book and any forms and agreements herein are intended for educational and informational purposes only.

Printed in the United States of America.

Library of Congress Cataloging-in-Publication Data

Haynes, Allyson W.
    Litigators on experts : strategies for managing expert witnesses from retention through trial / Allyson W. Haynes, Wendy Couture.
        p. cm.
    Includes bibliographical references and index.
    ISBN 978-1-60442-929-9
    1. Evidence, Expert—United States.   2. Examination of witnesses—United States.   3. Trial practice—United States.   I. Couture, Wendy.   II. Title.
    KF8961.H39   2010
    347.73'67—dc22

                                                                          2010028237

14   13   12   11   10   5   4   3

Discounts are available for books ordered in bulk. Special consideration is given to state bars, CLE programs, and other bar-related organizations. Inquire at Book Publishing, ABA Publishing, American Bar Association, 321 N. Clark Street, Chicago, Illinois 60654-7598.

www.ababooks.org

CONTENTS

FOREWORD

Gregory P. Joseph[1]

Taking testimony from adverse experts is a tricky proposition—extracting what you want and bottling up what you don't. Experts are advocates. They know more about their fields of expertise than you do. They can do real damage to your case. But you can do real damage to them, too. A strong cross-examination of adverse experts at trial can have a telling effect on the outcome of the case. Let's not dwell on the effect of a weak cross.

Experts are, therefore, quite dangerous. Not just the other side's experts—yours, too. Bad testimony from your expert will be used against your client. Consider the testimony of the plaintiff's expert in *Johnson v. SJP Management LLC*,[2] in which the plaintiff was suing for injury due to a defective elevator that allegedly closed on her arm:

Q: Can we agree that if there were a problem with the Lambda 3-D door detector, it would not fix itself?
A: No.
Q: We can't agree with that?
A: We cannot agree on that.
Q: It could just miraculously be better the next day?
A: Miraculously be better the next day. You don't understand all the things that are involved in that. ***I would have to be an expert to do that.***
Q: Well, why don't you tell me what specifically was wrong with the Lambda 3-D detector on the day of this accident, December 14, 2005?
A: I don't know.

Who needs help like that?

1. Mr. Joseph is a former Chair of the Section of Litigation of the ABA and President-Elect of the American College of Trial Lawyers. He practices in New York City, at Gregory P. Joseph Law Offices LLC, http://www.josephnyc.com.

2. Johnson v. SJP Mgmt., LLC, Case No. 07-5545, 2009 U.S. Dist. LEXIS 11272, at *11–12 (E.D. Pa. Feb. 12, 2009).

Even good expert testimony may be of no help—it still must satisfy *Daubert, Frye,* or whatever evidentiary hurdle has been erected in the governing jurisdiction. "Whatever may have been the standard in the pre-*Daubert* era, it is clear that an expert's opinions are not admissible merely because the expert says, in effect, 'trust me, I know.'"[3] In the memorable words of Judge William G. Young of the U.S. District Court for the District of Massachusetts, every federal judge performing the mandatory *Daubert* gatekeeping function "asks three preliminary questions: First, is this junk science?... Second, is this a junk scientist?... Third, is this a junk opinion?"[4] If the answer to any of these questions is "Yes," your expert's opinion is out, and your case may not survive the damage.

Expert evidence is a critical component of virtually every civil litigation. This volume collects the thoughts and experience of excellent advocates from around the country. It offers cogent insights and guidance from pre-engagement of the expert through preparation and testimony, or deposition and cross. It is an invaluable addition to every trial lawyer's library.

---

3. Mooring Capital Fund, LLC v. Phoenix Central, Inc., No. CIV-06-0006-HE, 2009 U.S. Dist. LEXIS 117799, at *18(W.D. Okla. Feb. 12, 2009).
4. McGovern v. Brigham & Women's Hosp., No. 07-10643, 2008 U.S. Dist. LEXIS 94403, at *12–13 (D. Mass. Nov. 5, 2008).

PREFACE

We would like to take this opportunity to share our goals as editors and to thank those who were instrumental in the completion of this book.

First, in choosing the topics that this book would cover, we endeavored to cover each step of working with an expert witness—from retention through trial. In addition to these broad-based topics, we identified specific types of experts (such as financial damages experts) and specific substantive areas of the law (such as securities litigation) that merited particularized attention. In the end, we have compiled an eminently practical book that contains elements relevant to the practice of every litigator.

Second, in soliciting authors, we looked for experienced litigators with diverse backgrounds and for junior attorneys with unique perspectives. Our goal was to combine tried-and-true tactics, modern angles, and accessibility. In addition, we chose attorneys with diverse practice experience and backgrounds. Our authors hail from 18 states and 43 different institutions, including international law firms, boutique law firms, consulting firms, accounting firms, law schools, and the bench.

Finally, we would like to thank Diane Sumoski and Art Justice, former cochairs of the Expert Witnesses Committee, for pioneering this project; Joan Archer and Jeffrey Beaver, current cochairs of the Expert Witnesses Committee, for supporting this project through completion; Sarah Orwig, executive editor of Book Development and Publishing at the American Bar Association (ABA), for believing in this project from the outset; and our families for their patience as we edited this book on weekends and holidays.

Wendy Gerwick Couture and Allyson W. Haynes

ABOUT THE EDITORS

WENDY GERWICK COUTURE is an Associate Professor of Law at the University of Idaho College of Law in Boise, and she previously served as an Assistant Professor of Law at the St. Mary's University School of Law in San Antonio, Texas. Before entering law teaching, she was an associate at Carrington, Coleman, Sloman & Blumenthal, LLP in Dallas, Texas, and she served as a law clerk for the Honorable Barbara M.G. Lynn, United States District Court for the Northern District of Texas. She earned her undergraduate degree from Duke University and graduated *summa cum laude* from the Southern Methodist University Dedman School of Law. She teaches and writes in the areas of business law, commercial law, and civil procedure.

ALLYSON W. HAYNES is an Associate Professor of Law at the Charleston School of Law in Charleston, S.C. She joined the CSOL faculty in 2004 after serving as Director of the Legal Department at Sony Corporation of America in New York. She also served as law clerk to the Honorable David C. Norton, United States District Court for the District of South Carolina, and was an associate in the New York firm of Cleary, Gottlieb, Steen and Hamilton. She received her undergraduate degree from Duke University and graduated *magna cum laude* from the University of South Carolina School of Law. She teaches Civil Procedure, Evidence, Information Privacy Law, and E-Discovery, and has published articles on internet privacy, internet contracts, and personal jurisdiction.

CHAPTER 1

Selecting and Retaining an Expert

SEARCHING FOR AN EXPERT WITNESS

Michael Brennan, David Dilenschneider,
Myles Levin, and Jim Robinson[1]

Expert witnesses are used in a wide range of litigation, and their opinions are often viewed as critical—frequently they can make or break a case. As a result, many trials have turned into a battle of the experts. Yet despite their importance, few attorneys take the time to use the proper resources to find effective expert witnesses. In our view, the search for an expert witness should involve four essential steps: (1) learn the subject matter of the expertise at issue, (2) identify a pool of experts in that field, (3) vet those experts, and also (4) analyze how courts are treating experts in this field. This subchapter addresses how to accomplish each of these steps.

Learn the Subject Matter

If you do not have a detailed knowledge of the subject matter, it will be difficult to determine if an expert is truly qualified in a particular specialty. Careful investigation of the topic at the outset will not only allow you to determine what questions to ask a potential expert but also possibly lead to the names of experts in that field. In short, the first two steps referenced above often go hand in hand.

---

1. Michael Brennan is a Research Analyst at the largest law firm in Michigan, Miller, Canfield, Paddock & Stone. David Dilenschneider is a Director, Client Relations, for Lexis-Nexis. Myles Levin is the CEO of Daubert Tracker™. Jim Robinson is the founder of Juris-Pro, Inc.

Libraries

Local libraries—particularly through their websites—are excellent places to begin the search to find information about the subject matter and even to find potential experts. Start by searching libraries' online catalogs for books and journals on the subject. Pay particular attention to the identities of the authors—someone who writes extensively on the subject may make an ideal candidate to serve as an expert in your case. In addition, many public libraries offer their patrons free access to some online pay databases, such as Reference USA and Standard & Poor's. Ordinarily, all you need to access these pay databases is a library card and an Internet connection.[2]

Broad Internet Search

Alternatively, you may want to conduct a broad-based Internet search to educate yourself and uncover potential experts. For instance, in a products liability case, conducting a search for the name of the product at issue will likely lead to information about it and, potentially, to the names of knowledgeable experts. Note, however, that search engines such as Google and Bing sometimes tend to be overinclusive unless the search query is very precisely tailored. For example, a search in quotes will look for the exact phrase entered, thereby yielding more precise search results than a search without quotes.

Moreover, other challenges exist when it comes to using such broad Internet searches. First, the information available through the Internet is almost always unpoliced, so you must recognize that it may be inaccurate. Second, even the best search engines cannot index all of the information that is continuously added to the Web. Finally, such searches can also miss information on the websites of colleges, universities, hospitals, and associations, which can be excellent sources for finding and evaluating experts.

Professional Associations

For virtually every field and interest an association exists—and within those associations are potential experts. For example, the Joint Commission on Accreditation of Healthcare Organizations' website[3] is a directory of thousands of health care organizations, including ambulatory care facilities, assisted living facilities, behavioral health-care facilities (such as chemical dependency centers and development disabilities organizations), Health

---

2. A comprehensive list of library websites can be found at http://lists.webjunction.org/libweb.

3. http://www.jointcommission.com.

Maintenance Organizations (HMOs), home care organizations, hospitals, laboratories, long-term-care facilities, and office-based surgeons.

The best place to find information about associations is through the Associations Unlimited Database (otherwise known as the Encyclopedia of Associations). You can access this database for free through the websites of some university libraries and public libraries. The Associations Unlimited Database contains information on thousands of international, national, regional, state, and local membership organizations in all fields. These listings provide information about each organization, its membership, and its leadership. Such a database can be extremely helpful for finding experts in rather obscure fields such as hang gliding or petroleum packaging.

Topic-Specific Websites

If you know that a particular medical condition or product will be at issue, consider conducting searches at subject-specific websites. For instance, the National Library of Medicine (NLM)[4] is an excellent place to find information, and the names of experts, in the areas of biomedicine and health care. The NLM houses books, journals, technical reports, and manuscripts. Moreover, it, along with its associated services PubMed and MedLine Plus, contains links to medical encyclopedias, full-text news stories, articles, and free publications listed on the Internet, as well as information on how to order articles that must be purchased. Information about specific products can be found at the ThomasNet site[5] (formerly known as Thomas Register), which has gathered company information from registrations of companies in its industrial buying guides. This free online directory contains information on thousands of products and companies and the names of potential experts.

Identify a Pool of Experts

Once you have a basic understanding of the subject matter of the expert testimony, myriad additional resources are available for identifying a pool of potential experts.

University Websites

Faculty members who teach or perform research in a particular area are potential expert witnesses. Some universities set up separate Web pages for their professors, including short videos of the professors, their curricula

---

4. http://www.nlm.nih.gov.
5. http://www.thomasnet.com.

vitae (CV), publications, class schedules, research projects, links the professors thought were interesting, and sometimes even their hobbies. But search these websites directly, as individual faculty members' biographies usually do not appear in search engine results.

Verdict Reports

A verdict report is a summary of a lawsuit that has either been tried to decision by a judge/jury or settled nonconfidentially. A verdict report usually contains the case name, case number, date of decision, topic (e.g., medical malpractice, employment discrimination), result (i.e., which party won?), the amount of the judgment (if any), the alleged injury, jurisdictional information (i.e., state and county where the lawsuit was tried), name of judge, names of attorneys, a brief summary of the facts, a listing of the experts who were used by the parties, and other miscellaneous information about the lawsuit. Obviously, such reports can be used to find experts in a particular field.

Over a million verdict reports are now online, and they can be searched, most-comprehensively—though for a fee—through commercial vendors such as LexisNexis. Alternatively, a few free, searchable nationwide jury verdicts websites exist. For instance, Morelaw.com has verdicts and settlements dating back to December 1996, and one may search that database by the terms "defendant's expert" or "plaintiff's expert." In addition, the National Association of State Jury Verdict Publishers website[6] is a portal for many jury verdict publications. The data from this site is organized from independent reporters responsible for publications across the United States. A table and a map show the jurisdictions covered and, according to the website, its expert witness directory contains the names of experts who have testified in civil trials across the United States.

Expert Witness Directories and Referral Companies

Expert witness directories allow you to browse for consultants in a particular area of expertise and then contact them directly. Whereas the experts usually pay a listing fee, your search is free. Such directory listings often contain valuable information about experts, including areas of expertise, educational background, professional experience, and information about the lawsuits in which they have testified (e.g., whether the expert typically testifies for plaintiffs or for the defense).

---

6. http://juryverdicts.com.

Many expert directories are available online. Of particular note, the JurisPro Expert Witness Directory[7] is a free national online directory of expert witnesses in thousands of categories. Visitors to JurisPro are able to view and download the experts' contact information; link to the expert's website; obtain the expert's full CV (available for download or print); read articles that the expert has written that discuss his areas of expertise; review the expert's background as an expert witness (how many times the expert has testified, how often for the plaintiff versus for the defense, etc.); and obtain contact information for the expert's references. Many of the large legal portals, such as Martindale-Hubbell[8] and Law.com, as well as specialized commercial sites, also have online directories with short biographies, contact information, and links to each expert's website. Finally, many bar associations, such as the Los Angeles County Bar Association[9] and the San Francisco Bar Association,[10] have online directories of experts.

Expert witness referral companies, such as ForensisGroup,[11] maintain databases of professionals who are available for expert witness assignments. The benefit of using these services is their large size and the variety of their databases, so you can save a lot of time looking for experts. The downside is that you have to contact the referral company to get information for the expert and then pay an additional fee to retain that expert.

Vet Potential Experts

Once a short list of potential experts has been identified, a thorough vetting is not only warranted, but necessary. Many judges expect that any expert presented before them will be free from significant character deficiencies. The words of United States District Court Judge Nancy F. Atlas speak volumes: "CAUTION: Never retain, use, or list in court pleadings an expert without thoroughly researching the individual."[12]

Moreover, it is possible that the failure to perform such due diligence could result in a claim of legal malpractice. For instance, a California court

---

7. http://www.jurispro.com.
8. http://www.martindale.com.
9. http://www.lacba.org.
10. http://www.sfbar.org.
11. http://www.forensisgroup.com.
12. Hon. Nancy F. Atlas & Scott J. Atlas, *Finding, Preparing, and Defending an Expert in the Age of Judicial Gatekeepers*, Tips from the Trenches (Dec. 19, 2001), http://jhguth1942 .tripod.com/sitebuildercontent/sitebuilderfiles/gatekeepers.pdf (an exclusive online publication for the ABA Section of Litigation).

of appeals recently ruled that an attorney has certain responsibilities with respect to the retention and handling of experts and that the failure to adequately discharge those responsibilities could subject that attorney to a claim of professional negligence.[13] Finally, it must be remembered that, with respect to an expert being considered for retention, it is likely that opposing attorneys will be conducting their own research, trying to find damaging information with which to discredit that expert.

As noted above, when conducting such research, it is sometimes tempting to simply do a broad-based Internet search and believe that is sufficient. It is true that an Internet search conducted through a powerful search engine (e.g., Google, Bing) may retrieve information—whether professional or personal—that might be of use when evaluating an expert. However, according to various studies, those searches access less than 5 percent of the information available through the World Wide Web.[14] Moreover, it cannot be emphasized enough that not everything found through such broad searches is true. You should verify all data before relying on it.[15]

Consider investigating the following categories of information about potential expert witnesses: (1) professional background, (2) prior experience as an expert, (3) public statements, and (4) public records. What follows are tips about how to research these categories of information.

Professional Background

Studies suggest that falsifying credentials on a resume is not a rare occurrence among professionals, and anecdotal stories about experts and other professionals bear that out. Accordingly, you need to determine whether the expert's claimed credentials are accurate, and this involves three distinct tasks. First, gather as much biographical information from as many

---

13. Forensis Group, Inc. v. Frantz, Townsend & Foldenauer, 130 Cal. App. 4th 14 (2005). *See also* Wendy L. Wilcox & Christopher J. Weber, *Department: Barristers Tips: Dodging the Pitfalls of Qualifying an Expert*, L.A. Law., Sept. 2005, at 10 ("Failure to monitor the expert and the expert's opinion could subject counsel to litigation on the other side of the table.").

14. In fact, an April 27, 2009, article put the number at about 1 percent. *See* Sarah Rodriguez, *Search Engines Besides Google? Who Knew?* Va. Law. Wkly., Apr. 27, 2009, *available at* http://valawyersweekly.com/blog/2009/04/27/search-engines-besides-google-who-knew/.

15. For example, in *Campbell v. Secretary of HHS*, 59 Fed. Cl. 775, 781 (2006), the judge determined that procedures employed by the special master were fundamentally unfair. In particular, the judge noted that articles the special master found on the Internet, including some from Wikipedia, WebMD, and other purportedly reputable sites, did not "remotely" meet the requirement of reliability—due primarily to those sites' "disturbing" disclaimers.

sources as possible. Second, sort and compare that information, looking for discrepancies and gaps. Third, verify all claimed credentials.

An expert's biographical information can potentially be uncovered in various places:

1. The resume or CV provided during the course of the lawsuit in question;
2. Resumes or CVs filed by the expert in prior or concurrent litigation (typically found by searching collections of court-filed documents such as those available from LexisNexis; in particular, be sure to look at witness lists and expert reports as resumes and CVs are often attached as exhibits);
3. Credentials listed by the expert in an expert (or other professional) directory;
4. Licensing and other credentials disclosed in various licensing directories (e.g., the American Board of Medical Specialties);
5. Online profiles the expert may have posted on a social networking site (e.g., LinkedIn, Facebook); and
6. Credentials displayed at the expert's website (and be sure to "capture" screenshots of any information found as websites can be changed).

After obtaining the various claimed credentials of the expert in question, cross-reference them, looking for discrepancies and changes. At some point, did the expert change his undergraduate institution from a state college to an Ivy League university? Has the expert included embellished information in a directory listing in an attempt to better market his services? A simple comparison of the aforementioned biographical information might reveal such discrepancies.

Even if such cross-referencing fails to reveal any discrepancies, you should still verify as much of the claimed credentials as possible. Verify educational background, claimed licenses (paying particular attention to whether the claimed license is still active, has lapsed, was revoked, or the like), authored works, and association memberships.

An expert's educational degrees can sometimes be verified by calling the registrar's office of the appropriate college or university. Note, however, that some universities and colleges require a release and Social Security number before they will verify an individual's attendance date and whether any degrees were conferred. Obviously, this will be easier to obtain from an expert you are retaining, as you can include the release form as part of the retention agreement. An alternative resource is one of the several online services that allow you to verify attendance and whether the expert received the degree claimed. Although these online services will not cover every college and university in the United States, they usually post a list of those institutions that participate in their service.

Licensing information can be found online for virtually all 50 states and can easily be searched to verify the current status for any licenses an expert claims to hold—and at minimal cost. Many organizations, such as the American Medical Association, the American Board of Medical Specialties, and the American Board of Surgery, have their own websites where you can check the certification status of experts. Search Systems[16] (a pay site) links to over 45,000 public record databases and allows you to run a search for the type of record (e.g., license or certification), the jurisdiction (e.g., Ohio), and the occupation (e.g., accountant) about which you are interested. Using the metasite Portico,[17] you can verify licenses for occupations such as doctors, contractors, architects, and more. Finally, many certifying organizations also have an online listing of expert certifications or are willing to verify an expert's certifications telephonically.

Nothing can be more discrediting to an expert than a reprimand or license revocation for professional misconduct, especially if the misconduct goes to his credibility, such as a fraud or perjury conviction. All state governments and some professional associations maintain records of professional misconduct, and these records are sometimes available via the Internet. Because of the myriad of possible sites to search, it is impractical to search them individually. Accordingly, the best approach to take when pursuing disciplinary records is to first use public records to identify both an expert's current or prior residences and professional licenses. Thereafter, focus your research on those states and the professions and organizations with which the expert is affiliated.

Finally, be sure to research articles, books, and other publications authored by the expert in question. First, double-check that the expert has indeed authored the articles that he claims to have authored and has acknowledged coauthorship where applicable. This practice proved revealing a couple years ago with respect to a prominent mold expert.[18] Second, be sure to read the articles to ensure that the expert has not stated anything contrary to the position you would like him to take in your case. In addition, search for authored works that the expert has not acknowledged, as an expert may not tout authorship if a particular work contradicts the opinion about which the expert is expected to testify in the lawsuit. Finally, read

---

16. http://www.searchsystems.net.

17. http://indorgs.virginia.edu/portico.

18. Daniel Fisher, *Why Sketchy Science Doesn't Stop Medical "Experts,"* FORBES, Apr. 11, 2005 (despite an expert's claim to have authored "hundreds" of scholarly articles, a search through the PubMed database turned up fewer than 70).

what other experts in the field are saying about the expert's publications to ensure that his work has not been discredited.

Prior Experience as an Expert

If your potential expert has previously served as an expert witness, you should research how he was perceived by each court, the content of the testimony, and the outcome of each lawsuit. The potential expert should provide you with a list of all previous cases in which he has appeared, but some experts, through mere negligence or outright deception—perhaps to hide bad results—fail to disclose some of the prior lawsuits in which they were involved. Accordingly, in the course of compiling information about the expert's prior testimony, watch for references to cases of which you were unaware. Of course, an expert's failure to fully disclose prior testimony would be, in and of itself, a red flag.

The first step in conducting such verification is to simply search a database of court opinions for the expert's name. Many court opinions mention experts' names, such as when analyzing whether to exclude their testimony or when assessing whether their testimony is sufficient to create a genuine issue of material fact. You should not forget to include international court opinions in your search. For instance, it is not that uncommon for an expert based in the United States to work on, and testify in, cases in Canada (and vice versa).

However, a typical Boolean search through opinions based on the expert's name is not enough—it must be supplemented. Not every case opinion specifically references an expert by name. An authoring judge, for instance, might only refer to the expert as "plaintiff's expert" and leave it at that. Moreover, many opinions exist in which an expert's name has been misspelled. A Boolean search based on an expert's name would fail to find the opinions that fall into either category.

You should, therefore, also consult a specialty expert database, such as Daubert Tracker, to ensure that none of the opinions about an expert have fallen through the cracks. Daubert Tracker Case Reports (DTCRs) summarize opinions addressing the admissibility of expert witness testimony. Each summary is put into a chart, which identifies the case name, the case number, the expert's name, the expert's area of expertise, the attorneys, the judge, a summary of the court's decision (e.g., testimony inadmissible), and more. These reports offer three significant advantages over a regular search through case opinions. First, they actually identify, by name, the expert referenced in the related case opinion—even when the opinion does not. Second, the researchers at Daubert Tracker conduct name verification—double-checking the spelling of each expert's name and correcting it if appropriate.

For example, it knows that the Allan Done referenced in *Blum v. Merrell Dow Pharmaceuticals, Inc.*[19] is actually Alan Done. Another benefit is that DTCRs cover more opinions than those typically available via online services. For instance, although very few state trial court opinions are currently available online, DTCRs cover some of those that are not. In the end, DTCRs are a powerful complement to searching regular case opinions.

Do not stop with just opinions, however, because many court cases do not produce any published opinion. It is imperative that you also research other types of case-related information. For instance, commercial vendors have made the federal dockets available through the Public Access to Court Electronic Records system (PACER), and similar state court systems are full-text searchable. Specifically, LexisNexis CourtLink gives you the capability of searching through dockets of cases filed in the federal courts (as well as various state courts), and some of those dockets go as far back as the mid-1980s. Westlaw's West Dockets offers a similar service (though with more limited coverage). So by simply searching for the expert's name, you might uncover a wide variety of information about an expert beyond just opinions, including motions (e.g., "Motion in Limine to Exclude the Testimony of Expert Smith"), reports, deposition transcripts, affidavits, declarations, and resumes. Importantly, such a docket search might uncover cases in which the expert has been involved, even if that expert failed to make that disclosure to you.

In addition, various vendors, such as LexisNexis, Westlaw, and even Daubert Tracker, offer full-text searchable databases of motions and briefs filed in both state and federal courts. You can search these databases to uncover court filings that mention the expert in their main text, even if the expert's name is not referenced in the caption of the document itself (and therefore could not be found via a docket search). For example, finding a brief filed in support of a motion *in limine* to exclude an expert can provide valuable information about someone else's assessment of the expert you are considering retaining.

Verdict reports, in addition to helping you uncover prior cases in which the expert has testified, can provide additional insight. For instance, after reviewing a number of verdict reports, you might uncover potential bias— the expert always seems to testify for plaintiffs or defendants, or the expert has testified for a particular party or attorney on numerous occasions. Moreover, data contained within a verdict report might lead you to additional information about the expert. For example, you could use the case

---

19. Blum v. Merrell Dow Pharms., Inc., No. 1027, 1996 WL 1358523 1996 Phila. Cty. Rptr. LEXIS 122 (Pa. Com. Pl. Dec. 13, 1996).

name and number listed in a verdict report, along with the jurisdictional information, to track down the file from the lawsuit to search for more information. Or, if the names of the attorneys are listed in the report, you might contact them to ask them for their impressions of the expert. Finally, if the potential expert has never been on the winning side of a case, you might not want to retain that expert. In short, how you use information found in a verdict report is only limited by your creativity.

You should also attempt to obtain copies of the transcripts of your potential expert's prior testimony. Several options exist for tracking down these prior statements, whether in a deposition or at trial. Although both LexisNexis and Westlaw now have large databases of transcripts, other options exist for those firms affiliated with either the plaintiffs' bar or the defense bar. Specifically, transcripts are available for a fee to defense attorneys who are members of the Defense Research Institute (DRI). On the plaintiff's side, the AAJ Exchange[20] makes available to its members a database of over 10,000 expert witnesses and over 15,000 transcripts. The commercial service TrialSmith,[21] jointly sponsored and contributed to by more than 52 trial lawyer associations and litigation groups, claims to have more than 350,000 transcripts. One can run a free search at the site for a particular expert and then view or download the transcripts immediately. As an alternative, try directly contacting lawyers who have worked with (or against) a particular expert and ask if they have transcripts or other background information. If the expert appeared in one or more of their cases, they probably did background research themselves. These treasure troves of prior vetting can sometimes save you hours of work.

Finally, you should recognize that case-related video may be available on the Internet. Some depositions and other materials regarding expert witnesses have begun showing up (though sometimes only briefly) on websites such as YouTube.com. Therefore, searches for video material on the Internet will become an ever more important part of your work and should not be overlooked. Bing, Google, and AltaVista have added tabs to allow users to search for video. For example, running a Yahoo video search for a computer forensic expert may retrieve extracts from videotaped depositions.

Expert's Prior Public Statements

Uncovering case-related information is essential to a thorough vetting of a potential expert. However, a wealth of non-case-related information is also

---

20. http://www.justice.org/cps/rde/xchg/justice/hs.xsl/677.htm.
21. http://www.trialsmith.com/TS.

available online and should be searched. Such information includes news, congressional information, postings on discussion boards, blog entries, patent information, agency decisions, law review articles, and even public records.

When it comes to an expert's prior opinions or statements on a topic, look beyond just opinions expressed in litigation. Statements made outside of litigation can sometimes be very damaging. For instance, experts often proffer opinions in articles, radio and television interviews, editorial commentary, and letters to the editor. Yet, despite the existence of such a potentially fruitful resource, many researchers fail to consider the news when they research experts.

A good first step is to search the news portion of a search engine site (e.g., Google or Bing). However, for two reasons, be aware that such searches may not provide complete results. First, the news databases available through noncommercial search engines are not as robust as those available from the commercial vendors. For instance, Google searches only about 4,500 news sources. When it comes to experts, this lack of coverage can be critical. For instance, a November 1992 article from the *Washingtonian* magazine relates a judge's ruling that a particular damages expert had given false testimony.[22] A search of that expert's name through Google News, however, fails to retrieve that article. Second, although these searches are often perceived as free, you still may have to pay to access some of the articles retrieved (e.g., it costs $2.95 to retrieve a 1999 article from the *Chicago Sun-Times*, found via Google).

Because you do not want to risk failing to find something damaging about your expert that your opponent could exploit at trial, take the second step of searching a commercially available news database. One of the largest such databases (available from LexisNexis and titled "Mega News, All (English, Full Text)") draws from over 22,000 sources, including much more than just newspaper and magazine articles. In fact, databases like this often contain transcripts from television and radio networks and shows (e.g., CNN, *60 Minutes*, *20/20*, *CBS Evening News*, National Public Radio), articles from specialized legal news sources, and other sources such as blogs.

You should also search congressional records and documents. Prominent experts often appear before Congress and testify or do work for congressional committees. Other experts, along with other professionals and scientists, sign letters on certain issues (sometimes within their specialty)

---

22. *See Doctors Cheer Olender Reversal*, WASHINGTONIAN, Nov. 1992.

that are sent to Congress. Insights as to an expert's political or religious position, even if not directly relevant to the issues involved in the pending lawsuit, may be of tactical value.

Discussion board postings and blogs are other potential sources of information. First, it may be possible to find an expert's opinion on a particular subject by searching postings on discussion boards. For instance, by clicking on the "Groups" tab on Google's home page, you can access more than 1 billion messages dating as far back as 1981. Second, many experts post their opinions on their own blogs, which are often linked to from an expert's website or discoverable through search engines. Because of the ease of their creation, postings and blog comments are often casual in nature, quickly written, and rarely peer reviewed. As such, you can sometimes find statements that are detrimental to the authoring expert—such unfiltered opinions can lead to strong cross-examination material by the opposing side. Also, comments posted by others to an expert's discussion board or blog entry may provide guideposts for attacking that expert's testimony.

For experts who are engineers, scientists, or the like, a search through patent information might yield damaging statements. In one of the ballot-contest lawsuits heard in Leon County, Florida, in 2000, then-Governor Bush's attorneys called to the stand an expert on voting machines. He had helped design the punch card voting devices used in many of the contested counties in Florida. The expert defended the use of the punch card voting devices and deemed them reliable. However, during his cross-examination, Gore's attorney confronted the expert with a patent he obtained on October 27, 1981, for a "new and improved" version of the voting devices used in the Florida election. In the "Background of the Invention" portion of the patent application, the expert had made the following statements:

> Incompletely punched cards can cause serious errors to occur in data processing operations utilizing such cards.

> If, however, the voter does not hold the voting punch straight up and down when punching, it is possible under certain temperature and humidity conditions to pull the template toward the voter a few thousandths of an inch, sufficient to prevent complete removal of the chad when the stylus is inserted. This can produce what is called a "hanging chad," as the chad-piece of the card is still attached to the card by one or two of the frangible holding points.

> It must be emphasized that the presence of even one incompletely punched chip in a run of several thousand tabulating cards is in most cases too great a defect to be tolerated.

Therefore, the material typically used for punch boards in punch card voting can and does contribute to potentially unreadable votes, because of hanging chad or mispunched cards.[23]

Gore's attorney used the expert's own words to support Gore's position:

> **Stephen Zack (attorney):** Any incompletely punched cards can cause serious errors to occur in data-processing operation utilizing such cards. Is that a fair statement of what you said?
>
> **The Expert:** That is correct.

As reported by the *New York Times*: "The effect of [the expert's] testimony was written plain in the strained facial expressions of the Bush legal team."[24]

Many experts (particularly doctors and economists) appear before various agencies, so you should consider searching through agency opinions. After identifying agencies before which an expert may have appeared, contact those agencies and ask for the expert's reports or transcripts of his testimony. Note, however, that although many agencies enable you to search their opinions on their websites, such an effort can be quite time consuming. An alternative is to use commercial vendors, which have databases that combine opinions from numerous agencies, thereby making all those various opinions searchable simultaneously.

Because authors of law review articles sometimes quote experts, cite to their works, and discuss their testimony, a database of law reviews can also be a good source of information. Not all law reviews are online for free, so, for a more comprehensive law review search, use a commercial site such as LexisNexis or Westlaw, or your library's free remote databases.

Finally, as with your search on prior experience of an expert, you should determine whether any video or audio recordings of the expert are available. These are important, both for the substance of the statements and as an indication of the expert's communication skills. Some experts have included streaming video of themselves on their own websites to enable attorneys to see them in action. In addition, at least one expert directory (i.e., JurisPro) allows you to both see and hear the listed expert. Another option is to search podcasts, which can be found (1) through an online directory of podcasts, such as Podcast Alley or Blawg (click on the "Podcast" category),

---

23. Pat. No. 4,297,566.

24. Katharine Q. Steele, *Contesting the Vote: The Vice President; Gore Reviews His Legal Options and Says He Remains Determined to Press His Case*, N.Y. TIMES, Dec. 4, 2000, at A15.

or (2) by simply using a search engine and adding the word "podcast" to your keyword search.

Public Records regarding the Expert

Public records can reveal a lot about an expert. For instance, an expert's financial situation might be revealed by how much his house cost, what type of car he drives, or a recent bankruptcy filing. Voter registration records may reveal a political party affiliation. A conflict of interest (e.g., the expert is related to a party) might be found by checking out real or personal property records, employment histories, or the like.

Note that a search through public records should include a search for civil and criminal matters in which the expert has been named as a party. Believe it or not, some experts have engaged in significant criminal activity. And on the civil side, many medical experts are parties to lawsuits because they are practicing doctors, and, as such, get sued. If a medical expert has been found liable for malpractice in a prior lawsuit, that information may prove valuable to the opposition when it comes to questioning that expert's claim to expertise in a certain area. And be sure to include not only case filings but also judgment and lien information when you make such inquiries.

If the jurisdiction where the expert practices is not available online or is not covered by one of the online legal services, consider calling the clerk of the court for the county where the expert practices. The clerk may be able to tell you over the telephone if there has been any litigation in which the expert was a named party. Some clerk's offices charge a fee, requiring that you send them your request and payment before they provide the requested information. If this is the case, then you need to plan ahead, as the response time can vary greatly from two days to (in the worst cases) well over two months.

Analyze How Courts Are Treating Experts in This Field

The background and specific qualifications of your prospective expert are crucial to the admissibility of the expert's testimony. Such information, however, should not be analyzed in a vacuum. Equally important is how courts are generally treating experts in the field of the claimed expertise.

In certain types of both civil and criminal litigation, experts from some professional disciplines are so commonly retained that the admissibility of their testimony is uncontroversial. In commercial litigation, for example, an accountant is usually retained if the case involves a claim of lost profits. In medical malpractice cases involving birth injuries, it is virtually inevitable that both sides will need to retain a pediatric neurologist. In such instances, you may be lured into thinking that you need not be concerned about thoroughly researching the entire class of expertise. But because there is no guarantee that the expert you are going to retain or depose in fact has demonstrated adherence to the generally accepted principles and methods of his discipline, presuming so could be quite dangerous. You must determine how the expert's methods and opinions conform to or deviate from those of other experts in the same discipline. In addition to employing all of the standard research tools previously discussed, a simple and useful practice is to have the prospective expert explain, in his own words, how questions about the science behind the methods used would be addressed. If the expert is unfamiliar with basic *Daubert*[25] or judicial gatekeeping concepts or cannot clearly articulate the basic methodology used to arrive at his opinions, you should think twice about retaining that expert.

This is particularly essential if the expert will be giving testimony involving a novel or emerging theory, or one with significant controversy concerning its scientific legitimacy. In such situations, you must research the entire class of the testimony relating to the theory. A good example of a class of expertise where the theory and science is emerging is trauma-induced fibromyalgia. Whereas fibromyalgia is an accepted and recognized diagnostic category and rheumatology, expert testimony that a physical trauma can cause fibromyalgia is highly controversial. Although numerous studies support a causative link between trauma and fibromyalgia, other studies do not support such a conclusion.[26] So, when researching an expert who will testify in an emerging area such as trauma-induced fibromyalgia, you must consider several factors:

- Know the science behind the theory: Attorneys presenting testimony in an emerging area should be thoroughly acquainted with all major studies performed and papers written on the topic.
- Know the case law: Every effort should be made to avail oneself of all major opinions and decisions that have been written on the admissibility of testimony in the emerging area.
- Know the jurisdiction: Standards for admissibility vary from one jurisdiction to the next, and those standards will have a significant impact

---

25 Daubert v. Merrell Dow Pharms, Inc., 509 U.S. 579 (1993).

26. *See* Michael Finch, *Judicial Evaluation of Traumatically Induced Fibromyalgia*, PSYCHOL. INJ. & L., Mar. 2009, *available at* http://www.springerlink.com/content/l60849t307u46626/fulltext.html.

on the tack taken in arguing for admissibility of novel or controversial testimony.

- Know the court/judge: The best indicator of future admissibility of a novel or controversial opinion is the established tendencies of the court or judge with respect to novel testimony in general and specifically the class of testimony at hand.
- Know the expert: When presenting novel testimony, it could be argued that the best safeguard against exclusion would be to select an expert whose testimony on the topic has already been admitted.

Conclusion

Know the subject matter. Find the right expert. Investigate the expert's background and credentials. Analyze how courts are treating expert testimony in this field. Each of these steps can be critical when it comes to ensuring that you have chosen the right expert for your client.

RETAINING AN EXPERT

Loren Kieve[1]

This subchapter assumes that (1) you have determined you need an expert witness, either as a consulting expert or a testifying expert, and (2) you have found an expert that you believe (a) is qualified, (b) is competent and has the necessary qualifications and credentials in the relevant field of expertise, (c) will provide valuable advice or present credible and convincing testimony, and (d) has no conflict of interest or other problem that would prevent the expert from providing advice to you and your client or testifying on behalf of your client.

Before you retain the expert, you will have interviewed him extensively to discuss the potential engagement. When you do so, you should confirm, preferably in a signed written agreement, that even the preliminary information you discuss with the expert is itself confidential and may not be disclosed without your and your client's written permission. This can avoid potential embarrassment and, worse, disqualification if the expert breaches this agreement.[2]

You should normally retain the expert initially as a consulting expert so that you can make sure that the expert's testimony will be helpful to your case and stand up to scrutiny under cross-examination by the other side before actually designating him as a testifying expert. If the expert remains a consulting expert, you can retain another expert to testify in the case. Again, however, that expert should also first be retained as a consultant.

The written retention agreement is key to setting forth a clear understanding of what the expert will—and will not—do as part of the expert's engagement, and what your and the expert's expectations will be going forward. A model retainer agreement is attached to this chapter as appendix A and is referenced throughout this subchapter.

---

1. Loren Kieve heads the firm of Kieve Law Offices, San Francisco, California. He has consistently been recognized as a Northern California "Superlawyer." Before moving to California in 2000, he was a partner with Debevoise & Plimpton in Washington, D.C., where he was also recognized as a leading lawyer.

2. *See, e.g.,* Western Digital Corp. v. Superior Court, 60 Cal. App. 4th 1471, 1471 Cal. Rptr. 2d 179 (1998).

Provide for the Confidentiality of the Retainer Agreement and Materials Produced to the Expert

You should label your retainer agreement as "Privileged and Confidential—Attorney Work Product," preferably in boldfaced type. However, this label may not necessarily protect the retainer agreement from discovery if the expert is designated as testifying. Under Federal Rule of Civil Procedure 26(a)(2)(B)(ii) and its state court analogues, the expert will be required to disclose "the data or other information considered by the expert" in forming his opinions. It is unclear whether a court would consider the expert's retainer agreement as falling within this language. If there is no controlling contrary case law in a particular jurisdiction, counsel should assume that there is a reasonable possibility that any communication with the expert, including the retainer agreement itself, will be fair game for inquiry by the other side.[3]

As of the date of this book, the Federal Civil Rules Advisory Committee has proposed a revision to this rule that would become effective in December 2010 and would provide greater protection to communications between counsel and an expert.[4] It would require that the expert disclose only those facts and data on which he is relying in forming an opinion.

Also keep in mind that sophisticated counsel often stipulate among themselves that work product and similar communications with an expert, as well as draft reports, are not discoverable.[5] Although a stipulation that there will be no waiver by sharing work product with an expert would probably protect the information in the particular case, there is no guarantee that it would protect it against nonparties in another setting.[6]

You will also want the expert to acknowledge the confidentiality of the retention itself. Confirm in the retention agreement that the expert will maintain the confidentiality of the assignment and will not broadcast that he has been retained in the greatest case since the Ringling Bros. and Barnum

---

3. *See* 8 CHARLES ALAN WRIGHT ET AL., FED. PRACTICE AND PROCEDURE § 2031.1, at 442 (2d ed. 1994 & Supp. 1999) ("It appears that counsel should now expect that any written or tangible data provided to testifying experts will have to be disclosed.").

4. *See infra* "Communicating with the Expert" in chapter 2.

5. *See* AMERICAN BAR ASSOCIATION, CIVIL DISCOVERY STANDARDS Standard 21(e) (Aug. 2004) ("Until there is a clear legal rule, the best way to deal with the issue is to try to obtain an agreement from all the parties to the case on how they will treat the issue or seek a ruling from the court on it.").

6. *See, e.g.*, Bank Brussels Lambert v. Crédit Lyonnais (Suisse) S.A., 160 F.R.D. 437, 448 (S.D.N.Y. 1995). (The test is whether disclosure is done in a way that "substantially increases the likelihood that the work product will fall into the hands of the adversary.")

& Bailey circus came to town—unless you want the expert to do that and agree to it in writing.[7]

Confirm That There Are No Conflicts

An expert may be disqualified because of conflict if he has previously given advice to or consulted with the opposing party or with a person or entity with an interest adverse to your client. Although not, strictly speaking, a legal disqualification, the expert may be practically disqualified if he has taken a position contrary to the one that is being taken in your case.

You should have the expert confirm in the retention agreement that he has told you about any previous assignments that may bear on the current assignment. You want to make sure that the expert has not testified that the moon is made of green cheese when your case is based on its being red. Rule 26(a)(2)(B)(iv) and (v) require an expert's report to include "(iv) the witness's qualifications, including a list of all publications authored in the previous 10 years," and "(v) a list of all other cases in which, during the previous 4 years, the witness testified as an expert at trial or by deposition." Your previous due diligence should include not only these bare minimums, but an extensive investigation into the expert's overall career and previous assignments, without any time limitation. The last thing you want to have happen is for your expert to be impeached by his own writings or previous positions.[8]

Confirm That the Expert Will Spend Sufficient Time on the Case

The retention agreement should confirm that the expert will devote sufficient time to the matter. You do not want to spend considerable resources on your expert only to find that he has taken on a new assignment that conflicts with yours.

It is not unusual for experts to be subpoenaed, not only in the case in which they are assisting you, but in other cases.[9] You should require your

---

7. *See* Model Agreement ¶¶ 5 and 6.

8. For more guidance on vetting your expert, see "Searching for an Expert Witness" *supra*.

9. *See, e.g.*, Ortiz-Lopez v. Sociedad Española de Auxilio Muto y Benefiencia de P.R., No. 00-1278-01A (D.P.R., May 3, 2001) (expert's credibility and qualifications, including prior testimony in cases involving similar claims, were "directly at issue"); Expeditors Int'l of Washington, Inc. v. Vaster, Inc., 2004 WL 406999 (N.D. Ill. Feb. 26, 2004) (Rule 26 does not preclude a Rule 45 subpoena *duces tecum* to an expert witness where the docu-

expert to inform you immediately if he is subpoenaed so that you can take appropriate action.[10]

Confirm That the Expert Will Return Provided Materials

You should ensure that, when the case is over, the expert does not retain any confidential client information or protected attorney work product. Some experts, particularly ones whose livelihoods are based on providing expert consultation or testimony, may want to retain their work papers for potential use in subsequent cases. Unless there are very good reasons for letting them do so, you should insist that "what goes on in Los Angeles, stays in Los Angeles" in your case.[11]

Address the Expert's Compensation

The preferred method for compensating an expert is the expert's standard hourly rate. This will permit the expert to testify that he is being compensated for the time spent on the case rather than for supplying a paid opinion. You should verify that this is, in fact, the expert's standard hourly fee that is charged for similar assignments. You never want to compensate an expert by a contingent fee. It is unethical because it turns the expert from a supposedly neutral opinion giver into someone who is aligned with a party and has his own "skin" in the outcome of the case.

Some experts, for example, university professors and professional lecturers, may, however, ask to be compensated for having committed their time in advance to your case when they could have appeared at one or more other engagements or seminars. If so, you may consider an engagement along the lines of paragraph 11(b) of the Model Agreement. If you have a scheduled trial date, the expert may also want an agreement along the lines of paragraph 11(c).

You should specify the names and rates of anyone assisting the expert whom you will be expected to compensate. You should also confirm that

---

ments requested pertained to the expert, as opposed to a party; requiring the production of the expert's deposition and trial testimony and reports for the past 10 years regarding trade secrets); *cf.* Alper v. United States, 190 F.R.D. 281, 283 (D. Mass. 2000) (subpoena not appropriate to obtain evidence from expert witnesses).

10. *See* Model Agreement ¶ 10.
11. *See* Model Agreement ¶ 9.

any of the expert's assistants will also abide by the terms of the expert's engagement agreement.[12]

Finally, because you have retained the expert, you should ensure that you receive the expert's statements.[13] They should be submitted monthly so you can keep track of what the expert is doing (and also make sure that the expenses do not get out of hand). It is not unusual, particularly in large cases, to have the client pay the expert directly, so that the lawyer or law firm does not end up financing the litigation. If, however, the case is on a contingent fee arrangement, then the lawyer or law firm will normally advance expert fees as the case progresses. As noted above, however, the expert will never be retained on a contingent fee basis.

Reference Any Protective Orders

Because the expert is assisting you and may be privy to material covered by a court protective order, it is essential that the expert (and any assistants) also agree to be bound by the order.[14]

Ensure That the Expert Preserves His Materials

As noted above, under the current (as of 2009) version of Rule 26(a)(2)(B) (ii), an expert's report is required to include "the data or other information considered by the [expert] witness in forming [her opinions]." Many state courts have similar provisions. The federal courts and these state courts have generally held that this language requires the expert to disclose everything that he "considered" during the course of the assignment as an expert witness. This means that every note an expert writes, and every draft, document, e-mail, or phone call you have with an expert is probably discoverable.[15] If your expert destroys any of these documents, you and your client may be subject to sanctions.[16]

Although you may be retaining the expert as a consulting expert—in which case these provisions would not apply—there is a possibility that you may later decide to have the expert testify. If so, then these provisions apply full force. It is therefore essential that the expert understand, from the outset, that he should keep (1) a careful record of everything he reviews during the

---

12. *See* Model Agreement ¶ 13.
13. *See* Model Agreement ¶ 15.
14. *See* Model Agreement ¶ 14.
15. American Fidelity Assurance Co. v. Ladonna Boyer & Comb. Ins. Co., 225 F.R.D. 520 (D.S.C. 2004); 6 MOORE'S FEDERAL PRACTICE § 26.80[1][a] (2009).
16. G. Joseph, *Expert Spoliation*, NAT'L L.J., Feb. 3, 2003, at B7.

assignment, and (2) copies of each of these materials. It is also essential that the expert understands that everything he prepares, including drafts, is fair game for the opposing side in discovery.

As also noted above, the Federal Civil Rules Advisory Committee is currently considering amendments to Rule 26(a)(2)(B)(ii) that would require the expert to disclose only material he actually relies on in forming an opinion. If these amendments are adopted, the expert will still have to maintain and identify the materials he is relying on—rather than everything he merely may have "considered." But the line between the two is not entirely clear, so the better course is make sure the expert retains everything so that, if a dispute arises, there will be no claim of improper "expert spoliation" of discoverable material.

Protect against Release of Drafts and Notes

Clarify with your expert that any documents he creates might be discoverable. First, confirm that the expert clearly understands that anything he writes is very likely to end up in the hands of opposing counsel.[17] Second, confirm that the expert will not commit *anything* (including so-called internal working papers) to paper in the way of an opinion or report without first discussing it with you. This ensures that no tentative or erroneous concepts become fair game for the other side to exploit. Third, make clear that the expert's opinion may evolve as additional information develops in the case.

As noted above, you may, however, also want to do what experienced counsel ordinarily do in cases where both sides retain experts: have a written stipulation that modifies the terms of Rule 26(a)(2)(B) to provide that (1) communications between counsel and any expert, including a testifying expert, are off bounds from discovery; and (2) it is only the expert's written report and materials or data the expert actually *relies on* in forming his opinion(s) and report(s) that are discoverable.[18]

Provide for the Expert's Continuing Obligation after the Case Is Concluded

You should confirm that the expert is to maintain the confidentiality, even after the case is over, of any information, including conclusions, that he receives

---

17. *See, e.g.*, W.R. Grace & Co.-Conn. v. Zotos Int'l, Inc., 2000 WL 1843258 (W.D.N.Y. Nov. 2, 2000).

18. *See* American Bar Association, Civil Discovery Standards Standard 21(e) (Aug. 2004).

or develops in the case.[19] You should also confirm that the expert is to continue to abide by the terms of any protective order entered in the case and to return or destroy any materials or information covered by a protective order.[20]

Conclusion

A written engagement letter is essential to (1) establish the terms on which the expert is retained, and (2) clearly define what the expert will and will not do during the course of the engagement. The paragraphs in the attached model agreement are meant to be guides, rather than diktats, for retaining an expert.

A signed engagement letter does not, however, resolve all the potential issues surrounding an expert. You must constantly engage with and supervise your expert to make sure that you and the expert are on the same page throughout the case.

---

19. *See* Model Agreement ¶ 23.
20. *See* Model Agreement ¶ 24.

WORKING WITH NONTESTIFYING EXPERTS

Matthew F. Prewitt[1]

Consulting experts labor without glory. Unless trial counsel has made a serious error, ordinarily the consulting expert will never take the witness stand, will never be deposed, and may never even be disclosed to opposing counsel. However, in any complex litigation, the consulting expert plays an essential supporting role for trial counsel. Even though you may never know his name, a consulting expert is assisting your opposing counsel to devise the unanticipated case theory or devastating cross examination that your litigation team may never consider—unless you too have retained a consulting expert.

The distinguishing characteristic of the consulting expert is confidentiality. Shielded by the attorney work product doctrine and, in some cases, by the attorney-client privilege, the consulting expert provides confidential advice to trial counsel regarding the specialized areas of knowledge that will provide the essential proof of the parties' claims and defenses at trial. Confidentiality affords the attorney and consultant the freedom to engage in a candid assessment of the potential strengths and weaknesses of both the client's and the adversary's case theories and to explore alternative case theories without fear of disclosure. This subchapter provides a practical guide to preserving the confidentiality of consulting expert work product and communications, and explains how to avoid the litigation pitfalls that may result in inadvertent waiver of the work product doctrine and attorney-client privilege for consulting experts.

---

1. Matt Prewitt is a shareholder in the Chicago office of Greenberg Traurig, LLP, where he practices in the litigation department. His practice encompasses a broad range of business disputes in the state and federal trial courts and the bankruptcy courts. He has represented clients in disputes arising from corporate acquisitions, enforcement of shareholder agreements, claims of successor and alter ego liability, creditor remedies, misappropriation of trade secrets, environmental and mass tort liabilities, and unfair competition. Matt is also an adjunct professor of law at the Chicago-Kent College of Law. He gratefully acknowledges the research assistance of Christopher Chubb (University of Michigan Law School, Class of 2010) while a summer associate for Greenberg Traurig.

The Two Bastions of Consultant Confidentiality

The confidentiality of consulting expert work product may be protected under both the work product doctrine and the attorney-client privilege. Preserving these protections requires careful planning and diligence throughout the attorney-consultant relationship.

Work Product Doctrine

Rule 26 of the Federal Rules of Civil Procedure draws a bright line between testifying experts and nontestifying consultants.[2] Under Rule 26(b)(4), a party may depose "any person who has been identified as an expert whose opinions may be presented at trial," but an expert who will not testify is generally shielded from discovery:

> Ordinarily, a party may not, by interrogatories or deposition, discover facts known or opinions held by an expert who has been retained or specially employed by another party in anticipation of litigation or to prepare for trial and who is not expected to be called as a witness at trial.[3]

This protection under Rule 26(b)(4)(B) for nontestifying experts is an extension of the attorney work product doctrine, which is codified by Rule 26(b)(3):

> Ordinarily, a party may not discover documents and tangible things that are prepared in anticipation of litigation or for trial by or for another party or its representative (including the other party's attorney, consultant, surety, indemnitor, insurer, or agent).[4]

The protection is available even if the only reason a party does not want the consultant to testify is that his opinion would be harmful to the client's case.[5] The very purpose of the rule anticipates that there will be instances in which the consulting expert reaches conclusions or provides advice that, if disclosed, would be damaging to the client's case. By ensuring confidentiality, the work product doctrine protects the advisor from becoming an involuntary

---

2. *But see* "The Future of Consulting Experts: The Proposed Amendment to Rule 26(b) (4)" *infra* for a discussion of proposed amendments to Federal Rule of Civil Procedure 26(b) (4) that would substantially eliminate the distinction between testifying and consulting experts.

3. FED. R. CIV. P. 26(b)(4)(B).

4. FED. R. CIV. P. 26(b)(3).

5. *See* Spearman Industries, Inc. v. St. Paul Fire & Marine Ins. Co., 128 F. Supp. 2d 1148, 1152 (N.D. Ill. 2001).

witness and encourages candid discussion between the attorney and the consulting expert.[6]

History of the Work Product Doctrine

The work product protection for attorneys was first recognized by the Supreme Court in the landmark decision *Hickman v. Taylor.*[7] In *Hickman*, the Court acknowledged that shielding attorney work product from discovery is essential to preserve the integrity of the attorney-client relationship and the adversary system.[8] When the Supreme Court subsequently expanded the work product doctrine to include expert consultants in *United States v. Nobles*,[9] the Court recognized the central role of nonattorney consultants in assisting counsel to prepare for trial.[10] In *Nobles*, defense counsel had hired an investigator to interview two witnesses. The defendant called the investigator as a witness at trial to impeach the witnesses' testimony but refused to disclose the investigator's report. The Court held that the report was protected by the work product doctrine, until the defendant waived the privilege by calling the investigator to testify.[11] The Court, therefore, affirmed the trial court's ruling that the investigator could not testify without also disclosing his report.

Exceptions to Work Product Protection

The work product doctrine is not an absolute privilege. Many attorneys incorrectly assume that the work product doctrine will shield facts and data collected by the consulting expert unless the protection is somehow waived. However, both Rule 26(b)(3) and Rule 26(b)(4) recognize a qualified right of the opposing party to obtain disclosure on a sufficient showing of need.

Under Rule 26(b)(4), the required showing is described as "exceptional circumstances under which it is impracticable for the party to obtain facts or opinions on the same subject by other means."[12] What qualifies as exceptional circumstances is an intensely factual inquiry that will vary from case

---

6. *Id.* (citing Eliasen v. Hamilton, 111 F.R.D. 396, 401 (N.D. Ill. 1986)).

7. Hickman v. Taylor, 329 U.S. 495 (1947).

8. *Id.* at 511 ("Inefficiency, unfairness and sharp practices would inevitably develop in the giving of legal advice and in the preparation of cases for trial.").

9. United States v. Nobles, 422 U.S. 225 (1975).

10. *Id.* at 238–39 ("[A]ttorneys often must rely on the assistance of investigators and other agents in the compilation of materials in preparation for trial. It is therefore necessary that the [work product] doctrine protect material prepared by agents of the attorney as well as those prepared by the attorney.").

11. *Id.*

12. Fed. R. Civ. P. 26(b)(4)(B).

to case. For example, in *White v. Cooper Industries, Inc.*,[13] a products liability case involving a broken metal chain, the trial court compelled disclosure of the results of testing performed on an unbroken link in the subject chain.[14] Similarly, in *Cooper v. Meridian Yachts, Ltd.*,[15] the court compelled disclosure of documents describing how an expert had "manipulated and disassembled components" during his investigation of an accident, finding "exceptional circumstances" because the opposing party would never have the opportunity to examine the objects in their original condition.[16]

Similarly, under Rule 26(b)(3), work product may be discovered if "the party shows that it has substantial need for the materials to prepare its case and cannot, without undue hardship, obtain their substantial equivalent by other means."[17] For example, in a securities class action, counsel for the defendant corporation had retained the services of an accounting firm to investigate the basis for the plaintiffs' claim and had then disclosed the final report produced by the accounting firm. The plaintiffs sought discovery of documents underlying the report, but the district court refused to compel discovery because the plaintiffs had failed to show that the information contained in those documents was unavailable from other sources, and the defendant had not disclosed the auditors as testifying experts.[18]

Even if the opposing party obtains an order compelling disclosure of protected work product, this disclosure ordinarily will be limited to the facts observed and recorded by the consultant. Although Rule 26(b)(4) expressly authorizes disclosure of either "facts or opinions," the work product doctrine as developed by the courts and as codified by Rule 26(b)(3) distinguishes between disclosure of factual materials and disclosure of mental impressions and opinions:

> If the court orders discovery of those materials, it must protect against disclosure of the mental impressions, conclusions, opinions, or legal theories of a party's attorney or other representative concerning the litigation.[19]

Courts have applied this distinction between fact and opinion work product to limit disclosure of expert work product, seeking to shield opinions and trial strategy even where the court compels disclosure of fact work product.

---

13. White v. Cooper Indus. Inc., No. CIV. 06-4272-KES, 2008 WL 3245461 (D.S.D. Aug. 6, 2008).
14. *Id.*
15. Cooper v. Meridian Yachts, Ltd., No. 06-61630-CIV, 2008 WL 2229552 (S.D. Fla. May 28, 2008).
16. *Id.* at *5–7.
17. FED. R. CIV. P. 26(b)(3)(A).
18. *In re* PolyMedica Corp. Sec. Litig., 235 F.R.D. 28 (D. Mass. 2006).
19. FED. R. CIV. P. 26(b)(3).

For example, in *White v. Cooper Industries, Inc.*,[20] discussed above, the court compelled disclosure of the data collected during the testing of the metal chain, but the court refused to compel disclosure of the opinions of the consulting expert who performed the test.[21] Similarly, in *Cooper v. Meridian Yachts, Ltd.*,[22] also discussed above, the court compelled disclosure of documents describing the expert's investigation, but the court protected from disclosure the investigator's opinions regarding the cause of the accident.[23]

Courts sometimes disregard the distinction between opinion and fact, however, especially where the retaining counsel fails to take adequate steps to prevent the consulting expert from becoming an indispensable witness with direct observation of disputed conditions within his expertise. For example, in *Delcastor, Inc. v. Vail Associates, Inc.*,[24] an engineer retained by the defendant ski resort investigated the cause of a mudslide by inspecting the site immediately after the incident.[25] His report contained both his observations and his opinions regarding the cause of the mudslide. The defendant disclosed the engineer solely as a fact witness and not as an expert. The plaintiffs, however, sought to examine the engineer on his opinions and to obtain a complete copy of his report. The trial court compelled disclosure of the report and his opinions because "effective cross-examination of his testimony regarding 'facts' surrounding the mudslide require[d] discovery of his opinions as to its cause."[26] The trial court found that "exceptional circumstances" warranted disclosure because the engineer was the only expert in a position to form opinions about the cause of the mudslide based on firsthand observations immediately after the incident. The plaintiffs would therefore be entitled to the report because "it [was] impracticable for [them] to obtain information similar to that contained in the [engineer's] report."[27] The defendant's mistake was in requesting a key fact witness for anticipated litigation to provide a candid opinion in a written report on a critical disputed issue.

Attorney-Client Privilege

Although the work product doctrine is typically the focus of disputes over disclosure and examination of nontestifying experts, counsel should not

20. *White*, 2008 WL 3245461.
21. *Id.*
22. *Cooper*, 2008 WL 2229552.
23. *Id.*
24. Delcastor, Inc. v. Vail Assocs., Inc., 108 F.R.D. 405 (D. Colo. 1985).
25. *Id.* at 407–09.
26. *Id.* at 408.
27. *Id.* at 409.

overlook the attorney-client privilege as an important additional protection against disclosure. Unlike the work product doctrine, the attorney-client privilege is not a qualified privilege, and communications shielded by the attorney-client privilege are thus protected from disclosure unless the privilege is waived.

Application of the attorney-client privilege is well illustrated by Judge Friendly's decision in *United States v. Kovel*.[28] In *Kovel*, counsel instructed his client to provide information to an accountant retained by the lawyer, and the accountant then communicated to counsel the information received from the client together with the accountant's analysis to assist counsel in representation of the client. Holding that the client's communications with the attorney and the attorney's communications with the accountant both could be protected by the attorney-client privilege, Judge Friendly analogized the work of the accountant to an interpreter assisting an attorney whose client speaks a foreign language, comparing the principles of accounting to a foreign language.[29] However, Judge Friendly warned that not all communications with consulting experts are protected by the attorney-client privilege:

> What is vital to the privilege is that the communication be made in confidence for the purpose of obtaining legal advice from the lawyer. If what is sought is not legal advice but only accounting service . . . or if the advice sought is the accountant's rather than the lawyer's, no privilege exists.[30]

Subsequent cases have applied Judge Friendly's interpreter analogy to limit application of the attorney-client privilege to consultant communications that facilitate communications between the attorney and client. For example, in *United States v. Ackert*,[31] although counsel had contacted an investment banker "in order to gain information and to better advise his client," the court rejected defendant's assertion of the attorney-client privilege to protect counsel's communications with the investment banker, instructing that that privilege does not protect "communications that prove important to an attorney's legal advice to a client."[32] Because the investment banker had not been asked to "clarify communications between attorney and client,"[33] the attorney-client privilege would not apply.

---

28. United States v. Kovel, 296 F.2d 918 (2d Cir. 1961).
29. *Id.* at 992.
30. *Id.*
31. United States v. Ackert, 169 F.3d 136 (2d Cir. 1999).
32. *Id.* at 139.
33. *Id.* (citing *Kovel*, 296 F.2d at 992).

Preserving Expert Consultant Confidentiality

To preserve the confidentiality of the consulting expert's communications and work product, the attorney and consultant must remain ever vigilant to the requirements of the work product doctrine and the attorney-client privilege, and they must establish a record that clearly supports assertion of the privileges. This process begins with the retention of the consulting expert and must be considered with all written communications and work product of the consulting expert.

Retention of the Consulting Expert

Retention by Counsel

In theory, a consulting expert could be retained by either the attorney or the client. In practice, however, most consulting experts are retained by counsel. Retention of the consulting expert by trial counsel helps to define clearly the expert's role as assisting counsel to prepare for litigation. An expert retained solely by the client may be confused with an expert retained in the ordinary course of business and may lose the protection of the work product doctrine.[34] In addition, trial counsel will be experienced in drafting an appropriate retention agreement.

Retention Agreement

A retention agreement with a consulting expert should clearly specify that the expert is retained solely to provide consulting services in connection with pending or anticipated litigation and, if possible, should provide examples of some of the specific tasks to be performed by the consultant.[35] If the intended role of the expert and his relationship with counsel or the client are subsequently disputed by a litigation adversary seeking discovery, the recitals in a retention agreement have been relied on by courts to sustain a claim of privilege.[36] The retention agreement should not include any provision that suggests that the consultant may be called as a testifying expert. If it subsequently becomes necessary to call the consultant as a testifying expert, the respective dates and contents of the first retention agreement as a consultant and the second retention agreement as a testifying expert can provide the court with

---

34. Fed. R. Civ. P. 26(b)(4)(B); Ngo v. Standard Tools & Equip., Co., 197 F.R.D. 263, 266–67 (D. Md. 2000).

35. *See* "Retaining an Expert" *supra* for additional guidance on drafting a retention agreement.

36. *See, e.g.,* Hartford Fire Ins. Co. v. Pure Air on the Lake LP, 154 F.R.D. 202, 207 n.8 (N.D. Ind. 1993).

useful benchmarks to distinguish between consultant work product that may be withheld and Rule 26(a)(2) materials that must be produced.

Documenting Informal Consultations

Instances may arise in which confidential communications precede an anticipated formal retention, but the consulting expert is never actually retained. It is well established that the work product doctrine will protect confidential communications preceding formal retention or in instances of an informal consultation.[37] Even in such cases, however, counsel would be well served to memorialize the purpose of the consultation in relation to pending or anticipated litigation and the participants' expectation of confidentiality through a letter or memorandum to the consultant, to avoid any future dispute. For example, in *Ngo v. Standard Tools & Equipment, Co.*,[38] plaintiff and his counsel conferred with plaintiff's treating physician regarding the disputed medical issues in the litigation, but no formal retention agreement or confidentiality agreement was ever signed, and the physician received no consulting fee.[39] The trial court rejected plaintiff's attempt to shield the physician's meeting with his attorney from discovery because the court held the treating physician was not a consulting expert.[40] The court suggested in dicta that a confidentiality agreement might have been sufficient to change the outcome of the discovery dispute.[41]

Joint Retention and Joint Defense Agreements

In some instances, a consulting expert may be jointly retained by two or more parties aligned against a common litigation adversary. In such cases, a formal retention agreement is even more important. It is well established that the joint defense privilege encompasses both the attorney-client privilege and the work product doctrine.[42] The joint defense privilege allows parties and their counsel to share documents and information without waiving any privilege that otherwise would be lost by voluntary disclosure, in-

---

37. Spearman Indus., Inc. v. St. Paul Fire & Marine Ins. Co., 128 F. Supp. 2d 1148, 1151 (N.D. Ill. 2001) (FED. R. CIV. P. 26(b)(4)(B) protects communications with experts informally consulted) (citing Advisory Committee note).
38. *Ngo*, 197 F.R.D. 263.
39. *Id.* at 265–66.
40. *Id.*
41. *Id.*
42. *See, e.g.*, Waller v. Fin. Corp. of Am., 828 F.2d 579, 583 n.7 (9th Cir. 1987) (attorney-client privilege); *In re* Grand Jury Subpoenas, 902 F.2d 244, 249 (4th Cir. 1990) (work product doctrine).

cluding communications with their shared expert consultants.[43] A written joint defense agreement is not a prerequisite to asserting the joint defense doctrine.[44] However, a clear agreement will do much to protect against any subsequent challenge to the privilege.[45] The potential confusion created when a consultant confers with multiple law firms and perhaps their respective clients may create ambiguity that could result in an unintended waiver. A written joint defense agreement and a written expert retention agreement that directly identify the purpose and scope of the consultant's retention and the parties and counsel included within the scope of the expert's confidential consultation will provide a clear record supporting nondisclosure in any subsequent discovery battle.[46]

Written Work Product and Communications

A consulting expert may produce extensive memoranda, reports, and correspondence. This written record of the consultant's work creates the possibility that protected consultant work product may be mistaken for nonprivileged, discoverable documents. The first risk is the inadvertent disclosure of consultant work product in discovery when a consultant document is mistakenly included by counsel in the party's document production as a nonprivileged document. The second risk is the possibility that the document will become the subject of a discovery dispute and may be ordered disclosed after *in camera* review if the privileged content is not apparent to the court.

Thus, any substantive document should be prepared in a manner that clearly indicates its privileged content to any reviewer. At a minimum, each document should include a boldface legend identifying the document as a consulting expert's confidential work product prepared for litigation, and the document should clearly identify the author, the date, and all recipients. As should be clear from the foregoing discussion, only in rare cases should the consulting expert's written communications and reports be addressed or delivered to anyone other than trial counsel. In addition, any substantial report or analysis prepared by the consulting expert should also include a brief preface reciting the facts that provide the basis for asserting the work

---

43. *See* United States v. Schwimmer, 892 F.2d 237, 244 (2d Cir. 1989) ("The protection afforded by the privilege extends to communications made in confidence to an accountant assisting lawyers who are conducting a joint defense.").
44. Lugosch v. Congel, 219 F.R.D. 220, 236 (N.D.N.Y. 2003).
45. *Id.*
46. *See* Minebea v. Pabst, 228 F.R.D. 13, 16 (D.D.C. 2005); City of Kalamazoo v. Michigan Disposal Serv. Corp., 125 F Supp. 2d 219 (W.D. Mich. 2000).

product doctrine or attorney-client privilege for the document. Finally, counsel must always remember that litigation is inherently unpredictable and that the work product doctrine is only a qualified privilege. Even documents bearing a "confidential" stamp may someday be disclosed to an adversary, and both counsel and the consulting expert must be mindful that placing too much trust in such labels can be a trap for the unwary.

Preserving the Distinction between Consulting and Testifying Experts

As discussed above, the Federal Rules of Civil Procedure draw a clear distinction between the testifying expert and the nontestifying or consulting expert. Preserving that distinction is essential to protect the confidentiality of consultant work product. In practice, however, a variety of circumstances can blur this distinction, leading to compelled disclosure of the consulting expert's communications and work product.

When Consultant Work Product Is Disclosed to a Testifying Expert

Rule 26(a)(2) requires the disclosure of "the data or other information considered by the witness in forming" his expert opinions.[47] This includes the work product of a consulting expert if reviewed and considered by the testifying expert.[48] Allowing the testifying expert to review and rely on a consulting expert's analysis blurs the distinction between the testifying and consulting expert and makes the consulting expert a target for discovery. Disclosure of the consultant's work product to the testifying expert ordinarily will waive the work product protection for the information and analysis disclosed to the testifying expert.[49] For example, in *Trigon Insurance Co. v. United States*,[50] nontestifying experts had participated extensively in the preparation, drafting, and editing of the testifying expert's report. Since the testifying expert considered and incorporated in his own report the work product of the consulting experts, Rule 26(a)(2) required the disclosure of the consultants' work product, including their draft reports.[51]

---

47. FED. R. CIV. P. 26(a)(2)(B).
48. Trigon Ins. Co. v. United States, 204 F.R.D. 277 (E.D. Va. 2001).
49. Heitmann v. Concrete Pipe Mach., 98 F.R.D. 740, 743 (E.D. Mo. 1983).
50. *Trigon Ins.*, 204 F.R.D. 277.
51. *Id.*

Not all communications between testifying experts and consultants will waive work product protection. In *Estate of Manship v. United States*,[52] the plaintiff presented evidence of a five-hour conference call between the consulting expert and testifying expert for the defendant two days before the deadline for submission of expert reports.[53] The testifying expert, however, submitted a declaration that he did not receive assistance from the nontestifying expert relating to his report and that he had completed his report before the conference call. The court refused to allow the deposition of the nontestifying expert. *Manship* and similar cases may suggest that Rule 26(a)(2) can be evaded simply by avoiding written disclosures of the consultant's opinions to the testifying expert. However, a testifying expert is bound to disclose oral communications to the same extent as written communications, even if the proof of a violation of Rule 26(a)(2) is more elusive for oral communications.

When the Consultant "Ghostwrites" the Testifying Expert's Report

The most experienced and highly qualified testifying experts may find the time demands of their practice to equal or exceed the time pressures of trial counsel. Notwithstanding the direction in Rule 26(a)(2)(B) that the expert report must be "prepared by" the testifying expert, in many cases, assistance in drafting the expert report is unavoidable. Any consulting expert who contributes to the drafting of the expert report becomes the legitimate target of discovery. A draft expert report prepared by the consultant is no less discoverable than any other source considered and relied on by the expert in preparing the report.[54] Disclosure of the consultant's draft, particularly if the draft is substantially similar to the testifying expert's final report, may result in the deposition of the consulting expert. In *Long Term Capital Holdings v. United States*,[55] for example, the opposing party sought to depose two nontestifying experts who had prepared a draft report that was reviewed by the testifying expert and that was similar to the testifying expert's final report.[56] The court granted the motion to compel their depositions but limited the scope of examination to include only their involvement in

---

52. Estate of Manship v. United States, 240 F.R.D. 229 (M.D. La. 2006).

53. *Id.*

54. In extreme cases, where the expert has merely signed a report prepared by another, the expert's testimony may be inadmissible at trial. *See Trigon Ins.*, 204 F.R.D at 294 (report must be "based on the expert's own valid reasoning and methodology.").

55. Long Term Capital Holdings v. United States, No. 01-CV-1290 (JBA), 2003 WL 21269586 (D. Conn. May 6, 2003).

56. *Id.*

preparing the expert report; the court did not allow discovery of the consulting experts' opinions beyond what was set forth in their draft report provided to the testifying expert.[57]

When Testifying and Nontestifying Experts Are from the Same Firm

The risk of waiving the work product protection through ghostwriting and other collaboration between the testifying expert and nontestifying consultants is often most acute when both testifying and consulting experts are from the same firm. With good reason, courts have warned against this practice and have described counsel who retain a single firm to provide both consulting and testifying experts as "playing with fire"[58] and proceeding "at their peril."[59]

Trigon Insurance again well illustrates the dangers of using a single firm. In that case, the testifying expert was a principal of the firm, and the non-testifying experts were employees of the same firm. This arrangement invited the ghostwriting issues discussed above. A decision from the Delaware Chancery Court in the *Chaparral Resources, Inc. Shareholders Litigation*[60] provides another good example of the pitfalls created by this approach. Applying Chancery Rule 26(b)(4)(B) (identical to Federal Rule of Civil Procedure 26(b)(4)(B)), the court's opinion describes the extensive interactions between the testifying expert and the consultants. The testifying expert had conversations with consultants and reviewed documents they prepared, and the consultants contributed to the testifying expert's report. The court deemed the consulting experts' opinions and work product to be subject to full disclosure as if they were testifying experts for purposes of discovery.[61]

An unpublished decision from the Tenth Circuit highlights a further risk of hiring consulting and testifying experts from the same firm. The trial court in *Master Palletizer Systems, Inc. v. T.S. Ragsdale Co.*[62] had issued a general sequestration order for all trial witnesses. Although permitting both parties' counsel to seat at counsel's table a nontestifying consultant, the trial court excluded from the courtroom all consultants from the same firm as any of the testifying experts, reasoning that "having a member of

57. *Id.*
58. *Trigon Ins.*, 204 F.R.D at 281–82.
59. *In re* Chaparral Resources, Inc. Shareholders Litig., C.A. No. 2001-VCL, 2007 WL 2998967, at *1 (Del. Ch. Oct. 11, 2007).
60. *Id.*
61. *Id.* at *3.
62. Master Palletizer Sys., Inc. v. T.S. Ragsdale Co., 937 F.2d 616 (10th Cir. 1991).

the same firm as the testifying expert witness be the technical advisor at the counsel table violated the spirit of the sequestration rule, because of the risk of collaboration and communication between the two."[63] The Tenth Circuit affirmed the ruling of the trial court. Thus, trial counsel was denied the assistance of his chosen consulting expert in a complex trial of technical engineering issues because of counsel's tactical error in relying on a single firm.

Although these cases highlight the risks of using a single consulting firm to provide both testifying and nontestifying experts, there is nothing per se improper about this approach. Some attorneys will retain a single firm and then go to extraordinary lengths to preserve the appearance of separateness by using separate engagement letters, requesting separate bills, instructing the consulting and testifying experts to use separate file management, and prohibiting any direct written or electronic communications between the consulting and testifying experts. These precautions may be sufficient to protect the consultants' work product from disclosure and may even exceed what some courts would require, but this approach begs the question whether there are any remaining benefits from hiring a single firm if the separateness of consulting and testifying experts is in fact so strictly preserved. Such precautions may only reinforce the appearance of sharp practice to skirt the disclosure requirements under Rule 26(a)(2).

When an Expert Attempts to Play a Dual Role as Consultant and Witness

In some instances, even the best prepared trial counsel may be forced to call a consulting expert as a testifying expert witness at trial. To limit the scope of disclosure required by Rule 26(a)(2), trial counsel may attempt to distinguish and withhold the witness's communications and work product created in his initial role as a consultant. Although possible in theory, in practice the distinction is very difficult to defend against scrutiny. In general, counsel should expect that all documents prepared or reviewed by the expert relating to the subject matter of his testimony will be ordered disclosed under Rule 26(a)(2).[64] Any uncertainty about a particular document typically will be construed in favor of the party seeking discovery.[65]

---

63. *Id.*

64. *See, e.g.,* Beverage Mktg. Corp. v. Ogilvy & Mather Direct Response, Inc., 563 F. Supp. 1013, 1014 (S.D.N.Y. 1983). For an example of the unusual case in which trial counsel successfully preserves the distinction, see *Grace A. Detwiler Trust v. Offenbecher,* 124 F.R.D. 545, 546 (S.D.N.Y. 1989).

65. B.C.F. Oil Ref., Inc. v. Consol. Edison Co. of N.Y., Inc., 171 F.R.D. 57, 61–62 (S.D.N.Y. 1997).

When attempting to withhold the testifying expert's consultant work product and communications, retaining counsel may prefer to focus on the task performed by the consultant when preparing or receiving the subject documents rather than the document's subject matter; in general, a task-based analysis instead of a subject matter analysis may justify a broader withholding of documents. For example, in *Securities & Exchange Commission v. Reyes*,[66] the court acknowledged that other courts had applied both standards but chose to focus on the content of the documents as the proper basis for an *in camera* review and on that basis ordered disclosed *all* documents relating to the subject matter of the expert's testimony.[67] By contrast, the court in *Messier v. Southbury Training School*[68] focused on the assigned task of the expert at the time he prepared the subject documents. On this basis, the court allowed the retaining party to withhold documents providing the expert's trial strategy recommendations.[69] Even if the court adopts a task-based analysis, any ambiguity in the recorded documents may be resolved against the retaining party, as illustrated by *B.C.F. Oil Refining, Inc. v. Consolidated Edison Co. of N.Y., Inc.*[70] Although the court allowed counsel to withhold documents prepared by the consultant to assist trial counsel with deposition examination outlines and document requests, the court ordered all other documents disclosed, including trial strategy memoranda, because assisting with depositions and document discovery were the only specific tasks that were easily distinguished from the expert's preparation to testify.[71]

The Future of Consulting Experts: The Proposed Amendment to Rule 26(b)(4)

As this book goes to press, proposed amendments to the Federal Rules of Civil Procedure that could materially impact the use of consulting experts in the federal courts have been transmitted by the Supreme Court to Congress and may soon be implemented.

---

66. SEC v. Reyes, No. C 06-04435 CRB, 2007 WL 963422 (N.D. Cal. Mar. 30, 2007).
67. *Id.*
68. Messier v. Southbury Training Sch., No. 3:94-CV-1706 (EBB), 1998 WL 422858 (D. Conn. June 29, 1998).
69. *Messier*, 1998 WL 422858 at *2.
70. *B.C.F. Oil Ref.*, 171 F.R.D. 57.
71. *Id.* at 61–62.

Proposed amendments to Rule 26(b)(4) would substantially eliminate the distinction between consulting and testifying experts by adding new subsections (B) and (C) that would shield all draft reports from disclosure by treating the draft reports as work product:

(B) Trial Preparation Protection for Draft Reports or Disclosures. Rules 26(b)(3)(A) and (B) protect drafts of any report or disclosure required under Rule 26(a)(2), regardless of the form of the draft.

(C) Trial Preparation Protection for Communications Between Party's Attorney and Expert Witnesses. Rules 26(b)(3)(A) and (B) protect communications between the party's attorney and any witness required to provide a report under Rule 26(a)(2)(B), regardless of the form of the communications, except to the extent that the communications:

(i) Relate to compensation for the expert's study or testimony;

(ii) Identify facts or data that the party's attorney provided and that the expert considered in forming the opinions to be expressed, or

(iii) Identify assumptions that the party's attorney provided and that the expert relied upon in forming the opinions to be expressed.[72]

As the Advisory Committee notes make clear, the intended purpose of these amendments in part is to greatly reduce the use of consulting experts and to level the playing field for parties unable to afford retention of both the consulting and testifying experts. The Advisory Committee also recognizes that similar stipulations excluding draft expert reports and attorney-expert communications from discovery already are widely employed by counsel to reduce litigation expense.

Even if the proposed amendments are adopted, it is too early to predict the scope of their impact.[73] The earliest that the proposed amendments might take effect is December 2010, and counsel no doubt will be reluctant to rely fully on the amendments until the courts have been given time to provide their own gloss on their meaning and effect.

One potentially significant gap in the proposed amendments is that, because only draft reports and attorney-expert communications are shielded from production, cautious trial counsel still will be reluctant to employ testifying experts in a true dual role. Nothing in the text of the proposed

---

72. Proposed Amendments to the Federal Rules of Civil Procedure, *available at* http://www.uscourts.gov/rules/.

73. On April 28, 2010, the Supreme Court issued orders adopting the amendments and transmitting the amendments to Congress. The amendments will take effect on December 1, 2010, unless Congress enacts legislation to provide otherwise under the Rules Enabling Act, 28 U.S.C. § 2074 (a).

amendments would shield from discovery a testifying expert's preliminary or tentative use of alternative testing methodologies or data sets that proved unfavorable to the retaining party's case if such data or analyses are material to the questions addressed by the expert's report. Nor can a testifying expert be expected to erase from his memory at deposition or trial the outcome of unfavorable alternative testing methods and analyses, simply because the results are presented only in a "draft" report that has never been disclosed to opposing counsel. Although the case law in time might yield a different result, the term "draft report" would, on its face, appear to encompass few of the litigation support tasks that typically have been entrusted to consulting experts. An attorney who seeks a thorough and candid development and assessment of alternative theories and scientific or technical methodologies to support the client's case will still rely on a consulting expert even if these proposed amendments are enacted and embraced fully by the federal courts.

COURT-APPOINTED EXPERTS

Mark S. Olson, Meghan Anzelc, Dennis Hansen, Tara Vavrosky Iversen, Archana Nath, and David Prange[1]

Court-appointed experts have long served a small but important role in federal and state courts. They have helped judges understand the scientific and technical basis of evidence to make admissibility decisions, and they have helped both judges and juries understand the relevance and weight or credibility of evidence to make merits decisions.[2] There are several types of court-appointed experts who can assist the trial court in making these admissibility and merits determinations: technical advisors, court-appointed expert witnesses, and special masters.[3] This subchapter will first address the role of court-appointed experts and how they are capable of assisting the courts. It will then discuss the nuts and bolts of Federal Rule of Evidence 706, which governs the appointment and use of court-appointed experts. The subchapter will then explore how court-appointed experts are used by courts as a practical matter, including how often they are used and the debate over the propriety of their use. The use of court-appointed experts by state courts is also briefly discussed, as well as the use of technical advisors as an alternative to court-appointed experts. This subchapter concludes with practical considerations when dealing with court-appointed experts or technical advisors.

---

1. The authors are members of the Business Litigation group at Oppenheimer Wolff & Donnelly LLP in Minneapolis, Minnesota. Mark Olson is a partner and focuses his practice on a wide variety of product liability, mass tort, and business litigation. Meghan Anzelc, Dennis Hansen, Tara Vavrosky Iversen, Archana Nath, and David Prange are associates in the Business Litigation group.

2. Sophia Cope, *Ripe for Revision: A Critique of Federal Rules of Evidence and the Use of Court-Appointed Experts*, 39 GONZ. L. REV. 163, 168 (2003–2004).

3. The role and utilization of special masters is outside the scope of this subchapter. For in-depth information about special masters, see FED. R. CIV. P. 53 and Michael Connelly & John Muir, *Special Masters, Court-Appointed Experts and Technical Advisors in Federal Court*, 76 DEF. COUNS. J. 77 (Jan. 2009).

The Role of a Court-Appointed Expert

A court-appointed expert is capable of assisting the court in at least three areas: (1) helping the judge understand the scientific and technical basis of evidence to make an admissibility decision, (2) aiding settlement, and (3) helping the trier of fact understand the relevance and weight or credibility of the evidence to make a merits decision.[4]

Assisting the Court in Its Gatekeeper Role

In 1993, in *Daubert v. Merrell Dow Pharmaceuticals, Inc.*,[5] the U.S. Supreme Court charged trial courts with the duty of acting as "gatekeepers" in determining when scientific evidence is properly admissible. The Court noted that trial courts should determine at the outset

> whether the expert is proposing to testify to (1) scientific knowledge that (2) will assist the trier of fact to understand or determine a fact in issue. This entails a preliminary assessment of whether the reasoning or methodology underlying the testimony is scientifically valid and of whether that reasoning or methodology properly can be applied to the facts in issue.[6]

Since *Daubert*, a major focus of the gatekeeper has been on the reliability of scientific and other technical and complex evidence. Although *Daubert* did list four nonexclusive factors that could be considered when evaluating scientific evidence, the Court did not provide a clear roadmap for the gatekeeper in determining whether to admit or exclude scientific evidence. It did, however, suggest several tools that a trial court could consider using in its admissibility determinations. One of the tools mentioned by the Court was Rule 706 of the Federal Rules of Evidence, which allows a court, in its discretion, to procure the assistance of an expert of its own choosing.[7] Four years later, in the second case of the *Daubert* trilogy, *General Electric Co. v. Joiner*,[8] Justice Breyer noted in his concurring opinion that as the number of cases presenting significant science-related issues had grown, judges were able to use both the Federal Rules of Evidence and the Federal Rules of Civil Procedure to find ways to assist them in dealing with difficult issues and making determinations about complicated scientific and technical evidence. Justice Breyer cited Rule 706 as one of the "Rules-authorized meth-

---

4. Cope, *supra* note 2, at 168.
5. Daubert v. Merrell Dow Pharms., Inc., 509 U.S. 579 (1993).
6. *Id.* at 592–93.
7. *Id.* at 596.
8. Gen. Elec. Co. v. Joiner, 522 U.S. 136 (1997).

ods" for accomplishing a court's task. Citing the amicus brief of the *New England Journal of Medicine*, Justice Breyer stated:

> [A] judge could better fulfill this gatekeeper function if he or she had help from scientists. Judges should be strongly encouraged to make greater use of their inherent authority . . . to appoint experts. . . . Reputable experts could be recommended to courts by established scientific organizations, such as the National Academy of Sciences or the American Association for the Advancement of Science.[9]

Encouraging Settlement

The use of a court-appointed expert may also encourage parties to settle before trial. An expert who works with the parties and their experts can provide clarity about the issues on which the parties disagree, thereby reducing the number of issues in dispute.[10] In addition, the expert may cause attorneys to reevaluate and change their extreme positions in the case, making it easier to reach a resolution without a trial.[11]

Assisting the Trier of Fact

Court-appointed experts can assist the trier of fact in understanding technical issues necessary to reach a well-informed decision in a complicated case.[12] Moreover, by filling in the gaps that the parties and their experts may leave, the expert can help the trier of fact in understanding the relevance, weight, and credibility of the evidence.[13] The expert can also provide an independent and neutral opinion, which could lessen the polarization of the parties' theories that the parties' experts sometimes create, or could allow for a more thorough presentation of the issues if either or both sides of the litigation fail to offer expert testimony.[14]

---

9. *Id.* at 149–50.

10. Karen Buther Reisinger, *Court-Appointed Expert Panels: A Comparison of Two Models*, 32 IND. L. REV. 225, 234 (1998).

11. *Id.*; JOE S. CECIL & THOMAS E. WILLGING, COURT-APPOINTED EXPERTS: DEFINING THE ROLE OF EXPERTS APPOINTED UNDER FEDERAL RULE OF EVIDENCE 706 538 (Federal Judicial Ct. 1993), *available at* http://www.fjc.gov/public/pdf.nsf/lookup/13.expert.pdf/$File/13.expert.pdf.

12. CECIL & WILLGING, *supra* note 11.

13. Buther Reisinger, *supra* note 10, at 234; Cope, *supra* note 2, at 177.

14. CECIL & WILLGING, *supra* note 11; Buther Reisinger, *supra* note 10, at 234; Cope, *supra* note 2, at 177.

Procedure for Appointing a Court-Appointed Expert

Federal Rule of Evidence 706 governs the appointment of a court-appointed expert. The rule was adopted in 1975, although a number of federal courts recognized the power before the Federal Rules of Evidence were enacted.[15] The mechanics and logistics of appointing an expert under Rule 706 are straightforward but, in most cases, the devil is in the details.

The Appointment Process

Under the rule, an expert may be appointed either by motion of a party or by the court on its own motion.[16] The court has discretion to request nomi-nations from the parties[17] or may simply select an expert of its own choos-ing.[18] Some courts have appointed law professors to aid the court in selecting a panel of knowledgeable and neutral experts.[19] If the parties cannot agree on an expert, the court may appoint the expert.[20]

A Federal Judicial Center study found that in a number of instances, judges tended to rely on their personal networks to locate or select a particular expert.[21] In addition to a judge's personal network, there are independent sources for potential experts. The American Association for the Advancement of Science established the Court Appointed Scientific Experts (CASE) pro-gram, which has attempted to match interested judges with scientific experts.[22]

---

15. *See Ex parte* Peterson, 253 U.S. 300 (1920); Scott v. Spanger Bros., Inc., 298 F.2d 928 (2d Cir. 1962). In 1946, Rule 28 of the Federal Rules of Criminal Procedure was adopted. It permitted a trial court to appoint an impartial expert in a criminal trial. In the civil context, courts before 1975 had the inherent authority to appoint an expert under appropriate cir-cumstances to aid the court in a just resolution of the case. *See, e.g.,* Danville Tobacco Ass'n v. Bryant-Buekner Assocs., Inc., 333 F.2d 202 (4th Cir. 1964) (appointing tobacco marketing expert in antitrust case); *Scott,* 298 F.2d 928 (appointing medical expert in personal injury case).

16. Fed. R. Evid. 706(a).

17. Gates v. United States, 707 F.2d 1141 (10th Cir. 1983) (directing the parties to sug-gest potential members for a panel of experts to be appointed).

18. *Id.; see* Students of Cal. Sch. for the Blind v. Honig, 736 P.2d 538 (9th Cir. 1984).

19. *See, e.g., In re* Joint E. and S. Dist. Asbestos Litig., 151 F.R.D. 540 (S.D.N.Y. 1993).

20. *Gates,* 707 F.2d 1141.

21. Cecil & Willging, *supra* note 11, at 31.

22. The Private Adjudication Center at Duke University School of Law maintained a Registry of Independent Scientific and Technical Advisors, but the center closed in 2003. For a discussion of the use of the Duke registry in *Soldo v. Sandoz Pharmaceuticals Corp.,* 244 F. Supp. 2d 434 (W.D. Pa. 2003), see Joe S. Cecil, *Construing Science in the Quest for 'Ipse Dixit': A Comment on Sanders and Cohen,* 33 Seton Hall L. Rev. 967 (2003).

Other sources of experts include universities and professional organizations.[23]

Communications with the Expert

Rule 706 requires the expert to be informed of his duties either in writing or at a conference in which the parties have an opportunity to participate.[24] In the event the court chooses to provide the requisite notice with a written order, the order should address topics such as the following:

1. The expert's responsibilities;
2. How the expert will communicate with the court and the parties;
3. The expert's compensation;
4. Communication of the expert's findings; and
5. Whether the expert will give deposition testimony, be required to attend the trial, and/or give trial testimony.[25]

The issue of ex parte communications between a party or the parties and the expert, or between the expert and the court, poses serious issues for the integrity of the process. Some courts have expressly prohibited such contact by the parties.[26] In *Edgar v. K.L.*,[27] a judge's ex parte meeting with a panel of court-appointed experts was grounds for disqualification of the judge. Ex parte communications with the expert should be discouraged, if not prohibited. In addition, every effort should be made to make as full and complete a record as possible of any communications among the court, the parties, and the expert.

The Expert's Findings

The expert must advise the parties of his findings. Courts have used a variety of means to facilitate this requirement. In some instances, the expert

---

23. American Bar Ass'n, Civil Trial Practice Standards 11(a)(ii) 29 (1988); William W. Schwarzer & Joe S. Cecil, Management of Expert Evidence in Moore's Federal Practice: Reference Manual on Scientific Evidence 39 (2d ed. 2000).
24. Fed. R. Evid. 706(a).
25. See Connelly & Muir, *supra* note 3, at 88.
26. See, e.g., Lessona Corp. v. Varta Batteries, Inc., 522 F. Supp. 1304, 1312 n.18 (C.D.N.Y. 1981) (providing in the court's order that all communication with the court expert was to be done through the court and all materials sent by the court to the expert were to be placed in the court's file).
27. Edgar v. K.L., 93 F.3d 245 (7th Cir. 1996).

has submitted a comprehensive written report.[28] In other cases, courts, in addition to having the expert prepare written reports, have permitted meetings with counsel to allow counsel to ask the expert questions and have also held hearings in which the experts testified and were subject to cross-examination.[29]

The Expert's Testimony

Before trial, a party may depose a court-appointed expert in a civil case.[30] In a criminal case, the issue of the interrelationship between Rule 706 and other statutes or rules regarding court-appointed experts is unclear.[31]

At trial, the expert may be called to testify by any party or the court. The parties may cross-examine the expert at any time, regardless of which party called the expert to testify.[32]

The Expert's Compensation

Under Rule 706(b), experts are entitled to reasonable compensation in whatever amount the court may permit. In civil cases, the parties may be responsible for payment of the expert's compensation in a proportion as the court determines and when the court directs.[33] Court-appointed expert fees are taxable as costs by the prevailing party,[34] although such taxation is within the discretion of the court.[35] In exercising that discretion, the court

---

28. *See, e.g.,* Computer Assocs. Int'l, Inc. v. Altai, Inc., 982 F.2d 693 (2d Cir. 1992); DeAngelis v. A. Tarricone, Inc., 151 F.R.D. 245 (C.D.N.Y. 1993).

29. *See, e.g., In re Joint Asbestos Litig.,* 151 F.R.D. 540.

30. FED. R. EVID. 706(a). But see *In re* Joint E. and S. Dist. Asbestos Litig., 982 F.2d 721 (2d Cir. 1992), in which the court prohibited depositions of court-appointed experts because it had provided extensive opportunities to the parties to learn about the experts' opinions through other means and because it thought that permitting depositions would undermine the Rule 706 process.

31. *See* JACK B. WEINSTEIN & MARGARET A. BERGER, 4 WEINSTEIN'S FEDERAL EVIDENCE § 706.06[4] (2d ed. 2001).

32. FED. R. EVID. 706(a).

33. FED. R. EVID. 706(b).

34. *Id.; see also* 28 U.S.C. § 1920(6).

35. *See* Con-Way Transp. Servs., Inc. v. Auto Sports Unlimited, Inc., No. 1:04-cv-570, 2008 WL 294596, at *2–3 (W.D. Mich. Jan 31, 2008) (declining to tax court-appointed expert witness fees as costs because both parties benefited from the court-appointed expert and did not expend money in retaining experts themselves); Assocs. Int'l, Inc. v. Altai, Inc., 775 F. Supp. 544, 573 (court not taxing expert witness fees to losing party), *vacated in part on other grounds,* 982 F.2d 693 (2d Cir. 1992).

may consider such factors as the nature of the case, the status of the parties, the need for the expert, and other circumstances.[36]

Disclosure of Court-Appointed Status to the Jury

Rule 706(c) gives the court discretion as to whether it will disclose to the jury the fact that the expert who testifies was appointed by the court.[37] One commentator noted that this provision was the most controversial provision during the rulemaking process and "[o]pponents of disclosure argued that the opinion of a court's expert would be decisive in any case in which it was offered because such an expert acquires from the court the mantle of both authority and impartiality."[38] The Federal Judicial Center study found that the trial judge commonly discloses the appointment to the jury.[39] One possible way to lessen the impact of any potential undue weight that a jury might give to a court-appointed expert's testimony would be to request a specific jury instruction dealing with the issue.[40]

Court-Appointed Experts in Practice

Courts have used court-appointed experts in a wide range and variety of cases and issues including product liability cases,[41] patent cases,[42] trademark cases,[43]

---

36. Aiello v. Town of Brookhaven, 149 F. Supp. 2d 11, 14–15 (E.D.N.Y. 2001) (citing B. WEINSTEIN & BERGER, *supra* note 31, § 706.06[4]).

37. FED. R. EVID. 706(c).

38. *See* 29 CHARLES ALAN WRIGHT & ARTHUR R. MILLER, FEDERAL PRACTICE AND PROCEDURE § 6305, at 481.

39. CECIL & WILLGING, *supra* note 11, at 49.

40. In *Monolothic Power Systems, Inc. v. O2 Micro International Ltd.*, 558 F.3d 1341, 1348 (Fed. Cir. 2009), the Federal Circuit affirmed the trial court's use of the following jury instruction:

> You should not give any greater weight to [the court appointed expert's] opinion testimony than to the testimony of any other witness simply because the court ordered the parties to retain an independent witness. In evaluating his opinion, you should carefully assess the nature of and basis for [the court appointed expert's] opinion just as you would do with any other witness' opinion.

41. *See, e.g.*, Nemir v. Mitsubishi Motors Corp., 381 F.3d 540 (6th Cir. 2004).

42. *See, e.g., Monolithic Power Sys.*, 558 F.3d 1341; NEC Corp. v. Hyundai Elects. Indus. Co., 30 F. Supp. 2d 546 (E.D. Va. 1998).

43. *See, e.g.*, Tillery v. Leonard & Sciolla, LLP, 521 F. Supp. 2d 346 (E.D. Pa. 2007).

copyright cases,[44] toxic tort cases,[45] DNA issues,[46] the interpretation and application of foreign law,[47] computer forensic investigation relating to discovery abuse and spoliation issues,[48] medical issues,[49] damage calculations,[50] mental capacity determinations,[51] and bankruptcy administration.[52]

An example of the use of formal Rule 706 court-appointed experts can be found in *In re Silicone Gel Breast Implants Product Liability Litigation.*[53] Multi-District Litigation ("MDL") judge, Sam C. Pointer, appointed a national science panel under Rule 706 to review the evidence related to issues of general causation. As a first step, Judge Pointer asked six people to serve on a panel to assist in the selection of neutral experts in each of four areas of expertise—toxicology, immunology, epidemiology, and rheumatology. The selection panel was also charged with assisting the national science panel in the preparation of reports and preparation of testimony.

After the experts were appointed, the court and the parties conferred regarding the experts' duties and topics to be addressed. In addition to prohibiting ex parte contact with any of the panel experts, Judge Pointer also appointed special counsel for the panel members. The panel heard three days of testimony from both sides' experts and later released a report in December 1998. The plaintiffs requested written discovery and depositions of the experts regarding their conclusion that there was no link between silicone breast implants and autoimmune disease and other claimed medical conditions. The court permitted depositions to proceed and further

---

44. *See, e.g.,* Harbor Software, Inc. v. Applied Sys., Inc., 952 F. Supp. 1042 (S.D.N.Y. 1996); *Computer Assocs.,* 982 F.2d 693.

45. *See, e.g.,* Renaud v. Martin Marietta Corp., 749 F. Supp. 1545 (D. Colo. 1990), *aff'd,* 972 F.2d 304 (10th Cir. 1992).

46. *See, e.g.,* United States v. Bonds, 12 F.3d 540 (6th Cir. 1993).

47. *See, e.g.,* Servo Kinetics, Inc. v. Tokyo Precision Instruments Co., 475 F.3d 783 (6th Cir. 2007) (appointing expert on Japanese law); Carbotrade S.P.A. v. Bureau Veritas, No. 92 Civ. 1459 (JGK), 1998 WL 397847 (S.D.N.Y. July 16, 1998) (appointing expert on Greek law).

48. *See, e.g.,* Gutman v. Klein, No. 03-1570, 2008 WL 4682208 (E.D.N.Y. Oct. 15, 2008) (appointing expert to analyze computer hardware relating to spoliation issues); Cerruti 181 S.A. v. Cerruti, Inc., 169 F.R.D. 573 (S.D.N.Y. 1996) (appointing expert to investigate unreliable data provided by party in discovery).

49. *See, e.g., In re* Breast Implant Cases, 942 F. Supp. 958 (S.D.N.Y. 1996); *see also* Walker v. Am. Home Shield Long Term Disability Plan, 180 F.3d 1065 (9th Cir. 1999); DeAngelis v. A. Tarricone, Inc., 151 F.R.D. 245 (S.D.N.Y. 1993).

50. *See, e.g.,* Eastern Air Lines Inc. v. McDonnell Douglas Corp., 532 F.2d 957 (2d Cir. 1976).

51. *See, e.g.,* United States v. Green, 544 F.2d 138 (3d Cir. 1976).

52. *See, e.g., In re Joint Asbestos Litig.,* 982 F.2d 721.

53. *In re* Silicon Gel Breast Implants Prod. Liab. Litig., 996 F. Supp. 1110 (N.D. Ala. 1997).

indicated that the videotaped depositions could be used in other breast implant cases.[54]

Frequency of Use of Court-Appointed Experts

The Advisory Committee's note to Rule 706 suggests that "experience indicates that actual appointment [of experts] is a relatively infrequent occurrence."[55] However, the Advisory Committee also noted that the trend is increasingly to provide for their use. In the post-*Daubert* world, several commentators have forecasted that there would be an increase in the use of court-appointed experts.[56] There is very little data available regarding courts' use of court-appointed experts, but what data exists suggests a gradual trend of increased use.

The 1993 Federal Judicial Center study about court-appointed experts was conducted by Joe S. Cecil and Thomas E. Willging.[57] One of the study's findings supported the notion suggested by the Advisory Committee's note that the rule was to be used sparingly. Eighty percent of the federal judges surveyed had never appointed a Rule 706 expert.[58] Of the 20 percent who had used the rule, half of them had only done so on one occasion.[59]

The two primary reasons given by the judges who invoked Rule 706 for appointing experts were to aid the court in its decision making and to aid in the settlement process.[60] The study found that even though many judges had not used the process, they were still open and receptive to it.[61] Among the reasons given by the judges for not appointing experts were (1) infrequency

---

54. For a more detailed and thorough discussion of the MDL experience, see Buther Reisinger, *supra* note 10, at 244–52, and Laural L. Hooper et al., *Assessing Causation in Breast Implant Litigation: The Role of Science Panels*, 64 LAW & CONTEMP. PROBS. 139, 140 n.3 (2001).

55. FED. R. EVID. 706, Advisory Committee's note.

56. *See* Michal J. Saks et al., *Admissibility of Scientific Evidence*, SJ081 ALI-ABA 1, 90 (Am. Law Inst. 2004) ("[T]he chorus of voices calling for judges to exercise Rule 706 has grown nearly deafening."); Timothy Hillman, *Using Court Appointed Experts*, 36 NEW ENG. L. REV. 587, 587 (2002) (noting as to the use of Rule 706, "[f]rankly, it's coming, and it's going to happen sooner than later").

57. CECIL & WILLGING, *supra* note 11.

58. *Id.* at 7.

59. *Id.* at 8.

60. *Id.* at 12–18.

61. *Id.* at 11–12 (finding that 87 percent of responding judges indicated that court-appointed experts are likely to be helpful in at least some cases).

of cases requiring extraordinary assistance, (2) respect for the adversarial system, (3) difficulty identifying an expert suitable for appointment, (4) difficulty securing compensation for an expert, (5) lack of early recognition that appointment is needed, and (6) lack of awareness of the procedure.[62]

In a similar 1998-1999 survey, 73.9 percent of federal judges reported that they would never use Rule 706 to appoint an expert, and 16.2 percent would only appoint an expert in cases with particularly difficult evidence.[63] A 1999–2000 study concluded that court-appointed experts "have been considered at a rate of approximately 2.7 cases per 10,000 in recent years (.027%)."[64]

A survey of the combination of state and federal judges and administrative officials involved in water disputes published in 2007 suggests that a greater percentage of judges are appointing experts now than in the past.[65] Of the judges surveyed who had the authority to appoint expert witnesses, 32 percent had appointed an expert within the previous five years.[66] However, because the survey did not distinguish between state and federal judges, it is difficult to determine whether the survey truly demonstrates an increase in the use of court-appointed experts in federal court from 1999 to 2007.[67]

Although it is unclear whether the actual use of court-appointed experts is on the rise, it is apparent that courts are discussing the topic with increasing frequency. A 2001 Westlaw search for federal court references to "court-appointed expert" in each year from 1983 to 2001 demonstrated that from 1983 to 1993 the number of citations to that term was between 17 to 43 times per year.[68] From 1994 to 2000, the range of citations was 48 to 72 times per

---

62. *Id.* at 18–23.

63. Shirley A. Donnin, *Federal and State Trial Judges on the Proffer and Presentation of Expert Evidence*, 28 JUST. SYS. J. 1, 8 (2007).

64. THOMAS E. WILLGING, SPECIAL MASTERS INCIDENCE AND ACTIVITY: REPORT TO THE JUDICIAL CONFERENCES' ADVISORY COMMITTEE ON CIVIL RULES AND ITS SUBCOMMITTEE ON SPECIAL MASTERS (Federal Judicial Center, 2000), http://www.fjc.gov/public/pdf.nsf/lookup/SpecMast.pdf/$file/SpecMast.pdf.

65. Mariam J. Masid, *Hydrology and the Courts: The Role of Expert Witnesses—A Study on Potential Reforms*, 11 U. DENV. WATER L. REV. 1, 38 (2007).

66. *Id.* Also of note, the majority of judges responding to the survey indicated that they are in favor of "reforms that would promote more frequent use of court-appointed expert witnesses." *Id.* at 43.

67. *See id.* State court judges appear to be more likely to appoint experts than federal judges. The 1998–1999 study posed the same question to state court judges; of the responding judges, 57 percent reported that they would never appoint an expert. Donnin, *supra* note 63, at 11. However, the 1993 study did not include state court judges, so there is no data with which to compare the 1999 result.

68. *Hooper, supra* note 54, at n.3.

year, "with a gentle upward trend."[69] To update this research, from 2001 to 2004 the number of cases using the term "court-appointed expert" ranged between 53 and 92. For the years 2005 to 2008 the range was 112 to 197, with 197 and 195 cases citing the term in 2007 and 2008, respectively. This quite obvious and dramatic increase in the discussion of the subject may signal that the use of court-appointed experts has or is about to become more frequent.

Debate over Propriety of Court-Appointed Experts

At the heart of the debate about whether to use court-appointed experts rest several reasons and crucial policy issues that proponents and opponents raise. Proponents of the process argue that the appointment of an expert by the court may enhance the information available to the fact finder and also "fill in gaps" in knowledge.[70] Court-appointed experts may also be helpful in facilitating settlement of a case.[71] In addition, where the parties' advocacy is inadequate or unbalanced, expert assistance may be necessary for a rational decision on a complex subject.[72]

On the other hand, opponents of the process suggest several reasons for rejecting the use of court-appointed experts. A fear exists that the designation of a witness as appointed by the court and as "impartial" may lead the jury to believe that the expert has been "cloaked with a robe of infallibility."[73] Critics also argue that the use of a court-appointed expert interferes with the deliberative process of the jury if it follows the so-called neutral opinion.[74] In addition, the process, it is argued, interferes with party autonomy.[75] Finally, the use of court-appointed experts is likely to increase the litigation costs and could even delay the proceedings.[76]

---

69. *Id.*

70. Buther Reisinger, *supra* note 10.

71. *Id.*

72. Ellen F. Deason, *Court-Appointed Expert Witnesses: Scientific Positivism Meets Bias and Deference*, 77 Or. L. Rev. 59, 94 (1998).

73. *See, e.g.,* Elwood S. Levy, *Impartial Medical Testimony—Revisited*, 34 Temp. L.Q. 416, 424 (1961).

74. *Id.*

75. Thomas E. Willging, Court-Appointed Experts 18 (1986).

76. *See* Buther Reisinger, *supra* note 10, at 237–38 (citing Ellen Relkin, *Some Implications of Daubert and Its Potential for Misuse: Misapplication to Environmental Tort Cases and the Abuse of Rule 706(a) Court-Appointed Experts*, 15 Cardozo L. Rev. 2255, 2255 n.3 (1994)). For a discussion of trial lawyers' objections to court-appointed experts, see Andrew MacGregor Smith, *Using Impartial Experts in Valuations: A Forum Specific Approach*, 35 Wm. & Mary L. Rev. 1241, 1281 (1994).

Court-Appointed Experts in the States

Thirty-one states[77] have adopted some version of Federal Rule of Evidence 706.[78] In most of these states, the rule is similar to the federal rule.[79] There are some differences, however. For example, in Alabama, the appointment of an expert by the court may not be disclosed to the jury.[80] In Tennessee, the court may appoint an expert for a bench trial but not for a jury trial.[81]

Another distinction between the state rules and the federal rule concerns the compensation provision.[82] Some states do not have such a provision,[83] while others have slightly altered the method of compensating court-appointed experts.[84] In Arizona, the court's power to appoint an expert is subject "to the availability of funds or the agreement of the parties concerning compensation."[85]

The vast majority of state court cases discussing court-appointed experts involve family or criminal law. In the family law context, court-appointed experts are most typically tasked with property valuations[86] or psychological evaluations.[87] In criminal cases, courts often appoint experts

---

77. The following states have adopted some form of the court-appointed experts rule: Alabama, Alaska, Arizona, Arkansas, California, Colorado, Delaware, Hawaii, Idaho, Iowa, Kentucky, Louisiana, Maine, Maryland, Michigan, Minnesota, Mississippi, Nebraska, New Mexico, North Carolina, North Dakota, Pennsylvania, South Dakota, Rhode Island, Tennessee, Utah, Vermont, Washington, West Virginia, Wisconsin, and Wyoming.

78. FED. R. EVID. 706.

79. See WRIGHT & MILLER, *supra* note 38, § 6301 nn.17–20 for a comparison of various state rules to Rule 706.

80. ALA. R. EVID. 706.

81. TENN. R. EVID. 706.

82. The compensation provision in the federal rule states as follows:
> Expert witnesses so appointed are entitled to reasonable compensation in whatever sum the court may allow. The compensation thus fixed is payable from funds which may be provided by law in criminal cases and civil actions and proceedings involving just compensation under the fifth amendment. In other civil actions and proceedings the compensation shall be paid by the parties in such proportion and at such time as the court directs, and thereafter charged in like manner as other costs.

FED. R. EVID. 706(b).

83. See, e.g., ALA. R. EVID. 706; LA. CODE EVID. 706.

84. See, e.g., VT. R. EVID. 706 (providing for compensation in civil cases to be paid by the parties, instead of as provided by law where available under the federal rule).

85. ARIZ. R. EVID. 706.

86. See, e.g., Pekarek v. Pekarek, 362 N.W.2d 394, 397 (Minn. Ct. App. 1985); Swilling v. Swilling, 404 S.E.2d 837, 838 (N.C. 1991); Sharp v. Sharp, 449 S.E.2d 39, 49 (N.C. Ct. App. 1994); Tallman v. Tallman, 396 S.E.2d 453, 457 (W. Va. Ct. App. 1990).

87. See, e.g., Helfenstein v. Schutt, 735 N.W.2d 410, 416 (N.D. 2007); Smith v. Smith, No. M2005-01688-COA-R3-CV, 2008 WL 1127855, at *1 (Tenn. Ct. App. Apr. 9, 2008);

for indigent defendants as a service ancillary to the defendants' right to appointed counsel and to present a defense.[88] State courts have also appointed experts to assist with foreign law issues,[89] property disputes,[90] trust and estate issues,[91] electronic discovery issues,[92] malpractice issues,[93] and evidentiary issues arising in the employment law context.[94]

Like the federal rule,[95] state court appointments of experts are reviewed for abuse of discretion.[96] Court appointments of experts are rarely reversed, although there have been reversals in situations where the court has failed to give the parties notice and an opportunity to be heard,[97] or where the court has permitted the appointed expert to usurp judicial functions.[98]

Alternative Appointment of a Technical Advisor

In contrast to appointing an expert under Rule 706, courts sometimes employ the more flexible approach of appointing a technical advisor when they are seeking assistance or education on particularly complex issues or evidence.

Mmoe v. MJE, 841 P.2d 820, 823 (Wyo. 1992); *In re* Welfare of Angelo H., 102 P.2d 822, 824 (Wash. Ct. App. 2004).

88. *See, e.g.,* People v. Young, 234 Cal. Rptr. 819, 825 (Ct. App. 1987) (holding that while an indigent felony defendant is entitled to the appointment of an expert, the defendant has no right to the appointment of any particular expert, and the defendant first has the burden to show that the expert is reasonably necessary to ensure presentation of a defense).

89. *See, e.g.,* Saudi Basic Indus. Corp. v. Mobil Yanbu Petrochemical Co., No. Civ. A. 00C-07-161JRJ, 2003 WL 22016864, at *2 (Del. Aug. 26, 2003).

90. *See, e.g.,* Durbin v. Bonanza Corp., 716 P.2d 1124, 1127 (Colo. Ct. App. 1986); Delany v. Canning, 929 P.2d 475, 479 (Wash. Ct. App. 1997).

91. *See, e.g., In re* Estate of Cooper, 913 P.2d 393, 402 (Wash. Ct. App. 1996).

92. *See, e.g.,* Authsec, Inc. v. Roberts, No. 13-C-06-067710, 2007 WL 2691845 (Md. Cir. Ct. July 17, 2007).

93. *See, e.g.,* Warren v. Eckert Seamans Cherin & Mellott, 45 Pa. D. & C. 4th 75, 77 (Ct. Com. Pl. Apr. 25, 2000).

94. *See, e.g.,* Dufhilo v. D'Aquin, 615 So. 2d 522, 525 (La. Ct. App. 1993).

95. A federal appellate court will review a trial court's decision to appoint a Rule 706 expert for an abuse of discretion. *Walker,* 180 F.3d 1065.

96. *See, e.g., In re the Welfare of Angelo H.,* 102 P.3d at 826; *see also* Wilson v. Kemp, 644 S.W.2d 306 (Ark. Ct. App. 1982); Hager v. Commonwealth, No. 2005-CA-002592-MR, 2007 WL 542814, at *5 (Ky. Ct. App. Feb. 23, 2007); Collins v. Los Angeles County, 74 Cal. App. 3d 47 (Ct. App. 1977); Philipbar v. Philipbar, 980 P.2d 1075, 1078 (N.M. Ct. App. 1999).

97. *See In re Welfare of Angelo H.,* 102 P.2d at 827; Commonwealth v. Byer, 173 S.W.3d 247, 249–50 (Ky. Ct. App. 2005).

98. *See, e.g.,* Petroutson v. First Nat'l Bank, 631 So. 2d 1172, 174 (La. Ct. App. 1994); *see also* Adams v. CSX R.R., 904 So. 2d 13, 20–21 (La. Ct. App. 2005); SAF Constr., Inc v. AKR & Assoc., No. 241980, 2004 WL 224421, at *2 (Mich. App. Feb. 5, 2004); Cede & Co. v. Technicolor, Inc., 758 A.2d 485 (Del. 2000).

This section compares the appointment of a technical advisor to the appointment of an expert witness.

The role of a technical advisor is to organize, advise on, and help the court understand relevant scientific evidence.[99] In that role, the technical advisor is a tutor who aids the court in understanding the "jargon and theory" relevant to the technical aspects of the evidence.[100] A technical advisor is not allowed to assume the role of an expert witness by supplying new evidence.[101] As well, the technical advisor may not usurp the role of the judge by making findings of fact or conclusions of law.[102]

The court has the inherent power to appoint a technical advisor.[103] A technical advisor is not subject to the provisions of Rule 706,[104] and thus the technical advisor is not subject to the rule's deposition requirements, being called at trial, or cross-examination.[105]

In a 2000 article, Campbell and Vale provided a handy comparison chart of the different characteristics of a technical advisor appointed pursuant to the court's inherent authority and an expert appointed under Rule 706:[106]

Technical Advisor	Rule 706—Court-Appointed Expert
Useful in a *Daubert* hearing where the qualifications or methodology of a party-selected expert have been challenged.	Most useful at trial where experts have survived *Daubert* scrutiny.
No testimony by advisor, therefore has limited utility in evaluating settlements.	Useful in evaluating settlements because the expert's testimony will be needed.
If challenged expert's opinions survive *Daubert* scrutiny, the advisor's opinion cannot be used at trial.	Useful, as in the breast implant cases, where the same issue arises in other cases and objective testimony is needed for trial.

99. Ass'n of Mexican-Am. Educators v. California, 231 F.3d 572 (9th Cir. 2000).

100. Reilly v. United States, 863 F.2d 149 (1st Cir. 1988).

101. A&M Records, Inc. v. Napster, 284 F.3d 1091 (9th Cir. 2002).

102. *Id.*

103. *Reilly*, 863 F.2d 149.

104. FTC v. Enforma Natural Prod., Inc., 362 F.3d 1204 (9th Cir. 2004); *Reilly*, 863 F.2d at 155–56.

105. *Reilly*, 863 F.2d at 155–56; *see also* Hemstreet v. Burroughs Corp., 666 F. Supp. 1096, 1124 (N.D. Ill. 1987) (holding no error in not allowing deposition of technical advisor because advisor did not provide findings to the court within the meaning of Rule 706(a)), *rev'd on other grounds*, 861 F.2d 728 (Fed. Cir. 1988).

106. Natasha I. Campbell & Anthony Vale, *Encouraging More Effective Use of Court-Appointed Experts and Technical Advisors*, 67 DEF. COUNS. J. 196, 206 (Apr. 2000).

Technical Advisor	Rule 706—Court-Appointed Expert
Less time-consuming than Rule 706 expert because no depositions. May be more attractive option for highly qualified advisors.	More time-consuming and more likely to delay trial than technical advisor because depositions will be taken. The time commitment may deter highly qualified experts from serving.
Less expensive than Rule 706 expert because no depositions will be taken.	More expensive than technical advisor because depositions will be taken.
No cross-examination, therefore more risk that flaws in advisor's opinions will not be exposed to the judge.	Parties have more opportunity to expose flaws in the expert's opinion during cross-examination.

In the Silicone Gel Breast Implant Litigation, Judge Robert E. Jones of the U.S. District Court for the District of Oregon appointed a panel of technical advisors to aid him in understanding scientific issues in connection with the defendants' motion *in limine* to exclude the plaintiffs' proffered expert testimony regarding any causal link between silicone breast implants and systemic disease.[107] In fulfilling his role as a gatekeeper, Judge Jones consulted with a former medical school president who helped screen potential advisors. Judge Jones then selected four experts in the necessary fields of epidemiology, rheumatology, immunology and toxicology, and biochemistry. The advisors reviewed the parties' materials as well as observed the parties' experts' testimony in court. During a preliminary hearing to address various expert issues under Federal Rule of Evidence 104, the parties presented their experts, and the court, counsel, and the technical advisors asked questions of the testifying experts.

Judge Jones permitted the parties to submit questions to be asked of the technical advisors that were designed to guide the advisors in evaluating the testimony and in preparing their reports.[108] After the technical advisors submitted their reports, which addressed the requested questions, the parties and the court were given an opportunity to question the advisors' findings.

Other courts have used technical advisors in other capacities. In several patent cases, technical advisors have been appointed to help the court address

---

107. Hall v. Baxter Healthcare Corp., 947 F. Supp. 1387 (D. Or. 1996).

108. For a comparison of the Jones methodology and the Pointer methodology, see the useful chart in *Hooper, supra* note 54, at 145.

complex scientific and technical issues.[109] In one medical malpractice case, a technical advisor was appointed to assist in the calculation of the future earnings capacity of an infant negligently injured at birth.[110] Technical advisors have also been appointed to help courts understand unusual issues such as psychometrics[111] and computer-generated legislative redistricting plans.[112]

Because of the lack of the procedural safeguards provided in Rule 706 in the arena of technical advisors, several courts have developed a list of guidelines for the use of technical advisors. The guidelines were initially set forth by Judge Tashima in his dissent in *Association of Mexican-American Educators v. State of California*.[113] Judge Tashima suggested that courts implement the following recommendations:

1. Use a fair and open procedure for appointing a neutral technical advisor;
2. Address any allegations of bias, partiality or lack of qualifications;
3. Clearly define and limit the technical advisor's duties;
4. Make clear to the technical advisor that any advice he or she gives to the court cannot be based on any extra-record information; and
5. Make explicit, either through an expert's report or a record of ex parte communications, the nature and content of the technical advisor's advice.[114]

A number of courts have endorsed Judge Tashima's recommendations.[115]

Finally, some of the same criticisms of court-appointed experts apply equally to the use of technical advisors. For example, some critics fear that judges uncomfortable with the issues may improperly delegate decision-making authority to technical advisors.[116] In addition, there are concerns that technical advisors may not always be neutral, and they may actually interfere with the adversarial process by providing evidence directly to the judge.[117]

---

109. *See, e.g.*, Data Gen. Corp. v. IBM Corp., 93 F. Supp. 2d 89 (D. Mass. 2000); TM Patents, L.P. v. IBM Corp., 72 F. Supp. 2d 370 (S.D.N.Y. 1999); Mediacom Corp. v. Rates Tech., Inc., 4 F. Supp. 2d 17 (D. Mass. 1998).

110. *Reilly*, 863 F.2d 149.

111. Ass'n of Mexican-Am. Educators v. California, 195 F.3d 465 (9th Cir. 1999).

112. Burton v. Sheheen, 793 F. Supp. 1329 (D.S.C. 1992).

113. *Ass'n of Mexican-Am. Educators*, 231 F.3d 572.

114. *Id.* at 611–14.

115. *See, e.g., Enformac*, 362 F.3d 1204; TechSearch LLC v. Intel Corp., 286 F.3d 1360 (Fed. Cir. 2002); Conservation Law Found. v. Evans, 203 F. Supp. 2d 27 (D.D.C. 2002).

116. Note, *Improving Judicial Gatekeeping: Technical Advisors and Scientific Evidence*, 110 HARV. L. REV. 941, 953 (1997).

117. *Id.*

Practical Considerations in Dealing with a
Court-Appointed Expert or Technical Advisor

When confronted with a situation in which a court might appoint an expert or technical advisor (or in which one of the parties may want to propose such an appointment), one of the first considerations is whether such an appointment will help your position, hurt your position, or be neutral with respect to your position. The following considerations may apply to your situation, depending on the strategic or tactical value of the appointed expert/technical advisor:

1. If the case involves complex scientific or technical issues or evidence, alert the court as early as possible, including at the Rule 16 Pretrial Conference,[118] of the potential need for court-appointed experts so that the judge will not be surprised later in the case if it is necessary to have such an expert retained or appointed and so that the process of selection and appointment can begin as early as possible.
2. Request that the court issue a written order detailing the retention of a technical advisor or the appointment of an expert. Take steps to ensure that the order specifies the precise role (e.g., technical advisor, court-appointed expert) and source of authority for the appointment.[119]
3. To the extent that the court relies on the parties to suggest names of potential experts to the court, you should keep in mind several considerations to evaluate to protect your client's position, including the following:
   a. Whether the candidate has a relationship to any of the parties;
   b. The candidate's experience serving as an expert, including testimonial experience;
   c. Relevant education, training, and experience;
   d. Familiarity with the parties, businesses, industry, products, or issues in the lawsuit; and
   e. The candidate's willingness to serve as an expert and his availability.[120]
4. Take an active role in the selection process.

---

118. *See* Fed. R. Civ. P. 16.

119. In *Peterka v. Dennis*, 764 N.W.2d 829 (Minn. 2009), the Minnesota Supreme Court held that a neutral evaluator appointed by the district court to evaluate marital property in the form of business assets in a divorce proceeding met all the requirements for a Rule 706 court-appointed expert even though the court's order did not make reference to Rule 706. The court also held that Rule 706 court-appointed experts were entitled to immunity for suits performed pursuant to the appointment.

120. NEC Corp. v. Hyundai Elec. Indus. Co., Ltd., 30 F. Supp. 2d 546, 559–60 (E.D. Va. 1998).

5. Take steps to prevent ex parte communication between the expert and any party or the court.
6. Seek to have input into the expert's methodology, including what materials the expert will review and what questions will be submitted to the expert.
7. Once a report or expert findings have been issued, request the right to conduct discovery, including a deposition.
8. If an expert's conclusions are adverse to your position, request a jury instruction that attempts to minimize the impact of the expert's testimony.[121]
9. If necessary, attempt to have the court use the expert in specific phases of the case rather than lumping all of the potential expert functions into a single role. For example, try to have the court first use the expert as a tutor. Then, have the court focus the expert's work on *Daubert*-related admissibility issues. You might even consider asking the court to allow the expert to assist in settlement activities. Finally, the court can direct the expert to provide testimony to the jury that initially attempts to educate and clarify for the jury what the differences in the expert opinion are and why they exist rather than simply providing the expert's own opinions and conclusions.
10. Work to establish a budget at the outset of the case to conserve resources and set a reasonable payment-sharing plan.

The specific steps you take in a particular case depend significantly on the case-specific facts with which you are dealing. However, if you can keep the procedural safeguards set out in Rule 706 and the principles recommended by Judge Tashima in his dissent at the forefront of your analysis,[122] they should guide you in making strategic and tactical decisions.

Conclusion

With the increasing number of cases involving complex scientific and technical issues, the use of court-appointed experts and technical advisors can serve as a useful tool for a trial judge faced with fulfilling his gatekeeping function. These experts can provide important educational benefits to both a trial judge and a jury faced with complex issues. Although there are no hard and fast rules for deciding whether or when a court-appointed expert or technical advisor might be used, there are reasonable steps you can take to protect or enhance your client's position if the court decides to appoint an expert.

---

121. *See supra* note 40.
122. *See supra* notes 113–14 and accompanying text.

Appendix A: Model Agreement

The following agreement is to be used as a model, but should be modified as appropriate to reflect the parameters of the particular expert engagement.

PRIVILEGED AND CONFIDENTIAL—ATTORNEY WORK PRODUCT

Professor Eager B. Expert
University of Northern Utopia
201 North Forest Road
South Bank, Utopia 00001

Southern Missouri River Dam Litigation
Civil Action No. 12345 (N.D. Iowa)

Dear Professor Expert:

This will confirm your agreement to provide professional services to assist us as attorneys for [name of client] ("our client") in the [describe the nature of the litigation or arbitration] (the "matter").

To make sure that both you and this firm understand what we expect of each other, we have set forth the terms of your engagement as an expert in this matter to make sure that you and we both have a clear understanding of what will be required of you.

1. You confirm that we have explained to you the nature of this dispute, the relevant parties and the issues involved in it,[1] and that (a) you have no conflict of interest in providing your services to us as counsel for [name of client] and being adverse to [name(s) of opposing party(ies)], (b) you believe you have the necessary expertise, as a result of your education, training, and experience, to provide advice to us and our client and, if necessary, to testify on behalf of our client, (c) you know of no reason why you cannot provide expert advice to us and our client and, if necessary, testify on behalf of our client, and (d) you can, consistent with your other obligations, devote sufficient time and attention to this matter to assist us and our client and will not take on additional assignments that would make it difficult for you to do so.

---

1. You may want to expand on this paragraph to provide more detail about the case and how the expert's advice or opinions will bear on it, but keep in mind that this agreement may be discoverable by the opposing party.

2. In taking on this assignment, you will be an independent contractor and not an employee of this firm or the client. Any staff or other person you engage to assist you will also be independent of and not an employee of the firm or the client. Neither the firm nor the client will withhold or pay Social Security, FICA, Medicare/Medicaid, unemployment insurance, or income or other taxes on your or your staff's or assistant's behalf.

3. The trial of this matter is currently scheduled for [date]. We will notify you if the date is changed. You agree to be available during the trial for your expert testimony. We would also expect that, in addition to working with us to develop your opinion(s) and report, you would have your deposition taken. Our best estimate is that this will be sometime in the months of [describe] of [year]. You agree to be available for deposition.[2]

4. You also confirm that you have disclosed to us any relevant publications, papers, and previous engagements where you provided expert opinion, advice, and/or testimony that may relate to your advice and potential testimony in this case in order for us to conclude that there is no impediment to your doing so in this case.

5. You understand the highly sensitive and confidential nature of this engagement and that you are serving as an agent of, and are providing assistance to, this law firm, which has a professional obligation to preserve the confidences and communications of our client. You will keep confidential your retention by this firm on behalf of our client, unless and until you are identified in court papers as a testifying expert or we otherwise authorize you in writing to disclose your retention.

6. To make certain there is no misunderstanding, at no time will you communicate to any other person (1) that you are assisting us, (2) the fact that you may have arrived at certain conclusions, or (3) the substance of your conclusions, in each case unless you have our prior permission, in writing, to do so.

7. Consistent with the nature of our relationship with our client, any communications between you and us or our client will be, and will remain, privileged and confidential as attorney-work product and attorney-client communications. Any materials or information provided to you are to be used by you solely to assist you in advising us on the matters for which you have been retained. By the same token, any conclusions

---

2. This paragraph gives you and the expert a mutual understanding of the likely time frame for the case. If you do not have a trial date, you can provide some estimate of when it is likely to be tried. The same goes for the deposition.

you may reach are to be provided solely to us as counsel for our client, and to no one else.[3]

8. To ensure that your assistance to us is fully protected, any materials you may prepare are to be labeled "Attorney work-product / Attorney-client communication / Privileged and Confidential."[4]

9. You understand that any notes or work papers you may prepare in connection with your assistance to us are the property of this firm. At the conclusion of this engagement, you will return all notes and work papers prepared by you during this engagement to us unless we otherwise agree in writing.

10. If, at any time during or after your engagement, you are served with legal process or any other form of request seeking testimony, information, or documents relating to your engagement with us, you agree that you will notify us immediately, and take instructions from us as to how you will respond to that process or request.

11a. You will be compensated for the time you spend on this matter at your standard rate of $____ per hour.

OR

11b. We understand that your standard daily seminar fee is [$] and that, by taking on this engagement, you will be foregoing those fees for any time you spend working on this engagement that you would otherwise have received from seminars. We therefore agree that you will be paid a daily fee of [$] for any full days you spend on this matter, and a pro-rated hourly fee of [$] for any time you spend that takes up less than a day.

OR

11c. The trial is scheduled to begin on [date] and will be held in [city]. We anticipate having you testify on or about [date]. If the case is settled before then, or the trial date is changed, you will be paid your outstanding fees as well as your daily rate of an additional [$] to account for the fact that you would have otherwise participated in another engagement or scheduled a seminar for that date.

---

3. You want to make sure that all communications are confidential, any materials you provide the expert are to be used solely in your case, and the expert will not provide any conclusions, tentative or otherwise, to anyone but you.

4. This is self-explanatory. As noted above, this label does not necessarily mean that these materials will be protected against discovery.

12. We understand that you will use the following additional persons to assist you and their respective rates per hour are set forth next to their names:

[List, with hourly rates]

13. If you use any other person to assist you in your engagement with us, you will first obtain our permission to do so, and will also have him/her sign and provide to us a copy of this letter agreement before he/she renders any assistance to you and, through you, to us.

14. One or more protective orders have been entered by the court or courts that govern the use of confidential or proprietary information in this case. A copy of each is attached to this letter agreement. Please read them and sign the certification at the end and return a copy to me. Also please have any of your staff who will be involved in your work read the protective orders and sign a copy of the certification and return it to me. If any additional staff are engaged in this matter, please also have them sign and return to me a copy of their certification.

15. Any statements for your professional services should be sent directly to me at the address above with sufficient time and expense descriptions so we and the client will have a clear picture of your activities. Please send us your statements on a monthly basis. If you have any additional out-of-pocket expenses, please provide us with a list of them, and receipts or invoices for any individual item in excess of $75. You will not incur any given expense in excess of [$] without our advance agreement. You understand that we will submit your statements to [name of client] and agree that you will be paid when we receive payment from [name of client] for these statements.

16. You will keep confidential all information obtained, or analyses developed, in connection with this litigation or any related litigations with respect to which we may seek your advice and you will use this confidential information solely in connection with your engagement by us on behalf of our client.[5]

17. You will preserve any written materials, including materials stored electronically and any e-mails, generated or received by you in connection with this engagement, because these materials are potentially discoverable in litigation. It is important that we know what documents you have received in connection with your serving as an

---

5. This ensures that the expert does not use material developed in your case for other assignments she may have. Some experts, particularly ones that testify regularly, may want to negotiate this provision.

expert witness. If you review any other materials, we also need to keep a record of them. We would therefore request that you please keep all documents that you receive or review in this matter as part of your engagement in one or more segregated files so we can keep track of them. Also please keep any materials you may prepare, including drafts. Under no circumstances are you to destroy any written materials or delete from your electronic files any of this information.

18. If we later designate you as a testifying expert, we would expect that you will provide a written report containing your opinion or opinions. We would also expect that that report would include all the information required by Federal Rule of Civil Procedure 26(a)(2)(B) regarding experts. You agree that you are familiar with that rule and have the necessary information and materials to be able to comply with its requirements.[6]

19. If we later designate you as a testifying expert, all documents you create, review, or receive, including any drafts or notes you have prepared prior to preparing your report, may be discoverable by the other side. At no time should you destroy any document that you have created or considered in arriving at any of your conclusions.[7]

20. You should keep any materials we send you, as well as all communications between us, strictly confidential. All materials that we supply to you, as well as your reports and work product, will remain our or our client's property and may not be disclosed without our or our client's consent.[8]

21. You agree that you will not in the future consult for, or represent, any other person or entity with an interest adverse to our client's interests

---

6. As noted above, FED. R. CIV. P. 26(a)(2)(B)(iv) and (v) require an expert's report to include "(iv) the witness's qualifications, including a list of all publications authored in the previous 10 years," and "(v) a list of all other cases in which, during the previous 4 years, the witness testified as an expert at trial or by deposition." Many state court rules contain the same or similar provisions. This provision is designed to make sure the expert understands these requirements and that she has maintained the necessary file of information to comply with them.

7. This provision underscores the importance of the expert retaining everything she creates, reviews, or receives during the assignment to avoid a charge of expert spoliation.

8. Because, at least under the current version of FED. R. CIV. P. 26(a)(2)(B)(ii), everything an expert looks at is discoverable, you should not send the expert any material, including your own work product, that you do not want the other side to obtain. You should nevertheless emphasize to the expert that everything you give him is presumptively confidential and may not be disclosed without your and the client's consent.

in or concerning the pending litigation, or the events or occurrences out of which the pending litigation arises.[9]

22. It is specifically understood that, because you may become a testifying expert, all documents you create may become discoverable, including drafts and notes prepared prior to the time that your opinion or report is finalized. In our experience, opposing counsel who obtain these documents in discovery often seek to use them in an unfair and misleading way, for example, to suggest that a change from an earlier draft to a later version has some sinister explanation. This is particularly unfair because you will be learning the case over time, and you may not know all relevant information prior to the time that you finalize your opinion and report. The preparation of draft opinions and reports is also expensive and should not be undertaken prematurely. Therefore, you agree that:

(a) You will not prepare any draft opinion or report unless we have specifically discussed this with you in advance and obtained our consent (regardless of whether the draft is for internal purposes or to share with others).

(b) You will not share any draft opinion or report, or any notes, with any other person without our consent.

(c) Every draft opinion or report will bear the following legend: "THIS IS A PRELIMINARY DRAFT. IT HAS BEEN PREPARED BASED ON PRELIMINARY INFORMATION AND ON ASSUMPTIONS. NO ONE MAY RELY ON THIS DRAFT. IT IS SUBJECT TO CHANGE AS ADDITIONAL INFORMATION BECOMES AVAILABLE OR IS CLARIFIED."

(d) All your notebooks or individual pages of notes will bear the following legend: "THESE NOTES ARE INCOMPLETE AND HAVE BEEN PREPARED FOR PERSONAL USE ONLY. NO ONE MAY RELY ON THEM FOR ANY PURPOSE. ALL VIEWS ARE SUBJECT TO CHANGE AS ADDITIONAL INFORMATION BECOMES AVAILABLE OR IS CLARIFIED."[10]

23. You understand that your obligation to maintain the confidentiality of your engagement—and any conclusions you may reach as well as any

---

9. You and the client do not want the expert to use information or expertise she may have obtained on behalf of your client in a future case against your client. It would also ordinarily be improper for the expert to be retained by someone else to provide advice regarding the very occurrences that are involved in your case. Some professional experts may want to negotiate the language and scope of this restriction.

10. The text of this paragraph, as well as selected other material, is taken from an article by Gregory P. Joseph, *Engaging Experts*, NATIONAL LAW JOURNAL, Apr. 18, 2005, at 12.

other matters communicated to you as our agent in a privileged setting—will continue after your engagement has been concluded.

24. You also understand that, if a protective order has been entered in the case, you (and your staff) are under an obligation to continue to comply with that order and not divulge or use any protected information you may have received as a result of that order for an indefinite period of time even after the case is over. If you have received any information or materials that you are required to return or destroy, you will do so and confirm to us in writing that you have done so.

Would you please countersign this letter-agreement below and return a copy to me.

We do want to thank you in advance for agreeing to assist [name of client] and us in this important litigation. We look forward to working with you.

Sincerely,
John Q. Lawyer

I have read the preceding letter-agreement and any attachments to it, I have had its meaning and effect explained to me, I understand its terms, and I agree to be bound by the restrictions set forth in it.

Dated: _____

_____
Eager B. Expert

CHAPTER 2

Communicating with Experts

FIRST MEETING WITH THE EXPERT

Ben J. Scott[1]

The first meeting with your expert witness is an important part of selecting and preparing an expert. Starting your relationship with the expert on the right foot will pay dividends over the life of the case, and paying close attention to your first impressions of the expert will give you valuable insight into the way in which the expert will appear to the jury. This subchapter contains eight guidelines to consider in preparing for and attending your first meeting with an expert witness.

Review Your Research on the Expert

It is in your and your client's best interests to identify any red flags or potential problems with an expert as early in the preparation process as possible. In the real world, there are invariably issues that you cannot predict that you are forced to deal with late in the game, but you should put early effort into identifying some of the more predictable pitfalls. Even an ideal expert will have certain vulnerabilities to address during your preparation.

As discussed previously in this book,[2] researching your potential experts before deciding with whom you want to meet is a vital step in the pro-

---

1. Ben J. Scott is a member of the litigation department of FedEx Express in Memphis, Tennessee. He has experience in employment litigation, commercial litigation, health care, and product liability.
2. *See supra* "Searching for an Expert Witness" in chapter 1.

cess, but the value of that research outlasts the selection process. Your initial research is precisely what your adversary will have in hand when preparing to depose or cross-examine your expert witness, so it is a valuable source of preparation material. Before meeting with your expert for the first time, review that information again. Guided, at least initially, by publicly available information on your expert, your adversary will have two goals in mind: (1) how to disqualify your expert, and (2) how to discredit your expert. Therefore, from the very start, you should work against your opponent's success on either point. If there are questions about the expert's expertise that may make him vulnerable to a *Daubert* or *Frye* challenge down the road, not only do you want to consider that from the very start, but you also want to strategically address that challenge throughout your work with the expert. Likewise, if an expert has a history of work, publications, or testimony that pose a possible credibility problem with the jury, you will want to know about and strategically address those points from the very start with your expert.

In addition, if you have not done so already during the selection process, you should speak with other lawyers about their experience with a specific expert. In some fields, experts are "frequent flyers" and are known quantities to certain members of the bar in particular specialties. For experts in more esoteric subject matter, you may need to call a lawyer across the country instead of down the street, but that effort can pay off—either in recognizing a problem early or in building your and your client's confidence that you have the right person for the job. Other lawyers may be able to give you a perspective on whether the expert is easy to work with, makes a compelling witness, and complies with deadlines. You may also learn helpful hints from previous cases as to how to work most effectively with the expert, such as whether the expert barely met the court's standard for an expert or whether there was no legitimate challenge to the witness's expertise. Information like this helps you to know where you will need to concentrate your time with the expert witness in your first and future meetings.

Call the First Meeting an Interview

In some cases, you may want to meet with many experts before picking one or several from the group. Often, in smaller matters, you will be fairly certain that you have zeroed in on the right witness before any face-to-face meeting. Either way, it is useful to meet with an expert witness as the first step in the process and to call that meeting an interview. Thus, do not formally retain the expert or send case materials in advance of this first meeting. Simply meet with the expert for an introductory review of his expertise and litigation experience and to discuss the basic facts of the case.[3]

There are several items to cover when you meet with an expert in the first interview, including the expert's fee, conflicts, the role of the expert, preferences for communication and file management, deadlines, and the proper means of communication between counsel and expert. We shall look at these areas in more detail below.

Fees

Confirm what the expert witness charges. Some witnesses charge a flat fee while others charge by the hour. Many experts charge different rates for file review, deposition testimony, and trial testimony. If the case will require the expert to travel for a site inspection, deposition, or trial attendance, be sure to address this early. When travel is involved, some experts who otherwise charge by the hour may charge by the day or simply assess a flat fee. Depending on how often the individual serves as an expert witness, there may be a well-honed fee structure, or the witness may have to come up with a fee structure for your case. While in the rare case money is no object, at other times, your client may be willing to pay only a certain amount for an expert to be involved in the case. Therefore, being able to predict the cost of retaining the expert is paramount and requires that you address issues of compensation on the front end to ensure smooth sailing throughout the life of the case. With regard to travel, some experts—as leading authorities in their fields—are exceptionally busy people. Arranging a necessary trip can be a daunting logistical undertaking. Thus, discussing travel requirements early will serve you well.

Potential Conflicts

Before the first meeting, provide the expert with case information and the identities of all parties and all law firms involved so that the expert can determine if any conflict exists. At the first meeting, confirm with the expert that he has examined the identity of each party and that no conflicts exist that prevent him from taking on the case. If there are any potential conflicts, catching them early is imperative. Sometimes the expert may have some level

---

3. This is, of course, a matter of preference. Depending on the case, your client's wishes, and scheduling concerns, you may elect to send the materials to the witness before the first meeting. This is certainly acceptable practice provided that you have a confidentiality agreement before providing the materials.

of knowledge about or acquaintance with a party that does not rise to the level of a formal conflict but may nonetheless cause some concern. For instance, an expert may not be comfortable with the potential effect of his testimony on one of the parties in the case. Alternatively, you may be concerned that the expert's relationships or familiarity with a party—though not a formal conflict—threaten to cause your expert to appear biased. Discuss any such matters with the expert and confirm that he feels comfortable in offering an objective opinion despite some familiarity with a party to the suit.

Willingness to Testify

This may sound unnecessary, but it is vitally important to ensure that an expert witness understands that he will be required to form an opinion, testify to that opinion under oath at a deposition and at trial, and withstand adversarial cross-examination from the other side's lawyer. You do not want your expert witness, on whom your client's case depends, to get cold feet about testifying on the eve of trial. Even some experienced experts may have only rarely—or never—testified from the stand during a trial and have a preference merely to review files and issue reports in cases where testimony is unlikely. It is best to discuss this issue—if only briefly—with the expert in frank terms and confirm that he is willing to testify under oath in a courtroom and face cross-examination from an adversarial lawyer just like he has seen on television. In some cases, you may just need an opinion from an expert to support a motion early in the life of the case, and you will have an opportunity to find a testifying expert at a later time. Each case dictates its own strategy, but always investigate and confirm the willingness of an expert whom you may need or want to testify to do so.

Communication and Note Taking

The first meeting is a good time to discuss whatever communication and documentation ground rules your strategy and the discovery implications of a given case dictate. You should explain the concept of discoverability to a witness who is not already familiar with it and instruct the expert as to what should or should not be communicated in e-mails or written correspondence, whether the expert should refrain from making written notes during review of the file, and whether the expert will be required to produce any draft reports.

Under the rules in many jurisdictions, any written correspondence between a lawyer and an expert is discoverable and must be produced to the other side. In situations where no agreement exists between the parties and the court to disallow such discovery, every e-mail, letter, and exchanged draft of a report between a lawyer and an expert is discoverable, will be read by the other side, asked about during a deposition, and—if admissible—discussed at trial. An expert's entire file is also typically discoverable. Thus, if your expert takes notes as he reviews the file or highlights sections of deposition transcripts, that, too, may be discoverable and used during a deposition and at trial. Life will be easier for you and your expert if you keep unnecessary documentation to a minimum.

Proposed Amendments to Federal Rule of Civil Procedure 26 expand the work product protection of certain communications—oral or written—between counsel and expert witnesses, including drafts of expert reports and communications between counsel and the expert regarding compensation. It is imperative that you know which rules apply to your case and that you instruct your expert witness accordingly. Subsequent sections of this subchapter offer a detailed analysis of these considerations.[4]

Setting these ground rules can avoid serious problems in the future with the expert's personal notes or confidential information being turned over to the other side. Having an expert produce a stack of handwritten notes that you wish did not exist to opposing counsel during a discovery deposition is not a good thing. At other times, you may not be particularly concerned about the other side having access to certain notes or correspondence from your expert. Whatever the situation, the first meeting can help you chart the course you want and ensure that your expert is fully informed as to your preferences.

Timing

Deadlines are ubiquitous in trial practice and some of the more troublesome deadlines can be those for disclosure of expert opinions and for making your experts available for deposition. Sometimes, expert testimony is optional, but in other cases, the lack of expert testimony can be fatal to the case. In medical malpractice cases, for example, expert testimony is typically a required part of each side's case in chief. Without an expert, a party loses the case as a matter of law. Having an expert disqualified for failing to meet deadlines can be quite a disappointment, so do your best to ensure that the expert will work with you to meet deadlines. While scheduling conflicts can never be entirely avoided, discuss the expert's schedule and flexibility to get a feel for whether this is an expert willing and able to do what needs to be done in a timely fashion. At the very least, you and your client will have early notice that scheduling will be a sensitive issue that needs to be handled diligently and far in advance.

---

4. *See* "Communicating with the Expert" *infra*.

Future Communication

Make sure your expert knows how to get in touch with you and—even more importantly—make sure you know how to get in touch with your expert. Some experts may handle their own affairs while others may have a specific employee or assistant who handles the expert's legal cases. To prevent headaches down the line should it become imperative to get in touch with your expert on short notice, you should obtain your expert's cellular phone number and the contact information of your expert's personal assistant.

Vet Your Expert

At this first meeting with the expert—the interview—discuss the expert's credentials and background with the goal of making sure all is in good order and to satisfy yourself that there are no skeletons in the closet. Although you have already vetted your expert during the selection process,[5] it is imperative that you verify your findings during the initial interview with the expert.

This can sometimes be a sensitive exercise with an expert. One of the easiest and most effective ways to structure the conversation is simply to say something to the effect of "When you give your deposition in this case, the lawyer for the other side is going to ask you a series of fairly detailed questions about your qualifications and background, so what I would like to do is go ahead and ask you those questions myself. Remember that you will be under oath and required to answer these questions truthfully. And, of course, none of this is being asked to embarrass or criticize you, it's just important to go through the truthful answers to all of these questions. Is that agreeable?"

With that, commence questioning the expert about his credentials and background. Begin with questions about the expert's curriculum vitae (CV). The CV is worth a fair amount of time because it is a representation by the expert that will be provided to the other side. You must do your best to ensure that the expert—even unintentionally—does not set any traps for himself with a less than perfectly accurate CV. Some areas to address include the following:

- Confirm each educational degree listed on the expert's CV and the date of each;
- Confirm all board certifications listed on the CV, including the current status of each;
- Confirm awards and distinctions listed on the CV; and
- Confirm the status of any current jobs, responsibilities, or positions listed on the CV.

---

5. *See supra* "Searching for an Expert Witness" in chapter 1.

Continue to question your expert about other areas of interest, including any of those skeletons in the closet in which you were interested while performing your own research. Regardless of whether you found any negative information, still question the expert about each area. Some questions that are typically called for include the following:

• Have you ever been suspended by any employer or licensing authority?
• Have you ever failed any licensure or board certification tests?
• Have you ever had a professional license revoked?
• Have you ever been subjected to professional or workplace discipline?
• Have you ever been sued?
• Have you ever been fired?
• Have you ever been arrested?
• Have you ever been convicted of a crime?
• Have you been involved in any divorce or custody proceedings?

If the answer to any of these questions is yes, then explore the facts and circumstances of the situation with the expert.[6] A yes answer to one or more of these questions does not mean that a particular expert is not the right witness for the job. For example, most medical doctors have been named in a medical malpractice suit at some point in their career. Similarly, many experts have been involved in family litigation. Still, you want to know the details of any of the above occurrences from the start so that you can (1) weigh them as part of your analysis as to whether to use the expert, (2) review any court filings, and (3) prepare to defuse whatever the opposing party may attempt to make out of the issue. As has been mentioned with regard to many of the topics discussed in this subchapter, the best time to learn any bad news about your expert or any information that needs to be managed throughout the life of the case is during your first meeting with the expert, not while you watch your expert being cross-examined.

It is also important to determine how often the expert has testified for the plaintiff or the defendant. A chemist who always testifies on behalf of industry may be seen as partial, while a doctor who has testified both for and against defendants in malpractice actions may appear to be more objective. This is one consideration among many but an important issue to discuss with your expert.

---

6. The Federal Rules of Evidence allow cross-examination as to any conviction subject to punishment of over a year, in addition to general impeachment via evidence of untruthfulness. FED. R. EVID. 608, 609.

Discuss the General Facts and Issues of Your Case

Once satisfied that your expert is qualified and will make a good witness, discuss generally the facts and issues involved in your case. If the expert does not have much experience with the process, explain the role that expert testimony plays in litigation, the issues on which expert testimony is required, and the nature and limits of an expert opinion. If you have not provided the expert with materials in advance of the first meeting, this may take a bit of time. Before the meeting, think about the details that are most relevant to the expert's future opinion and outline the case. Include and highlight the positive and negative details that will be critical issues for the expert to analyze.

Likewise, have the expert explain her preliminary impressions to you in as much detail as possible. Any case requiring an expert opinion likely involves at least a moderately complicated subject area. Beyond the primary purpose of this meeting—to investigate the suitability of the witness—a sit-down meeting with an expert witness is an excellent opportunity for you to learn more about the case, develop strategy, and study the technical details at issue. By asking the expert witness to teach you, you will (1) gain valuable knowledge about the technical issues in your case, (2) see and evaluate the reasoning and assumptions behind your expert's opinion, and (3) get an excellent preview of how this witness will perform on the stand. After all, at trial you will ask your expert to teach the jury about the technical aspects of the case in an accessible manner and to explain to the jury in a convincing and understandable way why your expert's conclusions are credible and trustworthy.

Obtain an Oral Preliminary Reaction

Whether your witness previously reviewed materials or has just listened to you describe the basic facts and circumstances at issue, ask for a preliminary reaction on the critical issues. Any expert worth his salt will, of course, need to delve further into the details before reaching an opinion, but in most cases, the expert's preliminary reaction is helpful. If the critical issue involves a particular document or piece of evidence—an X-ray alleged to have been read improperly, a disputed valuation of a piece of commercial property, or a contract alleged to be outside the usual course of business in a particular industry—bring those documents or pieces of evidence to the meeting and have the expert examine them and give you his reaction. There is no use in engaging an expert who is not going to further your client's case, so do not shy away from asking the critical questions or getting a preliminary reaction to a critical piece of evidence.

Some additional areas to explore at this juncture include the following:

- Does the expert actually hold and depend on this opinion in his day-to-day work in his profession?
- Would this opinion be commonly accepted in his profession?
- Is this an easy call or a close call?
- Has he ever testified to or publicized a similar opinion?
- Has he ever testified to or publicized a contrary opinion?[7]

Also, do not allow an initially positive general reaction to take your focus from the weak points of your case. Some expert witnesses, like many of the rest of us, like to please people and tell them what they want to hear. An expert eager to agree with you and give you a helpful opinion may have the same instinct when being questioned by an adversarial lawyer about the weak points of your case. Discuss your case's vulnerabilities with the expert and have the expert analyze the importance of negative facts and issues as well as explain how his opinion accounts for those problems. In this first meeting, you can establish a rapport with your expert by assuring the expert that you want him to give you a frank, honest assessment of what he sees as strong points and weak points in the case.

Once you have discussed the general facts of the case and the expert's general reactions, confirm that the expert feels qualified to offer an expert opinion in this case. Occasionally, a case that appeared to be about engineering standards may actually turn on a fine point of architecture, or a case that you anticipated would depend on the opinion of an ophthalmologist may actually require a neurologist's analysis.

Evaluate the Expert—Is This a Good Witness?

As you discuss the case with your expert, analyze what kind of witness the individual is likely to make at trial:

- Does the expert speak with confidence and authority?
- Is the judge likely to view this witness as a qualified expert?
- Is the witness likely to be credible and convincing to a jury?

---

7. Depending on the expert and the profession at issue, a given witness may have a dense testimonial history and prolific publications. In those cases, you may not be able to rely on the expert's memory as to past testimony and publications and will need to ensure that your team reviews the information carefully.

- Is the expert a teacher? Can the witness explain complicated concepts in everyday language?

An expert who speaks confidently, makes eye contact, speaks in a way that nonspecialists will understand, and who has a generally appealing and credible presentation will serve you well. An expert who has trouble making eye contact or speaking clearly, who depends on hypertechnical jargon, who comes across as an overly invested advocate, or who does not make an appealing witness for some other reason may be cause for concern. Of course, you may not have too many witnesses to choose from depending on the area of expertise, but—like many other areas addressed in this subchapter—weaknesses and vulnerabilities are best known early. If your first meeting reveals that your expert is less than ideal, you still may use the expert, but your trial strategy can evolve with the knowledge that the expert opinion may be not be a jury-motivating part of your case.

Most expert witnesses can perform successfully during direct examination. After all, the direct examination at trial will simply be a chance for the expert to teach the jury what is already in the expert's report, with your helpful questions structuring and pacing the explanation. The real test for an expert witness comes when that expert is cross-examined in front of the jury. For that reason, you need to pay special attention to the extent to which your expert is able to think on his feet, understand and navigate around "lawyer speak," stay on course when diverted to other issues, and stay firm and confident even when challenged. An expert who possesses the skills to nimbly handle direct challenges and changes of subject is one who stands a far better chance of surviving—or even strengthening your case—during cross-examination.

Certain experts may also be a particularly good or bad fit for a certain case. For instance, in a case regarding the effectiveness of a patented invention, world-class credentials may be far more important than the appeal of a witness who is charming and makes good eye contact with the jury. On the other hand, if your adversary accuses your client of taking a hypertechnical stance in the case, a personable expert who is comfortable speaking in layman's terms may greatly soften your client's position before the jury. The particular qualities you need in an expert witness will vary from case to case, but you should think critically about what your case requires when sizing up your expert at this first meeting.

Provide Your Expert with Case Materials

If you are satisfied with the expert, provide him with the case materials for review. In addition to those materials, provide a confidentiality agreement to be signed by the expert.[8] If you bring these materials to your first meeting, you can have the agreement read and signed on the spot. Keep a signed copy in your file, and provide the expert with a copy for her records as well. Guiding the expert as to which materials are most critical and will likely require the most analysis can help the expert, but you should also be mindful that the expert, in reviewing the entire file, may notice important technical details that you would not have found on your own, so do not be too quick to strictly limit an expert's review of the file. Also critical is an exact list of each and every item provided to the expert for future proof and confirmation of what the expert has been provided and on which he bases his opinion. When your adversary files discovery requests or issues subpoenas requesting that you identify everything the expert has been provided, a well-maintained and up-to-date list will resolve any confusion you or your expert may have in responding to those inquiries.

Address Vulnerabilities of an Experienced Expert Witness

Highly experienced experts come not only with great benefits but also with vulnerabilities of their own. Two of those are (1) a nonspecific approach to your case, and (2) the appearance of being a professional witness.

An experienced expert may not think it necessary to spend a great deal of time in an interview or may have an established method for review of files, correspondence with counsel, and billing practices. To the extent that your case will require a different approach, the first meeting is the time to set ground rules with the experienced expert. You may have to actively undo a certain way of doing things if the expert typically works in other jurisdictions or if it is critical for your case to be handled in a different fashion than the expert's usual course.

Highly experienced experts are also vulnerable to an attack by the opposition for being a professional witness or "opinion for hire." The intent of the other party is to devalue your expert's opinion by demonstrating that rather than a busy professional taking a brief time-out to discuss that profession in a court case, the witness has merely created a lucrative niche in the cottage industry of being a full-time witness. Such witnesses, the argument goes, depend on giving helpful opinions for their livelihood and thus

---

8. A basic model of a confidentiality agreement is attached to this chapter as appendix A. This agreement sets the parameters of your relationship and your expert and is separate and distinct from any global confidentiality order or agreement governing the case as a whole.

are biased to serve the interests of those who hire them. Therefore, you will want to ask such an expert about his financial background, how much he has earned by being an expert witness, and how many active cases he is involved in. These sorts of witnesses tend most often to be defense or plaintiff witnesses, testifying almost exclusively for one side or the other. An experienced expert may be exactly what your client needs in a given case, but it is important to address these particular vulnerabilities early and work with the witness as well as within your overall trial strategy to minimize them.

Conclusion

As stated above, every case is different, and expert testimony is more critical in some cases than others. But, in any case worth the time and effort of retaining an expert witness, you and your client want to ensure that the witness helps your case as much as possible. You can make great strides to that end in your first meeting with an expert by preparing carefully for the meeting, clearly laying out the ground rules, and examining your expert with a juror's eye.

PROVIDING MATERIALS TO THE EXPERT

Cynthia H. Cwik, Robert G. Knaier, and L. David Russell[1]

Once you have researched, chosen, and met with an expert,[2] you will need to educate that expert about the facts of your case. This is a crucial part of case preparation; only a well-informed expert can render a thorough, reliable, and useful opinion.[3] To educate your expert, you will need to consider not only the ways in which you communicate with him—whether in person, by telephone, or through written correspondence[4]—but also the materials you will provide to that expert. The latter consideration is the subject of this subchapter.

Specifically, this subchapter provides practical advice on providing materials to experts, focusing on two issues: (1) what materials you should provide to your expert, and (2) how you should provide those materials to your expert. In addition, this subchapter contains a brief preliminary comment about the ever-important topic of privilege,[5] which influences what

---

1. Ms. Cwik is a partner in the Litigation Department of Jones Day in San Diego, California. She has extensive experience in complex litigation, including multiplaintiff matters and class actions. She has special expertise in litigation involving health, science, and technology issues, including mass tort and product liability actions. Mr. Knaier is an associate in the Litigation Department of Latham & Watkins LLP, in San Diego, California. He has significant experience in mass tort litigation, class actions, commercial litigation, and appellate practice. Mr. Russell is an associate in the San Diego office of Latham & Watkins LLP.

2. *See* "First Meeting with the Expert" *supra.*

3. Indeed, failing to properly educate your expert about the nature of your case and the relevant facts can be fatal. *See, e.g.,* Storage Tech. Corp. v. Cisco Sys., Inc., 395 F.3d 921, 928 (8th Cir. 2005) (holding that because damages expert had insufficient knowledge of the personnel and technology involved in the transaction in question, the "district court was well within its discretion in deciding that [the expert's] testimony was so uninformed and baseless that it could not assist the jury in the task of fixing damages"); Kennecorp Mortgage & Equities, Inc. v. Cline, Bischoff & Cook Co., L.P.A., No. L-82-130, 1982 Ohio App. LEXIS 11583, at *8 (Ohio App. Dec. 17, 1982) (holding that the trial court correctly excluded expert evidence where the record indicated that the expert witnesses lacked "knowledge of various integral facts absolutely necessary" to the opinion offered).

4. *See* "Communicating with the Expert," *infra.*

5. This topic is addressed more fully elsewhere in this chapter. *See* "Privilege Issues," *infra.*

materials to provide and how to do so, and a reminder to obtain relevant materials *from* your expert.

The Problem of Privilege and Work Product

Communicating with experts and providing materials to experts raise a host of questions relating to the attorney-client privilege and the work product doctrine. Most jurisdictions follow rules similar to those set forth in the Federal Rules of Civil Procedure, which broadly require that an expert witness disclose all "data or other information considered by the witness in forming" an opinion.[6] Generally, you should assume that all communications with an expert hired to testify at trial must be produced to the other side.[7] Indeed, even if you send a testifying expert "core" attorney work product, be aware that you might lose the privilege shielding that work product.[8] In contrast, communications with so-called consulting (nontestifying) experts are privileged and need not be produced unless, of course, these communications are later given to testifying experts.[9] Thus, with regard to testifying experts, you should be extremely careful in what you say in written correspondence, what you send to your expert, and what an expert sends to you.

Obtaining Relevant Materials from Your Expert

While the focus of this subchapter is providing materials to your expert, you also should be diligent in obtaining *from* your expert anything relevant to your case—and to your expert's credentials and credibility.[10] For example, you will need your expert's curriculum vitae, so that you can educate yourself about such things as his educational and professional qualifications, any relevant articles or books he has written, any relevant studies he has performed

---

6. FED. R. CIV. P. 26(a)(2)(B)(ii).

7. *See, e.g.*, Reg'l Airport Auth. v. LFG, LLC, 460 F.3d 697, 715–16 (6th Cir. 2006); Lidle v. Cirrus Design Corp., No. 08-1253, 2009 U.S. Dist. LEXIS 33514, at *4–5 (S.D.N.Y. Mar. 24, 2009); SEC v. Reyes, No. 06-04435 CRB, 2007 U.S. Dist. LEXIS 27767, at *4 (N.D. Cal. Mar. 30, 2007).

8. *See In re* Pioneer Hi-Bred Int'l, Inc., 238 F.3d 1370, 1375–76 (Fed. Cir. 2001).

9. *See* Elm Grove Coal Co. v. Dir., OWCP, 480 F.3d 278, 303 n.25 (4th Cir. 2007). Given this distinction between testifying and nontestifying experts, you may on occasion wish to restrict your communications to nontestifying experts until such time as you are satisfied that it is sensible to begin communicating with your testifying expert.

10. *See supra* "Searching for an Expert Witness" in chapter 1 (detailing strategies for vetting a potential expert witness).

or with which he has otherwise been involved, and any cases in which he has consulted or testified. In many instances, your expert will be required to disclose such information.[11] But it also can be quite useful in preparing your case. Indeed, it is particularly important that you obtain copies of your expert's prior writings and transcripts of any prior deposition or trial testimony. By reviewing these materials, you can determine whether your expert has at some point in the past taken a position inconsistent or in tension with the position he is taking in your case—a fact your adversary could use to impeach your expert's credibility, either at deposition or at trial.[12]

What Materials to Provide to the Expert

Having educated yourself about your expert, you may then begin educating your expert about the facts of your case. What materials you should provide to an expert witness will depend, in part, on the nature of your case and the expert's particular area of concern. For example, if you are involved in a toxic tort case, in which the plaintiffs claim to have been harmed by exposure to a chemical agent, then an expert on medical causation will likely need to be familiar with plaintiff-specific information (e.g., the plaintiffs' medical records, their treating physicians' deposition transcripts, and other such materials). If, instead, you are involved in a securities class action, in which a representative shareholder alleges that a class of shareholders was harmed by an accounting fraud, then an expert on damages may have no need for such plaintiff-specific materials; rather, the expert's focus will likely be on factual information relevant to the entire class (e.g., the number of outstanding shares during the class period, the corporation's accounting data, and similar facts). And if you are involved in a commercial dispute that might turn on certain electronic data stored by your client or your client's adversary, then you may need to provide a forensic expert with hard drives, access to servers, and other means of evaluating such electronic data.

Nevertheless, you should consider providing some categories of materials to experts in nearly any kind of case. In nearly any case requiring an expert opinion, that expert should become familiar with the basic facts and

---

11. *See* Fed. R. Civ. P. 26(a)(2)(B)(iv)–(v) (requiring that an expert disclose "qualifications, including a list of all publications authored in the previous 10 years," and "a list of all other cases in which, during the previous four years, the witness testified as an expert at trial or by deposition").

12. This can be an effective strategy, and for that reason, you also should attempt to identify and obtain any of your adversary's expert's writings or testimony.

theories of the case. To accomplish this, you should provide your expert with relevant pleadings, key documents, electronic data, physical evidence, percipient witness deposition transcripts, other experts' reports and deposition transcripts, and, sometimes, relevant research. Below, we discuss these categories of materials, and then we provide a few tips on what you may not want to provide to an expert.

Relevant Pleadings

It is common for a witness, expert or otherwise, to be asked at his deposition whether he has reviewed the complaint and other pleadings in the action. The point of such questions is to probe the extent to which the witness has familiarized himself with the allegations and theories of liability at issue, as well as the defendant's responses to those allegations and theories. This is a particularly salient question for an expert witness. An expert who has not reviewed the pleadings may be viewed as untutored in—or even unconcerned with—the basic equities of the case. Indeed, a failure to review the pleadings may be used by counsel for the opposing party to suggest that the expert is merely a hired gun, ready to offer an opinion without fully understanding or caring about the reasons why the case came into being. For these reasons, you should consider providing your expert with materials such as the plaintiff's complaint, the defendant's answer, and certain motions, related motions such as motions to dismiss or motions for summary judgment.

Key Documents

In addition to providing your expert with the *allegations* of the case, you also should ensure that your expert is familiar with the *facts* of the case as developed, for example, through document discovery. This does not mean that you should provide your expert with every document produced in the case. Rather, if there are certain key documents that are relevant to your expert's opinion, be certain to provide them. This is true whether those documents support the expert's opinions or do *not* support those opinions. For example, suppose a case in which a plaintiff contends that exposure to a chemical agent caused her to develop breast cancer. Suppose also that the plaintiff's treating physician produces genetic testing results showing that the plaintiff was predisposed to develop breast cancer. Whether you represent the defendant or the plaintiff, you should provide this document to your expert. As the defendant's counsel, you want to make your expert aware of the existence of a potential alternative explanation for the plaintiff's illness—an explanation *other than* her alleged exposure. And as the plaintiff's counsel, you want to be sure that your expert is aware of these results, so that he can determine whether, despite a genetic predisposition, a plaintiff's exposure could have contributed to her illness. A failure to provide your expert with such documents may render his opinion significantly flawed, resting on an incomplete or inaccurate factual and scientific basis. Indeed, if the flaw is significant enough, your expert's opinion may be subject to exclusion for failure to rest on a reasonable foundation.[13] Thus, you should make every effort to see that your expert has reviewed all key documents relevant to his opinion, whether those documents support that opinion or not.

Electronic Data

You also might need to provide electronic data to your expert.[14] Hard drives, servers, laptop computers, and even cellular telephones and personal digital assistants may contain communications or other materials relevant to your case. Some of this data may be best relayed to your expert in its raw form rather than as a printout or other hard copy. For example, if your expert needs to evaluate the contents of a spreadsheet, he may need access to hidden formulae or data underlying the final product. Thus, it may be necessary to provide the actual source files.

Furthermore, if electronic data is implicated in your case, you may require an expert who specializes in accessing and evaluating such data. Forensic experts specializing in this sort of evidence-gathering and analysis are increasingly becoming common. When determining what type of electronic evidence to provide to a digital forensic expert, it is important to work closely with that expert as well as with information technology personnel. It is often helpful to engage a digital forensic expert at the beginning of any e-discovery. Together, you can locate electronic evidence of interest, on

---

13. *See* FED. R. EVID. 702 (explaining that an expert may testify "in the form of an opinion or otherwise, if (1) the testimony is based upon sufficient facts or data, (2) the testimony is the product of reliable principles and methods, and (3) the witness has applied the principles and methods reliably to the facts of the case"); *see also* Daubert v. Merrell Dow Pharms., Inc., 509 U.S. 579, 593–94 (1993) (establishing nonexclusive factors for trial courts to use in assessing whether expert testimony complies with FED. R. EVID. 702); Gen. Elec. Co. v. Joiner, 522 U.S. 136, 146 (1997) ("[N]othing in either *Daubert* or the Federal Rules of Evidence requires a district court to admit opinion evidence that is connected to existing data only by the *ipse dixit* of the expert. A court may conclude that there is simply too great an analytical gap between the data and the opinion proffered."); Kumho Tire Co., Ltd. v. Carmichael, 526 U.S. 137, 141 (1999) (holding that *Daubert* factors "appl[y] not only to testimony based on 'scientific' knowledge, but also to testimony based on 'technical' and 'other specialized' knowledge").

14. Issues involving electronic data are addressed more fully in a subsequent chapter. *See* "E-Discovery" *infra*.

whatever electronic media it may reside, and start to analyze this evidence early in the litigation. Such an expert also can help to retrieve, collect, and store the electronic information in a way that will preserve the chain of custody and maintain the data for future expert analysis.[15] Finally, a forensic expert can be helpful in determining what electronic media to demand from a producing party and can help to ensure that the producing party handles its electronic production in a forensically sound matter.

Physical Evidence

In addition to documents and data, electronic or otherwise, you may need to provide your expert with certain physical evidence. This can be true in a wide variety of cases. A DNA laboratory may need to evaluate samples found at a crime scene. A medical expert may need to test tissue samples for the presence of certain agents. An engineer may need to inspect a medical device or automotive part alleged to have failed. In any event, it is crucial that you preserve such evidence and provide it to your expert as early as possible, and, as discussed further below, in a way that maintains its integrity. Failing to do so could subject you to sanctions for "spoliation" of evidence.[16] Furthermore, providing your expert with important physical evidence will permit him to base his opinion on a proper and complete foundation. Thus, you should begin considering at an early stage whether physical evidence will be relevant to your case and whether you will require an expert to analyze and opine on it.

Percipient Witness Deposition Transcripts

To further familiarize your expert with the facts of the case, you also should provide him with relevant deposition testimony from percipient witnesses.

---

15. Courts have criticized digital forensic experts for processing electronic evidence in forensically unsound ways that compromise the data's authenticity or even *erase* evidence. *See, e.g.*, MGE UPS Sys. v. Fakouri Elec. Eng'g, Inc., No. 04-445, 2006 U.S. Dist. LEXIS 14142, at *5–8 (N.D. Tex. Mar. 14, 2006) (holding that accusations that plaintiff's expert used improper forensic methodology that deleted, contaminated, and otherwise altered electronic evidence could be considered when weighing that evidence); Gates Rubber Co. v. Bando Chem. Indus., Ltd., 167 F.R.D. 90, 112 (D. Colo. 1996) (finding that forensic expert's incorrect use of a forensic program erased 7 to 8 percent of a hard drive's information); Taylor v. State, 93 S.W.3d 487, 498–508 (Tex. Ct. App. 2002) (overturning a criminal conviction partly because officer-expert did not verify a forensic examination of a target hard drive and copied the target hard drive onto a contaminated hard drive).

16. *See* West v. Goodyear Tire & Rubber Co., 167 F.3d 776, 779 (2d Cir. 1999) ("Spoliation is the destruction or significant alteration of evidence, or the failure to preserve property for another's use as evidence in pending or reasonably foreseeable litigation.").

Again, this does not mean that you should provide your expert with every transcript available in the case. An expert's time is valuable—and correspondingly expensive—so you should think carefully about what testimony is truly important to your expert in formulating his opinion and whether you want to incur the expense of having him read lengthy transcripts. But if there is percipient witness testimony relevant to your expert's opinions, you should provide that testimony. In a medical malpractice action, for example, an expert may need to review the defendant's deposition testimony, as well as the testimony of other witnesses to the incident at issue, to determine exactly what occurred and whether the defendant's conduct was consistent with the relevant standard of care. Similarly, an expert on medical causation in a toxic tort case may need to review a plaintiff's deposition transcript to help determine the extent to which the plaintiff was exposed to a chemical agent, the nature of the harm alleged, and whether any alternative causes of that harm exist. Such an expert may not, however, need to review the testimony of a witness deposed on the subject of the defendant's corporate structure and ownership history. Be selective in what you provide to your expert in this regard.

Nevertheless, you should take care to provide your expert with *all* testimony necessary to permit him to render an informed opinion. As noted elsewhere in this subchapter, you should make every effort to avoid the appearance that you are providing your expert with a one-sided view of the facts. Accordingly, even if percipient witnesses have disagreed about what happened in a given case, you should provide your expert with all competing versions of the facts. Your expert should be prepared to defend his opinion even in the face of testimony unfavorable to your side of the case, or perhaps inconsistent with the opinion being offered. Indeed, if your expert has failed to review such testimony, then your opponent may use this omission to undermine the accuracy and credibility of your expert's opinion. Do not lay that trap for your own expert by failing to provide him with all relevant information.

Other Experts' Reports and Deposition Transcripts

Once your expert has reviewed the allegations of the case and has become familiar with the factual record, he can begin formulating an opinion. To be able to render a helpful, reliable opinion, however, your expert will need to be aware of other experts' opinions as well as the bases for those opinions. Just as your expert may provide a report describing his opinions, and likely will be deposed on the bases for those opinions, other experts in the case will do likewise.[17] Thus, if they are available, you should provide your expert with the

---

17. In federal court, experts are *required* to provide comprehensive reports, setting forth their opinions and the bases for those opinions. *See* FED. R. CIV. P. 26(a)(2)(B)(i)–(ii)

reports and deposition testimony on relevant issues of other experts in the case—whether those experts were retained by your adversary or by you.

Indeed, if you require an expert on a given topic, your adversary may very well retain an expert on that topic as well.[18] Thus, whether testifying in your case-in-chief or as a rebuttal witness, your expert will need to be intimately familiar with an opposing expert's opinions in relevant areas, so that he can either criticize the opposing expert's methodology and conclusions or defend his own methodology and conclusions against the opponent's criticisms. Reviewing an opposing expert's report is important in this regard, as it represents the opposing expert's considered view of the matter, based on his review of the facts. It is often the case, however, that the

---

(requiring testifying expert to produce a written report containing "a complete statement of all opinions the witness will express and the basis and reasons for them" and "the data or other information considered by the witness in forming them"). However, expert reports are not always required. For example, in state court, an expert often is required to provide only a concise statement of the topics on which he will testify. *See, e.g.,* CAL. CIV. PROC. CODE § 2034.260(c) (stating that parties must exchange a declaration containing "(1) A brief narrative statement of the qualifications of each expert"; "(2) A brief narrative statement of the general substance of the testimony that the expert is expected to give"; "(3) A representation that the expert has agreed to testify at trial"; "(4) A representation that the expert will be sufficiently familiar with the pending action to submit to a meaningful oral deposition concerning the specific testimony, including any opinion and its basis, that the expert is expected to give at trial"; and "(5) A statement of the expert's hourly and daily fee for providing deposition testimony and for consulting with the retaining attorney"); N.Y. C.P.L.R. § 3101(d)(1)(i) ("Upon request, each party shall identify each person whom the party expects to call as an expert witness at trial and shall disclose in reasonable detail the subject matter on which each expert is expected to testify, the substance of the facts and opinions on which each expert is expected to testify, the qualifications of each expert witness and a summary of the grounds for each expert's opinion."). Nevertheless, parties sometimes stipulate that their experts will provide reports that set forth their opinions and the bases for those opinions, as this can help both sides to a dispute to understand the strengths and weaknesses of a case at an early stage and may help in seeking or defending against summary judgment.

18. Failing to designate an expert on a topic for which your adversary has done so may leave you at a significant evidentiary disadvantage. A trier of fact generally is under no obligation to accept unrebutted expert testimony as true. *See* Sartor v. Ark. Natural Gas Corp., 321 U.S. 620, 627–28 (1944) ("The rule has been stated 'that if the court admits the testimony, then it is for the jury to decide whether any, and if any what, weight is to be given to the testimony. . . . even if such testimony be uncontradicted.'") (quoting Spring Co. v. Edgar, 99 U.S. 645, 658 (1879), and The Conqueror, 166 U.S. 110, 131 (1897)); Applied Med. Res. Corp. v. U.S. Surgical Corp., 147 F.3d 1374, 1379 (Fed. Cir. 1998) (holding that uncontested expert testimony does not automatically resolve a factual question in that party's favor). Nevertheless, "studies have shown that jurors give great weight to expert testimony." Carol Henderson, *Expert Witness: Qualifications and Testimony, in* ABA SCIENTIFIC EVIDENCE REVIEW: ADMISSIBILITY AND USE OF EXPERT EVIDENCE IN THE COURTROOM, MONOGRAPH NO. 6, 1, 10 (American Bar Ass'n ed., 2003). Thus, you should give serious thought to whether you need an expert, particularly if your adversary already has one.

bases for an expert's opinions—and potential flaws in those bases—are revealed only at a thorough deposition.[19] Thus, it is crucial that your expert also be familiar with what an opposing expert said at his deposition, under the light of difficult questioning.[20]

Furthermore, if your case requires it, you may retain more than one expert to testify on related topics. For example, in a toxic tort case, you may retain an epidemiologist to testify regarding the patterns and causes of diseases in human populations, and you may also retain a toxicologist to testify regarding the biological plausibility that a given chemical could have caused a given plaintiff's harm. These experts will need to be aware of each other's opinions, so that your case is coordinated and internally consistent. Thus, just as it is important for your expert to be aware of the reports and testimony of opposing experts, it is helpful that he be provided with the reports and testimony of other experts on the same side of the case. Again, though, be selective in this process. Do not overburden your expert with reports and testimony that are not relevant to his own opinion.[21]

Relevant Research

On occasion, it may be appropriate to provide an expert witness with research relevant to his opinion. To effectively work with an expert witness, you will need to become as knowledgeable and conversant as possible in that expert's field. Doing so has several benefits. You will better know what information and materials to provide to the expert, because you will understand

---

19. Indeed, in those instances in which an opposing expert does not need to prepare a report, see *supra* note 17, becoming familiar with the expert's deposition testimony may be the *only* way to discover and understand the expert's opinions.

20. Another way to accomplish this is to bring your expert to the opposing expert's deposition. Although you do not want your expert to be, or be seen as, an advocate, his presence at a deposition can serve a useful function. Your expert may be able to offer feedback on your preparations, can evaluate the opposing expert's opinions during the course of the deposition, and can gauge the credibility of the opposing expert in a way that a cold deposition transcript might not convey. Moreover, if your expert is well known and respected in the relevant field, his mere presence at the deposition may help to constrain what an opposing expert is willing to say. Most experts take their professional reputations seriously, and they are unlikely to want to alienate top minds in their area of expertise.

21. Furthermore, be careful to avoid excessively entangling your own experts with one another. While it is important for your experts to be consistent, it is just as important that they be independent and not be seen as mere sounding boards for one another or as crafting their opinions *to be* consistent with one another. Thus, it is often best to keep communications among experts to a minimum. Indeed, you may be able to undermine the credibility of an opponent's expert witnesses by demonstrating just this sort of interdependence among them.

what might be relevant to his opinion. You will be able to speak intelligently with the expert, asking relevant questions and being able to respond to the expert's inquiries. And you will be able to understand the expert's opinions and the bases for those opinions—which will prepare you not only to question your expert clearly at trial, but also to cross-examine your opponent's expert successfully.

To become knowledgeable in your expert's field—to become something of an expert yourself—requires researching the methodologies and conclusions accepted in that field. In performing that research, you likely will cover much of the same ground that the expert will in preparing his opinions. Indeed, to the extent that you have the time and ability, you are well served by conducting an independent review of the bases for an opinion in your case. For example, if you have retained an expert on accounting to provide an opinion on whether a defendant committed accounting fraud, you should familiarize yourself with the relevant accounting regulations and literature. In doing so, you may accumulate a significant amount of materials that could be helpful to your expert. Or, your expert may ask for assistance in gathering certain research materials, perhaps because you have more cost-effective ways to access those materials. For example, if you are at a large firm, you may have less expensive access to certain online databases. In any event, on occasion, you may wish to consider providing your expert with research materials relevant to his area of inquiry.

You should, however, exercise considerable caution here. First, remember that your communications with the expert are generally discoverable, absent stipulation to the contrary, so they should not contain case strategy or identify holes in your case.[22] Second, you should not do anything to suggest that you are shaping your expert's opinions by providing him with the bases for those opinions. Indeed, avoid being too involved in the work you are doing with an expert, as there is a risk that the work will be subjected to criticism for being biased. The authors of this subchapter were involved in a case in which the plaintiffs insisted that a study performed by one of their experts was "the single most significant piece of causation evidence available in the litigation." When the expert was deposed, he testified that the plaintiffs' counsel had provided him with a great deal of the data used to complete the study and that the best source for learning about the methodology used for certain aspects of the study was *the law firm for the plaintiffs*. Such testimony can significantly undermine the credibility of an expert's study. Remember, it is your expert's job to independently evaluate the facts of your case and apply the methodologies and

---

22. *See* "How to Provide Materials to the Expert" *infra.*

conclusions of his field. Do not usurp that role, in fact or appearance. If you do, you may subject your expert to the criticism that he is merely being fed his opinion by counsel, thereby undermining his credibility and effectiveness at trial.

Tips on What Not to Send to an Expert

In addition to advice about what materials to provide your expert, we offer some tips on the sorts of things you should not give to your expert. As noted above, you should avoid providing any materials that would suggest an excessive involvement with the formulation of his opinions. This can be particularly difficult in the context of providing feedback on drafts of your expert's reports. As discussed further elsewhere in this book,[23] materials provided to testifying experts generally are not protected by privilege or the work product doctrine. Thus, if your expert gives you a draft of his report, and you offer written feedback on that draft, your feedback ordinarily will be subject to disclosure to your adversary. Therefore, be careful if you provide your expert with written commentary on his draft reports.[24]

Of course, constraining communications in this way can make working with your expert difficult. To avoid such difficulty, it recently has become more common for both sides to a dispute to stipulate in advance to certain rules governing communications with, and discovery from, expert witnesses. For example, the authors of this subchapter have entered into stipulations in federal and state cases in which both sides agreed that they were not required to produce draft reports, draft studies, draft affidavits, or draft work papers; preliminary or intermediate calculations, computations, or data; other preliminary, intermediate, or draft materials prepared by, for, or at the direction of a testifying expert witness; and any written communications between counsel (or at counsel's direction) and the expert—as long as these materials were not substantively relied on by the expert in forming his opinions. Such stipulations may facilitate more efficient and rapid communications with experts and also reduce unnecessarily voluminous document productions from experts.[25]

---

23. See "Privilege Issues," *supra.*

24. Indeed, you may want to avoid creating and exchanging draft reports at all. Some federal courts that have addressed the issue have determined that preliminary drafts created by testifying experts (or by attorneys for these experts) must be turned over in discovery. *See, e.g.,* Krisa v. The Equitable Life Assurance Soc'y, 196 F.R.D. 254, 256–57 (M.D. Pa. 2000); County of Suffolk v. Long Island Lighting Co., 122 F.R.D. 120, 122 (E.D.N.Y. 1988); Hewlett-Packard Co. v. Bausch & Lomb, Inc., 116 F.R.D. 533, 536–37 (N.D. Cal. 1987).

25. Note, however, that you may not always wish to agree to such a stipulation. A review of an opposing expert's draft report or communications with counsel, produced

Absent a stipulation that precludes discovery of communications with an expert, however, you should proceed with caution in providing any materials to your expert. Do not provide work product such as attorney research and analysis to your expert. Indeed, do not provide anything to your expert that you do not want produced to your adversary. Of special note here is the ubiquitous e-mail. Given both the prevalence of e-mails as a form of communication and the casual way in which they ordinarily are drafted, you should heed their dangers. It simply is too easy for you and your expert to write something in an e-mail that, at the time, seems clever or humorous but does not sound quite as good when being read to a jury. It may thus be wise to adopt a general rule to avoid communicating with testifying experts via e-mail.

How to Provide Materials to the Expert

Having decided what to send to your expert witness, you should consider *how* to send those materials. In doing so, it is important to be mindful of the confidentiality of any materials you provide, the form that the materials take, whether and to what extent you and your expert keep track of them, and the method of providing them.

Maintaining Confidentiality

If you need to provide your expert with confidential material, you will be expected to take steps to preserve that confidentiality. For example, in a patent case, experts may need to view proprietary information to evaluate the validity of a claim. In an accounting fraud case, experts may need to analyze highly sensitive financial data. And in a toxic tort case, experts may need to review and assess private medical records. That confidential information may be relevant and material to a case, however, does not mean that it must become public knowledge. Accordingly, parties often enter into stipulations to ensure that if they produce confidential, trade secret, proprietary, or other sensitive information, it will remain confidential.

Such confidentiality agreements typically identify a limited group of people to whom confidential material may be shown—a list that generally includes relevant experts. For example, a confidentiality agreement may provide that confidential materials may be shown to consultants, experts, or advisors retained for the prosecution or defense of the litigation, provided

---

through the ordinary rules of discovery, may yield valuable information that can relate to issues such as the credibility and reliability of that expert's opinions.

that each such consultant, expert, or advisor shall have executed a copy of a certification attached to the confidentiality agreement. In the certification, the expert to whom confidential information will be shown can then declare that he has read, understands, and agrees to abide by the confidentiality agreement—and that he consents to the jurisdiction and venue of the court for purposes of enforcing the agreement. Thus, if you come to believe that your case requires expert review of confidential information, you should consider entering into a confidentiality agreement, providing your expert with a copy of that agreement, and obtaining your expert's assurance that he will abide by the agreement.

The Form of Materials Provided to an Expert

Whether you are providing deposition transcripts, key documents, electronic data, physical evidence, expert reports, or other relevant materials to your expert, you should provide them in an unadulterated form. For physical evidence, such as a suspect automotive part or a tissue sample, be careful to maintain its physical integrity. For electronic data, try to avoid modifying that data in any way before your expert receives it. For documents, when possible, provide nothing more than accurate copies. Do not give your expert copies adorned with your analysis or commentary. It cannot be overstated: this is discoverable work product, and it may suggest that you are inappropriately attempting to shape your expert's opinions.

Keeping Track of Materials

You and your expert should keep thorough, accurate records of the materials you provide, as well as of the chain of custody through which those materials pass. An expert should try to account for the evidence throughout the entire time he maintains custody of it. Indeed, if your expert is relying on analyses of electronic or physical evidence, such as hard drives or tissue samples, it is particularly important that he document what he receives. He should log in the evidence received, noting where it came from; when it was received; who delivered it; and where and how it was stored. For electronic data, for example, an expert must be certain that he tracks not only physical, tangible items (e.g., digital cameras, laptops, thumb drives), but also the intangible data (e.g., files, messages, metadata).[26]

---

26. Counsel should take particular care with electronic evidence, given its growing importance. When turning over electronic information to an expert, counsel should ensure that the data is processed in a way that will preserve the chain of custody and ensure that future analysis will be performed on forensically sound evidence. Ideally, counsel should

In any event, whether in connection with physical or electronic evidence, or with regard to documents, testimony, reports, or studies provided to your expert, accurate record keeping is important. For you, this can help to catalogue what may become a voluminous amount of documents, to avoid providing duplicative materials, and to reduce the possibility that evidence is corrupted along the way. For your expert, there is significant value in keeping a log of the materials received, including the documents, testimony, and other items on which he actually relied on in forming his opinions. Indeed, your expert may be *required* to list in his report, and perhaps to produce to the opposing party, all materials relied on in forming his opinion.[27] Furthermore, even if your expert is not required to disclose and produce such materials, doing so can helpfully demonstrate to the opposing party and to the court that he has actively participated in the case, is well informed on all relevant issues, and has formed an opinion with a thorough, reliable foundation.

The Method of Providing Materials to an Expert

Given that you should attempt to minimize the extent to which you provide attorney analysis and commentary with materials provided to an expert, and to minimize the potential for corrupting electronic data, likely the safest method for providing materials to that expert is by delivering unadulterated materials by ordinary U.S. mail, Federal Express, or hand delivery. If sent under cover of a letter, or as an attachment to an e-mail (caution!), avoid conveying in writing anything other than an inventory of the contents of the delivery. Do not characterize a deposition transcript as *the crucial testimony*. Do not refer to documents as *key*. Do not disparage the reports or testimony of opposing experts or downplay the import of documents unfavorable to your case. Let your expert impartially evaluate the evidence and formulate his opinion. The credibility of your expert, and the quality of your case, will be better off for it.

---

work with forensic experts to ensure that they make master copies or complete image backups of electronic evidence before initiating forensic analysis of electronic data. Counsel should also insist that forensic examiners audit the steps taken during their analysis, from intake through the completion of their task. Further, as with other kinds of physical evidence, an expert should keep sources of electronic evidence in a place where he can verify their location and where they will not be molested.

27. *See* FED. R. CIV. P. 26(a)(2)(B)(ii) (stating that an expert's written report must include "the data or other information considered by the witness in forming" his expert opinion).

In general, if you wish to provide your expert with your view on an issue, you may want to do so orally.[28] In addition, using a webinar, in which you and your expert can view the expert's report over an Internet connection and simultaneously discuss it on a conference call, provides an effective way to communicate without the time and cost of travel.

Conclusion

In a wide variety of matters, a well-informed expert who can provide a relevant, reliable opinion may be the key to victory. To ensure that your expert is well informed, however, you will need to provide him with several kinds of materials: pleadings, key documents, electronic data, physical evidence, deposition transcripts, expert reports, and other helpful documents. In doing so, you must be ever vigilant to avoid turning over attorney work product—and to avoid creating the appearance that you are inappropriately shaping your expert's opinions. You must provide a quantity and quality of material sufficient to help your expert demonstrate to a court that his opinions have a proper foundation, but you must not provide corrupted evidence or involve yourself so deeply in your expert's work that a trier of fact finds that that his opinions lack impartiality and credibility. Ultimately, accomplishing this requires being thorough and careful in evaluating and handling evidence, having confidence in the merits of your case, and having faith that you chose your expert well (i.e., that if provided with an uncorrupted, impartial, unbiased view of the facts, your expert will be able to provide a relevant, reliable opinion).

---

28. Opposing counsel is, of course, free to inquire into what you *say* to your testifying expert. Again, your communications are not privileged. Nevertheless, if you avoid committing your thoughts to the permanent written record, you may significantly reduce the likelihood that those thoughts will one day be read verbatim to court and jury.

COMMUNICATING WITH THE EXPERT

Charles R. Beans and Kevin A. Spainhour[1]

Throughout the steps that counsel takes in establishing a relationship with the expert, and throughout counsel's preparation of that expert, communication is key. Communicating with the expert is essential to advancing the theme and strategy of the case and fitting the expert into it. This communication must take place within the constraints of time and budget and with the recognition that it may be discoverable.

Communication will vary depending on the situation. Witnesses come in all experience types, ranging from wind-up "usual suspects" to persons who are completely unfamiliar and unprepared for the litigation procedures. The communication will also depend on the subject matter and complexity of the case, and how the expert's opinions fit the overall case strategy and theme. There is no one-size-fits-all approach for this, and like any element of strategy, communication with experts should be constantly evaluated and adapted. That said, here are six general guidelines to follow when communicating with an expert.

Get to Know Your Expert Better

Lawyers may learn about their expert in the selection process, or the witness may be an experienced, well-known testifier with a lengthy track record. This does not mean that the learning process ends at the start. As the litigator works with the expert, it is crucial to continue gathering information that may affect the expert's usefulness and effectiveness in the case and to update the information already obtained.

An obvious guide to evaluating an expert's background is to use the Litigator's Golden Rule: consider what tactics one would use against the

---

1. Charles R. Beans is a partner who defends corporations in general liability litigation, including product liability, toxic tort, insurance coverage, and appellate practice. Kevin A. Spainhour is an associate who practices in the area of civil litigation with an emphasis on insurance defense, professional malpractice, and product and premises liability. Both are with the firm Goodman McGuffey Lindsey & Johnson, LLP in Atlanta, Georgia.

other side's expert. Any sensitive or embarrassing information from the expert's history—education, training, professional career, academics, politics, social life, and testimony—must be discovered before the opponent. Most of this information is in the background, and it may already be known and, to a certain extent, already dealt with. But the advocate must at least try to update this information by asking the questions. The expert's continuing work—in other cases, in the subject area, on a professional level, in print, or in his personal life—may create new situations that the lawyer needs to know about. The expert may have made presentations in his field. He may have taken on new cases with similar issues. He may have had contact with other lawyers, experts, or witnesses. Any such information is vital to the presenting attorney, because it will invariably come to the attention of the opposing counsel.

Monitor the Ground Rules for the Engagement

Establish the ground rules for the engagement at the time of retention, but along the way the plan has to be monitored, fine-tuned, and executed. At the outset, give the witness a framework for the assignment. In particular, give the witness a schedule, a scope of work, and a budget of some sort, depending on the circumstances. The witness will know what is expected as far as work product, degree of documentation, and testing or other work to be done. There are several reasons to periodically revisit this framework: first, the expert's work may change the theme of your case (i.e., reveal an unknown affirmative defense or claim); second, the work may reveal flaws in your theory of the case. For either of the foregoing, the last thing one wants is to find out about the change during the expert's first testimony. Finally, your work may change the theme or theory of the case. Updating the expert avoids redundant or superfluous work.

Soon after retention, the expert should be given an overview of the legal principles involved in the case—the causes of action, defenses, and evidentiary issues. In addition, the lawyer should go over common issues applicable to experts, such as burden of proof and reasonable degree of certainty. Plan how to satisfy the *Daubert*[2] standard.[3] Finally, disclose information about the case as it develops. The issues rarely remain the same and may even become clearer as the litigation progresses. It is usual for the lawyer to learn more about the case, and the expert should be apprised of these revelations as soon as possible. The communication should take place with discovery

---

2. Daubert v. Merrell Dow Pharms., Inc., 509 U.S. 579 (1993).
3. *See infra* chapter 6.

and advocacy in mind; usually the information should be provided by oral means, not in writing or by e-mail.

Here is an example from our experience. The issue in a product liability case was the feasibility of an add-on, alternative safety device. No such product in the real world had such a device, and our expert was prepared to testify from his significant experience that not only was the device not required by the applicable regulations, but it would actually be a bad idea in actual use. However, while a *Daubert* motion was pending to exclude the opinion of the opposing expert, who had no such experience or knowledge, the client informed us that it was developing a prototype for exactly such a protective device, to be advertised as an after-market option. Needless to say, the case was settled as quickly as possible after that unhappy revelation and before any ruling.

No expert thinks that he is unqualified, but the lawyer and the expert should be confident with what the expert is being asked to do in the case. Particularly with relatively new experts, they should be aware of the distinctions between being professionally qualified, and being qualified under the *Daubert* standard. The scope of work should not exceed the qualifications of the expert. Likewise, the expert must be provided with sufficient information, including documents, from the litigation to have a sound factual footing for the opinions. Finally, the lawyer should work with the witness to ensure that the analysis leading to the opinions is based on the evidence in the case and is conducted in a reasonable fashion just as it would be in the real working world, outside of the needs of litigation. The expert, assisted by the retaining lawyer, should obtain and be prepared to discuss the industry and professional standards that support the expert's methods and opinions. Real-world experience and published information should support the opinions and the methods, to the greatest extent possible.

Prepare the Presentation of the Opinion

Experts are usually helpful to the litigator planning the case. They can help with factual and technical discovery, educate counsel about the issues of their expertise and related areas, assist with background and critique of the opposing expert, and provide referral to other experts. However, you should not be lulled into neglecting diligent inquiry merely because your expert refers another expert. Counsel should find out what each expert needs or considers useful and plan discovery accordingly.

All experts have certain experiences and preliminary bents, and after they have completed a certain amount of review of the case, they form opinions that later become testimony. That journey must be assisted by counsel.

Because discovery and analysis are ongoing, the expert should not memori-alize preliminary opinions. Marking notes as "draft" or "subject to change" is less preferable, because it may give an impression that the expert's opin-ions are malleable for improper reasons. The trial lawyer can determine how the preliminary opinions fit or shape the case themes, if more or differ-ent work needs to be done, and how best the opinions should be expressed. This latter concept includes how the opinions are stated: what order, termi-nology, demonstrative aids, or props may assist the effective and persuasive presentation of the opinions.

The first landmark for the presentation of opinion is disclosure to the opposing party in discovery. Whether a written report for federal court or an interrogatory response in some state courts, this presentation will intro-duce the opinions of the expert and guide (and even limit) the presentation of those opinions in court. The more this presentation is an informed col-laboration between the expert and counsel, the better, insofar as effective advocacy for the client is concerned.

In everyday life, some questions like "how did you meet your spouse?" and "did you ever use drugs when you were my age?" are better handled if planned for in advance. Likewise in litigation, counsel should try to antici-pate and preview usual tactics and areas of questioning for the expert. Even if an expert has been deposed many times, every lawyer is different and every case presents new issues.

Play Well with Others

If a case requires an expert at all, it may require more than one. Communi-cation with experts includes the concept of communication among experts. An effective tactic for cross-examining one opposing expert is to obtain an opinion or concession that is harmful or contradictory from another oppos-ing expert. Therefore, in preparation for testimony, counsel must coordinate his client's own experts so that they do not contradict or step on each other's areas of testimony. In addition, this type of discussion can help advance the case because the experts can share experiences, educate each other, identify weaknesses in each other's opinions, and otherwise synergize together.

In some areas of litigation, such as automotive product liability or toxic torts, this coordination is commonplace and formalized. In other areas, it is less common. An attorney may act as a go-between in an attempt to keep the communication privileged as a possible work product communication between the attorney and the expert.[4] The experts may communicate with

---

4. *See, e.g.,* McKinnon v Smock, 264 Ga. 375; 445 S.E.2d 526 (1994). *But see* Wilson v. Wilkinson, No. 2:04-CV-00918, 2006 U.S. Dist. LEXIS 32113 (S.D. Ohio May 19, 2006)

the attorney and each other on a telephone or video conference, or in a physical meeting. In any event, at the very least, each expert should have a general awareness of the subject matters and opinions of the other experts. A conservative approach to the discoverability of communications with experts is to assume that everything is discoverable and to plan accordingly. Some jurisdictions make all such communications discoverable, while others may determine whether the expert relied on the information in formulating his opinions.[5]

Counsel must be aware that the existence of such collaboration may be discovered and characterized as plotting or conspiracy by the opposing party. For example, while e-mail is convenient, it creates a record that may be discoverable, and it is a written form that is particularly subject to being misconstrued and misinterpreted, particularly by the opposing party seeking to cast it in a negative light. In general, written communications among the attorneys and the experts should be avoided or at least minimized. But the benefits of this collaboration usually outweigh these risks, and the downside of not coordinating the testimony of multiple experts can be disastrous to the case.

Present Your Expert in the Best Light

The next step in most jurisdictions is to present the expert for a discovery deposition. This is different than preparing for testimony at trial, as most lawyers see a deposition as something to be accomplished, survived, and left behind for trial. The expert needs to be told by counsel whether the deposition is a preliminary effort to persuade, a dry run for trial, or an exercise in holding the cards close. The expert needs a reasonable date, time, and place for the deposition, and the chance to be reasonably well prepared for the exercise. Finally, the lawyer must determine the expert's preferred billing practices in advance and shape those to reality if necessary. One of the authors encountered an unfortunate adversary expert who started a deposition by answering the standard question "please state your name" with "where's my check?"

Following the deposition, the testimony should be fine-tuned. In addition to the formality of the errata sheet, it must be determined if any course corrections for the expert, or the expert's part in the case, are necessary. Further support for the opinion, such as publications or standards, may need to be obtained and disclosed. If further work is needed, the expert

---

(holding all attorney-expert communications are discoverable but recognizing disagreement on this point among federal courts).

    5. *See* "Privilege Issues" *infra.*

needs directions, and the plan should be communicated to the opposing party as soon as is practicable. For trial, the planning that has been going on since retention should suggest the best way to present the testimony of the expert, including order and manner of testimony, and props or demonstrative aids.

Communicate the End Game

The case is over, whether by settlement, dispositive motion, or trial. It is not quite time to forget the expert witness. He needs to know how the case came out. He needs to have some critique of how he did and how he can improve. Indeed, sometimes he is in a position to return the favor of an evaluation of the case tactics and the result.

Other details that need to be handled are final billing and what the expert should do with the case materials and evidence. The expert, with assistance of counsel, needs to consider the pros and cons of keeping transcripts of depositions or other testimony, because retaining the expert's own transcripts may allow them to be discovered later.

Conclusion

Communicating with experts is like any other aspect of litigation: it must take place according to a plan, it must adapt as needs dictate, and it must be thorough enough to achieve the desired result. The better the communication, the more effective the advocacy, and the greater the likelihood of a favorable result.

PRIVILEGE ISSUES

Timothy N. Toler and Sherri G. Buda[1]

Communicating with your expert is fraught with peril. The reason is simple: how and what you communicate is potentially subject to complete disclosure to your opponent. This is particularly true for a testifying expert. Failure to carefully consider how and what you communicate to your testifying expert can have disastrous consequences for your case. The damage might include undermining the credibility of your expert, disqualifying your expert, and disclosing privileged client communications and attorney work product to your opponent.

Consider the following scenario. You are defending a client in federal court. In accordance with Rule 26(a)(2) of the Federal Rules of Civil Procedure, you have disclosed the identity of your testifying expert and submitted your expert's written report. Before taking your expert's deposition, your adversary requests production of the following:

- Your retainer agreement with your expert and all invoices submitted by your expert;
- All written communications between you and your expert, including e-mail;
- All writings, documents, and data you provided to your expert, including any summaries or evaluations prepared by you; and
- All writings, documents, and data generated by your expert, including all draft reports, marginalia, and notes of conversations with you or the client.

You have now entered the field of battle between the competing legal doctrines encompassed in Rule 26: the attorney-client privilege and work product doctrine versus mandatory and complete expert disclosure. The attorney-client privilege protects client confidences. The work product

---

1. Timothy N. Toler is a member of the construction litigation firm of Toler & Associates LLC located in Atlanta, Georgia. His practice focuses on resolving disputes for various participants in the construction process, including owners, general contractors, subcontractors, and industrial equipment suppliers. Sherri G. Buda is an associate with Toler & Associates LLC. She concentrates her practice in construction litigation and arbitration.

doctrine protects an attorney's mental impressions and trial preparation materials from discovery. The doctrine of full expert disclosure permits effective cross-examination and rebuttal of expert testimony at trial.

In most federal jurisdictions, you may soon learn that what you thought was protected is fully discoverable. While there remains some disagreement among jurisdictions, the recent trend of federal courts is toward allowing discovery of nearly all documents and information created or reviewed by testifying experts while preserving protection of documents and information created or reviewed by consulting experts who will not testify.[2]

Competing Doctrines of Rule 26

Rule 26 governs discovery in federal civil actions and is the model for most state discovery rules. The current substantive rules concerning expert discovery are based on the 1993 amendments to Rule 26.

Defining the permissible scope of expert discovery "requires an interpretation of the interaction between Rule 26(a)(2)(B), Rule 26(b)(3), Rule 26(b)(4), and the attorney client privilege."[3] Before 1993, parties were limited in what they could discover from testifying experts. Information and documents provided to the testifying expert were discoverable only if known and relied on by the expert in forming his opinion.[4] Attorney work product materials provided to a testifying expert generally retained protected status under Rule 26(b)(3) and were not discoverable.[5] This changed with the 1993 amendments. The 1993 amendments imposed mandatory disclosure obligations on testifying experts and broadened the scope of discoverable information.[6] Rule 26(a)(2)(B) was added to require testifying experts to submit a signed written report providing a complete statement of all opinions the expert will express and "the data or other information considered by the witness in forming" those opinions.

The Advisory Committee's notes to the 1993 amendments indicate that "considered" has a broader meaning than "relied upon." The Advisory Committee noted that under the obligations of Rule 26(a)(2)(B), "litigants should no longer be able to argue that materials furnished to their experts to be

---

2. It appears that much of the disagreement among jurisdictions will be resolved by a proposed amendment to Rule 26 that is expected to be approved and go into effect on December 1, 2010. *See* "Proposed Changes to Expert Discovery Rules" *infra*.

3. Synthes Spine Co. v. Walden, 232 F.R.D. 460, 462 (E.D. Pa. 2005).

4. *See* FED. R. CIV. P. 26(b)(4) (1992).

5. *See* Bogosian v. Gulf Oil Corp., 738 F.2d 587, 594–96 (3d Cir. 1984).

6. *See Synthes Spine*, 232 F.R.D. at 462.

used in forming their opinions—whether or not ultimately relied upon by the expert—are privileged or otherwise protected from disclosure when such persons are testifying or being deposed."[7] The Advisory Committee thus signaled a significant shift toward full disclosure of materials provided to or generated by testifying experts, even for materials that would otherwise receive privilege or work product protection. The majority of federal courts addressing Rule 26(a)(2) discovery disputes after the 1993 amendments have acknowledged the expanded scope of expert witness discovery.

The 1993 amendments did not modify Rule 26 discovery of an expert who has been retained or specially employed in anticipation of litigation or to prepare for trial but who is not expected to testify.[8] Nor did the amendments address discovery of experts not retained or specially employed in anticipation of litigation but who are expected, nonetheless, to give expert opinion testimony as an actor or viewer, with respect to the events in issue. These witnesses receive no protection from discovery of relevant information.

Privilege Issues concerning the Testifying Expert

The Majority View

Rule 26(a)(2)(A) requires that a party, without awaiting a discovery request, "disclose to the other parties the identity of any witness it may use at trial to present evidence under Federal Rules of Evidence 702, 703, or 705." Rule 26(a)(2)(B) mandates the submission of a written report from any witness "retained or specially employed to provide expert testimony in the case or one whose duties as the party's employee regularly involve giving expert testimony." This subchapter may refer to this person as a testifying expert or expert witness.

Since the 1993 amendments to Rule 26, the trend among federal courts has been to require the disclosure of all information and documentation provided by counsel to a testifying expert, including opinion work product and privileged attorney-client communications. Under the bright-line rule, when an expert witness considers confidential attorney-client communications in developing his testimony, offering of opinions constitutes waiver of attorney-client privilege for those communications: "[T]he disclosure of privileged materials to a testifying expert to formulate her testimony assumes that such materials will be made public or put at issue in the litigation, and

---

7. FED. R. CIV. P. 26(a)(2), advisory committee's note to 1993 amendments.
8. FED. R. CIV. P. 26(b)(4)(B).

effectuates a waiver to the same extent as any other disclosure."[9] Most federal courts hold that the opposing party is entitled to discover everything that went into an expert witness's opinion, whether or not the witness actually relied on the information. As one district court stated, "the drafters of the new Rule obviously contemplated that the term 'considered' was something different than the term 'relied' given that the drafters rejected an earlier draft version of subdivision (a)(2) that required the disclosure of 'the data or other information *relied upon* in forming such opinions.'"[10] These courts interpret "information considered" under Rule 26(a)(2)(B) to include "any information furnished to a testifying expert that such an expert generates, reviews, reflects upon, reads, and/or uses in connection with the formulation of his opinions, even if such information is ultimately rejected."[11] In the battle between the work product privilege afforded under Rule 26(b)(3) and the disclosure requirements of Rule 26(a)(2)(B), the disclosure requirements "were meant to trump all claims of privilege, mandating production of all information furnished to the testifying expert for consideration in the formulation of her opinions, regardless of privilege."[12] This would include claims of attorney-client privilege.[13]

Rationale of the Majority View

The trend toward full disclosure recognizes the increasing importance of expert testimony in determining the outcome of cases.[14] The policy considerations articulated by courts applying the bright-line rule are threefold. First, broad disclosure enables effective cross-examination of expert witnesses, which is essential to the integrity of the truth-finding process.[15] The scope of information provided and considered goes to the credibility of expert opinion.[16] An adverse party should be able to determine "to what extent counsel's observations, even if nothing more than opinions, affected the testimony of the expert."[17] Second, broad disclosure does not violate the core precepts of the work product doctrine. Counsel can protect work product

---

9. *Synthes Spine*, 232 F.R.D. at 463–64 (citing 2 Paul R. Rice, Attorney-Client Privilege in the United States § 9:33 (2d ed. 1999)).

10. Trigon Ins. Co. v. United States, 204 F.R.D. 277, 282 (E.D. Va. 2001).

11. *See Synthes Spine*, 232 F.R.D. at 463.

12. *Id.*

13. *Id.*

14. *See* Am. Fid. Assurance Co. v. Boyer, 225 F.R.D. 520, 522 (D.S.C. 2004).

15. *See id.* at 521 (citing Musselman v. Phillips, 176 F.R.D. 194 (D. Md. 1997)); B.C.F. Oil Ref. Inc., v. Consol. Edison Co. of N.Y., 171 F.R.D. 57, 66 (S.D.N.Y. 1997).

16. *See Boyer*, 225 F.R.D at 521.

17. *See B.C.F. Oil*, 171 F.R.D. at 64.

by simply not divulging it to his expert.[18] Third, the bright-line rule avoids disputes as to what information and documentation the expert "considered" in formulating his opinion.[19] Strict application of the rule requires the production of any and all information and documentation provided to one's expert witness without regard to privilege. This approach is attractive to trial courts because it lessens judicial involvement in discovery disputes and provides counsel with a clearly defined rule governing what must be produced to an adverse party.

Scope of Disclosure under the Majority View

Under the bright-line rule, a party must disclose all materials, regardless of privilege, that the testifying expert "generated, reviewed, reflected upon, read, and/or used in formulating his conclusions, even if these materials were ultimately rejected" by the expert in reaching his opinions.[20] This includes disclosure, in whatever form the expert received them, of all materials supplied by counsel, including e-mails, summaries, analyses, retainer letters, invoices, and draft reports.[21] Courts adhering strictly to the bright-line rule will not attempt to determine what was and was not considered by the testifying expert. If a party or its counsel provides information to a testifying expert, it must be produced.

Under the bright-line rule, all documents generated by a testifying expert are discoverable. This includes the expert's notes made during meetings with counsel, "regardless of whether these notes contain information that falls under the protection of the attorney-client privilege or the work product privilege."[22] All notes and draft reports generated by a testifying expert have been held discoverable.[23] It is less clear whether draft reports created by an expert but not shared with counsel are discoverable.[24]

---

18. *Id.*
19. *Id.* at 62.
20. *Synthes Spine*, 232 F.R.D. at 464.
21. *Id.*
22. *Id.*; *see also B.C.F. Oil*, 171 F.R.D. at 62.
23. *See, e.g., Am. Fid. Assurance Co.*, 225 F.R.D. 520.
24. *See Trigon Ins.*, 204 F.R.D. at 283 and n.8 (holding drafts that are not solely the product of the expert's own thoughts and work must be disclosed while declining to decide whether drafts prepared solely by that expert while formulating the proper language with which to articulate his own opinion must be disclosed); Krista v. Equitable Life Assurance Soc'y, 196 F.R.D. 254 (M.D. Pa. 2000) (holding that draft reports and other documents prepared by expert witnesses do not receive work product protection). *But see* Teleglobe Commc'ns Corp. v. BCE Inc., 392 B.R. 561 (Bankr. D. Del. 2008) (holding that expert drafts are not subject to disclosure).

There should be no distinction drawn between written communications between attorney and expert and oral communications between them, the latter being discoverable through depositions.[25] Attorney notes based on conversations with one's expert and not shown to the expert have been held not to be discoverable.[26]

The Minority View

A minority of courts take a less expansive view of the Rule 26(a)(2)(B) disclosure requirements in an effort to protect attorney-client communications and attorney work product. The minority view holds that the disclosure requirements of Rule 26(a)(2)(B) do not overcome the protection accorded to counsel's mental impressions, opinions, and legal theories disclosed to a testifying expert.[27] These courts rely primarily on two justifications.[28] The first is that the policy interests in protecting attorney work product outweigh the policy interests at stake in discovery.[29] The second is that Rule 26 lacks a "clear statement" waiving protection of attorney work product provided to an expert witness.[30] This rationale has been criticized as clearly inconsistent with the intent of the drafters of the 1993 amendments as reflected in the Advisory Committee notes.[31]

The minority view holds that where documents considered by a testifying expert contain both facts and legal theories of the attorney, only facts must be disclosed. Where both types of information exist in the same document, it is necessary to redact the document "so that full disclosure is made

---

25. *See* TV-3, Inc. v. Royal Ins. Co. of Am., 193 F.R.D. 490, 492 (S.D. Miss. 2000) (requiring disclosure of all documents and oral communications reviewed by experts in connection with formulating opinions, even those ultimately rejected or not relied on); *B.C.F. Oil*, 171 F.R.D. at 67 ("[T]here does not seem to be a principled difference between oral and written communications between an expert and an attorney insofar as discoverability is concerned."); Karn v. Ingersoll-Rand Co., 168 F.R.D. 633, 640 (N.D. Ind. 1996). *But see Synthes Spine*, 232 F.R.D. at 465 ("[P]laintiff's expert need not disclose the content of privileged communications that plaintiff's expert never considered in formulating his opinion . . . as such communications would not fall within the scope of Rule 26(a)(2)(B).").

26. *See B.C.F. Oil* 171 F.R.D. at 61–62.

27. *See, e.g., Krista*, 196 F.R.D. 254; *see also Teleglobe Commc'ns Corp.*, 392 B.R. 561 (holding that, although "considered" is more than "relied upon," work product protection still applies to "core" attorney work product).

28. *See* Stephen D. Easton & Franklin D. Romines, II, *Dealing with Draft Dodgers: Automatic Production of Drafts of Expert Witness Reports*, 22 Rev. Litig. 355, 389 (2003).

29. *Id.* (citing *Krista*, 196 F.R.D. at 259 and Ladd Furniture, Inc. v. Ernst & Young, 41 Fed. R. Serv. 3d 1633, 1640–41 (M.D.N.C. 1998)).

30. *Id.* (citing *Krista*, 196 F.R.D. at 260).

31. *Id.* at 391–93.

of facts presented to the expert and considered in forming his or her opinion, while protection is accorded the legal theories."[32] In addition, under the minority view, the mental impressions, conclusions, opinions, or legal theories of a party's attorney are discoverable in the deposition of a testifying expert only on a showing of exceptional circumstances.[33]

Privilege Issues concerning the Retained or Specially Employed Consulting Expert

The discovery rules governing communications with retained or specially employed experts who are not expected to testify at trial differ drastically from the rules for communications with testifying experts. Considering the distinct roles of testifying experts and nontestifying experts, often referred to as consulting experts, it makes sense that different discovery rules apply. Simply put, "while discovery with respect to testifying experts is essential to allow opposing counsel to adequately prepare for cross and to eliminate surprise at trial, 'there is no need for a comparable exchange of information regarding non-witness experts who act as consultants and advisors to counsel regarding the course litigation should take.' "[34]

In contrast to the rationale for allowing discovery of communications with testifying experts, policy considerations indicate that a consulting expert's communications with counsel should be shielded from discovery by an adversary. Such policy considerations include the following: (1) encouraging counsel to obtain expert advice without fear of such advice being turned over to his adversary, (2) preventing the unfairness that would result if an opposing party could reap the benefits of another party's efforts and expense, (3) preventing a chilling effect on expert consultants if their testimony could be compelled, and (4) preventing prejudice to the retaining party if the opposing party could call at trial an expert who initially provided an unfavorable opinion to the other party.[35]

Thus, unlike subsections (a)(2)(B) and (b)(4)(A) of Rule 26, which allow broad discovery from a testifying expert, Rule 26(b)(4)(B) creates a safe harbor for facts made known to and opinions developed by consulting experts in anticipation of litigation. Specifically, a party may discover facts known or opinions held by a consulting expert only as provided in Rule 35(b)

---

32. Smith v. Transducer Tech. Inc., 197 F.R.D. 260, 262 (D.V.I. 2000).

33. Haworth, Inc. v. Herman Miller, Inc., 162 F.R.D. 289 (W.D. Mich. 1995).

34. *See* Plymovent Corp. v. Air Tech. Solutions, Inc., 243 F.R.D. 139, 143 (D.N.J. 2007) (quoting Mantolete v. Bolger, 96 F.R.D. 179, 181 (D. Ariz. 1982)).

35. *See id.*

(concerning reports of experts conducting physical and mental examinations) or "on showing exceptional circumstances under which it is impracticable for the party to obtain facts or opinions on the same subject by other means."[36] Notably, the safe harbor provided by Rule 26(b)(4)(B) extends only to facts and opinions that the expert learns or develops in anticipation of litigation.[37] In this vein, information and opinions that an employee obtains or forms in the ordinary course of his work are freely discoverable.[38]

Federal district courts have split on the issue of whether the exceptional circumstances standard applies to discovery of the identity of nontestifying experts as well as their opinions.[39] Courts that allow discovery of a consulting expert's identity without a showing of exceptional circumstances have done so based on the plain language of Rule 26(b)(4)(B), which states that such a showing is required for discovery of "facts known or opinions held" by an expert who has been retained or specially employed but not expected to testify at trial.[40] On the other hand, a number of courts reason that "once the identities of retained or specially employed experts are disclosed, the protective provisions of the rule concerning facts known or opinions held by such experts are subverted."[41] Accordingly, those courts protect the identity of consulting experts under the exceptional circumstances standard.[42]

Privilege Issues concerning Experts Informally Consulted but Not Retained

While Rule 26(b)(4)(A) addresses discovery concerning testifying experts and Rule 26(b)(4)(B) addresses discovery of retained or specially employed experts who are not expected to testify, no provision is made anywhere in the rule for nontestifying experts who are informally consulted by a party in

36. FED. R. CIV. P. 26(b)(4)(B).
37. *See* Atari Corp. v. Sega of Am., 161 F.R.D. 417, 421 (N.D. Cal. 1994).
38. *See* 8 CHARLES ALAN WRIGHT, ARTHUR R. MILLER & RICHARD L. MARCUS, FEDERAL PRACTICE AND PROCEDURE § 2033 (2d ed. 2009).
39. *Compare In re* Pizza Time Theatre Sec. Litig., 113 F.R.D. 94 (N.D. Cal. 1986) (holding discovery of the identities of nontestifying experts is subject to the same exceptional circumstances standard as discovery of their opinions) *with* Eisai Co., Ltd. v. Teva Pharm. USA, Inc., 247 F.R.D. 440 (D.N.J. 2007) (holding discovery of the identity of a nontestifying expert, as opposed to his thinking, does not require a showing of exceptional circumstances) *and* Sea Colony, Inc. v. Cont'l Ins. Co., 63 F.R.D. 113 (D. Del. 1974) (same).
40. *See Sea Colony*, 63 F.R.D. at 114.
41. *See* Ager v. Jane C. Stormont Hosp. and Training Sch. for Nurses, 622 F.2d 496, 503 (10th Cir. 1980).
42. *Id.*

preparation for trial but not retained or specially employed in anticipation of litigation. Discovery concerning such experts is addressed only in the Advisory Committee's note to Rule 26, which suggests that neither the names nor the facts and opinions of informally consulted experts are discoverable under Rule 26,[43] and courts that have considered the issue have generally followed the committee's suggestion.[44] However, a party is not precluded from discovering the identity of an expert by independent investigative methods.[45]

Special Situations

Changing Designation of Expert from Testifying to Consulting Expert

It is not unusual for a party, after designating an expert as a trial witness, to later decide that it will not call the expert to testify. A majority of courts that have considered such a situation have held that once the expert is withdrawn as a witness, discovery from that expert is governed by the exceptional circumstances standard of Rule 26(b)(4)(B).[46] The exceptional circumstances standard has been held to apply even where the expert testified at an initial hearing or provided an expert report.[47] A few courts, however, have held that submitting an expert's report waives the protection of Rule 26(b)(4)(B) for that expert and subjects the expert to the possibility of being called as a witness by an opposing party.[48]

Using Employees to Provide Opinion Testimony

Courts have applied the rules concerning expert discovery to two common situations in which a party's employee will testify as an expert. On one hand, an employee who is a fact witness and also qualifies as an expert may be called to offer fact and opinion testimony. District courts are divided as to whether the documents provided to such hybrid fact and expert witnesses are discoverable.[49] On the other hand, courts appear to agree that employees

---

43. *See* Wright, Miller & Marcus, *supra* note 38; *see also Ager*, 622 F.2d 496.
44. *See, e.g.,* Procter & Gamble Co. v. Haugen, 184 F.R.D. 410 (D. Utah 1999).
45. *See id.*
46. *See, e.g., Plymovent Corp.*, 243 F.R.D. at 144.
47. *See, e.g.,* Estate of Manship v. United States, 240 F.R.D. 229 (E.D. La. 2006) (collecting case law).
48. *See, e.g.,* Penn Nat'l Ins. v. HNI Corp., 245 F.R.D. 190, 193 (M.D. Pa. 2007).
49. *Compare* R.J. *ex rel.* Ron J. v. McKinney Indep. Sch. Dist., No. 4:05-CV-257, 2006 WL 5111119, at *1 (E.D. Tex. Mar. 20, 2006) (holding because hybrid witnesses are essentially "actors" and "viewers," they are treated as ordinary fact witnesses for purposes of discovery) *with* Planalto v. Ohio Cas. Ins. Co., 256 F.R.D. 16, 21 (D. Me. 2009) (holding

who spend time developing opinions and preparing to testify are, in effect, specially employed within the meaning of Rule 26 and that, despite the rule's plain language, such employees are required to produce expert reports and subject to discovery as retained or specially employed experts.[50]

Practice Tips

1. Assume that anything given to or created by a testifying expert will be discoverable. While case law continues to evolve concerning how far Rule 26(a)(2)(B) goes in eliminating work product protection for attorney communication with a testifying expert, the majority of federal district courts faced with the problem hold in favor of mandatory disclosure over work product protection. It is best, therefore, to assume that the following will be discoverable:
   a. Your expert's retainer agreement;
   b. Your expert's notes of conversations with you or the client;
   c. Your expert's notes reflecting preliminary investigations, findings and conclusions;
   d. All drafts of your expert's Rule 26(a)(2)(B) written report, including your edits, comments, and marginalia;
   e. Your expert's invoices;
   f. All letters, e-mails, and memoranda that you exchanged with your expert; and
   g. All documents and data you provided to your expert in the manner provided.
2. Try to reach an early agreement among counsel for all parties about what is and is not discoverable. Attempt to draft an agreement specifying what must be produced and what may be withheld. The Rule 26(f) discovery conference provides a good opportunity to address expert discovery issues. Be mindful, however, of the possibility that later added parties may not agree to such ground rules.
3. Explain disclosure requirements to your expert at the earliest opportunity, and explain exactly what this means. Experienced testifying experts will have been given any manner of conflicting and inconsistent

---

unless an employee expert is "fed" facts and opinions to support his opinion testimony, documents given to a hybrid witness that are otherwise protected by the attorney work product doctrine or attorney-client privilege are not discoverable).

    50. *See, e.g.*, Minnesota Mining and Mfg. Co. v. Signtech USA, Ltd., 177 F.R.D. 459, 461 (D. Minn. 1998); Day v. Consol. Rail Corp., No. 95 CIV. 968 (PKL), 1996 WL 257654, at *1 (S.D.N.Y. May 15, 1996).

direction from previous counsel. Be sure your expert understands what you expect and why.

4. Consider minimizing the written record of communications with your expert by relying on verbal communication. Write letters and e-mail sparingly. Discourage your expert from excessive note-taking during meetings or telephone conversations. The greater the written record, the more to maintain and produce. The inherent advantages of productivity, efficiency, and clarity that written communications have over verbal communications must be weighed against the ramifications of eventual disclosure to your opponent. This analysis will vary from case to case.

5. If your jurisdiction mandates retention and production of draft expert reports, make sure this is fully understood by your expert. Discuss with your expert at what point in the process you will expect the creation of a written report, how drafts are to be designated and maintained, and whether preliminary drafts should carry some qualifying language emphasizing that the report is preliminary and subject to change as additional information becomes available or is clarified.[51]

6. Discuss with your expert how much or little detail should be included on invoices. Comprehensive narratives of all steps undertaken provide a nice roadmap for your adversary.

7. Consider initially retaining your expert as a consulting expert to be considered for designation as a testifying expert later. Communications with the expert should, of course, always assume he will become a testifying expert subject to full disclosure.

8. If you determine that the cross-examination of your testifying expert will disclose privileged communications or information that should not be disclosed, consider redesignating the expert as a nontestifying consultant or withdrawing the expert designation altogether. The consequences, however, will vary depending on jurisdiction.

9. If you do not want to waive attorney-client privileges and work product protection, do not provide the sensitive materials to your expert.

Proposed Changes to Expert Discovery Rules

Summary of Proposed Amendment to Rule 26

The Advisory Committee on the Federal Rules of Civil Procedure has recommended approval of a proposed amendment to Rule 26.[52] The

---

51. *See* Gregory P. Joseph, *Engaging Experts*, Nat'l L.J., Apr. 8, 2005, at 12.

52. *See* Report of the Civil Rules Advisory Committee (May 8, 2009) , *available at* http://www.uscourts.gov/uscourts/RulesAndPolicies/rules/Reports/CV05-2009.pdf [hereinafter May 8, 2009, Advisory Comm. Rep].

amendment is expected to be adopted and become effective on December 1, 2010.[53]

The proposed amendment has two distinct parts. The first requires counsel to produce a summary of the facts and opinions to be attested to by expert witnesses who are not required to file reports under Rule 26(a)(2)(B).[54] While important, this disclosure requirement does not affect any privilege or work product issues. The second part of the proposed amendment is highly relevant to our discussion and would substantially alter how we work with testifying experts.

The proposal generally adopts the minority rule for discovery concerning specially retained or employed expert witnesses by applying "work product protection to the discovery of draft reports by testifying expert witnesses and, with three important exceptions, communications between those witnesses and retaining counsel."[55] This change will affect how a majority of federal courts apply the attorney-client privilege and work product doctrine to communications between counsel and expert witnesses and documents prepared by those experts.

Rationale for the Proposed Changes to Expert Witness Discovery Rules

The proposed amendments to the expert discovery rules are intended to address problems created by the 1993 amendments to Rule 26, which have been widely interpreted to allow discovery of all communications between counsel and specially retained or employed expert witnesses as well as discovery of all draft reports prepared by such experts.[56] Not surprisingly, lawyers responded to the expanded scope of discovery under the 1993 amendments by taking elaborate steps to avoid creating discoverable documents while at the same time attempting to discover all communications and drafts of an opposing expert.[57] Commonly used discovery avoidance techniques include minimizing written communications between counsel and testifying experts, instructing experts to delay or avoid producing draft reports, and retaining separate consulting and testifying experts.[58]

---

53. Federal Rulemaking, http://www.uscourts.gov/rules/newrules6.htm.
54. *See* May 8, 2009, ADVISORY COMM. REP. at app. C-28.
55. REPORT OF THE JUDICIAL CONFERENCE COMMITTEE ON RULES OF PRACTICE AND PROCEDURE, at 10 (Sept. 2009), *available at* http://www.uscourts.gov/uscourts/RulesAndPolicies/rules/Reports/Combined_ST_Report_Sept_2009.pdf.
56. *Id.*
57. *See id.* at 11.
58. *See id.*

These practices have the undesirable effects of increasing the costs and burdens of discovery and reducing the quality and effectiveness of experts' work.[59] The proposed amendments are intended to make such inefficient practices unnecessary.

Changes to Expert Witness Discovery Rules

The proposed amendments clarify the interplay between the work product doctrine under Rule 26(b)(3) and the disclosures required of expert witnesses under Rule 26(a)(2) and (b)(4) by adopting what is presently the minority rule concerning expert witness discovery. The proposed rules for conducting discovery of specially retained expert witnesses or party employees who regularly provide expert testimony would revise Rule 26 as follows:

- Rule 26(a)(2)(B)(ii) would be revised to require that an expert report contain the "facts or data" considered by the witness in forming his opinions rather than the "data or other information" considered;[60]
- Rule 26(b)(4)(B) would be added to provide the work product protection of Rules 26(b)(3)(A) and (B) to drafts of any report or disclosure required under Rule 26(a)(2);[61] and
- Rule 26(b)(4)(C) would be added to provide the work product protection of Rules 26(b)(3)(A) and (B) to "communications between the party's attorney and any witness required to provide a report under Rule 26(a)(2)(B)" except to the extent the communications:
  - i. relate to compensation for the expert's study or testimony;
  - ii. identify facts or data that the party's attorney provided and that the expert considered in forming the opinions to be expressed; or
  - iii. identify assumptions that the party's attorney provided and that the expert relied on in forming the opinions to be expressed.[62]

The Advisory Committee's report provides guidance for interpreting the proposed amendments. The committee's report advises, among other things, that the change to require disclosure of "facts or data" rather than "data or other information" under Rule 26(a)(2)(B)(ii) complements the extended application of the work product doctrine expressed in Rule 26(b)(4)(B) and (C)[63]

---

59. *See id.*
60. May 8, 2009, Advisory Comm. Rep. at app. C-18.
61. *Id.* at app. C-24.
62. *Id.* at app. C-24–25.
63. *Id.* at app. C-3.

and "is meant to limit disclosure to material of a factual nature by excluding theories or mental impressions of counsel."[64] In addition, the Advisory Committee's report notes that Rule 26(b)(4)(C) will apply only to experts required to prepare a Rule 26(a)(2)(B) report and that for such experts, Rule 26(b)(4)(C) will apply to all forms of discovery, including depositions.

The proposed amendments should be a welcome change to those of us who regularly work with testifying experts. The revisions would eliminate the need for many of the cumbersome and highly inefficient practices that developed in response to the 1993 amendments and may even reduce expert-related costs. Although some will lament the move away from the transparency most courts have imposed over attorney-expert communications since the 1993 amendments, safeguards against abuse will remain. As with all rule revisions, only time will reveal how far the pendulum will swing back in this direction.

---

64. *Id.* at app. C-28.

E-DISCOVERY

Wendy Butler Curtis and Seth D. Rothman[1]

In today's electronic world, practitioners need to be more careful than ever in communicating with their experts. While the law varies from jurisdiction to jurisdiction, prudent practitioners operate under the presumption that all communications with a testifying expert are potentially discoverable. This includes e-mails and other forms of electronically stored information.

In this subchapter, we discuss the intersection of electronic discovery and testifying experts. Without meaning to be exhaustive, we have tried to provide useful advice to practitioners who are attempting to find their way through the thicket, from retaining the expert to preparing and submitting the expert's report. This subchapter overlays the preceding subchapters in the book, highlighting the importance of e-discovery when working with an expert witness.

Retention of the Expert—The Duty to Preserve Electronic Information

A party's duty to preserve potentially relevant evidence extends to its testifying experts.[2] This duty stems from the party's obligation, under Federal

---

1. Ms. Butler Curtis is eDiscovery of Counsel at Orrick, Herrington & Sutcliffe LLP and chair of its eDiscovery working group. Mr. Rothman is a partner at Hughes Hubbard & Reed LLP and co-chair of its eDiscovery Practice Group. The authors would like to express their gratitude for the substantial contributions of Lily Becker and Yohance Bowden.

2. *See* Trigon Ins. Co. v. United States, 204 F.R.D. 277, 287 (E.D. Va. 2001) (citing Vodusek v. Bayliner Marine Corp., 71 F.3d 148, 155 (4th Cir. 1995)). This subchapter does not address the obligations of nontestifying or consulting experts. Materials used by nontestifying experts are generally not discoverable, but there are some instances in which a duty to preserve those materials arguably exists. First, the federal rules provide that facts and opinions of a nontestifying expert may be discoverable on a showing of "exceptional circumstances under which it is impracticable for the party to obtain facts or opinions on the same subject by other means." FED. R. CIV. P. 26(b)(4)(B). Second, if the facts or opinions

Rule of Civil Procedure 26(a)(2)(B), to disclose the data and information considered by its expert in forming his opinions. Obviously, if the expert does not preserve the information, it will be unavailable for production and, if that happens, it is the party who suffers the consequences.[3] Thus, counsel must ensure that the expert retains this information.

When does the duty to preserve attach? Often, a party will work with an expert before deciding whether to designate that expert as a testifying expert under Rule 26(a)(2)(A). It is unclear whether the duty to preserve attaches as soon as the expert is retained, when he is actually designated as a testifying expert, or at some other time. At least one court has found that the duty to preserve did not attach until the opposing side requested the information.[4] But the best and safest practice is to instruct the expert from the outset that he must preserve all case-related materials.

Counsel should take care to issue preservation instructions before they start sending case materials to the expert. Your expert might jump the gun and start researching on his own, and you want to preserve any materials considered in that process. Indeed, it is especially important for the expert to retain the information considered during independent research because the expert is the only source of that information.

As a practical matter, preservation instructions should be put in writing and perhaps made part of the retention agreement. These instructions should be clear and unambiguous enough that the expert understands the nature and scope of the duty. Among other things, the expert should realize that he needs to save both materials found on his own and materials received from counsel, that he needs to be especially careful to preserve documents with handwritten notations, and that he needs to preserve both sent and received e-mails, as well as other types of electronically stored information.

In drafting the instructions, direct the expert to preserve everything relating to the engagement and then specify the particular items that should, at a minimum, be taken into account. These items might include the following:

- Computer(s) or laptop hard drives;
- Other electronic storage media, such as CDs, DVDs, and flash drives;

---

of a non-testifying expert are disclosed to a testifying expert, who in turn considers them, then those facts or opinions may be discoverable.

    3. *See, e.g.,* Nat'l Grange Mut. Ins. Co. v. Hearth & Home, Inc., No. 2:06-CV-54-WCO, 2006 U.S. Dist. LEXIS 97675, at *19 (N.D. Ga. Dec. 19, 2006) ("Due to the negligence of plaintiff's expert and/or adjuster in failing to preserve the evidence, the court concludes that culpability rests with plaintiff.").

    4. *See* Univ. of Pittsburgh v. Townsend, No. 3:04-CV-291, 2007 U.S. Dist. LEXIS 24620 at *11 (D. Tenn. Mar. 30, 2007) (finding that receipt of a document subpoena triggered the duty to preserve draft reports).

- Hard-copy documents;
- E-mails;
- Electronic documents, including word processing documents, text files, spreadsheets, and presentations;
- Statistical data, computations, summaries, and analyses;
- Text and instant messages; and
- Phone records and digital voice mails.

Rule 26 requires the disclosure of the materials that the expert considered in forming his opinions, but in many cases, parties request and courts require an expert to produce his entire file. Preservation instructions should be correspondingly broad and should encompass the following:[5]

- Documents and records provided to the expert;
- Pleadings and depositions;
- Corporate information;
- Communications relating to the case;
- Documents and communications relating to the expert's retention;
- Learned treatises;
- The expert's billing records or invoices; and
- Drafts of the expert's report (if any).

When issuing preservation instructions, counsel should determine whether the expert has any routine policies for document deletion or destruction, such as the automatic deletion of e-mails. An individual consultant may not have such policies, but institutional experts, like accounting and valuation firms, probably will. It is important to ensure that the expert suspends or otherwise circumvents such policies, so that discoverable information is preserved.[6]

---

5. Courts have required preservation of a broad range of information. *See In re* Zyprexa Prods. Liab. Litig., No. 1596, 2006 WL 3821491 (E.D.N.Y. Dec. 28, 2006) (ordering expert to "preserve any and all documents and information including, but not limited to, all computer(s), hard-drives, other electronic storage media, hardcopy documents, emails, e-documents, text messaging, instant messaging, phone records and voice mails . . . ; [and] billing records or invoices for services"); Synthes Spine Co., L.P. v. Walden, 232 F.R.D. 460, 464 (D. Pa. 2005) (ordering disclosure of materials supplied to plaintiff's expert "including e-mails, summaries of lost sales, summary spreadsheets, pleadings, corporate information, sales charts and breakdowns, time analyses, retainer letters and invoices, and draft expert reports"); *see also* THE SEDONA PRINCIPLES ADDRESSING ELECTRONIC DOCUMENT PRODUCTION cmt. 3.d. (The Sedona Conference, 2d ed. June 2007), *available at* http://www .thesedonaconference.org/content/miscFiles/publications_html. (discussing "requests for all of the electronic copies of expert witness reports, for access to the expert's hard drive to search for deleted data, or requests for access to all email accounts of the expert").

6. *See* Fiduciary Nat'l Title Ins. Co. v. Intercounty Nat'l Title Ins. Co., 412 F.3d 745, 750–51 (7th Cir. 2005) (expert accounting firm's "document-retention policy cannot trump

Do not send a testifying expert a copy of your document hold memorandum.[7] Some jurisdictions have found that the hold memorandum is privileged and work product,[8] and sending it to the expert may be viewed as a waiver of those protections. Even if a waiver is unlikely, sending the hold memorandum to an expert is not a good idea, as it may wind up in the expert's file and be inadvertently produced with the rest of the expert's materials.

Counsel need to take preservation seriously. An expert's failure to preserve discoverable evidence can lead to spoliation sanctions, even absent a court order requiring that the evidence be preserved.[9] Spoliation sanctions may include fines, exclusion of the expert's testimony, adverse inference instructions, and even dismissal.[10]

Communicating with Your Expert

Counsel should assume that communications with testifying experts will be produced to the other side—in most cases, they will. While the law varies from jurisdiction to jurisdiction, the general trend is toward finding that all communications between counsel and a testifying expert are discoverable.[11]

Rule 26(a)(2)(B)"); *Trigon Ins.*, 204 F.R.D. at 289 ("The document retention policies of AGE do not trump the Federal Rules of Civil Procedure or requests by opposing counsel.").

7. A document hold memorandum or legal hold is "a communication issued as a result of current or anticipated litigation, audit, government investigation or other such matter that suspends the normal disposition or processing of records" and "may encompass procedures affecting data that is accessible as well as data that is not reasonably accessible." THE SEDONA CONFERENCE GLOSSARY: E-DISCOVERY & DIGITAL INFORMATION MANAGEMENT (Working Group on Electronic Document Retention & Production (WG1) RFP+ Group, 2d ed. Dec. 2007) (on file with author), *available at* http://www.thesedonaconference.org/content/miscFiles/publications_html.

8. *See, e.g., In re* eBay Seller Antitrust Litig., No. C 07-01882 JF (RS), 2007 WL 2852364 at *2 (N.D. Cal. Oct. 2, 2007).

9. *See Trigon Ins.*, 204 F.R.D. at 285, 291 (sanctioning the defendant despite the absence of a court order to preserve specific documents).

10. *See id.* at 291 (imposing spoliation sanctions that included an adverse inference instruction, preclusion of the consultants working with the experts, and costs); *see also* United States v. Phillip Morris USA Inc., 327 F. Supp.2d 21 (D.D.C. 2004) (defendants' failure to suspend automatic deletion of e-mail precluded defendants from calling 11 key employees as fact or expert witnesses).

11. *See, e.g.*, Weil v. Long Island Sav. Bank FSB, 206 F.R.D. 38, 43 (E.D.N.Y. 2001) (ordering plaintiffs to turn over all communications between attorneys and experts that experts considered in forming their opinions); Univ. of Pittsburgh v. Townsend, No. 04-CV-291, 2007 U.S. Dist. LEXIS 24620, at *13–14 (D. Tenn. Mar. 30, 2007) (finding it was

When it comes to communications, e-mail is especially dangerous. Most people, including lawyers, are not as careful about what they say in an e-mail as they are in more formal forms of written communication. So the simple rule of thumb is not to use e-mail when communicating with experts. If you need to communicate with your expert, use the telephone.

Drill this lesson into the expert from the beginning of the retention. We prefer to use the phone or in-person meeting for all substantive communications with experts. But we also try to be practical. With some experts, no e-mail is an ironclad rule, while for others, we permit e-mail to be used to schedule meetings and for other nonsubstantive purposes. But even this makes us nervous. Once you start using e-mail, there is no telling when either you or the expert will slip and make a substantive remark that you would rather have back.

Providing Materials to Your Expert

In most cases, you will want to provide your expert with a set of case materials. These materials typically include the documents that you have received from your own client and the documents that you have received from the other side. We discuss both of these from the standpoint of electronically stored information.

The general rule is never to give a testifying expert a document that has not already been produced to the other side. In today's electronic age, however, it is not simply the document that is important, but its form. This often becomes an issue when the information comes from a database.

For example, suppose your client has a proprietary database in which it keeps certain types of information. The database has built-in functions that permit the documents to be searched and sorted, and your client considers the design of the database and its functions to be trade secrets. Your client does not want to make these features available to the other side or its expert. So, when it comes time to produce information from that database, you agree with the other side that you will run reports from the database and send these reports to them on a hard drive.

Your own expert now wants to work with the same information. He knows the client has a database and asks if he can use it. You have two

---

improper "for plaintiff's counsel to have instructed and/or otherwise suggested to the experts that such communications [with counsel] should be destroyed," because under Rule 26(a)(2), experts are required to disclose "data or other information considered by the witness in forming the opinions"); Karn v. Ingersoll Rand, 168 F.R.D. 633, 639 (N.D. Ind. 1996) ("[T]he requirements of (a)(2) 'trump' any assertion of work product or privilege.").

choices. First, you can refuse his request and give him the same hard drive of extracted data reports that you gave the other side. This is the safest way to proceed, but you may have to listen to your expert complain that with access to the actual database, he could do his work in half the time, produce exactly the reports you need, and be more certain about his analysis. Second, you can provide your expert with access to the actual database, but this runs the risk that you may have to provide your adversary's expert with the same access. As one of our adversaries so colorfully put it, "we should all be singing out of the same hymnal."

A related issue arises with whether to give your expert access to your litigation database, the database that you are using to host and review documents for purposes of the litigation. At any given time, your litigation database may contain documents in different stages of review and production. Early in the case, your litigation database will typically contain documents that have been collected from the client but have not yet been reviewed. Many of these documents will never be produced, while others will be produced in redacted form only. As the case progresses, the database will also contain documents that have been reviewed and subjectively coded. And, depending on the database, it may also contain documents in their produced form—essentially, a produced documents database that contains images of the documents exactly how they have been produced to the other side, with redactions, confidentiality legends, and Bates numbers intact.

It is this last category of documents that interests us the most. Parties sometimes grant an expert access to the produced document portion of its database for the purpose of investigating the case or preparing the expert report. When parties do so, they must be cautious. If proper security features and access authorizations are not properly enabled, the expert may wind up with access, not just to the produced documents, but also to subjective coding, to attorney comments, and possibly even to the entire document collection. This could have disastrous consequences, from waiving work product protections to making the entire database discoverable.

In *United States Fidelity & Guaranty Co. v. Braspetro Oil Services Co.*,[12] the defendants gave an expert access to a database with scanned images of 1.1 million documents. The expert did not view every document on the database, but he conducted searches across the entire database.[13] The court held that defendants "voluntarily relinquished whatever confidentiality attached to the contents of those discs, and thereby waived the attorney-client privilege with respect to everything on the discs."[14]

---

12. United States Fid. & Guar. Co. v. Braspetro Oil Servs. Co., No. 97 CIV. 6124JGK-THK, 2002 WL 15652 (S.D.N.Y. Jan. 7, 2002).
13. *Id.* at *5.
14. *Id.*

There are several possible ways to protect the privilege. First, consider whether an agreement can be reached with your adversary providing that the expert's use of the database will not waive privilege. Second, if an agreement cannot be reached, consider having an attorney conduct searches for the expert and provide the expert with the results. If these approaches are not possible, then you must familiarize yourself with the database and especially the security measures and restrictions that can be established. Once that is understood, you will be in a better position to decide whether to grant access to your expert.

One further consideration: you may have your adversary's productions stored on your litigation database, and these productions may have been made under a protective order or a confidentiality agreement. If this is the case, you must take care to ensure that your expert complies with any such order or agreement.[15]

The Expert's Own Materials

Many experts maintain their own libraries, create their own databases or analysis tools, conduct research on their own, or take custody of physical evidence related to the case. Counsel should encourage these activities as they make the expert appear more independent. But counsel must make sure that the expert keeps track of what he considers and preserves electronic evidence, especially evidence that is unique and central to the case.

In *Barnett v. Simmons*,[16] the plaintiff's expert took custody of a hard drive and then destroyed certain evidence. Although the trial court declined to impose sanctions, the Oklahoma Supreme Court reversed and remanded. The supreme court stated as follows:

> When an expert employed by a party or his attorney conducts an examination reasonably foreseeably destructive without notice to opposing counsel and such examination results in either negligent or intentional destruction of evidence, thereby rendering it impossible for an opposing party to obtain a fair trial; it appears that the court would not only be empowered, but required to take appropriate action, either to dismiss the suit altogether or to ameliorate the ill-gotten advantage.[17]

---

15. Of course, when drafting an agreed protective order or confidentiality agreement, counsel should make sure to include a provision permitting experts to review the produced documents.

16. Barnett v. Simmons, 197 P.3d 12 (Okla. 2008).

17. *Id.* at 19 (citing Holm-Waddle v. William D. Hawley, M.D., Inc., 967 P.2d 1180, 1182 (Okla. June 23, 1998)).

The Expert's Report

The drafting of the expert's report is perhaps the area where e-discovery and experts most often intersect. We take no position on whether and to what extent counsel should be involved in the drafting of the expert report. That determination depends on various factors and is beyond the scope of this subchapter. Instead, we discuss the e-discovery issues that arise concerning the drafts of the report and the electronic communications regarding those drafts.

Some courts have required parties to disclose the drafts of their testifying expert reports, while others have not, and there appears to be a split in authority over whether the disclosure requirement set forth in Rule 26(a)(2) trumps the work product protection set forth in Rule 26(b)(3).[18]

No matter which jurisdiction practitioners find themselves in, they should read the local rules. Many jurisdictions, courts, and individual judges have rules that cover this situation. For example, New Jersey makes it clear that "communications between counsel and the expert constituting the collaborative process in preparation of the report, including all preliminary or draft reports produced during this process, shall be deemed trial preparation materials discoverable only as provided in paragraph (c) of this rule."[19]

Many experts now draft their reports on a computer, making changes and revisions to a single electronic document. As the court recognized in *In re Teleglobe Communications*, this makes it impractical to compel the retention and production of all draft reports:

> For example, any time an expert added or subtracted a section, a paragraph, a sentence or even a word, the Defendants' reading of the Rules would require the expert to save the draft and preserve it for production later. This is a completely unworkable reading of the Rules and would mire the courts in battles over each draft of an expert's report. The Court concludes that this interpretation comports with neither the plain meaning of the Rule nor its policy.[20]

---

18. *Compare Trigon Ins.*, 204 F.R.D. at 282–83 (finding that drafts of reports are discoverable, where the drafts were not "solely the product of the expert's own thoughts and work") *with In re* Teleglobe Commc'ns Corp., 392 B.R. 561, 572–73 (Bankr. D. Del. 2008) (finding no obligation to produce drafts of reports). *See also* Weil v. Long Island Savings Bank, 206 F.R.D. 38 (E.D.N.Y. 2001) (finding that drafts of expert reports sent via e-mail to attorneys are discoverable, as are any comments prepared by an attorney in response to the draft).

19. N.J. Ct. R. 4:10-2(d)(1).

20. *In re Teleglobe Commc'ns Corp.*, 392 B.R. at 573.

Indeed, savvy experts who wish to avoid cross-examination concerning the different iterations of their reports know to write their reports on a computer and not to create any drafts. These experts are careful not to print out hardcopy drafts or send drafts by e-mail to counsel. Many practitioners encourage these practices and require that all discussions regarding the report be conducted in person, by telephone, or by Webex. In this way, they avoid creating discoverable drafts and communications.

Proposed Amendment to Rule 26

As we go to press, a proposed amendment to Rule 26 is pending, which, if approved, would go into effect on December 1, 2010. Citing the rising costs and "undesirable effects" resulting from the routine discovery of drafts, the Advisory Committee proposes to limit the discoverability of draft expert reports and clarify that "Rules 26(b)(3)(A) and (B) protect drafts of any report or disclosure required under Rule 26(a)(2) regardless of the form in which the draft is recorded."[21]

Moreover, the proposed rule specifically extends work product protections to communications between an attorney and his testifying expert, "regardless of the form" of the communications.[22] There are three exceptions. Communications are not protected if they (1) relate to compensation for the expert's study or testimony, (2) identify "facts or data" that the attorney provided to the expert and that the expert considered in forming opinions, or (3) identify assumptions that the attorney provided to the expert and that the expert relied on in forming opinions.[23]

What to Do in the Meantime

In 2006, the American Bar Association (ABA) passed a resolution recommending that, until the rules are amended, "counsel should enter voluntary stipulations protecting from discovery draft expert reports and communications between attorney and expert relating to an expert's report."[24] Indeed, The Sedona Conference encourages parties to meet and confer early in a litigation to determine what expert witness materials should be preserved and exchanged.[25] Meet and confers are an opportunity to reduce costs and burdens.

---

21. Report of the Civil Rules Advisory Committee Proposed Rule 26(b)(4)(C) (May 8, 2009).
22. *Id.* at 16.
23. *Id.*
24. *Discoverability of Expert Reports, in* ABA Report 120A, 4 (2006).
25. *See* The Sedona Principles, *supra* note 5.

As the Sedona Conference Cooperation Proclamation[26] and *Mancia v. Mayflower Textile Services Co.*[27] reflect, many judges expect the parties to meet and confer to resolve discovery disputes and craft creative solutions to ameliorate the ever-rising costs of e-discovery.

If the parties fail to agree on a protocol for dealing with the burden of e-discovery, the court may resolve the issue itself. For example, in *D.G. v. Henry*, the court crafted a unique solution to the problem of overly large document productions. Finding that "it would be unfair and wasteful to require Defendant Hendricks to scour the documents in an effort to anticipate which documents Plaintiff will use," the court ordered plaintiffs to provide defendants with a preliminary expert report identifying which documents the plaintiffs believed supported their contentions.[28] In this way, the defendant was relieved of the burden of performing a linear review of its own documents until after receiving the plaintiffs' preliminary expert report. This approach saves costs and narrows the universe of documents to a more manageable size.

Checklists

E-Discovery Tips for Use in Retaining an Expert

- Obtain a confidentiality agreement.
- Ensure that data security protections are in place.
- Communicate the preservation obligation in writing.
- Explain the scope of this duty: communications, documents received, draft reports, etc., but do not provide the expert with your client's document hold memorandum.
- If you have retained an expert to conduct testing to evaluate the merits of a claim, make that clear in the expert agreement. Obtain a written assurance from the expert that design testing is not specific to a particular item, but rather can be done and duplicated on identical items that are readily available.
- If the expert is working with original physical evidence, give very clear instructions on how to handle such evidence.

---

26. The Sedona Conference Cooperation Proclamation (2008), *available at* http://www.thesedonaconference.org/content/tsc_cooperation_proclamation/proclamation.pdf.

27. Mancia v. Mayflower Textile Servs. Co., 253 F.R.D. 354 (D. Md. 2008).

28. D.G. v. Henry, No. 08-CV-74-GKF-FHM, 2009 U.S. Dist. LEXIS 13739 (N.D. Okla. Feb. 20, 2009).

- If the expert is analyzing original information or computer hard drives, have a copy made. Preserve the original and give the copy to the expert so that if the expert alters or destroys information during testing, the original evidence is not altered or destroyed.
- Understand whether the expert is an independent contractor working on an individual PC or an employee of a company working on a network.
- Where applicable, ask that the expert suspend or circumvent routine policies for the destruction of documents, including systems that automatically delete e-mails.
- Determine whether the expert uses a personal e-mail account for work and ensure that he is comfortable producing e-mail from that account.
- Discuss whether the expert will create drafts of his report.
- Include a provision for the destruction of client information or the entire expert file at the conclusion of the matter. This avoids discovery requests in subsequent matters.
- Ensure that any destruction is completed in accordance with governing protective orders or confidentiality agreements.

Tips for a Meet and Confer

- Discuss with your adversary the scope of preservation obligations and the production of information from experts. Reduce agreements to writing.
- Remember that whatever you ask of your opponent's expert will likely apply to your expert.
- Consider whether you want to produce any of the following:
  - Draft reports;
  - Communications with counsel;
  - Information that is "relied upon" as opposed to "considered";
  - Metadata; or
  - Retention agreements.
- With respect to the collection of communications between expert and attorney, consider the following:
  - Agreements to collect from one but not both;
  - Agreements to limit preservation obligations to one but not both; and
  - Agreements to allow experts to search the production database or other databases without waiving privilege or objections.
- Reminder: always check the local rules, standing orders, and protocols.

Tips for Communicating with Experts

- Assume any communication with an expert should be retained.
- Assume any communication with the expert is discoverable.
- Communications should be by telephone or in person. Limit written communications with an expert, especially e-mail.
- Be cautious of exchanging draft reports. If draft reports are attached to correspondence to counsel, they should be retained and may be discoverable.
- Be hesitant to grant experts access to production databases. If they are to be granted access, be sure to double-check all security protections and levels of access. Document what access the expert was granted and consider using database functionality to track any and all documents opened or accessed by the expert.
- Once information from the expert is requested, notify the expert in writing of these discovery requests and remind the expert of the duty to preserve.
- Do not instruct an expert to destroy anything while still subject to the duty to preserve.

Checklist for Discovery Requests for Opposing Party Expert Disclosures

- Communicate your expectations to the opposing party as early as possible to trigger the duty to preserve. If expert preservation is not addressed at the meet and confer, consider sending a preservation letter to opposing counsel stating your intention to request all information considered by its experts, including communications with counsel and draft reports, and that you expect this information to be retained by expert and counsel.
- Make sure that all discovery requests are clear and well drafted. If you want all draft reports, ask for them. If you want all communications between counsel and the expert, ask for them.
- Finally, if opposing counsel or their expert claim that information was not preserved, consider moving to compel the production of all relevant computers or backup tapes. These can be used for restoration or for forensic inspection to locate relevant evidence.

Appendix A: Expert Confidentiality Agreement

This Confidentiality Agreement ("Agreement") is entered into by and between Law Firm, PLLC ("Law Firm") and A.B. Expert, Ph.D. ("Expert") (collectively, the "Parties").

WHEREAS, the Parties desire to enter into this Agreement.

NOW, THEREFORE, in consideration of the foregoing and for other good and valuable consideration, the receipt and sufficiency of which are hereby acknowledged, the Parties agree as follows:

(1) Law Firm shall provide copies of certain documents (including records, photographs, and medical records) to Expert. The terms of this agreement shall apply to all documents submitted to Expert by Law Firm;

(2) The Parties desire to meet their obligations under federal privacy regulations issued pursuant to the Health Insurance Portability and Accountability Act of 1996 and the federal standards for privacy of individually identifiable health information codified at 45 C.F.R. §§ 160 and 164. Expert is prohibited from using or disclosing protected health information for any purpose other than the litigation or proceeding for which such was submitted to Expert;

(3) Expert shall maintain the confidentiality of all documents provided to Expert by Law Firm; Expert is prohibited from providing copies of the documents, or disclosing their contents, to any other persons;

(4) Expert is required to return the records to Law Firm at the earlier of (a) the end of this litigation, and (b) request by Law Firm;

(5) Expert is required to notify Law Firm of any instance in which Expert is aware the confidentiality of the records and information has been breached.

Law Firm, PLLC   A.B. Expert, Ph.D.

By:_____   _____
Print Name:_____   Date:_____
Print Title:_____
Date:_____

CHAPTER 3

Ethical Issues in Dealing with Experts

Lawrence J. Fox and Bruce Green[1]

Can we dream? You help to fulfill your clients' dreams. Why not indulge in some of your own?

> Your case is a "big" one. Your firm is thrilled to be handling it and you are a heroine for bringing it in. Lots of documents. Close questions. Depositions galore. And a need for expert witnesses to wow the jury with the merits of your client's position.

Do not wake up yet.

> You locate the preeminent expert in the field. The expert is charming, presents well, is good-humored, has a curriculum vitae (CV) that knocks your socks off, but does not have a pretentious bone in her body. Speaks clearly. Just enough gray hair.

Still dreaming?

> And the expert endorses your position; no, she actually reinforces it with a line of analysis neither your client nor you ever considered.
>
> The expert prepares a report. Comprehensive. Understandable. To the point. Letter perfect. Just what the doctor ordered to bring the other side to its knees in the upcoming mediation. Alas, that does not work. The opponent just does not get it. They will be sorry later.
>
> The deposition prep lasts mere minutes. The testimony is better than expected. Still no settlement. But you need a good trial to get your sea legs back and your expert is your ace in the hole.

---

1. Lawrence J. Fox is a partner of Drinker, Biddle & Reath LLP in Philadelphia, where he practices primarily in the area of securities litigation. He is also the former chairman of the ABA Standing Committee on Ethics and Professional Responsibility and the Crawford Lecturer in Law at the Yale Law School. Bruce Green is the Louis Stein Professor at Fordham University School of Law, where he directs the Stein Center for Law and Ethics.

No need for trial prep. Just a slight tutorial for your benefit. And the jury loves your expert. No jargon. Great eye contact. Stands at the easel and teaches the "class." Even the judge asks questions that help your case along.

Only cross-examination can go wrong now, but, true to form, your expert remains calm, turns each question into an opportunity to reinforce the points made on direct, and returns to the easel to give a perfect summation. If you lose this case, it will be in spite of the dream expert.

Now open your eyes. We know that is what we seek to achieve. But we also know that it never happens quite that way. The path for lawyer and expert from identifying the right person (always flawed in some respect) to the final cross-examination in a windowless courtroom (featuring a cantankerous judge and a bored-to-tears jury, as well as two or three concessions you could do without) is a roadway filled with potholes, speed bumps, and detours, requiring enormous energy and good judgment, an activity that can present ethical challenges as well as strategic ones.

Others are filling this book with strategic guidance. This chapter aims to help you meet the professional responsibility requirements that pervade the expert witness process.

Do Not Forget the Client

You have decided you need an expert in a tax case. An accountant who can bless your client's challenged deductions. You need her to testify. You need her just as much to educate you. Your immediate impulse is to pick up the telephone and call an expert you think would be ideal. But not so fast!

Do not forget the client. It is the client's case. And it is the client's money you are about to spend. You are not a free agent (pun intended). You have ethical and fiduciary duties to communicate with the client, collaborate on the decision whether to hire an expert and who that expert should be, and accept the client's direction about how to proceed.[2] Clients can reject the use of an expert or have strong views on who should fill that role. And, of course, clients foot the bill for the expert's fees, which can be pretty steep. They need to know what is in store.

Client confidentiality is another important concern.[3] In talking to prospective experts, you will be sharing confidential information. But you, of course, are required to preserve the client's confidences—not just what you

---

2. *See, e.g.,* MODEL RULES OF PROF'L CONDUCT R. 1.2(a), 1.4(a), (b).
3. MODEL RULES OF PROF'L CONDUCT R. 1.6.

learned from the client but everything else "relating to the representation"—
that is, unless your client gives you "informed consent" to disclose them.[4]
Do not be tempted here to say that the client has "impliedly authorized"
you to disclose confidences to the expert "to carry out the representation;"
this is no time to rely on the client's implied consent. The client might not
recognize that disclosing client confidences is part of the process of choosing an expert and how extensive the disclosure may have to be for you to
accomplish the necessary work. So do not proceed into the expert witness
terrain without your client at your side giving approval along the way.

Shopping for the Right Expert

With the client's approval, you venture off in search of the perfect expert. It
can be an arduous task. You want someone with the right credentials, knowledge, experience, demeanor, presence, and personality. And, crucially, you
want someone whose opinions will help your client's case. As you conduct
the beauty contest and vet the expert, you want to proceed in a manner that
never comes back to haunt you. The ethical imperatives to be competent and
maintain confidentiality call on you to take precautions to prevent disclosures. The last thing you want to come out is the fact that you approached 11
different potential experts before you found the one you needed—even if you
rejected the first 10 not because of their opinions, but because they were total
geeks, brilliant, and hopeless candidates for witnesshood.

How can you keep your initial screening confidential? With respect to
experts who are not also lawyers, the best you can do is try, but there are no
guarantees. Your own screening efforts will be protected by the work product immunity, meaning that your role in the process of vetting potential
experts should not be the subject of inquiry by the opposing party. But
there is nothing you can do to prevent a potential expert who is never hired
from disclosing to the lawyers on the other side (should they later happen
upon her) that you contacted her first. Of course, when the time comes to
convey the news that there will be no second date, you may deliver a parting
admonition that you hope the proposed expert will not tell anyone that you
spoke. But the jilted expert is not duty bound to comply with your stern
instruction. If the prospective expert is contacted to testify for the other
side, the individual may have to disclose the contact to prevent these new
lawyers from getting into trouble.[5] A lawyer-expert, on the other hand, will

---

4. MODEL RULES OF PROF'L CONDUCT R. 1.0(e), 1.6(a).
5. *See* "Hiring an Opposing Expert from a Different Pending Case" *infra*.

have an ethical duty to maintain the prospective client's confidences,[6] a duty that will ordinarily continue unless and until she is designated as a testifying expert.[7]

Shopping for the Right Opinion

You have found a potential expert and are ready to move past the first date. Is this expert a keeper?

Who knows? At this early stage, you are probably not ready to vow to use this expert as a trial witness. Returning to the dream world, it is sometimes possible to decide on the expert's "witnessability" before the hiring has occurred. Maybe it is obvious, based on her prior writings, that she can support your position. Or maybe the issue in the case is easy enough to describe that the expert can evaluate it and reach at least a tentative conclusion before the engagement starts. But far more often the expert will have to learn a lot more about the case and undertake other research before reaching her tentative opinion. And that will generate not only fees for your client to pay, but also communications, both written and oral, that could later become grist for the other side's mill.

There are two confidentiality concerns regarding your communications with the potential testifying expert. The first arises if, alas, she is never designated to testify. Anticipating that possibility, you want to take steps to ensure that your communications are protected from prying eyes, never to become the topic of testimony in discovery or at trial. Toward this end, you should ensure that the expert's work remains subject to the protection of the work product doctrine to the greatest extent possible. This is likely to be so if the expert undertakes her work subject to your direction and control and neither of you shares it with anyone aside from your firm, your client, and those with whom you have a joint representation agreement. It also will require labeling documents generated by the expert as work product and limiting their distribution to those whose receipt of the documents will not destroy the assertion of work product immunity. In addition, you should ensure that the consulting expert contractually agrees that she recognizes the privilege, will not disclose any information relating to the matter unless

---

6. *See* Model Rules of Prof'l Conduct R. 1.18 ("Duties to Prospective Client").

7. A lawyer hired as a consulting expert ordinarily has a duty of confidentiality under the ethics rules. *See* ABA Committee on Ethics and Professional Responsibility, Formal Op. 97-407 (1997) (discussing lawyers' role and responsibilities as consulting and testifying experts).

you approve, and will notify you if she is contacted by anyone seeking information on the matter.

Second, and completely contrary to the simple edifice one can erect to protect all with respect to the consulting expert, is the concern that arises if the expert becomes a testifying expert. In many state courts (although no longer in federal court),[8] absent a contrary agreement between or among the parties, most or even all preparatory work by a testifying expert is subject to wholesale discovery. This includes notes, research, documents reviewed, conversations, e-mail and other written communications, drafts of reports or opinions, and materials reviewed and relied on. As a result, unless you know that the expert you are consulting will never testify or you are in a benighted jurisdiction that has adopted a narrower approach to expert discovery, it matters little that the expert's preliminary work initially might have work product protection.

Rather, you must learn the rules of the jurisdiction in which you are litigating. This is absolutely key. And the rules governing expert discovery are all over the place. Some allow just expert reports to be discovered. Some allow drafts. Some allow all documents *relied on*. Some allow all documents *reviewed*. Some allow all documents *received*. Some allow every communication between lawyer and expert. The rules on discovery are also ever-changing.

Suffice it to say for purposes of understanding your ethical obligations, your responsibility is to protect as much information as possible and at the same time advise the expert what her retention and production responsibilities are likely to be. If expert discovery is freewheeling, let your expert know that from the start, so that she can understand the need to conduct herself as if everything put in writing will be published on the front page of *The New York Times* (above the fold). If required under your rules, also advise the expert to keep every shred of paper. But note that the expert is under no obligation to write things down. And there may be more protection available in your jurisdiction for work the expert undertakes that is not shared with counsel than that which is. So you and your expert should be careful about the extent and content of your communications—particularly written communications that are most easily turned into a cause célèbre, the centerpiece of a withering cross-examination.

The issue of expert discovery creates a balancing act for the conscientious lawyer. It is good to limit the quantity of discoverable material vis-à-vis one's expert, but at the same time you do not want to limit communication

---

8. New Rule 26(a)(2)(B) of the Federal Rules of Civil Procedure, to become effective December 1, 2010 (assuming Congress does not act), requires disclosure of expert reports and allows depositions of experts in federal civil proceedings but does not require the disclosure of drafts.

(even written communication) that will prevent the expert's report and testimony from being as good as it can be. Stating the proposition from a professional responsibility point of view, the lawyer should deal with the expert in a way that maximizes privilege protections while minimizing the amount of discoverable communications. But the lawyer must do so in a manner consistent with the obligation of the lawyer to act competently in dealing with the expert. In other words, as in so many situations, wise judgment is the order of the day.

Hiring an Opposing Expert from a Different Pending Case

Your client is defending a Superfund case. Lots of experts are needed. Your client is particularly enthusiastic about a remediation expert who helped your client at another site reduce the client's contribution by half. Hire him, you are urged. But then you remember that this same expert is testifying against another client of the firm in a dispute between a seller and buyer over which entity is contractually responsible for some recently uncovered arsenic drums found in a junk pile down by the river. Can you hire this expert?

Not without difficulty. The cases may be totally unrelated. Nothing that happens in one will affect the other. That is, unless your colleague's cross-examination of this expert in the acquisition case materially undermines her ability to help your present client in the Superfund matter. As a result, it would be best to suggest an alternative expert.

If the client insists on using the expert, you have a hard question to answer. Are you reasonably certain that your firm will still be able to competently represent both the client in the Superfund case and the client in the contract action? Or will you be operating under a material limitation within the meaning of American Bar Association (ABA) Model Rule of Professional Conduct 1.7(a)(2)?[9] This means that you must be objectively convinced that your partner in the contract action will not pull punches to avoid creating a record that could be used to undermine the expert's credibility in your own case. Conversely, you must be objectively convinced that your partner will not have a need to create a devastating record of impeachment

---

9. Model Rule 1.7(a)(2) provides that there is a conflict of interest if "there is a significant risk that the representation of one or more clients will be materially limited by the lawyer's responsibilities to another client, a former client or a third person or by a personal interest of the lawyer." In that event, Rule 1.7(b)(1) and (4) allows a lawyer to undertake the representation only if "the lawyer reasonably believes that the lawyer will be able to provide competent and diligent representation to each affected client" and "each affected client gives informed consent, confirmed in writing." Model Rules of Prof'l Conduct R. 1.7.

material that would later lead your client to complain that your firm prejudiced it. If you are satisfied that neither client will be harmed, you still need the informed consent of both clients.[10] This will require two important considerations. First, you will be required to share the respective clients' confidential information. And second, to do that, you will be required to get each client's consent to that sharing. As a result, none of this may be achievable unless you manage to get permission from each client to disclose to the other its confidential information regarding both its case and its plans for expert assistance.

What if you have hired a pristine remediation expert, one who has never previously testified in your neck of the woods, but lo and behold, she is later designated as the expert by the opposing party in another case your firm is handling? Same problem. Can you anticipate and avoid it? Certainly. You can make it a term of the expert's retention agreement that, until your case is over, she will not accept engagements in cases in which your firm is on the other side. If she agrees, you avoid the conflict. If not, this may be a red flag about the expert's commitment to the engagement. In addition, even if the expert has a plausible explanation for objecting to the term, you will assume some risk by hiring the expert, and you have to decide whether the expert is so good that it is a risk worth running.

Hiring the Turncoat as an Expert

Your client knows of a disgruntled former employee of its adversary who can testify as an expert on adhesives. May you retain her to be your client's expert witness?

Putting aside that a jury may not consider a disgruntled employee to be particularly objective and that the jury may be distracted from the genuine credentials of this supposed expert, one must tread very carefully when contacting former employees, much less when hiring them. Some jurisdictions restrict communications with former key employees of the opposing organizational party. They subject these communications to Rule 4.2, which forbids communications with represented persons.[11] But even if you are free to contact this person, you still must proceed with caution. You may not

---

10. "Informed consent" means "the agreement by a person to a proposed course of conduct after the lawyer has communicated adequate information and explanation about the material risks of and reasonably available alternatives to the proposed course of conduct." MODEL RULES OF PROF'L CONDUCT R. 1.0(e).

11. MODEL RULES OF PROF'L CONDUCT R. 4.2; RESTATEMENT (THIRD) OF THE LAW GOVERNING LAWYERS § 99 (2000).

invade the other side's attorney-client privilege.[12] You also may not tor-
tiously interfere with any confidentiality agreement the employee has with
the former employer.[13] Moreover, you must not induce the former employee
to breach any fiduciary duties that he owes the old employer.[14] Rule 4.4(a)
requires you to respect the rights of third parties—including adversaries.[15]

Hiring the Other Side's Former Prospective Expert

You hired a superb expert. Everything is going well. You are on the cusp of
producing your expert report. How she will devastate the other side! Then,
in a final conversation, your expert mentions your opposing counsel. You
do not remember mentioning him before. "How do you know him?" you
ask. "Oh, I met with him a couple of weeks before you called me. Paid me
$5,000. A lot of money for me to tell him I couldn't help." "And you didn't
tell me?" you exclaim. "You never asked," is her response. The first lesson is,
of course, to have asked this question early on. If, however, you end up in
this situation, may you go ahead and retain her?

Your expert is obviously the expert of choice. The problem is, she's been
chosen twice. And in her first engagement, she may have learned the other
side's privileged information. That means that your expert could very well be
disqualified. The expert may have spoken to opposing counsel only briefly,
but you can imagine how that will be characterized in the other side's disqualification motion.

And if the other side revealed its privileged and work product information to this expert before deciding not to hire her, they will claim—and a
court may be inclined to assume—that she disclosed this information to you
after you did hire her. Communications between a prospective expert and a
potential hiring attorney can be considered privileged by the court and
should be protected from disclosure under the work product privilege.
Consequently, in *Shadow Traffic*,[16] the attorneys who hired an expert interviewed by the opposing party as a potential expert were disqualified, as

---

12. *See* Restatement (Third) of the Law Governing Lawyers § 102 (2000).
13. *See* Model Rules of Prof'l Conduct R. 4.4 cmt 1 ("[I]t is impractical to catalogue all such rights, but they include . . . unwarranted intrusions into privileged relationships, such as the client-lawyer relationship.").
14. *Id.*
15. Model Rules of Prof'l Conduct R. 4.4(a); Restatement (Third) of the Law
Governing Lawyers § 102 (2000).
16. Shadow Traffic Network v. Metro Traffic Control, Inc., 29 Cal. Rptr. 2d 693, 700
(Ct. App. 1994).

was their entire firm.[17] If you knowingly elicited the other side's privileged information, you will subject yourself to serious discipline. But even if you did so unintentionally and unwittingly, you still run the risk of being disqualified to prevent you from using what you learned.[18]

Hiring All the Available Experts

You have hired the very best of the available experts, but there still are several very good ones out there. You would not be thrilled to see any of them on the other side. So what about this idea? You identify the other four or five leading experts on the issue, contact them for possible retention, give them lots of confidential information, maybe even pay each one something, and that way your adversaries will either have to settle for second best or go far afield in search of their expert witness.

Although it is a creative idea, contacting experts just to make them unavailable to the other side would probably be a waste of money and effort and, worse yet, might violate the rules of professional conduct. As the court observed in *Paul v. Rawlings Sporting Goods Co.*, if the courts make it too easy to disqualify an expert, "unscrupulous attorneys and clients may attempt to create an inexpensive relationship with potentially harmful experts solely to keep them from the opposing party."[19]

Compensating Your Expert

Your client has a great claim. You have taken it on a contingency fee, in part because the client has no cash. You have found the ideal expert witness—a leader in the field of fluid dynamics. Nothing stands in the way of hiring her. She has never spoken to the other side. She has never been hired by one of your other opponents. Well, maybe there is one impediment. Money. The best do not come cheap. $850 per hour! And now your cash is running low, too. You explain your plight to the expert and she sympathizes. "No problem,"

---

17. *Id.* at 705.
18. Mayer v. Dell, 139 F.R.D. 1, 3 (D. D.C. 1991). *See, e.g.,* Connors v. Dawgert, 38 Pa. D. & C. 4th 367, 381 (1998) (finding that an expert who had received a solicitation letter from the plaintiff could serve as an expert witness for the defense where the expert did not remember receiving the letter and the letter contained no confidential information); Cordy v. Sherwin-Williams Co., 156 F.R.D. 575, 581–82 (D.N.J. 1994) (holding that an expert who had billed 28 hours and received confidential information could not act as a witness for the opposition).
19. Paul v. Rawlings Sporting Goods Co., 123 F.R.D. 271, 281–82 (S.D. Ohio 1988).

she says. "You took the case on a contingency. So will I. Promise me five percent of any recovery by the client. That is how much I think you are right."

You are entering more than treacherous terrain. You have solved your cash flow problem. But you have created a bigger one. It is unethical to pay testifying experts a contingent fee. The *Restatement (Third) of the Law Governing Lawyers* prohibits paying a witness a fee contingent on the outcome of the litigation or on the content of her testimony.[20] Otherwise, an expert may be paid for expenses she incurs as a result of testifying and a noncontingent fee.[21] While the Model Rules are a bit oblique in their discussion regarding expert witness fees,[22] almost all jurisdictions prohibit the payment of contingency fees to experts.[23]

The only proper way to proceed is to pay the expert for her time, without regard to the content of her testimony or the result of the proceeding. Even if it were not contrary to the ethical rules to make an expert's compensation contingent on the outcome of the trial, the arrangement would be bad lawyering. What credibility will your expert have once it is disclosed that her compensation is tied to victory? Juries start off viewing party-retained experts with some suspicion. Undermining your expert's credibility by entering into a contingent fee arrangement would border on malpractice—or cross that border—even if it were otherwise permissible.

Influencing the Expert's Opinion

Your case has multiple defendants. You represent one of them. Your job is to shift blame to the others. To support this effort, you have hired a renowned metallurgy expert—a professor from the M.I.T. of your state. But the good professor comes back with a tentative opinion that is not quite as helpful as you would have hoped. It leaves open the question of whether your client's product could have played a role, albeit minor, in the ultimate disaster that prompted the high-stakes litigation. Your client reviews the expert's preliminary conclusions with dismay. The client remains convinced that the catastrophe did not

---

20. Restatement (Third) of the Law Governing Lawyers § 117 (2000).

21. *Id.*

22. Model Rule 3.4(b) explains, "A lawyer shall not . . . offer an inducement to a witness that is prohibited by law . . . "

23. Restatement (Third) of the Law Governing Lawyers § 117 cmt. d (2000); *see* Model Rules of Prof'l Conduct R. 3.4 cmt. ("The common law rule in most jurisdictions is that it is improper . . . to pay an expert witness a contingency fee."). A few jurisdictions, however, do allow expert witness contingency fees. *See, e.g.,* D.C. Rules of Prof'l Conduct R. 3.4 cmt. 8 (2007) (allowing experts to be paid contingency fees but prohibiting the fee to be based on a percentage of any recovery).

result from its product. The client says that the professor should go back to the drawing board. And it wants you to help the professor see the light.

Is it ethical to work with (or over) the expert in an effort to shape her conclusions? Of course it is. In the end, your obligation of competence requires that you put on the stand an expert who is at ease with his or her opinions. It is perfectly legitimate to help the witness get to that point by identifying facts the expert might have overlooked, subject areas the expert has not addressed, or theories that might support a different opinion. Your client has been living the case for years; you have been engaged in the matter for months yourself; and, as a result of the well-trodden path you both have walked 100 times, you both may be able to help the expert.

Your expert must maintain her credibility and integrity. But that does not mean your expert must be cloistered from your influence, a monk who takes your client's original problem and returns, after an unguided journey to a sheltered expert temple, with some irrefutable truth. So *push* if you wish. The good expert will refuse to leave her comfort zone but could very well be persuaded to revisit initial opinions and address additional topics suggested by your client or you. The fact that these discussions could form the basis of cross-examination is, of course, one issue you must consider. But having your expert admit that, with the receipt of additional information, the expert's opinion was modified is far better than failing to have your expert address an important topic, allowing your expert to proceed from a flawed premise, or having your expert remain ignorant of some new development in her field of expertise.

Ghostwriting the Expert's Report

Your expert formulates her views and now it is time to set them down in an expert report to present to the opposing party. Your expert is a genius and fully supports your side, but she has written a draft report that is a disaster. No one without a Ph.D. in biochemistry and 20 years of National Institutes of Health–sponsored research lab experience could understand it. Can you rewrite her report? Is that ethical?

In many cases you may and, if you are being competent, perhaps you must. It is your responsibility to work with the expert to achieve a clear, concise, and comprehensive report. Translating her highfalutin language into something the judge, jury, and opponents will understand is critical. Maybe in the dream world your expert's report is letter perfect from the first draft. But in the real world, the expert's first draft will often need editing, even heavy editing. And, in some cases, the expert is simply incapable of producing a cogent report. So you can write away with three huge caveats.

First, you had better assure yourself that you are writing or rewriting a report that accurately reflects your expert's opinions. The touchstone of the rules is not whether the expert prepares the report in isolation from the lawyer, but whether the report accurately reflects the expert's opinions and findings.[24]

Second, the Federal Rules of Civil Procedure require that expert witnesses "prepare" their reports.[25] A lawyer may aid an expert witness in preparing his or her testimony, but the expert must substantially participate in the preparation.[26] If the lawyer prepares the expert's report from whole cloth and then asks the expert to sign the report, the expert fails in his duty to prepare the report.[27] Furthermore, if the lawyer prepares and submits a report that does not reflect the expert's actual opinion, then the lawyer violates Federal Rule of Evidence 702.[28] Consequently, a lawyer may participate in the preparation of an expert report, but the ultimate document must reflect the actual opinion of the expert.

Third, you have to be prepared for your role in editing, rewriting, or writing your expert's report to be disclosed in testimony. Only you can make the call whether the game is worth the candle. But there is certainly nothing unethical about your role as author or editor, that is, as long as your expert later answers questions truthfully about your invaluable assistance.[29]

Coaching Your Expert

You want to spend days preparing your expert's testimony for deposition or trial and girding your expert for cross-examination—maybe even videotaping the entire event and showing it to the expert and to your jury consultant, too, if the stakes are high and your client can afford it. Is that unethical?

Not at all. Your job is to prepare witnesses. It is your ethical obligation. Letting an unprepared witness on the stand might border on malpractice. This upcoming trial is a crucial event. Entering a courtroom is an intimidating experience. If your expert is new at this, you might even want to

---

24. *See* Standing Committee on Legal Ethics of the Virginia State Bar, Op. 1726 (1998) ("[A] lawyer may prepare a medical report for a physician who is his expert witness to review, and to sign if it accurately reflects the physician's own findings and opinions.").

25. Fed. R. Civ. P. 26(a)(2)(B).

26. Trigon Ins. Co. v. United States, 204 F.R.D. 277, 292–93 (E.D. Va. 2001).

27. *Id.* at 293 (citing Manning v. Crockett, No. 95 C 3117, 1999 WL 342715, at *2–3 (N.D. Ill. May 18, 1999)).

28. Fed. R. Evid. 702 (an expert witness may testify if . . . "the witness has applied the principles and methods reliably to the facts of the case"); *Trigon Ins.*, 204 F.R.D. at 294.

29. *Cf.* Resolution Trust Corp. v. Bright, 6 F.3d 336 (1993).

walk the expert down to the courthouse to watch a trial or two, at least to get the feel of the place. More important, it is crucial that you prepare the expert witness, this $1,000-per-hour genius, to deliver the truthful opinion testimony that is critical to your case in a way that is totally understandable to judge and jury.

This can be accomplished only through extensive preparation. Jettison the jargon. Simplify the sentences. Turn the lofty research professor on the cusp of a Nobel Prize into a junior high school teacher who makes no assumptions and delivers the key information in an accessible and understandable way. Does this take time? Of course it does. Does this take patience? Sure. But, the important lesson is that it is perfectly proper to so proceed.

Similarly, if your expert's testimony might be conveyed, in part, through demonstrative evidence, it is perfectly acceptable not only to suggest but also to assist the expert in developing such material. Decisions, for example, on how slick or folksy to make the expert's graphs and charts are perfectly appropriate topics for discussion between lawyer and expert witness.

All of this comes with two caveats, but they are the same caveats that apply to most witness preparation. First, the preparation of the expert, though arguably work product, may turn out to be an appropriate topic for cross-examination—and perhaps an embarrassing one. (You rehearsed how many times?) As with so many judgments the ethical lawyer must make, striking the right balance is a consideration that deserves careful attention. Second, and this is absolutely critical, you may not counsel the expert (or any other witness, for that matter) to testify falsely or allow her to do so.[30]

---

30. *See* RESTATEMENT (THIRD) OF THE LAW GOVERNING LAWYERS §116 cmt. b:
   In preparing a witness to testify, a lawyer may invite the witness to provide truthful testimony favorable to the lawyer's client. Preparation consistent with the rule of this Section may include the following: discussing the role of the witness and effective courtroom demeanor; discussing the witness's recollection and probable testimony; revealing to the witness other testimony or evidence that will be presented and asking the witness to reconsider the witness's recollection or recounting of events in that light; discussing the applicability of law to the events in issue; reviewing the factual context into which the witness's observations or opinions will fit; reviewing documents or other physical evidence that may be introduced; and discussing probable lines of hostile cross-examination that the witness should be prepared to meet. Witness preparation may include rehearsal of testimony. A lawyer may suggest choice of words that might be employed to make the witness's meaning clear. However, a lawyer may not assist the witness to testify falsely as to a material fact.

Squaring Off against an Expert Who Is Also
Your Client in Another Matter

The other side just identified its damages expert—an economist you know well. Indeed, you admire this individual's work with which you are way too familiar. Why the treasure trove of information? Because this expert—the person hired to force your client to pay triple any reasonable amount if your client loses—is your firm's client. So is her little consulting business, which your firm incorporated. How cozy is that?

Is this a problem? You bet! You have a conflict of interest. Actually, two. Without her informed consent, you may not cross-examine your firm's own client, even if she is just a third-party witness. How could you ever tear into her exaggerated credentials or accuse her of offering the best opinion money can buy? She is entitled to take offense. You may not act directly adverse to a client without her informed consent, and attempting to impeach your client on cross-examination is an example of direct adversity.[31] That is the first conflict.

The second is that, to spare the client-expert's feelings and reputation, there is a risk that you will pull your punches in cross-examining her. That is a problem for the party you represent in the lawsuit. You owe that party zealous, not half-hearted, advocacy. Even if you are confident that your cross-examination of the client-expert will be first rate, you may not conduct it without the informed consent of the client for whom you are litigating.

Does this mean you will have to give up the case? It is certainly a development you will have to discuss right away with your client in the litigation. Perhaps there will be no way around withdrawing from the representation so that your client in the litigation can hire a new lawyer who has nothing standing in the way of a devastating deposition and cross-examination of the opposing expert. But wait! The client wants you to remain on the case. All that time and money has been invested in educating you. And you are such a great trial lawyer. A switch now would work a severe hardship. The client happily will waive the conflict.

That, of course, only solves half the equation. Can you actually ask your expert client to waive the conflict as well? Rule 1.7(b)(1) certainly suggests the answer could very well be no. It provides that, before you even ask for a waiver, you must conclude that *each* representation will be able to proceed with diligence and competence. That is a difficult conclusion to reach when

---

31. Model Rules of Prof'l Conduct R. 1.7(a)(1); ABA Committee on Ethics and Professional Responsibility, Formal Op. 92-367.

any objective observer would conclude that your cross-examination of your own client must be circumscribed by your continuing loyalty to the client. This is not unlike asking a client for a waiver to sue it for a Racketeer Influenced and Corrupt Organizations Act (RICO) or securities fraud violation or for punitive damages. Yet one could imagine a case in which the nature of the testimony (and more important, the nature of the anticipated cross-examination) might make the seeking of a waiver a legitimate possibility, though if you proceed that way, you must keep in mind that the waiver may only be limited to the circumstances you now anticipate. If those circumstances change, a new waiver may need to be sought or, more likely, another solution found at that later date.

Can you put an end to your representation of the opposing expert, your once cherished client? That may be hard. Courts do not like it when you drop one client like a hot potato to represent another client.[32] Here, you might plead, the representation of the party to the lawsuit was well under way when the conflict arose. And you could not have anticipated it. The court may be sympathetic, especially if it thinks the client-expert will be harmed less than the party to the lawsuit if the former has to lose her lawyer of choice.[33]

Maybe there is an even better solution, though. There is at least a suggestion in the previously cited ABA Formal Opinion 92-367 that new counsel could be brought in to cross-examine the expert whom you represent in another matter. It would require that the area of your client's expert testimony be a discrete part of the matter and that you would not only *not* conduct the cross-examination, but also not participate in any way in the preparation for the cross-examination as well as the direct examination of your side's expert. The conflict-of-interest rules apply with equal vigor to what is done behind the scenes as to what occurs in the conference or courtroom.

Cozying Up to the Other Side's Expert

You know the other side's expert. Your kids go to the same school. You see her at PTA meetings and school plays from time to time. If you took her out to lunch, you would have a chance to persuade her of the error of her ways.

---

32. *See, e.g.,* Harte Biltmore, Ltd. v. First Pennsylvania Bank, N.A., 655 F. Supp. 419 (S.D. Fla. 1987).

33. *See* Model Rules of Prof'l Conduct R. 1.7 cmt. 5; *In re* Sandahl, 980 F.2d 1118 (7th Cir. 1992).

You have looked at Rule 4.2. It tells you that you may not contact represented persons. But she is not represented. She is a mere witness. So you wonder, why not?

There are two "why nots." First, if you contact this proposed expert to talk about this case, you could be violating Rule 4.4(a), which requires you to respect the rights of third parties. This includes the rights of your adversary. And one of those rights is the right to work product protection. Talking to the other side's expert would run an almost certain risk that you would be learning work product of the other side. Yet the meeting would be just a wasted, albeit pleasant, lunch, if you did not learn work product. Why else take the time?

It may be no excuse that if the other side's expert testifies at a deposition or at trial, this information will be discoverable anyway. First, the expert has not testified yet and may never testify. Second, if he does testify, it will be under circumstances that will permit the other side's lawyer to object and limit the inquiry. Many courts cabin the permissible areas of inquiry so that the only discovery of the other side's expert to which you are entitled is the discovery provided by the rules. In some jurisdictions, that means you get a report.[34] In others, you get a report and a deposition.[35] In still others, you get a report, a deposition, drafts, and all documents the expert received. Whatever the jurisdiction allows probably does not include a one-time ex parte lunch filled with intrusive or even subtle questioning and persuading.

Preventing Your Expert from Cozying Up to Opposing Counsel

Can you instruct your expert witness not to talk to the other side? It makes sense that you can do so—at least in those jurisdictions that limit the available discovery from experts. If the other side is entitled only to your expert's report, the instruction simply helps prevent opposing counsel from surreptitiously undermining the discovery rule. But if the jurisdiction does not prohibit a party's lawyer from communicating ex parte with the other side's expert, the instruction may run afoul of Rule 3.4(f),[36] though you may inform your expert that there is no requirement that she chat with the other side. It may also be a strategic error to give the forbidden instruction. The

---

34. Pa. R. Civ. Proc. 4003.5.
35. N.J. R. Civ. Proc. 4:10-2(d).
36. Rule 3.4(f) of the ABA Model Rules provides that a lawyer shall not "request a person other than a client to refrain from voluntarily giving relevant information to another party . . . "

jury may view your expert as overly partisan if it comes out on cross-examination that you instructed her not to talk with the opposing counsel. Still, you can at least warn your expert not to share any material with the other side that is covered by the work product protection or the attorney-client privilege. Again, the fact that the expert may testify by deposition or in open court does not open the expert to these informal inquiries because the expert might not testify and, even were the expert to testify, certain areas of inquiry could be the subject of sustainable objections.

The Prevaricating Proctologist

You are in the middle of defending a medical malpractice case. The plaintiff claims that your client, a doctor, misread the films and missed colon cancer. Your expert heads the radiology unit at State University Hospital. He is an impressive guy, and he obviously wowed the jury. You obtain a defense verdict, and now the case is up on appeal on a challenge to the jury instructions. You are not concerned. But wait! There is a problem with your expert's credentials. He is not board-certified and has been masquerading as such for 20 years. Unfortunately, you did not discover this fact when vetting your expert. Fortunately, your side already won, right?

Wrong. The case is still pending, and your duty to correct your witness's false testimony under Rule 3.3 continues until it is over.[37] So if this is materially false testimony, you have to supplement the record even now. Can you argue it is not material? We do not think so. Even if it were just one line on a 50-page CV, it is a material line. Board-certified means something. And he was your witness. You undoubtedly elicited his exalted credential right at the beginning of his direct testimony. What a shame, but life is too short, and your obligation is too clear.

---

37. Model Rules of Prof'l Conduct R. 3.3:
(a) A lawyer shall not knowingly:
    (1) make a false statement of fact or law to a tribunal or fail to correct a false statement of material fact or law previously made to the tribunal by the lawyer;
    (2) fail to disclose to the tribunal legal authority in the controlling jurisdiction known to the lawyer to be directly adverse to the position of the client and not disclosed by opposing counsel; or
    (3) offer evidence that the lawyer knows to be false. If a lawyer, the lawyer's client, or a witness called by the lawyer, has offered material evidence and the lawyer comes to know of its falsity, the lawyer shall take reasonable remedial measures, including, if necessary, disclosure to the tribunal. A lawyer may refuse to offer evidence, other than the testimony of a defendant in a criminal matter, that the lawyer reasonably believes is false.

Conclusion

From start to finish, your work with expert witnesses can present ethical challenges no less than strategic ones. Client counseling, confidentiality, competence, conflicts, candor, observing limits on communications with both represented and unrepresented persons—these ethical considerations and others may be implicated along the way. It is good to chart the straight and narrow path—and to stay on it. The reality may never be as good as your dream. But you certainly do not want to make it a nightmare.

CHAPTER 4

Expert Reports

John L. Tate, Clark C. Johnson, and Michael K. Kim[1]

If a party has retained or employed an individual who is expected to testify as an expert witness pursuant to Federal Rule of Evidence 702, Federal Rule of Civil Procedure 26 mandates that a pretrial disclosure be made in the form of a written report[2] signed and prepared by the witness. The requirements of Rule 26(a) are mandatory and self-executing.[3] This subchapter provides an overview of Rule 26(a), explains the rule's background, summarizes the penalties for failing to disclose an expert report, discusses which witnesses are required to produce a report, details the report's content, and outlines the obligation to supplement.

Overview of Federal Rule of Civil Procedure 26(a)

Rule 26(a)(2)(B) requires all expert witnesses "retained or specially employed to provide expert testimony in the case or whose duties as an employee of the party regularly involve giving expert testimony" to provide an appropriate written report.[4] Rule 26(a)(2)(A) requires that the report be served on "other parties" and not just the adversary. Unless the trial court orders otherwise, the expert report must be provided 90 days before trial or, for

---

1. The authors practice with Stites & Harbison PLLC in the firm's office in Louisville, KY. Mr. Tate is a Fellow of the American College of Trial Lawyers. Mr. Johnson is a member of the firm, and Mr. Kim is an associate, in the Business Litigation Group.

2. State rules of civil procedure may depart from the federal rules. The practitioner should be aware that some states do not require expert reports.

3. Nguyen v. IBP, Inc., 162 F.R.D. 675, 681 (D. Kan. 1995) ("If the expert is unable or unwilling to make the disclosures he should be excluded as a possibility for retention as an expert witness in the case.").

4. FED. R. CIV. P. 26(a)(2)(B).

experts whose testimony is intended solely to contradict or rebut other experts, within 30 days after the disclosure of the material to be rebutted.[5]

Rule 26 mandates full disclosure of expert witness testimony with the aim of reducing surprise and lowering litigation costs.[6] Furthermore, since Rule 26 reports must disclose all the topics and opinions to which an expert expects to testify,[7] depositions—if taken—are expected to be more focused and efficient.[8] The drafters of Rule 26(a)(2)(B) expressed the hope that fulsome reports could help further reduce the fees and costs associated with expert discovery.[9]

Background of Current Rule 26(a)

Before the 1993 amendments to the Federal Rules of Civil Procedure, parties were limited to the discovery methods listed in Rule 26(a) to obtain information about testifying experts. The pre-1993 rules generally limited an inquiring party's knowledge of an opposing expert to interrogatory answers or a discovery deposition or, most commonly, both.[10] The 1993 amendments introduced the concept of "required disclosures," that is, disclosures that a party must make "without awaiting a discovery request."[11]

Under the 1993 amendments, expert testimony became a "required disclosure" to be made in the form of a written report conforming to the specific content requirements of Rule 26(a)(2)(B). The purpose was to accelerate the exchange of information and eliminate unnecessary discovery requests.[12] Requiring a written and signed report setting forth the expert's proposed opinions and the reasons supporting them was intended to "focus and expedite the deposition, and even avoid any need for a deposition in some cases."[13] Accordingly, Rule 26(a) "imposes on parties a duty to disclose,

---

5. Fed. R. Civ. P. 26(a)(2)(C).

6. *See* Fed. R. Civ. P. 26(b)(4)(A) Advisory Committee's note (1993); Fielden v. CSX Transp., Inc., 482 F.3d 866, 871 (6th Cir. 2007).

7. *See* Fed. R. Civ. P. 26(a)(2)(B) (stating that a report must contain "a complete statement of all opinions the witness will express and the basis and reasons for them").

8. *See* Fed. R. Civ. P. 26(b)(4)(A) Advisory Committee's note (1993) ("Since depositions of experts required to prepare a written report may be taken only after the report has been served, the length of the deposition of such experts should be reduced, and in many cases the report may eliminate the need for a deposition.").

9. *See Fielden*, 482 F.3d at 871.

10. *See* Fed. R. Civ. P. 26(b)(4)(A) (1980) (amended 1993).

11. *See* Fed. R. Civ. P. 26(a)(1).

12. *See* Fed. R. Civ. P. 26(a) Advisory Committee's note (1993).

13. Civil Rules Advisory Committee, Meeting Minutes 15 (Sept. 7–8, 2006), *available at* http://www.uscourts.gov/RulesAndPolicies/rules/Minutes/CV09-2006-min.pdf.

without awaiting formal discovery requests, certain basic information that is needed to prepare for trial or make an informed decision about settlement."[14] Moreover, comprehensive expert reports ensure "that opposing parties have a reasonable opportunity to prepare for effective cross examination and perhaps arrange for expert testimony from other witnesses."[15] Rule 26 therefore is intended to help "focus the discovery that is needed, and facilitate preparation for trial or settlement."[16]

Penalties for Failing to Disclose Rule 26(a) Expert Reports

Along with the disclosure requirements of Rule 26(a)(2)(B) came the concept of mandatory sanctions under Federal Rule of Civil Procedure 37 for failing to make the required disclosures. The Advisory Committee explained that, before the 1993 amendments, information disclosed under Rule 26 about the substance of expert testimony "was frequently so sketchy and vague that it rarely dispensed with the need to depose the expert and often was even of little help in preparing for a deposition of the witness."[17] The possibility of sanctions under Rule 37 (along with Rule 702 of the Federal Rules of Evidence) now "provide[s] an incentive for full disclosure; namely, that a party will not ordinarily be permitted to use on direct examination any expert testimony not so disclosed."[18]

In its current form, "Federal Rule of Civil Procedure 37(c)(1) requires absolute compliance with Rule 26(a)—that is, it 'mandates that a trial court punish a party for discovery violations in connection with Rule 26 unless the violation was harmless or is substantially justified.'"[19] A party failing to make the requisite disclosure bears the burden of proving the omission was either harmless or substantially justified.[20] A violation is considered harmless only if there was an honest mistake by the disclosing party coupled with sufficient knowledge of the information by the opposing party to avoid unfairness.[21] The determination of whether a Rule 26(a)

---

14. FED. R. CIV. P. 26(a) Advisory Committee's note (1993).
15. FED. R. CIV. P. 26(a)(2) Advisory Committee's note (1993).
16. FED. R. CIV. P. 26(a)(1) Advisory Committee's note (1993).
17. FED. R. CIV. P. 26(a)(2)(B) Advisory Committee's note (1993).
18. *Id.*
19. Roberts v. Galen of Virginia, Inc., 325 F.3d 776, 782 (6th Cir. 2003).
20. *Id.; see also* Mitchell v. Ford Motor Co., 318 F. App'x 821, 824 (11th Cir. Mar. 9, 2009); Heidtman v. County of El Paso, 171 F.3d 1038, 1040 (5th Cir. 1999); Salgado v. Gen. Motors Corp., 150 F.3d 735, 741–42 (7th Cir. 1998).
21. *Roberts*, 325 F.3d at 783.

violation is harmless is entrusted to the broad discretion of the district court.[22]

The consequences of violating Rule 26 are severe: "[Any] party that without substantial justification fails to disclose information required by Rule 26(a) . . . is not, unless such failure is harmless, permitted to use as evidence at a trial, at a hearing, or on a motion any witness or information not so disclosed. In addition to or in lieu of this sanction, the court, on motion and after affording an opportunity to be heard, may impose other appropriate sanctions."[23]

When fashioning a remedy, the district court will consider, inter alia, the reason for noncompliance, the surprise and prejudice to the opposing party, the extent to which allowing the information or testimony would disrupt the order and efficiency of the trial, and the importance of the information or testimony.[24]

Witnesses Required to Produce Rule 26(a) Expert Reports

The straightforward language of the rule, requiring a written report from any expert witness "retained or specifically employed to provide expert testimony in the case or whose duties as an employee of the party regularly involve giving expert testimony,"[25] is intended to promote consistent application.[26] Under the plain meaning, the rule requires reports from individuals who are retained by a party to testify in a legal proceeding; employees of a party who qualify as expert witnesses but are not regularly engaged in testifying are not required to provide a Rule 26 report.[27]

---

22. *See* Neiberger v. FedEx Ground Package Sys., 2009 U.S. App. LEXIS 11161, at *18 (10th Cir. May 27, 2009).

23. *See* Canterna v. United States, 2008 U.S. App. LEXIS 16653, at *10–11 (3d Cir. Mar. 7, 2008) (quoting Fed. R. Civ. P. 37(c)(1)).

24. Wegener v. Johnson, 527 F.3d 687, 692 (8th Cir. 2008).

25. Fed. R. Civ. P. 26(a).

26. *See* Duluth Lighthouse for the Blind v. C.G. Bretting Mfg. Co., 199 F.R.D. 320, 325 (D. Minn. 2000) ("We are not empowered to modify the plain language of the Federal Rules so as to secure a result that we think is correct.").

27. GSI Group, Inc. v. Sukup Mfg. Co., 2007 U.S. Dist. LEXIS 18764 (C.D. Ill. Mar. 16, 2007) (denying motion to compel the production of privileged materials relied on in a submitted expert report because the report was not required by the expert employees); *see also* Bowling v. Hasbro, Inc., 2006 U.S. Dist. LEXIS 58910, at *5–6 (D.R.I. Aug. 10, 2006) (not requiring employee experts to submit an expert report because "the plain language of the Rule provides otherwise. Parties should have the certainty that the Court will construe the Federal Rules as written and not have to guess as to which line of conflicting authority the Court might follow in construing an unambiguous procedural Rule"); Adams v. Gateway, Inc., 2006

Courts aware of the policy considerations at play in Rule 26 often look to the Advisory Committee's notes for guidance,[28] in effect treating the notes as a form of legislative history to guide them in their interpretation.[29] Thus, "[t]he construction given the Advisory Committee is of weight,"[30] and the explanatory statements of the Advisory Committee should be considered when ascertaining a rule's meaning.[31]

The rule's clear language and the Advisory Committee's notes are not enough to eliminate all disputes, however. For example, the notes identify treating physicians as an example of expert witnesses who "can be deposed or called to testify at trial without any requirement for a written report."[32] The rule contemplates that treating physicians are not "retained or specifically employed to provide expert testimony," presumably because their opinions are developed without regard to litigation.[33] But this is not always true. Consequently, some courts have required reports from treating physicians.[34]

U.S. Dist. LEXIS 14413 (D. Utah Mar. 10, 2006) (not requiring employee of coplaintiff and expert on technical subject matter to submit expert report because he was not regularly involved in litigation and unaccustomed to preparing expert reports); Navajo Nation v. Norris, 189 F.R.D. 610, 613 (E.D. Wash. 1999) ("If the drafters had intended to impose a report obligation on all employee-experts, they could have and would have done so. . . . [But] the plain language of FRCP 26(a)(2)(B) requires the report only of experts in the two explicit categories stated.").

28. United States v. Watson, 485 F.3d 1100, 1107 (10th Cir. 2007) ("On one hand, the rulemakers were clearly concerned about the fulsome and efficient disclosure of expert opinions when they adopted the report requirement for most cases and experts. On the other hand, it is apparent that the rulemakers did not think reports should be required in all cases and seemed concerned, for example, about the resources that might be diverted from patient care if treating physicians were required to issue expert reports as a precondition to testifying.").

29. Reed v. Binder, 165 F.R.D. 424, 427 (D.N.J. 1996) ("The Advisory Committee Notes, though not conclusive, are a very important source of information and should be given considerable weight. They provide something akin to a legislative history of the Rules.").

30. Mississippi Publ'g Corp. v. Murphree, 326 U.S. 438, 444 (1946).

31. *Id.*

32. FED. R. CIV. P. 26(a)(2)(B) Advisory Committee's note (1993).

33. Fanning v. Target Corp., 2006 U.S. Dist. LEXIS 4804, at *4–5 (S.D.N.Y. Feb. 6, 2006) (treating physicians not required to provide a report in order to testify as to their examination and treatment of the plaintiff); Sullivan v. Glock, Inc., 175 F.R.D. 497, 500 (D. Md. 1997) (holding that the party wishing to offer a hybrid fact/expert witness need only provide the witness's identification to satisfy Rule 26(a)(2)); Lauria v. AMTRAK, 1997 U.S. Dist. LEXIS 3408, at *2 (E.D. Pa. Mar. 24, 1997) (treating physician basing opinion on facts gleaned during treatment of the plaintiff not required to file a Rule 26(a)(2)(B) report to offer opinion testimony).

34. Musser v. Gentiva Health Servs., 356 F.3d 751, 757–58 (7th Cir. 2004) (barring treating physicians from testifying as experts because "failure to disclose experts preju-

Similarly, some courts have required reports from party employees whose jobs do not involve testifying by reasoning that "a blanket exception for all employee expert testimony would 'create a category of expert trial witness[es] for whom no written disclosure is required' and should not be permitted."[35] Arguments that an employee's job does not regularly involve giving testimony have been rejected because excluding unretained employees from the requirements of the rule could create "a distinction seemingly at odds with the evident purpose of promoting full pre-trial disclosure of expert information."[36] Therefore, notwithstanding either the language of the rule or the Advisory Committee's notes, a few courts hold that Rule 26(a)(2)(B) imposes broad disclosure requirements on all trial experts.[37] Even an employee who does not regularly give expert testimony may still "fairly be viewed as having been 'retained' or 'specially employed' for that purpose."[38]

The divergent views on this issue prompted a proposed amendment to Rule 26(a) intended to clarify whether a report may be required from additional witnesses who will offer opinion testimony. The proposed amendment recognizes that requiring an expert report from every witness who presents opinion testimony could impose substantial burdens,

---

diced" defendants); Rodriguez v. Town of West New York, 191 F. App'x 166, 169 (3d Cir. 2006) (treating physician's testimony excluded because he was required to submit an expert report under Rule 26(a)); Harville v. Vanderbilt Univ., 2003 U.S. App. LEXIS 18053, at *15 (6th Cir. Aug. 27, 2003) (treating physicians' testimony excluded because their testimony regarding the standard of care fell within the category of expert testimony that is required to be disclosed under Rule 26).

35. Prieto v. Malgor, 361 F.3d 1313, 1318 (11th Cir. 2004) (requiring employee expert who did not regularly give expert testimony to file an expert report before testifying because he only reviewed the materials in preparation for trial and had no personal knowledge of the case); McCulloch v. Hartford Life & Accident Ins. Co., 223 F.R.D. 26, 27–28 (D. Conn. 2004) (requiring employee experts to file reports because "to find otherwise would risk encouraging corporate defendants to attempt to evade the report requirement by designating its own employees" as expert witnesses).

36. Day v. Consol. Rail Corp., 1996 U.S. Dist. LEXIS 6596, at *4 (S.D.N.Y. May 14, 1996); Innogenetics v. Abbott Labs., 2007 U.S. Dist. LEXIS 193, at *26–27 (W.D. Wis. Jan. 3, 2007) (noting that the purpose of Rule 26 is to make "discovery easier, faster and more efficient, as well as to avoid surprises at trial," and thus "it would thwart the Rule's purposes to allow exemptions from the report requirement").

37. *Day*, 1996 U.S. Dist. LEXIS 6596, at *4–5.

38. *Id.* at *7; Funai Elec. Co. v. Daewoo Elecs. Corp., 2007 U.S. Dist. LEXIS 29782, at *9 (N.D. Cal. Apr. 11, 2007) (requiring employees providing "technical evaluations of evidence reviewed solely in preparation for trial, who provide opinion testimony on the merits of the case, or who have no direct and personal knowledge of the facts to which they are testifying" to submit Rule 26(a) expert reports).

particularly given the concern that a treating physician may be reluctant to take part in discovery or trial, much less provide a report meeting the detailed requirements of Rule 26(a)(2)(B).[39] Under the proposed amendment, Rule 26(a)(2) would read as follows:

> (C) *Witnesses Who Do Not Provide a Written Report.* Unless otherwise stipulated or ordered by the court, if the witness is not required to provide a written report, the Rule 26(a)(2)(A) disclosure must state:
>
>> (i) the subject matter on which the witness is expected to present evidence under Federal Rule of Evidence 702, 703, or 705; and
>>
>> (ii) a summary of the facts and opinions to which the witness is expected to testify.

The amendment is intended to "resolve a tension that has sometimes prompted courts to require reports under Rule 26(a)(2)(B) even from witnesses exempted from the report requirement, reasoning that having a report before the deposition or trial testimony of all expert witnesses is desirable."[40] It is expected that "[w]ith the addition of Rule 26(a)(2)(C) disclosure for expert witnesses exempted from the report requirement, courts should no longer be tempted to overlook Rule 26(a)(2)(B)'s limitations on the full report requirement."[41]

Under the amendment, if a witness identified under Rule 26(a)(2)(A) is not required to provide a Rule 26(a)(2)(B) report, the party must disclose the subject matter of the expected expert testimony and a summary of the facts and opinions to which the expert is expected to testify.[42] This disclosure will support preparation for deposing the witness and may satisfy other parties that there is no need for a deposition.[43] According to the Advisory Committee, the disclosure should be "considerably less extensive than the report required by Rule 26(a)(2)(B). Courts must take care against requiring undue detail, keeping in mind that these witnesses have not been specially retained and may not be as responsive to counsel as those who have."[44]

---

39. Committee on Rules of Practice and Procedure, Report of the Civil Rules Committee, at 104, (May 9, 2008) (supplemented June 30, 2008), *available at* http://www.us courts.gov/RulesAndPolicies/Rules/Reports/CV06-2008.pdf.
40. FED. R. CIV. P. 26 Advisory Committee's note (2008).
41. *Id.*
42. *Id.*
43. *Id.*
44. *Id.*

Content of Rule 26(a) Expert Reports

If an expert report is mandated, Rule 26(a)(2)(B) sets out six elements that a report must contain:

1. A complete statement of all opinions to be expressed and the basis and reasons for them;
2. The data or other information considered by the witness in forming his opinions;
3. Any exhibits that will be used to summarize or support them;
4. The witness's qualifications, including a list of all publications authored in the previous 10 years;
5. A list of all other cases in which, during the previous four years, the witness testified as an expert at trial or by deposition; and
6. A statement of the compensation to be paid for the study and testimony in the case.[45]

The Advisory Committee's notes state that the report is expected in the first instance to "set forth the substance of the direct examination."[46] The report should be written in a manner that reflects the testimony to be given by the witness, which explains why it must be signed by the witness himself.[47] In addition, the report should include the data and other information considered by the expert as well as any exhibits or charts that summarize or support the witness's opinions.[48]

The attorney's task, therefore, is to ensure that the proffered report contains opinions that are properly articulated and thoroughly supported.[49] This section details how to ensure that an expert report contains all of the requisite information.

A Complete Statement of All Opinions to Be Expressed and the Basis and Reasons for Them

As courts recognize, "[t]he first and most important element of the Rule 26 analysis is whether the report prepared by [the expert] contains a complete statement of his opinions and the basis for his opinions."[50] The statement must be complete and detailed—"sketchy" or "vague" statements will not

---

45. Fed. R. Civ. P. 26(a)(2)(B).
46. *See* United States v. Kalymon, 541 F.3d 624, 638 (6th Cir. 2008).
47. *Id.*
48. *Id.*
49. *Salgado*, 150 F.3d at 742 n.6.
50. Campbell v. McMillin, 83 F. Supp. 2d 761, 764 (S.D. Miss. 2000).

suffice.[51] Conclusory and unsupported statements are likewise insufficient.[52] Courts disfavor reports providing opinions that something "could" have caused the harm at issue or that findings "suggest" a particular possibility.[53]

Moreover, "the report must provide the substantive rationale in detail with respect to the basis and reasons for the proffered opinions" and "must explain factually why and how the witness has reached them."[54] The report should contain not only the expert's ultimate conclusions, but it must also answer the question of how he came to such conclusions.[55] Merely stating that the expert relies on his education, experience, and training in reaching his opinions, without providing the substantive rationale for reaching the specific opinions, is insufficient.[56] A recognized exception is when a report, to effect the replacement of a previously disclosed witness, incorporates the conclusions and opinions already set forth in a previous report.[57]

The Advisory Committee's notes provide that others may assist the expert in the preparation of such reports, but the rule requires the expert to "substantially participate in the preparation of his report"[58] and mandates that "the final report must be that of the expert."[59] The few reported cases interpreting Rule 26(a)(2)(B) indicate that the preparation and signing requirement is designed to ensure that expert reports express "what the expert has freely authorized and adopted as his own" rather than expressing an opinion "merely for appeasement or because of intimidation or some undue influence by the party retained by him."[60]

The disclosure of all opinions to be expressed, including the basis and reasons for those opinions, is critical in light of the U.S. Supreme Court

---

51. Sierra Club, Lone Star Chapter v. Cedar Point Oil Co., 73 F.3d 546, 571 (5th Cir. 1996).

52. *See Campbell*, 83 F. Supp. 2d at 765 (finding report inadequate because it merely offered conclusory allegations without providing the basis of the opinions); *Reed*, 165 F.R.D. at 430 n.11 ("The insistence of Rule 26(a)(2)(B) on a 'complete statement of all opinions to be expressed and the basis and reasons therefore' has another salutary effect. Practitioners should no longer have to face what is referred to in the state courts as a 'net opinion.' This is defined as an expert's bare conclusion, unsupported by factual evidence.").

53. *See Campbell*, 83 F. Supp. 2d at 764–65.

54. Dunkin' Donuts, Inc. v. Patel, 174 F. Supp. 2d 202, 211 (D.N.J. 2001) (*quoting* Hilt v. SFC, Inc., 170 F.R.D. 182, 185 (D. Kan. 1997)).

55. *See Reed*, 165 F.R.D. at 428 n.5 ("In simple terminology, this means 'how' and 'why' the expert reached the conclusions and opinions to be expressed.").

56. *See Hilt*, 170 F.R.D. at 185.

57. *See Roberts*, 325 F.3d at 783–84.

58. Manning v. Crockett, 1999 U.S. Dist. LEXIS 7966, at *8 (N.D. Ill. May 18, 1999).

59. 4 Daniel R. Coquillette et al., Moore's Federal Practice § 26.23 (3d ed. 1999).

60. Marek v. Moore, 171 F.R.D. 298, 302 (D. Kan. 1997).

decisions in *Daubert v. Merrell Dow Pharmaceuticals, Inc.*[61] and *Kumho Tire Co., Ltd. v. Carmichael.*[62] Revised to reflect *Daubert* and its progeny, Federal Rule of Evidence 702 governs the admissibility of expert testimony.[63] This standard is discussed in detail in chapter 6.

In assessing whether a witness's proposed testimony is reliable under *Daubert*, the court undertakes an examination of the facts on which the witness relies, the method by which the witness draws conclusions from those facts, and how the witness applies the facts and methods to the case at hand.[64] *Daubert's* focus on a witness's methodology makes critical the content of expert reports because the rule requires a statement not only of an expert's opinions, but also the "basis and reasons" for them.[65] Analysis of an expert's methods under *Daubert* naturally correlates with the "basis and reasons" for an expert's proposed opinions. Rule 26 reports are arguably the single most important piece of evidence in a *Daubert* hearing.[66]

The Data or Other Information Considered by the Expert in Forming His Opinions

Practically speaking, this item is as important as the first. Failure to disclose all the data or other information "considered" is sufficient reason to preclude the expert's testimony.[67]

---

61. Daubert v. Merrell Dow Pharms., Inc., 509 U.S. 579 (1993).

62. Kumho Tire Co., Ltd. v. Carmichael, 526 U.S. 137 (1999).

63. *See* Smith v. Cangieter, 462 F.3d 920, 923 (8th Cir. 2006); Nelson v. Tennessee Gas Pipeline Co., 243 F.3d 244, 250 (6th Cir. 2001).

64. Heller v. Shaw Indus., 167 F.3d 146, 155 (3d Cir. 1999) ("The reliability analysis applies to all aspects of an expert's testimony: the methodology, the facts underlying the expert's opinion, the link between the facts and the conclusion, et alia."); City of Wichita, Kansas v. Trustees of APCO Oil Corp. Liquidating Trust, 306 F. Supp. 2d 1040, 1108 (D. Kan. 2003) ("Once an expert meets Rule 702's qualification requirements, his or her opinions must be based on sufficient facts or data. This is the rule's requirement for foundation.").

65. Synergetics, Inc. v. Hurst, 477 F.3d 949, 956 (8th Cir. 2007) (holding that as long as expert's methodology is sound, mere "disagreement with the assumptions" does not warrant exclusion).

66. *See, e.g.*, Reynolds v. Freightliner, LLC, 2006 U.S. Dist. LEXIS 97244, at *13–18 (E.D. Ky. June 21, 2006) (finding expert testimony inadmissible because expert report did not meet specificity requirement under Rule 26 and thus failed to use any methodology that could be tested or replicated for purposes of cross-examination or rebuttal).

67. *See, e.g.*, Olson v. Montana Rail Link, Inc., 227 F.R.D. 550, 551–53 (D. Mont. 2005).

Before the 1993 amendments, Rule 26 disclosure requirements applied to data and facts a witness "relied on."[68] As the 1993 Advisory Committee's notes state, however,

> The report is to disclose the data and other information considered by the expert and any exhibits or charts that summarize or support the expert's opinions. Given this obligation of disclosure, litigants should no longer be able to argue that materials furnished to their experts to be used in forming their opinions—whether or not ultimately relied upon by the expert—are privileged or otherwise protected from disclosure when such persons are testifying or being deposed.[69]

As one court observed, "'[c]onsidered,' which simply means 'to reflect on' or 'to think of: come to view, judge, or classify,' clearly invokes a broader spectrum of thought than the phrase 'relied upon,' which requires dependence on the information."[70] Another court essentially defined it the same way: "'Considered,' which simply means 'to take into account,' clearly invokes a broader spectrum of thought than the phrase 'relied upon,' which requires dependence on the information."[71]

This expansive scope serves a key purpose in discovery. As the court said in *Trigon*, "information considered, but not relied upon, can be of great importance in understanding and testing the validity of an expert's opinion."[72] Accordingly, when addressing motions to compel, courts commonly require the disclosure of all materials reviewed by the expert in forming his opinions.[73] Whether the witness relies on or deems the reviewed material relevant is not determinative.[74]

---

68. *See* Constr. Indus. Servs. Corp. v. Hanover Ins. Co., 206 F.R.D. 43, 50 (E.D.N.Y. 2001) ("Documents and information disclosed to a testifying expert in connection with his testimony are discoverable by the opposing party, whether or not the expert relies on the documents and information in preparing his report.").

69. FED. R. CIV. P. 26(a) Advisory Committee's note (1993).

70. Trigon Ins. Co. v. United States, 204 F.R.D. 277, 282 (E.D. Va. 2001).

71. Karn v. Ingersoll Rand, 168 F.R.D. 633, 635 (N.D. Ind. 1996).

72. *Trigon Ins.*, 204 F.R.D. at 282.

73. *See id.* at 283; *Karn*, 168 F.R.D. at 635.

74. Fidelity Nat'l Title Ins. Co. of N.Y. v. Intercounty Nat'l Title Ins. Co., 412 F.3d 745 (7th Cir. 2005) (upholding district court's ruling to exclude expert witness testimony as sanction for failing to produce notes that did not support the witness's expert opinion); Loff v. The Landings Club, Inc., 2006 U.S. Dist. LEXIS 97473, at *8 (S.D. Ga. July 17, 2006) (data was undoubtedly "'considered' by the expert witness in forming his opinion, even if the data he gathered merely verified the data he already had in his possession"). *But see* Flebotte v. Dow Jones & Co., Inc., 2000 U.S. Dist. LEXIS 19875 (D. Mass. Dec. 6, 2000) (refusing to sanction party for conducting several tests but not including them in the expert report).

Before 1993, there was general agreement that the Rule 26 expert witness disclosure requirements did not apply to attorney work product.[75] Post-1993, however, the rules are different. Attorneys are still expected to work with their expert witnesses: "Rule 26(a)(2)(B) does not preclude counsel from providing assistance to experts in preparing the reports, and indeed . . . this assistance may be needed."[76] But most federal courts hold that an attorney's mental impressions and other traditional work product—even trial strategy—will be subject to disclosure if provided to a testifying expert.[77]

A few courts hold that the disclosure requirements of Rule 26(a) do not trump the work product protections of Rule 26(b)(3).[78] As a practical matter, however, the observation that "Rule 26(a)(2)(B) does not preclude counsel from providing assistance to experts in preparing the reports" is arguably illusory because there is no protection for attorney work product. Anything the witness looks at or hears, including an attorney's input, is deemed to be "considered by the expert" and is fair game for discovery by the other side.[79]

---

75. *See, e.g.,* Toledo Edison Co. v. G A Techs., Inc., 847 F.2d 335, 339–41 (6th Cir. 1988); Bogosian v. Gulf Oil Corp., 738 F.2d 587, 595 (3d Cir. 1984).

76. *See* FED. R. CIV. P. 26(a)(2)(B) Advisory Committee's notes (1993).

77. Suskind v. Home Depot Corp., 2001 U.S. Dist. LEXIS 1349, at *11 (D. Mass. Jan. 2, 2001) ("It is worth noting that if the authors of the 1993 Amendments to Rule 26 intended the required expert disclosure pursuant to Rule 26(a)(2)(B) to be subject to either the attorney-client privilege and/or work product protection, they could have said so as they did with the required disclosure under Rule 26(a)(1)(C).").

78. Magee v. The Paul Revere Life Ins. Co., 172 F.R.D. 627, 642 (E.D.N.Y. 1997) (holding core work product considered by an expert need not be disclosed under Rule 26(a)(2)(B)); Ladd Furniture, Inc. v. Ernst & Young, 1998 U.S. Dist. LEXIS 17345, at *43 (M.D.N.C. 1998) (holding core attorney work product materials provided to an expert are not discoverable).

79. Mfg/Admin. and Mgmt. Sys., Inc. v. ICT Group, Inc., 212 F.R.D. 110, 111 (E.D.N.Y. 2002) ("Notwithstanding the disagreement in the courts and the literature, the text of Rule 26 mandates disclosure of [core] work product given to a testifying expert."); *In re* Pioneer Hi-bred Int'l, Inc., 238 F.3d 1370, 1375–76 (Fed. Cir. 2001) ("fundamental fairness requires disclosure of all information supplied to a testifying expert in connection with his testimony," even if such information falls under the attorney-client or core work product privilege); Colindres v. Quietflex Mfg., 228 F.R.D. 567, 571 (S.D. Tex. 2005) ("information that the expert creates or reviews related to his or her role as a testifying expert must be produced," even when materials are privileged); Am. Fid. Assurance Co. v. Boyer, 225 F.R.D. 520, 521 (D.S.C. 2004) (requiring disclosure of core attorney work product materials that were used or consulted in preparation of expert report); Cornell Research Found., Inc. v. Hewlett, 223 F.R.D. 55, 78–79 (N.D.N.Y. 2003) (disclosing work product materials to testifying expert overcomes privilege); CP Kelco U.S. Inc. v. Pharmacia Corp., 213 F.R.D. 176, 178–79 (D. Del. 2003) (requiring production of documents, which implicate the attorney-client privilege, reviewed by testifying expert because it would be "manifestly unfair to allow a party to use the privilege to shield information which it had deliberately chosen to use

This includes any communications such as e-mail,[80] oral communications,[81] and notes of phone conversations.

The case of *Haworth, Inc. v. Herman Miller, Inc.*[82] provides a good example of one court's attempt to balance the strong protection afforded attorney work product with the expansive discovery authorized under current Rule 26. The court drew a line between factual work product and opinion work product. On the one hand, the court held that "all factual information considered by the expert must be disclosed in the report," even if the attorney compiled that information.[83] On the other hand, the court held that opinion work product, even if provided to the expert, was protected from discovery: "Not even the most liberal of discovery theories can justify unwarranted inquiries into the files and mental impressions of an attorney."[84] The court rejected the argument that the disclosure of opinion work product is necessary to shed light on an attorney's attempt to unduly influence an expert's opinion. The court noted that the adversarial system already provides sufficient checks to ensure that a lawyer does not unduly influence the expert's opinion (e.g., the reasonableness of the expert's opinion is always subject to the evaluation of other experts and may be tested against basic knowledge of the expert's field).[85]

The *Haworth* court's interpretation is in the minority, however. Other courts and commentators point out that distinctions like those drawn in *Haworth* seriously undermine the 1993 amendments. The work product doctrine has never protected against the discovery of facts (as opposed to the documents on which an attorney has recorded those facts) and, even before the 1993 amendments, the consensus among federal courts was already "in favor of disclosure of factual information."[86]

---

offensively"); Vitalo v. Cabot Corp., 212 F.R.D. 478, 479 (E.D. Pa. 2002) ("Rule 26(a)(2) (B) . . . vitiates a claim of attorney work product with respect to any information considered by a party's expert, whether or not relied upon by that expert.").

80. Ass'n of Irritated Residents v. Dairy, 2008 U.S. Dist. LEXIS 57459, at *3–5 (E.D. Cal. June 18, 2008).

81. Synthes Spine Co., L.P. v. Walden, 232 F.R.D. 460, 465 (E.D. Pa. 2005) ("A plaintiff's expert must disclose the content of all oral communications that the expert considered in formulating his opinions as a testifying expert, regardless of whether the oral communications come from the plaintiff's counsel or the plaintiff itself."); B.C.F. Oil Ref., Inc. v. Consol. Edison Co. of New York, Inc., 171 F.R.D. 57, 67 (S.D.N.Y. 1997) ("There does not seem to be a principled difference between oral and written communications between an expert and an attorney insofar as discoverability is concerned.").

82. Haworth, Inc. v. Herman Miller, Inc., 162 F.R.D. 289 (W.D. Mich. 1995).

83. *Id.* at 295.

84. *Id.* (quoting Hickman v. Taylor, 329 U.S. 495, 510 (1947)).

85. *See Haworth*, 162 F.R.D. at 295–96.

86. *B.C.F. Oil Ref.*, 171 F.R.D. at 66.

In sum, prudent practice dictates that any materials provided to the expert (whether he relies on the documents or simply reviews and rejects them) be identified and produced.[87] This includes such items as notes taken during testing, measurements and calculations, photographs, computer calculations, and graphics.[88] Interview notes are also included.[89] Communications to and from counsel are likewise included, as are drafts of findings or conclusions: "in simple language, this means disclosure applies to 'what' the witness saw, heard, considered, read, thought about or relied upon in reaching the conclusions and opinions to be expressed."[90]

The Advisory Committee apparently recognizes that the discovery of draft expert reports and all communications between attorney and expert allowed by most courts often fail to yield useful information because lawyers and experts employ stratagems that generally defeat discovery efforts.[91] Accordingly, proposed amendments to Rule 26(a)(2)(B)(ii) and 26(b)(4) seek to correct the unforeseen consequences that have emerged in the wake of the 1993 amendments.

Rule 26(a)(2)(B)(ii) would be amended to require disclosure of only "the facts or data considered by the witness in forming" his opinions. The Advisory

---

87. *See Fidelity Nat'l*, 412 F.3d at 751 ("A testifying expert must disclose and therefore retain whatever materials are given him to review in preparing his testimony, even if in the end he does not rely on them in formulating his expert opinion, because such materials often contain effective ammunition for cross-examination."). *But see id.* ("He is not required to retain every scrap of paper that he created in the course of his preparation—only documents that would be helpful to an understanding of his expert testimony or that the opposing party might use in cross-examination.").

88. *See id.* at 551 (listing these as items included in the untimely supplementation of the report following counsel's "epiphany" that such information must be provided).

89. *See, e.g.*, Mems v. City of St. Paul, Dep't of Fire & Safety Servs., 327 F.3d 771, 779–80 (8th Cir. 2003) (affirming sanction of excluding testimony for failure to provide expert's interview notes in timely manner).

90. *Reed*, 165 F.R.D. at 428 n.6.

91. Fed. R. Civ. P. 26 Advisory Committee's note (2008). The Committee on Rules of Practice and Procedure identified the following issues: (1) experts and counsel often go to great lengths to avoid creating draft reports, creating drafts only in electronic or oral form, deleting all electronic drafts, and even scrubbing hard drives to prevent subsequent discovery; (2) lawyers and experts often avoid written communications or creating notes by the expert, encumbering attorney-expert communications and the formulation of effective and accurate litigation opinions; (3) litigants often engage in expensive discovery seeking to obtain draft reports or attorney-expert communications but gain nothing useful by it; (4) parties often retain two sets of experts, one for consultation and the other for testimony; and (5) lawyers and parties are reluctant to hire potentially superb experts who have not become professional witnesses, for fear that discovery of the necessary conversations that tell them how to behave as witnesses will destroy their usefulness. Report of the Civil Rules Committee, *supra* note 39, at 4.

Committee's notes state that the objective of striking the "data or other information" disclosure prescribed in 1993 is "to alter the outcome in cases that have relied on the 1993 formulation as one ground for requiring disclosure of all attorney-expert communications and draft reports."[92] The refocus on disclosure of "facts or data" is meant to limit the disclosure requirements to material of a factual nature, as opposed to theories or mental impressions of counsel.[93] The Advisory Committee's notes are also clear that "[a]t the same time, the intention is that 'facts or data' be interpreted broadly to require disclosure of any material received by the expert, from whatever source, that contains factual ingredients.[94] The disclosure obligation extends to any facts or data 'considered' by the expert in forming the opinions to be expressed, not only those relied upon by the expert."[95]

The Advisory Committee has also proposed to revise Rule 26(b)(4) by inserting subsections (B) and (C), which specifically extend work product protections to drafts of both expert reports and expert party disclosures under Rule 26(a)(2)(C) and to attorney-expert communications.[96] Under the proposed amendment, Rule 26(b)(4) would read:

> (B) *Trial Preparation Protection for Draft Reports or Disclosures.* Rules 26(b)(3)(A) and (B) protect drafts of any report or disclosure required under Rule 26(a)(2), regardless of the form of the draft.
>
> (C) *Trial Preparation Protection for Communications between Party's Attorney and Expert Witnesses.* Rules 26(b)(3)(A) and (B) protect communications between the party's attorney and any witness required to provide a report under Rule 26(a)(2)(B), regardless of the form of the communications, except to the extent that the communications:
>
> > (i) Relate to compensation for the expert's study or testimony;
> >
> > (ii) Identify facts or data that the party's attorney provided and that the expert considered in forming the opinions to be expressed; or
> >
> > (iii) Identify assumptions that the party's attorney provided and that the expert relied upon in forming the opinions to be expressed.

The protection afforded by proposed Rule 26(b)(4)(B) applies regardless of the form of the draft, whether oral, written, electronic, or otherwise. It

---

92. FED. R. CIV. P. 26 Advisory Committee's note (2008).
93. *Id.*
94. *Id.*
95. *Id.*
96. *Id.*

also applies to drafts of any supplementation under Rule 26(e).[97] Similarly, the protection under Rule 26(b)(4)(C) would apply to attorney-expert communications regardless of the form of communication whether oral, written, electronic, or otherwise.[98] While Rule 26(b)(4)(B) would apply to witnesses subject to Rule 26(a)(2)(B) or (a)(2)(C), the Advisory Committee's notes are explicit in that the Rule 26(b)(4)(C) protections afforded for attorney-expert communications would apply only to witnesses subject to Rule 26(a)(2)(B).[99]

The proposed amendment permits three exceptions to work product protection, to permit routine discovery of attorney-expert communications relating to (1) compensation, (2) identifying facts or data the attorney provided to the expert and that the expert considered in forming the opinions to be expressed, and (3) identifying the assumptions that the lawyer provided to the expert and that the expert relied on in forming his opinions.[100]

Discovery into compensation is not limited to compensation for work forming the opinions to be expressed but extends to all compensation for the study and testimony provided in relation to the action.[101] The Advisory Committee's notes caution that the exception is limited to those facts or data that bear on the opinions the expert will be expressing, not all facts or data that may have been discussed by the expert and counsel, and only to communications "identifying" the facts or data provided to counsel.[102] Under proposed Rule 26(b)(4)(C)(iii), discovery regarding attorney-expert communications is permitted to identify any assumptions that counsel provided to the expert and that the expert relied on in forming the opinion, but the exception is limited to those assumptions that the expert actually did rely on.[103]

The proposed rule does not absolutely prohibit discovery regarding attorney-expert communications on subjects outside the three exceptions in Rule 26(b)(4)(C) or draft expert reports or disclosures. Discovery may be permitted regarding attorney-expert communications or draft reports in limited circumstances and by court order. For example, a court may order discovery if a party can make the showing that it has a substantial need for the discovery and cannot obtain the substantial equivalent without undue hardship. The Advisory Committee's notes anticipate, however, that "[i]t

---

97. FED. R. CIV. P. 26 Advisory Committee's note (2008).
98. *Id.*
99. *Id.*
100. *Id.*
101. *Id.*
102. FED. R. CIV. P. 26 Advisory Committee's note (2008).
103. *Id.*

will be rare for a party to be able to make such a showing given the broad disclosure and discovery otherwise allowed regarding the expert's testimony."[104]

Any Exhibits to Be Used as a Summary of or in Support of the Opinions

A report should identify all exhibits the witness expects to use. Rule 26(a)(2)(B) requires that the expert report include "the data or other information considered by the witness in forming the opinions [and] any exhibits to be used as a summary of or support for the opinions," among other things. Merely including references to exhibits does not meet the requirement of Rule 26(a)(2)(B).[105] Failure to attach exhibits may warrant exclusion of an expert, even if a party attempts to cure the absence of exhibits in a supplemental report.[106]

The Qualifications of the Expert, Including a List of All Publications Authored by the Expert in the Previous 10 Years

This requirement is usually interpreted to require the witness's curriculum vitae (CV) and, as part of that disclosure, a listing of recent authorships. A CV that only lists a selection of publications, and not a list of all publications authored within the last 10 years, does not comply with the rules.[107]

The CV should be as complete as possible, establishing the expert's qualifications. First, a flimsy CV may form the basis for a *Daubert* challenge.[108] For example, an expert might be excluded if his CV fails to incorporate any professional experience in the area about which he will testify or fails to establish that he participates in recognized organizations or institu-

---

104. *Id.*

105. Pierce v. CVS Pharms., Inc., 2007 U.S. Dist. LEXIS 69006, at *8 n.1 (D. Ariz. Sept. 13, 2007).

106. Minebea Co. v. Papst, 231 F.R.D. 3 (D.D.C 2005).

107. Branche v. Zimmer, Inc., 2008 U.S. Dist. LEXIS 106789, at *5 n.2 (E.D. Tenn. Sept. 11, 2008).

108. Redding Linden Burr, Inc. v. King, 2009 U.S. Dist. LEXIS 8248, at *6–7 (S.D. Tex. Feb. 4, 2009) (quoting FED. R. EVID. 702). *But see* Soufflas v. Zimmer, Inc., 474 F. Supp. 2d 737, 745 (E.D. Pa. 2007) (rejecting argument that expert opinions must be excluded because his CV did not reveal his experience and therefore did not provide a reasonable opportunity to prepare for effective cross-examination in accordance with Rule 26(a)(2)(B)).

tions that establish the standards governing the area of expertise.[109] Second, a CV that evinces expertise or experience on the subject matter of the expert report may offset a sparse report.[110]

Inaccuracies in a CV are extremely dangerous. The practitioner should take the time to verify each item in an expert's CV. Although a minor mistake will not necessarily lead to the exclusion of an expert witness,[111] skilled opposed counsel can use such a mistake to cast doubt on an expert's overall credibility.

The Compensation to Be Paid for the Expert's Study and Testimony

Compensation information allows the opposing party to probe for bias or prejudice.[112] It is not enough merely to provide the expert's rate;[113] however, courts may limit the extent of inquiries into this matter when appropriate (e.g., to avoid harassment brought about by sifting through an expert's personal financial records).[114] Nevertheless, the court may strike a report that fails to list an expert's compensation information.[115]

---

109. Rosvold v. L.S.M. Sys. Eng'g, Inc., 2007 U.S. Dist. LEXIS 82061 (E.D. Mich. Nov. 6, 2007).

110. Meyer v. Christie, 2009 U.S. Dist. LEXIS 19955 (D. Kan. Mar. 12, 2009).

111. Jung v. Neschis, 2007 U.S. Dist. LEXIS 97173 (S.D.N.Y. Oct. 23, 2007) (refusing to exclude based on inaccuracies in expert's CV in light of his long and distinguished career).

112. Cary Oil Co. v. MG Ref. & Mktg., 257 F. Supp. 2d 751, 756 (S.D.N.Y. 2003).

113. *Id.*; *see* Baxter Diagnostics, Inc. v. AVL Scientific Corp., 1993 U.S. Dist. LEXIS 11798 (C.D. Cal. Aug. 6, 1993) (ordering production of "all invoices rendered by the trial experts in connection with this litigation"); County of Suffolk v. Long Island Lighting Co., 122 F.R.D. 120, 124 (E.D.N.Y. 1988) (ordering expert to disclose "best estimate" of the total income he received from plaintiff, as well as an estimate of the percentage of his professional income attributable to his work for plaintiff).

114. *See Cary Oil Co.*, 257 F. Supp. 2d at 756; Wacker v. Gehl Co., 157 F.R.D. 58, 59 (W.D. Mo. 1994) (refusing discovery into expert witness's income tax returns for the past five years reflecting the income he has received in matters in which he has been retained as an expert consultant or witness); Behler v. Hanlon, 199 F.R.D. 553, 561–62 (D. Md. 2001) (rejecting request to discover the total income earned by the defense expert for the last five years, the amount earned from providing independent medical examinations, copies of the expert's tax returns, a list of all cases in which the expert provided services, and a list of all insurance companies with whom the expert was affiliated); Rogers v. U.S. Navy, 223 F.R.D. 533, 535–36 (S.D. Cal. 2004) (holding that expert's financial information was not discoverable since the expert was willing to provide the compensation he received in the particular case at issue as well as estimates regarding the percentage of his work); Sullivan v. Metro N. R.R. Co., 2007 U.S. Dist. LEXIS 88938, at *5–6. (D. Conn. Dec. 3, 2007).

115. *See* Am. Gen. Life & Accident Ins. Co. v. Ward, 530 F. Supp. 2d 1306, 1311–12 (N.D. Ga. 2008).

A Listing of Other Cases in Which the Expert Has Testified as an Expert at Trial or by Deposition in the Previous Four Years

This portion of the disclosure should include, at a minimum (1) the name(s) of the court(s) or administrative agencies, (2) the names of the parties, (3) the case number, and (4) whether the testimony was by deposition or at trial.[116] Although the failure to disclose this information will not necessarily be fatal,[117] it can result in the exclusion of the witness's testimony.[118] If the expert has not testified in any other cases, there is no such information to disclose.[119]

Rebuttal and Supplemental Reports

Rule 26(a)(2)(C) permits parties to disclose expert opinions "intended solely to contradict or rebut evidence on the same subject matter identified by another party under paragraph (2)(B)." A rebuttal report must provide evidence that specifically contradicts, impeaches, or defuses the impact of evidence offered by the adverse party.[120] Thus, experts may submit rebuttal reports, but the contents of a rebuttal report may contain only evidence "intended solely to contradict or rebut evidence on the same subject matter identified" in another party's expert witness report."[121] The expert is "free to support his opinions with evidence not cited in [the expert report] so long as he rebuts the 'same subject matter' identified in those reports."[122] Parties

---

116. *Nguyen*, 162 F.R.D. at 682.

117. *See* Smith v. Baptist Healthcare Sys., 23 F. App'x 499, 501 (6th Cir. 2001) ("The Court may have been able to look past Plaintiffs' failure to provide the expert's publications, compensation for testifying and past testimony, but the absence of any signed report stating a specific opinion renders proceeding impossible.").

118. *See id.*

119. *Dunkin' Donuts*, 174 F. Supp. 2d at 211.

120. Peals v. Terre Haute Police Dep't, 535 F.3d 621, 630 (7th Cir. 2008).

121. FED. R. CIV. P. 26(a)(2)(C)(ii); *see also* City of Gary v. Shafer, 2009 U.S. Dist. LEXIS 41004, at *8 (N.D. Ind. May 13, 2009) (holding plaintiff's expert report was proper because each opinion it contained rebutted the "same subject matter" as that contained in the report of the defendant's expert); Procter & Gamble v. McNeil-PPC, Inc., 615 F. Supp. 2d 832, 838 (W.D. Wis. 2009) (striking paragraphs of expert rebuttal report identified as "Supplementation of My Opinion on Infringement" because "rebuttal reports are limited to responding to the issues raised by the opposing parties' experts").

122. MMI Realty Servs., Inc. v. Westchester Surplus Lines Ins. Co. 2009 U.S. Dist. LEXIS 18379, at *4 (D. Haw. Mar. 10, 2009); Sci. Components Corp. v. Sirenza Microdevices, 2008 U.S. Dist. LEXIS 92703, at *7–8 (E.D.N.Y. Nov. 13, 2008) ("It is not only permissible but also obligatory for the rebuttal expert report to provide technical background informa-

may attempt to file a "sur-rebuttal" report in response to a rebuttal report.[123] Courts have split on the permissibility of such reports.[124]

A party may file a rebuttal report "within 30 days after the disclosure made by the other party,"[125] but courts reach differing conclusions on the timeliness of a rebuttal report where a discovery plan does not provide for rebuttal reports. Certain courts conclude that in the absence of an order setting a deadline for expert rebuttal reports, the 30-day deadline set out in Rule 26(a)(2)(C) applies.[126] Other courts, however, find that "the thirty day requirement in Rule 26(a)(2)(C) only applies 'in the absence of other directions from the court or stipulation by the parties.'"[127]

---

tion adequate to illustrate the point. . . . Hence, technical information . . . that was not previously the subject of expert testimony . . . without which a non-scientist would be unable to evaluate [the rebuttal report], is not out of place in a rebuttal report.").

123. *See In re* Cardizem CD Antitrust Litig., 2000 U.S. Dist. LEXIS 18839, at *6 (E.D. Mich. Oct. 25, 2000) (granting request to submit sur-rebuttal expert report); TiVo Inc. v. EchoStar Commc'ns Corp., 2006 U.S. Dist. LEXIS 97135, at *4 (E.D. Tex. Apr. 3, 2006) (holding that even if the scheduling order did not provide for the service of sur-rebuttal reports, plaintiff should have filed one in accordance with Rule 26(a)(2)(C)).

124. *Compare* Houle v. Jubilee Fisheries, Inc., 2006 U.S. Dist. LEXIS 1408, at *5 n.4 (W.D. Wash. Jan. 5, 2006) ("The federal rules do not contemplate 'sur-rebuttal' experts.") *with In re* Fleming Cos., Inc., Contract Litig., 2000 WL 35612913, at *1 (W.D. Mo. Nov. 30, 2000) (concluding that Rule 26 permits sur-rebuttal reports).

125. Practitioners should also take note to check the local rules of a district court to determine how rebuttal reports are treated. *See, e.g.,* Campos v. MTD Prods., 2009 U.S. Dist. LEXIS 63846, at *25–26 (M.D. Tenn. July 24, 2009) (noting that despite the provision of Rule 26(a)(2)(C) requiring disclosure of rebuttal reports within 30 days after the other party's disclosure, Local Rule 39.01(c)(6)(d) states that "[t]here shall be no rebuttal expert witnesses, absent timely disclosure in accordance with these Rules and leave of Court").

126. *City of Gary,* 2009 U.S. Dist. LEXIS 41004, at *7–8; Dunn v. Zimmer, Inc., 2005 U.S. Dist. LEXIS 3505, at *3 n.1 (D. Conn. 2005) ("The court's scheduling order did not establish a time for the disclosure of rebuttal experts and therefore the Rule 26(a)(2)(C) applies as a default."); Aircraft Gear Corp. v. Marsh, 2004 U.S. Dist. LEXIS 15897, at *16 (N.D. Ill. Aug. 12, 2004) (finding that an expert rebuttal report was timely where filed within 30 days of the defendants' expert disclosure, even though the court had not set a deadline for rebuttal reports); Syringe Dev. Partners L.L.C. v. New Med. Tech., Inc., 2001 U.S. Dist. LEXIS 2843, at *104 n.7 (S.D. Ind. 2001) ("The [scheduling order] on the issue of expert disclosures and reports is sufficiently vague about rebuttal experts to allow for resort to Rule 26(a)(2)(C).").

127. Eckelkamp v. Beste, 315 F.3d 863, 872 (8th Cir. 2002) (affirming trial court's decision to deny the plaintiff's motion for leave to file a rebuttal expert report because "[t]he district court's case order set its management requirements and did not provide for rebuttal experts, and the court was entitled to hold the parties to that order"); Schablonentechnik v. MacDermid Graphic Arts, Inc., 2005 U.S. Dist. LEXIS 45982, at *7–8 (N.D. Ga. June 21, 2005) (excluding rebuttal expert reports where expert disclosure schedule did not provide for submission of rebuttal reports); Akeva L.L.C. v. Mizuno Corp., 212 F.R.D. 306, 310 (M.D.N.C. 2002) (holding rebuttal expert submissions impermissible where plaintiff

Rule 26(e)(1) may also require an expert witness to supplement an initial disclosure submitted pursuant to Rule 26(a)(2)(C). A supplemental report is required if the party learns that in some material respect the information disclosed is incomplete or incorrect. With respect to testimony of an expert from whom a report is required under subdivision (a)(2) (B), the duty extends both to information contained in the report and to information provided through a deposition of the expert. Any additions or other changes to this information is required to be disclosed by the time the party's pretrial disclosures are due.[128]

The rule contemplates that initial disclosures may contain partial or incomplete information.[129] Rule 26(e) thus permits—indeed requires—that an expert supplement his report and disclosures in certain limited circumstances when the party or expert learns that the information previously disclosed is incomplete or incorrect in some material respect.[130] Information "is incomplete or incorrect" in "some material respect" if there is an objectively reasonable likelihood that the additional or corrective information could substantially affect or alter the opposing party's discovery plan or trial preparation.[131]

A party may not, absent substantial justification, withhold information required by Rule 26(a).[132] Under such circumstances, a court may forbid a party from using that information as evidence at trial[133] unless the court finds that the failure to disclose is harmless.[134] At the same time, a court

---

participated in drafting the scheduling order, and the order did not include deadlines for rebuttal expert disclosures).

128. Fed. R. Civ. P. 26(e); Fed. R. Civ. P. 26(a), (e) Advisory Committee's notes (1993 amendments) ("Changes in the opinions expressed by the expert whether in the report or at a subsequent deposition are subject to a duty of supplemental disclosure.").

129. Caldwell-Baker Co. v. S. Illinois Railcar Co., 2001 U.S. Dist. LEXIS 9916, at *3 (D. Kan. June 5, 2001).

130. Cook v. Rockwell Int'l Corp., 580 F. Supp. 2d 1071 (D. Colo. 2006); Macaulay v. Anas, 321 F.3d 45, 50 (1st Cir. 2003) (once a mandatory disclosure is provided, it must be kept current).

131. Sender v. Mann, 225 F.R.D. 645, 653 (D. Colo. 2004).

132. Fed. R. Civ. P. 37(c)(1).

133. The factors applied by federal district court in deciding whether to exclude testimonial or equivalent evidence as a sanction for disobeying a court's order all generally consider the prejudice or surprise to the party against whom the evidence would be offered and the ability to cure the prejudice but differ slightly in other aspects according to the factors established by the circuit in which the district court sits. *See, e.g., In re* Paoli R.R. Yard PCB Litig., 35 F.3d 717, 791 (3d Cir. 1994); S. States Rack & Fixture, Inc. v. Sherwin-Williams Co., 318 F.3d 592, 597 (4th Cir. 2003); Price v. Seydel, 961 F.2d 1470, 1474 (9th Cir. 1992); Perry v. Winspur, 782 F.2d 893, 894 (10th Cir. 1986).

134. *Compare* NutraSweet Co. v. X-L Eng'g Co., 227 F.3d 776, 786 (7th Cir. 2000) (holding expert's testimony properly excluded due to failure to submit supplemental expert

may exclude a supplemental report if the report states additional opinions or rationales, or seeks to "strengthen" or "deepen" opinions expressed in the original expert report.[135] Permissible supplementation thus "means correcting inaccuracies, or filling the interstices of an incomplete report based on [unavailable] information at the time of the initial disclosure."[136]

A court may strike a supplemental expert report on the basis of an inadequate or incomplete initial report.[137] Courts recognize, however, that preclusion is a drastic remedy and generally order preclusion "only where the court finds that the party's failure to comply with the requirements was both unjustified and prejudicial."[138] Other common, but lesser, sanctions aimed at curing any prejudice include, among others, ordering depositions with the costs to be borne by the party submitting the improper report,[139] limiting the expert's testimony to the opinions expressed in the authorized reports,[140] granting the prejudiced party an opportunity to file a supplemental or rebuttal report,[141] forbidding the expert from expanding on the opinions expressed in the initial disclosure,[142] and granting a new trial.[143]

report); and Gallagher v. S. Source Packaging, LLC, 568 F. Supp. 2d 624, 630–31 (E.D.N.C. 2008) (excluding supplemental report due to surprise to plaintiff, which could not be cured without undue delay) *with* Mid-Am. Tablewares, Inc. v. Mogi Trading Co. Ltd., 100 F.3d 1353, 1363 (7th Cir. 1996) (finding no abuse of discretion in denying defendant's motion to exclude the testimony of plaintiff's expert where district judge correctly determined that defendant had sufficient time to prepare for the deposition of plaintiff's expert after receiving plaintiff's supplemented expert report).

135. *Cook*, 580 F. Supp. 2d 1071.

136. *Id.* (citing Keener v. United States, 181 F.R.D. 639, 640 (D. Mont. 1998); Beller v. United States, 221 F.R.D. 689, 694–95 (D.N.M. 2003)).

137. *Akeva*, 212 F.R.D. at 310 ("Rule 26(e) envisions supplementation when a party's discovery disclosures happen to be defective in some way so that the disclosure was incorrect or incomplete and, therefore, misleading. It does not cover failures of omission because the expert did an inadequate or incomplete preparation."); *Sierra Club*, 73 F.3d at 571 ("The purpose of rebuttal and supplementary disclosures is just that—to rebut and to supplement. These disclosures are not intended to provide an extension of the deadline by which a party must deliver the lion's share of its expert information.").

138. Virgin Enters. v. Am. Longevity, 2001 U.S. Dist. LEXIS 2048, at *6 (S.D.N.Y. Mar. 1, 2001).

139. Equant Integrations Servs. v. United Rentals, Inc., 217 F.R.D. 113, 118 (D. Conn. 2003).

140. Sandata Techs., Inc. v. Infocrossing, Inc., 2007 U.S. Dist. LEXIS 85176, at *25 (S.D.N.Y. Nov. 16, 2007).

141. Wilderness Dev., LLC v. Hash, 2009 U.S. Dist. LEXIS 19658, at *19 (D. Mont. Mar. 5, 2009).

142. *Id.* at *19–20.

143. Tenbarge v. Ames Taping Tool Sys., Inc., 190 F.3d 862, 865 (8th Cir. 1999).

A party may not circumvent the requirements governing rebuttal reports by arguing that a report is a supplementation, or vice versa.[144] An opposing party may thus challenge and seek to strike a report on the grounds that the report does not qualify as a rebuttal or supplemental report.[145] In those instances, a court will conduct a "careful examination" of the disputed report to determine whether the report qualifies as a rebuttal or a supplementation.[146] Because the timeliness of a report depends on whether the report is supplemental,[147] rebuttal,[148] or even an entirely new opinion,[149] the consequences of a court's decision to reclassify a report are significant.[150] Reclassification of a supplemental report to a rebuttal report can result in its exclusion if the report was not filed within 30 days of a report filed by the adverse party.[151] Conversely, a court may reclassify a rebuttal report as a supplemental report in instances where a court perceives that a party submitted a report in an effort to amend an initial expert report after the deadline for pretrial disclosures has passed.[152] If the deadline has passed, a court's reclassification can result in the exclusion of the report.[153]

---

144. *Equant*, 217 F.R.D. at 116 (quoting 6 Patrick E. Higginbotham, Moore's Federal Practice ¶ 26.23[3] (3d ed. 2002)).

145. Estate of Gaither v. D.C., 2008 U.S. Dist. LEXIS 108557 (D.D.C. Oct. 23, 2008).

146. Covington v. Memphis Publ'g Co., 2007 U.S. Dist. LEXIS 95842, at *9 (W.D. Tenn. Oct. 16, 2007).

147. Supplementations "must be disclosed by the time the party's disclosures under Rule 26(a)(3) are due." Fed. R. Civ. P. 26(e)(2).

148. Rebuttals must be filed "within 30 days after the other party's disclosure." Fed. R. Civ. P. 26(a)(2)(C)(ii).

149. Fed. R. Civ. P. 26(a)(2)(B) requires parties to serve expert disclosures containing a complete statement of all opinions to be expressed and the basis and reason therefore.

150. *Campos*, 2009 U.S. Dist. LEXIS 63846, at *27 (report reclassified as a rebuttal report, not a supplemental report, and thus "technically untimely"); *Sandata Techs.*, 2007 U.S. Dist. LEXIS 85176, at *14–17 (finding report submitted as a supplemental report was clearly a rebuttal report); Cooper Tire & Rubber Co. v. Farese, 2008 U.S. Dist. LEXIS 99667 (N.D. Miss. Dec. 9, 2008) (finding that an expert report was not a supplemental report, but rather an entirely new opinion, which should have been included in the initial report because information relied on in the new report was available to party at the time initial report was prepared).

151. *Covington*, 2007 U.S. Dist. LEXIS 95842, at *9.

152. Cooper Tire & Rubber Co. v. Farese, 2008 U.S. Dist. LEXIS 96729, at *7 (N.D. Miss. Nov. 26, 2008) (rejecting attempt to create a "procedural back door by labeling [the] report a rebuttal report as opposed to a supplemental report or new opinion").

153. *Id.* at *8.

Conclusion

Rule 26(a) requires any witness specifically retained or specially employed to provide expert testimony to produce a written report. The expert report and any rebuttal or supplemental report are subject to explicit requirements. Despite the clear language, courts have held that the rule imposes broad disclosure requirements on all trial experts, including treating physicians, who can generally be deposed or called to testify at trial without submitting a written report. To ensure that an expert's testimony will be admissible into evidence, the factors enumerated in Rule 26(a)(2)(B) must be satisfied. Misclassification of a witness or failure to comply with the requirements can have significantly negative consequences; trial courts have not been hesitant in excluding expert reports and testimony for failure to comply with Rule 26(a). Counsel should also work with the expert in crafting the expert report to ensure that any challenge under *Daubert* will be successfully repelled and that the report remains accessible to the layman. At the same time, counsel must work to protect attorney work product from becoming discoverable as a result of disclosure to an expert witness. The Civil Rules Advisory Committee has proposed amendments to Rule 26(a) meant to narrow the scope of discovery into attorney work product, but the expansive interpretation given to the rule's disclosure requirements by the courts cautions against free disclosure of attorney work product to an expert.

CHAPTER 5

Expert Depositions

DEFENDING YOUR OWN EXPERT'S DEPOSITION

John P. Phillips and Peter C. Meier[1]

To properly defend your expert's deposition, prepare for the worst. By now you have absorbed the advice in the preceding chapters, selected the best expert to address the issues that will control the result of your case, and spent the appropriate time working with your expert to develop his opinions and prepare any required reports. You have also become intimately familiar with your expert's opinions, files, past depositions and reports, and all of the work your expert did to prepare for the deposition. You understand the key literature and research that the expert may need to reconcile with your expert's opinions developed for the case. You also understand the factual foundation for your expert's opinions, so that you can object to questions that mischaracterize the record and underlying facts of the case. This work will be critical in helping your expert navigate the landmines and traps opposing counsel will try to lay.

This subchapter covers practical issues that you will want to address to ensure your expert's deposition goes as smoothly as possible. It also identifies steps you will want to take to protect your client's record as you head toward trial.

---

1. John P. Phillips and Peter C. Meier are litigation partners in the San Francisco, California, office of Paul Hastings Janofsky & Walker LLP. Both handle complex commercial disputes and class actions, trade secret disputes, product liability matters, and mass torts through trial and appeal.

Location and Logistics: The Days and Hours before the Deposition

Procedural Issues

Before you get to the deposition site, be sure to address any procedural issues. If the opposing party served your expert with a subpoena to obtain his files, ensure that an appropriate objection has been served and that you have compiled and reviewed responsive materials. If the court entered a case management order at the outset of the case that addresses expert discovery, review it again to ensure you have complied with its requirements. Bring copies of any deposition notice/subpoena objection with you to attach to the transcript if necessary, and be sure to think through any production issues (especially if your expert works mainly with electronic data) well in advance of the deposition. You also should be aware of the terms of any protective order in place in the case.

Exchange of Documents and Related Issues

Either through agreement, notice, or subpoena, your opponents will take appropriate steps to ensure they receive your expert's file materials before the deposition. Assess the volume and decide when and how to produce the materials. It is best to raise this issue early and negotiate an agreement that will work for both parties during expert discovery. In light of the federal seven-hour time limit for depositions,[2] you do not want to create an argument for the other side that materials were improperly or untimely produced, leading to a suspension or continuance of the deposition and additional expense for your client. Once a decision has been made (or an agreement reached) to produce an expert's documents before the deposition, carefully review those documents to ensure nothing inadvertently made its way into your expert's files. If you are producing electronic data, consider metadata and address formatting issues—again, to avoid an argument that the deposition should be suspended and resumed so that opposing counsel can decipher the electronic data. Simply put, work in advance with your expert to ensure your adversary obtains the documents and information he is entitled to before the deposition begins.

---

2. FED. R. CIV. PROC. 30(d)(1).

Videotaping and Court Reporter Issues

Counsel often videotape expert depositions. Videotaping in federal court is governed by the general provision of Federal Rule of Civil Procedure 30(b)(4). If the deposition is being videotaped, ask to look at the monitor—before the deposition begins—to see how the expert will look on camera. Similarly, talk with the court reporter in advance of the deposition (preferably outside of your expert's presence) if your witness is soft-spoken or if there are any other communication issues. It is critical to take every step to ensure the transcript is accurate. Instruct the court reporter to interrupt if it becomes difficult to hear or understand your expert. If the case involves complicated terms and it is possible to do so in advance of the deposition, develop a case dictionary and send it to the court reporter. You also should determine whether the party taking the deposition will be using LiveNote (or a similar deposition software program), so that you will be prepared to use LiveNote as well during the deposition if you so desire.

It is also wise to keep a sheet of paper handy to provide correct spellings to the court reporter during the break. The more technical the case, the more counsel needs to ensure that the court reporter understands the terms used and is taking them down properly. Only take notes, however, if it does not distract your expert or you from the more important goal of asserting appropriate objections and protecting the record.

Travel Schedules

Most experts do not work down the street from the courthouse or near opposing counsel's office. If your expert is traveling some distance for the deposition, make sure the schedule enables him to address any jet lag or potential travel delays and to start at a time when he is fresh.

Payment and Other Administrative Tasks

Depending on the jurisdiction and your agreement with plaintiff's counsel, ensure that your experts are paid for their time. Review all correspondence about the agreed-upon procedure for conducting expert discovery, confirm your agreement with plaintiff's counsel at the deposition, and ask the expert for any information (such as tax ID number) that opposing counsel will need to write the check.

Final Preparations: The Day of the Deposition

Emphasize the Key Guidelines for a Successful Deposition

During your brief meeting with your expert the day of the deposition, stress the *number one rule*: understand the question asked and answer only that question. As a corollary, do not volunteer information that is not responsive. Subject to very few exceptions discussed below, remind your expert that he is not there to win the case in deposition. That is what trials are for. If opposing counsel fails to ask the appropriate questions, that is his problem, not the expert's. Toward the end of the final preparation session, confirm that your expert understands what his role is and why he is being deposed. This is important so that your expert does not stray into areas that you have carefully reserved for other experts.

Confirm Guidance on Style and Demeanor

Stress again that demeanor is critical, especially if opposing counsel is videotaping the deposition or is likely to be aggressive during the deposition. Your expert should act professionally and maintain neutrality. If you have any concern about how your expert will comport himself, tell him to imagine he's giving a serious presentation to a group of distinguished scholars in his field and to act accordingly.

It also helps to arrive at the deposition site at least a half an hour early to give your expert time to set up and to familiarize himself with the space. (This also ensures you have extra time to locate the deposition site.) Talk with your expert about where he will be comfortable sitting in the room and coordinate with the court reporter, the videographer, and opposing counsel. Your expert should be permitted to sit wherever he is most comfortable.

Opposing counsel often pick a point in the deposition to try to rile the expert to see if a button can be pushed at trial. So be alert so you can assert the appropriate objection, and be sure to prepare your expert to stay calm and steady. In addition, remind your expert that sarcasm and jokes do not work well during a deposition and can be misunderstood when read aloud to the court or the jury.

Review Key Objections

Objections are discussed in more detail below, but review key objections with your expert so he understands the purpose behind each one. This will enable the expert to better formulate an answer or to explain why the question should be rephrased to permit an appropriate answer.

Control the Pace and Process: The Deposition Has Begun

Objections

Your main role during the expert's deposition is to protect the record—and the main way you do that is through objections. Often lawyers simply object without explaining to the expert why a particular objection is being made. But such objections help the expert see why a question is not particularly fair or appropriate, which in turn helps the expert understand the process.

As a legal matter, in most states, all objections as to form are waived unless timely made.[3] To properly defend any deposition, you need to know the rules of your particular jurisdiction. In some states you can only object as "to form." In others, it is permissible—or even necessary—to state the basis for the objection. Often, the court's local rules will address deposition procedures, so be sure to review those carefully before the deposition. If you have not committed Federal Rules of Civil Procedure 26 and 30 to memory, or if you are in state court and are not knowledgeable about all the rules in the jurisdiction that control the conduct of depositions, you should bring the text of those rules with you as well.

If you expect that objections, instructions to the witness not to answer questions based on a confidentiality or privilege issue, or other issues regarding the conduct of the deposition may become contentious for any reason, you should be prepared to state on the record the basis for your position on such issues. In federal cases in which the content of and basis for objections are challenged as improper by the party taking the deposition, that party is expected to suspend the deposition and seek an appropriate order under Rule 30(d)(3)(A). Opposing counsel may attempt to have the issue resolved by telephone if the assigned judge, magistrate judge, or special master (if one is appointed) is available. You must be prepared to present the basis for your objections or position on any other contested issue as succinctly as possible, with reference to the procedural rules, Advisory Committee notes (in the case of the Federal Rules of Civil Procedure), or local rules that support your position.

Key form objections include the following:

---

3. *See, e.g.*, FED. R. CIV. PROC. 32(d)(3).

Objection	Purpose
Vague and ambiguous (unintelligible)	Make this objection when something about the question does not make sense: a term was improperly used, testimony was misstated, or a reference in the question is unclear. This objection is likely to remind the expert to make sure he understands what is being asked and answer that question—the *number one rule* discussed above.
Compound	Make this objection when the question contains two separate questions. This is a particularly important objection to make sure the expert only answers the question asked. The expert should not hesitate to tell the questioner that he asked two questions and to break the question down so the record is clear.
Argumentative	Make this objection in a variety of settings, but mostly when a questioner uses unprofessional or harassing language, intentionally misstates an expert's prior testimony, or uses some term or pejorative that sounds more like a jury argument than a question aimed at understanding an expert's opinion or the basis for the opinion.
Misstates Testimony	Make this objection when a questioner attempts to "summarize an expert's testimony" and does so in either an improper or unfair way.
Incomplete Hypothetical	Make this objection when an expert is asked to answer a question based on an assumed set of facts. If the facts are incomplete or argumentative, assert this objection because the expert does not have sufficient information to answer the question. The watchwords for this question are "what if/I'd like you to assume." This objection is often combined with a "lacks foundation" objection.
Lacks Foundation	This objection often goes hand in hand with the incomplete hypothetical objection. It signals that opposing counsel has failed to establish a key foundational fact that is required to answer the pending questions. The objection should also be asserted if a question is aimed at a topic that is outside of the expert's area of expertise. If this occurs, be prepared to note for the record (if appropriate in your jurisdiction) that the question addressed an issue about which the expert was not disclosed to testify. You do not want your expert testifying about issues that he was not disclosed to address.

(*continued*)

Objection	Purpose
Legal Conclusions	In most jurisdictions, it is improper to ask an expert to address an ultimate legal conclusion that will be resolved by either the judge or jury. If this issue will arise during the deposition, research the relevant law in your jurisdiction before the deposition begins.

Protecting Work Product and Confidential Information

If your expert is asked about work or communications that are either confidential or subject to the work product objection, be prepared to advise the expert of his need to protect this information. For example, your expert may be engaged in another matter—not necessarily as a witness, not even necessarily for your firm. If the expert has not been disclosed in another matter, the expert's work in that matter may be protected. Further, in some jurisdictions, a testifying expert's communications with the attorney are subject to work product protection. Indeed, a proposed amendment to Federal Rule of Civil Procedure 26 to extend work product protection to some attorney-expert communications is currently under consideration.[4]

If any of the scenarios discussed above requires you to suspend the deposition, attempt to resolve the issue on the record so that you can make the proper representations to the court in your moving papers. The general rule is that you do not have the right to instruct an expert witness not to answer a question. The one exception is when you are protecting privileged information or work product.[5]

Lastly, in many cases, the parties negotiate a protective order to cover certain documents and testimony. If your expert has relied on confidential or confidential restricted documents (two standard designations in most matters), be prepared to designate the documents and testimony properly during the deposition. It is important to instruct the court reporter when testimony is subject to a confidentiality designation. Otherwise, you will be forced to resolve the issue after the deposition, which might result in unnecessary motion practice. The court reporter also will need to be informed of the procedures required by the protective order or under local rules for sealing of transcripts that have been designated as confidential.

---

4. *See* http://www.uscourts.gov/rules/jc09-2009/2009-09-Appendix-C.pdf; *see supra* "Privilege Issues" in chapter 2 and chapter 4.

5. *See* Fed. R. Civ. Proc. 30(c)(2).

Use of Documents

If opposing counsel uses a document to form the foundation of a question or as an exhibit, assess the document for completeness and make all appropriate objections. Often counsel will use snippets from documents, or refuse to mark exhibits or give the information required to locate the document once the expert has been questioned about it. Insist on full identification of documents for the record, along with page numbers or any other information that will ensure you can find the document afterwards. If opposing counsel has not provided you with a copy—too often because counsel "forgot to make extra copies"—insist that you obtain a copy on the break. More importantly, remind the expert that he can take his time to appropriately review the document on which a question is based—after all, the expert is the only person in the room under oath.

If your case involves the use of translated documents, ask opposing counsel for a standing objection to the use of any translation on the ground that it lacks foundation (i.e., the original document has not been translated correctly). Consult the relevant rules of evidence in your jurisdiction. Although this issue does not arise very often, there is a rule of long standing in the federal system that trials are to be conducted in English. The English-language requirement is confirmed further both by Federal Rule of Civil Procedure 43(d), which affords a trial court discretion to "appoint an interpreter of its choosing," and by Federal Rule of Evidence 604, which confirms that "[a]n interpreter is subject to the provisions of these Rules [of evidence] relating to the qualification as an expert and the administration of an oath or affirmation to make a true translation." Although there is some dispute about whether a foreign-language document is admissible without translation (the majority rule is that it is not), as a matter of prudence it is best to obtain translations from a certified translator of all the documents that might be used during a deposition. Be sure that the record is clear about which translation is related to which foreign-language original.

Prior Testimony and Publications

An expert will often be questioned about prior testimony and publications that relate to the opinions developed for litigation. As with the use of documents discussed above, if an incomplete transcript or article is shown to the expert, object because the record is incomplete. On a break, review the transcript with your expert to identify any areas that you might want to clarify at the end of the deposition. If snippets of the transcript are used unfairly, object that the question is argumentative.

Requests for Information/Documents during the Deposition

Opposing counsel often ask an expert to follow up and provide information or written materials that are identified during the deposition. If the requests are legitimate and within the scope of materials the parties agreed to exchange either before or during the deposition, follow up appropriately. All requests should be fielded and addressed by counsel. Do not permit the expert to agree to provide written responses when reviewing the transcript or to conduct any follow-up research after the deposition. If supplementation is required under Rule 26, take the appropriate steps, but prepare your expert to refer all requests for additional information or analysis to counsel.

Taking Appropriate Breaks

While paying attention to the procedural technicalities of the deposition, remember that a deposition can tax your expert's energy level and powers of concentration. For these reasons, it is important to take appropriate breaks, every hour or so, and to allocate a proper amount of time for a lunch break. Alternatively, if your goal is to finish the deposition in a short time period, discuss that with the expert in advance so that he can plan to push through lunch or breaks. If you decide that it is time for a break, the custom is to wait until opposing counsel has finished a line of questioning or is otherwise at a logical breaking point in the examination. At that point, simply ask to "go off the record and take a break." Substantively, be thoughtful about what you discuss on the break. These conversations are discoverable so ensure your expert understands that important fact. Never leave your expert alone in the room with opposing counsel. Leave and return to the deposition room together.

Addressing an Expert's Mistakes

Experts are human. At times, they will get confused or misunderstand a question. It is important, therefore, to remain attentive and identify those areas where the expert did not testify accurately. If it is a minor administrative matter (e.g., using the wrong exhibit number), clarify the record on the spot. If the mistake is substantive, the best approach is to find an appropriate spot for a break, discuss the issue with the expert, and have the expert correct the testimony as appropriate. Before going back on the record after the break, tell opposing counsel that the witness identified part of his prior testimony that needs to be addressed to ensure the record is accurate. It is better to correct the testimony while time remains for opposing counsel to ask questions about the modification than to make the correction in writing after the deposition and open the expert up to further cross-examination on the topic.

Dealing with a Frustrated Expert or Rude Opposing Counsel

If an expert becomes frustrated, the best remedy is to take a break and discuss the issue. Remind the expert of what you covered before the deposition and stress the need to retain a professional demeanor at all times. If the frustration is the result of opposing counsel's conduct, the best approach is to discuss counsel's inappropriate behavior off the record (unless it has to be addressed immediately) outside the presence of the other participants. If counsel's inappropriate behavior continues, consider adjourning the deposition to seek a protective order. Make an appropriate record. If counsel's behavior is part of an overall pattern of unprofessional conduct, consider videotaping opposing counsel or contacting your discovery magistrate or referee.

Seeking Intervention

For any number of reasons, it may become necessary for you to seek intervention from the court or from a special master appointed to resolve discovery disputes. Do so sparingly, and only after you have made every effort to resolve the matter informally (both on and off the record). If you have to contact the court to protect your client's interests, discuss this step with the court reporter so that he can prepare to read aloud the sections of the transcript that the court might need to consider.

Completing Your Record

Depending on how the testimony develops, it may be necessary for you to ask your expert questions at the end of the deposition. Remember that you will have the ability to develop opinions and identify other supporting literature or scientific materials when you call the expert to testify at trial. There are, however, three main situations that you should consider before the deposition begins that would require you (as part of your role defending the deposition) to ask questions of your expert:

1. To prepare for settlement. If your client intends to settle rather than take the case to trial, you may want to use the expert to educate your opponent about every weakness in his case. In that situation, if the questioner did not ask the right question to elicit the opinions from your expert, ask the expert to review the areas that were not covered.

2. To preserve testimony. Trial schedules are difficult to manage, and if your expert has professional obligations that create a meaningful risk that he may be unavailable for trial, you should ask questions to preserve the testimony that you would want to use in any pretrial setting or otherwise read/show to the jury.

3. To prepare for a *Daubert*[6] hearing. If you expect your expert to be subject to *Daubert* challenges, you may want the expert to clarify testimony or explain opinions to stave off any attack.[7]

Finishing Touches: Ending the Deposition

Future Work

Most depositions end with a series of questions designed to determine if your expert plans to conduct any future work. Cover this with your expert in advance of the deposition. If future work is warranted given the timing of the deposition and the overall state of fact discovery, ensure that your expert leaves the door open. Be careful, however, to do this only in rare situations because you may expose your expert to an additional deposition if he develops supplemental opinions after the deposition. Be mindful that you are also required to produce a supplemental report in federal court if your expert develops additional opinions.[8]

Final Logistics

Before the deposition is concluded, ensure any logistical issues relating to the copying and return of documents are clearly stated on the record. Make sure your expert does not leave the deposition room with original deposition exhibits. Ask for the opportunity to review and sign the transcript. Expert depositions are often taken close to trial: be prepared to address any requests to have the transcript reviewed on an expedited basis and negotiate a date that works for you and the expert.

Transcript Review

The last step to properly defend an expert's deposition is to review the final transcript for any areas that might require correction. Send the transcript

---

6. Daubert v. Merrell Dow Pharms., Inc., 509 U.S. 579 (1993).
7. *See infra* chapter 6 for a more thorough discussion of *Daubert* challenges.
8. *See* Fed. R. Civ. P. 26(e).

for review in a timely manner. Although the ultimate decision to change any testimony belongs to your expert, review the testimony and identify any answers that should be discussed with your expert.

Checklist for Defending Your Own Expert's Deposition

- Address logistics: confirm the schedule, your expert's availability, and ensure that you have adequate time to prepare.
- Review key witness rules/guidelines for a successful deposition.
- Address and resolve any document or data production issues before the deposition.
- Protect the record with appropriate objections—review key objections with your expert.
- Assess whether to complete the record with additional questions.
- Properly conclude the deposition.

TAKING THE DEPOSITION OF AN OPPOSING EXPERT

Peter C. Meier and John P. Phillips[1]

Preparing for the Deposition

Preparing for an expert witness deposition can be a daunting experience. You are unlikely to be thoroughly knowledgeable regarding the subject of the expert's testimony, and, therefore, before you can even prepare effective questions for the deposition, you will need to become conversant in the key scientific or technical terms used in the expert's field as well as become knowledgeable regarding the references the expert relies on. You will need to have a strong understanding of the factual record the expert relies on, any assumptions the expert makes in coming to his conclusions, and the opinions of any other experts in the case on whom the expert relies. Also, you will want to determine whether there is any scientific or technical literature that the expert does not rely on but that may support lines of cross-examination. An

---

1. Peter C. Meier and John P. Phillips are litigation partners in the San Francisco, California, office of Paul Hastings Janofsky & Walker LLP. Both handle complex commercial disputes, product liability, and mass tort cases through trial and appeal.

expert's failure to consider that literature may raise doubts about the thoroughness of his analysis or about his credibility, supporting an argument that the expert has cherry-picked only the literature that supports his opinions. In the typical compressed scheduled for expert discovery, there is little time to accomplish all of this, so it becomes necessary to identify the key goals of the deposition and to plan how to use your preparation time most effectively.

The Impact of Case Strategy on Your Preparation

The first question to ask in preparing for an expert deposition is, "What do I need to get from this witness, consistent with our strategy in the case?" Your underlying strategy in the case should determine the kinds of questions you prepare for the deposition.

For example, if you are representing a defendant, and you believe the plaintiff's case is vulnerable to a summary judgment motion, you may want to prepare a series of questions designed to yield concessions from the expert that will support your motion. Similarly, if you represent a plaintiff whose claim is vulnerable to summary judgment, you likely will want to use your time preparing questions that will yield concessions from the defense expert that will help you establish that there are disputed facts preventing summary judgment.

Whether you represent the plaintiff or defendant in this situation, you will not be able to yield concessions from the expert simply by asking open-ended questions. Rather, you will need to prepare a series of questions designed to pin the expert down on his opinion, drawing out the weaknesses in the expert's opinion that may impact the result of the summary judgment motion, whether these weaknesses are internal inconsistencies in the expert's report or inconsistencies with the factual record or scientific literature. Your audience for these questions and the expert's answers is the judge (or clerk) who will later read the motion for summary judgment, the supporting and opposing papers of which may quote directly from the expert's testimony in deposition.

But what if the defendant does not think he can file, or win, a summary judgment motion? Your tactics in the expert deposition in this situation should be very different, because there is little utility in aggressively questioning the expert in the deposition order to make him look foolish if all you will be doing in the process is giving the other side the outline of your trial cross-examination. In this situation, the most you may want to do is to tie down the expert's opinions and ask a limited number of set-up questions that can be used as the building blocks for the cross-examination.

Another consideration that will impact your preparation is whether you think the expert's testimony is subject to a *Daubert*[2] challenge or other challenge based on state law as to its admissibility. If you determine that the expert may lack the qualifications necessary to offer his opinions, or if you believe the expert's methodology is unreliable, the deposition gives you an opportunity to ask the expert questions that will support a motion to exclude his opinions on these grounds. To accomplish this goal, you should prepare questions that are based on the *Daubert* test (or other applicable test of admissibility). For example, if you believe that an expert professes to use a valid methodology, but you believe that he has not employed that methodology, your questioning should first pin the expert down regarding the steps in the analysis that the valid methodology requires. Then, you should push the expert to explain what he did to follow that methodology, looking for ways to draw out inconsistencies between what the expert claims to have done and what the expert really did in applying the methodology. If the questions are well prepared, the expert must make a decision in this situation as to whether to maintain at least some credibility by admitting that he did not follow particular steps in question or risk losing credibility by refusing to acknowledge ways in which the expert's true methodology differed from his professed methodology.

Another issue to consider is whether you believe the case can and should be settled well before trial begins. If you believe that an aggressive deposition of the other side's expert will yield admissions or expose weaknesses in the expert's testimony that will make it more likely that you can obtain an advantageous settlement for your client, you may be more willing to tip your hand in the deposition as to potential lines of cross-examination at trial.

Assistance from Consultants or Your Own Experts

In preparing for the deposition, you may need to rely on the expertise of a consultant or one of your own testifying experts. A consultant who is knowledgeable regarding the scientific or technical issues can make sure that your questions are scientifically and technically accurate, making it more difficult for the expert to quibble with them. You can also rely on one of your testifying experts to help you prepare for the deposition, but be aware that the expert's involvement in assisting you in this way may be disclosed when your expert is deposed. The opposing side is likely to claim that

---

2. Daubert v. Merrell Dow Pharms., Inc., 509 U.S. 579 (1993).

your expert's participation in preparation for the deposition demonstrates that your expert is an advocate or hired gun rather than an objective expert.

You may even want to consider having a trusted consultant sit in on the deposition with you. Such a consultant can help you make important decisions during the deposition as to whether to follow up with more questions on a particular subject. Sometimes, you may even find the presence of a good consultant will make it less likely that the other side's expert will attempt to get away with nonresponsive answers.

Logistical and Procedural Issues

As you prepare, you also need to think about which exhibits you will want to use in the deposition. If you are limited to seven hours of testimony (as in federal court), it is important to make sure that you do not attempt to use too many exhibits. Your list of potential exhibits must include documents in the expert's file. You will need to make sure you send a deposition notice or serve a subpoena for the expert's materials as soon as possible to ensure you will have adequate time to review the expert's materials before the deposition. Usually the parties reach an agreement regarding how and when each expert's materials will be provided to the other side before the expert's deposition.

Since you are the attorney taking the deposition, you want to be sure that the deposition will take place in a favorable environment. If you cannot depose the expert in your own office because the expert must be deposed in another city, consider using your contacts (or the contacts of your firm or other professional colleagues) to find a local law firm that can host the deposition. For example, you may need access to a printer during the deposition if you realize you need a hard copy of a document to question the expert or to use as an exhibit. In addition, you should try to obtain access to the location of the deposition the day before or at least an hour before the deposition starts, so that you can determine the best seats for the court reporter, the witness, and opposing counsel.

You also need to be prepared to pay for the expert's professional time during the deposition. If possible, obtain opposing counsel's agreement in advance that experts can be paid for their testimony within a few days after the deposition is concluded. Otherwise, it can be difficult to bring a check to the deposition in the correct amount, without knowing how many hours of testimony will be required.

You should also consider whether to videotape the deposition. At trial, videotaped testimony by an expert can be much more effective in impeaching that expert than simply reading from a transcript of the deposition. Also, videotaping of the deposition tends to bring out better behavior by the witness and opposing counsel, since the witness will likely be aware that evasive testimony will not come across well on the videotape, and opposing counsel will be aware that overly aggressive tactics in defending the deposition will look worse on videotape than on a printed transcript of the deposition. Of course if you videotape the other side's experts, the other side will likely want to videotape your own experts' depositions. In a case in which there are numerous expert depositions, videotaping can become a significant expense.

Conducting the Deposition

Issues to Cover during the Deposition

The Expert's Qualifications

In a typical deposition, there is little utility in spending your time having the opposing expert expound on his qualifications, eating up precious time by testifying about various academic and professional achievements. You should already have a copy of the expert's curriculum vitae (CV), and you can ask the expert to confirm that you have the most up-to-date version of the CV. Nevertheless, there are situations in which you will want to ask questions about the expert's qualifications.

First, on rare occasions, you may have grounds to challenge an expert witness under *Daubert* due to the expert's offering opinions regarding a subject beyond his expertise. It is more likely that this weakness in the expert's opinions will relate to only one or two different aspects of the testimony the expert proposes to offer at trial, as opposed to the entirety of the expert's opinion. For example, an expert regarding medical causation may propose to testify in a personal injury case regarding not only issues of general or specific causation, but also the defendants' conduct and whether it complied with industry standards. While the expert may have the qualifications to testify regarding medical causation, the expert should not be permitted to testify about the defendants' compliance with industry standards without first establishing the qualifications to do so.

In this situation, you should ask a series of questions to establish that the expert does not have the qualifications necessary to offer the testimony, such as the following:

- Do you have any educational background in [this subject]?
- What is that background?
- Have you published any articles regarding [this subject]?
- What research, if any, have you conducted regarding [this subject]?

- What are the leading professional organizations for experts in [this subject]?
- Are you a member of any of those organizations?

The second type of situation in which you may want to ask extensive questions regarding the expert's qualifications is where you believe the expert or opposing counsel has exaggerated the strength of the expert's background in the subject at issue, and you want to set up an effective cross-examination of the expert that will undercut the expert's credibility. For example, a medical doctor who diagnoses and treats patients with cancer might claim to be an authority regarding the causes and treatment of kidney cancer but may have published no articles regarding those subjects. While it may be unlikely that the judge would exclude the testimony of a medical doctor regarding cancer causation under *Daubert*, you still may be able to draw out facts from the expert that undercut his claim to be an authority on the subject. Thus, while you certainly could wait until trial to ask the expert questions that undermine his claims to authority, it may be less risky to establish the key weaknesses in the expert's qualifications during the deposition.

If you find a mistake or misrepresentation in the expert's CV, consider whether to ask about it in the deposition or to wait until trial to raise it. If you think the mistake is one that the expert will be forced to admit at trial, rather than of a type that he can quibble with you about on the witness stand, you may want to wait until trial to ask the question. Mistakes in the expert's CV might convey to the jury that the expert is exaggerating his credentials or is sloppy (or both).

Prior Testimony and Reports

In preparing your cross-examination of an expert, you likely will want to look for inconsistencies between the opinions the expert is offering in your case and in prior cases. For example, if the expert in your case is criticizing the methodology used by your own expert, it would be very powerful to demonstrate during cross-examination that the opposing expert adopted or approved of this same methodology in a prior case. Under Federal Rule of Civil Procedure 26, the expert must provide in the expert report a list of all other cases in which, during the previous four years, he testified as an expert at trial or by deposition. You should ask the expert whether he testified in any cases more than four years ago and obtain as much information about those cases as possible so that you can track down an existing transcript of the expert's testimony. Keep in mind as well that Rule 26 only requires the expert to disclose prior testimony, not prior expert reports. Therefore, be sure to ask the expert to identify all previous matters in which he prepared an expert report, and obtain information about those matters to assist you in obtaining a copy of the expert's report, if you think it will be useful in preparing for cross-examination. It also can be helpful for cross-examination to know whether the expert has tended to testify (or prepare expert reports) only on behalf of plaintiffs or defendants in various types of litigation.

Preparation of the Expert Report

If the expert prepared a report, you should find out how the report was prepared. Did the expert copy language from any previous expert reports prepared by the expert or someone else? Was all of the report prepared by the expert? Who assisted in its preparation? How much time did the expert spend on the report? You will also want to know whether and to what extent attorneys for the other side participated in the preparation of the report. It is common for an expert to claim that attorneys who reviewed the report only suggested minor wording changes here and there. Do not accept this as an answer without first probing for more information. What exactly did the attorney request be changed? Did the expert make the changes that the attorney requested? Why (or why not)? Were any e-mails exchanged with the attorney regarding the report and any proposed changes? Do not underestimate the effectiveness of questions at trial that demonstrate that the expert made extensive changes to his report—and therefore his opinions—at the request of counsel, indicating to the jury that the expert is basically no more than a mouthpiece for the opposing side's counsel.

You should also ask about preparation of draft reports, as long as you are prepared to have your own experts questioned about this subject. There are conflicting rules in various jurisdictions about whether draft expert reports are discoverable. If you think you are entitled to obtain previous drafts of the expert's report, and are willing to produce any draft reports prepared by your own experts, be sure to ask about the existence of prior drafts.

Contacts with Lawyers or Other Witnesses

In the same vein, you should ask about all of the expert's contacts with opposing counsel, not just contacts regarding the expert's report. You should find out whether the expert previously has been retained by opposing counsel, or the party, in a different case. An expert who at first blush may appear to be an unbiased seeker of truth might appear to be less so if he has testified on many occasions for the same lawyers, giving the same testimony.

You should ask a series of questions regarding how the expert became involved in your case. Who contacted him, and what did that person say was needed? What did the expert say in response? While these questions may seem mundane, they sometimes will yield useful information.

Some experts will also converse with other experts or colleagues in the course of their work in the matter. You should ask about those contacts. For example, in preparing his report, did the expert closely coordinate with experts testifying on behalf of the same party? If experts coordinate closely, it may appear that they are working collectively to weave together a consistent case for the attorneys, as opposed to engaging in an open-ended search for truth.

The Expert's Preparation for the Deposition

What did the expert do to prepare for the deposition? Once again, this question may seem mundane, but it often yields unexpected and useful information. For example, an expert in preparing for the deposition may discover errors in his own report that require additional work to shore up the opinions and preserve his credibility. Open-ended questions about the expert's effort to get ready for the deposition should yield any such efforts by the expert to bolster his opinions. This information can be useful because it may lead you to understand what the expert considers to be weaknesses in his opinions—after all, if the expert felt confident in the opinions, why was it necessary for him to conduct additional research for the scientific support for the opinions at the last minute?

You also should find out about the expert's conversations with opposing counsel leading up to the deposition. While some experts might claim to recall few details about discussions with counsel before the deposition, others may surprise you by recalling in great detail what was discussed. Ask a lot of follow-up questions regarding any meetings that occurred. Who exactly was present? How long did the meeting with counsel last? What questions did counsel tell you to expect would be asked in this deposition? Did you review any materials to prepare for the deposition? What did you review?

Closing Off Opinions

You also should consider whether to establish relatively early in the deposition that the report contains a complete statement of the expert's opinions, to prevent the expert from later claiming that it is necessary to supplement the report with new opinions. Some attorneys may be wary of eliciting additional opinions from the expert in the deposition, instead believing that it is best to rely on the Rule 26 report as a complete statement of the expert's opinions, subject to the duty to supplement the report under Rule 26(e)(1). But there are occasions when you are well served to make sure in the deposition that the expert does not have any additional opinions that he proposes to offer at trial.

As an illustration, imagine that you are representing the defendant in a personal injury matter, deposing an expert in medical causation. The expert's report discloses an opinion that your client's conduct caused the plaintiff's injury and refers to a large number of medical articles, as well as raw, unpublished government health statistics, for support. You face a question: do you ask the expert to explain how the unpublished government health statistics support his opinion, or do you consider that to be an undisclosed opinion that you might be able to keep out if you do not ask him about it in his deposition?

In the real case on which this example is based, the attorney chose to push the expert to explain how the unpublished data supported his opinion. The expert said in the deposition that he had not prepared an analysis of the data and how it supported his opinion. At trial, however, the expert attempted to testify at length regarding the government statistics and what they showed. After the jury rendered a verdict for the plaintiff, this testimony led to the court's granting a motion for a new trial because the court determined that the expert had not disclosed the opinions in his report and had testified in his deposition that he had not undertaken the type of analysis he tried to present at trial. Had the attorney not pressed the expert in the deposition regarding how the data allegedly supported his opinions, the result might have been different.

Often questions intended to close off the expert's opinions are met with resistance, because experts instinctively do not like to be boxed in to the opinions in their report. An expert may say that he is not prepared to answer a particular question because it would require additional investigation or research for the expert to do so. A response to this effort by the expert to leave the door open for additional opinions is to say: "I understand that you may review additional information in this case, but do you understand that I'm entitled to ask you in this deposition to tell me the opinions that you intend to offer at trial in this case?" You can follow this question by asking that the expert confirm his understanding that you intend to ask that any new, postdeposition opinions by the expert be excluded if those opinions were not provided in response to your questions in the deposition. Experts will sometime do a better job in answering your questions and not trying to leave the door open after they are forced to acknowledge this fact.

The Basis of Opinions and Supporting Data

Rule 26 requires that expert reports disclose the "basis" for the expert's opinions as well as "the data or other information considered by the witness in forming them." It is possible to spend an extensive amount of time in an expert deposition exploring the basis for the expert's opinions as well as whether and how data the expert considered supports the expert's opinions. You will need to a draw a line somewhere, however, in deciding how many questions to ask on this subject. If you are not trying to develop a *Daubert* motion, and the references cited by the expert generally seem to support the opinions in the report, there is not much point to extensive questions about those references, and you may simply be building the record for the other side.

On the other hand, if the expert appears to have cited references that are either of questionable validity or do not seem to support the expert's opinion, you will have to decide whether to save those weaknesses for cross-examination or instead try to ask set-up questions that will strengthen your ability to prepare an effective cross-examination. As an example, where an expert cites a scientific study as support for a causation opinion, but that study does not directly support the expert's opinion, you may want to put the study in front of the expert and ask him to explain how it supports the opinions in the report. The expert may struggle to do so and either admit that the study does not directly support his opinions or strain his credibility by insisting that it does.

Regarding data that the expert relies on, you should ask the expert to explain what exactly the data represents, who prepared it, and whether (and why) he considers the data to be reliable. While this line of questioning will not be fruitful in all situations, an expert will sometimes reveal ignorance about the source of data or how it was prepared.

Marking and Using Exhibits

Another decision you must make is what documents to mark as exhibits. Experts often cite dozens of references in their reports, and there may be dozens more articles or other documents that can be used to undermine the expert's opinions. But asking an expert about documents, especially complex articles published in the scientific literature, can be overly time-consuming. If you ask an expert a complex question relating to an article, the expert is likely to insist on reviewing the article before providing an answer. For example, if you ask the expert to admit that "the *Smith* article you reference in your report didn't find that Product X causes hair loss," the expert is likely to ask that you provide a copy of the article to answer the question. If you refuse to provide a copy, the savvy expert is likely to frustrate your effort to obtain useful testimony by saying something like "Well, I don't think you just want me to guess about that article and I assume you don't want this deposition to be simply a memory test. If you'd like my opinions about the article, I'm going to have to review a copy of it."

If you decide to provide the expert with the article, you must be prepared to direct the expert's attention to the particular part of the article about which you want to ask. Otherwise, you may find yourself seething at the loss of time while the expert slowly peruses the entire article looking for language he can reference in responding to your question. Also, opposing counsel is likely to ask that the document you ask about be marked as an exhibit to prevent confusion about what exactly the expert was referencing in the testimony.

Exploring Contradictions/Weaknesses in the Expert's Opinions

Once you have asked your questions about the expert's background, opinions in the case, the basis for the opinions, and any data or information that the expert considered in forming his opinions, you may decide you can conclude the deposition—or not.

The next question that confronts you is whether you should use the deposition to draw out contradictions and weaknesses in the expert's opinions. If you are in federal court and have not used up your seven hours, you may wish to devote the rest of your time to questioning the expert about evidence that he ignored in forming his opinions, about contradictions that you see in the expert's report, or about ways in which particular references may undermine the expert's opinions. This is a tactical decision that depends on numerous factors, among them the overarching strategic considerations that already have been discussed. Are you trying to set up or prepare to oppose a motion for summary judgment? Do you intend to challenge the expert's opinion under *Daubert*?

Another consideration, however, is how well prepared you think the expert is to answer your more difficult questions. If, based on the expert's answers to this point in the deposition you think that he is not well prepared for the deposition, why not test the expert's ability to answer some of your more difficult questions? This decision must be made on the fly, based on your assessment of your own level of preparation and that of the expert's. If the expert has been unflappable and has answered all of your questions about his opinions and the bases for those opinions without showing any hesitation or weakness and seems to be ready for whatever you might throw at him in the deposition, it might be best to save your best questions for cross-examination. If, on the other hand, you sense that the expert is not well prepared for the deposition and will have a difficult time dealing with your questions without further preparation, maybe it is time to ask a few of your best questions. The expert may give you testimony that he would not give at trial after better preparation.

There are no hard and fast rules that tell you how aggressively you should question the expert about weaknesses and contradictions in the expert's testimony. You simply have to make your best judgment based on your own sense of the benefits and drawbacks of asking those questions now rather than saving them for trial.

Taking and Using Breaks

One tactical question to consider during the deposition is when to take breaks. Ideally, you will not need to ask for any breaks during the deposition, but rather will wait until the expert requests one. Your goal should be to keep the process moving as swiftly as possible, so that the expert does not have extensive time for hallway conversations with opposing counsel about how he might improve on answers. If you need to leave the deposition room, you should be back in your chair and ready to resume questioning before the expert returns and is seated. That way, you keep the deposition moving along and give little opportunity for the expert to use breaks as an opportunity to think of ways to clean up his prior testimony with gratuitous and self-serving statements intended to help his own record rather than give answers to your questions.

Developing the Basis for *Daubert* Motions

As discussed above, you must make a strategic decision whether to use the deposition to develop strong *Daubert* issues or to save your best lines of attack for cross-examination at trial. You must decide in preparing for the deposition whether you believe you have a legitimate chance to have the expert's testimony excluded under *Daubert*. If you do believe you can win a *Daubert* motion, one purpose of the deposition will be to obtain testimony that will support your motion.

The relevant issues to consider in determining whether an expert's testimony should be excluded under *Daubert* include the following:

1. Does the expert have the necessary qualifications to offer opinions regarding the subject at issue?
2. Did the expert use a reliable methodology at arriving at his opinions?
3. What is the known or potential rate of error for the expert's methodology?
4. Has the expert's theory or methodology been subject to peer review.[3]

It is possible to develop extensive questions based on these requirements, but to be effective, the questions have to be tailored to the issues in the case. For example, if the expert is testifying regarding a technical issue that is not likely to be the subject of a peer-reviewed scientific journal, it is unlikely to matter much to the court that the expert's opinion on that subject is not likely to be subject to peer review. On the other hand, if the expert

---

3. *Daubert*, 509 U.S. 579; Fed. R. Evid. 702.

is making a novel scientific argument (e.g., that exposure to moonlight causes hair growth), you should ask for as much information as possible regarding whether those opinions have been subject to peer review.

More commonly, your questions regarding *Daubert* will focus on the expert's purported methodology and whether that methodology is reliable. Many experts will claim to follow a well-accepted methodology (e.g., the Bradford-Hill criteria for determining causation), but in fact the expert has been quite selective in how he has applied that methodology. One purpose of the deposition should be to establish the ways in which the expert has failed to follow the methodology.

If the expert applies a questionable methodology, you should ask a number of questions to establish that the expert's methodology is not reliable. For example, ask whether the methodology is supported by any other scientists in the expert's field. Ask if any professional or governmental organizations have endorsed the methodology. You also should ask the expert to explain how one could test the validity of the methodology. Where the expert's methodology is based on speculation and assumptions, there sometimes is no better way to demonstrate this fact to the judge than to show that the expert was unable in the deposition to explain how the methodology could be validated.

Dealing with Challenging or Difficult Witnesses

Now that you know the issues that you will need to cover in the deposition, you need to be prepared for the expert to do his best to frustrate your effort to obtain the testimony you need. There are many ways in which an expert may do this, including being evasive, argumentative, and excessively loquacious.

Dealing with an Evasive Expert Witness

Many experienced experts become expert in avoiding answering the questions asked. Instead, they use each question as an opportunity to state and restate various opinions and themes that are not responsive to the question. When an expert is not answering straightforward questions, you should restate your question, with a brief, nonargumentative preface: "Doctor, I don't believe that you answered my question. What I asked you is . . ." Do not let the expert draw you into an argument about whether a prior answer was responsive or not. Keep in mind that your duty is to press the expert for the information that you need.

If the expert continues to be evasive, you can respond with a politely stated warning: "Doctor, I am entitled to an answer to my question. I have been forced to ask this question several times, and I still do not have an answer from you. If I can't get an answer to this question, I will have to ask the court for an order compelling you to answer it, and I'll ask that opposing counsel be responsible for the cost of our having to return on another day so that you can answer it." If the expert is noncooperative, keep in mind that you are building a record that a judge or clerk or discovery master may someday read in support of a motion to compel further deposition testimony or for sanctions. You must be as professional and courteous as possible, while also standing your ground where you believe the expert is refusing to provide testimony.

Dealing with an Obstreperous Expert Witness

Some experts are not only evasive, they are downright nasty. Experts may be sarcastic, attempt to engage you in pointless arguments, storm out of the room, or even attempt to bully you. While this type of conduct is relatively rare from an expert, it does occur on occasion. Usually, your best protection against such conduct is to notice a videotaped deposition, since experts are less likely to misbehave if they know the worst of their behavior is being recorded. But if the presence of a video camera is not sufficient deterrence for the expert, do not let the expert's tactics cause you to lose control of your own emotions. The expert's sarcasm or anger is unlikely to translate well to the court (or a jury, if the testimony is ever played back in the courtroom), and you should not respond in kind.

Dealing with a Loquacious/Filibustering Expert Witness

One of the most frustrating techniques that experts may use to prevent you from obtaining valuable testimony is to use almost every question as an opportunity to launch into a long-winded answer that begins at the dawn of time and may not end until the lights are being turned off in the building. When an expert uses this tactic, you must be polite but forceful in putting a stop to it. One tactic is to interrupt a lengthy, nonresponsive answer by saying, "Excuse me, but I asked you about 'x,' and you are now instead telling me about 'y.' I would like to move on to my next question." Your interruption of the witness is likely to result in an objection from opposing counsel and perhaps even a claim that you are being "rude to the witness." But if your tone of voice is polite (as will be clear in a videotaped deposition) and you are careful not to say anything insulting to the witness, you need not be concerned about the accusation of rudeness.

If the witness continues to use such tactics, you may decide to make a more forceful warning, such as, "Doctor Smith, I have had to remind you numerous times during the course of this deposition that once you have answered my question, I will need to move on to my next question. You may have other things you wish to say regarding your opinions in this case, but I am asking the questions right now, and you are required to give only your answers to my questions. If you want to testify about other matters, you may do so after I am finished if the attorney who retained you decides to ask you questions about these other matters." You may wish to add: "If you refuse to cooperate with me in this request, I am going to be forced to request additional time to depose you, because you are preventing me from using the full [seven hours] I am entitled to use in questioning you."

Checklist for Deposing an Opposing Party's Expert

- Become thoroughly versed in the factual and scientific underpinnings for the expert's report.
- Review scientific or technical literature that the expert did not cite in his report to determine whether the expert has cherry-picked supporting literature.
- Determine the purpose of the deposition: will the deposition be necessary to bring or oppose a summary judgment motion, or is the intention solely to prepare for trial?
- Determine whether the expert's testimony is vulnerable to a *Daubert* or other admissibility challenge.
- Prepare questions and exhibits to be used for the deposition based on your objectives in taking the deposition.
- Be prepared for the witness to be evasive, difficult, and nonresponsive. Keep focused on the issues important to your case rather than letting the expert control the direction of the deposition.

CHAPTER 6

The *Daubert* Challenge and Hearing

DEFENDING YOUR EXPERT AGAINST A *DAUBERT* CHALLENGE

Sarah Jane Gillett, Stephanie T. Gentry, and Briana J. Clifton[1]

The adoption of Federal Rule of Evidence 702, followed some years later by the decision of the U.S. Supreme Court in *Daubert v. Merrell Dow Pharmaceuticals, Inc.*,[2] together sparked a veritable maelstrom of evidentiary issues surrounding expert witnesses. Rule 702 and pertinent case law set forth the applicable legal tests with more clarity and detail than before, when the *Frye v. United States* standard of "general acceptance" reigned supreme.[3] There is no question that the standard for admissibility of expert testimony has evolved since the enactment of Rule 702 in 1975; consequently, issues of expert admissibility hold heightened prominence. The practical effect of the evolution is not without irony, as the original intent of Rule 702 was to ease, rather than restrict, the admission of expert evidence.[4]

---

1. Ms. Gillett is a shareholder of Hall, Estill, Hardwick, Gable, Golden & Nelson, PC, headquartered in Tulsa, Oklahoma, where she is a member of the firm's complex litigation group and heads the electronic discovery practice group. Ms. Gentry and Ms. Clifton are associates at Hall, Estill, Hardwick, Gable, Golden & Nelson, PC.
2. Daubert v. Merrell Dow Pharms., Inc., 509 U.S. 579 (1993).
3. Frye v. United States, 293 F. 1013 (D.C. Cir. 1923) (premising admissibility on whether the scientific principle on which the expert evidence was based was generally accepted in the applicable scientific community).
4. *See* MANUAL FOR COMPLEX LITIGATION, FOURTH § 23.24, at 479 (Federal Judiciary Center 2009).

The stakes in this arena are high: especially in tort cases, the exclusion of expert testimony can, and often does, result in summary judgment for the defendant.[5] As a result, evidentiary challenges to all types of expert witnesses have increased exponentially in the past 10 years. For example, according to a 2007 PricewaterhouseCoopers study of reported federal decisions, in the year 2000, there were 251 *Daubert* challenges to experts; by contrast, in 2007, 704 such challenges were brought.[6]

As with any area of trial preparation, the key to overcoming a *Daubert* motion filed against your expert witness is early and adequate preparation. This subchapter guides you through the steps necessary to defend an expert against a *Daubert* challenge and includes practice tips along the way. Before delving into these practical strategies, a discussion about the *Daubert* standard itself, and how it is applied in federal courts, is in order.

---

5. In *Daubert*, the Supreme Court explicitly endorsed summary judgment motions based on deficient expert testimony. The Court said: "[I]n the event the trial court concludes that the scintilla of evidence presented supporting a position is insufficient to allow a reasonable juror to conclude that the position more likely than not is true, the court remains free to . . . grant summary judgment." *See, e.g.,* Vadala v. Teledyne Indus., 44 F.3d 36, 39 (1st Cir. 1995) (affirming district court entry of summary judgment for the defendant finding that proffered expert opinion could not sufficiently rule out the effect of the postcrash fire and holding the testimony inadmissible.); Allen v. Pennsylvania Eng'g, Inc., 102 F.3d 194, 197 (5th Cir. 1996) (excluding plaintiff's experts and entering summary judgment for defendants); Porter v. Whitehall Lab., Inc., 9 F.3d 607 (7th Cir. 1993) (granting summary judgment in favor of defendant pharmaceutical companies when plaintiff's causation expert disallowed under *Daubert* analysis); Buckner v. Sam's Club, 75 F.3d 290 (7th Cir. 1996) (plaintiff's sole causation expert witness disallowed, and summary judgment granted for defendant); Sorensen *ex rel.* Dunbar v. Shaklee Corp., 31 F.3d 638, 639 (8th Cir. 1994) (granting summary judgment where plaintiff's scientific evidence on causation did not satisfy *Daubert* test); *In re* Williams Sec. Litig., 558 F.3d 1130 (10th Cir. 2009) (granting summary judgment in securities fraud action after exclusion of expert testimony regarding "loss causation"); Miller v. Pfizer, Inc., 356 F.3d 1326 (10th Cir. 2004) (upholding summary judgment in favor of defendant pharmaceutical companies when plaintiff's causation expert disallowed under *Daubert* analysis); Wilson v. Merrill Dow Pharms., Inc., 160 F.3d 625 (10th Cir. 1998) (same); *see also* LLOYD DIXON & BRIAN GILL, CHANGES IN THE STANDARDS FOR ADMITTING EXPERT EVIDENCE IN FEDERAL CIVIL CASES SINCE THE *DAUBERT* DECISION (RAND Institute for Civil Justice 2001) (concluding that "[c]hallenges to expert testimony increasingly resulted in summary judgment after *Daubert*").

6. PRICEWATERHOUSECOOPERS, 2000–2007 FINANCIAL EXPERT WITNESS *DAUBERT* CHALLENGE STUDY (2008). According to the study, the highest number of challenges between the years 2000 and 2007 was in 2006, when there were 741.

Know the Daubert *Standard*

Federal Rule of Evidence 702 states as follows:

> If scientific, technical, or other specialized knowledge will assist the trier of fact to understand the evidence or to determine a fact in issue, a witness qualified as an expert by knowledge, skill, experience, training, or education, may testify thereto in the form of an opinion or otherwise, if (1) the testimony is based upon sufficient facts or data, (2) the testimony is the product of reliable principles and methods, and (3) the witness has applied the principles and methods reliably to the facts of the case.

In *Daubert*, the Supreme Court held that the adoption of Rule 702 overruled the standard previously set out by *Frye* regarding admissibility of scientific evidence. Using the language of Rule 702 as a backdrop, the Court set out a two-pronged test for admissibility.[7] First, the testimony must be reliable, meaning an expert's testimony "must pertain to scientific knowledge."[8] According to the Supreme Court, the "scientific knowledge" requirement means that the expert's opinion must be more than a mere subjective belief or unsupported speculation.[9] More importantly, "in order to qualify as 'scientific knowledge,' . . . [the testimony/opinion] must be derived by the scientific method," which is based on "generating hypotheses and testing them to see if they can be falsified."[10] Second, the testimony must be relevant, meaning that the testimony must "fit" the facts of the case.[11] This stems from the requirement of Rule 702 that the testimony must "assist the trier of fact" to be admissible.[12]

The focus of the *Daubert* inquiry is the particular methodology used by the expert witness to reach an opinion, as opposed to the actual conclusion. Rather than employing a bright-line test to discern the reliability of expert testimony, the Supreme Court set forth the following list of factors for courts to consider:

- Whether the expert's theories and techniques have been tested;
- Whether they have been subjected to peer review and publication;
- Whether they have a known error rate;

---

7. *Daubert*, 509 U.S. at 590.
8. *Id.*
9. *Id.*
10. *Id.* at 590, 593 (quoting Green, *Expert Witnesses and Sufficiency of Evidence in Toxic Substances Litigation: The Legacy of Agent Orange and Benedictin Litigation*, 86 Nw. U. L. Rev. 643, 645 (1992)).
11. *Id.* at 591.
12. *Id.*

- Whether the expert's particular discipline has enacted standards governing the methodology at issue; and
- Whether the methodology used by the expert enjoys widespread acceptance.[13]

Above all, the Court stressed flexibility, and stated that this list was not exhaustive and that other factors could come into play when evaluating expert testimony.[14]

Several years after the *Daubert* decision, the Supreme Court decided *Kumho Tire Co. v. Carmichael*.[15] *Kumho Tire* clarified that the standards enunciated in *Daubert* apply to all experts, whether their proposed testimony is scientific in nature or not.[16] This decision effectively set the stage for an explosion of pretrial motions *in limine* on the topic of expert testimony brought pursuant to the dictates of *Daubert*.[17]

Understand How the Daubert *Standard Applies in Your Court*

Federal Courts

As numerous commentators have noted, district courts and circuit courts around the country view *Daubert*—and apply the principles of *Daubert*—quite differently. The source of the differences among the courts with regard to *Daubert's* application is arguably *Daubert's* ambiguity and lack of any methodology to assist trial courts in deciding questions of admissibility.[18] This ambiguity, coupled with the fact that decisions as to admissibility at the circuit court level are reviewed under an abuse of discretion standard, generally means that the court in which you are litigating can affect whether your expert's testimony is admitted or excluded. Thus, how *Daubert*

---

13. *Id*. at 593–95.

14. *Id*. at 594.

15. Kumho Tire Co. v. Carmichael, 526 U.S. 137 (1999).

16. *Id*. at 147.

17. Evidentiary decisions rendered by state courts have been impacted as well. Many states have rules of evidence that mirror the Federal Rules of Evidence. In addition, state courts at times regard the Federal Rules of Evidence and decisions of the U.S. Supreme Court as persuasive authority. Thus, the *Daubert* trilogy raised the issue for state courts of whether to continue to rely upon existing standards for admitting expert testimony, which for most states was based on the *Frye* decision, or to adopt, or adapt, the new federal standard. As of this writing, 32 states have adopted the *Daubert* standard in some capacity or held *Daubert* to be instructive, while 18 states have rejected *Daubert*. *See* appendix B.

18. Cassandra Welch, *Flexible Standards, Deferential Review*, 29 Harv. J.L. & Pub. Pol'y 1085, 1091 (2006).

has been applied in the court where you are litigating can be an important consideration in developing your strategy for defending your expert against a *Daubert* challenge.

According to one commentator, "some courts rigidly investigate the four considerations identified in *Daubert*," while "others take seriously the Court's assertion that it is a flexible standard."[19] Another commentator has likewise noted that "[m]any judges have come to treat the factors set out in *Daubert* not as flexible criteria, but as technical hurdles, tests to be rigorously surmounted."[20] The Ninth and Eleventh Circuits have set particularly strict standards for the admission of scientific evidence and, not surprisingly, these courts "tend to produce defendant-friendly outcomes."[21] On the other end of the spectrum, taking a minimalist view of the gatekeeping function, the Eighth Circuit has held that expert testimony should be excluded only where it can be firmly established that the testimony is of no assistance whatsoever to the jury.[22] The Third Circuit, which falls somewhere in the middle, requires consideration of the *Daubert* factors, yet allows for other relevant factors to come into play as well.[23] Moreover, one commentator has noted that "hearsay-like considerations, rather than methodology" dominate the *Daubert* inquiry in the Ninth Circuit, such that the simple fact that an expert's opinions are unsubstantiated and undocumented is sufficient to deny admission of the expert's testimony even in the absence of any evaluation whatsoever of the expert's methodology.[24] Hearsay-like considerations are also given great weight in the Seventh Circuit, where the focus has been on scientists' "ordinary course of business." Appendix A sets forth some recent noteworthy cases from each circuit, illustrating both the differences and similarities in how the circuits apply *Daubert*.

State Courts

By way of state evidentiary rules and decisional law, the federal jurisprudence of *Daubert* and its progeny have slowly trickled into state courts. Nearly half the states have ruled *Daubert* to be controlling or instructive,

---

19. *Id.* at 1096–97.

20. David Crump, *The Trouble with Daubert-Kumho: Reconsidering the Supreme Court's Philosophy of Science*, 68 Mo. L. Rev. 1, 1–2 (2003) (citing illustrative cases).

21. Jennifer Wolsing, *Daubert's Erie Problem*, 82 Ind. l.j. 183, 183–84, 210 (2007).

22. Welch, *supra* note 18, at 1098 n.114 (citing Larson v. Kempker, 414 F.3d 936 (8th Cir. 2005)).

23. *Id.* at 1098 n.108 (citing Ruth Saunders, *The Circuit Courts' Application of Daubert v. Merrell Dow Pharmaceuticals, Inc.*, 46 Drake L. Rev. 407, 417 (1997)).

24. *Id.* at 1098 n. 112 (citing Jon Y. Ikegami, *Objection: Hearsay—Why Hearsay-Like Thinking Is a Flawed Proxy for Scientific Validity in the* Daubert *Gatekeeper Standard*, 73 S. Cal. L. Rev. 705, 710 (2000)).

although a significant number of states continue to adhere to the *Frye* standard. Among those states that have adopted *Daubert*, its application has been decidedly nonuniform and often incorporates local variations. For example, the Texas Supreme Court, in that state's seminal case *E.I. du Pont de Nemours & Co. v. Robinson*,[25] adopted the test for admissibility of scientific expert testimony formulated by the Supreme Court in *Daubert* but also added two additional primary factors.[26] Recent key decisions adopting *Daubert* into state jurisprudence are set forth in Appendix B.

Case Study: Judicial Acceptance of DNA-Typing Evidence

This case study, about judicial acceptance of DNA-typing evidence, highlights the importance of understanding how the *Daubert* standard applies in the court where your case is pending. The first DNA-based conviction in the United States occurred in 1988 when the Circuit Court in Orange County, Florida, convicted Tommy Lee Andrews of rape after DNA tests matched his DNA from a blood sample with that of semen traces found in the rape victim.[27] In the first years following this groundbreaking case, the admissibility of DNA evidence was largely undisputed. Courts carefully considered the expert testimony of scientists from the fields of molecular biology and genetics, concluded that the basis for DNA testing was the well-accepted proposition that "except for identical twins each individual has a unique overall genetic code" and consistently admitted DNA evidence. As DNA evidence became more widely used, attorneys began to challenge its admissibility.

People of New York v. Castro was a landmark murder case commonly cited as the first serious challenge to the admissibility of DNA evidence, under pre-*Daubert* standards.[28] The court determined that although DNA identification theory, practice, and techniques are generally accepted among the scientific community, pretrial hearings were required to determine whether the testing laboratory's methodology was in alignment with scientific

---

25. E.I. du Pont de Nemours & Co. v. Robinson, 923 S.W.2d 459 (Tex. 1995).

26. In Texas, counsel defending a *Daubert* challenge should think about (1) the extent to which the theory has been or can be tested, (2) the technique's potential rate of error, (3) whether the theory has been subjected to peer review and publication, (4) whether the underlying theory or technique has been generally accepted as valid by the relevant scientific community, (5) the extent to which the technique relies upon the subjective interpretation of the expert, and (6) the nonjudicial uses that have been made of the theory or technique. *Id.* at 557.

27. Andrews v. State, 533 So. 2d 841 (Fla. Dist. Ct. App. 1988); *see also* William C. Thompson & Simon Ford, *DNA Typing: Acceptance and Weight of the New Genetic Identification Tests*, 75 VA. L. REV. 45, 46 n.4 (1989).

28. People of New York v. Castro, 545 N.Y.S.2d 985 (1989).

standards and produced reliable results for jury consideration. A number of judicial challenges to the admissibility of DNA evidence followed and, where inadmissibility was found, it was largely due to questions about the validity of techniques used to derive or interpret the DNA profile (such as population statistics) or about the reliability of the lab or technician performing the analysis.[29]

In the post-*Daubert* world, yet another wave of cases challenging DNA typing came with advancements in DNA testing technology. Technological advances resulted in another opportunity to challenge the admissibility of DNA evidence by calling into question the new methodology's reliability for determining DNA identification. These issues were, for the most part, resolved in support of the admissibility of the new methods in a string of cases decided in 2001.[30]

Ultimately, courts accept DNA typing based on the fact that it is commonly recognized in all scientific disciplines that cells with nuclei contain DNA and that the structure of this DNA is different in all individuals except for identical twins. Yet when the particular methodology for testing DNA changed, courts rigorously examined the validity of the new testing technique. Today, courts continue to review whether the methods actually employed in any given case conform to accepted standards for that particular methodology. No matter how well-accepted the principle underlying a methodology, the particular method used must be valid, and the expert applying that method must do so in accordance with accepted standards. When a methodology employs several submethods drawn from distinct fields, each of those supporting methods must also be valid. Often the raw data produced by a test must be interpreted using statistical analysis. In such a case, both the testing method and the statistical method must be valid. Where methodologies are continually being improved on and refined through the introduction of new technologies or new processes, be prepared to show the validity of these refinements.

Deflect a Daubert *Challenge*

Especially if working with a novice or unseasoned expert, it is critical to contemplate Rule 702 and *Daubert* from the beginning of the expert retention. Many experts are unaware of or do not fully appreciate the mandates

---

29. *See, e.g.*, Commonwealth v. Curnin, 565 N.E.2d 440, 440 (Mass. 1991); State v. Bible, 858 P.2d 1152 (Ariz. 1993); State v. Schwartz, 447 N.W.2d 422, 428 (Minn. 1989).

30. People v. Hill, 107 Cal. Rptr. 2d 110 (2001); Lemour v. State, 802 So. 2d 402 (Fla. Dist. Ct. App. 2001); State v. Butterfield, 27 P.3d 1133, 1144 (Utah 2001).

of *Daubert*. In addition, while a critical mass of states have adopted *Daubert*, experts who typically testify in state court proceedings may lack a familiarity with the principles expressed in Rule 702. Your preparatory work should begin with the retention of a qualified expert. To be avoided at all costs is that uncomfortable moment during the expert's deposition when he admits that he is not qualified to perform the work in question.[31]

Once a qualified expert has been hired, your opponent has two primary vehicles through which to challenge the witness—the expert report and the deposition. Your focus must be on working with your witness to "*Daubert*-proof" the opinions that will eventually be expressed in the report and during deposition.

Formulation of Expert Opinion

While the expert must take the lead in identifying and reviewing the relevant factual information, utilizing the appropriate methodology, and arriving at an ultimate opinion, you are well advised to take an active role from the beginning of the expert retention. The expert needs two pieces of information from you: first, the scope of the engagement or, put another way, the issue on which he has been hired to opine and, second, any facts or assumptions he will need to render an opinion. It is helpful to enter into a written agreement with the witness, describing the scope of the assignment and taking into account the collaboration necessary to overcome any *Daubert* hurdles.

Once the preliminaries are out of the way, you need to know and understand the analysis your expert proposes to undertake to reach a conclusion. It is your job to make sure that the methods used by the expert are

---

31. Consider, for example, the impact of the inclusion of the following deposition testimony in a motion to exclude your expert made under *Daubert*:
Q: Do you consider yourself an expert in performing business valuations?
A: Yes, I do.
Q: How many have you performed?
A: Between three and five.
Q: Are your opinions in this case based solely on your own work?
A: It's all my work up to this point.
Q: Why the qualification? Do you anticipate others working with you?
A: I have thought about engaging a more experienced person to help me.
Q: What would that person be asked to do?
A: Just back me up, inform me if I've made mistakes and review my work. I think a second opinion would be helpful.
Q: Because you have performed very few actual valuations yourself?
A: Yes, I would feel more comfortable standing up in court and testifying if I had a second opinion.

scientifically valid, as defined by the case law interpreting *Daubert* in your particular jurisdiction. This holds true whether you are dealing with a biologist, an economist, or a car mechanic. The nonexclusive factors set forth in *Daubert* serve as your guide. If the witness's area of expertise has controlling industry standards or a governing body, the expert should refer to and follow those standards. When such guiding principles do not exist— either because the theory or technique is too new or relates to a discipline lacking a governing body or controlling principles—it is helpful if the methodology has undergone peer review or been published in a respected journal in the expert's field.

Sometimes, because of the nature of the testimony, the expert lacks the imprimatur of a third-party publication or governing body. These types of expertise—the auto mechanic, for example—may be supported simply through the experience and credentials of the expert.

The other prong of *Daubert*, relating to whether the proffered opinion fits the facts of the case, represents an inquiry into relevance. Rule 702 requires that the evidence "assist" the jury in resolving the case. Be mindful of this concept when guiding your expert as to the shaping of his opinion.

In any event, studying these issues in advance of completion of the expert's work and creation of the report will prove invaluable in avoiding a *Daubert* motion. The best advice is to ensure that the expert supports his work using the factors set forth by the Supreme Court—or analogous factors used by other courts considering expert evidence on the same subject matter. If that is not possible due to the nature of the technique or the newness of the discipline, know that the evidence is more vulnerable to potential exclusion on these grounds.

The Expert Report

Federal Rule of Civil Procedure 26(a)(2) governs disclosure of expert testimony in federal courts. A written report containing the expert's opinions, data considered by the expert, exhibits in support of the opinions, the expert's qualifications, a list of other testimony, and the compensation paid to the expert is required.[32] Compiling a thoughtful, detailed, and well-supported expert report can go a long way in heading off a potential *Daubert* challenge or in defending against such a challenge.

The heart of the report contains the expert's opinions. Some experts list and discuss each opinion separately; this format probably lends itself best to

---

32. Many states do not require written expert reports. *See, e.g.,* 12 OKLA. STAT. § 2705; FLA. STAT. § 1.280(4); KY. REV. STAT. ANN § 26.02(4); MONT. CODE. ANN. § 26(B)(4); NEB. REV. STAT. § 6-326(4). In these states, written discovery in the nature of document requests and interrogatories is the best vehicle for learning about an expert opinion before a deposition.

a logical and detailed report in accordance with Rule 26. Whether your expert has organized the report in that fashion, ask yourself the following questions to ensure that the report passes muster:

- Is each opinion that the expert will express clearly stated in the report?
- Is the basis for each opinion stated?
- Does the expert list all data he considered in forming the opinions?
- Has this data been produced to the other side? [33]

As the Supreme Court has clarified, the report must provide data or evidence in support of each and every conclusion: "Nothing in *Daubert* or the Federal Rules of Evidence requires a district court to admit opinion evidence that is connected to existing data only by the *ipse dixit* of the expert. A court may conclude that there is simply too great an analytical gap between the data and the opinion proffered."[34] One line of attack is to characterize particular conclusions as lacking in foundation. All conclusions, even basic truisms, should be supported with objective and scientific references as much as possible. If there are publications that are peer reviewed or otherwise well known in the expert's field and that mention the methods used by the expert, they should be referenced in some fashion within the expert report.

The *Daubert* factor that is failed most commonly by experts involves the need for support from scientific testing. The expert report should contain references to any sort of testing that the expert may have relied on to support the opinions in the report. Testing can include litigation testing that the expert performed for the case at issue, scientific testing that the expert performed in an academic setting, scientific testing others have performed in an academic setting, testing the parties have done, or testing the other side's experts have completed. No matter the source of the testing, it is important to specifically identify the testing supporting the expert's conclusion and provide those specific references in the expert's report. Further, testing is not limited to scientific experiments. For example, identifying publicly available products that include features from an alternative design might test the feasibility of the alternative.

In summary, avoid a subsequent dispute over admissibility by ensuring that your expert submits a logical, organized, and cogent report containing the following elements:

---

33. It is critical that you confirm that all information relied on by your expert has been produced to the other side. The failure to do so can be disastrous. *See, e.g.,* NutraSweet Co. v. X-L Eng'g, Inc., 227 F.3d 776, 785–86 (7th Cir. 2000); Yeti by Molly, Ltd. v. Deckers Outdoor Corp., 259 F.3d 1101, 1107 (9th Cir. 2007).

34. General Elec. Co. v. Joiner, 522 U.S. 136, 146 (1997).

- A clear and concise statement of all opinions to be expressed.
- The basis for each opinion.
- All data considered in the formation of each opinion.
- References to applicable third-party publications approving of the expert's method.
- Reference to the governing body for the discipline, if applicable.
- If the testimony is experiential rather than analytical, a robust section explaining the past work of the expert on projects of a similar nature.

The Expert Deposition

Your expert's deposition, while nominally an opportunity for your adversary to explore and understand the opinions rendered in the report, is the prime opportunity for the other side to learn whether your expert is *Daubert*-able. The submission of a well-reasoned and supported report is one important step in avoiding a deposition disaster. Your opponent should be on notice that you are aware of the mandates of *Daubert* and that you do not intend for your expert to fall victim to its traps. As in every case, preparation of the witness for deposition is key, especially if your expert does not have testifying experience. Within the context of *Daubert*, you should view the deposition as opposing counsel's opportunity to make your witness vulnerable. Consequently, your task is to foil that strategy.

The goal is straightforward testimony discussing proffered opinions, the reasons for the opinions, and the methods used to arrive at the opinions. Prepare your expert using a line of questioning that likely foreshadows a *Daubert* problem and assess the responses that are given. Make sure that references to testing, rate of error, governing principles, and publications approving of the expert's methodology are sprinkled throughout the answers. The expert must be clear as to the scope of the assignment and the assumptions you gave. Leave no room for your adversary to transform deposition answers into junk science.

As for the second prong of *Daubert* relating to relevancy, the expert must be skilled in relating his methods to the ultimate opinion expressed in the case. Because some courts may exclude testimony if there is "too great an analytical gap" between the conclusions and the data, opposing counsel will attempt to make the expert's conclusions sound unsupported.[35] Prepare your expert to respond carefully to questions intended to

---

35. *See* Rider v. Sandoz Pharms. Corp., 295 F.3d 1194, 1202 (11th Cir. 2002) ("Courts are cautioned not to admit speculation, conjecture, or inference that cannot be supported by sound scientific principles. The courtroom is not the place for scientific guesswork, even of the inspired sort.") (internal citations and quotations omitted).

elicit responses demonstrating that the expert's conclusions are either not pertinent to the case or insufficient to prove the matter for which they are offered.

One final point about depositions: guard against the natural proclivity of some experts to demonstrate superior competence, when baited by opposing counsel, by elaborating unnecessarily on the opinions in the report. If the expert is inexperienced, make sure he understands how a skilled examiner can use silence as a weapon to make the witness uncomfortable and perhaps to elicit on off-the-cuff remark as a result. If the expert digresses from the report and reveals even a potential inconsistency with the report, that is not only fodder for impeachment at trial but may wind up as support for a motion *in limine* under *Daubert.*

In conclusion, make sure that the expert deposition cements your defense against any *Daubert* challenge by following these practice tips:

- Prepare your expert for deposition as you would prepare any other witness.
- Engage in mock questioning so that your expert may practice explaining his methods.
- Encourage the witness to link conclusions to the case.
- Anticipate hypothetical questions and be wary of pitfalls.
- Advise the expert to avoid unnecessary explanation. Remember: silence is golden.

Use the Other Side's Expert

An opposing party's expert can sometimes be your best ally in defending against a *Daubert* challenge. Because *Daubert* motions frequently attack scientific methodologies that may have been used in previous cases by either side's expert, the opposing side's experts may be able to provide you with testimony in support of the methodology your expert has used. Use written discovery requests or subpoenas to learn about other cases where the opposing party's expert has testified, transcripts that may be available, and published articles. Do your research in advance of taking the other expert's deposition.

Be prepared at the deposition to ask questions about the methodologies the expert recognizes as scientific and commonly accepted. This strategy may provide you with valuable testimony to validate the methodology your own expert is using—either directly or indirectly. Likewise, if testing is not typically used in the field to verify certain conclusions, the opposing side's expert should testify about this.

Take advantage of kindly human nature. Experts, like other witnesses, are often reluctant to personally attack the expert on the other side, especially if they are professional colleagues in a relatively small field. With strategic questioning, you may enjoy admissions from defense experts that the methodology your expert employed was sound or that your expert is well respected in his field. If your expert has conducted testing that you suspect may be subject to a *Daubert* challenge, it may also be possible to protect this testing from challenge using testimony from the opposing side's expert. Frequently, experts will agree on the record that they do not have any specific criticisms of the *methodology* used to conduct the testing (as opposed to the actual conclusion). This admission will doom a *Daubert* motion. It may be that the expert actually used your testing to support his conclusions even though the expert disagrees with the ultimate conclusion your expert reached. These types of admissions can go a long way in defeating a *Daubert* challenge.

Turn the other side's expert into your best defense against a *Daubert* challenge by following these practice tips:

- Research the background of the opposing party's expert extensively.
- Be knowledgeable and conversant about the methods employed by your own expert so that you can explore whether the other side's expert has ever endorsed them—either explicitly or implicitly.
- Take advantage of human nature by soliciting admissions relating to your expert during the opposing expert's deposition.

Create a Record

Provide all the scientific material supporting the expert's opinion at the outset. If the record already includes the supporting evidence establishing the reliability of the expert's methodology, it will be more difficult for opposing counsel to challenge the expert. If the expert is ultimately challenged, then having ready access to all the evidence necessary to respond allows you to get started quickly.

When a *Daubert* motion is filed, it is also helpful to have the publications supporting the conclusions in the expert's report in your own files and on the record. This means gathering peer-reviewed studies and reports of scientific testing to include as part of the record. Do not limit yourself to case-specific information, but rather attach to the expert's report and mark as deposition exhibits all of the background information supporting the expert's methodology and conclusions. This way, if your expert does face a *Daubert* challenge, all the evidence supporting the expert's opinion will already be a part of the record and easily referenced in the response.

It is also helpful to have sections of the deposition that can be used to give the court a complete picture of the expert's methodology and conclusions. Your adversary may have asked your expert to provide detailed testimony about the scientific methodology employed and how that methodology compares with what is generally accepted in the field. If no such testimony exists, then your expert can prepare and submit a declaration, if necessary, to support your opposition to a *Daubert* challenge. This evidence should include any peer-reviewed literature and scientific studies supporting the expert's conclusions.

Prepare to defend against a *Daubert* motion by following these practice tips:

- Gather and disclose supporting materials for your expert's opinion early on.
- Mine the deposition of your expert for helpful testimony or, alternately, prepare a detailed declaration explaining the scientific method employed and comparing that method to industry standards.

Conclusion

The best recipe for avoiding the exclusion of expert testimony (and the possibility of summary judgment as a result) is to provide careful and thoughtful attention early in the life of a case to the *Daubert* factors, their anticipated impact on your expert, and your expert's intended methodology.

Summary of Practice Tips

Expert Report:
- A clear and concise statement of all opinions to be expressed.
- The basis for each opinion.
- All data considered in the formation of each opinion.
- References to applicable third-party publications approving of the expert's method.
- Reference to the governing body for the discipline, if applicable.
- If the testimony is experiential rather than analytical, a robust section explaining the past work of the expert on projects of a similar nature.

Expert Deposition:
- Prepare your expert for deposition as you would prepare any other witness.
- Engage in mock questioning so that your expert may practice explaining his methods.

- Encourage the witness to link conclusions to the case.
- Anticipate hypothetical questions and be wary of pitfalls.
- Advise the expert to avoid unnecessary explanation. Remember: silence is golden.

Use the Other Side's Expert:

- Research the background of the opposing party's expert extensively.
- Be knowledgeable and conversant about the methods employed by your own expert so that you can explore whether the other side's expert has ever endorsed them—either explicitly or implicitly.
- Take advantage of human nature by soliciting admissions relating to your expert during the opposing expert's deposition.

Create a Record:

- Gather and disclose supporting materials for your expert's opinion early on.
- Mine the deposition of your expert for helpful testimony or, alternately, prepare a detailed declaration explaining the scientific method employed and comparing that method to "industry standards."

CHALLENGING AN OPPOSING PARTY'S EXPERT

Steven J. Fram[1]

Expert testimony is essential in many cases and is important in many others. As a consequence, a party that successfully prevents its opponent from presenting expert testimony can sometimes prevail without ever proceeding to trial.

This subchapter discusses the principles that govern pretrial applications to bar expert testimony. It begins by briefly summarizing the evidentiary standards that govern expert testimony. It then describes the gatekeeping role that the federal courts play in assessing the admissibility of expert testimony, outlines the most common challenges raised, and discusses the procedures that trial courts employ in considering those challenges. During the course of discussing these issues, this subchapter attempts to highlight some of the tactical issues that counsel are called on to consider.

The Substance of a Daubert *Challenge*

In its well-known decision in *Daubert v. Merrill Dow Pharmaceuticals, Inc.*,[2] the U.S. Supreme Court held that federal trial courts are required to perform a gatekeeping function under Federal Rules of Evidence 702 and 703 in determining whether expert testimony is sufficiently reliable to be admissible.[3] *Daubert* identified four factors that typically bear on the inquiry of reliability but made clear that there is no "definitive checklist or test" for determining reliability and held that the inquiry is a "flexible one."[4] The four factors identified in *Daubert* are as follows: (1) whether the theory or technique can be and has been tested, (2) whether it has been subjected

---

1. Archer & Greiner, PC, Haddonfield, New Jersey. Steven J. Fram is the chairperson of the firm's Commercial Litigation Practice Group. He concentrates his practice on disputes concerning corporate governance and shareholder rights, professional liability, and breaches of fiduciary duty, and technology ownership and performance.
2. Daubert v. Merrill Dow Pharms., Inc., 509 U.S. 579 (1993).
3. *Id.*
4. *Id.* at 593–94.

to peer review and publication, (3) whether it has a "known or potential rate of error," and (4) whether it enjoys general acceptance in the relevant scientific community.[5]

In *General Electric Co. v. Joiner*,[6] the Supreme Court underscored the wide discretion that trial judges exercise in determining whether to admit or exclude expert testimony by ruling that such decisions are reviewed on appeal under an "abuse of discretion" standard.[7] The Court's opinion in *Kumho Tire Co. v. Carmichael*[8] laid to rest any doubts about whether its holding in *Daubert* was limited to expert testimony of scientists by holding that *Daubert* applies to all proposed expert testimony, including that of engineers and other experts who are not scientists.[9] In so holding, the Court again emphasized that the test for determining reliability is flexible, so that *Daubert*'s list of specific factors neither necessarily nor exclusively applies to all experts or in every case. A trial court, *Kumho Tire* held, "must have the same latitude in deciding *how* to test an expert's reliability . . . as it enjoys deciding *whether or not* that expert's relevant testimony is reliable."[10]

Federal Rule of Evidence 702 was amended in 2000 to incorporate this trilogy of cases and now provides the standards by which trial courts should assess the admissibility of expert testimony:

> If scientific, technical, or other specialized knowledge will assist the trier of fact to understand the evidence or to determine a fact in issue, a witness qualified as an expert by knowledge, skill, experience, training, or education, may testify thereto in the form of an opinion or otherwise, if (1) the testimony is based upon sufficient facts or data, (2) the testimony is the product of reliable principles and methods, and (3) the witness has applied the principles and methods reliably to the facts of the case.

In the years since *Daubert* was decided and Rule 702 was amended, the courts have interpreted *Daubert* as imposing three requirements on expert "testimony: "qualification, reliability and fit."[11] This section will discuss challenges based on each of these criteria.

---

5. *Id.*
6. Gen. Elec. Co. v. Joiner, 522 U.S. 136 (1997).
7. *Id.*
8. Kumho Tire v. Carmichael, 526 U.S. 137 (1999).
9. *Id.*
10. *Id.* at 152 (emphasis in original).
11. Schneider *ex rel.* Estate of Schneider v. Fried, 320 F.3d 396, 404 (3d Cir. 2003).

Challenging Qualifications

Rule 702 allows expert testimony from a witness who is qualified "by knowledge, skill, experience, training, or education."[12] Where expert testimony is helpful to the jury, the courts have held that the qualification requirement should be interpreted liberally to allow expert testimony. As one court has noted, "Rule 702 does not mandate that an expert be highly qualified in order to testify about a given issue. Differences in expertise bear chiefly on the weight to be assigned to the testimony by the trier-of-fact, not its admissibility."[13]

Attacks on witness qualifications can take many forms. For example, a witness may have some experience or expertise in a particular area but not enough to qualify as an expert. Or he may have general expertise in a discipline but insufficient experience in the relevant subspecialty to testify about that case. For example, a physician who is an expert in cardiology may be deemed unqualified to testify in a case against an orthopedic surgeon. On the other hand, in an action against an interventional cardiologist, testimony will not be barred simply because the proposed expert is an invasive cardiologist who diagnoses and treats heart conditions rather than an interventional cardiologist who performs angioplasties.[14]

The goal of an attorney challenging qualifications at a *Daubert* hearing must be to establish that the expert is not qualified to give opinions of the nature offered. Such a challenge might highlight that the expert lacks certain licenses or credentials that are available in his field; that he has not published or presented to the same degree as other experts; that he has been subjected to professional discipline or has failed professional examinations; that he was denied tenure or promotion; that his proposed testimony was excluded in other cases; that he has faced malpractice claims or judgments; or that he lacks

---

12. Fed. R. Evid. 702.

13. Huss v. Gayden, 571 F.3d 442, 452 (5th Cir. 2009). *See also* Quiet Tech. DC–8, Inc. v. Hurel-Dubois UK Ltd., 326 F.3d 1333, 1345–46 (11th Cir. 2003) (holding flaws in expertise will affect the expert's analysis' probative value, not its admissibility; identification of such flaws is "precisely the role of cross-examination"); Adams v. Ameritech Serv., Inc., 231 F.3d 414, 428 (7th Cir. 2000) (holding disputes arising over expertise and expert testimony go to the weight of evidence presented, not to its admissibility); Holbrook v. Lykes Bros. S.S. Co., 80 F.3d 777, 782 (3d Cir. 1996) ("[M]ost arguments about an expert's qualifications relate more to the weight to be given the expert's testimony than to its admissibility."); United States v. Garcia, 7 F.3d 885, 890 (9th Cir. 1993) ("[L]ack of particularized expertise goes to the weight accorded [to the expert's] testimony, not to the admissibility of her opinion as an expert.").

14. *See Schneider,* 320 F.3d at 407.

experience in the particular issue in dispute. Demonstrating that an expert has falsified or overstated his credentials or that the expert has given false or misleading testimony in other proceedings can be particularly devastating.

Practice Tip: Investigation of the proposed expert, both formal and informal, is crucial in uncovering information that may be helpful in addressing the issue of qualifications. If other courts have rejected testimony by the expert you are challenging, those decisions may be particularly helpful.

Challenging Reliability

Offering up a qualified expert is not enough. As one court has noted, "Qualifications alone do not suffice. A supremely qualified expert cannot waltz into the courtroom and render opinions unless those opinions are based upon some recognized scientific method and are reliable and relevant under the test set forth . . . in *Daubert*."[15]

Since *Daubert* was decided over 15 years ago, the courts have had occasion to consider reliability challenges to expert testimony in a wide range of cases, including cases dealing with engineering,[16] economics,[17] forensic agricultural economics,[18] financing,[19] insurance,[20] real estate appraisal,[21] accounting,[22] ergonomics,[23] statistics,[24] accident reconstruction,[25] survey

---

15. Lewis v. Citgo Petroleum Corp., 561 F.3d 698, 705 (7th Cir. 2009) (quoting Clark v. Takata Corp., 192 F.3d 750, 759 n.5 (7th Cir. 1999)).

16. Zaremba v. Gen. Motors Corp., 360 F.3d 355, 357–60 (2d Cir. 2004).

17. Stewart v. Rowan Cos., Inc., No. Civ. A. 01-0987, 2002 WL 362847, at *2–3 (E.D. La. Mar. 7, 2002).

18. Halimage Farms, LLC v. Westfalia-Surge, Inc., No. 4:01CV3327, 2003 WL 1868673, at *2–4 (D. Neb. Apr. 11, 2003).

19. ID Sec. Sys. Canada, Inc. v. Checkpoint Sys., Inc., 198 F. Supp. 2d 598, 620–23 (E.D. Pa. 2002).

20. Hangarter v. Provident Life & Accident Ins. Co., 373 F.3d 998, 1015–18 (9th Cir. 2004).

21. Cayuga Indian Nation of New York v. Pataki, 83 F. Supp. 2d 318, 321–28 (N.D.N.Y. 2000).

22. In re Joy Recovery Tech. Corp., 286 B.R. 54, 69–71 (Bankr. N.D. Ill. 2002).

23. Lovato v. Burlington N. and Santa Fe Ry. Co., No. Civ. A. 00-RB-2584CBS, 2002 WL 1424599, at *2–13 (D. Colo. Jun 24, 2002).

24. McReynolds v. Sodexho Marriott Servs., Inc., 349 F. Supp. 2d 30, 34–38 (D.D.C. 2004).

25. Babcock v. Gen. Motors Corp., 299 F.3d 60, 66–69 (1st Cir. 2002).

evidence,[26] handwriting analysis,[27] fire causation,[28] roof design,[29] market power,[30] and commercial rules.[31]

The purpose of the reliability requirement, *Kumho Tire* noted, "is to make certain that an expert, whether basing testimony upon professional studies or personal experience, employs in the courtroom the same level of intellectual vigor that characterizes the practice of an expert in the field."[32] Consistent with this inquiry, courts have noted that the focus of the *Daubert* reliability inquiry "must be solely on the principles and methodology, not on the conclusions they generate."[33]

Challenges to reliability can fairly be divided into three categories: challenges to the methodology itself, challenges to the application of the methodology in a particular case, and challenges to the reliability or adequacy of the facts used in applying the methodology. In many cases, expert testimony will be attacked based on a combination of these arguments.

Flawed Methodology

As suggested in *Daubert* itself, the courts have developed numerous additional factors to assess in determining the reliability of an expert's methodology. For example, the Third Circuit has identified the following factors as important in testing the reliability of a technique:

> (1) whether a method consists of a testable hypothesis; (2) whether the method has been subjected to peer review; (3) the known or potential rate of error; (4) the existence and maintenance of standards controlling the technique's operation; (5) whether the method is generally accepted; (6) the relationship of the technique to methods which have been established to be reliable; (7) the qualifications of the expert witness testifying based on the methodology; and (8) the non-judicial uses to which the method has been put.[34]

---

26. Tunnell v. Ford Motor Co., 330 F. Supp. 2d 707, 718–19 (W.D. Va. 2004).
27. Deputy v. Lehman Bros., Inc., 345 F.3d 494, 505–09 (7th Cir. 2003).
28. Allstate Ins. Co. v. Hugh Cole Builder, Inc., 137 F. Supp. 2d 1283, 1285–86 (M.D. Ala. 2001).
29. Spearman Indus., Inc. v. St. Paul Fire and Marine Ins. Co., 138 F. Supp. 2d 1088, 1095–96 (N.D. Ill. 2001).
30. *In re* Visa Check/Mastermoney Antitrust Litig., 193 F.R.D. 68, 77 (2d Cir. 2001).
31. Gray v. Briggs, 45 F. Supp. 2d 316, 323–25 (S.D.N.Y. 1999).
32. *Kumho Tire*, 526 U.S. at 152.
33. *Daubert*, 509 U.S. at 595.
34. *In re* Paoli R.R. Yard PCB Litig., 35 F.3d 717, 741–43 (3d Cir. 1994).

At the same time, it has cautioned that this list is "neither exhaustive nor applicable in every case" and has suggested that trial courts retain flexibility in determining what factors to assess.[35]

Misapplication of the Methodology

Even if a methodology is recognized by the courts as reliable, the parties often battle over whether a particular expert applied the methodology properly. For example, in the area of disease causation, most courts have recognized a technique known as differential diagnosis as a reliable methodology for forming opinions about causation.[36] Differential diagnosis has been defined as a "method by which a physician determines what disease process caused a patient's symptoms."[37] In conducting such a diagnosis, "[t]he physician considers all relevant potential causes of the symptoms and then eliminates alternative causes based on a physical examination, clinical tests, and a thorough case history."[38] All of the circuits to consider differential diagnosis have held that the methodology enjoys widespread acceptance in the medical community, has been subject to peer review and, if applied properly, is reliable.[39]

As a consequence, many of the challenges relating to the use of differential diagnosis focus on whether it was properly applied in a particular case or whether the data relied on was adequate or sufficiently reliable. Courts have identified a list of red flags that purportedly suggest lack of reliability in the application of differential diagnosis, including improper extrapolation, reliance on anecdotal evidence, reliance on temporal proximity, insufficient information about the case, failure to consider other possible causes, lack of testing, and subjectivity.[40] As one might expect, challenges to the use of this technique are enormously fact specific; given the wide discretion that trial courts have in assessing *Daubert* issues, there is little question that expert testimony based on this methodology that might be allowed by one court might be disallowed by other courts.

---

35. Pineda v. Ford Motor Co., 520 F.3d 237, 248 (3d Cir. 2008) *cert. denied*, 313 U.S. 1190 (1995) (quoting Kannankeril v. Terminix Int'l, Inc., 128 F.3d 802, 806–07 (3d Cir. 1997)).

36. Handyman v. Norfolk & W. Ry. Co., 243 F.3d 255, 260 (6th Cir. 2001) (quoting Reference Manual on Scientific Evidence 214 (Federal Judicial Center ed., 1994)).

37. *Id.*

38. *Id.*

39. *See, e.g.*, Best v. Lowe's Home Ctr., Inc., 563 F.3d 171, 179 (6th Cir. 2009); Ruggiero v. Warner-Lambert Co., 424 F.3d 249 (2d Cir. 2005); Glasteter v. Novartis Pharms. Corp., 252 F.3d 986, 989 (8th Cir. 2001); Westberry v. Gislaved Gummi AB, 178 F.3d 257, 263 (4th Cir. 1999); *Paoli*, 35 F.3d at 732.

40. *See* Downs v. Perstpro Components, Inc., 126 F. Supp. 2d 1090 (E.D. Tenn. 1999).

False Facts or Invalid Assumptions

In other cases, expert testimony can be challenged because it is based on inaccurate information or invalid assumptions. Numerous cases have rejected expert testimony on this basis.[41] In assessing both a methodology and the factual basis relied on, the courts have emphasized that it is not necessary for the proponent of the evidence to establish that all of the facts are correct or even that they are the best facts, particularly where factual disputes may exist. Instead, the courts have generally held that weaknesses or inadequacies in the factual foundation for an expert's reports go to the weight, rather than the admissibility, of the testimony, and that such matters should be the subject of cross-examination at the time of trial.[42]

Similarly, an expert's testimony can be attacked, not because it is based on demonstrably false premises, but because the expert did not take the time to investigate the matter thoroughly. Sometimes it can be shown, based on the expert's bills, that he spent only a minimal amount of time

---

41. *See, e.g.,* Feit v. Great-West Life & Annuity Ins. Co., 271 F. App'x 246, 253–55 (3d Cir. 2008) (holding expert's opinion that head and neck injuries caused death was unreliable because it was based on speculation as it could not flow from the data and methodology when no autopsy was performed on the head and neck); Heller v. Shaw Indus., Inc., 167 F.3d 146, 163 (3d Cir. 1999) (holding expert testimony was unreliable where substantial differences existed between emission rates and studies and expert's estimates); Player v. Motiva Enter., LLC, No. Civ. 02-3216(RBK), 2006 WL 166452 (D.N.J. Jan. 20, 2006) (holding expert's contaminated property figures were unreliable because methodology relied on sending an e-mail with a misleading hypothetical to lenders and receiving four responses).

42. United States v. Mitchell, 365 F.3d 215, 244 (3d Cir. 2004); Keller v. Feasterville Family Health Care Ctr., 557 F. Supp. 2d 671, 678–80 (E.D Pa. 2009). *See also Daubert,* 509 U.S. at 596 ("[V]igorous cross-examination, presentation of contrary evidence, and careful instruction on the burden of proof are the traditional and appropriate means of attacking shaky but admissible evidence."); *Best,* 563 F.3d at 182 ("Any weakness in [the expert's] methodology will affect the weight that his opinion is given at trial, but not its threshold admissibility."); Structural Polymer Group, Ltd. v. Zoltek Corp., 543 F.3d 987, 997 (8th Cir. 2008) ("As a rule, questions regarding the factual underpinnings of the expert's opinion affect the weight and credibility of her testimony, not its admissibility."); Liquid Dynamics Corp. v. Vaughan Co., 449 F.3d 1209, 1221 (Fed. Cir. 2006) (noting that attacks on expert's testimony and analysis go "more to the weight of the evidence than its admissibility"); SR Int'l Bus. Ins. Co. v. World Trade Ctr. Props., LLC, 467 F.3d 107, 134 (2d Cir. 2006) ("To the extent that there are gaps or inconsistencies in [expert] testimony, those issues 'go to the weight of the evidence, not to its admissibility.'" (quoting Campbell v. Metro. Prop. & Cas. Ins. Co., 239 F.3d 179, 186 (2d Cir. 2001)); United States v. Moreland, 437 F.3d 424, 431 (4th Cir. 2006) (holding that significant gaps in expert's knowledge were relevant to the weight of her testimony, not its admissibility); Goebel v. Denver & Rio Grande W. R.R. Co., 346 F.3d 987, 998–99 (10th Cir. 2003) (holding that the failure to rule out all possible alternative explanations "did not affect the admissibility of the testimony, although it was an issue the fact finder could consider when assigning weight").

investigating the facts. In other cases it can also be demonstrated that the expert did not spend adequate time investigating the facts because he was "given" the facts by counsel.[43]

Hearsay Not of the Type Relied On by Experts in the Field

Federal Rule of Evidence 703 allows an expert to base his opinion on facts or data "perceived by or made known to the expert at or before the hearing."[44] The rule further provides that those facts or data need not be admissible in evidence if they are "of a type reasonably relied upon by experts in a particular field in forming opinions or inferences upon the subject."[45] One of the dangers of this provision is that it potentially allows an expert to present hearsay and otherwise inadmissible information to the jury based solely on the expert's representation that the evidence is of a type "reasonably relied upon" by experts in the particular field.[46] As a consequence, if the testimony of a proposed expert is based on out-of-court statements or other information, the accuracy or completeness of which can reasonably be questioned, counsel should inquire closely into whether experts in the field reasonably rely on such information and should consider a *Daubert* challenge on this basis.

---

43. *See, e.g.,* Domingo v. T.K., M.D., 289 F.3d 600, 607 (9th Cir. 2002) ("'[N]othing in either *Daubert* or the Federal Rules of Evidence requires a district court to admit opinion evidence that is connected to existing data only by the *ipse dixit* of the expert.' A trial court may exclude evidence when it finds that 'there is simply too great an analytical gap between the data and the opinion proffered.'") (quoting *Joiner,* 522 U.S. at 146)); Bowers v. Nat'l Collegiate Athletic Ass'n, 564 F. Supp. 2d 322, 344–45 (D.N.J. 2008) (excluding expert testimony based on draft expert reports belatedly turned over to opposing counsel that strongly suggested that the experts "shored up" their opinions after consulting with counsel); Solaia Tech. LLC v. ArvinMeritor, Inc., 361 F. Supp. 2d 797, 805 (N.D. Ill. 2005) ("Reiteration of parties' argument and substantial block quoting of the patent or another witness's deposition testimony are improper additions to an expert's opinion; these are properly reserved for the attorneys' legal briefs."); Crowley v. Chait, 322 F. Supp. 2d 530, 542 (D.N.J. 2004) (barring parts of expert report that were based solely on selections of deposition testimony made by counsel; "experts should conduct independent analysis, which ultimately may or may not confirm what various deponents have said"); Manning v. Crockett, No. 95-C-3117, 1999 WL 342715, at *3 (N.D. Ill. May 18, 1999) (holding that "ghost writing" by an attorney for an expert's report and testimony is impermissible); Intermedics, Inc. v. Ventritex, Inc., 139 F.R.D. 384, 396 (N.D. Cal. 1991) ("[R]eal harm to the truth finding process, as well as to public confidence in the integrity of our system of justice, can be done even when the influence a lawyer has on an expert's testimony" is subtle and seemingly noninflammatory.); Occulto v. Adamar of N.J., Inc., 125 F.R.D. 611 (D.N.J. 1989) (holding where expert deposition revealed that expert did not write his own report, trial testimony would be barred).
44. FED. R. EVID. 703.
45. *Id.*
46. *Id.*

The Second Circuit's 2008 decision in *United States v. Mejia*[47] had occasion to consider the limits of Rule 703 in a case involving expert testimony by police officers.[48] In *Mejia*, a criminal case, the prosecution presented Hector Alicea, an investigator with the New York State Police, to testify regarding the structure of MS-13, a nationwide criminal gang. In discussing the history, structure, and operations of the gang, Alicea relied on a broad range of hearsay, including statements by MS-13 members given in interviews, both custodial and noncustodial, statements by other law enforcement officers, and statements made in intercepted telephone conversations among gang members and print and online materials. Alicea testified that his reliance on such materials was consistent with ordinary practices of law enforcement officers, who "routinely and reasonably rely upon hearsay in reaching their conclusions."[49]

The Second Circuit held that Alicea's testimony crossed the "thin line" that separates "the legitimate use of an officer expert to translate esoteric terminology or to explicate an organization's hierarchical structure from the illegitimate and impermissible substitution of expert opinion for factual evidence." The court explained the danger that such testimony poses:

> The officer expert transforms into the hub of the case, displacing the jury by connecting and combining all other testimony and physical evidence into a coherent, discernable, internally consistent picture of the defendant's guilt. In such cases, it is a little too convenient that the government has found an individual who is expert on precisely those facts that the government must prove to secure a guilty verdict—even more so when that expert happens to be one of the government's own investigators. . . . When the government skips the intermediate steps and proceeds directly from internal expertise to trial, and when those officer experts come to court and simply disgorge their factual knowledge to the jury, the experts are no longer aiding the jury in its fact finding; they are instructing the jury on the existence of the facts needed to satisfy the elements of the charged defense.[50]

Mejia held that Alicea's testimony should have been limited by the district court because much of that testimony concerned material "well within the grasp of the average juror and became little more than a vehicle for transmitting otherwise inadmissible hearsay to the jury."[51] Such a practice, the

47. United States v. Mejia, 545 F.3d 179 (2d Cir. 2008).
48. *Id.*
49. *Id.* (quoting United States v. Dukagjini, 326 F.3d 45, 57 (2d Cir. 2003)).
50. *Mejia*, 545 F.3d at 192.
51. *Id.* at 197.

Second Circuit held, is particularly problematic in a criminal case because the jury is never given an opportunity to assess the reliability of the information relied on by the witness. Instead, the agent provides evidence to the jury without giving the jury the information it needs "to factor into its deliberations the reliability (or unreliability) of the particular source."[52] Such testimony therefore violates Rule 703.[53]

Practice Tip: Do not pursue a *Daubert* challenge unless you are confident of your chances of prevailing. A motion that is designed to *educate* the judge may backfire if the judge affirms the admissibility of the challenged testimony or if your challenge educates the opposing party and its expert to your planned attack at trial. Moreover, a *Daubert* motion can be very expensive.

Practice Tip: If you do believe that you should prevail in your challenge, pursue the motion vigorously by attacking the opposing expert and by highlighting that your motion, if successful, will eliminate the need for a trial and end the litigation. If the exclusion of expert testimony will not resolve the case and a trial will still be necessary, the trial court may perceive little benefit in conducting a hearing and may simply defer your challenge to the time of trial.

---

52. *Id.*

53. *Id. See also* United States v. Flores-De-Jesus, 569 F.3d 8, 21 (1st Cir. 2009) ("While there is no prohibition against a witness testifying as both an expert and a fact witness, 'courts must be mindful when the same witness provides both lay and expert testimony,' because of the heightened possibility of undue prejudice. The problem is especially acute where the dual roles of expert and fact witness are filled by a law enforcement official, in part because 'the jury may unduly credit the opinion testimony of an investigating officer based on a perception that the expert was privy to facts about the defendant not presented at trial.'") (quoting United States v. Upton, 512 F.3d 394, 401 (7th Cir. 2008)); *Dukagjini*, 326 F.3d at 58 ("Incorporating the *Daubert* standard, the amended Rules of Evidence require that expert testimony be based on 'sufficient facts or data' and on 'reliable principles and methods' that the expert 'witness has applied reliably to the facts of the case.' . . . When an expert is no longer applying his extensive experience and a reliable methodology, *Daubert* teaches that the testimony should be excluded.") (quoting FED. R. EVID. 702); United States v. Brown, 776 F.2d 397, 401 n.6 (2d Cir. 1985) (observing that the risk of a jury conflating expert and fact testimony "is increased when the opinion is given by the very officers who were in charge of the investigation").

The Procedure of a Daubert *Challenge*

A *Daubert* hearing is an *in limine* hearing that focuses on the admissibility of expert testimony. Like all *in limine* hearings, it is governed by Federal Rule of Evidence 104(a), which provides in relevant part that "preliminary questions concerning the qualification of a person to be a witness . . . shall be determined by the court" and which further provides that, in making its determinations, the court "is not bound by the rules of evidence except those with respect to privileges."[54] Although the party seeking to exclude expert testimony at a *Daubert* hearing is generally the moving party, the proponent of the expert testimony bears "the burden of establishing that the pertinent admissibility requirements are met by a preponderance of the evidence."[55]

Timing of the Challenge

While the analysis required by *Daubert* is most often associated with *in limine* hearings conducted on the eve of trial, the same requirements apply when expert opinions are offered in the context of pretrial proceedings, including class certification motions[56] and summary judgment motions.[57] For example, in *Brainand v. American Skondin Life Assurance Corp.*,[58] the plaintiffs had opposed a defense motion for summary judgment by arguing, among other things, that their expert report established the individual who allegedly defrauded them was an agent of the defendant insurer.[59] The trial court, after employing a *Daubert* analysis, rejected the expert's opinion as conclusory and devoid of substance or analysis. The Sixth Circuit affirmed,

---

54. FED. R. EVID. 104(a).

55. FED. R. EVID. 702 Advisory Committee's notes to 2000 amendments.

56. *See, e.g., In re* Hydrogen Peroxide Antitrust Litig., 552 F.3d 305, 322–25 (3d Cir. 2009) (holding where parties submitted conflicting expert testimony in support of and in opposition to motion for class certification, district court must assess admissibility under *Daubert* of expert testimony in undertaking analysis of Federal Rule of Civil Procedure 23); *Blades*, 400 F.3d at 569–70, 575.

57. *See, e.g., Lewis*, 561 F.3d at 704 ("[I]t was entirely proper for the district court to determine the admissibility of the plaintiff's expert testimony at the same time that it decided the defendant's motion for summary judgment."); Major League Baseball Prop., Inc. v. Salvino, Inc., 542 F.3d 290, 311 (3d Cir. 2008) (holding that the *Daubert* gatekeeping function applies to expert testimony "whether proffered at trial or in connection with a motion for summary judgment"; affirming determination of district court to disregard plaintiff's expert testimony and grant summary judgment).

58. Brainand v. Am. Skondin Life Assurance Corp., 432 F.3d 655 (6th Cir. 2005).

59. *Id.*

noting that trial courts have broad discretion in considering the admissibility of expert testimony.[60]

Whether There Will Be a Hearing

The federal appellate courts appear to be divided about whether an actual evidentiary hearing is necessary to assess the admissibility of expert testimony. Most of the circuit courts to address the issue directly have held that district courts are not required to conduct hearings and instead have wide discretion in determining how to assess the admissibility of expert testimony.[61] The Fifth Circuit, on the other hand, has suggested that a hearing is generally appropriate.[62] The *Manual for Complex Litigation* appears to echo the position taken by most of the circuits by discouraging the use of *Daubert* hearings:

> Although a number of judges have provided for extensive *Daubert* hearings in some cases, the general consensus seems to be that neither the party proffering the testimony nor the party opposing it is entitled to a Rule 104(a) hearing. One alternative is to hold an evidentiary hearing only where, despite the affidavits and evidence submitted by the parties, there are still questions that have not been addressed.[63]

In a bench trial, there is considerable support for the position that a hearing is generally unnecessary and that the admissibility of expert evidence can be decided at trial along with the parties' merits presentation. As the Seventh Circuit has noted:

> It is not that evidence may be less reliable during a bench trial; it is that the court's gatekeeping role is necessarily different. Where the gatekeeper and the factfinder are one and the same—that is, the judge—the need to

---

60. *Id.*

61. *See, e.g.,* Millenkamp v. Davisco Foods Int'l, Inc., 562 F.3d 971, 979 (9th Cir. 2009) ("District Courts are not required to hold a *Daubert* hearing before ruling on the admissibility of scientific evidence. . . . The parties provided the District Court with briefing on his scientific expertise and proposed testimony before trial. The District Court could properly determine that this information comprised an adequate record from which the Court could make its ruling."); *Lewis,* 561 F.3d at 704 ("[W]e have not required that the *Daubert* inquiry take any specific form and have, in fact, upheld a judge's *sua sponte* consideration of the admissibility of expert testimony.") (citing Kirstein v. Parks Corp., 159 F.3d 1065, 1067 (7th Cir. 1998)).

62. *See* Huss v. Gayden, 571 F.3d 442, 459–60 (5th Cir. 2009) ("Strangely, the parties did not request, and the court did not conduct, a *Daubert* hearing. . . . Upon retrial, such a hearing will be essential.").

63. 4 MANUAL FOR COMPLEX LITIGATION § 23.353, at 694–95 (Federal Judicial Center ed., 2008).

make such decisions prior to hearing the testimony is lessened. . . . That is not to say that the scientific reliability requirement is lessened in such situations; the point is only that the court can hear the evidence and make its reliability determination during, rather than in advance of trial. Thus, where the factfinder and the gatekeeper are the same, the court does not err in admitting the evidence subject to the ability later to exclude it or disregard it if it turns out not to meet the standard of reliability established by Rule 702.[64]

After the filing of a motion *in limine* to bar expert testimony, the court will determine whether to decide the motion on the papers, to conduct a *Daubert* hearing under Rule 104, or to consolidate issues relating to the admissibility of expert testimony with the trial on the merits. In federal court, depending on the nature of the issues raised, many judges will conduct a pretrial hearing only if a ruling on a challenge to expert testimony may result in dismissal of the case or will substantially abbreviate the nature of the proceedings that will be conducted before the jury.

A number of courts have required parties to submit *Daubert / Kumho Tire* "worksheets" to assist them in determining what types of proceedings to schedule. For example, in *Samuel v. Ford Motor Co.*,[65] the court noted that it had required defense counsel to complete the following form to facilitate its review of its *Daubert* motion:

Daubert / Kumho Tire **Worksheet**

1. **Name of expert challenged.**
2. **Brief summary of opinion(s) challenged** (*if more than one, designate separately*), **including reference to the source of the opinion** (*i.e., Rule 26(a)(2)(B) disclosure, deposition transcript references, interrogatory answers*). *Attach a highlighted copy of source materials as exhibit.*
3. **Briefly describe methodology/reasoning used by expert to reach each opinion which is challenged.** *Include reference to source of challenged methodology/reasoning, and attach a highlighted copy as an exhibit.*

---

64. *In re* Salem, 465 F.3d 767, 776–77 (7th Cir. 2006); *see also* Gibbs v. Gibbs, 210 F.3d 491, 500 (5th Cir. 2000) ("Most of the safeguards provided for in *Daubert* are not as essential in a case such as this where a district judge sits as the trier of fact in place of a jury."); Magistrini v. One Hour Martinizing Dry Cleaning, 180 F. Supp. 2d 584, 596 n.10 (D.N.J. 2002) ("[W]here the Court itself acts as the ultimate trier of fact at a bench trial, the Court's role as a gatekeeper pursuant to *Daubert* is arguably less essential."); Volk v. United States, 57 F. Supp. 2d 888, 896 n.5 (N.D. Cal. 1999) (Where "the 'gatekeeper' and the trier of fact were one and the same," it "was particularly reasonable for the judge to admit the [expert] evidence . . . knowing that she would be responsible for assessing the probative value of this evidence at trial.").

65. Samuel v. Ford Motor Co., 96 F. Supp. 2d 491 (D. Md. 2000).

4. **Briefly explain the basis for the challenge to the reasoning/ methodology used by the expert** *(for example, methodology unreliable; methodology reliable, but not valid for application to this case; failure to use standardized or accepted methodology (for example, with a standardized test); etc.). Attach a highlighted copy of affidavit or other source material supporting challenge to methodology/reasoning as an exhibit.*
5. **Is the challenged methodology/reasoning subject to a known or potential error rate? If so, briefly describe it.** *Attach a highlighted copy of any relevant source material as an exhibit.*
6. **Summarize relevant peer review materials relating to methodology/ reasoning challenged.** *Attach a highlighted copy of any relevant source material as an exhibit.*
7. **If the challenge to the opinion is based upon a contention that the methodology/reasoning has not been generally accepted within the relevant scientific or technical community, briefly explain the basis for this contention.** *Attach a highlighted copy of any relevant supporting materials as an exhibit.*[66]

Practice Tip: Do not assume that the trial court will conduct a *Daubert* hearing. File a formal written motion, consistent with the court's procedures, that outlines in detail the basis for your challenge and that explains why a hearing would be helpful to the court.

Logistics of the Hearing

When trial judges do schedule hearings, they have considerable discretion in the conduct of those hearings. Because hearings conducted under Rule 104 are not subject to the rules of evidence (other than privileges), including the hearsay rule, it should be borne in mind that the court can consider information other than live testimony, including affidavits of experts who do not appear to testify, transcripts of hearings in other matters, and articles and other publications. As a consequence, depending on the nature of the arguments that have been advanced, the expert whose testimony has been challenged may be called as the first witness or, if the court is satisfied that it understands the proposed testimony based on the submissions made in advance of the hearing, the court may allow defense experts or "attack" experts to testify first.

---

66. *Id.* at 504.

Although it has been suggested that the moving party (i.e., the party challenging the testimony), has the right to present its witnesses first,[67] in some cases this may mean that the moving party will be calling the opposing party's expert as an adverse witness. In some cases, such as where the challenging party hopes to establish that an expert failed to consider certain facts or data, was sloppy in his investigation, or relied on facts that are false or unreliable, it may be more effective to call the challenged expert as an adverse witness. In other cases, such as where the deposition testimony of the challenged expert has already been submitted to the court, the moving party may desire to call its own witnesses. Thus, if the line of attack focuses on the methodology, and the deposition testimony of the challenged expert has already been submitted with the moving papers, it may be unnecessary for the challenged expert to be the first witness at the hearing.

The Use of Attack Experts

In many cases it will be practically necessary or tactically helpful to rely on experts who have not been designated as testifying experts to challenge the reliability of an opposing party's expert. For example, where a scheduling order requires the plaintiff to serve its expert reports before the service of the defense reports, the plaintiff's expert will obviously not be able to address, in his report, issues relating to the reliability of the defense methodology.

If issues relating to the admissibility of the other party's expert are not addressed in your expert's report, must you seek leave to supplement your reports to address the issue of reliability? Or if you prefer not to have your trial experts become embroiled in a *Daubert* hearing, is it necessary to request permission to submit rebuttal reports? In many cases, counsel will prefer to have separate experts address issues relating to the admissibility of the opposing party's experts. Experts who are presented solely to challenge the reliability of the methodology used by the opposing party's experts have been referred to as attack experts.[68]

The courts have articulated differing views about the admissibility of evidence from attack experts who submit reports or affidavits for the first time after a deadline for expert reports has passed. A number of courts have allowed such testimony. In *In re Paoli Railroad Yard PCB Litigation*,[69] the

---

67. *See* Robert J. Shaughnessy, *Daubert after a Decade*, 30 Litig. 19, 68 (Fall 2003) ("By convention, the moving party [in a *Daubert* hearing] presents its witnesses first.").

68. *See* Shaughnessy, *supra* note 67, at 22–23 (describing the use of "attack" experts in *Daubert* challenges).

69. *Paoli*, 35 F.3d 717.

district court issued a scheduling order that required the defendants to designate "all trial expert witnesses" by a certain date.[70] After this deadline, the defendants submitted affidavits from a new set of experts and indicated that they intended to have these experts testify at a Rule 104 hearing concerning the admissibility of the plaintiffs' experts, but not at trial. Because discovery was closed, the plaintiffs were unable to depose the new experts. Although the plaintiffs moved to bar the experts from testifying at the hearing, the district court never ruled on this motion, allowed the experts to testify at the hearing, and relied on their testimony in excluding much of the plaintiffs' evidence.

On appeal, the Third Circuit noted, as a technical matter, that defendants did not violate the trial court's scheduling order because that order "setting deadlines for the identification of experts was only directed at trial witnesses and said nothing about witnesses who were to testify only at the *in limine* hearing."[71] The Third Circuit explained, though, that such a "conclusion does not settle the question" because

> [P]laintiffs' more significant claim of error is encapsulated in a recent law review article by Professor Berger, who argues that "[c]ourts should not permit the Defendant to obtain a hearing on a *motion in limine* by relying on Affidavits from experts unless their identity and reports have been supplied to the Plaintiff in the course of discovery and the Plaintiff had an opportunity to depose [them]."[72]

Although the Third Circuit ultimately held that the district court did not abuse its discretion in allowing the defendants' attack experts to testify at the *in limine* hearing without being deposed, it made clear that adequate discovery of such experts should generally be permitted:

> [W]e generally agree with Professor Berger that because under *Daubert*, a judge at an *in limine* hearing must make findings of fact on the reliability of complicated scientific methodologies and this fact-finding can decide a case, it is important that each side have an opportunity to depose the other side's experts in order to develop strong critiques and defenses of their expert's methodologies. . . . Given the "liberal thrust" to the federal rules . . . it is particularly important that the side trying to defend the admissibility of evidence be given an adequate chance to do so. Moreover, fairness suggests that each side should have an equal opportunity to depose the other side's experts.[73]

---

70. *Id.*
71. *Id.* at 739.
72. *Id.* at 739 (quoting Margaret A. Berger, *Procedural Paragons for Applying the Daubert Test*, 78 MINN. L. REV. 1345, 1372 (1994)).
73. *Id.*

Since the Third Circuit's decision in *In re Paoli*, a handful of unreported district court decisions have addressed the admissibility of attack experts. In *United Phosphorus, Ltd. v. Midland Fumigant, Inc.*,[74] the plaintiff sought leave, apparently after the deadline for the submission of expert reports, to supplement its expert witness disclosures to identify a rebuttal witness for a *Daubert* hearing that the court had scheduled.[75] The plaintiff explained that it did not intend to call that witness as an expert at trial. The trial court granted the plaintiff's motion, noting that the case was not scheduled to proceed to trial for another 11 months, the defendants had not demonstrated any prejudice, and the plaintiff had shown good cause for the additional testimony.

Likewise, in *Night Light Systems, Inc. v. Nitelites Franchise Systems, Inc.*,[76] the plaintiffs identified a potential expert witness for the first time after the deadline for submission of expert reports.[77] In response to a motion to exclude, plaintiffs represented that they did not intend to offer the expert witness at trial but only as part of a *Daubert* hearing challenging the admissibility of defense expert testimony. The plaintiffs argued that because they did not intend to offer their expert's testimony at trial, it was not necessary for them to identify him during the discovery period.

The district court expressed some reservations about this argument, based on a local court rule that required all anticipated expert testimony to be designated during the discovery period:

> The Rule dealing with the disclosure of expert witnesses, Federal Rule of Civil Procedure 26(a)(2), states that a party must disclose the identity of any expert witnesses who may be used "at trial to present expert evidence." It says nothing regarding the disclosure of an expert witness to be used at a *Daubert* hearing. Local Rule 26.2(C), however, does not contain the limiting language "at trial." It states, "[a]ny party who desires to use the testimony of an expert witness shall designate the expert sufficiently early in the discovery period to permit the opposing party the opportunity to depose the expert. . . ." By not disclosing the identity of Dr. Bernhardt, therefore, the plaintiffs appear to have violated Local Rule 26.2(C), but arguably have not violated Federal Rule of Civil Procedure 26(a)(2).[78]

---

74. United Phosphorus, Ltd. v. Midland Fumigant, Inc., No. Civ. A. 91-2133-EEO, 1997 WL 38112 (D. Kan. Jan. 24, 1997).

75. *Id.*

76. Night Light Sys., Inc. v. Nitelites Franchise Sys., Inc., Civ. A. No. 1:04-CV-2112-CAP, 2007 WL 4563875 (N.D. Ga. May 11, 2007).

77. *Id.*

78. *Id.* at *7.

Nevertheless, based on the Third Circuit's decision in *In re Paoli*, and after noting the dearth of other authority concerning the issue, the court ultimately held that the expert could testify at the *Daubert* hearing but not at trial. As a condition to his testimony, the district court required the plaintiffs to serve an expert report or affidavit outlining the expert's views and further required the plaintiffs to make him available to the defendants for a deposition.[79]

Other courts have been unreceptive to the designation of attack experts after expert deadlines have passed. In *Jeffries v. Centre Life Insurance Co.*,[80] the defendant sought leave to present testimony at an upcoming *Daubert* hearing from a previously undisclosed expert on infectious diseases.[81] The defendant argued that it was not required to disclose that witness under Federal Rule of Civil Procedure 26(a)(2)—which refers to disclosures for experts who may testify at "trial"—because the witness would only testify during the *Daubert* hearing and not at the trial. The court rejected the argument that Rule 26 does not apply to witnesses who are expected to testify only at *Daubert* hearings:

> Although a *Daubert* hearing is not a trial per se, it is an integral part of the trial proceedings because it will determine the admissibility of evidence at trial. In turn, the court's rulings on inadmissibility will certainly affect, in one way or another, the outcome of trial. [Defendant's] literal interpretation of Rule 26(a)(2)(A) evades the purpose and spirit of discovery and the Rules of Civil Procedure themselves.[82]

Moreover, the *Jeffries* court made clear that it was troubled by what appeared to be deliberative delay on the part of its defense counsel in disclosing their attack expert:

> [Defendant] provides no justification for its failure to disclose Dr. Halsey in accordance with Rule 26. Indeed, [Defendant's] non-disclosure of Dr. Halsey appears to be a conscious tactical decision. At this late date in the proceedings, having had no prior opportunity to examine Dr. Halsey

---

79. *Id.* at 8. *See also* Lyman v. St. Jude Med. S.C., Inc., 580 F. Supp. 2d 719, 725 n.3 (E.D. Wis. 2008) (rejecting defendant's objection to declaration filed for purposes of a *Daubert* hearing in support of the reliability of plaintiff's challenged expert: "Dr. West's testimony only became relevant in response to [defendant's] *Daubert* challenge, so there was no requirement of prior disclosure").
80. Jeffries v. Centre Life Ins. Co., No. 1:02-CV-351, 2004 WL 5506494 (S.D. Ohio Jan. 28, 2004).
81. *Id.*
82. *Id.* at *1.

regarding his opinions, Plaintiffs would be severely prejudiced at the *Daubert* hearing.[83]

The result in *Jeffries* may have been justified, given that defense counsel received the plaintiff's expert report and had the opportunity to address any *Daubert* issues it desired to raise when it served its own expert reports. But would the same result have been warranted if the plaintiff, who did not see the defense reports until after serving its own reports, attempted to present attack experts? Probably not.

Some courts have endeavored to avoid similar disputes by anticipating the potential need for experts who will participate only in *Daubert* proceedings and by setting two sets of dates—one for trial experts and a second for *Daubert* experts—in their pretrial scheduling orders.[84]

Practice Tip: If you anticipate that your case will involve disputes over expert methodology and the possible involvement of *Daubert*-only attack experts, flag that issue for the court at the initial conference and request that a separate schedule be set for reports from such experts. If this issue of *Daubert*-only experts is not addressed in the court's scheduling order, raise the issue expeditiously if you determine, based on reports received from the other side, that you may decide to rely on such experts. If you disclose your reliance on attack experts for the first time as part of a *Daubert* motion and the other side objects and claims prejudice, explain to the court why you did not make an earlier disclosure, and consider offering your attack expert up for a deposition to blunt any suggestion that you are attempting to gain an unfair advantage.

The Use of Court-Appointed Experts[85]

Pursuant to Federal Rule of Evidence 706, which allows federal trial judges to appoint experts, federal courts have appointed experts not only to testify at trial regarding the merits of a case, but also to provide opinions regarding

---

83. *Id.*

84. *See generally Magistrini*, 180 F. Supp. 2d at 591 (noting that the magistrate judge, in a pretrial order, had set a separate date, after the date for submission of reports from testifying experts, for the designation of "additional experts solely for the purposes of the *Daubert* hearing").

85. For additional guidance on working with a court-appointed expert, see *supra* "Court-Appointed Experts" in chapter 1.

the reliability of expert evidence in Rule 104 hearings.[86] In *Daubert*, the Supreme Court specifically suggested that trial judges consider exercising their power under Rule 706 to appoint their own experts.[87]

Federal courts have also relied on Rule 706 to engage technical advisors on complex and technical issues, a technique suggested by Justice Breyer in his concurring opinion in *Joiner*.[88] Such technical advisors generally do not issue reports available to the parties, are not deposed, and do not testify.[89]

The district court's decision in *Renaud v. Martin Marietta Corp.*[90] demonstrates the benefit of court-appointed experts in Rule 104 hearings. *Renaud* involved a toxic tort action concerning injuries due to contaminated water. The court appointed experts for a Rule 104 hearing to aid in its assessment of the reliability of the scientific sampling evidence presented. In that case, only one sample of the water was provided to show what the nor-

---

86. *See* Ford v. Mercer County Corr. Ctr., 171 F. App'x 416, 420 (3d Cir. 2006) ("Rule 706 affords the trial judge broad discretion to appoint an independent expert answerable to the court, whether *sua sponte* or on the motion of a party. The policy behind the rule is to promote the jury's fact-finding ability."); Carranza v. Fraas, 471 F. Supp. 2d 8, 11 (D.D.C. 2007) ("Rule 706 allows the court to appoint an expert witness to assist the court, not to assist a party. . . . Quite simply, 'litigant assistance' is not the purpose of Rule 706."); Reid v. Albemarle Corp., 207 F. Supp. 2d 499, 505 (M.D. La. 2001) (holding that court may rely on court-appointed expert's opinion regarding qualifications, or lack thereof, of plaintiffs' expert). Panels of experts have also been allowed. *See* Gates v. United States, 707 F.2d 1141, 1144 (10th Cir. 1983); Fund for Animals, Inc. v. Florida Game & Fresh Water Fish Comm'n, 550 F. Supp. 1206, 1208 (S.D. Fla. 1982); Lightfoot v. Walker, 486 F. Supp. 504, 506 (S.D. Ill. 1980).
87. *Daubert*, 509 U.S. at 595.
88. *Joiner*, 522 U.S. at 147–50 (Breyer, S., concurring).
89. *See, e.g.,* Ass'n of Mexican-Am. Educators v. California, 231 F.3d 572, 590 (9th Cir. 2000) ("In those rare cases in which outside technical expertise would be helpful to a district court, the court may appoint a technical advisor."); Reilly v. United States, 863 F.2d 149, 157–58 (1st Cir. 1988) (analogizing the technical advisor to a neutral law clerk who can guide the untrained judge through a complex subject matter); Allison v. McGhan Med. Corp., 184 F.3d 1300, 1311 (11th Cir. 1999) (noting that judges should "enlist outside experts to assist in [the] sometimes very difficult question" of reliability and relevance of scientific methodology so as "to quell the pseudo-scientist criticism" of judges who make decisions completely outside their field of expertise); Hall v. Baxter Healthcare Corp., 947 F. Supp. 1387 (D. Or. 1996) (using court-appointed technical advisors under Rule 104 to help evaluate the "reliability and relevance" of the scientific evidence in 70 cases brought against breast implant makers during an extensive *Daubert* hearing); *In re* Silicone Gel Breast Implant Prods. Liab. Litig., 1996 WL 34401813, 1996 WL 34401813, at *5 n.6 (N.D. Ala. May 31, 1996) ("Findings by the court-appointed experts may, however, be relevant to, and be considered by trial courts in ruling on, issues raised under Rule 104 . . . regarding admissibility of expert testimony and published research offered by the parties.").
90. Renaud v. Martin Marietta Corp., 749 F. Supp. 1545 (D. Col. 1990), *aff'd*, 972 F.2d 304 (10th Cir. 1992).

mal contaminant concentration of a certain pond was during the 11-year exposure period. It was the court-appointed expert who pointed out to the court that "it is unsound scientific practice to select one concentration measured at a single location in point and time and apply it to describe continuous releases of contaminants over an eleven-year period." On that basis, the court refused to admit the evidence of exposure and, given the absence of any other evidence, granted the defendant's motion for summary judgment.

Court-appointed experts are only likely to be helpful in certain types of cases, principally those where questions exist about whether a methodology is generally accepted or whether the methodology has been properly applied. In other cases, such as where the challenge focuses on the expert's qualifications, a court-appointed expert is less likely to be helpful.

A survey of federal judges conducted some years ago by the Federal Judicial Center (FJC) to determine the use of court-appointed experts found that only 20 percent of judges had relied on court-appointed experts. The FJC study cited two factors for the judges' failure to seek expert assistance. First, many judges view the appointment of experts as generally unnecessary and as helpful only in unusual circumstances.[91] Second, "a significant number of judges expressed their warranted belief that the adversarial process should be relied upon, and that court-appointed experts would take the matter away from the able hands of the parties."[92]

Practice Tip: Court-appointed experts will add expense to the litigation process and, in a close case, may sway the court in favor of one side or the other. So be careful what you wish for. As a general matter, it is wise to press for a court-appointed expert only if you are highly confident that your position is likely to be vindicated by that expert.

Conclusion

Expert testimony is essential in many cases, not only at trial, but also to survive key pretrial milestones such as class certification and summary judgment. Judges play a unique and enormously powerful role in determining

---

91. 1 Modern Scientific Evidence: The Law and Science of Expert Testimony § 1:38, at 113 (David L. Faigman et al. eds., 2008).
92. *Id.*

the admissibility of expert testimony. Unconstrained by the rules of evidence under Rule 104, they have enormous discretion, both in how they proceed and in their ultimate judgments about admissibility. Careful preparation and sound judgments in preparing for and participating in *Daubert* proceedings will maximize your chances of successfully excluding harmful expert testimony.

Checklists

Discovery Issues to Consider When Preparing to Challenge an Expert

1. Is the witness qualified to serve as an expert for the issues in this case?
2. Is the expert using a methodology that is recognized in the professional literature?
3. Did the expert properly apply applicable standards?
4. Did the expert adequately investigate the facts?
5. Are the expert's assumptions reasonable?
6. Are the facts or data on which the expert relied the type of facts or data relied on by other experts in the field?
7. Is the expert merely speculating?
8. Has the expert adequately explained the basis for his opinion?
9. Is the expert offering a net opinion?
10. Will the expert's testimony be helpful to the jury?
11. Does the expert's theory or technique fit the facts of the case?
12. Does the probative value of the expert's testimony outweigh its danger of unfair prejudice?
13. Is the expert impermissibly offering testimony about legal issues?

Preparation for the *Daubert* Hearing

- Obtain informal discovery concerning the expert;
- Serve a document request on opposing counsel;
- Serve a subpoena on the expert;
- Depose the expert;
- Research the expert's trial record;
- Have your own expert or consulting expert review and critique the opposing expert's work;
- Research the technical or scientific literature;
- Research other cases dealing with similar issues;
- Identify issues worth pursuing;

- Prepare and file a written motion; and
- Request a hearing.

Goals of the *Daubert* Hearing

- Exclude or limit the scope of the expert's testimony;
- Reveal critical weaknesses in the expert's analysis; and
- Set up for cross-examination at trial.

Possible Arguments for Exclusion

- The expert is not qualified;
- The expert is offering opinions beyond his area of expertise;
- The opinions offered are not those of the expert;
- The methodology employed is not reliable;
- The methodology may be reliable, but it has not been properly applied by the expert;
- The expert is relying on unreliable facts or data;
- The expert is relying on factual assumptions that are false;
- The expert is relying on inadmissible evidence that is not the type of evidence relied on by experts in the field;
- The expert is offering opinions on issues of law;
- The expert is offering opinions that are not helpful to the trier of fact;
- The expert's opinions are unduly prejudicial; and
- The expert's opinions are cumulative or duplicative.

Strategies for an Effective *Daubert* Attack

- Use concessions made by the expert being attacked;
- Use prior court rulings involving the expert being attacked;
- Use prior court rulings concerning the methodology being attacked;
- Use your own experts and their opinions;
- Use attack experts;
- Rely on other judicial decisions;
- Present scientific or technical literature;
- Request that the court appoint its own expert;
- Request that the court retain a law clerk with specialized knowledge;
- Request a hearing;
- Request specific findings of fact on key issues;
- Highlight weaknesses and qualifications; and
- Submit a written motion.

Appendix A: Key Decisions by Circuit

Circuit	Recent Noteworthy Cases
First	• *Chadwick v. Wellpoint*, 561 F.3d 38 (1st Cir. 2009). The plaintiff, who claimed employment discrimination, appealed the trial court's exclusion of proposed testimony by a Ph.D. in sociology with expertise in employment discrimination and sex-based stereotypes in the workplace. The First Circuit upheld the district court's exclusion of the testimony, stating that, while Rule 702 is to be liberally interpreted in favor of the admission of expert testimony, a district court's ruling is reviewed only for an abuse of discretion. The district court's ruling was based on the fact that "there was a mismatch between the expert's knowledge and qualifications and her ability to helpfully opine on the specifics of th[e] case." *Id.* at 48–49. • *First Marblehead v. House*, 541 F.3d 36 (1st Cir. 2008). The plaintiff sued his former employer because he had not been informed that his incentive stock options would lapse within three months of his resignation. The defendant employer sought to introduce testimony of a lawyer/accountant that the plaintiff's stock options were not worth anything during the three-month period in which the options could have been exercised. The trial court's decision to admit the expert testimony was not an abuse of discretion because his comments were limited to expressing an opinion regarding financial risk and did not attempt to address the credibility of the plaintiff's testimony. • *United States v. Malone*, 453 F.3d 68 (1st Cir. 2006). A footwear impression expert testified that footprints found at the scene of a bank robbery matched shoes found nearby that contained the defendant's DNA. In affirming the trial court's admission of the expert's testimony, even though she was not a qualified footwear expert through the International Association of Identification, the First Circuit noted that the district court had "explicitly considered the four guiding factors laid out as guidance by the Supreme Court in *Daubert*: (1) whether the underlying method can be or has been tested; (2) whether the method has been subject to peer review and publication; (3) the method's known or potential error rate; and (4) the level of the method's acceptance within the relevant discipline." • *Akerson v. Falcon Transport Company*, No. CV-06-36-B-W, 2006 WL 3377940 (D. Me. Nov. 21, 2006). *Akerson* addressed whether a physician's assistant was qualified as an expert witness in her field. The court held that there is a growing trend of scarcity in regard to the number of practicing physicians throughout the country, especially in rural areas, and if "this Country's medical system has sufficient confidence in the expertise of physician extenders to entrust the treatment of its citizens to them, this Country's legal system should have sufficient confidence to allow them to testify as experts[.]" *Id.* at *5.

Circuit	Recent Noteworthy Cases
Second	• *United States v. Williams*, 506 F.3d 151 (2d Cir. 2007). In upholding the trial court's ruling admitting the testimony of a ballistics expert, the Second Circuit noted that "[a] decision to admit scientific evidence is not an abuse of discretion unless manifestly erroneous." *Id.* at 160. The court further held that the trial court had fulfilled its gatekeeping function under *Daubert* even though it denied a separate evidentiary hearing because, before admitting the testimony, it considered the use of ballistic expert testimony in other cases, and because the government had provided an exhaustive foundation for the expert's expertise. "The formality of a separate hearing was not required," and there was no abuse of discretion. *Id.* at 161. • *In re Ephedra Product Liability Litigation*, 393 F. Supp. 2d 181 (S.D.N.Y. 2005). In a case that dealt with the possible side effects of Ephedra, the district court held that the plaintiffs could put forth expert testimony claiming that Ephedra "may be a contributing cause of stroke, cardiac injury, and seizure in some people" but that the experts could not testify with "medical certainty" that Ephedra caused the alleged injuries. *Id.* at *1. The court went on to state that "to hold the opinions of scientists inadmissible unless backed by statistically significant results from tightly controlled (and very expensive) experiments would set a separate, higher standard for scientists than for other witnesses with specialized knowledge." *Id.* at 4.
Third	• *Pineda v. Ford Motor Co.*, 520 F.3d 237 (3d Cir. 2008). Pineda involved an automobile technician who was injured when the rear liftgate glass of a sports utility vehicle shattered. The plaintiff brought a products liability action against the vehicle's manufacturer and sought to introduce expert testimony from an engineer that Ford had failed to provide proper warnings and instructions regarding the appropriate hinge removal sequence. *Id.* at 241–42. The court held that a trial court should consider several factors in evaluating whether a particular methodology is reliable: "(1) whether a method consists of a testable hypothesis; (2) whether the method has been subject to peer review; (3) the known or potential rate of error; (4) the existence and maintenance of standards controlling the technique's operation; (5) whether the method is generally accepted; (6) the relationship of the technique to methods which have been established to be reliable; (7) the qualifications of the expert witness testifying based on the methodology; and (8) the non-judicial uses to which the method has been put." *Id.* at 247–48 (citing United States v. Downing, 753 F.2d 1224 (3d Cir.1985)). The court further noted, however, that these factors are neither exhaustive nor applicable in every case. *Id.* at 248. In holding that the district court had improperly excluded the testimony of a design defect/warnings expert, the court found that the district court "did not demonstrate the

(continued)

Circuit	Recent Noteworthy Cases

appropriate level of flexibility required by Rule 702" and "focused too narrowly on [the expert's] failure either to offer proposed alternative language for a warning or to test the effectiveness of alternative warnings." Id.

- *Gutierrez v. Johnson & Johnson*, No. 01-53022006, U.S. Dist. LEXIS 80834 (D.N.J. Nov. 6, 2006). The court was faced with competing expert opinions regarding how to properly certify a class in a proposed employment discrimination scenario. Because the Third Circuit had yet to be faced with this issue, the court applied the Second Circuit's analysis to arrive at its decision. *See In re* Visa Checking/Master Money Anti-Trust Litig., 280 F.3d 124 (2d Cir. 2001). The court in *Gutierrez* determined that, when dealing with *Daubert* inquiries at the class certification stage, the court should apply a more lenient standard and that *Daubert* inquiries should focus on whether the expert opinions are "so fatally flawed as to be inadmissible as a matter of law." *Id.* at *6.

Fourth	- ***Richmond Medical Center for Women v. Herring***, 527 F.3d 128 (4th Cir. 2008). In a case involving the constitutionality of a Virginia statute banning "partial birth abortion," the trial court did not abuse its discretion in excluding the testimony of an obstetrician/gynecologist/perinatologist. That doctor, while credentialed and experienced as an obstetrician/gynecologist/perinatologist, did not have specialized knowledge or experience about the specific procedure at issue.

- ***Bryte ex rel. Bryte v. American Household, Inc.***, 429 F.3d 469 (4th Cir. 2005). The plaintiff died in a fire while using an electrically heated throw. Plaintiffs alleged that the heated throw had a defective safety circuit, which had caused the fire. The Fourth Circuit upheld the trial court's exclusion of the plaintiffs' proposed fire cause and origin expert, because the expert had failed to independently evaluate other possible causes of the fire.

- ***TWFS, Inc. v. Schaefer***, 325 F.3d 234 (4th Cir. 2003). A liquor retailer brought an action against the state comptroller alleging that Maryland's statutory scheme regulating wholesale pricing of liquor and wine violated the Sherman Act. In support of its defense, the state attempted to introduce testimony from a professor of economics that Maryland's liquor prices were actually higher than in other states. The Fourth Circuit upheld the district court's rejection of the plaintiff's contention that the economist's empirical evidence on state-by-state liquor price comparisons is so unreliable as to be inadmissible under *Daubert*. According to the Fourth Circuit, the plaintiff had not mounted a true *Daubert* challenge, because it did not argue that the expert's methods had not been tested, had not withstood peer review and publication, had excessive rates of error, had no standards for their application, or had not been accepted in

Circuit	Recent Noteworthy Cases
	their field. *Id.* at 240. Rather, the plaintiff only argued that the state's expert's calculations did not support his conclusion that Maryland has higher alcohol beverage prices than most other states. *Id.* The Fourth Circuit agreed with the trial court that plaintiff's challenge to the state's expert was really "a challenge to the proper weight to be given to [the expert's] evidence, not to its admissibility." *Id.*
Fifth	• ***Huss v. Gayden*, 571 F.3d 442 (5th Cir. 2009).** The defendant medical providers sought to introduce expert testimony to rebut the plaintiff's expert's testimony that the drug Terbutaline caused cardiomyopathy. In excluding the defendant's expert, the trial court incorrectly focused on the fact that the defendant's expert had less training and experience with the drug than did the plaintiff's expert. The court noted that this focus "missed the purpose for which defendants sought to elicit [the expert's] opinion," and that "the most important question is not whether one party's expert is more qualified that the other's, but, rather, whether an expert's testimony is reliable." The court held that the trial court's ruling excluding the testimony was an abuse of discretion.
	• ***Chan v. Coggins*, 294 F. App'x 934 (5th Cir. 2008).** In *Chan*, the Fifth Circuit held that the record "amply" supported the trial court's exclusion of the opinion of plaintiff's accident reconstruction expert about the cause of the accident that was the subject of the suit. That opinion lacked a scientific basis and was contrary to the facts in evidence, and the expert was therefore not qualified under Federal Rule 702 to opine as to whether the driver was negligent. The court also stated that the plaintiff's reliance on the fact that the expert had testified as an expert in other cases was misplaced, stating that "being qualified as an expert in the circumstances of one case does not qualify one as an expert in all future cases."
	• ***Knight v. Kirby Inland Marine, Inc.*, 482 F.3d 347 (5th Cir. 2007).** The plaintiff filed a claim against his former employer, for whom he had worked as a tankerman, for exposure to various toxic chemicals during his employment, which he claimed had caused his Hodgkins lymphoma. Plaintiff sought to introduce the testimony of an epidemiologist and physician on both general and specific causation. The court upheld the district court's exclusion of the doctor's proffered testimony on the basis that his opinions were unreliable because "the analytical gap between the studies on which he relied and his conclusions was simply too great." The court noted that "[d]istrict courts have an important role as gatekeepers in determining whether to admit expert testimony" and "must carefully analyze the studies on which experts rely for their opinions before admitting their testimony."

(continued)

Circuit	Recent Noteworthy Cases

Sixth

- *Sigler v. American Honda Motor Co.*, 532 F.3d 469 (6th Cir. 2008). The court held that the district court abused its discretion in excluding the testimony of the plaintiff's doctor regarding whether trauma resulting from an automobile accident in which plaintiff was involved exacerbated her preexisting seizure disorder. The court held that, in excluding the testimony, the district court "clearly abused its discretion because the factual record contradicts the court's analysis, which was infected by reliance on unsworn materials submitted by Honda." *Id.* at 481.

- *Surles v. Greyhound Lines, Inc.*, 474 F.3d 288 (6th Cir. 2007). A passenger sued the bus line for injuries she sustained after a terrorist incident. The plaintiff was injured when another passenger attacked the bus driver with a box cutter, causing the bus to drive off the road and crash into a ditch. The plaintiff suffered severe injuries to her spinal cord, leaving her a paraplegic. *Id.* at 291–92. The plaintiff offered testimony from two experts, one a former Los Angeles police officer, and the other a forensic engineer. The plaintiff claimed the officer had the requisite qualifications to testify based on his work in a threat management unit that dealt with potentially violent situations involving mentally ill individuals. The threat management unit had dealt with Greyhound before, and the officer offered testimony of other incidents involving the bus line and Greyhound's failure to react appropriately to these situations. The forensic engineer offered testimony regarding the feasibility of installing a protective unit around the bus driver to protect the driver from passengers. The plaintiff received a large jury verdict awarding her $8 million. Greyhound appealed.

  Greyhound brought *Daubert* challenges on the grounds that the plaintiff's two experts were not qualified or reliable. The Sixth Circuit held that there had been no abuse of discretion by the trial court and that the police officer's background allowed him the qualifications to "assist the trier of fact to make sense of the prior incident reports" and that his lack of expertise affected the weight of the evidence, not the admissibility. *Id.* at 294. The forensic engineer had previously designed a protective barrier for bus drivers; therefore, the Sixth Circuit readily agreed with the trial court's decision regarding the qualifications of the second expert. Due to the reliability of the forensic engineer, the Sixth Circuit applied a more relaxed standard based on the finding that the engineer's testimony was not scientific testimony, instead stating it was considered "technical or other specialized knowledge." As such, the court held that strict adherence to the *Daubert* factors was not applicable. *Id.* at 295.

Circuit	Recent Noteworthy Cases
Seventh	• *United States v. Pansier,* 576 F.3d 726 (7th Cir. 2009). The defendants, Pansier and his wife, refused to pay income and property taxes for many years. In an attempt to dodge his tax bills, Pansier submitted as payment for taxes owed to the Internal Revenue Service, the Wisconsin Department of Revenue, and the Treasury of Marinette County, Wisconsin, phony financial instruments that appeared to be "sight drafts" issued under the authority of the U.S. Department of the Treasury. Pansier was ultimately indicted on 31 counts, and in support of its case, the government offered the testimony of William Kerr, a bank examiner with the Office of the Comptroller of the Currency, who testified that the sight drafts submitted by Pansier were worthless financial instruments purportedly drawn on a Treasury direct account at the Treasury Department. The Seventh Circuit upheld the trial court's decision to allow Kerr's testimony. Pansier argued that the trial court did not properly consider the reliability of Kerr's testimony, that Kerr was not qualified, that his testimony was directly contradicted by an employee of the Bureau of Public Debt, and that the court erred in allowing Kerr to testify as to an ultimate issue involving a legal conclusion. The Seventh Circuit rejected all of these arguments. With regard to the argument that Kerr impermissibly testified regarding an ultimate legal issue, the court stated that, although Kerr testified as to the ultimate issue that the sight drafts were fictitious financial instruments and were purportedly drawn on a Treasury direct account, he did not testify as to Pansier's state of mind or intent to defraud, and therefore the district court did not abuse its discretion in allowing the testimony. • *United States v. Ozuna,* 561 F.3d 728 (7th Cir. 2009). In a case involving a hearing to suppress evidence of cocaine found at the defendant's tractor-trailer, the court held that a *Daubert* analysis was not required of a handwriting expert during a reopening of the suppression hearing. The court noted that the primary rationale behind *Daubert* (namely, for the court to serve as gatekeeper to the jury) is not applicable in a suppression hearing because judges are far less likely than juries to be swayed by experts with insufficient qualifications. • *United States v. Mikos,* 539 F.3d 706 (7th Cir. 2008). In a murder case, the Seventh Circuit held that the trial court did not abuse its discretion in permitting an FBI ballistics agent to give expert testimony that rifling on the bullets that killed the decedent did not rule out the type of revolver that the defendant allegedly used, even though the FBI's rifling database was incomplete. *Id.* at 711. The court held that "[d]istrict judges may admit testimony resting on 'scientific, technical or otherwise specialized knowledge' that will assist the trier of fact" and that, even though testimony based on the FBI's rifling database may not have been "scientific," it was both "technical" and "specialized." *Id.* (quoting FED. R. EVID. 702).

(*continued*)

Circuit	Recent Noteworthy Cases

Eighth
- *Allen v. Brown Clinic*, 531 F.3d 568 (8th Cir. 2008). The plaintiff in a medical malpractice case sought to preclude the testimony of the defendant's expert, whom the plaintiff claimed was an expert in laparoscopic but not open hernia repair surgery and because the doctor did not opine as to the proximate cause of the plaintiff's perforated esophagus, which the plaintiff contended was the open hernia repair surgery he had undergone. In rejecting the plaintiff's argument that the testimony was inadmissible because the expert did not opine as to an alternative proximate cause, rather than simply alternate possible causes, the court noted that, in a medical malpractice case, the plaintiff has the burden to show whether the doctor deviated from the required standard of care and that the plaintiff's argument would essentially shift the burden of proof to the defendant. Therefore, the court held, admission of the expert's testimony was proper, even though the expert had not testified regarding the proximate cause of the plaintiff's torn esophagus.
- *United States v. Spotted Elk*, 548 F.3d 641 (8th Cir. 2008). The defendants, who were engaged in a large drug-trafficking operation on the Pine Ridge Sioux Reservation, were convicted of various drug-related offenses. At trial the court admitted the testimony of a fingerprint expert. The defendants appealed, contending the court had erred in failing to hold a *Daubert* hearing on the proposed expert testimony. The court held the trial court had not erred in failing to hold a hearing, because fingerprint evidence and analysis is generally accepted and reliable.
- *Sappington v. Skyjack, Inc.*, 512 F.3d 440 (8th Cir. 2008). The Eighth Circuit reversed a trial court decision that excluded testimony from plaintiffs' accident reconstruction experts and awarded summary judgment to defendants. The district court relied in part on differences between conditions in the experts' testing and during the accident. Those differences were not so substantial, the appellate panel held, as to render the experts' opinions unreliable.
- *Larson v. Kempker*, 414 F.3d 936 (8th Cir. 2005). The plaintiff was a prison inmate who brought an action complaining that he was being exposed to environmental tobacco smoke (ETS). In support of his claim, he offered testimony from a doctor on the adverse health effects of ETS, which was excluded by the district court. The Eighth Circuit reversed, stating that an expert's testimony should be excluded only if it is so fundamentally unsupported that it could not offer any assistance to the jury. *Id.* at 941.

Ninth
- *United States v. Calderon-Segura*, 512 F.3d 1104 (9th Cir. 2008). In upholding the trial court's ruling admitting the testimony of a fingerprint identification expert, the court held that there was no merit in the defendant's arguments that the district court abused its discretion in

Circuit	Recent Noteworthy Cases

failing to conduct a more searching examination of the *Daubert* factors or in declining his request for a full *Daubert* hearing. The court stated that "[g]iven the familiar subject matter and the defense's failure to show cause for questioning the evidentiary reliability for exemplar fingerprint identification methods, this [was] just the sort of routine case where evidentiary reliability was properly taken for granted." *Id.* at 1110.

- *United States v. Reed,* 575 F.3d 900 (9th Cir. 2009). The defendant, who had been convicted of manufacture and distribution of the drug known as PCP, appealed his convictions, arguing that the district court erred in allowing testimony from a detective as to the meaning of certain drug jargon. After noting that "drug jargon" is a proper subject for expert testimony, the court held that the detective was qualified and helpful to the jury, since certain terms used in the trial were outside the knowledge of lay jurors.
- *United States v. Sandoval-Mendoza,* 472 F.3d 645 (9th Cir. 2006). The defendant, who was convicted of conspiracy to sell methamphetamine, appealed his conviction on entrapment grounds, stating that the district court erroneously excluded medical testimony proving the existence of a brain tumor that affected his inhibitions, memory, decision-making capabilities, judgment, and overall intellectual capacity, making him susceptible to suggestion and vulnerable to entrapment.

During the trial, the district court held an *in camera Daubert* hearing, allowing testimony from both the government's and the defendant's expert witnesses. The government's experts stated that the defendant did in fact have a very large pituitary tumor, but that he was purposefully underperforming on memory tests, and that while some brain tumors did cause disinhibition, pituitary tumors did not, unless they were much larger than the defendant's. After hearing expert witnesses from both sides, the district court excluded the testimony, claiming that it was not relevant to the entrapment defense and also due to a "lack of scientific validity" and "absence of ability to make a causal connection" between the tumor and the inducement by the government. *Id.* at 654. The Ninth Circuit reversed the conviction, holding that the testimony was relevant to the entrapment defense and further stated that "[w]hen credible qualified experts disagree, a criminal defendant is entitled to have the jury, not the judge, decide whether the government has proved its case." *Id.* The Ninth Circuit has also refused to apply a "*Daubert*-quality evidence" requirement to government action, stating that it would "impose an unreasonable burden on the legislative process." Gammoh v. City of La Habra, 395 F.3d 1114, *amended on denial of rehearing,* 402 F.3d 875 (9th Cir. 2005) (citing G.M. Enterprises, Inc. v. Town of St. Joseph, 350 F.3d 631, 640 (7th Cir. 2003).

(continued)

Circuit	Recent Noteworthy Cases

Tenth
- *Attorney General of Oklahoma v. Tyson Foods, Inc.*, 565 F.3d 769 (10th Cir. 2009). The plaintiff alleged that "poultry litter" produced by poultry growers who contracted with Tyson Foods was polluting the Illinois River Watershed (IRW) and sought a preliminary injunction to enjoin Tyson from applying or allowing to be applied any poultry waste to IRW lands. The district court, which denied the preliminary injunction request, had excluded the testimony of the plaintiff's proffered experts on the basis that the testimony was insufficiently reliable. The plaintiff argued on appeal that the district court had erred because it had found the testimony was admissible but then subsequently held it was unreliable. The court rejected this argument, noting that a judge conducting a bench trial maintains greater leeway in admitting questionable evidence, weighing its persuasive value on presentation. The court further noted in affirming the district court's decision that, "when experts employ established methods in their usual manner, they need not take issue under Daubert; however, where established methods are employed in new ways, a district court may require further indications of reliability." *Id.* at 780.
- *United States v. Nacchio*, 555 F.3d 1234 (10th Cir. Feb. 26, 2009). The defendant was convicted of insider trading and, three days before trial, had disclosed for the first time a professor of law and finance to provide expert testimony in support of his defense. The district court excluded the expert's testimony, largely on grounds that the defendant had failed to establish the reliability of the proffered expert's opinions. The court upheld the trial court's decision rejecting the defendant's argument that the admissibility and reliability of the expert's opinion could be established on the witness stand.
- *McDonald v. North American Specialty Ins. Co.*, 224 F. App. 761 (10th Cir. 2007). A structural engineer who could not account for alternative causes was allowed to testify. The Tenth Circuit deferred to the trial court's broad discretion regarding proof of alternative causes on the admissibility of expert witness testimony.
- *United States v. Lauder*, 409 F.3d 1254, 1263 (10th Cir. 2005). In *Lauder*, the Tenth Circuit emphasized that the development of a sufficient record is an important part of the district court's gate-keeping function.

Eleventh
- *Boca Raton Community Hospital v. Tenet Health Care Corp.*, 582 F.3d 1227 (11th Cir. 2009). The plaintiff, a Palm Beach County, Florida, hospital, brought suit against Tenet Health Care Corporation for allegedly engaging in "turbocharging" the Medicare/Medicaid

Circuit	Recent Noteworthy Cases

system, which resulted in the plaintiff receiving less money from the system for care it provided than it would have received if not for Tenet's alleged turbocharging. The court upheld the district court's exclusion of the plaintiff's proffered damages expert because the expert's damages theory "did not fit" its liability theory. The plaintiff's proffered expert had held Tenet to a stricter standard for injury and damages than its liability theory did for culpability. Specifically, for purposes of its liability theory, certain overcharges by Tenet were not considered unlawful, but those same over-charges were included in computing the plaintiff's damages even though they were not unlawfully obtained. The court described the expert's damages theory as "an oversized coat" that "covered too much" and stated that "[h]aving tailored a trim-fitting liability theory for the body of its case against Tenet, Boca cannot hang a baggy injury and damages theory on it. Whatever expert opinion Boca provided had to be suitably proportioned." *Id.* at 15.

- *Wilson v. Taser International, Inc.*, 303 F. App'x 708 (11th Cir. 2008) (unpublished). The plaintiff, a Georgia state trooper, was injured after volunteering to be shocked with a TASER gun during a training class. He offered the testimony of his physician in support of his claim that the shock had caused two compression fractures on his thoracic spine. The district court excluded the physician's testimony on the basis that it was unreliable, a decision that the Eleventh Circuit affirmed. The court stated that "in addressing the reliability of expert methodology, '[d]istrict courts "have substantial discretion in deciding how to test an expert's reliability."'" *Id.* at 713 (quoting Rink v. Cheminova, Inc., 400 F.3d 1286, 1292 (11th Cir. 2005); United States v. Majors, 196 F.3d 1206, 1215 (11th Cir. 1999)). The Eleventh Circuit noted that the four *Daubert* factors "may guide a district court's reliability inquiry, but the district court ultimately has 'broad latitude' as to how it determines reliability.'" *Id.* at 714 (quoting *Kumho Tire*, 526 U.S. at 152). Ultimately, the court stated that the plaintiff's physician had not demonstrated that his opinion that TASER exposure could cause compression fractures was testable, had not offered an error rate for his opinion, and his opinion had not been peer reviewed or shown to be generally accepted.
- *Corwin v. Walt Disney Co.*, 475 F.3d 1239 (11th Cir. 2007). The plaintiff sued Disney, claiming copyright infringement. He claimed that the EPCOT theme park at Walt Disney World Resort in Florida was copied from a painting he had inherited, which depicted an international theme park in miniature, and that the painting had been presented to Disney representatives in 1962 or 1963, and the company

(continued)

Circuit	Recent Noteworthy Cases

had rejected it. In support of his claims, the plaintiff sought to introduce the testimony of four expert witnesses in the areas of design, history, and organizational principles underlying theme parks, among others, in an attempt to prove that EPCOT had been copied from the plaintiff's painting. The court upheld the trial court's exclusion of portions of all four experts' reports on the basis that the reports focused on the concepts and ideas behind EPCOT rather than on the expression of those concepts and ideas. Therefore, the court held, the district court did not abuse its discretion in excluding the reports.

Appendix B: Key Decisions by State[93]

State	Daubert Adopted	Daubert Adopted, but Limited	Daubert Is Instructive	Daubert Rejected	Statute or Seminal Case
Alabama		X			Alabama Code section 36-18-30 mandates that the *Daubert* test be applied to "[e]xpert testimony or evidence relating to the use of genetic markers contained in or derived from DNA for identification purposes." The Alabama Supreme Court has refused to apply *Daubert* outside this specific circumstance. AAA Cooper Transp. v. Philyaw, 842 So. 2d 689, 690 n.1 (Ala. 2002).
Alaska	X				*State v. Coon*, 974 P.2d 386 (Alaska 1999) (discussing at length why *Frye* is inconsistent with Alaska Rule of Evidence 702, adopting *Daubert* and limiting *Frye*).
Arizona				X	*Logerquist v. McVey*, 1 P.3d 113 (Ariz. 2000). The court retained *Frye* and rejected *Daubert* on the grounds that *Daubert* permits "judicial activism" because it grants "the judge authority to preclude evidence because the judge disagrees with the methodology used by the witness or believes the methodology is unreliable or the witness is less credible than the witness produced by the other side." Under the common law of evidence and the Federal Rules of Evidence, the trial judge "had authority to exclude evidence when it violated some rule of law, such as the best evidence rule or the hearsay rule."
Arkansas	X				*Farm Bureau Mut. Ins. Co of Ark. v. Foote*, 14 S.W.3d 512 (Ark. 2000) (adopting *Daubert*).

93. For an additional discussion of the states' treatment of *Daubert*, see *infra* chapter 7.

(continued)

State	Daubert Adopted	Daubert Adopted, but Limited	Daubert Is Instructive	Daubert Rejected	Statute or Seminal Case
California				X	*Cooley v. Superior Court*, 57 P.3d 654 (Cal. 2002) (holding that *Daubert* does not displace People v. Kelly, 549 P.2d 1240 (Cal. 1976), which construed the California Evidence Code in adopting its standard for admissibility).
Colorado			X		*People v. Shreck*, 22 P.3d 68, 77 (Colo. 2001) (adopting a "totality of the circumstances" test for scientific expert evidence that focuses on whether the evidence involved is both relevant and reliable. In assessing reliability, courts are directed to conduct a broad inquiry and may consider the factors set forth in *Daubert*). Reaffirmed in *Golob v. People*, 180 P.3d 1006, 1011 (Colo. 2008).
Connecticut	X				*State v. Porter*, 698 A.2d 739, 746 (Conn. 1997) (adopting *Daubert*).
Delaware	X				*M.G. Bancorporation, Inc. v. LeBeau*, 737 A.2d 513 (Del. 1999) (adopting *Daubert*).
Florida				X	*Ibar v. State*, 938 So. 2d 451, 467 (Fla. 2006) ("Florida courts do not follow *Daubert*, but instead follow the test set out in *Frye v. United States*, 293 F. 1013, 1014 (D.C. Cir. 1923).").

Georgia	X	*Mason v. Home Depot U.S.A.*, 658 S.E.2d 603 (Ga. 2008) (holding that because it is proper to consider and give weight to constructions placed on the federal rules by federal courts when applying or construing a statute based on those rules and the Georgia rule regarding expert testimony was based on Federal Rule of Evidence 702, the trial court's application of the standards of *Daubert* was proper).
Hawaii	X	*State v. Vliet*, 19 P.3d 42, 53 (Haw. 2001) (expressly refraining from adopting *Daubert* but holding that because the Hawaii Rules of Evidence are patterned after the federal rules, *Daubert* is "instructive" in interpreting the state rule).
Idaho	X	*Weeks v. Eastern Idaho Health Serv.*, 153 P.3d 1180 (Idaho 2007) ("The Court has not adopted the *Daubert* standard for admissibility of an expert's testimony but has used some of *Daubert's* standards in assessing whether the basis of an expert's opinion is scientifically valid."). Idaho's test for admissibility of expert evidence is simply to follow the language of Idaho Rule of Evidence 702. *State v. Merwin*, 962 P.2d 1026, 1029-30 (Idaho 1995). Because this standard is vague, the Idaho Court of Appeals has looked to *Daubert* for guidance on several occasions. *See, e.g., State v. Siegal*, 50 P.3d 1033, 1042-43 (Idaho Ct. App. 2002); *State v. Parkinson*, 909 P.2d 647, 652 (Idaho Ct. App. 1996). However, the Idaho Supreme Court has reaffirmed its rejection of the application of *Daubert* to expert testimony and cited with approval a "bare analysis" of expert testimony conducted by a trial court. *Carnell v. Barker Mgmt., Inc.*, 48 P.3d 651, 656-57 (Idaho 2002).

(continued)

State	Daubert Adopted	Daubert Adopted, but Limited	Daubert Is Instructive	Daubert Rejected	Statute or Seminal Case
Illinois				X	*People v. McKown*, 875 N.E.2d 1029 (Ill. 2007) (noting that the Illinois courts have not addressed the issue of whether *Daubert* should supplant *Frye* and hinting that this issue is ripe for its consideration). In the meantime, Illinois case law is replete with references that Illinois law is "unequivocal" in that the exclusive test for the admission of expert testimony is the general acceptance test of *Frye*. See, e.g., *Donaldson v. Cent. Ill. Pub. Serv. Co*, 767 N.E.2d 314 (Ill. 2002) ("Illinois law is unequivocal: the exclusive test for the admission of expert testimony is governed by the standard first expressed in *Frye*.").
Indiana			X		*Malinski v. State*, 794 N.E.2d 1071, 1084 (Ind. 2003) (holding that *Daubert* is "helpful, but not controlling" in interpreting its rule of evidence). Indiana Rule of Evidence 702(b), unlike the pre-2000 Federal Rules of Evidence, provides that expert scientific evidence may be admitted only if "the court is satisfied that the scientific principles upon which the expert testimony rests are reliable." IND. R. EVID. 702(b).
Iowa			X		*Leaf v. Goodyear Tire & Rubber Co.*, 590 N.W.2d 525, 533 (Iowa 1999) (holding that Iowa courts are not required to consider the *Daubert* factors, but they may do so if they find that the factors are "helpful," especially in complex cases).

State				
Kansas	X			*Kuhn v. Sandoz Pharms. Corp.*, 14 P.3d 1170 (Kan. 2000) (rejecting *Daubert* and reaffirming *Frye*). *Kuxhausen v. Tillman Partners*, 197 P.3d 859 (Kan. 2008) (applying the *Frye* standard).
Kentucky		X		*Mitchell v. Commonwealth*, 908 S.W.2d 100 (Ky. 1995) (adopting *Daubert*), *overruled on other grounds by Fugate v. Commonwealth*, 993 S.W.2d 931 (Ky. 1999).
Louisiana		X		*State v. Foret*, 628 So. 2d 1116 (La. 1993) (adopting *Daubert*).
Maine			X	Maine has not adopted *Daubert*. *State v. Bickart*, 963 A.2d 183 (Me. 2009) ("In evaluating the reliability of Smith's testimony, the court correctly noted that we have not adopted the *Daubert* standard applied by federal courts."). However, its analysis of its own version of Rule 702 parallels *Daubert*, and the Maine Supreme Court cites *Daubert* along with its own cases. *See State v. MacDonald*, 718 A.2d 195, 198 (Me. 1998).
Maryland		X		*Burral v. State*, 724 A.2d 65, 80 (Md. 1999) ("We have not abandoned *Frye* or *Reed*."); *Clemons v. State*, 896 A.2d 1059 (Md. 2006) ("Maryland has continued to adhere to the *Frye* test rather than the *Daubert* standard.").
Massachusetts	X			*Commonwealth v. Lanigan*, 641 N.E.2d 1342 (Mass. 1994) (adopting *Daubert*).

(continued)

State	Daubert Adopted	Daubert Adopted, but Limited	Daubert Is Instructive	Daubert Rejected	Statute or Seminal Case
Michigan	X				*Gilbert v. Daimler Chrysler Corp.*, 685 N.W.2d 391 (Mich. 2004). Michigan Rule of Evidence 702 has "been amended explicitly to incorporate *Daubert's* standards of reliability. But this modification of MRE 702 changes only the factors that a court may consider in determining whether expert opinion evidence is admissible . . . Thus, properly understood, the court's gatekeeper role is the same under *Davis-Frye* and *Daubert*." *Id.*
Minnesota				X	*Goeb v. Tharaldson*, 615 N.W.2d 800 (Minn. 2000) (reviewing the cases and commentary surrounding the issue, reaffirming adherence to *Frye* and rejecting *Daubert* because "*Frye-Mack* is more apt to ensure 'objective and uniform rulings' as to particular scientific methods or techniques—our primary concern in previously refusing to abandon *Frye-Mack* in *Schwartz*").
Mississippi	X				MISS. R. EVID. 702; *Jones v. State*, 918 So.2 d 1220, 1226 (Miss. 2005) (holding that after years of applying the *Frye* standard on the issue of admissibility of expert testimony, the court would now apply the *Daubert* standard).
Missouri			X		*State Board of Reg. for Healing Arts v. McDonagh*, 123 S.W.3d 146 (Mo. 2003). To the extent that section 490.065 (of the Missouri Rules of Evidence) mirrors Federal Rules of Evidence 702 and 703, as interpreted and applied in *Daubert* and its progeny, the cases interpreting those federal rules provide relevant and useful guidance in interpreting and applying section 490.065.

State			Case
Montana	X		*State v. Moore*, 885 P.2d 457 (Mont. 1994) (adopting *Daubert*).
Nebraska	X		*Schafersman v. Agland Coop.*, 631 N.W.2d 862 (Neb. 2001) (adopting *Daubert*).
Nevada		X	*Krause Inc. v. Little*, 34 P.3d 566 (Nev. 2002) ("We have previously declined to adopt the *Daubert* standard. We now take this opportunity to reaffirm our existing legal standard concerning the admissibility of expert testimony."). Nevada follows a liberal test for the admission of expert testimony. *Dow Chem. Co. v. Mahlum*, 970 P.2d 98, 108 n.3 (Nev. 1998). While the Nevada court has not adopted *Daubert*, it has stated that *Daubert* and the federal court decisions discussing it may provide persuasive authority in determining whether expert testimony should be admitted in Nevada courts. *Hallmark v. Eldridge*, 189 P.3d 646 (Nev. 2008) (citing *Dow*).
New Hampshire	X		*Baker Valley Lumber, Inc. v. Ingersoll-Rand Co.*, 813 A.2d 409 (N.H. 2002) (adopting *Daubert*).
New Jersey	X		*State v. Chun*, 943 A.2d 114 (N.J. 2008), *cert denied*, 129 S. Ct. 158 (2008) (applying the *Frye* standard).
New Mexico	X		*State v. Alberico*, 861 P.2d 192 (N.M. Ct. App. 1993) (adopting *Daubert*).
New York	X		*Parker v. Mobil Oil Corp.*, 857 N.E.2d 1114 (N.Y. 2006) (applying the *Frye* standard).

(continued)

State	Daubert Adopted	Daubert Adopted, but Limited	Daubert Is Instructive	Daubert Rejected	Statute or Seminal Case
North Carolina	X				*State v. Goode*, 461 S.E.2d 631 (N.C. 1995) (adopting *Daubert*).
North Dakota				X	*State v. Hernandez*, 707 N.W.2d 449, 453 (N.D. 2005) (explaining that the court "has a formal process for adopting procedural rules after appropriate study and recommendation by the Joint Procedure Committee" and declining to adopt *Daubert* by "judicial decision"). The North Dakota standard "envisions generous allowance of the use of expert testimony if the witnesses are shown to have some degree of expertise in the field in which they are to testify." *Hamilton v. Oppen*, 653 N.W.2d 678, 683 (N.D. 2002). This standard is far more liberal than *Daubert*. *Id.*
Ohio	X				*State v. Nemeth*, 694 N.E.2d 1332 (Ohio 1998) (adopting *Daubert*).
Oklahoma	X				*Christian v. Gray*, 65 P.3d 591 (Okla. 2003) (adopting *Daubert* for civil cases); *Harris v. State*, 13 P.3d 489 (Okla. Crim. App. 2000) (applying *Daubert*).
Oregon			X		*State v. O'Key*, 899 P.2d 663, 680 n.7 (Or. 1995) (expressly holding that *Daubert* is not binding but adopting a similar gatekeeping rule for scientific evidence).
Pennsylvania				X	*Grady v. Frito-Lay, Inc.*, 839 A.2d 1038, 1044-45 (Pa. 2003) (holding, "after careful consideration," that "the *Frye* rule will continue to be applied in Pennsylvania," because in the court's

State			
Rhode Island	X		view, "*Frye's* 'general acceptance' test is a proven and workable rule, which when faithfully followed, fairly serves its purpose of assisting the courts in determining when scientific evidence is reliable and should be admitted"). *Gregg v. V-J Auto Parts, Co.,* 943 A.2d 216 (Pa. 2007) ("We first adopted the *Frye* test in *Commonwealth v. Topa,* 369 A.2d 1277 (Pa. 1977) and more recently reaffirmed it in *Grady v. Frito-Lay,* 576 Pa. 546, 839 A.2d 1038 (2003), notwithstanding the United States Supreme Court's departure from *Frye* in *Daubert v. Merrell Dow Pharms., Inc.,* 509 U.S. 579, 113 S.Ct. 2786, 125 L.Ed.2d 469 (1993)."). *Raimbeault v. Takeuchi Mfg. (U.S.), Ltd.,* 772 A.2d 1056 (R.I. 2001) (adopting *Daubert*).
South Carolina		X	South Carolina's test, like *Daubert,* imposes a gatekeeping requirement for scientific evidence. *State v. Council,* 515 S.E.2d 508 (S.C. 1999). However, South Carolina's test uses different factors to assess reliability: "(1) the publications and peer review of the technique; (2) prior application of the method to the type of evidence involved in the case; (3) the quality control procedures used to ensure reliability; and (4) the consistency of the method with recognized scientific laws and procedures." *Id.* at 517. Unlike the *Daubert* factors, which are merely illustrative, South Carolina courts must apply their state's four factors. *Id.* at 517–18. *See also State v. Jones,* 681 S.E. 2d 580, 590 (S.C. 2009) (noting that "this state has not adopted the standards set forth in *Frye v. United States,* 293 F. 1013 (D.C. Cir. 1923) or *Daubert v. Merrell Dow Pharmaceuticals, Inc.,* 509 U.S. 579 (1993).").

(continued)

251

State	Daubert Adopted	Daubert Adopted, but Limited	Daubert Is Instructive	Daubert Rejected	Statute or Seminal Case
South Dakota	X				*State v. Hofer*, 512 N.W.2d 482 (S.D. 1994) (adopting *Daubert*).
Tennessee			X		*McDaniel v. CSX Transp., Inc.*, 955 S.W.2d 257, 265 (Tenn. 1997) (stating that "[a]lthough we do not expressly adopt *Daubert*, the non-exclusive list of factors to determine reliability are useful in applying our Rules 702 and 703").
Texas	X				*E.I. du Pont de Nemours & Co., Inc. v. Robinson*, 923 S.W.2d 549 (Tex. 1995) (adopting *Daubert*).
Utah				X	In *State v. Crosby*, 927 P.2d 638, 642 (Utah 1996), the Utah Supreme Court determined that its long-held standard was similar to, although less flexible than, *Daubert*. Under Utah's standard, the court must determine whether scientific evidence is "inherently reliable" before it can be admitted. Such a determination involves exploration of "the correctness of the scientific principles underlying the testimony, the accuracy and reliability of the techniques used in applying the principles to the subject matter before the court and in reaching the conclusion expressed in the opinion, and the qualifications of those actually gathering the data and analyzing it." *State v. Rimmasch*, 775 P.2d 388, 403 (Utah 1989). The trail court should "carefully explore each logical link in the chain that leads to the expert testimony given in court and to determine its reliability." *Id.* However, the Utah test applies only to expert testimony "based on newly discovered

State			
Vermont	X		"principles" or testimony based on "novel scientific methods and techniques." *Alder v. Bayer Corp, AGFA Div*, 61 P.3d 1068, 1083–84 (Utah 2002). *State v. Streich*, 658 A.2d 38 (Vt. 1995) (adopting *Daubert*).
Virginia		X	Virginia imposes a duty on the trial court, as in *Daubert*, to make a threshold finding of reliability whenever "unfamiliar" scientific evidence is offered. *Satcher v. Commonwealth*, 421 S.E.2d 821, 835 (Va. 1992). However, Virginia has expressly left open the question of whether the *Daubert* factors could be applied to this determination. *John v. Im*, 559 S.E.2d 694, 698 (Va. 2002).
Washington		X	*State v. Copeland*, 922 P.2d 1304, 1320 (Wash. 1996) (holding that "*Frye* remains the standard for admissibility of novel scientific evidence in Washington").
West Virginia	X		*Wilt v. Buracker*, 443 S.E.2d 196 (W.Va. 1993) (adopting *Daubert*).
Wisconsin		X	Wisconsin, while not ruling out the possibility that it will someday adopt *Daubert*, for now eschews any substantive test for admissibility of expert testimony, instead considering credentials sufficient. *Conley Publ'g Group Ltd. v. Journal Commc'ns, Inc.*, 665 N.W.2d 879, 892 (Wis. 2003).
Wyoming	X		*Bunting v. Jamieson*, 984 P.2d 467 (Wyo. 1999) (adopting *Daubert*).

CHAPTER 7

Experts in State Court

W. Michel Pierson[1]

This chapter provides a thumbnail sketch[2] of some of the salient features of state evidence law that relate to expert witnesses. To do this, a series of 11 topics are presented, each of which involves an issue that commonly arises in the course of presenting expert evidence and/or litigating questions relating to expert evidence in the course of a trial. Within each topic, an attempt is made to catalogue the position of each state on the issue by the citation of representative authority from that state in the form of an appellate

---

1. W. Michel Pierson has served as associate judge of the Circuit Court for Baltimore City, Maryland, since January 2004. He previously engaged in a litigation practice, including trial and appellate work in federal and state courts. He served as law clerk to Hon. C. Stanley Blair, U.S. District Judge, District of Maryland from 1973 to 1974, after graduating from the University of Maryland School of Law in 1973, where he was editor in chief of the *Maryland Law Review* and elected to the Order of the Coif. He is an elected member of the American Law Institute, a member of the Maryland Court of Appeals Standing Committee on Rules of Practice and Procedure, a member of the American College of Business Court Judges, and an adjunct faculty member at the University of Maryland School of Law.

2. The confines of this treatment do not permit an extended commentary or any exploration of doctrinal subtleties. Most states have an abundance of expository material concerning evidentiary law, including periodical articles, handbooks, and treatises; even a bibliography of these items would expand beyond the space limitations of this chapter. The objective here is to provide you with an entry into each state's doctrine. There is no attempt at analysis, nor at completeness. Insofar as any choice is made, there is a preference for recent authority.

Restrictions of space have also required the exclusion of other topics that affect the presentation of expert evidence. There has been no attempt to cover state decisional authority concerning the qualifications of experts. For the most part, there is no significant diversity among the states in this regard. Nor is there any attempt to cover the requirements for pretrial disclosure. Every state has such rules, and the state decisional authority is consistent concerning the consequences of noncompliance with these rules. Similarly, there is no treatment of other discovery issues relating to experts that have been the subject of much litigation, such as work product issues or the permissible scope of discovery concerning facts that might bear on expert bias. The focus here is on trial and evidence.

case or a state rule of evidence. The choice of topics focuses on practical subjects that the litigator will face in the course of presenting expert evidence in the courts of the particular state. In particular, this chapter addresses the following topics:

- Does the state have procedural rules for expert testimony comparable to the federal rules?
- Does the state follow *Frye*[3] or *Daubert*?[4]
- What is the appellate standard of review for a *Frye/Daubert* decision?
- What is the state law concerning (1) permissible bases of expert opinion and admissibility of those bases, and (2) the need for disclosure of the basis of the expert's opinion?
- What is the state law concerning opinions on ultimate issues?
- May the proponent of expert testimony introduce the expert's deposition at trial without a showing of unavailability?
- May the expert remain in the courtroom despite a rule excluding witnesses?
- Must the expert be formally tendered?
- What is the rule concerning use of learned treatises?
- Must the expert's opinion embody a specific degree of certainty?
- What is the state rule concerning admission of expert opinion in documents?

The two phenomena that have driven the development of state evidence law in recent decades are the adoption of rules or codes of evidence that displace or supplement the common law of evidence and the evolution of standards for assessing the reliability of expert evidence. These developments, which have generated a body of law governing evidence in federal courts, have fostered a movement toward greater uniformity among the states, although significant variations still exist. Here, these subjects are used as tools to frame the outline of state law relating to experts, by comparing the states' treatment of an issue to the pertinent federal rule or doctrine, which facilitates an abbreviated sketch of each state's doctrine on that point. Where possible, the state variations are presented through tables, to permit ready reference, with brief explanations of the state differences.

Even with the increasing commonality of state evidence principles, the brevity of this treatment necessarily requires the omission of important variations that may have a bearing on specific types of cases. Many states have statutory provisions that may affect presentation of expert testimony in a particular case. For example, it is quite common for states to have

---

3. Frye v. United States, 293 F. 1013 (D.C. Cir. 1923).
4. Daubert v. Merrell Dow Pharms. Inc., 509 U.S. 579 (1993).

special provisions relating to expert testimony in medical malpractice cases or other types of professional negligence cases. Likewise, statutes have been enacted in many states that regulate the presentation of evidence relating to DNA. You must be alert for such provisions.

Does the State Have Procedural Rules for Expert Testimony Comparable to the Federal Rules?

Forty-two states have adopted rules of evidence based on the Federal Rules of Evidence and/or the Uniform Rules of Evidence. With a few exceptions, the numbering of the state rules tracks the numbering system of the federal rules. Most of the provisions of Article VII relating to opinions and expert testimony have been adopted by the states, with a relatively limited number of significant variations.

In the federal rules, Article VII encompasses six rules:

Rule 701. Opinion Testimony by Lay Witnesses
Rule 702. Testimony by Experts
Rule 703. Bases of Opinion Testimony by Experts
Rule 704. Opinion on Ultimate Issue
Rule 705. Disclosure of Facts or Data Underlying Expert Opinion
Rule 706. Court Appointed Experts

Article VII of the 1974 version of the Uniform Rules of Evidence[5] closely tracked the Federal Rules of Evidence. As a result, those states that adopted the Uniform Rules of Evidence essentially adopted the federal rules. Other states patterned their rules directly on the federal rules through the work of drafting committees.

The Article VII provisions of the federal rules were amended in several respects in 2000. Rule 701 (Opinion Testimony by Lay Witnesses) was amended to add an express provision that lay opinions could not include opinions based on scientific, specialized, or other technical knowledge within the scope of Rule 702.[6] Rule 702 (Testimony by Experts) was amended for the purpose of explicitly incorporating the *Daubert*[7] test. Rule 703 (Bases of Opinion Testimony by Experts) was amended to provide that facts relied on

---

5. Uniform Rules of Evidence (1974), 13A UNIFORM LAWS ANNOTATED 210 (2004) [hereinafter U.L.A.].

6. 192 F.R.D. 398, 400 (2000).

7. *Daubert*, 509 U.S. 579.

by an expert that were otherwise inadmissible should not be disclosed to the jury unless the court determines that their probative value in assisting the jury to assess the expert's opinion substantially outweighs their prejudicial effect.[8] Some states have adopted some of the 2000 amendments and some have not.

Rule 702 of the Uniform Rules was amended in 1999 to provide a test for admission of expert opinion that adopted a reliability standard incorporating both *Frye*[9] and *Daubert*.[10] No state has yet adopted this version of Rule 702.

Nine jurisdictions have not adopted rules of evidence: California, the District of Columbia, Georgia, Illinois, Kansas, Massachusetts, Missouri, New York, and Virginia. Of those nine jurisdictions, several have one or more statutory provisions that parallel some of the rules contained in Article VII.

Tables A-E in appendix A list the state rules that are comparable to the Article VII rules.

Does the State Follow Frye *or* Daubert?

Reliability standards for expert testimony have been the subject of extensive discussion, revolving around the issues discussed in *Frye, Daubert,* and *Kumho Tire Co. v. Carmichael*.[11] There is great diversity among the states on this subject. Some states have adopted the *Daubert* standard for all types of expert testimony, while others have adopted *Daubert* only for testimony based on scientific principles. Some states continue to apply *Frye*. Other states apply neither.

Although the Supreme Court opinion in *Daubert* stated that its conclusions were derived from the language of Federal Rule of Evidence 702, not all courts in states with rules based on Rule 702 have followed this reasoning. As a result, the language of the state counterpart of Rule 702 does not govern whether the state has adopted the *Daubert* standard.

The following list describes the position of each state on this topic. However, labeling a state as a *Daubert* state or a *Frye* state does not adequately convey the variations in the different positions of the states or express the complexities of each state's doctrine. There are many additional nuances encompassed within each state's general stance. For example, *Frye* states

---

8. 192 F.R.D. at 400.
9. *Frye,* 293 F. 1013.
10. *Supra* note 6; Unif. R. Evid. 702 (1999), 13A U.L.A. 140 (2004).
11. Kumho Tire Co. v. Carmichael, 526 U.S. 137 (1999).

may end their inquiry with the question of whether the general methodology enjoys general acceptance or may require a showing of the reliability of the individual expert's application of the general principle to the specific facts of the case. Similar variations exist within states' *Daubert* analyses. Where the *Frye/Daubert* examination is confined to scientific evidence, there remains the issue of what reliability standards apply to other evidence. The cases listed in this section must be regarded as starting points for research into the state's law on this topic.

- Alabama has not adopted *Daubert*. *Frye* applies to opinions that are based on a scientific principle, method, or procedure.[12] Some standards have been adopted by statute for specific principles; for example, *Daubert* applies to DNA testing.[13]
- Alaska has adopted *Daubert*.[14] However, it has limited its application to expert testimony based on scientific principles.[15]
- Arizona has expressly declined to follow *Daubert* and held that *Frye* applies to novel scientific principles but not to other forms of expert testimony, which are governed by the literal terms of Rule 702.[16]
- Arkansas has adopted *Daubert*.[17] Rule 702 applies to all types of expert testimony.[18]
- California continues to adhere to its version of *Frye*, which is the *Kelly-Frye* test.[19] This test applies only to evidence based on novel scientific principles.[20]
- Colorado has expressly abandoned *Frye*, holding that Colorado Rule 702 mandates a reliability analysis applicable to all types of expert evidence. The standard is flexible, and may or may not involve *Daubert* factors.[21]
- Connecticut adopted *Daubert* for scientific evidence in *State v. Porter*.[22] The court has declined to extend its use beyond scientific evidence.[23]

---

12. ArvinMeritor, Inc. v. Johnson, 1 So. 3d 77 (Ala. App. 2008).
13. Turner v. State, 746 So. 2d 355 (Ala. 1998).
14. State v. Coon, 974 P.2d 386 (Alaska 1999).
15. Marron v. Stromstad, 123 P.3d 992 (Alaska 2005).
16. Logerquist v. McVey, 1 P.3d 113 (Ariz. 2000).
17. Farm Bureau Mut. Ins. Co. v. Foote, 14 S.W.3d 512 (Ark. 2000).
18. Coca-Cola Bottling Co. v. Gill, 100 S.W.3d 715 (Ark. 2003). *But see* Turbyfill v. State, S.W.3d 557 (Ark. App. 2005) (*Daubert* factors apply only to novel opinion).
19. People v. Leahy, 882 P.2d 321 (Cal. 1994).
20. People v. Stoll, 783 P.2d 698 (Cal. 1989).
21. People v. Shreck, 22 P.3d 68 (Colo. 2001).
22. State v. Porter, 698 A.2d 739 (Conn. 1997).
23. State v. Sorabella, 891 A.2d 897 (Conn. 2006).

- Delaware follows *Daubert* and applies it to all expert testimony in accordance with *Kumho Tire*.[24]
- The District of Columbia applies *Frye* to novel scientific evidence.[25]
- In Florida, the *Frye* test applies to novel scientific evidence, and where expert testimony is deduced from a scientific principle, the principle must have general acceptance. This does not apply to "pure opinion testimony."[26]
- In Georgia, *Daubert* was adopted by statute in civil cases.[27] In other cases, the standard is whether the principle has reached a scientific state of verifiable certainty.[28]
- Hawaii employs a reliability analysis that follows that of *Daubert* and *Kumho Tire*.[29] It applies to all expert testimony based on specialized knowledge.
- Idaho has rejected *Frye*.[30] It employs a reliability analysis based on Rule 702.[31] Idaho has not, however, adopted *Daubert*.[32]
- Illinois follows *Frye*.[33] It applies only to novel scientific principles.[34]
- Indiana has adopted *Daubert* analysis for expert testimony based on scientific principles.[35] It does not extend to expert testimony not based on scientific principles.[36]
- Iowa has declined to adopt *Daubert*, applying instead an "expansive test" under which trial judges have discretion to determine reliability by assessing factors that may include *Daubert* factors.[37]
- Kansas applies *Frye* to new or experimental scientific techniques.[38] It does not apply to pure opinion testimony developed from inductive

24. M.G. Bancorporation v. Le Beau, 737 A.2d 513 (Del. 1999).
25. Roberts v. United States, 916 A.2d 922 (D.C. 2007).
26. Flanagan v. State, 625 So. 2d 827 (Fla. 1993); Marsh v. Valyou, 977 So. 2d 543 (Fla. 2007).
27. GA. CODE ANN. § 24-9-67.1(f); Mason v. Home Depot U.S.A., Inc., 658 S.E.2d 603 (Ga. 2008).
28. Mann v. State, 645 S.E.2d 573 (Ga. App. 2007).
29. State v. Vliet, 19 P.3d 42 (Haw. 2001).
30. State v. Faught, 908 P.2d 566 (Idaho 1995).
31. Weeks v. East Idaho Health Servs., 153 P.3d 1180 (Idaho 2007).
32. Swallow v. Emergency Med. of Idaho, P.A., 67 P.3d 68 (Idaho 2003).
33. Donaldson v. Cent. Ill. Pub. Serv. Co., 767 N.E.2d 314 (Ill. 2002).
34. *In re* Marriage of Alexander, 857 N.E.2d 766 (Ill. App. 2006).
35. McGrew v. State, 682 N.E.2d 1289 (Ind. 1997).
36. Fueger v. Case Corp., 886 N.E.2d 102 (Ind. App. 2008).
37. Leaf v. Goodyear Tire & Rubber Co., 590 N.W.2d 525 (Iowa 2007).
38. Kuxhausen v. Tillman Partners, L.P., 197 P.3d 859 (Kan. App. 2008).

reasoning based on the expert's own experience, observation, or research.[39]

- Kentucky follows *Daubert*.[40] It applies to all expert testimony based on technical or specialized knowledge.[41]
- Louisiana has adopted *Daubert*.[42] It applies to all expert testimony, not just scientific.[43]
- Maine does not apply *Frye*.[44] It has declined to adopt *Daubert*.[45] Expert testimony must meet a threshold level of reliability; where expert testimony "rests on newly ascertained, or applied, scientific principles," a trial court may consider a series of indicia of scientific reliability.[46]
- Maryland applies *Frye* to novel expert scientific testimony.[47]
- Massachusetts adopted *Daubert* in *Commonwealth v. Lanigan*.[48] *Daubert* is equally applicable to expert testimony based on technical or other specialized knowledge.[49]
- Michigan has expressly adopted *Daubert*, as indicated in the amendments to Michigan Rule 702.[50] *Daubert* was also adopted by statute for actions involving injury to person or property.[51]
- Minnesota continues to apply the *Frye* test to evidence based on novel scientific techniques.[52]
- Mississippi applies *Daubert*.[53]
- In Missouri, neither *Frye* nor *Daubert* governs the assessment of reliability. Missouri Revised Statute section 490.065 is the standard for admitting expert testimony in civil cases. That section requires the court to consider whether experts in the field reasonably rely on the type of

39. Kuhn v. Sandoz Pharms. Corp., 14 P.3d 1170 (Kan. 2000).
40. Toyota Motor Corp. v. Gregory, 136 S.W.3d 35 (Ky. 2004).
41. Goodyear Tire & Rubber Co. v. Thompson, 11 S.W.3d 575 (Ky. 2000).
42. State v. Foret, 628 So. 2d 1116 (La. 1993).
43. Independent Fire Ins. Co. v. Sunbeam Corp., 755 So. 2d 226 (La. 2000).
44. State v. Williams, 388 A.2d 500 (Me. 1978).
45. Searles v. Fleetwood Homes of Pennsylvania, Inc., 878 A.2d 509 (Me. 2005).
46. *Id.*
47. Montgomery Mut. Ins. Co. v. Chesson, 923 A.2d 939 (Md. 2007).
48. 641 N.E.2d 1342 (Mass. 1994).
49. Canavan's Case, 733 N.E.2d 1042 (Mass. 2000).
50. Gilbert v. DaimlerChrysler Corp., 685 N.W.2d 391 (Mich. 2004).
51. MICH. COMP. LAWS ANN. § 600.2955.
52. Goeb v. Tharaldson, 615 N.W.2d 800 (Minn. 2000); Jacobson v. $55,900 in United States Currency, 728 N.W.2d 510 (Minn. 2007).
53. Mississippi Transp. Comm'n v. McLemore, 863 So. 2d 31 (Miss. 2003); Smith v. Clement, 983 So. 2d 285 (Miss. 2008).

facts and data used by the expert or if the methodology is otherwise reasonably reliable.[54] *Frye* continues to apply in criminal cases.[55]

- Montana did away with the *Frye* test before *Daubert*.[56] It subsequently adopted *Daubert* but applies it only to expert testimony based on novel scientific evidence.[57]
- Nebraska has adopted *Daubert* for all types of expert evidence.[58]
- Nevada has not expressly adopted *Daubert* but regards it as persuasive authority.[59]
- New Hampshire has adopted *Daubert*.[60] In addition, *Daubert* is enacted by statute.[61]
- New Jersey continues to apply the *Frye* test in criminal cases for determining the reliability of scientific expert testimony.[62] In civil cases, scientific evidence is admissible if it derives from a reliable methodology supported by some expert consensus.[63]
- New Mexico has adopted a standard similar to *Daubert*.[64] It is limited to testimony that requires scientific knowledge.[65]
- New York follows *Frye*.[66] Its application is limited to novel scientific evidence.[67]
- North Carolina has rejected *Daubert* in favor of a "less mechanistic and rigorous" flexible approach to determining reliability.[68] Nor does North Carolina apply *Frye* as such.[69]

---

54. State Bd. of Registration for the Healing Arts v. McDonagh, 123 S.W.3d 146, 153 (Mo. 2003); *cf.* Goddard v. State, 144 S.W.3d 848 (Mo. App. 2004) (opining that *Daubert* applies to testimony based on scientific principles).

55. State v. Daniels, 179 S.W.3d 273 (Mo. App. 2005).

56. Barmeyer v. Montana Power Co., 657 P.2d 594 (Mont. 1983).

57. State v. Moore, 885 P.2d 457 (Mont. 1994); State v. Price, 171 P.3d 293 (Mont. 2007).

58. Schafersman v. Agland Coop, 631 N.W.2d 862 (Neb. 2001).

59. Hallmark v. Eldridge, 189 P.3d 646 (Nev. 2008); Dow Chem. Co. v. Mahlum, 970 P.2d 98 (Nev. 1998).

60. Baker Valley Lumber v. Ingersoll-Rand, 813 A.2d 409 (N.H. 2002).

61. N.H. REV. STAT. ANN. § 516:29-a; *see* Baxter v. Temple, 949 A.2d 167 (N.H. 2008).

62. State v. Harvey, 699 A.2d 596 (N.J. 1997); State v. Moore, 902 A.2d 1212 (N.J. 2006).

63. Hisenaj v. Kuehner, 942 A.2d 769 (N.J. 2008); Kemp v. State, 809 A.2d 77 (N.J. 2002).

64. State v. Alberico, 861 P.2d 192 (N.M. 1993).

65. State v. Torres, 976 P.2d 20 (N.M. 1999).

66. People v. Wesley, 633 N.E.2d 451 (N.Y. 1994).

67. People v. Whitaker, 734 N.Y.S.2d 149 (2001).

68. Howerton v. Arai Helmet, Ltd., 597 S.E.2d 674 (N.C. 2004).

69. State v. Goode, 461 S.E.2d 631 (N.C. 1995).

- North Dakota has not expressly adopted *Daubert*.[70] Rule 702 imposes on the trial court the duty to determine whether expert testimony is reliable and relevant.[71]
- Ohio has adopted *Daubert*.[72]
- Oklahoma adopted *Daubert* for novel scientific evidence in criminal cases in *Taylor v. State*.[73] It held that it applied to all expert testimony in *Christian v. Gray*[74] and *Harris v. State*.[75]
- Oregon has not expressly adopted *Frye* or *Daubert*. The trial court must act as gatekeeper to screen scientific testimony to determine whether it is sufficiently valid, as a matter of science, to legitimately assist the trier of fact. There are 18 factors for the court to consider in performing this task.[76]
- Pennsylvania has expressly rejected *Daubert* in favor of continued adherence to *Frye*.[77] *Frye* applies only to novel scientific evidence.[78]
- Rhode Island has adopted principles similar to *Daubert* for novel or complex scientific testimony.[79] These principles do not apply to other types of expert testimony.[80]
- South Carolina does not apply *Frye* or *Daubert*. Reliability of scientific evidence is measured under a standard involving several factors, including the following: (1) the publications and peer review of the technique, (2) prior application of the method to the type of evidence involved in the case, (3) the quality-control procedures used to ensure reliability, and (4) the consistency of the method with recognized scientific laws and procedures.[81] Rule 702 imposes a reliability requirement for all types of expert evidence, whether or not scientific, but the court has declined to outline a formula that will apply to all types of expert evidence.[82]

---

70. State v. Hernandez, 707 N.W.2d 449 (N.D. 2005); Hamilton v. Oppen, 653 N.W.2d 678 (N.D. 2002).

71. Myer v. Rygg, 630 N.W.2d 62 (N.D. 2001); State v. Burke, 606 N.W.2d 108 (N.D. 2000).

72. Miller v. Bike Athletic Co., 687 N.E.2d 735 (Ohio 1998); Terry v. Caputo, 875 N.E.2d 72 (Ohio 2007).

73. Taylor v. State, 889 P.2d 319 (Okla. Crim. App. 1995).

74. Christian v. Gray, 65 P.3d 591 (Okla. 2003) (civil cases).

75. Harris v. State, 84 P.3d 731 (Okla. Crim. App. 2004) (criminal cases).

76. Marcum v. Adventist Health Sys./W., 193 P.3d 1 (Or. 2008).

77. Grady v. Frito-Lay, Inc., 839 A.2d 1038 (Pa. 2003).

78. Commonwealth v. Dengler, 890 A.2d 372 (Pa. 2005).

79. DiPetrillo v. Dow Chem. Co., 729 A.2d 677 (R.I. 1999).

80. State v. Briggs, 886 A.2d 735 (R.I. 2005).

81. State v. Jones, 259 S.E.2d 120 (S.C. 1979); State v. Council, 515 S.E.2d 508 (S.C. 1999).

82. State v. White, 676 S.E.2d 684 (S.C. 2009).

- South Dakota has adopted *Daubert.*[83] It applies to all varieties of expert opinion based on specialized knowledge.[84]
- Tennessee has abandoned *Frye.* Although it did not expressly adopt *Daubert*, noting language differences between the Tennessee and federal rules, it held that the list of factors in *Daubert* may be employed in Tennessee.[85] These factors also apply to nonscientific expert testimony.[86]
- Texas has adopted the *Daubert* analysis and applies it to all types of expert evidence.[87]
- Utah has discarded *Frye* and follows a standard under which scientific evidence must be shown to have "inherent reliability" to be admitted.[88]
- Vermont has adopted *Daubert.*[89] It applies to all types of expert evidence.[90]
- Virginia has not adopted *Frye* and has not decided whether to adopt *Daubert.*[91] The trial court must make a finding as to whether scientific evidence is reliable based on the testimony of experts.[92]
- Washington adheres to *Frye.*[93] Evidence that does not involve new scientific principles is not subject to *Frye.*[94]
- West Virginia has adopted *Daubert.*[95] It has declined to extend it beyond scientific evidence.[96]
- Wisconsin has not adopted *Frye* or *Daubert*, leaving reliability for the jury.[97]
- Wyoming has adopted *Daubert* and applies it to all types of expert testimony.[98]

83. State v. Hofer, 512 N.W.2d 482 (S.D. 1994).
84. State v. Guthrie, 627 N.W.2d 401 (S.D. 2001).
85. McDaniel v. CSX Transp., Inc., 955 S.W.2d 257 (Tenn. 1997).
86. Brown v. Crown Equip. Corp., 181 S.W.3d 268 (Tenn. 2005).
87. Kelly v. State, 824 S.W.2d 568 (Tex. Crim. App.1992); Gammill v. Jack Williams Chevrolet, 972 S.W.2d 713 (Tex. 1998).
88. State v. Rimmasch, 775 P.2d 388 (Utah 1989); State v. Butterfield, 27 P.3d 1133 (Utah 2001).
89. State v. Brooks, 643 A.2d 226 (Vt. 1993).
90. USGen New England, Inc. v. Town of Rockingham, 862 A.2d 269 (Vt. 2004).
91. John v. Im, 559 S.E.2d 694 (Va. 2002).
92. Spencer v. Commonwealth, 393 S.E.2d 609 (Va. 1990).
93. State v. Copeland, 922 P.2d 1304 (Wash. 1996); State v. Gregory, 147 P.3d 1201 (Wash. 2006).
94. State v. Roberts, 14 P.3d 713 (Wash. 2000).
95. Wilt v. Buracker, 443 S.E.2d 196 (W. Va. 1993).
96. West Virginia Div. of Highways v. Butler, 516 S.E.2d 769 (W. Va. 1999).
97. Conley Publ'g Group Ltd. v. Journal Commc'ns, Inc., 665 N.W.2d 879 (Wis. 2003); State v. Donner, 531 N.W.2d 369 (Wis. 1995).
98. Bunting v. Jamieson, 984 P.2d 467 (Wyo. 1999).

What Is the Appellate Standard of Review
for a Frye/Daubert Decision?

In all states, the abuse of discretion standard applicable to most evidentiary rulings also typically applies to decisions concerning admissibility of expert evidence. However, courts have applied differing standards to decisions concerning reliability of scientific (and sometimes other) evidence. The nature of reliability issues may also affect other facets of appellate review, such as whether the appellate court will take judicial notice of scientific discourse without regard to customary constraints on the appellate record. A list of representative cases from each state follows:

- Alabama: abuse of discretion.[99]
- Alaska: abuse of discretion.[100]
- Arizona: *de novo.*[101]
- Arkansas: abuse of discretion.[102]
- California: mixed question of law and fact subject to limited *de novo* review, with deference to findings of fact.[103]
- Colorado: abuse of discretion; specific findings required.[104]
- Connecticut: abuse of discretion.[105]
- Delaware: abuse of discretion.[106]
- District of Columbia: *de novo.*[107]
- Florida: *de novo.*[108]
- Georgia: abuse of discretion.[109]
- Hawaii: the trial court's decision as to reliability is reviewed under an abuse of discretion standard; decision as to relevance is reviewed *de novo.*[110]
- Idaho: abuse of discretion.[111]
- Illinois: *de novo.*[112]

---

99. ArvinMeritor, Inc. v. Johnson, 1 So. 3d 77 (Ala. App. 2008).
100. State v. Coon, 974 P.2d 386 (Alaska 1999).
101. State v. Tankersley, 956 P.2d 486 (Ariz. 1998).
102. Houston v. State, 906 S.W.2d 286 (Ark. 1995).
103. People v. Hill, 89 Cal. App. 4th 48 (2001).
104. People v. Shreck, 22 P.3d 68 (Colo. 2001).
105. State v. Pappas, 776 A.2d 1091 (Conn. 2001).
106. M.G. Bancorporation v. Le Beau, 737 A.2d 513 (Del. 1999).
107. United States v. Porter, 618 A.2d 629 (D.C. 1992).
108. Arnold v. State, 807 So. 2d 136 (Fla. 2002).
109. Mason v. Home Depot U.S.A., Inc., 658 S.E.2d 603 (Ga. 2008).
110. State v. Vliet, 19 P.3d 42 (Haw. 2001).
111. State v. Crea, 806 P.2d 445 (Idaho 1991).
112. People v. Simons, 821 N.E.2d 1184 (Ill. 2004).

- Indiana: abuse of discretion.[113]
- Iowa: abuse of discretion.[114]
- Kansas: *de novo*.[115]
- Kentucky: abuse of discretion.[116]
- Louisiana: abuse of discretion.[117]
- Maine: abuse of discretion.[118]
- Maryland: *de novo* review, with deference to findings of fact.[119]
- Massachusetts: abuse of discretion.[120]
- Michigan: abuse of discretion.[121]
- Minnesota: *de novo* standard.[122]
- Mississippi: abuse of discretion.[123]
- Missouri: abuse of discretion.[124]
- Montana: abuse of discretion.[125]
- Nebraska: *de novo* standard applies to whether the trial court abdicated its gatekeeping function; decision to admit or exclude the evidence subject to abuse of discretion.[126]
- Nevada: abuse of discretion.[127]
- New Hampshire: independent determination of general acceptance without regard to the findings of the trial court.[128]
- New Jersey: abuse of discretion (civil);[129] *de novo* (criminal).[130]
- New Mexico: abuse of discretion.[131]
- North Carolina: abuse of discretion.[132]
- North Dakota: abuse of discretion.[133]

113. Ford Motor Co. v. Ammerman, 705 N.E.2d 539 (Ind. App. 1999).
114. State v. Brown, 470 N.W.2d 30 (Iowa 1991).
115. Kuhn v. Sandoz Pharms. Corp., 14 P.3d 1170 (Kan. 2000).
116. Toyota Motor Corp. v. Gregory, 136 S.W.3d 35 (Ky. 2004).
117. Corkern v. T.K. Valve, 934 So. 2d 102 (La. App. 2006).
118. State v. Bickart, 963 A.2d 183 (Me. 2009).
119. Blackwell v. Wyeth, 971 A.2d 235 (Md. 2009).
120. Canavan's Case, 733 N.E.2d 1042 (Mass. 2000).
121. People v. Dobek, 732 N.W.2d 546 (Mich. App. 2007).
122. State v. Bailey, 677 N.W.2d 380 (Minn. 2004).
123. Webb v. Braswell, 930 So. 2d 387 (Miss. 2006).
124. McGuire v. Seltsam, 138 S.W.3d 718 (Mo. 2004).
125. State v. Moore, 885 P.2d 457 (Mont. 1994).
126. Zimmerman v. Powell, 684 N.W.2d 1 (Neb. 2004).
127. Hallmark v. Eldridge, 189 P.3d 646 (Nev. 2008).
128. State v. VandeBogart, 616 A.2d 483 (N.H. 1992).
129. Hisenaj v. Kuehner, 942 A.2d 769 (N.J. 2008).
130. State v. Harvey, 699 A.2d 596 (N.J. 1997).
131. State v. Alberico, 861 P.2d 192 (N.M. 1993).
132. Howerton v. Arai Helmet, Ltd., 597 S.E.2d 674 (N.C. 2004).
133. State v. Hernandez, 707 N.W.2d 449 (N.D. 2005).

- Ohio: abuse of discretion.[134]
- Oklahoma: mixed standard for a decision involving law and factual determinations;[135] for novel scientific evidence, independent review not limited by deference to the trial judge's discretion.[136]
- Oregon: *de novo.*[137]
- Pennsylvania: abuse of discretion.[138]
- Rhode Island: abuse of discretion.[139]
- South Carolina: abuse of discretion.[140]
- South Dakota: abuse of discretion.[141]
- Tennessee: abuse of discretion.[142]
- Texas: abuse of discretion.[143]
- Utah: abuse of discretion.[144]
- Vermont: abuse of discretion.[145]
- Virginia: abuse of discretion.[146]
- Washington: *de novo.* [147]
- West Virginia: *de novo.*[148]
- Wisconsin: not applicable (reliability determined by the jury).[149]
- Wyoming: abuse of discretion.[150]

What Is the State Law concerning (1) Permissible Bases of Expert Opinion and Admissibility of Those Bases, and (2) the Need for Disclosure of the Basis of the Expert's Opinion?

Federal Rule of Evidence 703 provides that an expert may base his conclusions on facts that need not be admissible in evidence if those facts are of a

---

134. Lewis v. Alfa Laval Separation, 714 N.E.2d 426 (Ohio App. 1998).
135. Christian v. Gray, 65 P.3d 591 (Okla. 2003).
136. Taylor v. State, 889 P.2d 319 (Okla. Crim. App. 1995).
137. State v. Brown, 687 P.2d 751 (Or. 1984).
138. Grady v. Frito-Lay, Inc., 839 A.2d 1038 (Pa. 2003).
139. In re Mackenzie C., 877 A.2d 674 (R.I. 2005).
140. State v. White, 676 S.E.2d 684 (S.C. 2009).
141. State v. Guthrie, 627 N.W.2d 401 (S.D. 2001).
142. McDaniel v. CSX Transp., Inc., 955 S.W.2d 257 (Tenn. 1997).
143. Kelly v. State, 824 S.W.2d 568 (Tex. App. 1992).
144. Brewer v. Denver & Rio Grande W. R.R., 31 P.3d 557 (Utah 2001).
145. USGen New England, Inc. v. Town of Rockingham, 862 A.2d 269 (Vt. 2004).
146. John v. Im, 559 S.E.2d 694 (Va. 2002).
147. State v. Gregory, 147 P.3d 1201 (Wash. 2006).
148. State v. Leep, 569 S.E.2d 133 (W. Va. 2002).
149. *Conley,* 665 N.W.2d 879; *Donner,* 531 N.W. 2d 369.
150. Bunting v. Jamieson, 984 P.2d 467 (Wyo. 1999).

type reasonably relied on by experts in the particular field. Rule 703 was amended in 2000 to provide that facts that are otherwise inadmissible shall not be disclosed to the jury by the proponent of the evidence unless the court determines that their probative value in evaluating the expert's opinion outweighs their prejudicial effect. Federal Rule of Evidence 705 provides that an expert may express an opinion without first testifying to the underlying facts, unless the court requires otherwise, but that the expert may be required to disclose the underlying facts on cross-examination.

States have taken a variety of approaches to these issues. The majority of states have adopted rules that follow Rule 703 and Rule 705. A few states have adopted the 2000 amendment to Rule 703. Several states have rules that are substantially different. Even in states that have adopted Rule 703, there remains a significant concern about permitting an expert's testimony simply to supply a conduit for otherwise inadmissible evidence.[151]

Tables C and E in Appendix A to this chapter list the variations.

What Is the State Law concerning Opinions on Ultimate Issues?

At common law, opinions were often excluded on the basis that they were opinions on the ultimate issue, which invaded the province of the jury. Although this rubric applied to both lay and expert opinions, it proved particularly troubling as applied to expert opinion. Even before the adoption of the Federal Rules of Evidence, many courts had discarded the most rigid form of the ultimate opinion rule.

Federal Rule of Evidence 704(a) provides that "[t]estimony in the form of an opinion or inference otherwise admissible is not objectionable because it embraces an ultimate issue to be decided by the trier of fact." The great majority of state rules are virtually identical to Rule 704(a). Three state rules add the word "merely" to the rule: Delaware, Indiana, and Maryland. Four state rules add the word "solely" to the rule: Louisiana, New Hampshire, Ohio, and West Virginia. Five states have provisions that exclude specific types of expert opinions: Connecticut, Indiana, Maryland, and Utah have provisions like Rule 704(b),[152] and Louisiana Rule 704(b) excludes opinions on the issue of guilt or innocence.

---

151. *See, e.g.,* C.S.I. Chem. Sales v. Mapco Gas Prods., Inc., 557 N.W.2d 528 (Iowa App. 1996); State v. Lundstrom, 776 P.2d 1067 (Ariz. 1989); Linn v. Fossum, 946 So. 2d 1032 (Fla. 2006); Martin v. Mississippi Transp. Comm'n, 953 So. 2d 1163 (Miss. App. 2007).

152. Rule 704(b) provides that no expert witness testifying with respect to the mental state or condition of a defendant in a criminal case may state an opinion or inference as to whether the defendant did or did not have the mental state or condition constituting an

Two states do not have rules like Rule 704. Alabama's Rule 704 expressly provides that ultimate opinions are not admissible. Kentucky has no version of Rule 704, although its Supreme Court has since indicated that it follows the modern authority under which opinions are not excluded solely because they embrace an ultimate issue.[153] One common law state, Virginia, excludes expert testimony on the ultimate issue of fact because it invades the province of the fact finder.[154]

Notwithstanding the reported demise of the ultimate issue rule, state courts continue to exercise significant vigilance over expert opinions that seem to advise the jury how to decide. Often these opinions are excluded under Federal Rule of Evidence 403, on the premise that the opinion does not satisfy Rule 701 because it is not of assistance to the jury, or because the opinion invades the province of the jury.

An illustrative list of state authority on this issue follows. Table D in Appendix A lists the state rules.

- Arizona: Comment to Rule 704.
- Arkansas: *Gramling v. Jennings*, 625 S.W.2d 463 (Ark. 1981).
- California: *Schauf v. Southern California Edison Co.*, 243 Cal. App. 2d 450 (1966).
- Colorado: *Hines v. Denver & R. G. W. R. Co.*, 829 P.2d 419 (Colo. App. 1991).
- District of Columbia: *Lampkins v. United States*, 401 A.2d 966 (D.C. 1979).
- Georgia: *Carlock v. Kmart Corp.*, 489 S.E.2d 99 (Ga. App. 1997).
- Hawaii: *State v. Kahakai*, 36 P.3d 812 (Haw. 2001).
- Illinois: *Swanigan v. Smith*, 689 N.E.2d 637 (Ill. App. 1998); *C.L. Maddox, Inc. v. Royal Ins. Co.*, 567 N.E.2d 749 (Ill. App. 1991).
- Kansas: *State v. Mullins*, 977 P.2d 931 (Kan. 1999).
- Mississippi: *Quitman County v. State*, 910 So. 2d 1032 (Miss. 2005).
- New Jersey: *State v. Reeds*, 962 A.2d 1087 (N.J. 2009).
- New York: *People v. Ingram*, 770 N.Y.S.2d 294 (2003).
- North Dakota: *First Trust Co. v. Scheels Hardware & Sports Shop*, 429 N.W.2d 5 (N.D. 1988).
- Ohio: Staff notes to Rule 704.
- Pennsylvania: *Houdeshell v. Rice*, 939 A.2d. 981 (Pa. Super. 2007).
- South Dakota: *State v. Guthrie*, 627 N.W.2d 401 (S.D. 2001).

---

element of the crime charged or of a defense thereto. Such ultimate issues are matters for the trier of fact alone.

153. Stringer v. Commonwealth, 956 S.W.2d 883 (Ky. 1997).

154. Ward v. Commonwealth, 570 S.E.2d 827 (Va. 2002).

- Tennessee: *State v. Turner*, 30 S.W.3d 355 (Tenn. Crim. App. 2000).
- Utah: *State v. Tenney*, 913 P.2d 750 (Utah App. 1996).
- Washington: *State v. Baird*, 922 P.2d 157 (Wash. App. 1996).
- West Virginia: *State v. Edward Charles L.*, 398 S.E.2d 123 (W. Va. 1990).
- Wyoming: *Cockburn v. Terra Resources, Inc.*, 794 P.2d 1334 (Wyo. 1990).

May the Proponent of Expert Testimony Introduce the Expert's Deposition at Trial without a Showing of Unavailability?

There is a growing trend to permit the presentation of an expert's testimony through a deposition regardless of whether the state's rule relating to admissibility of depositions would otherwise permit such use of the deposition. A number of states have such provisions; some allow such use in the case of any expert witness, while others are limited to members of certain professions. A list of these provisions follows.

- Alabama: A deposition may be used on a showing that the witness is a licensed physician or dentist.[155]
- Alaska: The deposition of a witness may be used by any party for any purpose if the court finds that the witness's testimony has been recorded on videotape.[156]
- Arizona: There is not an unavailability requirement for any witness.[157]
- California: A statute permits the use of deposition of treating or consulting expert witness.[158]
- Connecticut: A rule permits the use of the deposition of a "physician, psychologist, chiropractor, natureopathic physician or dentist licensed under the provisions of the general statutes."[159]
- District of Columbia: A videotape deposition of a treating or consulting physician or of any expert witness may be used for any purpose, unless otherwise ordered for good cause shown, even though the witness is available, if the notice specified that it was to be taken for use at trial.[160]
- Florida: A deposition may be used by any party for any purpose if "the witness is an expert or skilled witness."[161]

---

155. Ala. R. Civ. P. 32(a)(3)(D).
156. Alaska R. Civ. P. 32(a)(3)(F).
157. Ariz. R. Civ. P. 32(a).
158. Cal. Civ. Proc. Code § 2025.620(d).
159. Conn. Gen. St. Ann. § 52-149a.
160. D.C. Super. Ct. R. Civ. P. 32(4).
161. Fla. R. Civ. P. 1.330(a)(3)(F).

- Georgia: A deposition may be used by any party for any purpose if the court finds that "because of the nature of the business or occupation of the witness it is not possible to secure his personal attendance without manifest inconvenience to the public or third persons." In addition, the deposition of any witness may be used in the discretion of the trial judge, even though the witness is available to testify in person at the trial.[162]
- Illinois: The evidence deposition of a physician or surgeon may be introduced in evidence at trial on the motion of either party regardless of the deponent's availability.[163]
- Indiana: The rules make no express provision for expert witnesses, but a rule does permit the use of depositions for any purpose "upon agreement of the parties."[164]
- Iowa: A deposition may be used for any purpose if it was taken of an expert witness specially retained for litigation or if the deponent was a health care provider offering opinions concerning a party's physical or mental condition.[165]
- Kentucky: A rule permits the use of depositions if the court finds that the deponent is a practicing physician, dentist, chiropractor, osteopath, podiatrist, or lawyer.[166]
- Louisiana: Any party may use the deposition of an expert witness for any purpose on notice to all counsel of record, who may require live testimony by paying the expert's fee and expenses in advance. The court may permit the use of the deposition, notwithstanding an objection, if it finds that, under the circumstances, justice so requires.[167]
- Maryland: A videotaped deposition of a treating or consulting physician or of any expert witness may be used for any purpose even though the witness is available to testify if the notice specified that it was to be taken for use at trial.[168]
- Massachusetts: On motion or by stipulation unless the court orders otherwise, any party intending to call a treating physician or expert witness as that party's own witness may take an oral deposition by audio visual means for the purpose of its being used as evidence at trial in lieu of oral testimony.[169]

---

162. Ga. Code Ann. § 9-11-32(a)(3)(E).
163. Ill. Sup. Ct. R. 212(b).
164. Ind. R. Civ. P. 32.
165. Iowa R. Civ. P. 1.704(4).
166. Ky. R. Civ. P. 32.01(vi).
167. La. Code Civ. Proc. art. 1450A(5).
168. Md. R. 2-419.
169. Mass. R. 30A(m).

- Michigan: Testimony given as a witness in a deposition taken in the course of the same proceeding is admissible if the court finds that the deponent is an expert witness and if the deponent is not a party to the proceeding.[170]
- Mississippi: A rule permits the use of depositions when "the witness is a medical doctor."[171]
- Missouri: No requirement of unavailability for any witness. Any part of a deposition that is admissible under the Rules of Evidence, applied as though the deponent were testifying in court, may be used against any party who was present or had notice. Depositions may be used in court for any purpose.[172]
- New Jersey: A videotaped deposition of a treating physician or expert witness may be used at trial in lieu of testimony regardless of whether the witness is available to testify, on conditions.[173]
- New Mexico: There is no express provision for experts, although the deposition of a witness who is within 100 miles may be used if "an order was entered prior to the deposition permitting the use of the deposition at trial and the notice of deposition sets forth that the proponent intended to use the deposition at trial."[174]
- New York: The deposition of a person authorized to practice medicine may be used by any party without the necessity of showing unavailability or special circumstances, subject to the right of any party to move to prevent abuse.[175]
- North Carolina: The deposition of a witness, whether or not a party, may be used by any party for any purpose if the court finds that the witness is an expert witness whose testimony has been procured by videotape as provided for under Rule 30(b)(4).[176]
- Ohio: A rule permits the use of depositions when "the witness is an attending physician or medical expert, although residing within the county in which the action is heard."[177]
- Oklahoma: A rule permits the use of depositions when "the witness is an expert witness, who for purposes of this section is a person educated

---

170. Mich. R. Evid. 803(18).
171. Miss. R. Civ. P. 32 (a)(3)(E).
172. Mo. R. Civ. P. 57.07(a).
173. N.J. Ct. R. 4:14-9 (e).
174. N.M. R. Civ. P. 1-032.
175. N.Y. C.P.L.R. 3117(a)4.
176. N.C. Gen. Stat. § 1A-1, Rule 32(a)(4).
177. Ohio R. Civ. P. 32(a)(3)(E).

in a special art or profession or a person possessing special or peculiar knowledge acquired from practical experience."[178]

• Pennsylvania: A deposition on oral examination of a medical witness, other than a party, may be used at trial for any purpose whether or not the witness is available to testify.[179]

• Rhode Island: A deposition of a medical witness, or any witness called as an expert, other than a party, which has been recorded by videotape by written stipulation of the parties or pursuant to an order of court, may be used at trial for any purpose whether or not the witness is available to testify.[180]

• South Dakota: The rule makes no express provision for expert witnesses but does provide that a deposition may be used by any party, if the court finds that the witness is unable to attend because of occupational commitments, if the deposition was taken for purposes of use at the trial because of such commitments.[181]

• Virginia: The deposition of a physician, surgeon, dentist, chiropractor, or registered nurse, who in the regular course of his profession treated or examined any party to the proceeding, is admissible at trial.[182]

• Washington: The deposition of an expert witness may be used as follows: (1) the discovery deposition of an opposing party's expert witness, who resides outside the state of Washington, may be used if reasonable notice before the trial date is provided to all parties and any party against whom the deposition is intended to be used is given a reasonable opportunity to depose the expert again; (2) the deposition of a health care professional, even though available to testify at trial, taken with the expressly stated purpose of preserving the deponent's testimony for trial, may be used subject to certain conditions.[183]

• Wisconsin: The deposition of a medical expert may be used by any party for any purpose without regard to the limitations otherwise imposed by the rule.[184]

---

178. Okla. R. Civ. P. 32(a)(3)(E).
179. Pa. R. Civ. P. 4020(a)(5).
180. R.I. R. Civ. P. 32(a)(3)(E).
181. S.D. Codified Laws § 15-6-32 (a)(3)(C).
182. Va. R. 4:7(a)(4)(E).
183. Wash. Super. Ct. R. 32 (a)(5).
184. Wis. Stat. Ann. § 804.07(1)(c)2.

May the Expert Remain in the Courtroom despite a Rule Excluding Witnesses?

Federal Rule of Evidence 615 provides that "[a]t the request of a party the court shall order witnesses excluded so that they cannot hear the testimony of other witnesses, and it may make the order of its own motion." The rule provides for the exception of several categories of persons from the rule of exclusion, including "a person whose presence is shown by a party to be essential to the presentation of the party's cause." The Advisory Committee's note states that this category "contemplates such persons as an agent who handled the transaction being litigated or an expert needed to advise counsel in the management of the litigation."[185] The language of the note does not explicitly cover an expert witness.

Most states that have adopted rules of evidence have a rule similar to Rule 615 (although some states have substituted "may" for "shall"), and most have an exception like that quoted from the federal rule. States have exhibited varying degrees of receptivity to excepting experts from the exclusion provision of the rule. Many state courts, like the federal courts, have identified a variety of considerations that support excepting expert witnesses from orders excluding witnesses. They draw a distinction between expert witnesses and percipient witnesses, whose presence in the courtroom during the testimony of other witnesses may affect their testimony. Furthermore, the provision of Rule 703 that an expert may base his opinion on evidence presented at trial implies the necessity for the expert witness's presence to hear the testimony. On the other hand, as the following survey shows, some states do not favor excepting experts from exclusion. In those states that do favor excepting experts, courts commonly hold that excepting an expert witness from the exclusion order is reviewed for abuse of discretion.

- Alabama: *Camp v. General Motors Corp.*, 454 So. 2d 958 (Ala. 1984) (upholding exclusion, but suggesting expert witnesses should be permitted to remain).
- Alaska: *Johnson v. State*, 511 P.2d 118 (Alaska 1973) (prerule) (no abuse of discretion in permitting an expert witness to testify after reading the testimony of the opposing party's expert witnesses).
- Arkansas: *McGraw v. Weeks*, 930 S.W.2d 365 (Ark. 1996) (permitting expert to remain); *Parker v. Holder*, 867 S.W.2d 436 (Ark. 1993) (exclusion not error where no showing that expert would base testimony on other witnesses).

---

185. Fed. R. Evid. 615 Advisory Committee's note.

- California: *People v. Valdez*, 177 Cal. App. 3d 680 (1986) (discretionary but favors excepting expert from exclusion).
- Colorado: *Martin v. Porak*, 638 P.2d 853 (Colo. App. 1981) (no reason to exclude the physician from the courtroom where the physician testified in an expert capacity only and not to the facts of the case).
- Connecticut: *State v. Sherman*, 662 A.2d 767 (Conn. App. 1995); *Donaghue v. Nurses Registry, Inc.*, 485 A.2d 945 (Conn. Super. 1984) (no exceptions for experts).
- Delaware: Comment to Rule 615 states that state drafters recognized "that it is sometimes desirable not to sequester a particular witness, especially an expert witness."
- District of Columbia: *Johnson v. District of Columbia*, 655 A.2d 316 (D.C. 1995) (favoring excepting experts from exclusion order).
- Florida: *Hernandez v. State*, 4 So. 3d 642 (Fla. 2009) (discretionary, favoring exception where expert needs to hear testimony).
- Georgia: *Bean v. Landers*, 450 S.E.2d 699 (Ga. App. 1994); *Gray v State*, 476 S.E.2d 12 (Ga. App. 1996) (excepting expert from sequestration rule is acceptable but not automatic).
- Hawaii: *Bloudell v. Wailuku Sugar Co.*, 669 P.2d 163 (Haw. App. 1983) (referring to the exception for essential witnesses, the court states that the exception requires the witness to have specialized expertise or intimate knowledge of the facts of the case).
- Idaho: *State v. Christensen*, 603 P.2d 586 (Idaho 1979) (refusal to exclude testimony of expert witnesses who remained despite order of exclusion within court's discretion).
- Illinois: *Friedman v. Park District of Highland Park*, 502 N.E.2d 826 (Ill. App. 1986) (trial court's discretion, no automatic exception).
- Indiana: *R. R. Donnelley & Sons Co. v. North Texas Steel Co.*, 752 N.E.2d 112 (Ind. App. 2001) (trial court abused discretion by excluding experts in complex case requiring that they hear testimony).
- Kentucky: *Johnson v. Mutual Benefit Health & Accident Association*, 229 S.W.2d 758 (Ky. App. 1950) (allowing expert to remain despite exclusion order).
- Louisiana: Advisory commentary to Article 615 states that ordinarily expert witnesses should not be sequestered except when failure to do so would be manifestly unfair to another party.
- Maryland: Maryland Rule 5-615(b)(3) explicitly excepts experts who are to render opinions based on testimony given at the trial.
- Massachusetts: *Zambarano v. Massachusetts Turnpike Authority*, 215 N.E.2d 652 (Mass. 1966) (exclusion of expert witness within judge's discretion).

- Michigan: *People v. Martin*, 192 N.W.2d 215 (Mich.1971) (refusal to sequester expert witness not an abuse of discretion).
- Minnesota: Committee comment to Rule 615 states that the rule leaves the issue subject to the trial court's discretion and that experts essential to advise counsel in litigation should not be excluded.
- Mississippi: *Northup v. State*, 793 So. 2d 618 (Miss. 2001) (experts may remain to hear testimony of other witnesses).
- Missouri: *Klaus v. Deen*, 883 S.W.2d 984 (Mo. App.1994) (concurring opinion suggests experts should be exempted).
- Montana: *State v. Riggs*, 113 P.3d 281 (Mont. 2005) (given the preference expressed in Rule 615, for excluding witnesses, whether lay or expert, no abuse of discretion in excluding expert).
- Nebraska: *In re Dennis W.*, 717 N.W.2d 488 (Neb. App. 2006) (no error in permitting witness to remain to hear testimony of other side's experts).
- Nevada: *Wallace v. State*, 447 P.2d 30 (Nev. 1968) (prerule) (no abuse of discretion in permitting psychiatrist to remain during defendant's testimony).
- New Jersey: *State v. Popovich*, 964 A.2d 804 (N.J. App. Div. 2009) (Rule 615 does not authorize routine sequestration of experts).
- New Mexico: *State v. Simonson*, 669 P.2d 1092 (N.M. 1983) (no abuse of discretion in permitting expert to remain).
- New York: *R.J. Cornelius, Inc. v. Cally*, 551 N.Y.S.2d 20 (1990); *People v. Medure*, 683 N.Y.S.2d 697 (1998) (permitting experts to remain).
- North Dakota: *Nesvig v. Nesvig*, 712 N.W.2d 299 (N.D. 2006) (no error in permitting expert to remain to hear testimony of plaintiff's witnesses).
- Ohio: *Oakwood v. Makar*, 463 N.E.2d 61 (Ohio App. 1983); *Meyer v. Fisher*, No. 1999CA00302, 2000 WL 502676 (Ohio App. Apr. 17, 2000) (no abuse of discretion in excluding expert notwithstanding reasons to except them).
- Oklahoma: *Clark v. Continental Tank Co.*, 744 P.2d 949 (Okla. 1987) (permitting experts to remain).
- Oregon: *Siegfried v. Pacific Northwest Development Corp.*, 793 P.2d 330 (Or. App. 1990) (approval of expert remaining).
- Pennsylvania: *Commonwealth v. Albrecht*, 511 A.2d 764 (Pa. 1986) (expert may state his opinion on evidence he heard in the courtroom; decision whether to sequester a witness will not be reversed absent a clear abuse of discretion).
- Rhode Island: *State v. Perez*, 882 A.2d 574 (R.I. 2005) (where testimony of expert witness was essential to prosecution's rebuttal case, trial court properly held that Rule 615 would not permit the exclusion of the expert from the courtroom).

- South Dakota: *State v. Traversie*, 387 N.W.2d 2 (S.D. 1986) (if a witness is to base his expert opinion on facts or data presented at trial, the expert should be exempt from sequestration).
- Tennessee: *State v. Bane*, 57 S.W.3d 411 (Tenn. 2001) (trial court erred by refusing to allow expert witness to remain in the courtroom without considering the purpose of Rule 615).
- Texas: *Drilex Systems, Inc. v. Flores*, 1 S.W.3d 112 (Tex. 1999) (while essential person exemption often will cover experts, they are not automatically exempt).
- Utah: *Astill v. Clark*, 956 P.2d 1081 (Utah App. 1998) (purposes of sequestration do not apply to experts, but no harm shown to result from exclusion).
- Vermont: *State v. Beattie*, 596 A.2d 919 (Vt. 1991) (no error in allowing an expert, after testifying, to remain in the courtroom and then to be called in rebuttal).
- Virginia: VA. CODE § 8.01-375 (Where expert witnesses are to testify in civil cases, the court may, at the request of all parties, allow one expert witness for each party to remain in the courtroom.).
- Washington: *Sanderson v. Moline*, 499 P.2d 1281 (Wash. App. 1972) (prerule) (in dental medical malpractice case, no error in the trial court's refusal to exclude all the dentists from the courtroom because within the court's discretion).
- Wisconsin: *State v. Evans*, 617 N.W.2d 220 (Wis. App. 2000) (showing that expert's presence would have been helpful did not equal showing that presence essential).
- Wyoming: *Stone v. State*, 745 P.2d 1344 (Wyo. 1987) (showing that expert's presence would have been helpful did not equal showing that presence essential).

Must the Expert Be Formally Tendered?

In every jurisdiction, it is necessary for the proponent of expert testimony to demonstrate that the witness is qualified to testify as an expert. A practical question that may arise is whether the proponent must formally tender the witness as an expert for an express determination by the trial court. The following list collects reported cases in which state courts have ruled on this issue. Also included are cases in which courts have considered whether this announcement should be made in the presence of the jury. Beyond the scope of this treatment is the issue of how courts treat the use of Federal Rule of Evidence 104 with respect to litigating issues of reliability and other preliminary issues outside the presence of the fact finder.

- Colorado: Admission of expert testimony amounts to implied finding by trial court that witness was qualified as expert; absence of request or finding that witness was qualified as expert does not affect defendant's substantial rights.[186]
- Georgia: Proponent should expressly ask, after laying foundation, that the court deem the witness qualified to testify as an expert.[187] However, although much preferred for the sake of clarity and certainty and to preclude question, it is not required that an expert be formally tendered; tender may be implied by permission to proceed with or without objection, after laying foundation.[188]
- Indiana: Advisory comment to Indiana Rule 702 states that the rule does not require a formal tender of the witness as an expert. The committee believes that judges normally should not announce their ruling that a witness is qualified as an expert, because the jurors may misinterpret such a ruling as an endorsement of the witness's testimony. In *Campbell v. Shelton*,[189] the court expressed disapproval of counsel's request that the trial court expressly accept a witness as an expert and stated that a court should refrain from recognizing a witness as an expert before the jury.
- Kansas: KAN. STAT. ANN. § 60-456(c): Unless the judge excludes the testimony, he is deemed to have made the finding requisite to its admission.
- Kentucky: Where proponent made no motion to have witness qualified as an expert to render an opinion, and the trial court did not make an express finding that she was an expert who was qualified to render an opinion, the trial court's admission of the opinion "under the circumstances of this case" constituted an abuse of discretion.[190] All rulings recognizing the expert should be made outside the hearing of the jury, and there should be no declaration that the witness is an expert.[191]
- Louisiana: There is no requirement that a party formally tender an expert witness or that a court formally declare that a witness is accepted as an expert.[192]

---

186. People v. Lomanaco, 802 P.2d 1143 (Colo. App. 1990).

187. Ingram v. State, 342 S.E.2d 765 (Ga. App. 1986).

188. Morrow v. State, 495 S.E.2d 609 (Ga. App. 1998); Mayer v. Wylie, 535 S.E.2d 816 (Ga. App. 2000).

189. Campbell v. Shelton, 727 N.E.2d 495 (Ind. App. 2000).

190. Wilson v. Commonwealth, No. 2005-SC-0014-MR, 2006 WL 2707451, 1 (Ky. Sept. 21, 2006).

191. Luttrell v. Commonwealth, 952 S.W.2d 216 (Ky. 1997).

192. Square Deal Siding Co., Inc. v. Thaller, 3 So. 3d 71 (La. App. 2008).

- Maine: Judge's announcement that he found expert qualified and evidence reliable should not have been made in presence of jury.[193]
- Maryland: Before a witness properly may be asked a question that calls for expert testimony, the witness's qualifications must be proved and the witness proffered to the court and accepted by it as an expert in the relevant field.[194]
- Massachusetts: Although it is for the court to determine whether a witness is qualified to testify as an expert, there is no requirement that the court specifically make that finding in open court on proffer of the offering party. Such an offer and finding by the court might influence the jury in its evaluation of the expert, and the better procedure is to avoid an acknowledgement of the witness's expertise by the court.[195]
- Mississippi: An expert should be formally tendered in order for expert testimony to be accepted.[196]
- New Hampshire: The fact that a witness is permitted to give expert testimony implies a finding by the trial court that he was qualified to testify in that capacity.[197]
- New York: The court properly permitted witness to give expert testimony after it was established that the witness possessed the requisite training and experience to qualify as an expert. The court was not required to formally declare or certify the witness to be an expert.[198]
- North Carolina: In the absence of a request for a finding by the trial court as to the qualification of a witness as an expert, it is not essential that the record show a specific finding on this matter, the finding being deemed implicit in the ruling admitting or rejecting the opinion testimony of the witness.[199] However, the better practice is for counsel to tender the witness as an expert and for an express finding.[200]
- Ohio: Where witness's qualifications were demonstrated, failure to tender him as an expert is of no consequence.[201]

193. State v. Goyette, 407 A.2d 1104 (Me. 1979).
194. State v. Blackwell, 971 A.2d 296 (Md. 2009).
195. Commonwealth v. Richardson, 667 N.E.2d 257 (Mass. 1996).
196. Cowan v. Mississippi Bureau of Narcotics, 2 So. 3d 759 (Miss. App. 2009).
197. Emery v. Tilo Roofing Co., 195 A. 409 (N.H. 1937).
198. People v. Leung, 712 N.Y.S.2d 88 (2000).
199. State v. Bullard, 322 S.E. 2d 370 (N.C. 1984); Cato Equip. Co. v. Matthews, 372 S.E.2d 872 (N.C. App. 1988).
200. State v. Stallings, 419 S.E.2d 586 (N.C. App. 1992); State v. Greime, 388 S.E.2d 594 (N.C. App. 1990).
201. State v. Davis, 880 N.E.2d 31 (Ohio 2008).

- Rhode Island: Where witness's qualifications were sufficient to refute any allegation of abuse of discretion in allowing him to render expert opinions, the lack of a formal tender of the witness as an expert and a specific ruling thereon before treating him as an expert and allowing him to testify as such did not constitute prejudicial error.[202]
- Tennessee: There is no requirement in Tennessee for formal tender of a witness before the giving of expert testimony.[203]
- Vermont: Permitting witness to testify as an expert after he had been examined and cross-examined as to his experience and knowledge constituted an implied finding as to competency of the witness.[204]
- West Virginia: The trial judge should not advise the jury that he has determined reliability.[205]

What Is the Rule concerning Use of Learned Treatises?

Federal Rule of Evidence 803(18) provides an exception to the rule excluding hearsay, as follows:

> To the extent called to the attention of an expert witness on cross-examination or relied upon by the expert witness in direct examination, statements contained in published treatises, periodicals, or pamphlets on a subject of history, medicine, or other science or art, established as a reliable authority by the testimony or admission of the witness or by other expert testimony or by judicial notice. If admitted, the statements may be read into evidence but may not be received as exhibits.

This exception differs from the common law. At common law, statements in learned treatises could be used to impeach the testimony of experts only if the expert admitted that they were authoritative. The federal rule expanded the use of treatises in several respects, including permitting them to be established as a reliable authority by other expert testimony or by judicial notice, and permitting their limited use as substantive evidence by allowing them to be read into evidence. The state rules vary in which, if any, of these expanded uses they follow.

Twenty-four states have adopted the exact text of Rule 803(18). Among the common law jurisdictions, California, the District of Columbia, and Virginia have similar rules.

---

202. State v. Ashness, 461 A.2d 659 (R.I. 1983); State v. Abdullah, 967 A.2d 469 (R.I. 2009).

203. Tire Shredders, Inc. v. ERM-N. Cent., Inc., 15 S.W.3d 849 (Tenn. App. 1999).

204. Smith v. De Metre, 118 A.2d 346 (Vt. 1955).

205. State v. Leep, 569 S.E.2d 133 (W. Va. 2002).

Five states have adopted Rule 803(18) with minor variations. Hawaii has an additional provision in Rule 702.1 that does not seem to alter its meaning. Louisiana states that the material may be received as an exhibit but not taken to the jury room. New Jersey adds "or, if graphics, may be shown to the jury." South Carolina has an additional sentence referring to statutes (and the only applicable statute was since repealed). South Dakota's language is slightly different.

Five states permit the statements to be received as exhibits: Colorado, Connecticut (implicitly through omission of last sentence), Idaho (on motion and for good cause shown), Nevada (implicitly through omission of last sentence), and New Hampshire (if court finds that their probative value outweighs their prejudicial effect).

Ten states allow the use of the statements only for cross-examination: Florida, Georgia, Illinois, Maine (may be read in evidence), Massachusetts (may be read in evidence), Michigan, Missouri, New York, Oregon (for impeachment only), and Tennessee (impeachment only).

Indiana allows only statements "that contradict the expert's testimony." Kansas explicitly allows such statements to prove the truth of the matter stated there. Mississippi requires prior disclosure of treatises used in direct examination. Pennsylvania provides that "limited use" may be made on direct or for impeachment on cross. And Wisconsin explicitly allows such statements to prove the truth of the matter stated there and requires prior disclosure.

Table G in Appendix A contains the citations to the rules provisions and cases for common law states.

Must the Expert's Opinion Embody a Specific Degree of Certainty?

It is commonplace for courts to require that some or all types of expert opinions be stated to a degree of reasonable certainty or reasonable probability. It has been observed that the antecedents of this practice are questionable, as are the functions that it purportedly serves.[206] However, the practice became widespread, particularly insofar as opinions by expert medical witnesses were concerned, and especially for issues of causation or future consequences. In some trial courts, the requirements of the usage have spread beyond medical opinions to other experts, requiring that experts be asked to state opinions to a reasonable degree of scientific certainty.

---

206. Jeff L. Lewin, *The Genesis and Evolution of Legal Uncertainty about "Reasonable Medical Certainty,"* 57 MD. L. REV. 380 (1998).

However, in recent years, courts have begun to jettison such a requirement. Following are cases from those jurisdictions that have expressly opined on the issue. It should be noted that the admissibility of the expert's opinion is not necessarily the same as whether the evidence is sufficient to support a verdict; the cases listed here relate to admissibility.

- Arkansas: The standard is reasonable degree of medical certainty or probability.[207]
- California: A doctor testifying as to future results of an injury is not required to state that such results are "reasonably certain" to occur before his testimony is admissible.[208]
- Colorado: Reasonable medical probability or certainty standard has been abrogated by the adoption of the Colorado Rules of Evidence.[209]
- Connecticut: The standard is reasonable medical probability.[210] Whether an expert's testimony expresses a reasonable probability does not depend on semantics or use of a particular term or phrase but is determined by looking at the entire substance of the expert's testimony.[211]
- Delaware: The standard is a reasonable medical probability or a reasonable medical certainty.[212]
- District of Columbia: The standard is reasonable medical certainty standard.[213]
- Florida: The standard is reasonable medical probability.[214]
- Georgia: Expert need not use the magic words "reasonable degree of medical certainty."[215] An expert is not required to prove within a reasonable degree of scientific certainty his opinion of how an accident occurred.[216]
- Hawaii: Medical opinion must be based on reasonable medical probability.[217]
- Idaho: The standard is reasonable degree of medical probability.[218]

---

207. Rose Care, Inc. v. Ross, 209 S.W.3d 393 (Ark. App. 2005).

208. Bauman v. San Francisco, 108 P.2d 989 (Cal. App. 1940).

209. People v. Ramirez, 155 P.3d 371 (Colo. 2007).

210. Eisenbach v. Downey, 694 A.2d 1376 (Conn. App. 1997).

211. State v. Nunes, 800 A.2d 1160 (Conn. 2002).

212. Floray v. State, 720 A.2d 1132 (Del. 1998); Rizzi v. Mason, 799 A.2d 1178 (Del. 2002).

213. Robinson v. Group Health Ass'n, 691 A.2d 1147 (D.C. 1997).

214. Dutcher v. Allstate Ins. Co., 655 So. 2d 1217 (Fla. App. 1995); Shearon v. Sullivan, 821 So. 2d 1222 (Fla. App. 2002).

215. Beasley v. Northside Hosp., Inc., 658 S.E.2d 233 (Ga. App. 2008).

216. B. Hunt Transp. v. Brown, 512 S.E.2d 34 (Ga. App. 1999).

217. Barbee v. The Queen's Med. Ctr., 194 P.3d 1098 (Haw. 2008); Craft v. Peebles, 893 P.2d 138 (Haw. 1995).

218. Bloching v. Albertson's, Inc., 934 P.2d 17 (Idaho 1997).

- Illinois: There is no magic in the phrase "based upon a reasonable degree of medical certainty," and failure to use it does not render the expert's testimony inadmissible.[219]
- Indiana: The cases reject the notion that the admissibility of medical testimony is dependent on expert's ability to state conclusions regarding reasonable medical certainty.[220]
- Iowa: Buzzwords like "reasonable degree of medical certainty" are not necessary.[221]
- Kansas: No particular words of art are necessary; it is sufficient if the expert's words can be interpreted to show reasonable probability.[222]
- Kentucky: An expert medical witness does not need to use the magic words "reasonable probability."[223]
- Louisiana: The cases eschew use of reasonable medical certainty.[224]
- Maryland: An expert witness must base opinion on "reasonable probability or reasonable certainty" and not on "mere possibilities."[225]
- Minnesota: Reasonable probability standard.[226]
- Mississippi: The standard is reasonable medical certainty, but particular phrase is not dispositive.[227]
- Missouri: The standard is reasonable degree of certainty.[228]
- Montana: Evidentiary standards are satisfied if medical testimony is based on an opinion that it is more likely than not.[229]
- Nebraska: A medical expert's testimony need not be couched in the magic words "reasonable degree of medical certainty or a reasonable probability."[230]
- Nevada: The standard is reasonable medical probability.[231]
- New Jersey: The standard is reasonable medical probability or certainty.[232]

---

219. Hahn v. Union Pac. R.R. Co., 816 N.E.2d 834 (Ill. App. 2004).
220. Noblesville Casting Div. of TRW, Inc. v. Prince, 438 N.E.2d 722 (Ind. 1982).
221. Hansen v. Central Iowa Hosp. Corp., 686 N.W.2d 476 (Iowa 2004).
222. Tamplin v. Star Lumber & Supply Co., 836 P.2d 1102 (Kan. 1992).
223. Turner v. Commonwealth, 5 S.W.3d 119 (Ky. 1999).
224. Lasha v. Olin Corp., 625 So. 2d 1002 (La. 1993).
225. Farley v. Allstate Ins. Co., 733 A.2d 1014 (Md. 1999).
226. Block v. Target Stores, Inc., 458 N.W.2d 705 (Minn. 1990).
227. Catchings v. State, 684 So. 2d 591 (Miss. 1996).
228. Tompkins v. Cervantes, 917 S.W.2d 186 (Mo. App. 1996).
229. Dallas v. Burlington Northern, Inc., 689 P.2d 273 (Mont. 1984).
230. Shahan v. Hilker, 488 N.W.2d 577 (Neb. 1992).
231. Morsicato v. Sav-On Drug Stores, Inc., 111 P.3d 1112 (Nev. 2005).
232. Schrantz v. Luancing, 527 A.2d 967 (N.J. Super. 1986); Vitrano v. Schiffman, 702 A.2d 1347 (N.J. Super. 1997).

- New Mexico: The standard is medical probability; whether magic word is used is not determinative, but opinion is viewed as a whole.[233]
- New York: The standard is reasonable degree of medical certainty.[234] Requirement is not to be satisfied by a verbal straightjacket but by any formulation from which it can be said that the whole opinion reflects an acceptable level of certainty.[235]
- North Carolina: The standard is reasonable medical certainty.[236]
- North Dakota: Hypertechnical words are not necessary; the test for admissibility is whether the expert's testimony demonstrates the expert is expressing a medical opinion that is more probable than not.[237]
- Ohio: An expert opinion is competent only if it is held to a reasonable degree of scientific certainty, which means probability.[238]
- Oregon: Cases adopt a probability standard.[239]
- Pennsylvania: Reasonable degree of medical certainty, but experts are not required to use "magic words" when expressing their opinions.[240]
- Rhode Island: Admissibility of expert testimony does not require the use of "magic words;" if expert's testimony is given with the requisite degree of certainty, that is, "some degree of positiveness," it matters not what words are used to convey that certainty.[241]
- South Carolina: Testimony must satisfy the "most probably" rule.[242]
- South Dakota: There are no magic words needed to express an expert's degree of medical certainty; the test is whether the expert's words demonstrate that he was expressing an expert medical opinion.[243]
- Tennessee: That expert's testimony is "reasonably certain" is a prerequisite to admissibility.[244]
- Texas: The standard is reasonable medical probability.[245]
- Utah: The standard is probability.[246]

---

233. Regenold v. Rutherford, 679 P.2d 833 (N.M. 1984).
234. Jacques v. State, 487 N.Y.S.2d 463 (1984).
235. Matott v. Ward, 48 N.Y.2d 455 (1979).
236. Ferrell v. Frye, 424 S.E.2d 197 (N.C. App. 1993).
237. Klimple v. Bahl, 727 N.W.2d 256 (N.D. 2007); Kunnanz v. Edge, 515 N.W.2d 167 (N.D. 1994).
238. Cunningham v. St. Alexis Hosp. Med. Ctr., 758 N.E.2d 188 (Ohio App. 2001); State v. Benner, 533 N.E.2d 701 (Ohio 1988).
239. Gregg v. Oregon Racing Comm'n, 588 P.2d 1290 (Or. App. 1979).
240. Welsh v. Bulger, 698 A.2d 581 (Pa. 1997).
241. Morra v. Harrop, 791 A.2d 472 (R.I. 2002).
242. Payton v. Kearse, 495 S.E.2d 205 (S.C. 1998).
243. Stormo v. Strong, 469 N.W.2d 816 (S.D. 1991).
244. Miller v. Choo Choo Partners, L.P., 73 S.W.3d 897 (Tenn. App 2001).
245. Duff v. Yelin, 721 S.W.2d 365 (Tex. App. 1986).
246. Dalebout v. Union Pac. R.R. Co., 980 P.2d 1194 (Utah App. 1999).

- Virginia: The standard is reasonable degree of medical probability.[247]
- Washington: The standard is reasonable degree of medical certainty.[248]
- West Virginia: The standard is reasonable degree of medical certainty.[249]
- Wisconsin: No particular words of art are necessary to express the degree of medical certainty required to remove an expert opinion from the realm of mere possibility or conjecture.[250]
- Wyoming: Does not require that an expert use the magic words "reasonable medical probability" in order for his opinion to be considered a competent medical opinion.[251]

What Is the State Rule concerning Admission of Expert Opinion in Documents?

Federal Rule of Evidence 803(6) is the business records exception to the hearsay rule. It provides that opinions and diagnoses contained in business records are admissible, "unless the source of information or the method or circumstances of preparation indicate lack of trustworthiness." Most states that have adopted the Federal Rules of Evidence have adopted Rule 803(6) in the same form as the federal rule. Some states, however, have expressly declined to include opinions in the material that may be admitted under this exception or imposed conditions or restrictions. Table F in Appendix A details these variations. In addition, courts have applied the lack of trustworthiness language to assess whether medical opinions in hearsay documents should be admitted in particular cases.[252]

Conclusion

The use of expert testimony in civil and criminal trials of all varieties continues to increase. It can be expected that principles of state evidence law that apply to this testimony will continue to evolve. Indeed, this survey represents a snapshot of the law at the current moment, and you should be vigilant for changes in the law. Furthermore, while the development of rules of evidence has transformed trial practice in state courts, it is clear

---

247. Pettus v. Gottfried, 606 S.E.2d 819 (Va. 2005).
248. Reese v. Stroh, 907 P.2d 282 (Wash. 1995).
249. Bennett v. Walton, 294 S.E.2d 85 (W. Va. 1982).
250. Drexler v. All Am. Life & Cas. Co., 241 N.W.2d 401 (Wis. 1976).
251. Weber v. McCoy, 950 P.2d 548 (Wyo. 1997).
252. *See, e.g.,* Shpigel v. White, 741 A.2d 1205 (Md. 1999); Arkansas Dep't of Human Servs. v. Huff, 65 S.W.3d 880 (Ark. 2002).

that these principles are not susceptible to rote application, but often demand subtle and complex analysis. It is hoped that this survey is a useful tool for that analysis.

Appendix A: State Variations on Article VII of the Federal Rules of Evidence

This appendix contains seven tables, labeled A through G, showing the states' variations on Federal Rules of Evidence 701–705, 803(6), and 803(18).

Table A: Federal Rule 701 (Opinion Testimony by Lay Witnesses)

States that are similar to Federal Rule 701 BEFORE the 2000 amendment	States that are similar to Federal Rule 701 AFTER the 2000 amendment	States with significant differences from Federal Rule 701
Alabama R.E. 701	Colorado R.E. 701	Florida Stat. § 90.701
Alaska R.E. 701	Delaware R.E. 701	(lay opinion permitted
Arizona R.E. 701	Idaho R.E. 701	(1) when the witness
Arkansas R.E. 701	Kentucky R.E. 701	cannot readily, and
Connecticut C.E. § 7-1	Mississippi R.E. 701	with equal accuracy
Hawaii R.E. 701	New Mexico R.E. 11-701	and adequacy,
Indiana R.E. 701	12 Oklahoma Stat. §	communicate what he
Iowa R.E. 5.701	2701	has perceived to the
Louisiana C.E. art. 701	Pennsylvania R.E. 701	trier of fact without
Maine R.E. 701	South Carolina R.E. 701	testifying about
Maryland R. 5-701	Vermont R.E. 701	inferences or opinions
Michigan R.E. 701	Washington R.E. 701	and the witness's use of
Minnesota R.E. 701		inferences or opinions
Montana R.E. 701		will not mislead the
Nebraska Rev. Stat. § 27-701		trier of fact to the
Nevada Rev. Stat. Ann. § 50.265		prejudice of the objecting party; and (2)
New Hampshire R.E. 701		the opinions and
New Jersey R.E. 701		inferences do not
North Carolina R.E. 701		require a special
North Dakota R.E. 701		knowledge, skill,
Ohio R.E. 701		experience, or
Oregon R.S. § 40.405 (R 701)		training.)
Rhode Island R.E. 701		

(continued)

States that are similar to Federal Rule 701 BEFORE the 2000 amendment	States that are similar to Federal Rule 701 AFTER the 2000 amendment	States with significant differences from Federal Rule 701
South Dakota Codified Laws § 19-15-1		
Tennessee R.E. 701		
Texas R.E. 701		
Utah R.E. 701		
West Virginia R.E. 701		
Wisconsin Stat. Ann § 907.01		
Wyoming R.E. 701		

Table B: Federal Rule 702 (Testimony by Experts)

States that are similar to Federal Rule 702 BEFORE the 2000 amendment	States that are similar to Federal Rule 702 AFTER the 2000 amendment	States with significant differences from Federal Rule 702
Alabama R.E. 702	Delaware R.E. 702	Alaska R.E. 702[a]
Arizona R.E. 702	Kentucky R.E. 702	Florida Stat. §9 0.702[b]
Arkansas R.E. 702	Michigan R.E. 702	Hawaii R.E. 702[c]
Colorado R.E. 702	Mississippi R.E. 702	Indiana R.E. 702[c]
Connecticut C.E. § 7-2	Vermont R.E. 702	Maryland R. 5-702[d]
Idaho R.E. 702		Minnesota R.E. 702[c]
Iowa R.E. 5.702		Nevada Rev. Stat. Ann. § 50.275[e]
Louisiana C.E. art. 702		North Carolina R.E. 702[g]

[a]Alaska adds (b) and (c) regulating number of experts and standard-of-care testimony.
[b]Florida has language that the opinion is admissible only if it can be applied to evidence at trial.
[c]Hawaii, Indiana, Minnesota, and Utah all add language establishing a reliability prerequisite.
[d]Maryland has different phraseology, which also requires the court to determine the appropriateness of expert testimony and whether a sufficient factual basis exists.
[e]Nevada adds language that a witness may testify to matters "within the scope of his knowledge."
[f]New Hampshire Revised Statutes Annotated section 516:29-a establishes reliability requirements for expert testimony, including the language of Federal Rule of Evidence 702 after the 2000 amendment.
[g]North Carolina adds a series of provisions relating to testimony concerning HGN tests, drug testing, and medical malpractice.
[h]Ohio adds a reliability requirement and a requirement that the testimony relate to matters beyond the knowledge of laypersons.
[i]Pennsylvania adds that the knowledge must be "beyond that possessed by a layperson."
[j]Tennessee requires that the testimony "substantially" assist the trier of fact.

States that are similar to Federal Rule 702 BEFORE the 2000 amendment	States that are similar to Federal Rule 702 AFTER the 2000 amendment	States with significant differences from Federal Rule 702
Maine R.E. 701		Ohio R.E. 702[h]
Montana R.E. 702		Pennsylvania R.E. 702[i]
Nebraska Rev. Stat. § 27-702		South Dakota Codified Laws § 19-15-2
New Hampshire R.E. 702[f]		Tennessee R.E. 702[j]
New Jersey R.E. 702		Utah R.E. 702[c]
New Mexico R.E. 11-702		
North Dakota R.E. 702		
12 Oklahoma Stat. § 2702		
Oregon R.S. § 40.410 (R 702)		
Rhode Island R.E. 702		
South Carolina R.E. 702		
Texas R.E. 702		
Washington R.E. 702		
West Virginia R.E. 702		
Wisconsin Stat. Ann. § 907.02		
Wyoming R.E. 702		

Table C: Federal Rule 703 (Bases of Opinion Testimony by Experts)

States that are similar to Federal Rule 703 BEFORE the 2000 amendment	States that are similar to Federal Rule 703 AFTER the 2000 amendment	States with significant differences from Federal Rule 703
Arizona R.E. 703	Colorado R.E. 703	Alabama R.E. 703[a]
Arkansas R.E. 703	Idaho R.E. 703	Alaska R.E. 703
Connecticut C.E. § 7-4(b)	New Mexico R.E.	Delaware R.E. 703[b]
Florida Stat. § 90.704	11-703	Hawaii R.E. 703[c]
Indiana R.E. 703	North Dakota R.E.	Kentucky R.E. 703[d]
Iowa R.E. 5.703	703	Maryland R. 5-703[d]
Louisiana C.E. art. 703	Vermont R.E. 703	Michigan R.E. 703[e]
Maine R.E. 703		Minnesota R.E. 703[f]
Mississippi R.E. 703		Ohio R.E. 703[a]
Montana R.E. 703		Tennessee R.E. 703[g]
Nebraska Rev. Stat. § 27-703		
Nevada Rev. Stat. Ann. § 50.285		
New Hampshire R.E. 703		
New Jersey R.E. 703		
North Carolina R.E. 703		
12 Oklahoma Stat. § 2703		
Oregon R.S. § 40.415 (R. 703)		

[a]Alabama and Ohio eliminate the second sentence of Federal Rule of Evidence 703. Ohio also changes phraseology.

[b]Delaware adds a third sentence that facts otherwise inadmissible shall not be disclosed unless the court determines that probative value outweighs prejudicial effect.

[c]Hawaii adds a third sentence permitting the court to disallow testimony if the underlying facts indicate lack of trustworthiness.

[d]Kentucky and Maryland add identical subsections (b) and (c) allowing facts not admissible in evidence to be disclosed to the jury in the court's discretion and providing that the rule does not limit the right of an opposing party to cross-examine an expert.

[e]Michigan adds a proviso that the rule does not restrict the court's discretion to receive an expert opinion subject to the condition that the factual bases be admitted in evidence thereafter.

[f]Minnesota adds a second subsection requiring allowing admission of otherwise inadmissible facts in civil cases when cause is shown and the underlying data is "particularly trustworthy."

[g]Tennessee adds a proviso that inadmissible facts shall not be disclosed by the proponent unless the court determines that their probative value outweighs the prejudicial effect and a proviso that the court shall disallow the opinion if the underlying facts indicate lack of trustworthiness.

States that are similar to Federal Rule 703 BEFORE the 2000 amendment	States that are similar to Federal Rule 703 AFTER the 2000 amendment	States with significant differences from Federal Rule 703
Pennsylvania R.E. 703		
Rhode Island R.E. 703		
South Carolina R.E. 703		
South Dakota Codified Laws § 19-15-3		
Texas R.E. 703		
Utah R.E. 703		
Washington R.E. 703		
West Virginia R.E. 703		
Wisconsin Stat. Ann. § 907.03		
Wyoming R.E. 702		

Table D: Federal Rule 704 (Opinion on Ultimate Issue)

States that are *similar* to Federal Rule 704(a)	States that *differ* from Federal Rule 704
Alaska R.E. 704	Alabama R.E. 704
Arizona R.E. 704	Delaware R.E. 704(a)
Arkansas R.E. 704	Indiana R.E. 704(a)
California Evid. Code § 805	Louisiana C.E. art. 704(a)
Colorado R.E. 704	Maryland R. 5-704(a)
Connecticut C.E. § 7-3(a)	New Hampshire R.E. 704
Florida Stat. § 90-703	Ohio R.E. 704
Hawaii R.E. 704	West Virginia R.E. 704
Idaho R.E. 704	
Iowa R.E. 5.704	
Maine R.E. 704	
Michigan R.E. 704	
Minnesota R.E. 704	
Mississippi R.E. 704	
Missouri R. St. §490.065.2	
Montana R.E. 704	
Nebraska Rev. Stat. § 27-704	
Nevada Rev. Stat. Ann. § 50.295	
New Jersey R.E. 704	
New Mexico R.E. 11-704	
North Carolina R.E. 704	
North Dakota R.E. 704	

(continued)

States that are *similar* to Federal Rule 704(a)	States that *differ* from Federal Rule 704
12 Oklahoma Stat. §2704	
Oregon R.S. § 40.420 (R. 704)	
Pennsylvania R.E. 704	
Rhode Island R.E. 704	
South Carolina R.E. 704	
South Dakota Codified Laws § 19-15-4	
Tennessee R.E. 704	
Texas R.E. 704	
Utah R.E. 704 (a)	
Vermont R.E. 704	
Washington R.E. 704	
Wisconsin Stat. Ann. §907.04	
Wyoming R.E. 704	

Table E: Federal Rule 705 (Disclosure of Facts of Data Underlying Expert Opinion)

States that are *similar* to Federal Rule 705	States that *differ* from Federal Rule 705
Alabama R.E. 705	Alaska R.E. 705[a, b]
Arizona R.E. 705	Connecticut C.E. § 7-4(a)
Arkansas R.E. 705	Delaware R.E. 705[a]
Colorado R.E. 705	Florida Stat. § 90.705[a]
Indiana R.E. 705	Hawaii R.E. 705[c]
Iowa R.E. 5.705	Idaho R.E. 705[c]
Kentucky R.E. 705	Louisiana C.E. art. 705[d]

[a]Alaska Rule 705(b), Delaware Rule 705(b), Florida Statutes section 90.705(2), Maine Rule 705(b), and Texas Rule 705(b) all permit an adverse party to obtain a determination of the basis of the opinion before the expression of the opinion.
[b]Alaska Rule 705(c) and Texas Rule 705(d) provide for a balancing test for inadmissible facts if the danger that they will be used for an improper purpose outweighs their value as support for the expert's opinion. They also provide for a limiting instruction.
[c]Hawaii and Idaho add provisos that the underlying facts and data must have been disclosed in discovery proceedings.
[d]Louisiana requires that in a criminal case an expert witness state the facts on which the opinion is based.
[e]New Jersey, North Carolina, and Ohio expressly provide that questions need not be hypothetical.
[f]Ohio, Pennsylvania, and Rhode Island all require that the expert disclose the facts or data on which the opinion is based.
[g]Texas Rule 705(c) provides that if the court determines that the underlying facts do not provide a sufficient basis for the expert's opinion, the opinion is inadmissible.

States that are *similar* to Federal Rule 705	States that *differ* from Federal Rule 705
Maryland R. 5-703	Maine R.E. 705[a]
Michigan R.E. 705	New Jersey R.E. 705[e]
Minnesota R.E. 705	North Carolina R.E. 705[e]
Mississippi R.E. 705	Ohio R.E. 705[e, f]
Montana R.E. 705	Pennsylvania R.E. 705[f]
Nebraska Rev. Stat. § 27-705	Rhode Island R.E. 705[f]
Nevada Rev. Stat. Ann. § 50.305	Texas R.E. 705[a, b, g]
New Hampshire R.E. 705	
New Mexico R.E. 705	
North Dakota R.E. 705	
12 Oklahoma Stat. § 2705	
Oregon R.S. §40.425 (R. 705)	
South Carolina R.E. 705	
South Dakota Codified Laws § 19-15-5.1	
Tennessee R.E. 705	
Utah R.E. 705	
Vermont R.E. 705	
Washington R.E. 705	
West Virginia R.E. 705	
Wisconsin Stat. Ann. § 907.05	
Wyoming R.E. 705	

Table F: Federal Rule 803(6)

States that are *similar* to Federal Rule 803(6)	States that *differ* from Federal Rule 803(6)
Alabama R.E. 803(6)	California[a]
Alaska R.E. 803(6)	Connecticut C.E. § 8-4[b]
Arizona R.E. 803(6)	District of Columbia[c]
Arkansas R.E. 803(6)	Florida Stat. §90.803(6)[d]
Colorado R.E. 803(6)	Georgia§ 24-3-14[e]
Delaware R.E. 803(6)	Louisiana C.E. art. 803(6)[i]
Hawaii R.E. 803(6)	Massachusetts[j]
Idaho R.E. 803(6)	Missouri[k]
Illinois[f]	Montana R.E. 803(6)
Indiana R.E. 803(6)	Nebraska Rev. Stat. § 27-803(5)[l]
Kansas[g]	New Jersey R.E. 808[m]
Kentucky R.E. 803(6)[h]	New York[n]
Maine R.E. 803(6)	Ohio R.E. 803(6)[o]
Maryland R. 5-803(6)	Pennsylvania R.E. 803(6)[p]
Michigan R.E. 803(6)	South Carolina R.E. 803(6)[q]
Minnesota R.E. 803(6)	Virginia[r]
Mississippi R.E. 803(6)	Washington[s]
Nevada Rev. Stat. Ann. § 51.135	
New Hampshire R.E. 803(6)	
New Mexico R.E. 11-803(f)	
North Carolina R.E. 803(6)	
North Dakota R.E. 803(6)	
12 Oklahoma Stat. § 2803(6)	
Oregon R.S. § 40.460 (Rule 803(6))	
Rhode Island R.E. 803(6)	
South Dakota Codified Laws § 19-16-9	
Tennessee R.E. 803(6)	
Texas R.E. 803(6)	
Utah R.E. 803(6)	
Vermont R.E. 803(6)	
West Virginia R.E. 803(6)	
Wisconsin Stat. Ann. §908.03(6)	
Wyoming R.E. 803(6)	

[a] California: California Evidence Code section 1271 does not expressly mention opinions. People v. Beeler, 891 P.2d 153 (Cal. 1995) (Opinion admissible only if it is a statement of a fact or condition.).

[b] Connecticut: Connecticut Code of Evidence section 8-4 (business records) does not expressly speak to opinions. Opinions would be admissible only if person making entry were shown to be qualified to give that opinion in testimony. Cavallaro v. Hosp. of St. Raphael, 882 A.2d 1254 (Conn. App. 2005).

Table F (*continued*)

[c]District of Columbia: Opinions in business records are admissible if they involve routine observations about which expert witnesses are not likely to disagree. Lyons v. Barrazotto, 667 A.2d 314 (D.C. 1995).

[d]Florida: Florida Statutes section 90.803(6) permits opinions but has a clause stating that the opinion is inadmissible unless it would be admissible under sections 90.701-90.705.

[e]Georgia: Official Code of Georgia Annotated section 24-3-14 does not mention opinions. Duncan v. State, 515 S.E.2d 388 (Ga. 1999) (opinions in business records not admissible).

[f]Illinois: Opinions in medical records are admissible. Troyan v. Reyes, 855 N.E.2d 967 (Ill. App. 2006). The court may conclude that opinions should be presented by live testimony. Kelly v. HCI Heinz Constr. Co., 668 N.E.2d 596 (Ill. App. 1996).

[g]Kansas: Kansas Statutes Annotated section 60-460(m), the business records exception, allows opinions in hospital records. *In re* Estate of Bernatzki, 460 P.2d 527 (Kan. 1969).

[h]Kentucky: Rule 803(6)(B). No evidence in the form of an opinion is admissible under this paragraph unless such opinion would be admissible under Article VII of these rules if the person whose opinion is recorded were to testify to the opinion directly.

[i]Louisiana: Louisiana Code of Evidence article 803(6) applies only to civil cases.

[j]Massachusetts: Opinions in business records generally not admissible. Burke v. Memorial Hosp., 558 N.E.2d 1146 (Mass. App. 1990); Julian v. Randazzo, 403 N.E.2d 931 (Mass. 1980). By statute, medical records containing opinions are admissible under certain conditions. General Laws of the Commonwealth of Massachusetts ch. 233, § 79G.

[k]Missouri: Missouri Revised Statutes § 490.680. Opinions in business records admissible. Sigrist v. Clarke, 935 S.W.2d 350 (Mo. App. 1996). The appropriate test for admissibility of specific portions of medical records is whether the person whose opinions are recited in the record could have testified regarding those portions if present at trial.

[l]Nebraska: Rule 803(5) permits a business record "other than opinions or diagnoses."

[m]New Jersey: Under Rule 808, expert opinion that is included in an admissible hearsay statement shall be excluded if the declarant has not been produced as a witness unless the trial judge finds that the circumstances involved in rendering the opinion, including the motive, duty, and interest of the declarant, whether litigation was contemplated by the declarant, the complexity of the subject matter, and the likelihood of accuracy of the opinion, tend to establish its trustworthiness.

[n]New York: Where records meet the statutory qualifications for business records, opinions are admissible. Wilson v. Bodian, 519 N.Y.S.2d 126 (1987).

[o]Ohio: Rule 803(6) omits opinions and diagnoses. Prerule authority admitted opinions under certain circumstances. *See* Hytha v. Schwendeman, 320 N.E.2d 312 (Ohio App. 1974).

[p]Pennsylvania: Rule 803(6) omits opinions and diagnosis.

[q]South Carolina: Rule 803(6) omits the word "opinions" but includes "diagnoses." It has an express proviso that "subjective opinions and judgments found in business records are not admissible."

[r]Virginia: Opinions in business records are not admissible. Ward v. Commonwealth, 217 S.E.2d 810 (Va. 1975).

[s]Washington: There is no Rule 803(6). Revised Code of Washington section 5.45.020 does not mention opinions. *But see* Fox v. Mahoney, 22 P.3d 839 (Wash. App. 2001), admitting them under Washington Rule of Evidence 904.

Table G: Federal Rule 803(18)

States that are *similar* to Federal Rule 803(18)	States that *differ* from Federal Rule 803(18)
Alabama R.E. 803(18)	Colorado R.E. 803(18)
Alaska R.E. 803(18)	Connecticut C.E. § 8-3(8)
Arizona R.E. 803(18)	Florida Stat. §90.706
Arkansas R.E. 803(18)	Georgia: *Pound v. Medney*, 337 SE. 2d
California Evid. Code § 721(b)	772 (1985)
Delaware R.E. 803(18)	Idaho R.E. 803(18)
District of Columbia: *Hill v. Medlantic*	Illinois: *Downey v. Dunnington*, 895
Health Care Group, 933 A.2d 314	NE.2d 271 (2008)
(2007)	Indiana R.E. 803(18)
Hawaii Rule 702.1, 803(18)	Kansas St. Ann. 60-460(cc)
Iowa R.E. 803(18)	Maine R.E. 803(18)
Kentucky R.E. 803(18)	Massachusetts: *Commonwealth v.*
Louisiana R.E. 803(18)	*Sneed*, 597 NE.2d 1346 (1992)
Maryland Rule 5-803(18)	Michigan R.E. 707
Minnesota R.E. 803(18)	Mississippi R.E. 803(18)
Montana R.E. 803(18)	Missouri: *Wilson v. ANR Freight*
Nebraska Rev. Stat. § 27-803(17)	*Systems, Inc.*, 892 SW.2d 658 (1994)
New Jersey R.E. 803(18)	Nevada Rev. Stat. § 51-255
New Mexico R.E. 11-803	New Hampshire R.E. 803(18)
North Carolina R.E. 803(18)	New York: *Lipschitz v. Stein*, 781
North Dakota R.E. 803(18)	N.Y.S. 2d 773 (2004)
Ohio R.E. 803(18)	Oregon R.S. § 40.430 (Rule 706)
12 Oklahoma Stat. § 2803(18)	Pennsylvania: *Aldridge v. Edmunds*,
Rhode Island R.E. 803(18)	750 A.2d 292 (2000)
South Carolina R.E. 803(18)	Tennessee R.E. 803(18)
South Dakota Codified Laws § 19-16-22	Wisconsin Stat. § 908.03(18)
Texas R.E. 803(18)	
Utah R.E. 803(18)	
Vermont R.E. 803(18)	
Virginia Code § 8.01-401.1	
Washington R.E. 803(18)	
West Virginia R.E. 803(18)	
Wyoming R.E. 803(18)	

CHAPTER 8

Experts at Trial

PREPARING YOUR EXPERT FOR TRIAL TESTIMONY

Carl Robin Teague[1]

Sometimes expert witnesses are clueless about how and when to prepare for trial and about what to do in preparing for trial. Sometimes experts intentionally wait until the last minute to prepare. Some experts are just like some trial lawyers: they expect the case to settle and think that the effort to prepare will be wasted. Others might think that they already know all they need to know and therefore do not need to prepare: "Been there, done that." Seasoned trial lawyers know there is a rude awakening for those who are unprepared and for those who start too late to get prepared. The other side can sense lack of preparation and will take advantage of the unprepared trial team in settlement negotiations or at trial.[2]

Experts need leadership. Trial lawyers must provide that leadership. The buck stops with you.[3] Some of us are fortunate to have paralegals, legal assistants, legal secretaries, or in-house staff members who are skilled at getting cases ready for trial and have the time to get ready. But the legal assistant might become ill, or the paralegal might have a personal emergency.

---

1. Carl Robin Teague is a sole practitioner based in San Antonio, primarily serving as defense counsel for large, self-insured manufacturers in products liability suits brought in Texas.

2. The Honorable Mark Drummond, *The Trial Notebook*, Litigation News, Spring 2009, at 18.

3. *See* Nora Lockwood Tooher, *Trade Secrets: Tips for Witness Preparation*, Law. U.S.A., Jan. 14, 2009 (reporting American Bar Association (ABA) audio seminar given by Stephen D. Susman), *available at* http://lawyersusaonline.com/blog/2009/01/14/trade-secrets-tips-for-witness-preparation.

Trial lawyers should know how to get the case ready for trial and how to make sure the expert witnesses are going to be ready.

When should you start getting ready? Scheduling orders and other pretrial orders under Federal Rule of Civil Procedure 16 might provide a good guide for developing a pretrial and trial plan. Establish deadlines consistent with scheduling and other pretrial orders. If you delegate any of these pretrial preparations to associates or support staff, follow up to make sure that each deadline is met.

This subchapter addresses the following pretrial issues: (1) supplementing your expert's testimony, (2) responding to motions to limit your expert's testimony, (3) taking care of courtroom logistics, (4) ensuring your expert's attendance at trial, (5) educating your expert about courtroom procedure, (6) honing your expert's communication skills, (7) preparing your expert to testify on direct, and (8) preparing your expert to stand up under cross-examination.

Pretrial Supplementation of Expert Testimony

Well understood is the duty to disclose expert testimony.[4] A more difficult subject is the duty to supplement disclosures of expert testimony. A collection of rules governs the scope of the duty to supplement and the deadline for supplementation. Failure to timely and completely disclose might result in sanctions under Rule 37(c), including exclusion of the expert's testimony.

The scope of the duty to supplement is defined in Federal Rule of Civil Procedure 26(e):

> For an expert witness whose report must be disclosed under Rule 26(a)(2) (B), the party's duty to supplement extends to both information included in the report and to information given during the expert's deposition.[5]

The next sentence in that rule refers to "additions or changes to this information," indicating the supplemental disclosure should include additional information collected and changes made in information previously disclosed.

The trial lawyer's responsibility is to determine whether the information in the expert's report requires supplementation. Experts often continue investigations after preparing written reports or testifying by deposition, sometimes without notifying the trial attorney. For example, some experts perform litigation tests after preparing the report or testifying by deposition. Similarly, as discovery proceeds, additional "facts or data . . . may be . . .

---

4. *See* Fed. R. Civ. P. 26(a)(2).
5. Fed. R. Civ. P. 26(e)(2).

perceived by or made known to the expert"[6] after he has prepared the report or testified by deposition. "Facts . . . made known" would of course include information provided by the trial lawyer.

Scheduling orders may govern the deadline for supplementing expert disclosures. Rule 16(b)(3)(B) provides that "[t]he scheduling order may: (i) modify the timing of disclosures under Rules 26(a) and 26(e)(1)." Scheduling orders often require that supplemental disclosures be served at least 30 days before trial.

If the scheduling order does not establish the deadline for supplementing disclosures of expert testimony, then Rule 26(e)(2) and 26(a)(3) require that supplemental disclosures be made at least 30 days before trial. Under Rule 26(e)(2):

> Any additions or changes to this information [included in the report and . . . given during the expert's deposition] must be disclosed by the time the party's pretrial disclosures under Rule 26(a)(3) are due.

Rule 26(a)(3), in turn, provides as follows:

> (B) Time for Pre-Trial Disclosures; Objections. Unless the court orders otherwise, these disclosures must be made at least 30 days before trial.

The "at least" language leads to a cautionary note: a failure to timely and completely supplement an expert report *before* a deposition, even if the disclosure is made at least 30 days before trial, might lead to an objection or motion under Federal Rule of Civil Procedure 37(c)(1) that the failure is harmful because the objecting party did not have an adequate opportunity to depose the expert on the supplemental information. Waiting until the deadline might not be the best policy.

There is a final cautionary note: the question of whether a party has a *right* to supplement is different from the question of whether the party has a *duty* to supplement. For example, a party might want, for strategic reasons, to expand the scope of the expert's testimony via supplementation.[7]

Pretrial Evidentiary Motions

As with other evidence, expert witness testimony is the subject of pretrial evidentiary motions. The most common pretrial evidentiary motion is the

6. *See* FED. R. EVID. 703.

7. *See* Carl Robin Teague, *Is There a Right to Supplement Expert Witness Disclosures Under Rule 26(e)? published in* American Bar Association, Section of Litigation, EXPERT WITNESSES COMMITTEE ANNUAL REVIEW, at 7 (2009).

motion *in limine*, but, as discussed below, motions to admit or exclude may also be used with respect to expert testimony.

Many judges take a dim view of general motions *in limine*, including those relating to expert witnesses. Therefore, you should avoid general motions and be ready to object to them. Consider asking the court not to refer to the expert witnesses as "experts" and to instruct the parties and the witnesses to refrain from doing so. The Advisory Committee's notes to the 2000 amendments to Federal Rule of Evidence 702 provide support for such a motion:

> The amendment continues the practice of the original Rule in referring to a qualified witness as an "expert." . . . The use of the term "expert" in the Rule does not, however, mean that a jury should actually be informed that a qualified witness is testifying as an "expert." Indeed, there is much to be said for a practice that prohibits the use of the term "expert" by both parties and the court at trial.[8]

This kind of motion *in limine* might be a good idea if you are concerned that a reference by the judge to the opposing party's expert witness as an "expert" might be interpreted by the jury as a stamp of approval and a comment on the weight of the evidence. A competing consideration, however, is that stamping the opposing party's expert witness with the label expert might make it easier to attack the witness as a hired gun.

If the opposing party moves to limit your expert's testimony, consider filing a motion to admit the evidence. Taking the offensive might give you a psychological advantage over your opponent. It might also draw out an opponent who is "laying behind the log,"waiting to make the real objection when you make the offer during trial—when you might be under fire and not as prepared as you might be in a pretrial hearing.

Determine whether an affidavit by your expert witness is necessary to support your motion to admit or your response in opposition to a motion *in limine* or to exclude. Federal Rule of Civil Procedure 43 provides as follows: "When a motion relies on facts outside the record, the court may hear the matter on affidavits or may hear it wholly or partly on oral testimony or on depositions."[9] Local rules might require that affidavits in support be filed with the motion and that affidavits in opposition be filed with the response. Advise your expert, however, that testimony in person during a hearing

---

8. Fed. R. Evid. 702 Advisory Committee's notes to 2000 amendments; *see* United States v. Bartley, 855 F.2d 547, 552 (8th Cir. 1988).
9. Fed. R. Civ. P. 43(c).

might be required or more persuasive and that the expert should be prepared to testify at a pretrial hearing.[10]

Finally, consider asking the court to make a pretrial evidentiary ruling definitive rather than merely *in limine*. Since the 2000 amendments, Federal Rule of Evidence 103(a) has provided: "Once the court makes a definitive ruling on the record admitting or excluding evidence, either at or before trial, a party need not renew an objection or offer of proof to preserve a claim of error for appeal."[11] The Advisory Committee's notes to Federal Rule of Evidence 103 caution that "[t]he amendment imposes the obligation on counsel to clarify whether an *in limine* or other evidentiary ruling is definitive when there is doubt on that point."

Courtroom Logistics

Do the trial lawyer, expert witness, and litigation support team expect to walk into the courtroom, plug in, and begin? If so, you might be expecting too much and be surprised by what you find when the trial begins. For example, in a recent case, I found that some monitors worked and some monitors did not. In another situation, I found that one laptop was compatible with the courtroom system, but another, newer laptop was incompatible.

Your trial team, including expert witnesses, should visit the courtroom before the trial begins. Contact the courtroom deputy to arrange the visit. If your expert cannot visit the courtroom before testifying, consider sending the expert a video recording or still photographs and sketches of the courtroom and its systems.

Here is a checklist of issues to investigate when you visit the courtroom:

- Where are the electrical connections located?
- Is the courtroom high tech or low tech?
- If the courtroom is high tech, with what audio/visual systems is it equipped? Projector? Speakers? Screen? Monitors? Document camera?
- If the courtroom is high tech, is your equipment compatible with the system with which the courtroom is equipped? (For example, are adjustments in resolution on your or the expert witness's laptop required before images will properly project on a screen? Do laptop settings need to be changed so the laptop screens can be projected on the screen?)

---

10. *See generally In re* Paoli R.R. Yard PCB Litig., 35 F.3d 717, 736, 739 (3d Cir. 1994) (discussing the use of *in limine* hearings).

11. Fed. R. Civ. P. 103(a).

- Will there be enough room for all the equipment that the opposing parties plan to use? Or, because of space or other limitations, must the parties agree to cooperate and share some components?
- Is the expert bringing any large objects (such as part of an automobile in a product liability case or a large visual aid)? If so, will the objects fit through the doors of the courthouse and courtroom? If not, should a request be made for the trial to be conducted in a courtroom that can accommodate large objects? Or can the objects be disassembled so that the parts may fit into the courthouse and courtroom?
- Will there be a problem bringing any of your electronic equipment or visual aids through the court security? If so, what special arrangements must be made to allow passage?

Witness Availability

First, it is your responsibility to ensure that your expert witness attends the trial. Inform the expert witness about pretrial deadlines and the trial date as soon as the court renders the scheduling order. Monitor the witness so that the witness does not make conflicting plans.

Assist the expert in making travel arrangements. Do not rely entirely on experts to timely and adequately plan for travel to the trial. Do not wait until the last minute, when flights might be full or inconvenient, or airfares more expensive. Also assist the expert in arranging for accommodations, local travel, and shipment of tangible things (such as a product or exemplar product, test apparatus and fixtures, and visual aids).

Second, plan ahead for the possibility that your expert will be rendered unavailable. Lots of trial lawyers do not ask questions during depositions of their experts by the other side. (Routinely they end the deposition with, "We'll reserve our questions until the time of trial.") If there is a chance that your expert will not be available at trial, you should establish the witness's testimony at the deposition. You might even consider noticing the deposition of your own expert witness. A game is sometimes played between plaintiff and defense counsel regarding treating physicians in a personal injury or disease case. Plaintiff lawyers routinely wait for the defense to notice the depositions of those kinds of witnesses. Sometimes defense counsel does not do so. Do not wait until too late, when the expert witness is unavailable even for a deposition, or the deadline for completion of discovery has come and gone.

Finally, if your expert is suddenly unable to attend the trial, consider whether video or telephone conferencing is available where the witness is located and in the courtroom. Make arrangements for video or telephone conferencing ahead of time. Under Federal Rule of Civil Procedure 43(a), file and present a motion for permission to present "testimony in open court by contemporaneous transmission from a different location."

Courtroom Procedure

Trial lawyers often forget that the courtroom is a foreign place for many expert witnesses and that it is our job to make sure that our experts understand courtroom procedure. Specifically, you should explain the identity and role of court personnel and emphasize the importance of complying with an order excluding witnesses from the courtroom.

Court Personnel

If the expert witness is not experienced in courtroom testimony, information about courtroom personnel might be helpful. Consider providing information about the duties and roles to be played by the courtroom deputy, bailiff, and law clerks. Inform the expert witness about the formalities observed and required by the courtroom personnel.

Exclusion of Witnesses under Federal Rule of Evidence 615

At least one party usually requests that the court "order witnesses excluded so that they cannot hear the testimony of other witnesses."[12] Often, this request is made in this manner: "Your Honor, we invoke the rule." Federal Rule of Evidence 615 does not authorize exclusion of "a person whose presence is shown by a party to be essential to the presentation of the party's cause."[13] The question is whether this exception applies to expert witnesses. The Advisory Committee's notes indicate it might: "The category contemplates such persons as . . . an expert needed to advise counsel in the management of the litigation."[14] The exception does not, however, automatically apply to expert witnesses.[15] The burden is imposed on the party requesting application of the exception to show that the court should apply it.[16] The

---

12. *See* Fed. R. Evid. 615.
13. Fed. R. Evid. 615(3).
14. Fed. R. Evid. 615 Advisory Committee's notes to 1972 proposed rules.
15. *See* United States v. Seschillie, 310 F. 3d 1208, 1213–14 (9th Cir. 2002), *cert. denied*, 538 U.S. 953 (2003) ("We decline to conclude . . . that an expert witness will *always* meet the criteria of Rule 615(3).") (emphasis in original); Opus 3 Ltd. v. Heritage Park, Inc., 91 F.3d 625, 629 (4th Cir. 1996); Drilex Sys., Inc. v. Flores, 1 S.W. 3d 112, 118 (Tex. 1999).
16. *See Seschillie,* 310 F.3d 1208.

rule "vests in trial judges broad discretion to determine whether a witness is essential."[17] Appellate courts "review the district court's ruling regarding the applicability of Rule 615(3) for an abuse of discretion."[18]

Thus, the party requesting application of the exception to an expert witness should not always expect the opposition will agree and should be prepared to show that the expert's "presence [is] essential to the presentation of the party's cause."[19] But the opposition should not routinely object to the application of the exception since some appellate courts have held that the trial court abused its discretion in excluding an expert.[20] The party requesting application of the exception should not wait until the rule is invoked before preparing for a request for application of the exception.

Counsel should appropriately advise expert witnesses if the court refuses to apply the exception or if counsel decides that the expert witness should be excluded. The consequences of a violation of the rule can be severe. The trial court might order that the witness be disqualified.[21] If the court allows the witness to testify, the court might allow opposing counsel to cross-examine the witness about the violation[22] or instruct the jury to consider the violation in determining the credibility of the witness.[23]

Expert's Communication Skills

If the jury does not trust your expert witness, the substance of the witness's testimony is irrelevant. You should work with your expert before trial to ensure that he is complying with any unwritten dress code in the venue, that your expert does not have distracting habits, and that your expert understands how to answer questions clearly.

Dress Code

If you are trying a case in West Texas, you do not want your expert, "a Connecticut Yankee," to walk in wearing a brand new ten-gallon Stetson, lizard-skin boots, and a western suit. If you are prepared, this situation will happen only to your opponent—and to your amusement.

---

17. *Opus*, 91 F.3d 625.
18. *Seschillie*, 310 F.3d 1208.
19. *See* FED. R. EVID. 615.
20. *See Seschillie*, 310 F.3d 1208; Malek v. Fed. Ins. Co., 994 F.2d 49, 54 (2d Cir. 1993).
21. *See* United States v. Wilson, 103 F.3d 1402 (8th Cir. 1997).
22. United States v. Hobbs, 31 F.3d 918, 921 (9th Cir. 1994).
23. Holder v. United States, 150 U.S. 91 (1893); Hill v. Porter Mem'l Hosp., 90 F.3d 220 (7th Cir. 1996).

Talk to your expert if you have not been together several times, enough to get an understanding of the expert's style of dress. Talk to your expert before depositions, and before trial, because a visual record of a deposition will reveal inappropriate clothing worn then.

Visit the courtroom during a trial. Such a visit should lead you to learn about any informal dress code in that court for expert witnesses. Unless there is a reason to be formal, however, the expert should be dressed comfortably so that testimony will not be affected.

Bad Habits

Review the recording of the expert witness's deposition to identify any bad habits that you can help the witness break. First, look for distracting body language, such as rocking back and forth in the witness chair, covering the face with hands, fidgeting with hands, and playing with a necklace or other jewelry. Also look for communication problems, such as speaking too quickly or saying "uh huh" instead of "yes, ma'am," or "nuh uh," instead of "no, sir." (I try to cure the problem during the deposition: "Did you mean 'no'?" or "Was that a 'yes'?") Finally, listen for the expert's tendency to use obscure words. Physicians are especially prone to use uncommon words like "distal," "medial," and "proximal," which mean nothing to the typical juror and, when used, will lead to frustration. The trial lawyer who retained the expert should try to convince the witness to use understandable language. Experts might use technical terms, to show expertise, but should immediately explain and give examples.

Importance of Responsiveness

Some cross-examiners just love an unresponsive witness. You know that type of witness, the one who, when asked about the defendant's conduct, testifies instead about the plaintiff's conduct, or vice versa. Trial lawyers can make the unresponsive witness look like a fool. As Professor Jim McElhaney recently wrote, "Whenever you're evasive or argumentative, you lose credibility, and the judge and jury won't trust anything you say."[24] The trial lawyer should caution the expert to answer the question asked, not the question the expert wants to answer, and to apologize for misunderstanding the question if there is truly a misunderstanding. The lawyer should advise the expert that failing to answer the questions might lead to some of these embarrassing moments:

---

24. Jim McElhaney, *On Good Behavior*, A.B.A. J., Feb. 2009, at 28.

Q. Did you hear my question?
A. Yes.
Q. What was my question?
A. I don't remember.
Q. I'll ask the question again.
A. Okay.
Q. Did you hear my question that time?
A. I must not have. Please ask it again.
Q. Here goes for the third time.
A. Okay.
Q. Did you understand my question?
A. Yes.
Q. Sir, I know you want to answer *that* question (whether _____) but I want you to answer *this* question.
A. I thought I answered it.

And impress on the witness that the cross-examiner may not even need to ask the judge for help. The judge will finally get impatient and take action without request:

The Judge: The witness is instructed to just answer the question.

Answer: Yes, your Honor. I am so sorry (for playing games).[25]

Engaging the Jury

Trial lawyers and expert witnesses should be prepared to try to keep jurors awake. One way is to create motion in the courtroom. Normally, witnesses are required to testify from the witness chair, and often trial lawyers are required to ask questions from counsel tables or a podium. But many judges will permit a witness to leave the chair or the lawyer to leave the table or podium for the purpose of, for example, discussing an exhibit, showing an exhibit or visual aid to the jury, drawing on a chalk board or pad, or presenting a PowerPoint presentation. You should check the court's website for guidance or ask the court for instructions during the pretrial conference.

There are other methods for keeping jurors awake. One is to get to—and stick to—the point. Preparation might require practice "Q and A" with the witness so that one prone to verbosity will learn how to be concise.

Another trial technique is to make sure the jobs of the judges and jury are easy. Avoid making their jobs more difficult. Can the jury and judge see

---

25. *See* Fed. R. Evid. 611(a).

the witness? Exhibit A? Can they hear the witness? The sound and visual record of the deposition? Prepare for these situations with the expert witness.

Can the jury understand the witness? In a case involving some complex or uncommon subjects, the witness should be prepared to use analogies and examples. Once, in the trial of a product liability case involving a fall from a scaffold, a question was whether the scaffold platform could deflect, so that it was not level, causing the user to lose his balance. Trial preparation led to the discovery that the amount of deflection could be calculated using the Pythagorean Theorem. On direct examination, the question was asked, "Is there any theory which enables you to determine the amount of any deflection?" The answer was, "Yes. The Pythagorean Theorem." The high school math teacher on the front row of the jury box smiled and nodded her head in agreement and in recognition of a true expert. The witness then explained the theorem in layman's terms. The witness should be prepared to impress the jury but also to make sure the jury understands what the expert is talking about.

The witness should be prepared to talk directly to individual jurors. Some jurors are put off by watching a witness who pays attention only to the lawyer asking the questions. The witness should be prepared to involve the jury in the story.

Demeanor on Cross-Examination

Have you ever cross-examined an expert witness who, after being so pleasant and forthcoming on direct examination, became argumentative with you and evaded your (hopefully well-formed) questions? Prepare your expert witness to avoid this mistake. Make sure the witness knows the proper role of a witness, which is not to pick fights with opposing counsel, but rather to let opposing counsel pick a fight with the witness, if there is to be a fight. This advice does not, however, mean the witness should roll over for the cross-examiner. It is essential that the witness stand up under aggressive cross-examination.

A witness should be prepared to know the difference between holding one's ground and going out on a limb. The trial lawyer should prepare the witness to listen for that sound of the saw, cutting the limb off after the witness has gone out to the end of it. An example of going out on a limb is testimony by a defense expert in a product liability suit that the product is safe under all circumstances.

Preparation of Witness for Direct Examination

The Role of Expert Witnesses

Sometimes experts forget the proper role of an expert witness. There is the tendency of some experts to become advocates for or against one party, usually, of course, for the party that retained the expert. Advocacy by an expert is a matter considered by the jury in determining credibility and by the cross-examiner in showing the jury that the expert is taking sides. Other expert witnesses just enjoy playing games, like "hide the ball," or picking fights with the cross-examiner, not paying attention to the judge and jury, who are grading their papers.

So what is the proper role? In preparation for trial, the trial lawyer should inform or remind the expert witness about the Federal Rules of Evidence, which provide a guideline for the proper role:

> If scientific, technical, or other specialized knowledge will assist the trier of fact to understand the evidence or to determine a fact in issue, a witness qualified as an expert . . . may testify thereto.[26]

Thus, the rule indicates the proper role is twofold:

1. Assist or help the jury to understand the evidence; or
2. Assist or help the jury to determine a fact in issue.

The trial lawyer should advise the expert on those two roles and make sure that the expert realizes credibility might be damaged if the expert steps outside of those two roles.

The direct examiner and expert must decide on the scope or nature of the trial testimony by the expert. Will the expert testify on "an ultimate issue to be decided by the trier of fact," as permitted under Federal Rule of Evidence 704?[27] Or will the expert just try to "assist the trier of fact to understand the evidence?" Or assist the trier of fact to do both, "understand" *and* "determine?"

The Advisory Committee's notes provide an explanation of the difference between the expert as educator, through exposition, and the expert as advocate, through opinions:

---

26. FED. R. EVID. 702; *see also* FED. R. EVID. 701 ("If the witness is not testifying as an expert, the witness' testimony . . . is limited to those opinions or inferences which are . . . helpful to a clear understanding of the witness' testimony or the determination of a fact in issue .").

27. *See also* FED. R. EVID. 702 (permitting the "witness qualified as an expert" to "assist the trier of fact to . . . determine a fact in issue").

Most of the literature assumes that experts testify only in the form of opinions. The assumption is logically unfounded. The rule accordingly recognizes that an expert on the stand may give a dissertation or exposition of scientific or other principles relevant to the case, leaving the trier of fact to apply them to the facts.

[I]t seems wise to recognize that opinions are not indispensable and to encourage the use of expert testimony in non-opinion form when counsel believes the trier can itself draw the requisite inference. The use of opinions is not abolished by the rule, however. It will continue to be permissible for the experts to take the further step of suggesting the inference which should be drawn from applying the specialized knowledge to the facts. See Rules 703 to 705.[28]

Review of Materials in Preparation for Direct Examination

The witness and trial lawyer should, of course, read the transcript of the deposition. The lawyer should make sure the witness has timely corrected errors and returned the corrected transcript to the court reporter.

The lawyer should ask the witness to be self-critical. Some experts will recognize problems such as rambling answers, unresponsive answers, or confusing or unclear answers. To the extent that the witness does not recognize the problems, the lawyer should give advice, based in part on the written record of the testimony. The advice might be about the substance of the testimony. The advice might also be about techniques used by the lawyer taking the deposition.

The lawyer and witness should also view the sound and visual records of the deposition. Here the lawyer and witness may be helped by a third-person nonlawyer, who can provide feedback about mannerisms and clarity.

Preliminary Questions concerning Qualification of a Person to Be an Expert Witness

Prepare the expert witness for preliminary questions. Preliminary questions involve both substance and procedure. The substance is controlled by Federal Rule of Evidence 702:

---

28. Fed. R. Evid. 702, Advisory Committee's notes to 1972 proposed rules; *see also* 1 David L. Faigman et al., Modern Scientific Evidence: The Law and Science of Expert Testimony §§ 3:5–3:10 (2008) (discussing experts as "pure educators," as "assistant advocates," and as "hired guns").

If scientific, technical, or other specialized knowledge will assist the trier of fact . . . , a witness qualified as an expert by knowledge, skill, experience, training, or education, may testify thereto.

The procedure to be followed is based on several rules. Federal Rule of Evidence 104(a) provides as follows:

Preliminary questions concerning the qualification of a person to be a witness . . . shall be determined by the court.

"Consequently, the admissibility of all expert testimony is governed by the principles of Rule 104(a)."[29] The Advisory Committee's notes to 1972 Proposed Rule 104 provide an example of such a preliminary question: "Is the alleged expert a qualified physician?"[30] In other words, is the witness an expert? In making that determination, the court will also be generally guided by Federal Rule of Evidence 611, which provides for control by the court of interrogation of witnesses. The rules do not, however, "set forth procedural requirements for exercising the trial court's gate keeping function over expert testimony."[31]

The witness should be prepared for opposing counsel to break into the direct examination with an objection to the qualifications of the witness to testify as an expert ("Objection, lack of foundation."), and a request to take the witness on voir dire. Although the federal rules do not expressly provide for voir dire examination of a witness,

[c]ounsel objecting to introduction of evidence on the grounds of lack of introduction of a sufficient foundation will, if requested, frequently be given an opportunity to cross-examine the witness at the time of offer limited solely to the question of the sufficiency of the foundation. The process is referred to as "voir dire."[32]

During a voir dire examination involving qualifications, the witness should be prepared to testify about education, training, and experience; the knowledge, skill, and expertise the witness claims to have which are based thereon; and how that knowledge, skill, and expertise relates to the evidence or facts in issue. The trial lawyer should also prepare as exhibits the expert's written report and supplemental reports, resume, bibliography, and fee statements, which are required to be disclosed under Federal Rule of Civil Procedure 26(a)(2)(B).

---

29. FED. R. EVID. 702 Advisory Committee's notes to 2000 amendment.

30. FED. R. EVID. 104 Advisory Committee's notes to 1972 proposed rule.

31. *See* FED. R. EVID. 702 Advisory Committee's notes to 2000 amendments.

32. 2 MICHAEL H. GRAHAM, HANDBOOK OF FEDERAL EVIDENCE § 611.9 (6th ed. 2006).

The Outline for Direct Examination: Topical and Chronological

The expert should assist the trial lawyer in preparing an outline for direct examination at trial. Brainstorming can be useful. A good starting point might be the expert's written reports and supplemental reports. In addition, the outline should include the requirements for expert testimony discussed above: proof that the witness is qualified as an expert and that the specialized knowledge of the expert will assist the jury—that is, that the knowledge is relevant and that the testimony is reliable.[33]

The court may set forth requirements pursuant to Federal Rule of Evidence 705, relating to disclosure of underlying facts or data. But the rules otherwise leave to the trial lawyer and expert witness the decision as to when and how to disclose such data.[34] Normally, the expert is prepared to disclose during direct examination the "underlying facts or data,"[35] that is, the "facts or data in the particular case upon which an expert bases an opinion or inference"[36] and the reasons for opinions or inferences.[37] Failure to fully disclose during direct might lead to unpleasant disclosures during cross.

The outline should enable the trial lawyer to give headlines to the jury and judge so that they know what subject is going to be addressed next. ("Ms. Expert, I'd like to ask you some questions about your investigation. Did you investigate the accident?" Surprisingly, some witnesses will answer, "no," requiring rehabilitation, so make sure the witness is prepared to answer the questions you plan to ask.) The headings should enable the trial lawyer and expert to stay on point until the point is finished.

Disclosure of Inadmissible Facts or Data

The direct examiner and expert should consider whether they should disclose to the jury facts or data that are "otherwise inadmissible" on which the expert relied. Federal Rule of Evidence 703 governs the disclosure of otherwise inadmissible facts or data in this circumstance:

> Facts or data that are otherwise inadmissible shall not be disclosed to the jury by the proponent of the opinion or inference unless the court determines their probative value in assisting the jury to evaluate the expert's opinion substantially outweighs their prejudicial effect.

---

33. *See* Fed. R. Evid. 702.
34. *See* Fed. R. Evid. 705.
35. *See* Fed. R. Evid. 705.
36. *See* Fed. R. Evid. 703.
37. *See* Fed. R. Evid. 705; Fed. R. Civ. P. 26(a)(2)(B)(i).

The cross-examiner should be prepared to object to the disclosure, unless the cross-examiner plans to take advantage of the "otherwise inadmissible" facts or data. The direct and cross-examiner should not take each other or the court by surprise but should consider this matter in motions *in limine*.

Stealing Thunder

In every case, the expert's potential testimony has problems, whether they relate to underlying facts or to qualifications. In preparing for trial, the trial lawyer and expert should discuss those problems and decide whether to attempt during direct examination to steal the thunder from the cross-examiner, that is, to remove the sting, before the expert gets stung on cross-examination.

Open-Ended Questions

The expert should be prepared for leading questions on cross-examination. But in preparing for direct examination, the direct examiner should advise the expert not to expect to be fed the answers by leading questions from the trial lawyer. In preparing for trial, the trial lawyer should advise the expert witness about the rule governing leading questions:

> Leading questions should not be used on the direct examination of a witness except as may be necessary to develop the witness' testimony. Ordinarily leading questions should be permitted on cross-examination. When a party calls a hostile witness, adverse party, or a witness identified with an adverse party, interrogation may be by leading questions.[38]

Both direct examiner and expert should be careful to avoid leading questions or reliance on them because the court will probably sustain opposing counsel's objection ("Don't lead, counsel."), and the jury might get the impression the expert witness is a mere puppet of the direct examiner. Moreover, repeated objections will lead to the embarrassing revelation that the direct examiner is not prepared to ask the questions the right way or that the expert is not prepared to answer the questions without help.

Documents to Be Used during Direct Testimony

In preparation for trial, the direct examiner should ask the expert about documents the expert plans or wants to use while testifying (or before

---

38. FED. R. EVID. 611(c).

testifying). The trial lawyer and witness should prepare to use the previously disclosed documents during direct examination or be ready to produce the documents during cross-examination. The trial lawyer should also prepare to prove that the documents and other evidence were timely disclosed.

Visual Aids

Most trial lawyers know the science of a trial. We realize that each cause of action and affirmative defense consists of an element or elements that must be proved by the evidence. And most trial lawyers also realize the more persuasive case is the more artful case. The more artful case usually involves visual aids.

The terms "demonstrative evidence" and "visual aids" do not appear in any evidence code in the United States,[39] but Federal Rule of Evidence 1006 provides guidance:

> The contents of voluminous writings, recordings, or photographs which cannot conveniently be examined in court may be presented in the form of a chart, summary or calculation. The originals, or duplicates, shall be made available for examination, copying, or both, by other parties at a reasonable time and place. The court may order that they be produced in court.

Charts are a form of "demonstrative evidence,"[40] which serve "merely as a visual aid to the jury in comprehending the verbal testimony of a witness or other evidence."[41]

You should keep a record of the disclosure of visual aids. An adequate record might include a letter of transmittal containing a detailed list of documents and tangible things produced.

You should also consider whether the visual aids will be offered into evidence and whether a request will be made that the exhibit be sent to the jurors during deliberations:

---

39. *See* Robert D. Brain & Daniel J. Broderick, *The Derivative Relevance of Demonstrative Evidence: Charting Its Evidentiary Status*, 25 U.C. Davis L. Rev. 957, 962 n.13 (2002). *But see* Fed. R. Evid. 401 Advisory Committee's notes to 1972 proposed rules ("Evidence which is essentially background in nature . . . is universally offered and admitted as an aid to understanding. Charts, photographs, views of real estate . . . and many other items fall in this category."); Fed. R. Evid. 611 Advisory Committee's notes to 1972 proposed rules ("Item (1) . . . covers such concerns as . . . the use of demonstrative evidence.").

40. *See* 1 Graham, *supra* note 32, § 401.2.

41. *Id.*

While it is a common practice for demonstrative evidence to be displayed and referred to without formally being admitted into evidence, the formal offering and introduction of demonstrative evidence into the record as part of the witnesses' testimony is preferred.[42]

Some experts and some trial lawyers like in-court demonstrations and experiments. For example, sometimes a physician or surgeon will conduct part of a physical examination of a plaintiff/patient to show restrictions on range of motion (physical impairment) or to show disfigurement. Another example, in a product liability suit, is the disassembly of a product or part, such as a control, using a visual presenter to project enlarged images of the disassembly onto a screen. Still another example in a product liability suit is the use of a product, or an exemplar of a product, such as a ladder or scaffold, which is allegedly unsafe.[43]

Trial preparation also includes consideration of whether a demonstration may be more efficiently and effectively shown to the jury through a video record of an out-of-court demonstration. Practice of the experiment or demonstration might indicate to the trial lawyer whether the visual record of an out-of-court demonstration is preferable to an in-court demonstration.

Compensation

Expert witnesses should be prepared to explain why they charge so much, relative to the amounts earned by jurors. One way to explain is to detail the nonreimbursable costs and overhead expenses an expert incurs in providing the service. The trial lawyer should also prepare the expert to testify about the expense of expertise. Without bragging, the expert who charges high fees should show the jury just what was required to reach the point where the expert accumulated the expertise necessary to solve the problem.

Objections

The direct examiner should instruct the witness to pay attention to the other attorneys. The witness should stop talking when another attorney rises to make an objection or to otherwise address the court. Most judges have little patience with aggressive witnesses who rush to complete an answer during an objection. Jurors will take that behavior into consideration in determining credibility.

---

42. *Id.*
43. See the discussion about the in-court demonstration relating to a fall from an allegedly defective ladder in *Schmude v. Tricam Industries, Inc.*, 556 F.3d 624 (7th Cir. 2009).

The Order in Which Witnesses Should Be Called

The trial lawyer should consult with the expert witness about the preferred order for calling witnesses. Some trial lawyers believe calling a damages expert to testify before liability witnesses is putting the cart before the horse. The reasoning is the jury might not be ready to hear about damages from an expert until after they think the defendant is liable.

A decision should be made about whether to call expert witnesses to testify before lay-fact witnesses. In a case involving an amputation resulting from the use of a power saw, the plaintiffs called the expert to testify about alleged failure to adequately guard the blade and later called the plaintiff's son as a damages witness. After the trial, my cocounsel and I discussed whether the more effective and persuasive way for the plaintiffs to try the case would have been to call the son as the first witness to describe the scene, where the father burst through the door, holding the remains of his hand, screaming for someone to call an ambulance and to help him find his fingers. We both thought the plaintiffs might have won the case if the son had testified first and the expert next, instead of the other way around.

Preparation of Witness for Cross-Examination

Weight and Credibility

The direct examiner should prepare the expert for a cross-examination that involves an attack on credibility. The expert should be informed that under Federal Rule of Evidence 611(b), the scope of cross-examination includes the weight of the testimony and the credibility of the witness. Both the witness and trial lawyer should be prepared for harassment and undue embarrassment, from which the court should protect the witness under Rule 611(a). The trial lawyer should also be prepared to move *in limine* or object under Federal Rule of Evidence 403, on the ground that the evidence should be excluded because the "probative value is substantially outweighed by the danger of . . . confusion of the issues, or misleading the jury, or by consideration of undue delay, waste of time, or needless presentation of cumulative evidence."

An example of a question to one of my expert witnesses which I found effective is a question asked right at the outset of cross-examination: "Just how much are they paying you for your testimony?" (Prepare the witness to avoid looking bug-eyed.) Other favorites include questions about the relationship between the witness and the party, and between the witness and the attorneys: "How many times have you testified for the plaintiff attorney?" "Did you used to work for the defendant company?" "Have you consulted for the defendant?" "And what percentage of your income is derived from testifying as an expert witness?" Remember that, under rules in effect for years, the party or attorney retaining the expert must disclose the compensation to be paid to the expert,[44] so a professional witness should expect that question and be ready to answer it. Another is, "Do you do anything other than testify for attorneys?"[45]

The rules and opinions in *Daubert* and *Kumho Tire* suggest other lines of attack for which to prepare the witness:

- Have you tested your theory? (By what standards or under what controls did you test your theory?)
- Have you published any learned treatises about your theory?
- What does peer review mean? Has your theory been peer reviewed?
- Has your theory been generally accepted in the (scientific) community?
- Have you ever conducted research about your opinions (principles, methods) independent of litigation?
- Did you develop your opinions expressly for the purpose of testifying?
- Did you consider any explanations for the situation other than the explanation you gave? (Why did you rule out the other explanation?)
- Did you base your opinion on any facts or data discovered by you in your investigation—or did you base your opinion only on facts or data made known to you by the attorney who paid you to testify? (An expert witness may, however, appropriately testify on the basis of facts or data made known to the expert.)[46]

In a product liability case, the expert should be prepared for these types of questions:

- Have you ever used a product like that?
- Have you ever designed a product (or part) like that?
- Have you ever manufactured a product like that?
- Have you ever prepared an instruction manual for a product like that?
- Have you ever prepared a product safety label for a product like that?
- Have you built (and tested) a product (prototype) according to your design and specification (for what you contend is a safer alternative) to determine whether the alternative product design is actually safer? Effective?
- Have you tested the warning (instruction) you propose for determining whether it is effective?

---

44. *See* Fed. R. Civ. P. 26(a)(2)(B)(vi).
45. *See generally* 3 Graham, *supra* note 32, § 705.3.
46. See Fed. R. Civ. P. 703.

Impeachment by Prior Inconsistent Statements

Prior inconsistent statements may be used at the trial under Federal Rules of Evidence 613 and 801(d)(1). The trial lawyer should advise the expert about the use of prior inconsistent statements. At least to the extent prior statements by the expert witness were not already reviewed by the trial lawyer and expert before the deposition of the expert, prior statements should be reviewed in preparation for trial.

Prior inconsistent statements might be contained in several sources, including the written report by the expert witness, publications by the witness, and written reports and depositions in other cases. The trial lawyer should be wary of cross-examiners who do not question about prior inconsistent statements during depositions but wait for a later ambush at trial. Thus a thorough review of written statements by the witness should be made, even if the cross-examiner did not cover them during the deposition. Sometimes the trial lawyer should simply ask, "Are there any bad documents out there?" One kind of statement that will obviously not have been reviewed in preparation for the deposition is a statement made at the deposition. In preparing for trial, the trial lawyer and expert must determine whether the expert is going to change at trial any deposition testimony. If so, both should expect that the cross-examiner will attempt to impeach by prior inconsistent statements made by the expert during the deposition.

The expert should be prepared to explain the prior statement. If the expert will not deny the statement, a decision should be made in advance of trial about whether to remove the sting or steal the thunder during direct examination.

Leading Questions

You should prepare your expert not to get swept along by leading questions and, if possible, to interrupt the flow of the cross-examiner and slow the cross-examiner down to a pace comfortable to the witness. The witness should avoid appearing to obstruct the other lawyer but should be thoughtful to not jump to conclusions and to not make mistakes that are usually made while in too big a hurry.

Conclusion

One time I was cross-examining a mechanical engineer who had been called by the plaintiff to testify that a valve was defectively designed, causing a leak of hydrofluoric acid, which badly injured a worker at a chemical plant. Clearly he was qualified as an expert by education (and training). But was he prepared for this case and this trial? Based on the deposition and my investigation, I had compiled a substantial notebook for the cross-examination. I planned for the cross-examination to last a couple of hours.

I started by attacking the credibility of the witness ("Have you conducted any tests for this case?" Answer: "No.") About 30 minutes later, the trial judge almost shouted, "Shut it down, counsel!" Stunned, I soon "shut it down." The judge declared a recess and excused the jury. I nervously approached the judge and asked, "Did I do something wrong?" The judge replied with a question: "Have you ever been in the oil business?" I replied, "No, I have not." He looked back at me as he left the bench: "There's a saying in the oil business. When you strike oil, stop drilling."

Take the time to prepare your expert for trial so that opposing counsel does not strike oil.

DIRECT EXAMINATION OF YOUR EXPERT AT TRIAL

John Hutchins[1]

Direct examination of your expert at trial, in many ways, should be similar to a good direct examination of any other witness. Above all, direct examination should contribute to the telling of your client's story. Direct examination should include clear and identifiable themes that are compatible with the overall themes of your case and that the jury (or other fact finder) will be able to use as guideposts in the story that the presentation of your case is designed to tell.

Use Direct Examination to Help Tell Your Story

Generally speaking, the best direct examinations give the jury a feeling that they are merely eavesdropping on a conversation between the witness and the lawyer. This conversation between the lawyer and the witness should readily fit into the overall story of the case, and both the lawyer and the witness should use language that the jury can easily understand. If the lawyer and the witness do their jobs well, a direct examination should flow so freely that the lawyer almost disappears, merely asking questions to which the jury members themselves want the answers. In a skillful direct examination like this, any interruption by opposing counsel—such as an objection—will be viewed negatively by the jury, breaking up what is otherwise a helpful part of the bigger picture that the jury is tasked with grasping.

The expert witness and the lawyer, therefore, should play similar roles in this regard, as is true with any other witness. Witnesses, quite simply, tell what they know. Lawyers should generally act as a guide—there to help the

---

1. John Hutchins is a partner in the Atlanta, Georgia, office of Troutman Sanders LLP. He regularly handles a variety of commercial disputes but has substantial expertise in cases involving computer hardware and software development projects, government procurement, protection of trade secrets and proprietary business information, the Internet and e-commerce, privacy and data security, trademark and copyright infringement, and restrictive covenants. He has been lead counsel in numerous jury trials and bench trials in state and federal courts as well as arbitration and mediation proceedings.

jury navigate through the story. The only real difference between an expert witness and any other witness is that a special foundation must be laid during direct examination in order for the expert witness to tell what he knows. Federal Rule of Evidence 702 explains the required foundation:

> If scientific, technical, or other specialized knowledge will assist the trier of fact to understand the evidence or to determine a fact in issue, a witness qualified as an expert by knowledge, skill, experience, training, or education, may testify thereto in the form of an opinion or otherwise.

Thus, you must first establish that the expert's specialized knowledge will be helpful to the jury. Second, you must establish that the witness is qualified.[2] Generally speaking, once these two elements are established, the court will allow the witness's testimony as an expert who can offer opinion, even on the ultimate issue.

Let the Jury Hear Your Witness's Ultimate Opinion as Soon as Possible

It is important to note that, despite the requirements of Rule 702, most courts do not require rigid adherence to any particular order in laying this foundation. It is a condition of the expert witness's testimony, but most judges will generally grant lawyers significant leeway in the order of proof, expecting that the examining lawyer can meet these basic requirements before the witness's testimony is ultimately "tendered" to the jury. Lawyers should capitalize on this leeway by making sure that the most important information in an expert witness's testimony—the ultimate opinion—is presented to the jury as soon as possible.

Start with the Way You Call Your Witness to Testify

Your introduction of your witness's opinion to the jury should begin with the way you call your expert witness to the stand. Many lawyers squander this opportunity to enlighten the jury, and they call an expert witness to the stand the same as any other witness—"Your honor, we would like to call [name of expert] witness to the stand." But there is no rule that limits you to this boring, nondescript method.

Instead, when it is time to call your expert witness, give the jury a preview of the importance of your expert's testimony, and point out that this

---

2. Qualification of expert witnesses is covered in detail in chapter 6.

next witness is not just any witness—he's an expert. So, consider using very plain language to introduce your expert using this format:

> Your honor, we would like to call [expert's name], an expert in [topic of testimony], to testify to her opinion about [ultimate issue in dispute].

There are three key characteristics of this proposed method that should not go unnoticed. First, notice the suggestion to use the general topic of the expert's testimony when describing the expert's field. Second, the expert's opinion should be described with reference to the ultimate issue. Third, the language that you use must be understandable to your audience.

As an example, imagine you are handling a complex commercial case involving a business loss claim by your client, a multilocation retail chain. You are calling an expert in business valuation to give an opinion as to the amount of the loss your client claims. Attempting to follow the advice above, you could simply say,

> Your honor, we would like to call Mr. John Doe, an expert in forensic accounting, to testify to his opinion about business loss valuation.

Although this introduction is better than merely calling "Mr. John Doe" to the stand, there are two main problems with this introduction. First, by focusing on your witness's field of expertise, you have squandered your opportunity to be a good guide to the jury and tell them what they really want to know—what is this person going to tell me that helps me make my decision? Second, you have described the subject matter of your witness's testimony in a way that gives the jury only minimally more information about what is coming than they had when you stood up. So, consider this instead:

> Your honor, we would like to call Mr. John Doe, an expert in determining business damages, to testify to his opinion about the amount of money my client lost.

Now the jury knows that someone you consider an expert on a topic that should be helpful to them is coming to the stand to offer an opinion on something about which they must ultimately make a decision. This introduction might ruffle opposing counsel's feathers as slightly argumentative, but as a practical matter, it is extremely unlikely that opposing counsel will choose to highlight the introduction for the jury by objecting.

When Qualifying Your Expert, Less Is Sometimes More

Once your expert witness is sworn, you know you have got to get him qualified as an expert and lay the proper foundation for his testimony, but you should not let your duty to meet these requirements enslave your presentation of this expert to the jury. You have already told the jury that this witness is going to give them something that will be helpful to them—an opinion regarding the all-important issue of damages. You want to play the role of a good guide and deliver on your promise, so it is important for you to get that opinion before the jury as soon as possible and while the jury is paying attention. In most courts, it is not required that you lay the entire foundation underlying your expert's opinion before you offer the opinion itself. Rather, most courts will allow you to offer the opinion first. Remember that many courts or judges require that *Daubert* challenges be made pretrial.[3] Most often, all *Daubert* issues will have been dealt with by the time you call your witness. So, your most important challenge at trial is to get your witness qualified and accepted by the court so that you can offer your witness's opinion as quickly as possible. Once the opinion is offered, you can backfill the bases for the opinion.

Introduce your expert to the jury in a way that confirms what you have already told them—that this is a witness who can help them. But avoid getting so bogged down in your expert's qualifications that, by the time you tender the witness as an expert, the jury has forgotten why they ever thought this witness could help them. Regarding qualifications, do what you need to do to get your witness qualified, but do not overdo it. You should obviously cover the basics of specialized training, knowledge, education, and experience, and if there are cases in which your expert has been accepted by a court that are similar to your case, you should definitely bring that out on direct. But beware of too much of a good thing. There is always a risk that some jurors may perceive an expert witness who testifies at length about his qualifications as a braggadocio. In any event, most jurors probably make up their mind about whether an expert is qualified pretty quickly and may tune out an excessively long recitation of publications, presentations, and prior service as an expert. And a little humility goes a long way. Keep in mind that the other side is likely going to have an expert on the same subject matter, and that expert is likely going to be similarly well qualified. Once the judge accepts your expert and the opposing side's expert, the jury will likely credit their qualifications roughly equally. The judge has said that both are experts, and that is probably as far as the jury is going to go in deciding the issue of the weight of their qualifications. Instead, the jury is going to credit

---

3. *See, e.g.,* http://www.cod.uscourts.gov/Documents/Judges/JLK/jlk_pre_ord.pdf (requiring *Daubert* challenges before trial or deemed waived); Club Car, Inc. v. Club Car (Quebec) Import, Inc., 362 F.3d 775, 780 (11th Cir. 2004) ("A *Daubert* objection not raised before trial may be rejected as untimely."). *See also* 1 WEINSTEIN'S FEDERAL EVIDENCE ch. 104 (2d ed. 1997); EDWARD J. IMWINKELRIED & DAVID A. SCHLUETER, FEDERAL EVIDENCE TACTICS § 1.04 (1997).

your expert's opinion mostly based on its collective assessment that the opinion makes sense.

In establishing your expert's qualifications, therefore, focus on the expert's specialization as it relates particularly to the question the jury is looking for help in answering. Taking the example of the business loss expert, although it is important to cover a fact like your expert's Master's Degree from Columbia University, this is not as helpful to the jury in understanding your witness's expertise as the fact that he has been accepted by other courts as an expert on business losses in cases involving multilocation retail establishments. In choosing which qualifications to emphasize to the jury, be as specific as possible in bringing out the qualifications that relate to the jury's need for help in grappling with the question you are offering the witness to help answer.

Use Permissible Leading on Direct

At this point, it is helpful to remember the rule on leading a witness on direct examination. Contrary to popular belief, Rule 611(c) of the Federal Rules of Evidence does not say that it is impermissible to lead a witness on direct examination. Rather, it only says, "Leading questions should not be used on the direct examination of a witness *except as may be necessary to develop the witness's testimony.*" Most judges will allow a lawyer on direct examination to use simple, leading questions that will speed a witness through perfunctory testimony. This is a far better practice than starting any direct examination with questions that are phrased as only lawyers phrase questions, such as, "Please state your full name for the record." Especially with an expert witness, making wise use of a few, permissibly leading questions can speed your witness's testimony and give your witness some cover to protect against the braggadocio label.

Your Witness's Opinion Is Credited or Not Based on Its Reasonableness to the Jury

Regardless of your expert's qualifications, the jury will credit his opinion only if they find it reasonable. With this in mind, get the witness qualified as quickly as possible, and then go directly to the heart of the expert's opinion. This is critical because if the jury is going to credit your expert's opinion mostly based on its collective assessment that the opinion makes sense, it cannot possibly begin assessing the reasonableness of your expert's opinion until it has heard the opinion. Once you get the opinion before the jury, you should spend the remainder of your direct examination establishing the reasonableness of your expert's opinion. An example of a direct examination of the damages expert discussed above, showing how to get the expert qualified quickly and get his opinion before the jury promptly, is attached as Appendix A.

With your expert's opinion out in the open and no longer a mystery to the jury, it is time to remember why you called your expert witness in the first place. Under Rule 702, an expert witness can only be called "[i]f scientific, technical, or other specialized knowledge will assist the trier of fact to understand the evidence or to determine a fact in issue." So guide the witness through questions that will assist the jury in understanding, and remember that no jury can find an opinion reasonable unless it can understand the opinion. Help your expert teach the jury, and ask the expert the questions the jury wants to know about how the expert arrived at the opinion already given. Remember the lesson of humility. Avoid using lawyerly sounding phrases like, "please tell the ladies and gentlemen of the jury." Instead, ask questions that make you sound curious, just as the jury is curious. "Who?" "What?" "Where?" "When?" "How?" And, most important, "Why?" If you have properly revealed your expert's opinion as soon as you have qualified the witness, then the key points that remain are (1) how your witness arrived at this opinion, and (2) why it is worthy of being accepted.

Avoid using big or technical words, and do not let your witness use a big or technical term that you do not take the time to explain to the jury. In the business loss expert example, for instance, your expert may need to explain that his opinion was derived from an application of the "discounted lost future cash flow." But you will want to ask your expert what he means by "cash flow" and what it means that it is "discounted." Throughout your direct examination, talk like a real person, not like a lawyer. Keep your questions short and in plain English, and your expert's answers will more likely be short and in plain English. Most importantly, pay close attention to the verbs you use in questioning your expert. Use verbs like "teach," "explain," and "help." Never use verbs like "elucidate," "enlighten," or "edify." Your jury may not understand your questions (and hence, likely not understand the answers), but you also risk coming off as pompous, arrogant, and pretentious. And because your expert understands your big-worded questions and some members of the jury do not, your expert will go down alongside you.

Remember These Tricks of the Trade

Hopefully, you will be prepared enough that you will not need to write out your questions in advance. Doing so will likely lead to a direct examination that is stilted and sounds rehearsed, and this could damage your witness's credibility with the jury, as well as yours. If you are well prepared, you should have a very firm grasp of what specific testimony you need to elicit from your expert, your expert should know the information that it is critical for you to get, and you should keep to one or more themes that help both of you stay on course. Careful and thorough preparation will enable most lawyers to conduct the direct examination without prewritten questions and maybe even without notes. But if you need to make written notes, consider writing down the answers that you must get from the expert witness, rather than the questions.

Another important tactic to remember is to use topic headlines to announce to the judge, the jury, and your witness what is coming next. "Mr. Doe, I'd like to turn your attention to your experience in cases dealing with business losses suffered by multilocation retail chains." This is especially helpful on direct examination in avoiding impermissible (as opposed to permissible) leading questions. Headlines allow you to maintain control over your direct examination. If the witness wanders too far off the farm, do not be afraid to rein him in: "Mr. Doe, I don't want us to get ahead of ourselves. I'm focused right now on your experience in dealing with business losses suffered by multilocation retail chains. We'll get to those other issues in a few minutes. Although I appreciate your answer, I am asking a question that's a little different."

Also consider special tactics you can use to help your expert witness's testimony remain interesting. Use as many charts, graphs, photographs, and other visual aids as possible.[4] Consider the best medium to present this material, however, and be careful that you have scoped out the courtroom ahead of time before choosing your medium. The jurors and the judge need to be able to see your demonstratives clearly, without having to be inconvenienced. If this is not possible because of the space confines of the courtroom, it is better not to use them. Lawyers have made seriously bad mistakes in this regard, such as a trial in which the witness's timeline was so large that, when blown up on foam-backed boards, it had to be trifolded, and the only place in the courtroom big enough to spread it out was the front of the bench, forcing the judge to come down off the bench to be able to see it. These kinds of snafus are very distracting and, instead of making the direct examiner invisible, they will make him look unprepared at best and incompetent at worst.

Although forcing the judge down from the bench is not to be desired, getting your expert witness off the witness stand to draw on a white board

---

4. The use of demonstratives is discussed further in "Demonstrative Exhibits" *infra*.

or flip chart can often make otherwise difficult to understand technical or scientific testimony come alive. This kind of movement, however, should be carefully planned and done in the live trial only after you and your expert witness have walked through the steps beforehand so that both of you know exactly where everyone is going. Make sure, in advance, that this kind of off-witness-stand movement is okay with the judge. And, again, it is not good if the judge and the jury cannot see it. The best preparation for the placement of demonstratives or things such as white boards is to visit the courtroom where your case will be tried, well before the start of the trial, plan very carefully where you plan to place the chart, graph, or flip chart, and then sit in every seat in the jury box and make sure you can see it.

Deal with Negative Testimony in Direct in Preparation for Cross-Examination

Nearly every expert witness will have given deposition testimony that creates vulnerability on cross-examination. A key strategy question that needs to be answered with every witness is whether you should bring out the negative testimony on direct examination or simply prepare the witness to deal with it on cross. The advantage of bringing it out on direct examination is that it allows you the opportunity to deal with it on your terms. The question cannot be answered in the abstract, and every case is different, but if you decide to bring out negative testimony on direct, the main questions are (1) how, and (2) when. There are two basic tactical options:

1. Take into account the effect of primacy and recency (or at least the arguments regarding primacy and recency). It is widely believed that jurors remember what they hear first and what they hear last. Based on these principles, you might consider disclosing the negative testimony somewhere in the middle of your direct examination.

2. The flipside of the primacy/recency tactic is that, in order for the disclosure of negative testimony to have the desired result of taking the wind out of the opposing party's sails, the jury has to hear it and grasp that you dealt with this negative testimony first. Otherwise, when the opposing party begins cross-examination of your expert by jumping on the negative testimony out of the gate, your attempt at a preemptive strike may not work. So, if you opt to bury the disclosure of negative testimony deep in the middle of your direct examination, consider confronting your witness about it directly and providing an opportunity for a full and complete explanation of the negative testimony. Remember the rule on leading questions here—a few, quick leading questions might

get the negative information out succinctly and packaged in such a way that your expert can more easily explain it away. It is unlikely that opposing counsel will object to your leading questions, as you are probably asking the same questions you expect him to ask. If what you are doing is previewing potential harmful deposition testimony, leading questions may be particularly "necessary to develop the witness's testimony." When considering timing in regard to this tactic, you might wish to wait until near the end of your expert's testimony. Once the negative testimony (or other negative information) is out in the open, ask the witness the question that you know your opponent probably will not ask—"Mr. Doe, taking this information into account, does it change your opinion regarding the damages suffered by the plaintiff?" Give the witness a full opportunity to explain any impact on his opinion, and remember to ask the all important "How?" and "Why?" questions.

Conclusion

Direct examination of an expert witness should contribute to telling your client's story, just like any good direct examination. Use it to highlight themes that are compatible with the overall theme of your case. You and your expert should play the role of trusted guide. Let the jury hear your expert's ultimate opinion as soon as possible, and do not overdo it on your expert's qualifications. Help the expert do what experts are supposed to do—"assist the trier of fact to understand the evidence or determine a fact in issue." Teach, guide, explain, and help. And do it all with confident humility, and with big signposts along the way.

PREPARING FOR AND CROSS-EXAMINING THE OPPOSING EXPERT AT TRIAL

John F. Stoviak and Christina D. Riggs[1]

Preparing to cross-examine the opposition's expert at trial is a daunting challenge. Often, experts are experienced witnesses with the skills necessary to be persuasive to jurors and unyielding to cross-examiners. As a result, a realistic goal for cross-examining the opposition's expert is to simply diffuse and reduce the force and impact of the expert's direct testimony. There are numerous ways to meet this goal. For example, you may show that the expert failed to consider certain key facts or that one of the bases for the expert's opinion is incorrect or unsupported by facts in your case. Alternatively, you may show that the expert is not an independent witness but is instead a biased hired gun prepared to say anything for a fee. You can show bias by establishing that the expert regularly works for opposing counsel. You can also show bias by highlighting the expert's overzealous opinions or pejorative choice of language.

Overall, preparation and planning are the key to an effective cross-examination. While this golden rule applies to any cross-examination, it is especially applicable to cross-examination of an expert witness. An expert witness will likely know more than you about the subject matter. Therefore, to be adequately prepared, you must learn everything you can about the subject matter—and the expert. Mastering this information is necessary to conduct an effective cross-examination.

This subchapter begins by highlighting the key information to obtain before cross-examining an expert witness. It then describes how to organize and prepare for the examination. Finally, this subchapter concludes by addressing key points for conducting the cross-examination of the expert witness.

---

1. John F. Stoviak is a litigation partner in the Philadelphia, Pennsylvania, office of Saul Ewing LLP. He focuses his practice on trying complex business disputes and environmental litigation. He formerly served as managing partner of Saul Ewing for seven years and chair of its litigation department for five years. Christina D. Riggs is a litigation associate in the Philadelphia, Pennsylvania, office of Saul Ewing LLP.

Information Gathering

The first step in preparing to cross-examine your opposition's expert is to obtain a copy of the expert's report.[2] Carefully read this report to understand the assumptions and bases for each opinion, including mathematical calculations and formulas. If this seems like an overwhelming task, consult with other lawyers in your firm who are knowledgeable in the subject area. If the area of expertise is highly technical or complex, hire a consulting expert[3] to review the opposing expert's report and provide you with proposed areas of questioning to challenge the opposing expert.

Once you have a complete understanding of the facts and bases for the expert's opinion, you must determine whether the expert has written or testified previously in a manner inconsistent with this opinion. To make this determination, locate and digest every book, article, treatise, editorial, seminar, or presentation authored by the expert. Start with the expert's resume or curriculum vitae (CV), as it will often provide a list of presentations and publications. Check the accuracy of the expert's resume and CV regarding schools attended, degrees earned, and job history.

Beyond the resume or CV, Internet search engines are a great source of information. For example, if the expert is employed by an academic institution, the institution's Web page generally provides information on the expert. In addition, experts often participate in Web pages, blogs, or webcasts. Carefully review each writing or presentation to determine whether inconsistent positions have been taken. You often will find that an expert soon forgets what he has said previously.

Next, locate any prior testimony of the expert witness, including deposition and trial transcripts. For each case in which the opposing expert has testified (either in deposition or at trial), reach out to the counsel who opposed the expert to learn what kind of witness the expert was and any particularly fertile areas of questioning to challenge the expert's qualifications or opinions. Also, with these prior cases, make sure you precisely understand the area of expertise for which the expert was tendered. Determine whether this matches or overlaps the area of expertise on which the expert is being tendered in your case.

---

2. Disclosure of expert testimony, including the expert's report, is governed by Federal Rule of Civil Procedure 26(a)(2)(B).

3. A consulting expert is a person retained in preparation for litigation but who will not testify at trial. Unlike a testifying expert, his identity, theories, mental impressions, and opinions are generally nondiscoverable, unless there is a showing of exceptional circumstances. *See* FED. R. CIV. P. 26(b)(4).

Other attorneys are also able to provide insight into the expert's demeanor and personality. Knowing what type of expert to expect in a deposition or trial will help you prepare more effectively. Indeed, information on the expert's personality and demeanor will help you to decide what tone, attitude, and questioning style to use in your cross-examination. Beyond the expert's demeanor, find out whether the expert is a detailed person who understands and writes his own opinions or whether the expert is a big-picture person who relies on associates and assistants to perform research and prepare reports. In short, does this expert get his hands dirty with details?

Preparation

Once you have obtained the above information, you must not only master it, but you must also decide how to effectively use it in your cross-examination. To control this daunting task, organize the information into the following categories:

- The expert's qualifications;
- The expert's potential bias;
- Prior inconsistent statements; and
- The scope, formation, and basis of the expert's opinion in your matter.

Taking it one step at a time will keep you from missing key information.

Qualifications

First, the expert's qualifications should include any information capable of establishing that this witness is not qualified to opine on this particular subject, including any evidence that he lacks experience in the particular field. You will be able to use this information not only during your cross-examination, but also before trial if you choose to file a motion to exclude the expert's testimony.

Potential Bias

Second, the potential bias category should include any information sufficient to establish that this witness has a stake in the outcome of the litigation. It may also include information to show that this witness is a hired gun, and will say whatever he is asked to say, or that this witness always testifies on the same side, and thus lacks objectivity. This information will help to discredit the expert's testimony.

Prior Inconsistent Statements

Third, prior inconsistent statements should include any testimony from any source where the expert took a position—on an issue material to your case—that is inconsistent with the expert's current position. This information will be key to an effective impeachment during your cross-examination.

Scope, Formation, and Basis for Expert's Opinion

The fourth and final category is the most important. Fully understanding the scope, formation, and basis of the expert's opinion in your matter is essential. This category should include any and all documents provided to or reviewed by the expert in forming his opinion.[4] Determine whether there are any key documents that were not provided to or reviewed by the expert.

In the last few years, it has become very fruitful to get discovery of all communications between a testifying expert and those who hired him.[5] Under current law,[6] you can obtain drafts of the expert report, the expert's notes of telephone calls, and e-mail traffic between the expert and the side that hired him. Accordingly, you should obtain all drafts of reports and all communications—oral and written, preliminary and final—created by the expert. Note any revisions or additions to the reports. Consider why these revisions were made and why certain sections were not included in the initial drafts.

Deposing the Expert

After you have obtained and mastered all of this information, if the applicable rules allow you to depose the expert before trial, be certain to do so. Under Federal Rule of Civil Procedure 26(b)(4), you may depose the opposition's expert any time after you receive the expert's report. By contrast,

---

4. *See* FED. R. CIV. P. 26(a)(2).

5. *See, e.g.*, South Yuba River Citizens League v. Nat'l Marine Fisheries Serv., 257 F.R.D. 607, 611–15 (E.D. Cal. 2009) (discussing scope of discovery under Federal Rules of Civil Procedure when "protected work product is communicated to a testifying expert and considered in the formation of the expert's opinions").

6. Note that proposed revisions to Rule 26 would extend work product protection to most communications between an attorney and a testifying expert. *See* U.S. Courts, Federal Rulemaking, http://www.uscourts.gov/rules/index.html (last visited Nov. 4, 2009). If these revisions are adopted by the Supreme Court and not rejected by Congress, the scope of communications available for review in preparation for cross-examination will be more limited.

some states require permission from the court before one may depose an expert.[7]

Use the deposition to learn as much as possible about the expert's opinions and positions—do not do your anticipated cross-examination unless you anticipate settling the case before trial. If you are going to cross-examine the expert before a jury, you do not want to show your hand during the deposition. Rather, use the deposition to pin down the expert on precisely what his opinion is and to force the expert to identify every basis for his opinion and all facts relied on. You also need to force the expert to explain painstakingly his methodology. Draw out as much as possible and make certain the expert fully answers your inquiries.

Also use the deposition to learn as much as possible about the expert's style. Observe how articulate the expert is: is the expert controlled, wordy, or clear in his explanations? Use two or three cross-examination vignettes during deposition to see how the expert deals with the press and stress of pointed, challenging questions. Finally, observe the expert's demeanor, body language, wording, and presentation skills, as well as his ability to deal with a challenging question. These observations will help you plan your cross-examination at trial.

Another helpful tip in taking the expert's deposition is to use enough of the jargon and terminology to show the expert that you are prepared and know the issues. For example, if you are examining a hydrogeologist expert who is opining about the impact of certain chemicals on groundwater, you want to let the expert know that you know what chemicals are considered SVOC (semivolatile organic chemicals) or PAHs (polycyclic aromatic hydrocarbons) and what types of processes naturally attenuate certain chemicals, such as adsorption, absorption, cation exchange, and oxidation. A few questions using these terms will signal to the opposing expert that you know your stuff and he cannot sneak things past you. However, try to save "gotcha's" or clear mistakes made by the expert for cross-examination at trial.

After you take the deposition, obtain a copy of the transcript. Review the transcript for each opinion about which the expert can be expected to testify and, equally important, determine the subject matter on which the expert has no opinion. This will help you control the testimony at trial. Further, reexamine whether the expert based his opinion on unreliable facts or faulty assumptions. Also, consider whether the expert's position would change if those facts or assumptions changed. Use this information to begin crafting key questions for your examination.

---

7. *See, e.g.*, PA. R. CIV. P. 4003.5.

Conducting the Cross-Examination at Trial

When planning your cross-examination, remember two basic rules: (1) keep in mind the key themes of your case; and (2) keep it simple. These rules apply to every aspect of your case from your opening to closing statements—and your cross-examination of the expert witness is no different. This examination should be carefully crafted to support your theories. Determine exactly what you are trying to gain with this expert witness, create a list of objectives, and understand how these objectives play into the theories of your case.

Challenging the Expert's Admissibility

While this issue is covered in detail in a previous chapter,[8] a few points should be emphasized here about the qualification of the expert to testify at trial. Generally, a witness may qualify as an expert by knowledge, skill, experience, training, or education.[9] You will want to challenge the admissibility of this witness as an expert, but to do so you must know the applicable test. The two most commonly applied tests to determine the admissibility of expert testimony are *Frye*[10] and *Daubert*.[11] Under *Frye*, the admissibility of expert testimony depends on the general acceptance of its validity by those scientists active in the field to which the evidence belongs. By contrast, under *Daubert*, expert scientific testimony is admissible if (1) the testimony relates to scientific knowledge, thereby establishing a standard of evidentiary reliability, which will be based on scientific validity; and (2) the testimony is relevant. While experts are often challenged based on their qualifications, expert testimony can also be inadmissible if it improperly usurps the role of the court and amounts to nothing more than an attempt to substitute the expert's judgment for that of the court.[12]

If, however, you are not able to exclude the expert entirely, you should, at least, try to limit the expert's impact. To do this you should seek to limit the areas for which this expert may be tendered. Generally, the first part of any

---

8. *See supra* chapter 6.

9. *See* Fed. R. Evid. 702.

10. Frye v. United States, 293 F. 1013 (D.C. Cir. 1923).

11. Daubert v. Merrell Dow Pharms., Inc., 509 U.S. 579 (1993).

12. *See, e.g,* United States v. Lumpkin, 192 F.3d 280, 289 (2d Cir. 1999); United States v. Duncan, 42 F.3d 97, 101 (2d Cir. 1994); Harris v. Key Bank Nat'l Ass'n, 193 F. Supp. 2d 707, 716 (W.D.N.Y. 2002) ("[E]xpert testimony on . . . purely legal issues is rarely admissible.") (internal quotation marks omitted).

expert examination is voir dire.[13] Listen carefully during opposing counsel's voir dire of the expert to precisely determine the area for which this expert is being tendered. During your voir dire of the expert, precisely establish the areas in which this witness is *not* an expert. To accomplish this, point to problems in his CV, such as lack of specific degrees or lack of experience. This will help limit the impact of the forthcoming testimony. For example, assume the expert is tendered as a business valuation expert in a case involving the value of a professional services firm. If the expert's experience is limited to valuation of industrial business, not professional services firms, you must bring this point out in your voir dire.

After the voir dire process, the next important step will be your actual cross-examination. Overall, the purpose of this examination should be to undermine the value of the expert's testimony, slowly chipping away at the bases on which the expert's opinions stand.

Undermining the Substance of the Expert's Testimony

Undermining the substance of the expert's testimony is crucial to an effective cross-examination. The substance of an expert's testimony can be undermined in the following five ways:

1. Use your cross-examination to establish that the logic of the expert's opinion is fundamentally flawed;
2. Use your cross-examination to establish that the expert's opinion is premised on certain points or bases that are not true or not in evidence in your case;
3. Show that the expert ignored certain key facts in reaching his expert opinion;
4. Show that the expert's testimony is inconsistent with either prior writings or prior testimony by that expert; or
5. Show that the expert is an overzealous advocate for the opposition.

Flawed Logic

To establish that the logic of the expert's opinion is fundamentally flawed, commit the expert to certain simple, basic facts on a one-by-one basis. Asking the expert to agree with a statement that has multiple parts will allow the astute expert to focus on the parts with which he disagrees. Therefore,

---

13. Voir dire is a term used to describe the process by which expert witnesses are questioned about their backgrounds and qualifications to test their competency as an expert witness. BLACK'S LAW DICTIONARY 1605 (8th ed. 2004).

ask the expert to commit to a series of individual, narrowly tailored facts that you can later use in direct examination of your own expert.

For example, you might start by asking the opposing expert if he agrees with Fact A, Fact B, Fact C, and Fact D. Then, you can ask your own expert the following questions:

Q. You heard when Dr. X agreed that Fact A, Fact B, Fact C, and Fact D exist in this case?

A. Yes.

Q. So if Facts A, B, C, and D are true in this case as admitted by Dr. X, does that impact the conclusion that Dr. X reached?

A. Yes. It shows that his opinion is flawed and not possible in light of Facts A, B, C, and D because . . .

Inaccurate or Unsupported Bases

To show that the expert's testimony is predicated on inaccurate or unsupported facts, you must first establish every basis for the expert's opinion. Second, commit the expert to those bases. In other words, try to get the expert to agree that each basis is a crucial premise of his opinion. If one of the "crucial premises" for his opinion is not part of the trial record, the impact of the expert's testimony should be diluted.

Unfortunately, these key issues are often lost on the jury. Therefore, to explain the significance to the jury, create a picture. Explain that the expert's opinion is like a beach house built on a series of stilts or pilings; if you remove one of the pilings, then the beach house tips over. Here, the absence of any proof on any one of the crucial premises will cause the opposing expert's opinion to tip over as well.

Ignoring Key Facts

To show that the opposing expert failed to consider certain key facts, first establish each fact the expert *did* consider in reaching his expert opinion. Second, get the expert to acknowledge that facts running contrary to his opinion must also be evaluated and considered. After obtaining that admission, go through the litany of facts the expert failed to consider, highlighting the weakness in his opinion.

Q. You have now told us all the facts that you considered in reaching your opinion, is that correct?

A. Yes.

Q So you considered Facts M, N, O, P, Q, and R in reaching your opinion, correct?

A. Yes.

Q. You agree that it is important for an expert to consider all facts be-
fore reaching his opinion, even including facts that do not support
your conclusion?
A. Yes.
Q. But you did not consider Fact S, correct?
A. Yes.
Q. But you did not consider Fact T, correct?
A. Yes.

This simple and direct line of questioning will help you show the jury
that the expert's opinion is flawed because he failed to consider all the facts.

Prior Inconsistent Statements

To show that the opposing expert is taking a position inconsistent with
prior testimony, first lock in the expert to his current position. Then, con-
front the expert about the prior statement. For example, assume the expert
is offering an opinion on how to value a business and uses Method A for
valuation. Now assume this expert has previously testified or written that
Method B is the *preferred* valuation method. To undermine the credibility
of this expert's testimony, first commit the expert to his use of Method A
in your case. Only after committing the expert to Method A should you
question the expert about his prior statements about Method B. Failing to
follow this order will allow the expert to explain the discrepancy.

When addressing the prior statement, use the exact language from the
previous transcript or article and, if necessary, ask the court for permission
to show the transcript or article to the expert.[14] For example, ask the following questions:

Q. You used a method of valuing a business based on current revenue
times a multiplier, correct?
A. Yes.
Q. This is a different method than discounted cash flow analysis, cor-
rect?
A. Yes.
Q. You did not use a discounted cash flow analysis in valuing the busi-
ness in this case, correct?
A. Yes.
Q. Did you write an article in *XYZ Litigation Journal*, which was pub-
lished in October 2006?
A. Yes.

---

14. *See* FED. R. EVID. 613.

Q. You personally wrote the article and approved all of the statements in your article?

A. Yes.

Q. Has anything changed in the last three years that would cause you to change your views on preferred valuation methodologies?

A. No.

Q. Is Exhibit 321 a copy of your 2006 article on valuation methods?

A. Yes.

Q. Did you state in the very first paragraph of your 2006 article that the preferred method for determining the value of a business is to use the discounted cash flow model?

A. Yes.

Q. But you chose not to use this preferred valuation method in this case, correct?

A. Yes.

Overzealous Expert

Another potential option for undermining the opposing expert's testimony arises in situations where the opposing expert tries to be too much of an advocate for his side. The overzealous expert may get pejorative in his testimony or may make demeaning comments about your client. For example, if an expert offers an opinion about your client using colorful language, you could use the expert's language choice against him. For example, assume your client, Mr. X, has already testified and made a good impression on the jury as a decent, honest person:

Q. On direct examination, you accused Mr. X of "essentially stealing money" from his current employer because he kept coming to work when he was planning on leaving his job, isn't that right?

A. Yes.

Q. So you are accusing Mr. X of committing a crime? Being a thief?

If the expert answers "yes," and the jury does not believe that Mr. X is a bad guy, the opposing expert has lost his credibility. If the expert answers "no," you can simply continue to ask why he accused Mr. X of "essentially stealing money." The overzealous expert also may be too willing to offer opinions on a number of decidedly weaker or less supportable points. Attacking these opinions will help your argument to the jury that this expert's testimony should be given little weight.

Controlling the Witness

In attempting to undermine the expert's testimony, carefully plan your approach to cross-examination. Experts are often excellent witnesses who are prepared to fence with counsel or avoid answering questions directly. Your questions must, therefore, be precise and leading. Generally, no attorney should ever be stuck to a script. For expert witnesses, however, it is imperative that you take the time to, at least, frame each of your questions in advance.

In most jurisdictions, you are allowed to ask experts leading questions designed to elicit a yes or no answer.[15] You must be persistent in obtaining a yes or no answer to your question. If the expert tries to avoid answering your question, try asking the exact same question a second time. If opposing counsel objects on grounds of "asked and answered," note that the prior answer from expert was not responsive. If the expert continually fails to answer your question, ask the court to restrict the witness to yes or no responses.[16] Nevertheless, before seeking such admonitions or instructions, carefully determine how your jury will perceive your actions. In other words, will the jury think you are trying to prevent them from hearing the expert's entire testimony? If so, you may reconsider asking the court for such limiting instructions. Unfortunately, there is no bright-line rule for when to ask for such admonitions or instructions; this is a judgment call based on your reading of the jury.

Conclusion

When faced with the task of preparing for and cross-examining an expert witness, remember two points. First, preparation is the key to a successful cross-examination. Second, your goal is to diffuse and reduce the force and impact of the expert's direct testimony—anything else is icing on the cake. Follow these two simple rules, and your cross-examination will be clean, focused, and effective.

---

15. *See* Fed. R. Evid. 611(c).
16. *See* Fed. R. Evid. 611(a).

DEMONSTRATIVE EXHIBITS

Joan K. Archer[1]

In today's technology-filled world, a demonstrative aid is an essential tool for illuminating all aspects of a case, including expert testimony.[2] After all, seeing is believing. A picture or other aid can illustrate in a more meaningful way the magnitude of a problem or can make an expert's opinion more understandable and memorable. Visual aids carry so much power that, when properly prepared and displayed, they can substantially impact, if not alter, how jurors assess testimony.[3]

At the same time, poor demonstrative aids can be a terrible distraction.[4] For example, instances abound of attorneys using demonstrative posters or PowerPoint slides with too many words, text that is not large enough to be seen by all, or misspellings. In other cases, complicated diagrams or flow charts may be used that are confusing to even the most knowledgeable viewers. In these examples, the demonstratives will not assist the testimony but, by potentially distracting the viewer, actually may render it less effective than if none had been used at all. Thus, an important part of any expert's trial preparation should include time spent creating quality visual aids and practicing using them.

This subchapter addresses the importance of visual aids to expert testimony, the selection of appropriate visual aids, admissibility of visual aids, and the proper use of visual aids. In addition, Appendix B contains examples of effective demonstrative exhibits.

---

1. Joan K. Archer, Ph.D., J.D., is an attorney at Lathrop & Gage LLP's Kansas City, Missouri, office. Ms. Archer practices in intellectual property (trademarks, patents, copyrights, and trade secrets) and business litigation. She also prosecutes trademarks and counsels clients in branding, marketing, and Internet issues. Her doctoral degree is in communications and jury behavior, and she frequently consults on trial presentation issues.
2. *See, e.g.*, Jacob D. Fuchsberg, *Cool Advocacy in a Hot Court*, TRIAL, July 1983 at 44, 46.
3. L. O'Toole, *Admitting that We're Litigating in the Digital Age: A Practical Overview of Issues of Admissibility in the Technological Courtroom*, 59 FEDERATION OF DEFENSE AND CORPORATE COUNSEL QUARTERLY 3, 5 (2008).
4. *See, e.g.*, Eugene A. Cook, *Improving Your Oral Advocacy before the Supreme Court*, TEX. B.J. 243, 243 (1990).

Importance of Visual Aids to Expert Testimony

The content of expert witness testimony can overwhelm and confuse even the most educated juror. Complex topics are often presented through a vocabulary of specialized terms. The most persuasive trial lawyers spend a substantial amount of time educating jurors.[5] Thus, carefully created visual aids presented through good communication techniques can radically alter a juror's comprehension and recollection of an expert's testimony.

Graphics can increase jurors' retention and understanding. In general, jurors retain little of what they hear at trial.[6] But visual aids can increase the rate of retention.[7] This particularly holds true when a trial lasts several days or weeks. As the court noted in *Verizon Directories Corp. v. Yellow Book USA Inc.*, "Although rudimentary, the [graphic] images are effective in clarifying sometimes dense expert testimony, statistical surveys and theories."[8] As Charles Babcock and Jason Bloom have explained:

> As every good teacher knows, visual aids, by allowing jurors to see abstract concepts and relationships, significantly enhance both understanding and retention. Trial lawyers must remember that most jurors receive their primary information from television and are conditioned to learn more from visual images than from words alone. On the average, jurors watch six hours of television each day, during which they are bombarded with visual information. CNN, for example, which currently markets itself as the "get-to-the-point news network" and uses many graphics to illustrate the news, has been the number one source of news information for many jurors. News programs such as those on CNN succinctly spoon-feed information to viewers in bits. These programs make strategic use of flashy charts and graphics to illustrate the thrust of a news story. As lawyers, we should learn from the success of television in capitalizing on how people want to learn and receive new information.[9]

It is, therefore, important that attorneys and experts meet jurors' expectations for presentation of information by using mixed media to facilitate message comprehension.

---

5. G.C. RITTER, CREATING WINNING TRIAL STRATEGIES AND GRAPHICS 5 (2004).

6. C. Babcock & J. Bloom, *Getting Your Message Across: Visual Aids and Demonstrative Exhibits in the Courtroom*, 27 No. 3 LITIG. 41 (Spring 2001).

7. *Id.* at 41 ("The retention rate goes up significantly, to as high as 60 percent, when they [jurors] see something, and research has proven that jurors retain over 80 percent of what they simultaneously hear and see."); *see also* D. VINSON, JURY PERSUASION: PSYCHOLOGICAL STRATEGIES AND TRIAL TECHNIQUES 184 (1993).

8. *See* Verizon Directories Corp. v. Yellow Book USA Inc., 331 F. Supp. 2d 136, 139 (E.D.N.Y. 2004).

9. Babcock & Bloom, *supra* note 6, at 41.

Selection of Appropriate Visual Aids

Several factors should influence whether use of a visual aid is appropriate. A visual aid should be used if it can simplify otherwise difficult material, make the importance or impact of an event clearer, or attract the interest of the judge and jury and enhance their understanding. In particular, consider using a visual aid with your expert when the following circumstances exist:

- Unfamiliar concepts or terms will be used during the expert's testimony that need to be understood to make sense out of it;
- A scientific relationship, rule, or phenomena plays a key role in informing the expert's opinions;
- The expert is talking about an item, thing, technology, or part of the human body;
- The expert is explaining an event that occurred in the past that can be better understood through photos or a diagram; or
- Statistical information, formulas, or other data are essential to the opinions being stated.

If one of these criteria is met, the best presentation means should then be considered. A visual aid should enhance and explain complicated opinion testimony in the most succinct manner possible under the circumstances. This means that the nature and substance of the content determines which type of visual aid should be used to communicate a particular message. There are a variety of visual aids available for use in connection with an expert's testimony. Here are some of the primary types to consider:

- Photographs;
- Text (definitions and excerpts from treatises);
- Scale models;
- Product/product parts and samples;
- Charts or graphs with statistical information;
- Computer simulations and animations;
- Drawings;
- Evidentiary objects;
- Personal objects;
- Timelines;
- Records excerpts (i.e., transcripts, police reports, etc.); and
- Medical test records and X-rays.

It is particularly important to use a variety of exhibit types. This is necessary to keep the jurors' attention. Monotonous exhibit types can be as ineffective as a flat speaking tone, so choose types with diversity in mind. That said, do not overuse visuals. They should enhance the expert's testimony, not become the sum and substance of it! An expert who needs too many exhibits to explain a point could be perceived as less credible because jurors may believe the witness does not have a good command of the subject matter.

Also, work with the expert in creating visual aids. Do not simply prepare them for the witness. The exhibits you may select might not be ones the expert finds useful. Too much attorney involvement can lead to exhibits that sound like the attorney talking, not the expert.

Some experts prefer to create visual aids on their own. These can be quite effective if they are high quality and understandable. It is wise, however, to preview samples of an expert's work before agreeing to permit them to create visuals on their own. And, even if the expert is allowed to proceed with creating visuals, counsel should still be deeply involved in the process. Content should be carefully selected and assessed so that it will be useful to the judge and jury at trial. Work collaboratively with the expert so the most powerful and effective visuals are created.

Thus, the media and visual images should be presented in a professional manner.[10] Otherwise, the many hours of preparing for an expert's testimony at trial may be for naught. Most attorneys are not equipped to do this on their own. It may, therefore, be necessary to employ a graphic artist to help create professional quality images. Moreover, significant time should be spent with each expert selecting content for visual presentation as well as the type of visual aids to be employed.

Admissibility of Demonstrative Exhibits

An obvious important consideration is ensuring that the court allows you to use the visual aids you have worked to create. As a preliminary matter, demonstrative exhibits must be relevant (in that they must accurately reflect the underlying facts) to be admissible under Federal Rule of Evidence 402.[11] In the context of expert testimony, counsel should ensure that it can establish the foundation for the demonstrative exhibit, meaning that it accurately reflects evidence that is already part of the record so that "the matter in question is what its proponent claims" under Federal Rule of Evidence 901(a).[12]

---

10. *See* RITTER, *supra* note 5, for an excellent and detailed discussion of the various factors that impact the creation of trial graphics, along with the various types that can be employed.

11. *See* United Nat'l Ins. Co. v. Aon Ltd., Civ. No. 04-539, 2008 WL 4384455 (E.D. Pa. Sept. 19, 2008).

12. *See* Tritek Techs., Inc. v. U.S., 67 Fed. Cl. 727, 734 (Fed. Cl. 2005) (agreeing with the argument that "allowing the demonstrative exhibit and the supporting affidavits into

The primary objection made to admission of demonstrative exhibits is that their probative value is outweighed by the danger of unfair prejudice, cumulative effect, or likelihood of confusion under Federal Rule of Evidence 403,[13] so counsel should be prepared to meet that objection. Some courts allow the admission of demonstrative exhibits under Federal Rule of Evidence 611, which provides for trial court discretion over the mode of interrogation of witnesses.[14] Courts also allow the admission of demonstrative exhibits as a chart, summary, or calculation under Federal Rule of Evidence 1006 if "[t]he contents of voluminous writings, recordings, or photographs . . . cannot conveniently be examined in court." The trial court's decision as to admissibility is crucial, since that decision will be reversed only for abuse of discretion.[15]

Proper Use of Visual Aids

The following communication rules ensure that visual aids are as effective as possible:

1. **A visual aid should enhance and explain complex opinion testimony in the most succinct manner possible.** Visuals should add clarity not confusion. A well-drafted graphic, for example, can be essential to helping a jury understand a complex technology.
2. **Make sure that use of the visual aid is feasible in the courtroom and meets the rules of the court.** Today, many but not all courtrooms are equipped for electronic presentations. If yours is not, arrangements should be made for the necessary equipment. The precise size and layout of the courtroom should be considered in selecting equipment types, the number of screens and easels used, and their placement. Even a courtroom's existing screens, for example, may require supplementation if visuals are to be seen by all.

---

evidence would constitute the admission of unreliable, undisclosed and unsupported expert testimony").

13. *See Tritek Technologies*, 67 Fed. Cl. 727; Lorraine v. Markel Am. Ins. Co., 241 F.R.D. 534 (D. Md. 2007).

14. *See* United States v. Harms, 442 F.3d 367, 375 (5th Cir. 2006) ("[A]llowing the use of charts as 'pedagogical' devices intended to present the government's version of the case is within the bounds of the trial court's discretion to control the presentation of evidence under Rule 611(a).") (citations omitted); *see also id.* ("If a summary or chart is introduced solely as a pedagogical device, the court should instruct the jury that the chart or summary is not to be considered as evidence, but only as an aid in evaluating evidence.").

15. Gordon v. Lewistown Hosp'l., 423 F.3d 184, 215 n.21 (3d Cir. 2005).

3. **The aid should be large enough to be seen by all and should create visual interest.** In some circumstances, two easels or multiple screens with copies of the aid may be required in order for everyone in the courtroom to see it clearly. Obviously, visual material also should be clean and attractive. Lettering on posters should be prepared professionally in a way that is clear and appealing. Also, pay attention to color, scale, and contrast.

4. **The attorney needs to be careful not to use the visual aid in such a fashion that the judge and jury could be distracted.** That means that a visual aid should be kept covered until it is used or referred to and then should be covered again following use. This is especially true of Power-Point slides. If a slide is left up on the screen while counsel has moved on to the next topic, jurors may actually be still reading the last slide and thinking about the last topic instead of moving their attention to the next. Thus, whole bits of presentation content may be lost for some jurors. So, be mindful of what is being shown—if you are not using the visual in connection with specific testimony, it should be covered or replaced with a blank slide.

5. **The examining attorney may want to have an associate or assistant help with the visual aid.** It is embarrassing to drop a poster because it is too big for one person to handle. It may be helpful for the person providing assistance to use a pointer to direct the court's attention to particular aspects of the visual aid.

6. **Prepare backup visuals if technology is used.** Some technical difficulties just cannot be avoided, so backups are important. There is nothing more embarrassing than moving to a computer to show a graphic only to reveal a blank screen. Although jurors often are sympathetic to such technical glitches, counsel may become flustered and distracted from the line of examination at hand. An ounce of prevention in the form of having backup equipment available is well worth it!

7. **If equipment of any type is to be used in conjunction with the visual aid, it should be tested in the courtroom the day before trial to ensure that everything is in working order.** Burned out light bulbs can be found and words that appear too small on the screen can be revealed in advance and corrected. Problems can easily be avoided through careful planning and trial runs. Also, previewing graphics in the courtroom is important because lighting conditions, room set up, and other variables can alter how a poster or PowerPoint slide appears in use. For example, glare from a window may render a poster difficult to see. At that point, the visual could become a distracting hindrance. Obtaining a window covering may be an easy solution, but this is one solution that is not so easy in the middle of trial. Pretesting visuals in the courtroom can, therefore, provide time for solutions to be found for any problems encountered.

8. **Given the various problems associated with visual aid use, the attorney should practice with the visual aid before the expert's examination.** This means that not only should the witness be prepared to assist with the presentation of visual content at trial, but also any visual aids should be incorporated into the actual practice session. Both counsel and the expert should be comfortable with use of the visuals. Experts who want to point to specific parts of a diagram, for example, should actually practice doing so in order for timing and other issues to be addressed. Practice does make perfect in the context of expert witness testimony and use of visual aids.

Conclusion

Visual and other aids can be of great assistance in making expert testimony understandable and memorable. But visual aids are often misused, and they may detract from the testimony. Therefore, attorneys need to be very careful in preparing adequately for their use with experts.

Appendix A: Sample Qualification of Expert

[Basics]

Q. Your name is John Doe?

A. Yes, that's correct.

Q. And do you live in this state? *[Establish local residency or other connection to jurisdiction, if possible.]*

A. Yes.

Q. What is your profession?

A. I am a forensic accountant and business appraiser, and I make my living by helping clients with calculations of things like business losses and other complicated financial issues that come up, mostly in the context of lawsuits and other types of disputes.

Q. You work with the firm of Doe & Smith, LLC?

A. Yes.

Q. And you're a partner in that firm? *[Use opportunities to emphasize every meaningful qualification.]*

A. Yes.

Q. How long have you been a partner in that firm?

A. Since I founded it in 1978.

Q. What does your firm do? *[Notice the simple language.]*

A. We are mostly Certified Public Accountants and other experts providing financial analysis and investigation in litigation and other complicated business problems. *[Notice the uncomplicated description and "self-identification" as an expert.]*

Q. Do have any professional designations?

A. Yes, I am a CPA, that stands for Certified Public Accountant.

Q. What is involved in getting that certification? *[Don't rely merely on designations—emphasize the work that goes into obtaining/keeping such designations.]*

A. A number of things, including a college degree in a specific field like accounting, passing a national exam, and licensure by the state.

Q. So you have to be licensed by the state?

A. Yes.

Q. You have your license? *[Emphasize any designations granted by governments.]*

A. Yes.

Q. In what state(s)?

A. Georgia, South Carolina, and New York.

Q. Do you have any other licenses or certifications?

A. Yes. I am also accredited in Business Valuation by the AICPA, which is the American Institute of Certified Public Accountants.

Q. What is involved in obtaining that certification?

A. Specific types of training, a certain amount of education, specialized courses, and actual work experience.

Q. Does any of the required training relate particularly to analyzing financial statements and other financial data related to income of businesses?

A. Yes, quite a lot of it is focused on the particular topic of how to analyze income and predict future income.

Q. Do you have any other certifications?

A. Yes, I am also an Accredited Senior Appraiser of the American Society of Appraisers and also a Certified Fraud Examiner.

Q. What is involved in obtaining these last two certifications?

A. Similar to the others—specific types of training, a certain amount of education, specialized courses, and actual work experience.

Q. Do you have any requirements regarding keeping these licenses and certifications up to date?

A. Yes: ongoing training, learning, study, and reporting.

Q. In terms of hours per year, how much time do you invest in keeping it all up to date?

A. Approximately 80 hours per year.

Q. Can you give me a short summary of your work history?

A. *[Summary of work history]*

Q. In those various positions, how much of your time has been spent doing the kind of analysis of lost income and business losses that you have described today?

A. The vast majority. I would estimate 75–85 percent of my time is spent doing this kind of analysis.

Q. In addition to your professional designations and your work history, what is your formal education?

A. I have a college degree in business from Harvard Business School and a master's degree in accounting from Columbia University.

Mr. Doe, I want to turn your attention now to your experience as an expert witness in the area of Business Loss Damages. *[Use topic "headlines" to alert the jury that this is experience that really matters.]*

Q. How many matters in this area—business loss damages and valuation—have you worked on in your career? *[Give the jury some easy statistics to hang on to.]*

A. Hundreds if not thousands.

Q. Who normally hires you?

A. Law firms, receivers, trustees, and sometimes courts.

Q. Have you ever testified under oath before in cases where you have offered your opinion as to business loss damages and valuation issues?

A. Yes—probably 40 times.

Q. Have any of those been at trial?

A. Yes—probably 20 times.

Q. How is it that you are qualified to offer an opinion in this case in the area of business loss damages?

A. Well, I am a recognized expert in the area of financial analysis—in other words understanding the financial statements of businesses and my understanding is that, in this case, the plaintiff claims that he was stopped from locating a business at this particular location . . . so first I am qualified to analyze business results based on financial statements. Second, with regard to analyzing the loss that stemmed from the circumstances here, I relied on the same concepts that I use every day in other matters, matters where we are calculating the expected future earning from businesses, making projections, valuing companies, and other disputes requiring the calculation of the expected future results for the company. Business losses are calculated in many types of disputes.

Q. Have you ever been accepted by a court, where you have been allowed to testify in front of a judge or a jury, as an expert on business loss damages or valuation issues?

A. Yes, both.

Q. In any federal courts?

A. Yes.

Q. Which ones?
A. I can give some examples: the Northern District of Georgia—in Rome in front of Judge Murphy and in Atlanta in front of Judge Schoob; in the District of Washington, in Seattle, in front of Judge Bryan; also in the District of South Carolina, in Greenville, in front of Judge Anderson. Those are a few I can think of. There are others. *[Encourage the witness to give specific examples of courts and judges. Although the jury will not recognize the courts or judges, it gives the witness credibility.]*
Q. Have you also testified in state court?
A. Yes, in Fayette County in front of Judge Miller, in Fulton County in front of Judge Moore, and in Gwinnett County in front of Judge Oxendine. Those are some examples.
Q. Have you ever testified as an expert on business loss damages in a case dealing with a retail establishment? *[Bring the subject matter back to the subject matter from this case as often as possible.]*
A. Yes.
Q. Can you describe for the jury a couple of those matters?
A. *[Short description]*
Q. Did the court accept you as an expert in those cases?
A. Yes.

Your honor, I offer Mr. Doe as an expert on calculating business loss damages, especially with respect to damages suffered by an owner that is a multilocation retail chain.

Q. Mr. Doe, do you have an opinion on the amount of business losses suffered by the plaintiff in this case as a result of the fact that it was not able to locate a business at the location it sought to purchase from defendant in this case?
A. Yes. It is $4,095,000.

Appendix B: Selected Examples of Demonstrable Visual Aids

The following demonstrative exhibits, used with the permission of Navigant Consulting, Inc., exemplify the appropriate and effective use of visual aids:

- "Event Timeline"
- "Stripping"

Event Timeline

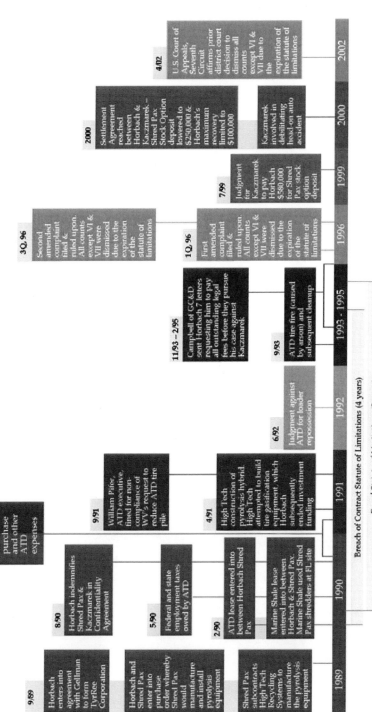

Navigant Consulting

STRIPPING

As-Built

As-Planned Shoring

Added Shoring

Perimeter Wall

Navigant Consulting

CHAPTER 9

Expert Issues Unique
to Types of Expertise

E-DISCOVERY

Wendy Butler Curtis and Shannon Capone Kirk[1]

E-discovery is an amorphous term generally used in reference to the discovery of Electronically Stored Information (ESI). ESI differs from paper information in its volume, variety of sources, and dynamic quality.[2] As a result of the unique legal and technical issues associated with ESI, e-discovery has evolved into both a substantive area of the law and area of specialized technical and scientific expertise. In this subchapter, we analyze the various roles played by e-discovery experts and the various types of e-discovery experts. In addition, we provide practical advice about dealing with unique challenges posed by e-discovery experts such as privilege considerations.

First, it is critical to understand the myriad potential roles played by an e-discovery expert. E-discovery experts can be effective in minimizing disputes, reducing burdensome e-discovery costs, and explaining to opposing

---

1. Ms. Butler Curtis is E-Discovery of counsel at Orrick, Herrington & Sutcliffe LLP and chair of its eDiscovery Working Group. Ms. Capone Kirk is E-Discovery counsel at Ropes & Gray LLP. Orrick has 22 offices in 8 countries. Ms. Butler Curtis is based in Orrick's Washington, D.C., office. Ropes & Gray has 9 domestic and international offices. Ms. Capone Kirk is based in Ropes's Boston office. The authors would like to express their gratitude for the substantial contributions of Lily Becker (Orrick) and Trent Christensen (Ropes & Gray).
2. Barbara J. Rothstein, Ronald J. Hedges & Elizabeth C. Wiggins, Managing Discovery of Electronic Information: A Pocket Guide for Judges 3 (Federal Judicial Center, 2007), *available at* http://www.fjc.gov/public/pdf.nsf/lookup/eldscpkt.pdf/$file/eldscpkt.pdf.

parties and the courts technical issues, challenges, and limitations. E-discovery experts ordinarily perform one or more of the following general functions:

- Resolve e-discovery disputes as a mediator or a special master;
- Advise counsel or court on a variety of technical issues related to preservation, collection, processing, culling, and review of ESI;
- Investigate forensic data for alterations, deletions, or embedded information;
- Attend "meet and confer" sessions with counsel;
- Provide declarations or testimony in support of discovery motions practice;
- Assist with the development of defensible preservation and collection plans; and
- Assist with the development of defensible search (key words and beyond) and culling techniques.

Once an attorney has identified the function of the e-discovery expert, the next step is to determine the type of expert to best perform this function. In making this determination, it is important to understand the distinctions among e-discovery experts. E-discovery is an evolving area of the law, and the market is full of self-proclaimed subject matter experts. By way of comparison, in medical malpractice claims, it would be improper to proffer a general internist to testify about brain surgery. It is the same with the wide-ranging field of e-discovery. If an expert is not properly selected and vetted, a party may find out, too late, that its expert is unqualified for the specific e-discovery task at hand. As with all legal service providers, counsel is responsible for selecting and supervising competent consultants and experts.[3] E-discovery experts fall into the following general categories, each of which is addressed below in detail:

- Legal experts, those who understand the legal obligations of parties and nonparties, including special masters and mediators;
- Forensic experts, those who conduct scientific examination and analysis of computer data, including the identification of hidden, fragmented, deleted, altered, or stolen data and the origin, storage, and genesis of data;
- E-discovery vendor experts knowledgeable in e-discovery technology, best practices, industry norms, and the costs of e-discovery; and

---

3. *In re* Seroquel Prods. Liab. Litig., 244 F.R.D. 650, 664 n.14 (D. Fla. 2007) ("'[U]ltimate responsibility for ensuring preservation, collection, processing, and production of electronically stored information rests with the party and its counsel, not with the nonparty consultant or vendor.") (quoting The Sedona Principles, Second Edition: Best Practices Recommendations & Principles for Addressing Electronic Document Production 40 cmt. 6d (2007), *available at* http://www.thesedonaconference.org/content/miscFiles/TSC_PRINCP_2nd_ed_607.pdf) [hereinafter Sedona Second Edition].

- Search and retrieval experts, those versed in how to isolate and retrieve, via technology and search terms, the most relevant information.

Finally, as discussed below in more detail, when evaluating whether to retain an expert, remember the following:

1. Will this expert reduce cost and risk?
2. Is this expert qualified in the issues specific to your case?
3. Are you remaining vigilant on distinctions between experts hired to consult on legal issues or provide expert opinions and e-discovery vendors hired to execute preservation, collection, or production?
4. Have you ensured that all agreements contemplate privilege and confidentiality?

Legal E-Discovery Experts

Given the increase and complexity of e-discovery, it should come as no surprise that courts and parties have turned to special masters and private mediators to resolve e-discovery disputes. This trend is reflected in recent case law, local rules,[4] court protocols,[5] and recommendations for the use

---

4. Some district court guidelines lay out the need for some sort of intermediary during ESI discovery, whether that be a special master or otherwise, to "promote communication and cooperation between the parties." *See* U.S. District Judge Colleen McMahon's Rules Governing Electronic Discovery § 2 (S.D.N.Y.), *available at* http://www.nysd.us courts.gov/cases/show.php?db=judge_info&id=262 (requesting "E<->discovery liaisons"). That party need not be an attorney but could be "a third party consultant, or an employee of the party," and must be, among other things, "knowledgeable about the technical aspects of e-discovery . . . [and] prepared to participate in e-discovery dispute resolutions." *Id.; see also In re*: Default Standard for Discovery of Electronically Stored Information, Admin. Order No. 174 (M.D. Tenn.), *available at* http://www.tnmd.uscourts.gov/files/ AO_174_E-Discovery.pdf (making no mention of special masters but encouraging the use of an "e-discovery coordinator" to "promote communication and cooperation between the parties" regarding ESI discovery).

5. *See* Suggested Protocol for Discovery of Electronically Stored Information ("ESI"), (D. Md.), *available at* http://www.mdd.uscourts.gov/news/news/ESIProtocol.pdf. Though there is no specific discussion of special masters included in this protocol, one topic covered in the "Topics To Discuss At Rule 26(F) Conference" section is whether the parties could come to "[a]ny agreement concerning retention of an agreed-upon Court expert, retained at the cost of the parties, to assist in the resolution of technical issues presented by ESI." *Id.* In addition, the District of Kansas's Guidelines for Discovery of Electronically Stored Information point to the possible use of a special master. *See* Guidelines for Discovery of Electronically Stored Information (ESI), App. 1 (D. Kan.), *available at* http://www.ksd.uscourts .gov/guidelines/electronicdiscoveryguidelines.pdf (encouraging litigants to ask, among other things, whether there is "a need for an e-discovery special master").

of experts or liaisons to resolve e-discovery issues. Special masters and private mediators can address any one or combination of the following:

- Developing case-specific e-discovery protocols and case management orders;
- Advising on a variety of technical issues related to preservation, collection, processing, culling, and review of ESI;
- Coordinating, monitoring, and enforcing compliance with discovery obligations and deadlines;
- Reviewing privilege logs and adjudicating related disputes;
- Adjudicating common discovery motions, including motions for protective orders and motions to compel; and
- Assessing sanctions for spoliation of evidence and other discovery disputes.

Whether agreeing to a special master or mediator, it is essential that the parties ensure that the legal expert has the requisite expertise. In an e-discovery context, it is sometimes important that this quasi-judicial function be executed by someone who understands not only e-discovery legal standards, but also the technical issues surrounding the ESI at issue. Many questions of e-discovery turn on the probative value of the evidence and the proportionality of the cost of the requested discovery as compared against the total value of the case.[6] Therefore, an e-discovery legal expert should also have sufficient understanding of the subject matter of the case to make this assessment. Finally, for the process to be successful, the parties should be sufficiently informed and prepared for conferences and negotiations with the special master or mediator. A successful special master or mediator must have the presence, authority, and respect necessary to ensure such behavior by the parties and their counsel.

Special Masters

Special masters are used when agreed to by the parties or ordered by the court pursuant to Federal Rule of Civil Procedure 53.[7] A court may appoint

---

6. *See* FED. R. CIV. P. 26(b)(2)(B):
   A party need not provide discovery of electronically stored information from sources that the party identifies as not reasonably accessible because of undue burden or cost. On motion to compel discovery or for a protective order, the party from whom discovery is sought must show that the information is not reasonably accessible because of undue burden or cost. If that showing is made, the court may nonetheless order discovery from such sources if the requesting party shows good cause, considering the limitations of Rule 26(b)(2)(C). The court may specify conditions for the discovery.

7. As the current Rule 53 is much more flexible than its predecessor, it "now permits the use of special masters on an as-needed basis, with the parties' consent, or, when excep-

a special master to "perform duties consented to by the parties" or "address pretrial and post-trial matters that cannot be effectively and timely addressed by an available district judge or magistrate judge of the district."[8] A special master has the authority to "regulate all proceedings; . . . take all appropriate measures to perform the assigned duties fairly and efficiently; and . . . if conducting an evidentiary hearing, exercise the appointing court's power to compel, take, and record evidence."[9] Special masters are generally appointed to coordinate, monitor, and enforce compliance with discovery; assist the court with privilege issues; or provide neutral opinions on technical and forensics issues.

Special Master to Coordinate, Monitor, and Enforce Compliance with Discovery Obligations

Courts may use e-discovery special masters to coordinate, monitor, or enforce compliance with discovery obligations. In complex cases, these tasks can take hundreds of hours of court time, and the appointment of special masters conserves valuable judicial resources.[10] Courts have also used special masters as a sword or "severe intervention" to motivate parties to cooperate or otherwise comply with their discovery obligations.[11] This approach is the result of the growing trend to encourage parties to be more cooperative and

---

tional conditions require, by court order." *See* Shira A. Scheindlin & Jonathan M. Redgrave, *Special Masters and E-Discovery: The Intersection of Two Recent Revisions to the Federal Rules of Civil Procedure*, 30 Cardozo L. Rev. 347, 352 (2008).

8. *Id.*

9. *Id.* In addition, a court "may use its inherent authority . . . to appoint an expert as a special master to advise the court." *See* James S. DeGraw, *Rule 53, Inherent Powers, and Institutional Reform: The Lack of Limits on Special Masters*, 66 N.Y.U. L. Rev. 800, 824–25 (1991) (citing Reilly v. United States, 863 F.2d 149, 154–55 (1st Cir. 1988)) (stating that the district court has inherent authority to appoint an expert). Appointing a special master is usually "deemed proper and is similar to a judge's consultation of other outside authorities, such as legal treatises and technical surveys. Indeed, such advice is within the traditional ambit of the special master and generally remains so today." *Id.*; *see also* Hart v. Cmty. Sch. Bd., 383 F. Supp. 699, 767–68 (E.D.N.Y. 1974) (discussing how the courts developed the inherent power to appoint experts).

10. *See* Bro-Tech Corp. v. Thermax, Inc., No. 05-CV-2330, 2008 WL 5210346, at *1 (E.D. Pa. Dec. 11, 2008) (after discovery became too complex, the court appointed a "special electronic discovery master" to manage discovery of electronically stored information).

11. In *Hohider v. United Parcel Service, Inc.*, the court appointed a special master because the plaintiff alleged that "UPS was not forthright in informing plaintiffs and the court about the nature and scope of UPS's preservation efforts." Hohider v. United Parcel Serv., Inc., No. 04-363, 2009 WL 1163931, at *2 (W.D. Pa. Apr. 28, 2009). Regarding the claims of spoliation, UPS maintained that "it had no duty to preserve relevant ESI until the case was certified." *Id.* at *3. The special master, however, recommended the court to reject this position and find that the "defendant's duty to preserve included ESI." *Id.* Further, in *S.E.C. v. Collins & Aikman*, Judge Scheindlin required the parties to "meet and confer forthwith and develop a workable search protocol that would reveal *at least some* of the information

committed to the "meet and confer" process.[12] With a dedicated special master overseeing discovery, the parties may become more collaborative and communicative earlier in the life of the case. It goes without saying that by reaching agreement before expenses are incurred and information is produced, parties may better avoid or limit discovery disputes. In addition, the perceived informality of special masters might allow for issues to be raised promptly, early in the process, and without the preparation of expensive motions.[13]

Utilizing a Special Master to Assist with Privilege Issues

Courts have voiced frustration with vague privilege logs that require *in camera* review of individual documents to make determinations of privilege. This *in camera* review can be time consuming and tedious. Thus, in some circumstances, special masters are appointed[14] to encourage compliance by the parties.[15] Such appointments "may be able to speed the resolution of disputes by fashioning fair and reasonable discovery plans based upon specialized knowledge of electronic discovery and/or technical issues."[16] In addition, when special masters are active in the meet and confer process, a well-informed special master may encourage the parties to

---

defendant seeks" and warned that "[i]f the parties cannot craft an agreement, the Court will consider the appointment of a Special Master to assist in this effort." S.E.C. v. Collins & Aikman, No. 07 Civ. 2419(SAS), 2009 WL 94311, *9 (S.D.N.Y. Jan. 13, 2009).

12. *See* THE SEDONA CONFERENCE COOPERATION PROCLAMATION, *available at* http://www.thesedonaconference.org/content/tsc_cooperation_proclamation/proclamation.pdf [hereinafter COOPERATION PROCLAMATION]; *see also* Mancia v. Mayflower Textile Servs. Co., 253 F.R.D. 354, 356–57 (D. Md. Oct. 15, 2008).

13. *See* Practical Tips to Ensure Cost Confers Sufficient Benefit *infra*.

14. *See* E.I. Du Pont de Nemours and Co. v. Cardinal Health, Inc., No. 3:03-848, 2005 WL 2218847 (M.D. Tenn. May 27, 2005) (Magistrate Order) (appointing a special master and outlining duty to review documents claimed to be privileged). Likewise, after a special master was appointed to manage production of ESI in *Medtronic Sofama Danek, Inc. v. Michelson*, the parties stipulated that they would submit any disputed privilege log entries to the special master for *in camera* review to determine whether the disputed documents were discoverable. Order Overruling Plaintiff's Objections To Special Master Balaran's Mar. 19, 2004 Order, Medtronic Sofama Danek, Inc. v. Michelson, No. 01-2373 MlV (W.D. Tenn. Apr. 19, 2004), *available at* http://www.tnwd.uscourts.gov/JudgeVescovo/opinions/338.pdf.

15. For example, in *Forest Guardians v. Kempthorne*, after the Fish and Wildlife Service failed to complete interrogatories and provide a comprehensive privilege log as ordered by the court, it was "afforded a final opportunity to 'get it right' . . . [but was] caution[ed] that any further instances of what has been observed to be dilatory tactics and recalcitrant behavior will result in increasingly severe intervention, including the possibility of . . . the appointment of a special master." Forest Guardians v. Kempthorne, No. 06CV2560-L(LSP), 2008 WL 4492635, at *4 (S.D. Cal. Sept. 29, 2008).

16. SEDONA SECOND EDITION, *supra* note 3, at 53 cmt. 10c.

include "clawback agreements"[17] or other privilege agreements in agreed orders, a step in obtaining the full protections of Federal Rule of Evidence 502.[18] They may also include, in the discovery protocol or scheduling order, agreements related to the format of the privilege log, timing of the production of the log, privilege search terms, and agreements regarding the reasonableness of a proposed privilege review methodology, all of which might reduce the costs and rises associated with privilege review among gigabytes, or even terabytes, of data.[19] A special master charged with organizing the parties on privilege review should be focused on such protocols and agreements.

Special Master on Technical and Forensics Issues

Special masters have also been appointed in cases involving unique sources of information,[20] forensic services,[21] including potentially deleted,[22]

---

17. "In a clawback agreement, the producing and receiving parties agree to return inadvertently produced privileged or protected information upon prompt demand by the producing party." THE ATTORNEY-CLIENT PRIVILEGE IN CIVIL LITIGATION: PROTECTING AND DEFENDING CONFIDENTIALITY 169 (Vincent S. Walkowiak ed., 4th ed. 2008). *See also* FED. R. CIV. P. 26(b)(5)(B).

18. FED. R. EVID. 502(d) ("A Federal court may order that the privilege or protection is not waived by disclosure connected with the litigation pending before the court—in which event the disclosure is also not a waiver in any other Federal or State proceeding.").

19. For example, in *Bray & Gillespie Mgmt. LLC v. Lexington Insurance Co.*, when a plaintiff produced ESI "without conducting a privilege review in an effort to comply with the court's orders requiring expedited production of that information," the special master "did not require [the defendants] to search out and segregate what might be considered privileged documents from the production . . . [but if], in the ordinary course of trial preparation, [defendants] encounter what appears to be a privileged document, normal ethical standards would be followed to resolve that situation." Bray & Gillespie Mgmt. LLC v. Lexington Ins. Co., No. 6:07-cv-222-Or-35KRS, 2009 WL 71678, at *1 (M.D. Fla. Jan. 8, 2009). *See also* FED. R. EVID. 502(b) (providing that disclosure will not operate as a waiver if "the holder of the privilege or protection took reasonable steps to prevent disclosure" and "the holder promptly took reasonable steps to rectify the error").

20. *See* RGIS, LLC v. A.S.T., Inc., No. 2:07-CV-10975, 2008 WL 186349, at *1 (E.D. Mich. Jan. 22, 2008) (special master assigned to assess whether the parties' source codes were substantially similar); *see also In re* Subpoena to Chronotek Sys., Inc., No. SACV 06-374 ODW (RNBX), 2007 WL 2177013, at *2 (S.D. Tex. July 27, 2007) (adopting the special master's expert conclusion that a third party's source code was relevant to a patent dispute).

21. *See* Square D Co. v. Scott Elec. Co., No. 06-00459, 2008 WL 2779067, at *7 (W.D. Pa. July 15, 2008) (finding that additional discovery disputes regarding forensic inspection of computers could result in the appointment of a special master).

22. *See* Koninklijke Philips Elec. N.V. v. KXD Tech., Inc., No. 2:05-cv-01532-RLH-GWF, 2007 WL 879683, at *5 (D. Nev. Mar. 20, 2007) (noting the court's power to appoint a computer forensic expert as a special master to "inspect, investigate and assess any alleged damage to the Defendants' computer servers or hard drives").

altered,[23] or stolen data, or other complex technical issues.[24] The contributions of the special master will depend on the timing of his or her appointment, mastery of the technical challenges at issue, and the involvement of other technical experts. If involved early in a matter, the special master may help craft appropriate protocols for complex technical challenges, assess the proportional value of inaccessible sources of information, or craft tiered discovery plans, allowing for sampling and other potentially cost-saving alternatives. These same efficiencies, however, might also be achieved through the use of technical experts retained by the parties or a neutral technical expert retained by the court without the additional cost of the special master. Nonetheless, if the parties can agree to a special master with the necessary technical expertise, they may save costs by simply splitting the cost of the special master rather than each incurring the cost of retaining an independent technical expert.

If the appointment of a special master is not raised until a dispute has arisen, a similar cost-benefit analysis should apply. On the one hand, the special master might adjudicate the dispute,[25] something the court could do at no cost. If, on the other hand, the relief sought is additional discovery or re-collection under a new discovery protocol, a technologically qualified special master may offer technical efficiencies in drafting the contours of the relief requested. If, however, the special master will require guidance from a neutral party or technical expert, the parties increase their costs by paying both the special master and the relied-upon expert(s). In this situation, the parties should weigh the need of retaining, in essence, two or more experts.

Additional Considerations When Deciding
Whether to Appoint a Special Master

A consistent concern when using a special master is who will pay for the special master's services. Rule 53 directs courts to "consider the fairness of

---

23. *See* Inventory Locator Serv. LLC v. Partsbase, Inc., No. 02-2695 Ma/V, 2006 WL 1646091, at *2 (W.D. Tenn. June 14, 2006) (granting a motion to appoint a special master to review a large amount of electronic data that plaintiff's expert testified contained fabricated evidence).

24. *See* United States v. Simels, No. 08-CR-640 (JG), 2008 WL 5383138, at *3 (E.D.N.Y. Dec. 18, 2008) (parties sought the appointment of a special master to review computer files and data seized during a search using the Drug Enforcement Agency's forensic computer laboratory).

25. *See* Eastman Kodak Co. v. Sony Corp., Nos. 04-CV-6095T, 04-CV-6547T, 2006 WL 2039968, at *1 (W.D.N.Y. July 20, 2006) (adopting a special master report recommending that defendant's motion to compel specifically correlated electronic information be denied).

imposing the likely expenses on the parties."[26] Thus, the "court must allocate payment among the parties after considering the nature and amount of the controversy, the parties' means, and the extent to which any party is more responsible than other parties for the reference to a master."[27] In addition, courts may also require one party to pay a disproportionate amount of the costs if that party's conduct required the appointment of the special master.[28]

Other concerns, such as an increased discovery burden, may dissuade parties from agreeing to use a special master for e-discovery issues. For example, a special master may require parties to address not only collection, processing, and production issues, but also preservation.[29] These preservation negotiations may result in a preservation order, something generally disfavored both by the Federal Rules of Civil Procedure and parties with the greater discovery burden.[30] The use of a special master should, as in all cases, be considered in proportion with the demands of the case and the amount in controversy.

In light of the cost and increased burdens of appointing a special master, experts on the issue agree that "appointments likely will remain the exception, and not the rule, as most parties should be able to address electronic discovery issues through cooperative efforts in the disclosure and discovery process, and any remaining disputes often can be decided by an available district court or magistrate judge of the district."[31]

---

26. FED. R. CIV. P. 53(a)(3).
27. FED. R. CIV. P. 53(g)(3).
28. *See Koninklijke Philips, supra* note 22, at *5 (based on the special master's findings as to whether ESI was purposely destroyed, the court could require either party to bear the costs of the special master); B. Padgett v. City of Monte Sereno, No. C 04-03946 JW, 2007 WL 878575, at *4 (N.D. Cal. Mar. 20, 2007) (despite the defendant's allegations to the contrary, the court found the defendant spoliated evidence and ordered that the defendant bear the costs of the special master); In re Gosman, 326 B.R. 889, 892 (Bankr. S.D. Fla. 2005) (ordering that the fees for a special master be paid by the trustee who sought to have allegedly "inherently valuable" documents seized); Medtronic Sofama Danek, Inc. v. Michelson, 229 F.R.D. 550, 559 (W.D. Tenn. 2004) (holding that "the parties will equally bear the cost of the special master's services.").
29. *See* Wm. T. Thompson Co. v. Gen. Nutrition Corp., Inc., 104 F.R.D. 119, 121 (C.D. Cal. 1985) ([T]he "Special Master made an oral document preservation order . . . upon which monetary sanctions could be awarded.").
30. FED. R. CIV. P. 26 Rules and Commentary, App. A (2006) ("The requirement that the parties discuss preservation does not imply that courts should routinely enter preservation orders. A preservation order entered over objections should be narrowly tailored. Ex parte preservation orders should issue only in exceptional circumstances.").
31. SEDONA SECOND EDITION, *supra* note 3, at 53 cmt. 10.c.

E-Discovery Mediators

In addition to court-appointed special masters, there is an emerging trend among private mediators to market their ability to resolve e-discovery issues. One area of particular focus is the meet and confer requirement of Federal Rule of Civil Procedure 26(f).[32] Rule 26(f) requires parties to engage in a formal or informal conference[33] to plan for discovery, including issues related to preservation, privilege, and the discovery of ESI.[34] After a meet and confer conference, Federal Rule of Civil Procedure 16(b) requires the court to then enter a scheduling order that addresses the discovery of ESI and any agreements between the parties regarding privilege.[35] Organizations like JAMS are now offering mediation within this meet and confer and scheduling process.[36] Further, the Sedona Conference organization pledged "to help create a network of trained electronic discovery mediators available to parties in state and federal courts nationwide, regardless of technical sophistication, financial resources, or the size of the matter."[37]

Comparing Special Masters and Private Mediators

The greatest difference between a private mediator and a special master is that the special master is imbued with the authority of the court. The appointing order from the district judge for a special master must state "the master's duties, including any investigation or enforcement duties," "any limits on the master's authority," and "the standards for reviewing the master's orders, findings, and recommendations."[38] Rule 53, therefore, presupposes that special masters will have investigative and enforcement duties.[39]

---

32. Fed R. Civ. P. 26(f).

33. This conference is mandatory unless exempted by Rule 26(a)(1)(B) or the court orders otherwise.

34. Fed. R. Civ. P. 26(f) (stating that "the parties must consider the nature and basis of their claims and defenses . . . ; discuss any issues about preserving discoverable information; and develop a proposed discovery plan," which would include language regarding ESI).

35. Fed. R. Civ. P. 16(b)(3)(B) ("The scheduling order may:. . . (iv) include any agreements the parties reach for asserting claims of privilege or of protection as trial-preparation material after information is produced; (v) set dates for pretrial conferences and for trial; and (vi) include other appropriate matters.").

36. See JAMS Arbitration, Mediation, and ADR Services, http://www.jamsadr.com.

37. Cooperation Proclamation, *supra* note 12.

38. Fed. R. Civ. P. 53(b)(2).

39. A district court, in a nonjury trial, "applies the same standard of review to the master's findings as a court of appeals applies to the district court's findings—conclusions of fact are presumed to be correct unless clearly erroneous." James S. DeGraw, *Rule 53, Inherent Powers, and Institutional Reform: The Lack of Limits on Special Masters*, 66 N.Y.U. L.

While a mediator may work with the blessing of the court, a private mediator cannot ordinarily require action by the parties.

Practical Tips to Ensure Cost Confers Sufficient Benefit

It is not a foregone conclusion that e-discovery legal experts, such as special masters and mediators, are more effective than a judge or that they lower discovery costs.[40] However, parties should consider the use of a special master or mediator when the complexity and quantity of e-discovery issues, conduct of opposing party or counsel, or lack of sophistication of the opposing party or counsel suggest the need for more extensive e-discovery case management and negotiation. In circumstances that justify the use of these quasi-judicial experts, the parties should take affirmative steps to ensure the experts are effective in reducing costs and avoiding disputes because an ineffective or overused special master or mediator could increase the costs of litigation.

To avoid inefficiencies, counsel should consider including, if appropriate, the following precautions in agreements with opposing counsel:

- Parties will confer with special master/mediator before any written submissions;
- Parties agree that there is a preference for informal submissions with page limits; and
- Parties agree that necessary players[41] will participate in meetings and conferences.

E-Discovery Forensic Experts

E-discovery issues range from legal issues to technical challenges and evidentiary offerings. Technical or forensic experts generally perform analysis

---

REV. 800, 800–01 (1991) (citing Liptak v. United States, 748 F.2d 1254, 1257 (8th Cir. 1984) (utilizing clearly erroneous standard)). *Cf.* Jenkins v. Sterlacci, 849 F.2d 627, 631 (D.C. Cir. 1988) ("[A] special master occupies a position functionally indistinguishable from that of a trial judge.").

40. *See The Final Report on the Joint Project* 18 (American College of Trial Lawyers Task Force on Discovery & The Institute for The Advancement of The American Legal System, Mar. 11, 2009) (revised Apr. 15, 2009), *available at* http://www.actl.com/AM/Template .cfm?Section=Home&template=/CM/ContentDisplay.cfm&ContentID=4008.

41. Depending on the specific dispute, necessary players may include e-discovery vendors, in-house information technology (IT) representatives, in-house counsel, e-discovery technical experts, e-discovery counsel, outside counsel, litigation services, or in-house e-discovery teams.

to determine whether information was altered, deleted, or properly preserved and collected.[42]

In practice, computer forensics experts are typically retained to do any of the following in litigation:

- Make forensic copies of certain media, primarily company laptops and computers;[43] (A forensic copy is an exact copy of an entire physical storage media, such as a hard drive, including all active[44] and residual[45] data, and unallocated[46] or slack[47] space on the media.);

---

42. *See* Mintel Int'l Group, Ltd. v. Neergheen, No. 08 c 3939, 2009 WL 1033357, at *2–3 (N.D. Ill., Apr. 17, 2009) (finding that more expert testimony was needed before ruling on plaintiff's spoliation motions). Courts have also recognized an emerging need for such experts in criminal cases. *See* United States v. Comprehensive Drug Testing, Inc., 579 F.3d 989, 1006 (9th Cir. 2009) (Future warrant applications to examine or seize forensic data must include provisions requiring that "[s]egregation and redaction [of forensic data] must either be done by specialized personnel or an independent third party" who agrees not to "disclose to the investigators any information other than that which is the target of the warrant." The warrant must include a protocol designed to uncover only information for which the government has probable cause, and only that information "may be examined by the case agents.").

43. *See* Simon Prop. Group v. mySimon, Inc., 194 F.R.D. 639, 641 (S.D. Ind. 2000) (requiring expert to inspect computers and create a mirror image of hard drive); *see also* Playboy Enters. v. Welles, 60 F. Supp. 2d 1050, 1055 (S.D. Cal. 1999) (requiring appointment of a computer expert to create a "mirror image" of the defendant's hard drive).

44. "Active Data" is "[i]nformation residing on the direct access storage media (disc drives or servers) that is readily visible to the operating system and/or application software with which it was created. It is immediately accessible to users without restoration or reconstruction." The Sedona Conference Glossary: E-Discovery & Digital Information Management 2 (Working Group on Electronic Document Retention & Production (WG1) RFP+ Group, 2d ed. Dec. 2007), *available at* http://www.thesedonaconference.org/dltForm?did=TSCGlossary_12_07.pdf [hereinafter Sedona Glossary].

45. Residual data or ambient data is "data that is not active on a computer system," including "(1) data found on media free space; (2) data found in file slack space; and (3) data within files that has functionally been deleted in that it is not visible using the application with which the file was created, without use of undelete or special data recovery techniques," and "[m]ay contain copies of deleted files, Internet files and file fragments." *Id.* at 44.

46. Unallocated space is "[t]he area of computer media, such as a hard drive, that does not contain normally accessible data. Unallocated space is usually the result of a file being deleted. When a file is deleted, it is not actually erased, but is simply no longer accessible through normal means. The space that it occupied becomes unallocated space, i.e., space on the drive that can be reused to store new information. Until portions of the unallocated space are used for new data storage, in most instances, the old data remains and can be retrieved using forensic techniques." *Id.* at 52.

47. Slack/slack space is "[t]he unused space on a cluster that exists when the logical file space is less than the physical file space. Also known as file slack. A form of residual data, the amount of on-disc file space from the end of the logical record information to the end of

- Examine unallocated computer space for missing or deleted files, folders, or other activity;
- Examine allocated and unallocated computer space for suspicious or fraudulent activity;
- Examine computer data for serial numbers and origin information for authentication or tampering;[48]
- Confirm that documents and data once existed but are no longer recoverable;
- Determine whether documents have been backdated;[49]
- Discover the timing of deletion or other suspicious activity as it relates to "intent;"[50]
- Determine whether certain documents or data have been modified and, if so, when;

---

the physical disc record. Slack space can contain information deleted from the record, information from prior records stored at the same physical location as current records, metadata fragments, and other information useful for forensic analysis of computer systems." *Id.* at 48.

48. *See* White v. Graceland Coll. Center for Prof'l Dev. & Lifelong Learning, Inc., No. 07-2319-CM, 2009 WL 722056, at *5 (D. Kan. Mar. 18, 2009) (ordering defendants to produce Microsoft Outlook personal file folders (PSTs or personal storage tables) and offline storage tables (OSTs) after the plaintiff's computer forensics expert reported discrepancies between creation and sent dates of e-mails already produced by the defendants); Morales-Arcadio v. Shannon Produce Farms, Inc., No. CV605-062, 2007 WL 5703959, at *3 (S.D. Ga. Mar. 27, 2007) (granting a motion to compel an inspection of the defendants' computer records after evidence was presented that the initial production of records was so redacted that neither plaintiff or defendants' own computer experts could read the files).

49. *See* Rivet v. State Farm Mut. Auto. Ins. Co., No. 07-1864, 2009 WL 614766, at *2 (6th Cir. Mar. 12, 2009) (upholding a jury finding of knowing and material misrepresentations by defendants since, among other things, the court-appointed computer expert testified that several settlement agreements had been backdated); *Graceland Coll.*, 2009 WL 722056, at *5 (finding that e-mails were backdated after testimony by plaintiff's computer forensics expert).

50. A computer forensic expert may provide "opinion" testimony that certain data was "intentionally" destroyed or taken. *See* Smith v. Slifer Smith & Frampton/Vail Assoc. Real Estate, LLC, No. 06-cv-02206-JLK, 2009 WL 482603, at *7 (D. Colo. Feb. 25, 2009) (granting an adverse inference instruction, the court found that defendants destroyed evidence in "bad faith" based on the plaintiff's computer forensic experts' opinion); Ed Schmidt Pontiac-GMC Truck, Inc. v. Chrysler Motors Co., LLC, 575 F. Supp. 2d 837, 840 (N.D. Ohio 2008) (denying summary judgment on a spoliation claim after the defendant's computer expert provided expert opinion testimony that destruction of a computer's system registry files did not result "from deliberate human action, but from 'corruption' of the registry."); Galaxy Computer Servs., Inc. v. Baker, 325 B.R. 544, 562–63 (Bankr. E.D. Va. 2005) (finding that opinion testimony of computer forensics expert was relevant since, among other things, it would permit jury instructions on spoliation of evidence and consciousness of guilt or wrongdoing).

- Validate dates and logged authors/editors of documents;
- Certify key elements of documents or hardware for legal purposes;
- Discover whether wiping or scrubbing software was used, such as Sure Delete, BC Wipe, Evidence Eliminator, Ultimate Cleaner, or Ultimate Defender;[51]
- Determine whether Universal Serial Bus (USB) drives or other external media were attached to computers or printers, and if so, when and whether documents or data were downloaded to such media;
- Analyze computer/server log files, such as Internet and firewall use; and
- Per stipulation, execute discovery protocols, and examine data.[52]

As with all experts, it is important to determine whether your potential forensic expert is sufficiently qualified in computer forensics.[53] Otherwise, he may be susceptible to a *Daubert* challenge.[54] Well-credentialed forensic

---

51. *See* Oz Optics v. Hakimoglu, No. 4:05CV230-D-A, 2009 WL 1017042, at *11 (Cal. App. 1 Dist. Jan. 14, 2009) (Plaintiff's computer forensic expert testified that plaintiff ran the Sure Delete program on relevant computer, explained difference between wiping and deleting, and analyzed, confirmed, and explained that files could not be recovered after scrubbing.); Nucor Corp. v. Bell, No. 2:06-CV-02972-DCN, 2008 WL 4442571, at *1 (D.S.C. Jan. 11, 2008) (Both parties offered testimony from computer forensics experts on the use of Ultimate Cleaner and Ultimate Defender, file data and erasing programs. Due to the unreliability of the methods of plaintiff's expert, the defendants' motion to exclude under *Daubert* was granted.).

52. As a practical matter, in this situation it is important to ensure that the protocol addresses evidence of wrongdoing and to whom the forensic expert should report this evidence. *See* Technical Sales Assocs., Inc. v. Ohio Star Forge Co., Nos. 07-11745, 08-13365 (E.D. Mich. May 1, 2009). In *Technical Sales*, a forensic examiner, Midwest Data Group, was engaged by stipulated order to search for a specific e-mail and to then report findings of actual data to the defendant to review to avoid privilege waiver. Midwest found no actual data but did find evidence of data deletion. Nothing in the stipulated order addressed the situation where examination revealed evidence of data loss. Midwest chose to report its findings not to defendant, but to plaintiff, who filed a motion for sanctions against defendant. In turn, the defendant filed a motion for contempt against Midwest for disclosing its opinion regarding deleted data to plaintiff. The court denied defendants' motion for contempt but not without a motion practice. This could have been avoided with an order detailing lines of communication. *Id.*

53. "Computer Forensics is the use of specialized techniques for recovery, authentication and analysis of electronic data when an investigation or litigation involves issues relating to reconstruction of computer usage, examination of residual data, authentication of data by technical analysis or explanation of technical features of data and computer usage." SEDONA GLOSSARY, *supra* note 44, at 10.

54. Daubert v. Merrell Dow Pharms., Inc., 509 U.S. 579 (1993). *See* Mintel Int'l Group, Ltd. v. Neergheen, No. 08 c 3939, 2009 WL 1033357, at *1 (N.D. Ill. Apr. 17, 2009). In *Mintel*, the defendant sought to exclude the plaintiff's qualified computer forensics and electronic discovery experts from testifying, arguing that the expert failed to meet the ap-

experts typically have some combination of the following qualifications and backgrounds:

- Law enforcement;
- Certifications in fraud investigations;
- Information technology/computer science degree or experience;
- Accounting degree or experience; and
- Experience testifying.

In retaining a computer forensic expert, counsel should be aware that local law may require computer forensics experts to hold a private investigator license. Some states have legislated that a computer forensic expert must be a licensed private investigator (PI) to legally copy or collect data from a computer.[55] Other states have interpreted existing laws requiring PI licenses to include computer forensic examiners.[56] Interestingly, at least one state, Texas, has taken the position that because attorneys in Texas are expressly exempted from laws requiring a PI license, anyone working under the direct supervision of an attorney does not need a PI license.[57]

---

propriate standards. *Id.* The court held that to testify as a Rule 702 opinion witness, the test is whether the witness "(i) is qualified to offer opinion testimony under Rule 702, (ii) has employed a reliable methodology, (iii) proposes to offer opinions that follow rationally from the application of his 'knowledge, skill, experience, training, or education,' and (iv) presents testimony on a matter that is relevant to the case at hand, and thus helpful to the trier of fact." *Id.* at *4 (internal citations omitted). Thus, the court decided to "hear the testimony of the experts and . . . then judge that testimony against the standards set forth above in deciding what weight, if any, to give the experts' views." *Id.*

55. *See* Gilbert F. Whittemore, *American Bar Association House of Delegates Recommendation, August 11–12, 2008*, A.B.A. Sec. Sci. & Tech. L. Rep. 301, *available at* www .abanet.org/scitech/301.doc (listing which states require a PI license for computer forensic examiners, states where a regulatory body has opined or it is common knowledge that such a license is required, and states where a license is possibly required but no agency has specifically articulated a need for the license); *see also* John J. Barbara, *The Case Against P.I. Licensing for Digital Forensic Examiners*, Forensic Magazine, April/May 2009, *available at* http://www.forensicmag.com/articles.asp?pid=273 (analyzing current laws in Arizona, Arkansas, California, Florida, Michigan, and South Carolina to demonstrate the ambiguity and lack of uniformity among such laws).

56. S.C. Code Ann. § 40-18-70 (1976); *see also* Op. S.C. Att'y Gen., 2007 WL 1302770, at *3 (April 23, 2007) (interpreting § 40-18-70 to require that "an individual or company selling their services in South Carolina as 'computer forensics' experts secure licenses as private investigators," including anyone who accepts "fees to examine and copy computer hard-drives to extract information to be reported to clients and to be presented in courts as evidence and/or testimony in civil and criminal actions").

57. Op. Tex. Att'y Gen. GA-0275, 2004 WL 2678849, at *3 (Nov. 24, 2004).

E-Discovery Vendors

E-discovery vendors may perform, based on credentials, background, and experience, the following functions as experts:

- Attend meet and confer conferences;
- Testify about the cost, time, and other burdens associated with proposed discovery;
- Craft and implement document retention policies; and
- Consult on document retention policies, identification of e-evidence, collection, preservation, review, and production.

More and more, courts are requiring parties to appear with their e-discovery expert to discuss e-discovery case management orders. In one case, a judge held an "experts only" conference in which the court directed the experts "to develop a protocol to address problems with electronic discovery."[58] The experts, without input from counsel, then "announced a protocol for discovery and preservation of responsive ESI."[59] The challenge with such an order is determining who falls within various courts' definitions of an e-discovery expert. The Seventh Circuit recently defined an e-discovery liaison as:

> [A]n attorney (in-house or outside counsel), a third party consultant, or an employee of the party . . . [who] must:
>
> (a) be prepared to participate in e-discovery dispute resolution;
>
> (b) be knowledgeable about the party's e-discovery efforts;
>
> (c) be, or have reasonable access to those who are, familiar with the party's electronic systems and capabilities in order to explain those systems and answer relevant questions; and
>
> (d) be, or have reasonable access to those who are, knowledgeable about the technical aspects of e-discovery, including electronic document storage, organization, and format issues, and relevant information retrieval technology, including search methodology.[60]

If the technical manner of preservation or collection is the primary issue before the court, a forensic expert may be most helpful.[61] However, it is usu-

---

58. John B. v. Goetz, 531 F.3d 448, 453 (6th Cir. 2008).

59. *Id.*

60. Seventh Circuit Electronic Discovery Committee, Seventh Circuit Electronic Discovery Pilot Program, Phase One, Statement of Purpose and Preparation of Principles, Prin. 2.02 (Oct. 1, 2009–May 1, 2010), *available at* http://www.ilcd.uscourts.gov/Statement %20-%20Phase%20One.pdf.

61. *See* Playboy Enters. v. Welles, 60 F. Supp. 2d 1050, 1055 (S.D. Cal. 1999) (requiring appointment of a computer expert "who specializes in the field of electronic discovery to create a 'mirror image'").

ally the court's intention simply to encourage, if not mandate, the parties to agree to a discovery protocol on collection, review, and production. In this scenario, the appropriate participants or experts are more likely the party's e-discovery vendor, IT representative, e-discovery counsel, or law firm litigation services personnel.

In addition, when litigating a motion to compel, a motion for protective order, or motion for sanctions, counsel may benefit from presenting the expert testimony of an e-discovery vendor on a variety of topics, including the following:

- Cost and burden associated with the proposed discovery;
- Time required to comply with the proposed discovery, including time to collect, process, and review data; and
- The reasonableness and best practices deployed by the client for preservation, collection, processing, culling, or review.

The case law is clear that when asking for relief, parties must be specific in articulating their objections and burden arguments. Using an e-discovery process expert can be an effective way of meeting the specificity requirements and arguing a compelling case. Using the e-discovery vendor expert to offer this evidence might also insulate the client's IT and firm legal personnel from serving as a declarant or witness.

In addition to retaining vendors in active litigation, many companies also retain service providers and consultants to implement e-discovery and preservation policies and practices, bring e-discovery technology in-house, improve the defensibility of litigation response practices, reduce overretention of information, avoid unintentional destruction of information subject to preservation obligations, and otherwise reduce e-discovery costs.[62] The expertise of these service providers vary greatly.

When retaining one of these service providers, counsel should consider the possibility that the service provider may, in subsequent litigation, be asked to serve as a Federal Rule of Civil Procedure 30(b)(6) witness, sign a declaration, or, if he is providing ongoing services, serve as a fact witness. For example, a vendor hired to implement litigation readiness protocols before litigation would have knowledge of those processes and whether the company adhered to them—facts that may be germane to subsequent litigation.[63] In light of this reality, even when a service provider is retained

---

62. *See* Sedona Second Edition, *supra* note 3, at 40 cmt. 6d. ("[M]any organizations rely on consultants to provide a variety of services, including discovery planning, data collection, specialized data processing, and forensic analysis.").

63. The guidelines warn that "even if a vendor is retained to serve in a non-testifying capacity, everyone should be aware of the potential need for testimony if forensic or other

independently of any active litigation, counsel should evaluate whether that service provider could serve as either a Rule 30(b)(6) witness, fact witness, or expert witness. When evaluating these capabilities, counsel should ask about the service provider's testifying experience and about which employee the vendor company recommends serve in this capacity. Many service providers aggressively market their ability to serve as expert witnesses. However, counsel should inquire whether the proposed expert's qualifications are limited to testifying to the vendor's own processes, practices, and technologies. An expert's testimony about his knowledge of his own company's practices and technologies is very different from his testifying to the details of a client's processes, practices, and technologies and whether they are reasonable or in line with industry best practices. Counsel should evaluate whether the expert's qualifications are sufficient for the task at hand and for future needs.

Search and Retrieval Experts

Finally, to ensure defensible search and retrieval of a large body of ESI, counsel may consider hiring a search and retrieval expert. For example, in *Victor Stanley, Inc. v. Creative Pipe, Inc.*, Judge Grimm discussed ways in which a lawyer should anticipate defending searches in court: "[T]hey should expect to support their position with affidavits or other equivalent information from persons with the requisite qualifications and experience, based on sufficient facts or data and using reliable principles or methodology."[64]

There are numerous search methodologies,[65] but this field is still in its infancy, with technology constantly changing and new case law emerging.[66]

---

technical expertise is required to prepare electronically stored information for review or production. Additionally, care should be taken to ensure that the vendor does not assume the role of a legal advisor, and that all persons involved understand what communications are protected under the attorney-client privilege and what information may be protected as attorney work product." *Id.*

64. Victor Stanley, Inc. v. Creative Pipe, Inc., 250 F.R.D. 251, 261 (D. Md. 2008).

65. For a discussion of available search methodologies, see Michael Swarz, *Concept Searching for Managing Mountains of Electronic Data*, PROOF, J. TRIAL EVIDENCE COMMITTEE, at 2 (Summer 2009), *available at* http://www.abanet.org/litigation/committees/trialevidence/newsletter.html.

66. *See, e.g., Victor Stanley, Inc.*, at 262 (noting that, in the context of privilege review, "[s]election of the appropriate search and information retrieval technique requires careful advance planning by persons qualified to design effective search methodology"); William A. Gross. Constr. Assocs., Inc. v. Am. Mfrs. Mut. Ins. Co., No. 07 Civ. 10639(LAK)(AJP), 2009 WL 724954 at *2 (S.D.N.Y. Mar. 19, 2009) (disapproving of keyword searches "in the

Indeed, studies have shown the potential for inaccuracy of ineffective search methods.[67] As Judge Facciola stated in *United States v. O'Keefe,* "whether search terms or 'keywords' will yield the information sought is a complicated question involving the interplay, at least, of the sciences of computer technology, statistics and linguistics. . . . This topic is clearly beyond the ken of a layman."[68]

The question is what qualifications should a search and retrieval expert have? Some have suggested that this person have background as a linguist or a mathematician. Some have suggested that the proper search and retrieval expert is a person who has developed actual searches in the context of real litigation—perhaps experienced e-discovery attorneys or vendors. Some courts may be confused as to what constitutes a search and retrieval expert, and court orders may confuse parties as to their requirements. For example, a court might order parties at the inception of discovery to retain forensic experts to design an agreed-upon search and retrieval protocol for all of the relevant ESI. Here, based on the court order, the parties might retain a computer forensic expert. The more appropriate expertise, however, likely lies in an e-discovery or practiced attorney, a litigation technology professional, an e-discovery vendor, or an e-discovery process or protocol expert. It is clear, in the very least, that transparency and cooperation in the search and retrieval process is a growing requirement of courts.[69]

How search and retrieval experts will be defined and used in litigation remains to be seen as this is an emerging e-discovery topic. At a minimum, when selecting such an expert, counsel may wish to test the expert's familiarity with *The Sedona Conference Best Practices Commentary on the*

---

dark, by the seat of the pants, without adequate . . . discussion with those who wrote the emails.").

67. *See* Jason Krause, *In Search of the Perfect Search,* ABA J., Apr. 2009, *available at* http://abajournal.com/magazine/in_search_of_the_perfect_search (discussing that while typical keyword searches found only roughly 20 percent of the responsive documents, there is a 78 percent efficiency when using combined searches with various protocols).

68. United States v. O'Keefe, 537 F. Supp. 2d 14, 24 (D.D.C. 2008).

69. *See generally* COOPERATION PROCLAMATION, *supra* note 12. *See, e.g.,* Covad Commc'ns Co. v. Revonet, Inc., No. 06-1892 (CKK/JMF), 2009 WL 1472345, at *9 (D.D.C. May 27, 2009) ("[C]ourts can, with the sincere assistance of the parties, manage e-discovery efficiently and with the least expense possible."); Ford Motor Co. v. Edgewood Props., Inc., No. 06-1278 (HAA), 2009 WL 1416223, at *5 (D.N.J. May 19, 2009) (following the principles of the COOPERATION PROCLAMATION, *supra* note 12); Newman v. Borders, Inc., No. 07-492 (RWR/JMF), 2009 WL 931545, at *4 n.3 (D.D.C. Apr. 6, 2009) ("Counsel should become aware of the perceptible trend in the case law that insists that counsel genuinely attempt to resolve discovery disputes."); William A. Gross Const. Assoc., Inc. v. Am. Mfrs. Mut. Ins. Co., 256 F.R.D. 134, 136 (S.D.N.Y. 2009) ("This Court strongly endorses The Sedona Conference Cooperation Proclamation.").

Use of Search and Information Retrieval Methods in E-Discovery[70] and the
Text Retrieval Conference.[71]

Privilege Considerations

All experts, including e-discovery experts, can be retained as either a consultant or a retained or testifying expert. To preserve privilege with respect to e-discovery experts, counsel should consider the following:

• Ensure that a "confidentiality and privilege" provision is included in the retainer agreement;
• Be aware that any and all written communications with testifying experts could be discoverable; and
• Create a clear separation between the consulting e-discovery expert and the person who collects and processes data in order to support a chain of custody for evidence production.

Forensic experts, in particular, often encounter unique privilege challenges. The information collected by a forensic expert may be privileged. This may be true both for information from the party retaining the expert as well as information from an opposing party. For example, one party's expert may collect an opposing party's data after the requesting party prevails on a motion to compel certain data. In that situation, courts have permitted a requesting party's expert to forensically collect data from the producing party. Here, the producing party often raises concerns that the requesting party will have unlimited access to privileged material through the requesting party's expert. Courts have addressed this problem in a number of ways, including ordering that the producing party have the opportunity to review the collection for privilege before review by the requesting party.[72]

---

70. THE SEDONA CONFERENCE BEST PRACTICES COMMENTARY ON THE USE OF SEARCH AND INFORMATION RETRIEVAL METHODS IN E-DISCOVERY, *available at* http://www.thesedonaconference.org/content/miscFiles/Best_Practices_Retrieval_Methods_revised_cover_and_preface.pdf.
71. TREC 2009 Legal Track, *available at* http://trec-legal.umiacs.umd.edu; *see also* http://trec.nist.gov/pubs/trec17/papers/LEGAL.OVERVIEW08.pdf. The Text Retrieval Conference was started in 1992 to support research within the information retrieval community by providing the infrastructure necessary for large-scale evaluation of text retrieval methodologies. TREC is overseen by a program committee consisting of government, industry, and academic representatives. *See generally* http://trec.nist.gov.
72. *See* Koosharem Corp. v. Spec Personnel, LLC, No. 6:08-583-HFF-WMC, 2008 WL 4458864, at *2–4 (D.S.C. Sept. 29, 2008) (articulating a 20-step protocol for the forensic collection of defendant data); Ferron v. Search Cactus, L.L.C., No. 2:06-CV-327, 2008 WL

Other courts have appointed a forensic expert to serve as an "Officer of the Court" so that, "to the extent that [the] computer expert has direct or indirect access to information protected by attorney-client privilege, such disclosure will not result in any waiver of the privilege."[73]

Conclusion

E-discovery has become an expensive and ever-present reality of litigation. As a result, e-discovery experts now play an important role in case-determinative strategy, motions practice, and trial evidence. They can also be an effective tool in reducing risk as well as cost. Sophisticated litigants now look to e-discovery experts both to defend their e-discovery conduct as well as to attack the opposing party. E-discovery experts also can serve in the place of magistrates and judges in adjudicating party disputes and issuing discovery protocols and orders. Regardless of the circumstances, because this industry has only recently reached a level of maturity, it is important to thoroughly vet any expert and ensure he has the requisite expertise for your case-specific issues.

1902499, at *1 (S.D. Ohio Apr. 28, 2008) (memorializing "the protocol for viewing and preserving information contained on Plaintiff's computer systems."); *In re* Honza, 242 S.W.3d 578, 582–84 (Tex. App. Dec. 28, 2007) (affirming forensic collection by opposing party's expert and including detailed discussion on case law on point from multiple jurisdictions).

    73. Bank of Mongolia v. M & P Global Fin. Servs., Inc., No. 08-60623-CIV, 2009 WL 1117312, at *7 (S.D. Fla. Apr. 24, 2009).

SCIENTIFIC EXPERTS

Heather L. Hodges[1]

Scientific consultants and experts perform essentially the same function in pretrial case development and at trial as any other expert witness: they assist the attorneys and the trier of fact to better understand evidence that requires specialized and scientific expertise. Scientific expert witnesses pose some unique challenges, however. This subchapter addresses these challenges. First, the subchapter recommends how to identify an appropriate scientific expert for retention. Second, the subchapter addresses how to ensure that your scientific expert's testimony is admissible at trial.

Retention of a Scientific Expert

Set forth below are some recommendations for identifying and locating an appropriate scientific expert and evaluating his academic and professional credentials.

Deciding Whether to Retain a Scientific Expert

Not every case requires a scientific expert but, because of the breadth of recognized scientific disciplines and the number of scientists working in new interdisciplinary or cross-disciplinary fields, careful thought and consideration should be given to retention of a scientific expert as an element of your trial strategy. The use of scientific experts is a common feature of modern litigation, and a wide range of scientific experts is routinely used in a variety of civil and criminal cases. The key question you should ask yourself is whether the trier of fact will be called on by any party in the case to understand evidence obtained or tested using scientific methods. If the answer

---

1. Heather L. Hodges is an attorney in private practice in Washington, D.C., with experience in all aspects of drug and medical device litigation, including the development of scientific, medical, and economic expert witness testimony.

is "yes" or "maybe," you should consider retaining a scientific consultant or expert.

Scientific experts can come from hundreds of recognized scientific disciplines, and you should think creatively about the specific type of scientific expertise that will be useful in your particular case. The Bureau of Labor Statistics has categorized scientists and the nature of their work into hundreds of different types. For example, the job description entry for "conservation scientists" states the following:

> Manage, improve, and protect natural resources to maximize their use without damaging the environment. May conduct soil surveys and develop plans to eliminate soil erosion or to protect rangelands from fire and rodent damage. May instruct farmers, agricultural production managers, or ranchers in best ways to use crop rotation, contour plowing, or terracing to conserve soil and water; in the number and kind of livestock and forage plants best suited to particular ranges; and in range and farm improvements, such as fencing and reservoirs for stock watering.[2]

These entries and occupational descriptions are a great starting point for brainstorming about potential types of scientific experts.

Armed with this information, you can search for potential experts on websites for educational institutions that offer courses and degrees in these areas of expertise. Many scientists work across disciplines or are highly specialized. University Web pages are useful sources of information about how scientists in the field are deploying their specialized expertise in both traditional and novel ways. For example, if you were looking for an expert in the aforementioned area of conservation, the University of California-Davis offers a certificate in conservation management, and its faculty members claim expertise in conservation genetics, aquatic ecology, disease ecology, ecosystem ecology, and wildlife ecology.[3]

Finally, as you begin your search, you may find it helpful to consult the numerous reference works—across many scientific disciplines—that can arm you with a basic understanding of the discipline. Helpfully, some are geared specifically toward attorneys. The Federal Judicial Center, for example, has published guides on the use of statistical, toxicological, and epidemiological evidence at trial.[4] Once you understand the type of expertise a particular scientist can bring to bear, you can quickly assess whether and how to use him in a case.

---

2. U.S. Department of Labor, Bureau of Labor Statistics, *Occupational Employment and Wages* (May 2008), http://www.bls.gov/oes/current/oes191031.htm.
3. *See* http://ecology.ucdavis.edu/programs/Conservation_Management/faculty.html.
4. These guides can be found at http://www.fjc.gov.

Evaluating Potential Scientific Experts

To evaluate and compare a scientific expert's credentials, it is important to have a deep understanding of the educational requirements particular to his field of expertise and the various markers of training, prestige, and professional success. Using the example of a biochemist, the following are helpful questions to ask someone familiar with the scientific field before you embark on your search. They are also a useful starting point for developing an interview outline for potential scientific experts.

What Is the Standard Educational and Career Path for the Scientific Field?

A top-tier biochemist, for example, will normally obtain a Ph.D. in this discipline, from one of a handful of nationally regarded universities such as the University of California at Berkeley, Massachusetts Institute of Technology, Stanford, Harvard, the University of Texas, Scripps, or the University of California at San Diego. As this list demonstrates, the most prestigious programs in a particular scientific field are not always located at the highest-ranked universities overall. You must conduct independent research to determine which programs are well respected.

Following the Ph.D. program, a well-regarded biochemist will do a post-doctoral fellowship under the supervision of a highly regarded professor. Subsequently, the academically oriented biochemist will begin to rise through the academic ranks, obtain his own lab, and make a name for himself through prolific publication. An alternate career path may take a biochemist out of basic science research and into the realm of applied research in private biotechnology firms.

What Are the Key Scientific Journals in the Field and What Does the Scientist's Publication List Tell You about His Qualifications?

Generally speaking, an academic scientist will have more frequent and recent publications listed on his curricula vitae (CV). If the candidate appears as the first author, this likely means he did the primary research. If he appears as the last author, that is an indication that he is being credited because the work was performed in his research laboratory. The most prestigious journals vary by subspecialty, but the common denominator among the most highly regarded journals is that the articles are peer reviewed by experts in the field.

What Does the Scientist Do on a Daily Basis?

In the case of a biochemist, it is more prestigious to run a laboratory at a major research university than to teach. While many biochemists do teach, the activities listed on a biochemist's CV should generally reflect a greater emphasis on research and scholarship in his field of expertise.

Is the Scientific Field One in Which the Opinions Offered
May Be Difficult for a Lay Person to Understand?

In the case of a complex scientific field such as biochemistry, it may be advantageous to avoid using an academic and to look for candidates with industry or consulting experience who are accustomed to interpreting and communicating pure or applied scientific concepts and research results to a lay audience (e.g., venture capitalists or in-house counsel). Depending on the issues of your case, it might also be helpful to use a biochemist who is engaged in a particular and relevant type of applied research.

Admissibility of a Scientific Expert's Testimony

While practitioners are encouraged to be creative in their deployment of scientists as experts, the law does place limits on the admissibility of scientific evidence. Although the admissibility limitations on expert testimony apply to nonscientific testimony as well as scientific testimony, the issue of admissibility is especially complicated and contentious in the context of scientific experts.

In *Daubert v. Merrell Dow Pharmaceuticals, Inc.*,[5] the Supreme Court described the inquiry that trial courts should undertake when considering the admissibility of a scientific expert's opinion into evidence. Before the expert's opinion is permitted to reach the jury, the trial judge must decide if the scientist's reasoning and methodology are scientifically valid and can be properly applied to understand or determine the facts at issue in the case. The Court cautioned that the inquiry should be a flexible one and that it should focus "solely on principles and methodology" and not on the expert's conclusions.[6] In doing so, the Court identified several considerations as relevant to the inquiry into the scientific validity of an expert's reasoning and methodology, including the following:

---

5. Daubert v. Merrell Dow Pharms., Inc., 509 U.S. 579 (1993).
6. *Id.* at 580.

- Whether the theory or technique can be or has been tested;
- Whether the theory or technique has been subjected to peer review and publication;
- The theory or technique's known or potential error rate and the existence and maintenance of standards controlling its operation; and
- Whether the methodology has attracted widespread acceptance within a relevant scientific community.[7]

These considerations have since hardened into a set of criteria that scientific testimony is often evaluated against, despite the fact that the Court cautioned against applying these criteria rigidly.[8]

When this standard is applied to scientific experts, courts often inquire into the extent to which an expert's opinions are securely anchored in the data. For example, in *General Electric Co. v. Joiner*,[9] the Supreme Court affirmed the exclusion of an expert's causation testimony because the scientist had failed to provide reliable, scientific evidence of a link between exposure to a chemical and the plaintiff's injury. The Court rejected the plaintiff's argument that under *Daubert* it was precluded from rejecting the expert's conclusions. The Court explained that conclusions and methodology were connected: experts routinely extrapolate their conclusions from data. However, such conclusions—in the form of expert opinions—were inadmissible if they were only connected to the data by the *ipse dixit* of the expert. Thus, practitioners are cautioned to guard against relying on an opinion that their opponent could persuasively argue is merely unsupported speculation cloaked in the guise of expert opinion.

Numerous resources are available to practitioners for investigation into whether a particular scientist or scientific methodology has ever been the subject of a *Daubert* motion. Westlaw has databases relating to scientific expert issues, opinions, and related court documents including a "Daubert-Citator" database. Lexis/Nexis also has a *Daubert* case tracker and a news service for *Daubert*-related developments. In addition, there are numerous written publications and websites that are useful tools for staying abreast of current developments relating to the admissibility of scientific evidence across the nation. For example, the American Bar Association (ABA) Section of Litigation's Expert Witness Committee publishes "News and Developments" as well as a regular newsletter on expert-related issues. Even for the most complex scientific issues, there is a wealth of resources available to help attorneys forecast potential *Daubert* challenges as well as to assist in identifying *Daubert* weaknesses in their opponents' experts' opinions.

---

7. *Id.*
8. *Id.* at 588.
9. General Elec. Co. v. Joiner, 522 U.S. 136 (1997).

Conclusion

Scientific experts can form an important arrow in your trial quiver. The identification and development of scientific experts lends itself to dynamic and creative thinking that can both invigorate and augment your trial strategy.

FINANCIAL DAMAGES EXPERTS

Richard G. Placey and Ronald P. Forster[1]

Financial damages experts are unusual in that their expertise and testimony are used in almost all types of litigation—contract cases, tort cases (including personal injury), family law cases, statutory tort cases like securities, antitrust and discrimination actions, appraisal and other corporate valuation cases, and many others. Moreover, the damage theories and expertise used to calculate damages in one type of case can often be applied to establish damages under a totally different legal theory. As an example, the manner of calculating lost profits damages in a contract case can usually be applied to establish lost profits in an appropriate tort or patent case—or in any case where counsel can make a substantive claim to recover lost profits as an element of damages. Damages are damages, so to speak, and while

1. Richard G. Placey is a partner at Montgomery, McCracken, Walker & Rhoads, LLP, in Wilmington, Delaware, where he concentrates on commercial, financial and bankruptcy litigation matters; he is admitted in Delaware, Pennsylvania, New Jersey, and Illinois. Ronald P. Forster is a partner at KPMG LLP, in Philadelphia, Pennsylvania, where he concentrates on providing assistance to legal counsel in the areas of accounting and misconduct investigations, fraud risk assessments, and economic and accounting aspects of litigation and arbitration matters, including deposition and trial testimony. He is a Certified Public Accountant in Pennsylvania and is certified in financial forensics. This article represents the views of the authors only and does not necessarily represent the views or professional advice of Montgomery, McCracken, Walker & Rhoads, LLP and/or KPMG LLP. ©2009 Montgomery, McCracken, Walker & Rhoads, LLP, and KPMG LLP, a U.S. limited liability partnership and a member firm of the KPMG network of independent member firms affiliated with KPMG International, a Swiss cooperative. All rights reserved.

they cannot be removed from the context of the substantive legal theory giving rise to the right to such damages, many legal theories share the same financial damages concepts. This subchapter explores the uses of financial damages experts, the various types of such experts, the challenges in presenting such experts, and typical areas of focus and controversy when such experts are presented.

Uses of Financial Damages Experts

Financial damages experts pose unique challenges because their uses are so varied. They are retained to testify about a wide variety of damage calculations in myriad types of cases. Financial damages experts consult and testify about the following types of damages, among others:

- Lost earnings or profits (gross, net, before/after tax, etc.);
- Profits earned by the liable party;
- Lost revenues or lost income streams;
- Lost wages or earnings;
- Value of an intangible asset lost or damaged (e.g., a trademark, a business or product line, natural resources, contract rights);
- Historical consequential damages, such as increased costs, overcharges, underpayments, costs of cover, warranty claims, reinsurance claims, increased borrowing or capital costs, or trading losses;
- Reasonable royalty amounts;
- Net loss on the purchase of an asset, particularly in the context of securities fraud claims;
- Damages allocation, particularly in class action settlements;
- Settlement fairness, particularly in class actions or other matters requiring court approval like bankruptcy settlements and wrongful death settlements; and
- Compliance with damages limitations or caps.

Moreover, as society and the economy become more complex—or perhaps as lawyers become more creative—the cases in which financial damages experts are needed appear to be growing. Financial damages experts often testify in the following types of cases, among others:

- Contract cases;
- Tort cases;
- Securities and other statutory tort cases;
- Stock appraisal actions;
- Divorce/equitable distribution actions; and
- Business valuations.

This section first identifies two general categories into which financial damages can be grouped and discusses the advocacy issues raised by each category. Then, this section examines several of the most significant legal theories pursuant to which financial damages experts are used to establish damages. Incorporated into the discussion of each theory is an analysis of the most frequent measures of damages for each theory.

Two General Categories of Financial Damages

While the types of financial damages that can be proven through expert testimony are quite varied, it can be useful for the advocate to view them as falling into two categories for advocacy purposes: (1) calculations of historical damages using historical data, simply to make computations of what did happen (but should not have); and (2) calculations of projected (or "what if") damages using hard data to make an estimate of that which did not happen (but which should have). Each category generates its own controversies, disputes, and issues, but usually they differ and require that counsel's attention be focused on different areas and concerns.

Historical losses include the amount of an overcharge in a contract case or antitrust case, rescission damages in securities cases (where the amount paid is simply returned), repair or replacement costs in breach of warranty cases, payments due under reinsurance treaties for historical claims, or the costs of buying replacement products or supplies in a Uniform Commercial Code (UCC) breach of contract case.

When litigating a case involving historical damages, an attorney often must address which specific items (costs, charges, etc.) are properly included in damages, which items should be excluded, and how to summarize, organize, and present an often significant amount of data or computations.

The classic example of projected (or "what if") damages is lost profits that, as discussed below, can be awarded in contract cases, tort cases, patent cases, and many other types of cases. Lost future income in personal injury or death cases is a similar example. Asset valuations of intangible assets, like stock, royalty streams, or other income-producing assets, are in many ways similar in that they require a projection of an income stream (and then a way to value it).

For trial counsel, it is useful to view projected damages as more of an estimate than a pure calculation. Viewed in that light, they also present another set of advocacy issues for each side's counsel: those arising from the judgments made by the damages experts in making the estimate. These issues are explored in some detail at the end of this subchapter.

Contract Damages

Contract law has for years allowed recovery of expectation damages and consequential damages.[2] Although these calculations are simple in some cases (the amount of an unpaid account receivable being a stark example), in other cases they are often quite complicated. Financial damages experts are routinely used to establish expectation and consequential damages.

Expectation damages often include lost profits.[3] An award of lost profits typically requires a showing that the profits can reasonably be determined, that profits were contemplated by the parties to the contract, and that the lost profits can be causally related to the breach.[4] Since most jurisdictions require that such profits be capable of "reasonable determination" and then proven with "reasonable certainty," a financial expert can be pivotal to recovery of lost profits. For example, in a dispute over failure timely to construct a factory, economists were used to testify to $845,000 in lost profits based on statistical evidence.[5] In a case involving the breach of a strategic alliance agreement in which the parties had agreed to jointly serve certain customers, the court sifted through the competing damages testimony of an accountant for one party and an economist for the other before awarding $8 million in lost profits.[6] In a case involving an established business and a wealth of applicable historical data as to use, a financial analyst's testimony was sufficient to support an award of $247,000 in lost profits in a breach of franchise agreement case.[7] Of course, use of a damages expert does not guarantee an award. In a case alleging lost profits arising from breaches of various cable TV contracts, both industry executives and Certified Public Accountants (CPAs) testified to the alleged lost profits arising from breaches of various cable TV contracts, although the lost profits claim was ultimately rejected.[8]

Contract expectation damages can also include the value of the asset or assets being sold pursuant to the allegedly breached contract. Sometimes, these assets are intangible, such as a trademark,[9] a business that can be sold

---

2. *See, e.g.,* Restatement (second) of Contracts § 344.

3. *See, e.g.,* U.C.C. § 2-708.

4. *See* McDermott v. Middle East Carpet Co., 811 F.2d 1422 (11th Cir. 1987) (applying Georgia law); Kenford Co. v. County of Erie, 493 N.E. 2d 234 (N.Y. 1986); Chas. R. Combs Trucking, Inc. v. Int'l Harvester Co., 466 N.E. 2d 883 (Ohio 1984).

5. *McDermott,* 811 F.2d at 1427–28.

6. Honeywell Int'l Inc. v. Air Prods. & Chems., Inc., 858 A.2d 392, 425–34 (Del. Ch. 2004).

7. Burger King Corp. v. Barnes, 1 F. Supp. 2d 1367 (S.D. Fla. 1998).

8. Schonfeld v. Hilliard, 218 F.3d 164 (2d Cir. 2000).

9. Nestle Holdings, Inc. v. Comm'r, 152 F.3d 83 (2d Cir. 1998).

in the marketplace,[10] a natural resource,[11] or a contract right. Where the asset is intangible, financial experts such as CPAs, financial analysts, business valuation experts, or economists can be and often are used to value the asset.[12] For example, in a case involving contracts to supply cable television programming, the court allowed a CPA to testify about the market value of the programming contracts.[13] There is also law to the effect that the owner of intangible assets is competent to testify as to their value,[14] but from counsel's viewpoint as an advocate, competence and persuasiveness are two very different things. Often, an expert's valuation is more persuasive, especially if the opposing side has retained a testifying expert.

Consequential damages awarded for a breach of contract include not only easily calculated items like cover costs, but also other costs such as increased administrative costs, maintenance costs, borrowing costs, or costs of capital. As to these types of consequential damages, financial experts are routinely used (and may be required) to establish the amount of increased costs. For instance, an expert's testimony helped the plaintiff to obtain a $116 million verdict in a breach of energy contract case,[15] to obtain an award of the costs of new financing in a case against the Federal Savings and Loan Insurance Corporation (FSLIC) alleging breach of a bank assistance agreement,[16] and to obtain an award of damages for additional operational/administrative costs and costs of borrowing in a case involving the breach of a contract to expand a cement plant.[17]

Tort Damages

As in contract cases, tort damages can also require complex financial analysis, and a financial expert is often invaluable (if not outright required) to prove those damages. Tort cases can involve some of the same types of damages as contract cases—such as lost profits—but also use additional damages measures.

As in the contract cases, lost profits, sales, or earnings claims are regularly presented through the testimony of an accountant, an economist, a

---

10. Indu Craft, Inc. v. Bank of Baroda, 47 F.3d 490 (2d Cir. 1995).
11. Central Dover Dev. Corp. v. Town of Dover, 680 N.Y.S.2d 668 (App. Div. 1988).
12. An appraiser is often used to value a tangible asset, for example, real property.
13. *Schonfeld*, 218 F.3d at 183.
14. Commerzanstalt v. Telewide Sys., Inc., 880 F.2d 642 (2d Cir. 1989).
15. Tractebel Energy Mktg. Inc. v. AEP Power Mktg., Inc., 487 F.3d 89, 107–08 (2d Cir. 2007).
16. Bluebonnet Sav. Bank v. United States, 266 F.3d 1348 (Fed. Cir. 2001).
17. Havens Steel Co. v. Randolph Eng'g Co., 813 F.2d 186 (8th Cir. 1987).

financial analyst/Master's Degree in Business Administration (MBA), or similar financial expert. In a tortious interference case, for example, lost profits of $1 million were awarded based on the analysis and testimony of a CPA specializing in plaintiff's industry.[18] In a civil contempt action for violation of the automatic stay in bankruptcy, extensive expert testimony established lost profits.[19]

In personal injury cases, future lost earnings or lost earning power damages are an "amorphous area combining law and economics,"[20] where experts, usually economists, "are commonly used by plaintiffs to present their case."[21] For example, in a wrongful death case, an economist testified about future lost earnings damages for five decedents.[22] This approach is not limited to wrongful death cases—economists are also called on to determine future lost wages claims for injured plaintiffs.[23]

In addition, consequential damages are also available in tort, particularly for business torts and fraud. Thus, where a tort case calls for damages that include lost profits, lost earnings, and consequential losses, the damages can often be most effectively proven using a financial expert.

Damages in Securities and Other Statutory Actions

Financial damages experts are often invaluable in cases that arise under certain types of remedial statutes, including the securities statutes, the antitrust laws, the racketeering statute, and the employment discrimination laws, which often require detailed and complex calculations. This is particularly so in class action cases, which almost always involve class members whose damages are calculated using different dates, time frames, or prices.

18. G.M. Brod & Co., Inc. v. U.S. Home Corp., 759 F.2d 1526 (11th Cir. 1985).

19. Elder-Beerman Stores Corp. v. Thomasville Furniture Indus., Inc., 206 B.R. 142 (Bankr. S.D. Ohio 1997), aff'd in part, rev'd in part, 250 B.R. 609 (Bankr. S.D. Ohio 1998), appeal denied, 201 F.3d 440 (6th Cir. 1999).

20. Aldridge v. Baltimore & Ohio R.R. Co., 789 F.2d 1061, 1067 (4th Cir. 1986), on re-hearing 814 F.2d 157 (1987), on remand, 866 F.2d 111 (1989).

21. Mecca v. Lukasik, 530 A.2d 1334, 1339 (Pa. Super. 1987).

22. Id. at 1338–40.

23. See Delmarva P&L Co. v. Burrows, 435 A.2d 716 (Del. 1981) (future lost earnings awarded where plaintiff could not work due to brain damage from his injury); Aldridge 789 F.2d at 1066–67 (future lost earnings award in Federal Employer's Liability Act (FELA) injury case). Aldridge highlights the debate over whether future lost earnings must be reduced to present value, and whether doing so requires a concomitant increase for inflation. Regarding this important debate as to the rules for calculating lost earnings damages, see St. Louis Southwestern Railway v. Dickerson, 470 U.S. 409 (1985). Determining such a present value generally should not be attempted without an expert.

For example, section 11(e) of the Securities Act generally provides for use of a complex damages calculation involving the difference between the amount paid for the security (not exceeding the public offering price) and either (1) the security's value when the suit is filed, (2) the price at which it was sold if sold presuit, or (3) the price at which it was sold postsuit if sold postsuit but prejudgment (if that reduces the damages from the damages as measured when suit was filed).[24] Section 12 provides for a rescission (i.e., refund) remedy, as well as damages.[25] In litigation under Securities and Exchange Commission Rule 10b-5, a comparison of the price paid or received with the value of the security is made to estimate damages.[26] Moreover, since the Private Securities Litigation Reform Act, there is now an additional cap on damages (with an exception) based on the market price of a security, providing that the damages "shall not exceed the difference between the purchase or sale price . . . and the mean trading price of that security during the 90 day period beginning on the date [the misstatement or omission is corrected]."[27]

These types of damages can theoretically be calculated by a lay person. However, the volume of calculations required often makes the use of an accountant or other expert desirable from a clarity and persuasiveness standpoint, particularly in class actions. Even if the damages involve simple calculations that are just voluminous, the expert can more easily provide his conclusions in a summary table or chart under Federal Rules of Evidence 705 and 1006.

Under the antitrust laws, a plaintiff is entitled to "recovery of actual damages," a very open-ended approach that has given rise to a broad range of damage theories and calculations.[28] As a result, financial damages experts are used to calculate antitrust damages under a variety of measurements. For example, an economist was recently used to determine the underpayment to scrap metal generators resulting from an antitrust conspiracy by brokers of the metal,[29] and the expert's testimony supported class damages of $11 million. Similarly, a financial expert was used to determine the lost profits of a sawmill operator resulting from a competitor's antitrust

24. 15 U.S.C. § 77k.
25. 15 U.S.C. § 77e.
26. Alley v. Miramon, 614 F.2d 1372, 1387 (5th Cir. 1980) (discussing measure of damages under section 10(b) of Securities Exchange Act, 15 U.S.C. section 78j(b), and Rule 10b-5).
27. 15 U.S.C. § 78u-4(e).
28. 15 U.S.C. § 15.
29. *In re* Scrap Metal Antitrust Litig., 527 F.3d 517 (6th Cir. 2008).

violations.[30] Such experts have also been useful in calculating and explaining racketeering damages[31] and are used to calculate future lost wages in some discrimination cases (using models similar to those used in the personal injury lost earnings cases).

Damages experts also can help prove damages in patent infringement cases, where damages should be "adequate to compensate for the infringement" but "in no event less than a reasonable royalty."[32] Financial experts are routinely employed in infringement cases to testify about the infringer's profits, the patent holder's lost profits,[33] and a reasonable royalty.[34]

Stock Appraisal Actions, Divorce/Equitable Distribution Actions, and Other Business Valuations

Most corporate law statutes grant appraisal rights in certain circumstances. In an appraisal, the fair value of the shares is determined and paid to stockholders dissenting from mergers or other corporate actions.[35] Such cases are often focused exclusively on the financial analysis, and in many circumstances, the determination of fair value involves a classic battle of the experts involving investment bankers, financial analysts, accountants, and others.

Many of these appraisal cases express the view that "[t]here is no inflexible test for determining fair value as [v]aluation is an art rather than a science."[36] Accordingly, appraisal cases often include several financial experts and competing valuation approaches. For example, in *M.G. Bancorporation, Inc. v. Le Beau*,[37] three separate financial experts provided opinions as to the fair value of the business (and therefore the amount of damages to

---

30. Confederated Tribes of Siletz Indians of Oregon v. Weyerhaeuser Co., 411 F.3d 1030 (9th Cir. 2005), *vacated*, 549 U.S. 312 (2007), *on remand*, 484 F.3d 1086 (9th Cir. 2007) (the Ninth Circuit initially upheld a $26 million lost profits damages award based on plaintiff's economic model but the award was vacated by the Supreme Court).

31. *See* Abell v. Potomac Ins. Co., 858 F.2d 1104, 1139–40 (5th Cir. 1988).

32. 35 U.S.C. § 284; *see also* Rite-Hite Corp. v. Kelley Co., 56 F.3d 1538 (Fed Cir. 1995).

33. *See* DSU Med. Corp. v. JMS Co., Ltd., 296 F. Supp. 2d 1140, 1144–58 (N.D. Cal. 2003) (a CPA with a doctorate in finance testified as to the patent holders' lost profits); Muniauction Inc. v. Thomson Corp., 502 F. Supp. 2d 477 (W.D. Pa. 2007), *rev'd in part*, 532 F.3d 1318 (Fed. Cir. 2008).

34. *See* Cargill Inc. v. Sears Petroleum & Transp. Corp., 388 F. Supp. 2d 37 (N.D.N.Y. 2005) (competing academic experts were offered to establish royalties and other damages).

35. *See* DEL. CODE ANN. tit. 8, § 262(h).

36. Casey v. Amboy Bancorporation, 2006 WL 2287024, at *3 (N.J. Super App. Div. Aug. 10, 2006).

37. M.G. Bancorporation, Inc. v. Le Beau, 737 A.2d 513 (Del. 1999).

be awarded) using various market comparison approaches and a discounted cash flow approach.[38] Similarly, *Casey v. Amboy Bancorporation* involved not just a half dozen different financial experts, including a court-appointed expert, but also numerous competing valuation methodologies, including the discounted cash flow approach and the comparable earnings approach.[39] In many of these cases, the debate is as much about the applicability of the expert's model (e.g., valuation by market comparisons versus valuation by cash flow) as it is about the other judgment calls that must, of necessity, be made in the analysis.[40]

Equitable distributions in divorce cases sometimes require business valuations similar to stock appraisals. For example, in *Steneken v. Steneken*, the court upheld an equitable distribution award based on the trial court's valuation of one spouse's closely held business.[41] In *Steneken*, the New Jersey Supreme Court approved valuing a business using the capitalized earnings method, the market comparison method, or the cost (apparently book value) method, which are to be applied with "flexibility."[42] In support of these valuations, an accountant, a business valuation expert, and an appraiser testified. In another divorce situation, three accounting experts (one court-appointed) were used to value the husband's medical practice for equitable distribution purposes.[43] Thus, financial damage experts can be useful in statutory appraisal cases and equitable distribution cases, in addition to other cases where the value of a business must be determined. In many ways, this damages analysis is similar to valuing intangible assets in contract and tort cases.

Types of Financial Damages Experts

The selection of a financial damages expert is a critical determination made by counsel and the client in the planning and execution of a case. The selection of an expert is typically driven by the type of damages, the relevant industry, and the complexity of the issues at hand. Financial damage experts often include, but are not limited to, professionals with one or more of the following credentials: CPA, Ph.D. economist, MBA with finance

---

38. *Id.* at 518–26.
39. *Casey*, 2006 WL 2287024, at *8–20.
40. *See* Doft & Co. v. Travelocity.com, Inc., No. Civ.A. 19734, 2004 WL 1152338 (Del. Ch. May 20, 2004).
41. Steneken v. Steneken, 873 A.2d 501 (N.J. 2005).
42. *Id.* at 505.
43. Agarwal v. Agarwal, 2009 WL 1650161 (N.J. Super. App. Div. June 15, 2009).

concentration, Certified Valuation Analyst (CVA), and actuary. This section addresses each of these credentials, explaining what standards govern opinions proffered by experts with these credentials, and providing guidance about the types of cases in which these credentialed experts are most helpful.

CPA

CPA is the statutory title of qualified accountants in the United States who have passed the Uniform Certified Public Accountant Examination (a four-part test provided on a state-by-state basis) and have met additional state education and experience requirements for certification as a CPA.[44] Some CPAs have completed an additional test and demonstrated professional experience to be Accredited in Business Valuation (ABV) by the American Institute of Certified Public Accountants (AICPA). A CPA with an ABV has demonstrated knowledge and training in business valuation. This knowledge and training can be useful in measuring economic damages, including diminution of business value and lost profits. Many CPAs provide attest services, such as audits of financial statements, or go on to be financial analysts, controllers, or even chief financial officers at corporations. However, some may decide to specialize in litigation support and are used by counsel as damages experts.

Cpas hold various expert roles depending on the practitioner's expertise. Such services may include the computation of economic damages, analysis of complex financial, governmental, or cost accounting data, analysis of the varying results from the interpretation and application of accounting principles, quantification of damages due to intellectual property infringement, and the valuation of a business or stock values. According to the AICPA,[45] litigation services are consulting services provided by CPAs and their employees, and, therefore, require adherence to the Statement on Standards for Consulting Services (SSCS). In addition to the SSCS, a CPA engaged in litigation services must comply with the general standards of the accounting profession contained in the AICPA Code of Professional Conduct. CPAs must also adhere to the professional standards set by their respective states and any standards governing other professional organizations to which the CPA may belong.

---

44. *See* DEL. CODE ANN. tit. 24, § 107 (Certificate and Permit Requirements for Certified Public Accountants).

45. AICPA MEMBER INNOVATION TEAM, LITIGATION AND APPLICABLE PROFESSIONAL STANDARDS (2009), *available at* http://fvs.aicpa.org.

Economist

As discussed, counsel may decide to use an economist, who will often hold a Ph.D. in economics. Economists may provide expertise in cases involving antitrust matters, production economics, analysis of market conditions and the impact on a company's financial performance, commercial damages, damages resulting from the infringement of intellectual property (copyright, patent, trademark, or trade secret infringement), cost performance issues, cost structures, and transfer pricing. Economists may also provide reports and testimony regarding lost earnings, lost profits (including the likelihood of loss and costs associated with the disruption in economic activity experienced by a business), and economic research. Economists tend to be used more frequently in cases requiring economic modeling, forecasts, statistical analyses, and market assessments, whereas accountants tend to be used more in matters involving the analysis of accounting or cost data and any tax implications. The two roles can be highly complementary, especially in cases that involve substantial data processing in response to an economic theory of damages, such as wage and hour dispute issues. In large cases, it is not uncommon for counsel to use both economists and accountants to determine the methodology and quantification of damages.

Expert with an MBA

The core courses in an MBA program are typically designed to introduce students to the various areas of business such as accounting, finance, marketing, human resources, operations management, etc. Many MBA students select an area of concentration as part of their graduate program and focus approximately one-third of their studies in this area.

Practitioners with an MBA may be selected in matters requiring expertise dealing with complex financial analysis, financial futures trades, analysis of various financial planning scenarios, corporate and structured finance issues, and financial projections. MBAs may give expert witness testimony in cases concerning fraudulent conveyances, guarantees, holders of interest, interest-rate risk, lease lending, letters of credit, lender liability, as well as other aspects of finance.

Valuation Expert

Valuation experts can hold several different credentials, including the ABV, the CVA, and the Accredited Valuation Analyst (AVA). The National Association of Certified Valuation Analysts (NACVA) is the governing body that certifies CVAs to perform business valuations. CVAs must pass a two-part exam to test knowledge and applied experience. Counsel may call on CVAs to provide expertise in cases determining the fair value of a business or the valuation of specific assets (intangible and tangible) in dispute, such as investment portfolios or the value of a security in security litigation cases.

Actuary

An actuary deals with the financial impact of risk and uncertainty. Actuaries evaluate the likelihood of events and quantify the contingent outcomes to minimize losses, both emotional and financial, associated with uncertain undesirable events. Actuaries typically have mathematical backgrounds and must pass a series of examinations to gain full professional status.

Actuaries are often brought on as experts involving actuarial disputes, including pricing and reserving practices of insurance companies, benefit plan provisions and corresponding benefit quantification in an employer setting, personal injury or wrongful death cases, and actuarial appraisals. While the overall dispute may involve broader issues (e.g., the price paid by one insurer for another), the role of the actuary is to focus on issues that fall within his area of expertise.

Financial experts may also act as the trier of fact, when the case involves complex accounting or financial issues that the financial expert's background equips him to understand and the parties agree to resolution by an expert arbitrator. Often in this role, the expert will serve as an arbitrator and will determine financial remuneration between parties. The arbitrator may resolve disputes over variances in the calculation of accounts receivable, accounts payable, accrued expenses, customer liabilities, or other working capital considerations. For example, parties often consider the role of an arbitrator in purchase or merger agreements in the event the parties are unable to agree on the final working capital calculation.

Challenges of Presenting the Financial Expert

One significant challenge in presenting any financial expert is the variation in jurors' and judges' knowledge of and comfort with math. Some potential jurors (and judges) start out hating and avoiding even basic arithmetic. Others may like numbers, and still others may be fascinated by them. This divergence creates a tension in how the financial damages testimony is presented—a problem made worse by what the Federal Reserve and other agencies call limited financial literacy in major parts of our society.[46]

---

46. *See* 2008 Report of the President's Council on Financial Literacy, *available at* www.jumpstartcoalition.org/PACFL_ANNUAL_REPORT_1_16_09.pdf; Federal Reserve

In a jury trial, given the different levels of financial knowledge and sophistication among jurors, gearing the presentation toward the lowest common denominator is probably unavoidable in most circumstances. Brilliant expert testimony on financial damages that goes over the heads of all but one or two jurors is not likely to be effective. An expert and presentation appropriate for an introductory college course is often the default choice in these cases, and the presentation is often geared to counsel's best guess as to the likely level of financial knowledge of the jury.

In a bench trial, the identity of the individual judge who will try the case is known well in advance in most jurisdictions. In this context, particularly with the rise of specialty courts and business courts, gearing the expert and presentation to the precise audience is more attainable and more important. A generalist judge on a state trial court or a federal district court typically hears from experts in a broad range of fields—almost certainly including medicine and probably including accounting. Thus—unless the judge has business credentials—while the theory and presentation can be sophisticated, the expert should educate the generalist judge on some of the concepts, be careful to define terms and acronyms, and, in short, probably should not be too much of an egghead. The expert and the presentation directed to a generalist judge as a fact finder is most often one appropriate for a graduate level course in the financial subjects at issue.

In a specialty court or business court, the considerations are different. The best-known example of such a court is probably the Delaware Court of Chancery; other examples are the federal bankruptcy courts and the business (or commerce) courts that have been established in other states.[47] In such courts, the level of financial sophistication is high. The courts' opinions rival many damages experts' reports, and some members of these courts write for scholarly journals on financial concepts.[48] Moreover, the court has probably heard and decided cases involving similar financial concepts and perhaps even the same damages models and concepts—something counsel and experts alike would want to know and take into consideration when putting on the case. In such a court, the financial experts probably do not have to be overly careful about terms and acronyms or spend much time giving the court background on the underlying concepts. However, they may well have to explain how the damages models and concepts at issue are

---

Personal Financial Education Initiatives (2004), *available at* http://www.federalreserve.gov/pubs/bulletin/2004/autumn04_fined.pdf.

47. *See* National Center for State Courts, Specialized Courts—Business Courts and Complex Litigation, *available at* http://www.ncsconline.org/WC/courtopics/StateLinks.asp?id=10.

48. *See* Henke v. Trilithic, Inc., No. Civ.A. 13155, 2005 WL 2899677, at *5–14 (Del. Ch. Oct. 28, 2005); *Elder-Beerman Stores Corp.*, 206 B.R. at 161–73.

the same as—or are different from—similar models employed in past cases that the court has considered. In addition, the financial expert should expect very sophisticated questions from the court. This expert and presentation is often one that would be appropriate for presenting and defending the analysis to the expert's peers, perhaps at the MBA or Ph.D. level.

In addition to gearing the expert and presentation to the trier of fact, trial counsel also faces substantial advocacy issues with regard to how to make the financial damages presentation simple, understandable, and clear. Often, an expert can present damages testimony via a summary or a set of conclusions.[49] Use of such summaries can keep the fact finder from being overwhelmed by the volume of data.

Moreover, if the damages involve numerous, repetitive calculations—lost profits calculations or claims calculations for multiple periods are good examples—there is a very real risk that the presentation will run on forever. This risk can be managed, and the presentation can be simplified, by picking one calculation to present thoroughly. The financial expert can go through one set of calculations in detail and then testify that the same methodology was employed in each set of calculations for the follow-on products, periods, or the like.[50] Moreover, grouping items in particular ways can simplify the presentation—for example, if a particular item or items of damages are disputed, spreading those items throughout the calculation makes it much harder to isolate them, while separating them and grouping them together makes their effect easier to see. This choice can have the effect of either highlighting or downplaying the disputed items.

Areas of Focus for the Advocate[51] Presenting or Cross-Examining Financial Damages Experts

When calculating and presenting historical financial damages, the debate at trial is typically over whether an item (or items) should be included in the list of claimed damages or excluded from it. These are not usually items as to which the expert is exercising judgment; usually the controversy is over causation of that damage item, mitigation, or factual support for the

---

49. *See, e.g.,* Fed. R. Evid. 705, 1006.

50. Of course, if the methodology is slightly different, even in unimportant ways, the risks to credibility and on cross-examination have to be weighed against the benefit of simplification—often a difficult judgment call.

51. The expert, of course, does not act as an advocate; that role is typically reserved for counsel and, indeed, the ethics codes applicable to certain experts limit or prohibit them from taking on an advocacy role.

item. While not directly related to the use and role of the expert, the advocate's goal in this regard is typically to make clear through the expert the effect on total damages—and thus the award—of including or excluding such items.

In the calculation of other types of damages, experts must often make judgment calls. As will be illustrated below, the judgments made in some of these areas can significantly affect the total damages, and thus they play an important role in the outcome of the damages case. Counsel (and sometimes the client) are typically aware of and involved in these judgments, and when cross-examining an expert, some or all of the judgment areas provide fodder for cross-examination. Some significant examples of these areas of focus are explored below.

Earnings and Profits—Gross, Net, After-Tax, Etc.

Because different cases or claims require that profits be measured in different ways, the issue of whether the appropriate type of profit is being measured arises in lost profits/lost earnings cases. For example, many consulting contracts require that the gross profit on a consultant-employee be paid to the consulting firm if the employee is hired away by the consultant's client.[52] In addition, certain cases involving lost sales of a specific product have awarded lost profits as measured by revenues less only the variable costs associated with the product sold.[53] In other circumstances, particularly where a business as a whole is being valued, net profits, EBITDA (earnings before interest, taxes, depreciation, and amortization), or even after-tax profits are used.[54]

Since gross profit, net profit, and after-tax profit can differ substantially, the type of profit to be calculated greatly affects the damages award. The advocacy issue for trial counsel is matching the earnings/profits calculation being made by the expert to the form of profits recoverable in the case. That type of profit may be explicit in the contract (in an easy case) or may be detailed by the relevant case law, or may require a decision by the trial court (in a difficult case).

---

52. Gross profit is generally the revenue produced, less only the variable costs attributable to the item sold—overhead costs are not used to reduce gross profit.

53. *See, e.g.,* Honeywell Int'l Inc. v. Air Prods. & Chems. Inc., 858 A.2d 392, 425–31 (Del. Ch. 2004), *aff'd in part, rev'd in part,* 872 A.2d 944 (Del. 2005).

54. In the context of lost wages, particularly in death or long-term disability cases, the question of whether after-tax earnings can and should be used has been a controversial one. *See, e.g., Delmarva Power & Light,* 435 A.2d at 721. This issue is arguably affected by whether the damages award itself is taxable.

Rates—Interest, Discount, Capitalization, Etc.

To determine the present value, at the time of trial, of a future income stream or of a business, an interest discount or capitalization rate is often used. Specific examples of the use of such rates are the determination of present value of a business in light of earnings,[55] and present valuation of lost wages/earnings in a personal injury case.[56]

This is another area involving judgment, as the Delaware Chancery Court explained in *Henke, Inc. v. Trilithic, Inc.*, a case in which the court explored in detail the components used to estimate the discount rate in that case.[57] It is also an area in which the judgment made can dramatically affect the ultimate award. In that regard, *Casey* contains an extensive discussion of the discount rates—varying from 11 percent to 18 percent—proposed by the parties and experts in that case.[58]

To illustrate the potential effect on an award, consider a perpetual income stream of $100, representing the expected income from an asset continuing in perpetuity. If the rate used to determine the present value of that income stream is 5 percent, then the present value is $2,000 (100/.05). Increasing the rate used for the present value from 5 percent to 6 percent reduces the present value from $2,000 to $1,667.

The decision about which rate to use, or the procedure to use to determine the rate, obviously varies from case to case. This issue is the subject of numerous opinions, including *Henke* and *Casey*, as well as many analytical articles. For counsel in a case that requires a present value calculation, the advocacy point is that small changes in the rate can lead to large changes in total damages. Thus, both the advocates and the experts (on all sides) can expect that the choice of rates used will be an area of focus and potential controversy.

Starting and Measuring Points

In making estimates of lost profits, lost sales, future lost wages, and many other items, the choice of a base or starting point is another decision that can significantly affect the damages award. Consider the lost wages claim in *Delmarva Power*, in which the future wage loss calculation was based only on the plaintiff's years of work in a high-paying deckhand job, omitting the years that he did not work or in which he worked in a restaurant.[59]

---

55. *See, e.g., Casey*, 2006 WL 2287024, at *18–20,
56. *See* St. Louis Southwestern Ry. Co. v. Dickerson, 470 U.S. 409, 411–12 (1985).
57. *Henke, Inc.*, 2005 WL 3578094, at *9–10.
58. *Casey*, 2006 WL 2287024, at *8–20.
59. *See Delmarva Power & Light*, 435 A.2d at 720–21.

The parties debated at some length whether the use of those years was a fair choice or a distraction.[60] To illustrate the effect on the damages, consider a hypothetical plaintiff, who over the last five years had the following history:[61] the worker earned $100,000 as a deckhand (including overtime) last year, was intermittently employed at other jobs for two years (making $10,000 each year), and was employed full time for the other two years in a restaurant (making $50,000 each year). If last year's deckhand wages are used, they were $100,000 annually, and 10 years of lost income totals $1 million. However, if the average wages for five years are used, they are $44,000 annually, and 10 years lost income is $440,000. Similar variations can occur with businesses, particularly if business expansions or recessions occurred in the year or years used to measure the income or profits—rendering certain years at least arguably unrepresentative.[62] Claims of cherry-picking—on the high side or the low side—are common with regard to such starting or measuring points.

There is usually some case law guidance in specific areas as to what constitutes a reasonable or comparable measuring point for calculation purposes, which will obviously be important in guiding the choice of a starting or measuring point.[63] However well the case law in a particular jurisdiction and type of case may (or may not) guide counsel, the advocacy concern and issue is that the choice of a starting or measuring point can significantly affect the damages calculation.

Indexes

When lost income, profits, wages, and the like have to be projected over several years, often the year-over-year increase is estimated by references to an index. For example, in *Amboy*, one of the debates was over the "earnings growth rate" of the business. The different experts used rates varying from 4.86 percent to well over double that, and testimony was presented that the "median earnings growth rate" for the type of business involved was 11.9 percent.[64] There was an extensive debate over what index (and modifications) to use in making this calculation.

---

60. *Id.*

61. The numbers are hypothetical because the *Delmarva Power & Light* opinion does not contain the plaintiff's income history in this level of detail.

62. Another potential issue in this area is seasonality, in which a large percentage of sales or earnings occur in a particular season —such as the holiday season for a toy store.

63. *See* McDermott v. Middle East Carpet Co., 811 F.2d 1422, 1427–28 (11th Cir. 1987) (finding that 1983 was a representative year for lost profits calculation given its similarity to the years being measured for lost profits in that case).

64. *Amboy*, 2006 WL 2287024, at *14–20.

For growth in business profits or income, measures of economic growth ranging from the increase in overall gross domestic product down to industry-specific growth indexes based on SIC (Standard Industrial Classification) codes—or even state and local growth indexes—have been used. In other circumstances, a price index (the Consumer Price Index (CPI) (national, state or local), Producer Price Index (PPI), or an index specific to the item involved) is used.[65] For example, in cases involving future lost wages, such as wrongful death or discrimination cases, the base wage is often inflated by an estimate of wage inflation (based on an index), plus an estimate of wage increases likely to have been given to the plaintiff based on promotions, seniority, and the like.

The choice of which index to use is another judgment item that can significantly affect the total damages. The case law in most areas provides at least some guidance as to what index (or indices) is sufficiently comparable for the task at hand. For example, in *Dobler v. Montgomery Cellular Holding Co.*,[66] the Delaware Court of Chancery held that use of a generic growth rate (gross domestic product (GDP) growth in that case) is "inherently flawed and unreasonable" and that industry-specific rates were more appropriate. Similarly, in *Nebula Glass International Inc. v. Reichhold, Inc.*,[67] the Eleventh Circuit Court of Appeals upheld a damages award based on product-specific revenue growth estimates. The advocacy point for trial counsel is that because there are potentially a wide range of indexes that could be used, this is another judgment that can have a significant effect on the total damages.

Use of Comparables

Earnings, lost profits, growth, and even asset values are often estimated by using comparables—data for a supposedly comparable company, industry, product, geographic region, or asset. The issue of whether the comparable data is, in fact, comparable to the circumstances in the case at bar is often hotly litigated. It goes without saying that counsel, often with expert assistance, will want to examine and possibly test the true comparability of the data being used to the damages case being tried.

---

65. Many of these are available for the U.S. Department of Commerce and industry associations (sales and economic growth), the Federal Reserve (economic growth and inflation), or the Bureau of Labor Statistics (wage growth and inflation).

66. Dobler v. Montgomery Cellular Holding Co., No. Civ.A. 19211, 2004 WL 2271592, at *10–12 (Del. Ch. Sept. 30, 2004).

67. Nebula Glass Int'l Inc. v. Reichhold, Inc., 454 F.3d 1203, 1218–19 (11th Cir. 2006).

Replacement Cost, Depreciated Value, Book Value, Fair Market Value, or Other Basis for Determining Cost of Assets

In various types of tort and insurance cases, the damages include the value of tangible assets—cars, buildings, houses, equipment—where the asset has been destroyed, lost, stolen, or damaged. The value of such an asset for damages purposes can differ based on the type of case or claim.

For example, fair market value is regularly used for many types of contract and tort damages:[68] "when a defendant's breach of contract deprives plaintiff of an asset, the courts look to compensate plaintiff for the 'market value' of the asset."[69] However, insurance claims will use the method of property valuation set by the policy—which may be replacement cost, depreciated value, or market value. In contrast, a stock purchase agreement may use book value if a single asset (out of many) is destroyed before closing. In other circumstances, the basis on which the asset is to be valued for damages purposes may be ambiguous and require judicial resolution.

While the substantive right answer will depend on the case, the contract, and the law, from an advocacy perspective, the answer becomes important because the approach used can have a significant effect on the damages award. This can be seen in the example of a hypothetical building destroyed by fire. It had been acquired for $100,000 10 years earlier; has been depreciated for tax purposes by $3,333/year (for a depreciated value of $67,000); has a market value for the building alone of $150,000; but will cost $175,000 to rebuild. In this circumstance, the potential valuations range from a low of $67,000 for depreciated value, to a market value of $150,000, to a replacement value of $175,000. In a tort case, to recover damages for the negligently caused fire, many jurisdictions will look to the market value, though in some, an argument could be made for replacement value. The damages on the fire insurance claim will be the replacement value if (but only if) the policy involved offers full replacement value coverage, but otherwise will be limited to whatever (probably lesser) value the policy involved covers.

For trial counsel, this is another area that calls for matching the damages expert's approach with the valuation method required by the contract or the law applicable to the case at hand.

---

68. This is assuming the cost of repair exceeds the fair market value.
69. *Schonfeld*, 218 F.3d at 178.

Conclusion

Financial damages experts, including accountants, economists, MBAs, and financial analysts, are used in a wide range of cases to prove historical and projected financial damages. In offering such testimony, experts must often make judgment calls, which can significantly affect the damages calculation. For counsel, a key advocacy concern is the need to identify and vet the judgments being made in such areas.

CHAPTER 10

Experts Unique to Substantive Areas of the Law

EXPERTS IN SECURITIES LITIGATION

Adriaen M. Morse Jr. and David S. Karp[1]

The past decade has seen a plethora of regulatory activity by the SEC and the U.S. Department of Justice (DoJ). Companies whose activities are under review by these entities are, in turn, vulnerable to private class action civil securities litigation lawsuits. Indeed, it is often the announcement of these investigations or their conclusion that is the catalyst for securities litigation. The complexity of the issues in SEC and DoJ investigations and related securities litigation makes it important for counsel representing companies or individuals facing potential criminal or civil liability under the federal securities laws, or counsel representing putative plaintiffs in civil actions arising from the alleged criminal or civil liability of a company or its officers, directors, or employees, to consider retaining an expert early on in the

---

1. Adriaen M. Morse Jr. is a partner in the Washington, D.C., office of Murphy & McGonigle, PC. Mr. Morse's practice focuses on representing financial services firms, accounting firms, public companies, and individuals in investigations and litigation before the U.S. Securities and Exchange Commission (SEC), Financial Industry Regulation Authority (FINRA) (formerly NASD and NYSE Enforcement), Public Company Accounting Oversight Board (PCAOB), and other federal and state securities industry regulators. He also represents clients in civil litigation, arbitration, and criminal matters involving the federal securities laws. David S. Karp joined the staff of the SEC in February 2009. This subchapter was written before he joined the staff of the Commission. The SEC, as a matter of policy, disclaims responsibility for any private publication or statement by any of its employees. The views expressed herein are those of the authors and do not necessarily reflect the views of the Commission or of the authors' colleagues upon the staff of the Commission.

investigation or litigation, either as a consultant, as a testifying witness, or as both.

Selecting an Expert

The defense of SEC and DoJ investigations and related securities litigation usually will involve issues of accounting, finance, economics, or valuation. Most securities matters require the assistance of an expert to analyze and explain these issues to regulators, courts, or juries. Retaining an expert early in the process forces counsel to develop an early understanding of the case and the appropriate strategy, as experts should be matched to issues as closely as possible. In analyzing the issues, counsel should evaluate which issues will benefit from expert analysis and determine whether more than one expert is required or whether a single expert can address multiple issues.

Counsel may also decide to use different kinds of experts for different purposes. Counsel may employ a nontestifying expert as a consultant to help understand the complex and technical issues related to a client's business. Counsel may also employ a testifying expert to prove (or disprove) an element in the case such as damages.

Expert as Consultant

One should not assume that an expert is only necessary after an action has been commenced. In numerous instances, it will be advisable for counsel to obtain an expert before the filing of a complaint, particularly if the client is being scrutinized by government regulators. A consulting expert working at the direction of a lawyer is useful in many ways. A good consulting expert can (1) serve as a sounding board for theories of the case; (2) assist in locating and interviewing prospective testifying experts; (3) help draft and review declarations or affidavits for use in the investigative, discovery, and trial phases of a case; (4) aid in developing productive questions for depositions of lay or expert witnesses; and (5) support the development of fruitful areas of investigation and inquiry throughout the representation. In describing the benefits of securing a consulting expert, this subchapter will use as an example the circumstance where the client is under investigation by the SEC and DoJ.

As is noted elsewhere in this book, consulting experts can serve an invaluable role in helping attorneys to shape a client's defense. This is particularly true in the context of securities-related investigations and litigation. The types of issues that arise in SEC and related DoJ investigations often require expert knowledge beyond that possessed by most lawyers, even most securities practitioners.

For example, few securities litigators possess a depth of knowledge about the rules governing disclosure of an oil and gas company's proved reserves, as defined in SEC Rule 4-10, Regulation S-X.[2] Nevertheless, in an investigation into a large international oil and gas company's 2004 recategorization of significant amounts of its proved oil and gas reserves, that rule and its application to the reserves that were written down proved to be central to the SEC's investigation and to the defense of the company's executives.[3]

In investigations and anticipated litigation involving specialized SEC rules, such as Rule 4-10, lawyers should endeavor early in the representation to locate and retain subject matter experts to assist them in understanding the rules and formulating theories. In addition to the assistance that an expert may provide to the lawyer in thinking about the case, an early search and retention is of paramount importance if there are a limited number of experts with the necessary background and experience to address the issues. Some situations lend themselves to using more than one expert. In our example, it might be appropriate to employ a petroleum engineer to deal with the engineering aspects of the rule and an accountant to analyze the accounting impact of its application on the company's financial statements.

As lawyers, our role is often to explain the relevant rules and their application to the facts of a case to a regulator, a prosecutor or a jury. The fact is, as much as we may learn about the issues we address in the matters we handle, and as persuasive as we may become in explaining them, very few lawyers are, in fact, expert in the nonlegal aspects of the cases they become involved in. Accordingly, when additional professional expertise is warranted, consulting experts should be brought in as early as possible.

Experts as Witnesses

Parties often rely on expert testimony in securities class actions. Securities litigation typically involves issues of accounting, finance, economics, or valuation. Because these issues tend to be complex and difficult to explain to laypeople, expert testimony is likely to be necessary in most securities cases, and the assistance of experts should be sought early in the pretrial process.

---

2. 17 C.F.R. § 210.4-10 (following public notice and comment, the rule was revised by the SEC with an effective date of January 1, 2010); *see* Securities Act Release No. 33-8995 (Dec. 31, 2008), *available at* http://www.sec.gov/rules/final/2008/33-8995.pdf; *see also* Joseph I. Goldstein, Comment Letter (Feb. 5, 2008), *available at* http://www.sec.gov/comments/s7-29-07/s72907-9.pdf.

3. *See* Watts v. SEC, 482 F.3d 501 (D.C. Cir. 2007); Press Release, Watts Dismissed From Securities Class Action Lawsuit (Feb. 20, 2008), *available at* http://mayerbrown.com/news/article.asp?id=4204&nid=5 (Google cache version available).

Under Federal Rules of Evidence 702, 703, and 705, a witness may offer opinion testimony if that witness has "specialized knowledge" that will assist the trier of fact in understanding the evidence or determining a fact at issue. In assisting the trier of fact, an expert witness may offer an opinion on the ultimate facts at issue in the case.[4] A qualified expert also is permitted to base an opinion regarding an ultimate fact at issue on information that would not itself be admissible as evidence at trial.[5] Experts may even supply a measure of damages for the trier of fact, and the basis for the expert's calculations need not be admissible into evidence or even disclosed at trial.[6] Given these relaxed standards and the complexity of economic and other issues that arise in securities litigation, parties commonly use experts.

Types of Expert Witnesses

Different types of experts may be needed depending on the nature of the alleged misrepresentation. Two of the more common types of experts—accountants and economists—are discussed below.

Accountants

Both plaintiffs and defendants need to consider employing an accounting expert if the alleged misrepresentation concerned financial results or financial statement disclosures. Because accounting is the language of business, accountants can often clarify business transactions, explain the records reflecting them, and discuss how they are recorded in a company's books.

Indeed, if the SEC or DoJ has investigated the company, the company may already have retained the services of such an expert for several reasons. First, the SEC has its own accountants, who will take a view about the proper accounting treatment or audit process that was followed. Second, SEC and DoJ lawyers often deal with accounting rules and are familiar with generally accepted accounting principles (GAAP), generally accepted auditing standards (GAAS), and other accounting concepts, whereas a defense lawyer's views rarely will be regarded as better, or even equally, informed. Accordingly, a declaration or testimony provided by a respected accounting or auditing expert that a particular accounting treatment conformed with GAAP or that a particular audit step complied with GAAS serves the dual purposes of alerting the agency that a different perspective on the issue

---

4. FED. R. EVID. 704(a).
5. FED. R. EVID. 705.
6. FED. R. EVID. 703–705.

exists and that a qualified expert is willing to provide an opinion to that effect. If nothing else, it raises the litigation risk for the agency should the issue be pushed to trial.

Accounting experts have been found to be useful in the following types of cases:

- *Channel stuffing.* Channel stuffing occurs when a company or the company's sales department inflates its sales figures by forcing more products through a distribution channel than that channel is capable of selling into the marketplace.
- *Expense deferral.* Expense deferral is the failure of companies to recognize current expenses within the proper period. In such cases, management attempts to defer the recognition of expenses to later periods and, in the process, boosts current-period earnings using one of three general methods: (1) failing to write down assets whose fair value has fallen below the fair market value; (2) neglecting to establish reserves despite estimable, probable contingent events that will impair the value of assets if they occur; and (3) capitalizing expenses that the company should recognize in the current period.
- *Premature revenue recognition.* Companies can recognize revenue prematurely by engaging in transactions that have the effect of increasing revenue on the company's books while providing no underlying economic benefit to the company.
- *Burying liabilities.* This occurs when a company hides liabilities or other obligations off the books by shifting them to some other entity, such as the special purpose entities made famous by Enron.
- *Inadequate disclosure.* Companies may omit or understate important required disclosures in required filings, including within footnotes to financial statements.

Economists

Economists are most useful as damage experts, particularly in fraud-on-the-market cases. Setting the true value of publicly traded securities in the hypothetical absence of a misrepresentation is complex. Although a simple measure is available—the change in price once a misrepresentation is revealed—a wide number of variables that can influence stock prices must be analyzed and explained. Because economists help companies apply the principles of market definition, price theory, economic modeling, and market risk, they can interpret the market's reaction to the release of information and define the extent to which that reaction is attributable to the release of corrective information or to market forces, the industry, or other business factors. For cases involving the value of publicly traded securities, plaintiffs and defendants tend to use the same type of experts: securities professionals, economists, or, occasionally, an attorney qualified in financial analysis.

To calculate damages, economic experts typically study the movement of the security at issue, comparing it to other securities in its industry group and to the market as a whole. Such experts also analyze the effect on the price of the security wrought by disclosures about the company, the industry, and economic factors in general. Based on these analyses, the expert offers opinions on whether the disclosure of certain information had an effect on the market price and, if so, in what amount. Those opinions, in turn, bear on whether the statement was material as well as the amount of damages per share.

Other Types of Experts

Other experts may be needed depending on the nature of the alleged misrepresentation. Sometimes an expert may be useful to describe the process of preparing annual or quarterly reports and the disclosure requirements of the federal securities laws. In cases brought under section 11 of the Securities Act of 1933, both parties should consider retaining experts who can opine on the underwriting process and the due diligence responsibilities of the participants.

Stages of Litigation Where Expert Witnesses May Be Useful

Expert witness assistance can be valuable at all phases of a securities fraud action. Parties have employed expert assistance at the motion to dismiss phase, on class certification issues, to assist with calculating damages, and on the important issue of loss causation, which typically is first tested in the summary judgment phase. The use of expert witnesses in each of these phases is discussed below.

Motions to Dismiss

Securities fraud complaints must overcome several hurdles to survive the motion to dismiss stage. First, all allegations in a securities fraud complaint must satisfy Rule 8(a) of the Federal Rules of Civil Procedure. That rule requires a plaintiff to allege "a short and plain statement of the claim showing that the pleader is entitled to relief." In *Bell Atlantic Corp. v. Twombly,*[7] the Court stated that under Rule 8(a), plaintiffs must allege "enough factual matter" to "raise a reasonable expectation that discovery will reveal evi-

---

7. Bell Atlantic Corp. v. Twombly, 550 U.S. 544 (2007).

dence" of the claim.[8] The Court went even further in *Ashcroft v. Iqbal*[9] and held that a court evaluating a motion to dismiss must first identify allegations that "are not entitled to the assumption of truth" because they are no more than conclusions.[10] The court must then determine whether the remaining allegations "plausibly give rise to an entitlement to relief."[11] Thus, "[w]here a complaint pleads facts that are merely consistent with a defendant's liability, it stops short of the line between possibility and plausibility of entitlement to relief."[12]

Second, allegations of fraud and misstatements in securities fraud actions are subject to heightened pleading requirements under Federal Rule of Civil Procedure 9(b), the Private Securities Litigation Reform Act of 1995 (the PSLRA),[13] and *Tellabs Inc. v. Makor Issues & Rights.*[14] Rule 9(b) requires that "[i]n alleging fraud . . . , a party must state with particularity the circumstances constituting fraud." Practically, Rule 9(b)'s requirement means that a securities fraud complaint based on misstatements must (1) specify the statements that the plaintiff contends were fraudulent, (2) identify the speaker, (3) state where and when the statements were made, and (4) explain why the statements were fraudulent.[15] Under the PSLRA, plaintiffs must identify in the complaint "each statement alleged to have been misleading, the reason or reasons why the statement is misleading, and if an allegation regarding the statement or omission is made on information and belief, the complaint shall state with particularity all facts on which that belief is formed."[16] The PSLRA requires a plaintiff to allege that the defendant acted with scienter (i.e., that the defendant knew the challenged statement was false at the time it was made or was reckless in not recognizing that the statement was false).[17] In alleging scienter under the PSLRA, the plaintiff must "with respect to each act or omission alleged to violate this chapter, state with particularity facts giving rise to a strong inference

---

8. *Id.* at 556.
9. Ashcroft v. Iqbal, 129 S. Ct. 1937 (2009).
10. *Id.* at 1950–51.
11. *Id.* at 1950.
12. *Id.* at 1949 (internal quotation marks and citations omitted). The Supreme Court in *Iqbal* made it clear that *Twombly* applies to all civil actions. *Id.* at 1953 (citations omitted).
13. Private Securities Litigation Reform Act of 1995, Pub. L. No. 104-67, 109 Stat. 737 (codified as amended in scattered sections of 15 U.S.C.).
14. Tellabs Inc. v. Makor Issues & Rights, 551 U.S. 308, 315 (2007).
15. *See, e.g.*, Novak v. Kasaks, 216 F.3d 300, 306 (2d Cir. 2000) (citations omitted).
16. 15 U.S.C. § 78u-4(b)(1).
17. 15 U.S.C. § 78u-4(b)(2).

that the defendant acted with the required state of mind."[18] In *Tellabs*, the Supreme Court ruled that

> to determine whether a complaint's scienter allegations can survive threshold inspection for sufficiency, a court governed by [the PSLRA] must engage in a comparative evaluation; it must consider, not only infer-ences urged by the plaintiff, . . . but also competing inferences rationally drawn from the facts alleged. To qualify as "strong" within the intend-ment of [the PSLRA], we hold, an inference of scienter must be more than merely plausible or reasonable—it must be cogent and at least as compel-ling as any opposing inference of nonfraudulent intent.[19]

In a securities class action case, Rule 8(a), *Twombly*, and *Iqbal* typically apply to loss causation and materiality, whereas Rule 9(b), the PSLRA, and *Tellabs* govern misleading statements and scienter.

In the wake of these decisions, plaintiffs have begun to rely on declara-tions and affidavits from experts, containing both facts and opinions, at the motion to dismiss stage to meet the pleading bar *Twombly*, *Iqbal*, Rule 9(b), the PSLRA, *Tellabs*, and their progeny have set.[20] In doing so, plaintiffs must pass several hurdles: (1) how the plaintiffs submit the expert's analysis and the expert's evidentiary issues, (2) whether the plaintiffs have sufficiently pled the basis for the expert's analysis, and (3) whether the expert is pro-viding an opinion or facts.

SUBMISSION OF ANALYSIS AND EXPERT EVIDENTIARY ISSUES   To put ex-pert opinions before the court in the motion to dismiss phase, some plain-tiffs have inserted the analysis directly into the pleading or appended it to the complaint. At least one court has denied a motion to dismiss where an expert affidavit was submitted and the court noted in dicta that the com-plaint was supported by "sworn expert analysis."[21] Other courts have re-fused to consider expert analysis annexed to the complaint because it is not a "written instrument" under Federal Rule of Civil Procedure 10(c).[22] Still

---

18. *Id.*
19. *Tellabs*, 551 U.S. at 315.
20. *See, e.g.*, Roth v. OfficeMax, Inc., 527 F. Supp. 2d 791 (N.D. Ill. 2007); *In re* Charles Schwab Corp. Sec. Litig., 257 F.R.D. 534 (N.D. Cal. 2009); *In re* Jones Soda Co. Sec. Litig., No. C07-1366RSL, 2009 WL 330163 (W.D. Wash. Feb. 9, 2009); Flaherty & Crumrine Pre-ferred Income Fund, Inc. v. TXU Corp., 565 F.3d 200 (5th Cir. 2009); *In re* Wash. Mut., Inc. Sec. Litig., No. C08-387MJP, 2009 WL 1393679 (W.D. Wash. May 15, 2009); Brodsky v. Yahoo!, Inc., 630 F. Supp. 2d 1104 (N.D. Cal. 2009).
21. *See, e.g.*, Barrie v. Intervoice-Brite, Inc., 397 F.3d 249, *modified and reh'g denied*, 409 F.3d 653 (5th Cir. 2005).
22. Rule 10(c) of the Federal Rules of Civil Procedure provides that "[a] copy of a writ-ten instrument that is an exhibit to a pleading is a part of the pleading for all purposes."

other courts have refused to consider expert reports at the motion to dismiss stage on the ground that their submission at that time is an attempted end-run around the PSLRA's discovery stay.[23]

ATTACKING THE BASIS FOR EXPERT ANALYSIS   Defendants should closely parse the expert analysis to see if it complies with the PSLRA requirements that all allegations (1) regarding the misleading nature of statements or omissions that are based on information and belief state "with particularity" all facts on which that belief is formed, and (2) state with particularity the facts giving rise to a strong inference of scienter.[24] Courts will not accept conclusory statements or lists of purported sources of information.[25]

FACTS VERSUS OPINION   Finally, defendants should review whether plaintiffs are offering the expert for factual analysis or to give an opinion on the underlying issue. The court may entirely disregard an expert's opinion if it is an attempt to substitute for facts.[26] However, courts usually will consider nonconclusory factual portions of expert affidavits in evaluating motions to dismiss.[27]

Class Certification

The motion to dismiss stage may be critical in a securities class action because many cases that survive a motion to dismiss are settled. If the court

---

Courts disagree about whether an expert affidavit or declaration is considered a "written instrument." For instance, one court stated that written instruments are only those documents "on which [a party's] action or defense is based . . . ." Rose v. Bartle, 871 F.2d 331, 339 n.3 (3d Cir. 1989) (internal quotation marks and citation omitted). Because it is highly unlikely that an expert's affidavit or analysis could ever form the basis of a claim in a securities case, courts may refuse to consider them on that basis. *See, e.g.,* DeMarco v. DepoTech Corp., 149 F. Supp. 2d 1212, 1220 (S.D. Cal. 2001); In re Viropharma, Inc. Sec. Litig., No. CIV.A. 02-1627, 2003 WL 1824914, at *2 (E.D. Pa. Apr. 7, 2003); Benzon v. Morgan Stanley, No. 3:03-0159, 2004 WL 62747, at *2 (M.D. Tenn. Jan. 8, 2004). Many courts, however, do not view Rule 10(c) as an impediment to reviewing the information contained in an expert's affidavit. *See, e.g., Roth,* 527 F. Supp. 2d at 801.
    23. *See, e.g., In re* Viropharma, 2003 WL 1824914, at *2.
    24. 15 U.S.C. § 78u-4(b)(1); *see also Roth,* 527 F. Supp. 2d at 801 (discounting opinion as "not based on any facts whatsoever").
    25. *See, e.g.,* Maldonado v. Dominguez, 137 F.3d 1, 12 (1st Cir. 1998) (expert's affidavit concluding that defendants "would have known" about certain facts not enough to allege scienter).
    26. *See, e.g.,* Fin. Acquisition Partners, LP v. Blackwell, 440 F.3d 278, 286 (5th Cir. 2006) (holding that expert's "opinions cannot substitute for facts under the PSLRA"); *In re* Jones, 2009 WL 330163, at *4 n.6 (industry expert's opinion disregarded).
    27. *See, e.g., Fin. Acquisition Partners,* 440 F.3d at 285.

denies the motion to dismiss and if the case does not settle at that stage, the next most important stage of the litigation is class certification.

Under Federal Rule of Civil Procedure 23(a), a court may not certify a lawsuit as a class action unless the named plaintiff demonstrates that the central facts of the case are capable of proof on a class-wide basis. In recent times, the named plaintiff has attempted to satisfy the requirements of Rule 23(a) through an expert witness, and defendants invariably put forth their own expert in response.

Both plaintiffs and defendants in the class action phase of securities litigation who plan to put forth expert witnesses need to consider two Supreme Court trilogies. The first Supreme Court trilogy involves the level of proof required to warrant certification under Rule 23. In *Eisen v. Carlisle & Jacquelin*, the Court stated that the district court may not conduct a "preliminary inquiry into the merits" in deciding whether to certify the class.[28] Four years later, in *Coopers & Lybrand v. Livesay*, the Court clarified that the class-certification inquiry "generally involves considerations that are enmeshed in the factual and legal issues comprising the plaintiff's cause of action."[29] Then, in *General Telephone Co. of Southwest v. Falcon*, the Court required district courts to undertake a "rigorous analysis" of the facts offered at the class certification stage, "prob[ing] behind the pleadings" to discern whether the case could be effectively adjudicated as a class.[30]

The second Supreme Court trilogy involves whether and under what circumstances expert testimony may be used in a motion for class certification. In *Daubert v. Merrell Dow Pharmaceuticals, Inc.*, the Supreme Court emphasized that courts must look beneath the surface of expert opinions, closely examine the expert's methodologies, and exclude testimony that is irrelevant or unreliable.[31] The Court ruled that to be helpful to the trier of fact, a district court must not only conclude that there is a "fit" between the expert's opinion and the facts presented, but also that the expert's reasoning and methodology is both scientifically valid and has been properly applied.[32] In *General Electric Co. v. Joiner*,[33] the Court expanded on *Daubert*'s allocation of the preliminary question of expert testimony admissibility to the province of the district court by requiring appellate courts to review such questions under the deferential abuse-of-discretion standard. Finally,

---

28. Eisen v. Carlisle & Jacquelin, 417 U.S. 156, 177 (1974).
29. Coopers & Lybrand v. Livesay, 437 U.S. 463, 469 (1978).
30. Gen. Tel. Co. of Southwest v. Falcon, 457 U.S. 147, 160–61 (1982).
31. Daubert v. Merrell Dow Pharms., Inc., 509 U.S. 579, 592–93 (1993).
32. *Id.* at 591–93.
33. Gen. Elec. Co. v. Joiner, 522 U.S. 136 (1997).

in *Kumho Tire Co. v. Carmichael*,[34] the Court rejected the argument that *Daubert* applies only to scientific testimony and held that *Daubert* applied to all expert testimony.

Together, these two trilogies erect three hurdles for a party wishing to offer expert testimony at the class certification stage: (1) the expert's opinions must fit with the facts of the case; (2) the expert's opinions must be derived from reliable principles and methods; and (3) the expert's opinions must be subject to some level of probing in connection with the district court's analysis of whether the requirements for class certification are satisfied under *Eisen, Livesay,* and *Falcon.*

The federal circuits have adopted two different approaches to class certification where the parties present expert evidence, the *Daubert*-only approach and the *Daubert*-plus rigorous analysis:

- Daubert-*only approach.* The First Circuit appears to apply the *Daubert* framework to ensure that the expert testimony a class proponent uses to support preliminary Rule 23 findings passes muster. In *In re Poly-Medica Corp. Securities Litigation*,[35] the First Circuit stated that "[t]he question of how much evidence of efficiency is necessary for a court to accept the fraud-on-the-market presumption of reliance at the class-certification stage is . . . one of degree."[36] The court acknowledged that its "generalities" on the issue "are the best [it could] do."[37]
- Daubert-*plus rigorous analysis.* The Second, Third, Fourth, Fifth, Seventh, Eighth, and Eleventh Circuits treat the *Daubert* inquiry as separate from—and preliminary to—the Rule 23 inquiry.[38] In fulfilling *Daubert*'s gatekeeper role, the district court determines whether expert evidence is relevant to Rule 23's requirements and is based on a reliable methodology. *Daubert* determines whether the expert opinion is admissible. If the expert opinion is admissible, then the district court considers the expert testimony along with all the other admissible evidence presented at the class certification hearing. Where class certification would be appropriate under one set of facts but not another, the district court

---

34. Kumho Tire Co. v. Carmichael, 526 U.S. 137 (1999).

35. *In re* PolyMedica Corp. Sec. Litig., 432 F.3d 1 (1st Cir. 2005).

36. *Id.* at 17.

37. *Id.*

38. *See, e.g., In re* Initial Pub. Offerings Sec. Litig., 471 F.3d 24, 40–41 (2d Cir. 2006); Blades v. Monsanto Co., 400 F.3d 562, 575 (8th Cir. 2005); Unger v. Amedisys, Inc., 401 F.3d 316, 319 (5th Cir. 2005); Gariety v. Grant Thornton, LLP, 368 F.3d 356, 366 (4th Cir. 2004); Newton v. Merrill Lynch, Pierce, Fenner & Smith, Inc., 259 F.3d 154, 166 (3d Cir. 2001) (citation omitted); Szabo v. Bridgeport Machines, Inc., 249 F.3d 672, 676 (7th Cir. 2001); Love v. Turlington, 733 F.2d 1562, 1564 (11th Cir. 1984) (citation omitted).

makes "whatever factual and legal inquiries are necessary" to determine whether Rule 23's requirements are met.[39]

Calculating Damages

The PSLRA limits damages in securities class actions by imposing a recovery cap that is based on the movement of a company's stock in the 90 days following "the date on which the information correcting the misstatement or omission that is the basis for the action is disseminated to the market."[40] If a plaintiff holds the security through the 90-day period, "the award of damages to the plaintiff shall not exceed the difference between the purchase or sale price paid or received, as appropriate, by the plaintiff for the subject security and the mean trading price of that security during the 90-day period."[41] If a plaintiff sells or repurchases the security before the expiration of the 90-day period, "the plaintiff's damages shall not exceed the difference between the purchase or sale price paid or received, as appropriate, by the plaintiff for the security and the mean trading price of the security during the period beginning immediately after dissemination of information correcting the misstatement or omission and ending on the date on which the plaintiff sells or repurchases the security."[42] The PSLRA defines "mean trading price" of the security as "an average of the daily trading price of that security, determined as of the close of the market each day during the 90-day period."[43] Given the many factors that go into the calculation of a stock's price other than a misstatement or omission, and the PSLRA's use of a cap rather than a specified damages measurement, the PSLRA leaves fertile ground for expert testimony. The following diagram of the hypothetical movement of a company's stock price illustrates the continued value of expert testimony after the PSLRA.

In this diagram, P1, P2, and P3 all represent purchases of securities before the beginning of the 90-day damage window, which begins with the disclosure of the misstatement or omission. The curving line represents the movement of the company's stock price. The horizontal dotted line that begins the 90-day damage window is the date on which the misstatement or omission was disclosed to the market. The immediate price drop following that disclosure is a typical starting point for examining the "inflation per share"—that is, the extent to which the stock price was inflated by the alleged fraud before the supposed truth was disclosed. (We say "starting

---

39. *Szabo*, 249 F.3d at 676.
40. 15 U.S.C. § 78u-4(e)(1).
41. *Id.*
42. 15 U.S.C. § 78u-4(e)(2).
43. 15 U.S.C. § 78u-4(e)(3).

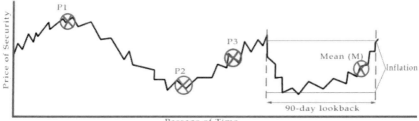

point" because depending on the facts of a given case, all, some, or none of the price drop could be properly attributable to the corrective disclosure instead of unrelated market, industry, or business factors.) For simplicity, we assume that each purchased share is held through the end of the 90-day lookback period.

- The 90-day cap for shares purchased at P1 is calculated by subtracting the mean from the P1 purchase price. The difference is greater than the range of inflation, and thus places no cap on P1's damages. This leaves fertile ground for expert testimony on the correct measure of inflation per share—that is, the extent of the range of inflation that is attributable to the release of corrective information (for which recovery is available) as opposed to other factors (for which recovery is not).
- The 90-day cap for shares purchased at P2 is calculated by subtracting the mean from the P2 purchase price. The difference is a negative number. Since P2 bought below the mean, P2's damages are zero, regardless of the correct measure of inflation per share.
- The 90-day cap for a share purchased at P3 also is calculated by subtracting the mean from the purchase price. In this case, the difference is less than the range of inflation, but (for the reasons discussed above) it will not necessarily be less than the correct measure of inflation per share. Because the 90-day cap would apply only in this latter instance, expert testimony would continue to be important in assessing the extent of P3's damages.

Loss Causation

Loss causation is a concept that repeatedly arises in securities fraud litigation. It is especially amenable to expert advice; in fact, the expert witnesss's opinion can be a crucial element in the outcome of a securities fraud action. Although a complete discussion of loss causation could be the subject of a treatise by itself, counsel considering whether to bring in an expert witness on loss causation should be aware of the following general guidelines.

The PSLRA includes a provision on loss causation that provides as follows: "In any private action arising under this chapter, the plaintiff shall have the burden of proving that the act or omission of the defendant alleged to violate this chapter caused the loss for which the plaintiff seeks to recover damages."[44] Following the enactment of the PSLRA, this provision engendered some confusion among the federal circuit courts regarding what plaintiffs had to demonstrate in order to prove loss causation. The Ninth Circuit held that a plaintiff need only show "that the price on the date of purchase was inflated because of the misrepresentation."[45] Other circuits held that an "allegation of a purchase-time value disparity, standing alone, cannot satisfy the loss causation pleading requirement."[46] The Supreme Court resolved the split in the circuits in *Dura Pharmaceuticals, Inc. v. Broudo* by rejecting the Ninth Circuit approach and holding that "in cases such as this one (i.e., fraud-on-the-market cases), an inflated purchase price will not itself constitute or proximately cause the relevant economic loss."[47] Alleging that price has been inflated as a result of a misrepresentation is not enough—even if the plaintiff has suffered a loss—unless the plaintiff can identify a "causal connection" between the loss and the misrepresentation.[48]

In dicta, the Court elaborated on what a plaintiff must show in order to show loss causation: first, the plaintiff must show that the decline occurred "after the truth ma[de] its way into the marketplace;" second, the plaintiff must show that the decline was not caused by "changed economic circumstances, changed investor expectations, new industry-specific or firm-specific facts, conditions, or other events, which taken separately or together account for some or all of that lower price."[49]

CORRECTIVE DISCLOSURES   Expert assistance can be useful in litigating *Dura*'s first requirement—that a plaintiff show a decline occurred "after the truth ma[de] its way into the marketplace." One category of cases involves allegations that the stock price declined due to a "corrective disclosure" that explicitly revealed some previously omitted material fact or corrected a misrepresented fact. These cases can involve numerous alleged corrective disclosures that precipitated a decline in share price. An expert can help

---

44. 15 U.S.C. § 78u-4(b)(4).
45. Knapp v. Ernst & Whinney, 90 F.3d 1431, 1438 (9th Cir. 1996) (citations omitted).
46. *See, e.g.,* Emergent Capital Inv. Mgmt. v. Stonepath Group, Inc., 343 F.3d 189, 198 (2d Cir. 2003).
47. Dura Pharms., Inc. v. Broudo, 544 U.S. 336, 342 (2005).
48. *Id.* at 347.
49. *Id.* at 342–43.

counsel sort through the disclosures and select the ones that they believe proximately caused the decline.

Counsel who plan to use an expert witness to select the appropriate disclosure should be aware of some of the hurdles that may arise. Some of them are similar to those present in the pleading stage such as the selected disclosures not including new information.[50] In a recent opinion, the Tenth Circuit in *In re Williams Securities Litigation—WCG Subclass*[51] affirmed the district court's granting of summary judgment where the plaintiffs or their expert witness were unable to present evidence linking the plaintiffs' losses to a revelation of fraud.[52] The *Williams* court observed that although the expert had submitted a 1,300-page compendium of news articles, reports, and SEC filings to support his conclusion that a number of tiny disclosures occurred each and every day of the class period, which had the cumulative effect of gradually disclosing the alleged fraud, the expert was unable to pinpoint a single date or selection of dates on which the fraud allegedly was revealed.[53] Similarly, in another case, the district court excluded an expert's report because the expert excluded a relevant event date from his study, which he admitted included a corrective disclosure.[54]

CHANGED ECONOMIC CIRCUMSTANCES   *Dura*'s second requirement—that the plaintiff be able to foreclose other causes for the decline—poses particular challenges to experts retained by the plaintiffs, as the *Williams* decision demonstrated. *Williams* held that the plaintiff's expert did not sufficiently account for the plaintiff's contention "that the declines in price were the result of the revelation of the truth and not some other factor."[55] It noted that there were "too many intervening factors at play" for the plaintiff's expert to attribute the decline to a materialization of risk, without analysis of "the mechanism by which fraud was revealed to the market."[56] The Tenth Circuit faulted the expert for not doing a regression analysis in considering the losses at issue and noted that because of this failure, the

---

50. *See, e.g., In re* Omnicom Group, Inc. Sec. Litig., 541 F. Supp. 2d 546, 551–54 (S.D.N.Y. 2008).

51. *In re* Williams Sec. Litig.—WCG Subclass, 558 F.3d 1130 (10th Cir. 2009).

52. *Id.* at 1143.

53. *Id.* at 1138–40.

54. *In re* Xcelera.com Sec. Litig., No. 00-1649-RWZ, 2008 U.S. Dist. LEXIS 77807, at *3 (D. Mass. Apr. 25, 2008).

55. *Williams*, 558 F.3d at 1143.

56. *Id.* at 1142.

expert "did not attempt to remove market and industry effects" from his analysis.[57]

DURA IMPOSES A HIGH BURDEN ON PLAINTIFFS   The *Williams* decision is one of the first pronouncements by circuit courts after *Dura* to consider the quality of expert evidence needed to satisfy *Dura*'s requirements.[58] *Williams* demonstrates that a plaintiff's burden under *Dura* is a high one. Counsel in securities fraud actions should be mindful of the expense likely needed to do the studies and analysis *Williams* would require and factor those issues into settlement considerations.

Strategic Considerations regarding Expert Witnesses

Expert Disclosures

Federal Rule of Civil Procedure 26(a)(2) governs the disclosures that a party employing a testifying expert must make to the other side before trial. Under that rule, in addition to identifying all testifying witnesses that the party may use at trial, the party employing the services of a testifying expert witness must provide the other side with a written report that includes the following:

- A complete statement of all opinions the witness will express and the bases and reasons for them;
- The data or other information the witness considered in forming the opinions;
- Any exhibits that will be used to summarize or support the opinions;
- The witness's qualifications and a list of all publications the witness authored in the past 10 years;
- A list of all cases during the previous four years in which the witness testified as an expert at trial or by deposition; and
- A statement of the compensation to be paid to the expert.[59]

The rule specifically applies to testifying expert witnesses and does not contain any disclosure requirements for nontestifying experts.

---

57. *Id.* at 1135 n.3.

58. At least one district court has similarly held that a plaintiff may not rely solely on a revelation of a company's true financial condition when attempting to defeat summary judgment. In *In re Retek Inc. Securities Litigation*, 621 F. Supp. 2d 690 (D. Minn. 2009), the court granted the defendants' motion for summary judgment where the plaintiffs' evidence, which included an expert declaration, failed to demonstrate a genuine issue of material fact between the alleged corrective disclosure and the alleged misrepresentation, or that any such link caused the decline in the company's stock.

59. FED. R. CIV. P. 26(a)(2).

Disclosure of Communications with Expert Witnesses

TESTIFYING EXPERTS   Rule 26(a)(2)(B)'s disclosure requirements effectively remove any question that, absent a stipulation among the parties to the contrary, all communications between the attorney and his expert will be discoverable.[60] Accordingly, counsel should take care in communicating with the expert, even from the very first interview. This does not mean that counsel should avoid talking about the legal theories of the case with the expert. Instead, this means that counsel should present the legal issues in as objective a manner as possible. In addition, when written communications occur, they should be drafted with the expectation that they will be produced. This precaution includes comments on drafts of the expert report. Counsel may wish to consider communicating comments on the draft to the expert orally.

NONTESTIFYING CONSULTING EXPERTS   Consulting experts have much greater protection from discovery than testifying experts.[61] Rule 26(b)(4)(B) requires a party seeking discovery from nontestifying consulting experts to demonstrate "exceptional circumstances under which it is impracticable for the party to obtain facts or opinions on the same subject by other means." In practice, a court's decision to grant or deny discovery from a consulting expert turns on fairness—in essence, where the party seeking disclosure has "a basic lack of ability to discover the equivalent information."[62] Examples of circumstances where courts have permitted a party to obtain discovery from a consulting expert include where (1) the consulting expert's report serves as a basis for the testifying expert's report;[63] or (2) the consulting expert is the only available expert on the subject matter or in the field

---

60. On September 15, 2009, the Judicial Conference approved proposed amendments to Federal Rule of Civil Procedure 26(b)(4), which would extend trial-preparation protection to many communications between attorneys and testifying experts. If the proposed amendment is approved by the Supreme Court, and not overruled by Congress, counsel will have more leeway when discussing the legal theories of a case with a testifying expert. For further discussion of this proposed amendment, *see infra* chapter 2(d).

61. *See, e.g.,* Mfg. Admin. & Mgmt. Sys., Inc. v. ICT Group, Inc., 212 F.R.D. 110, 118 (E.D.N.Y. 2002) (noting that mandatory disclosure requirement "creates an incentive for a party additionally to retain a non-testifying expert, to whom an attorney may speak freely about litigation strategies and opinions without falling prey to the powerful jaws of mandatory disclosure").

62. Hartford Fire Ins. Co. v. Pure Air on the Lake Ltd. P'ship, 154 F.R.D. 202, 208 (N.D. Ind. 1993) (citation and internal quotation marks omitted).

63. *See, e.g., id.* at 208; Pinal Creek Group v. Newmont Min. Corp., No. CIV-91-1764-PHX-DAE-(LOA), 2006 WL 1817000, at *7 (D. Ariz. June 30, 2006) (requiring disclosure of consulting expert's work files where testifying experts formulated their opinions in reliance on consultant's work).

in question.[64] Because the standard for disclosure of communications with a nontestifying consulting expert is so high, an attorney who employs both a nontestifying consulting expert and a testifying expert should segregate the nontestifying consulting expert from the testifying expert so that communications with the consultant and his work product will not become discoverable. This can be accomplished by requiring that all communications between the consultant and the testifying expert go through counsel.

Preparing to Depose the Testifying Expert Witness

The key to successfully deposing any expert is preparation. This is particularly the case when deposing an expert with a seemingly impressive list of credentials in complex subject matters. Without adequate preparation, counsel will not be able to probe the strengths and weaknesses of the expert's opinion. Although the strategic considerations involved in deposing an expert could (and does) take up volumes, the examining attorney should consider taking the following steps:

- *Thoroughly review the expert's qualifications.* One of the first steps that the examining attorney should take is to review the expert's qualifications, publications, and the cases in which the expert previously testified. These materials often provide key fodder for cross-examining the expert on the substantive opinions expressed in the expert's report as well as his qualifications to render those opinions.

  The examining attorney should review every publication authored by the expert. Even though the publications may seem opaque to someone who is not schooled in the particular academic or industrial discipline, the attorney may be able to glean certain themes from the publications. For example, if the attorney is preparing to depose an oil and gas expert, the attorney may discover through a review of the publications that, although the expert has written extensively on oil and gas, he has not written on the issue present in the case or has written an article advocating a position different from the one taken in the report.

  In addition, the attorney should make every effort to obtain the prior testimony of the expert to see if the expert previously expressed opinions that may contradict the opinion the expert is offering in the present case. The attorney also should try to speak with the attorneys who deposed the expert in those cases because the attorneys generally will be willing to talk and provide helpful advice.

---

64. *See, e.g.,* Spearman Indus., Inc. v. St. Paul Fire & Marine Ins. Co., 128 F. Supp. 2d 1148, 1152 (N.D. Ill. 2001).

- *Search online databases and the Internet.* The examining attorney should exhaustively search online databases, such as Lexis/Nexis and Westlaw, and the Internet for information on the expert. The expert may also patronize chat rooms, post on blogs, or have a publicly available Facebook or LinkedIn page. The examining attorney should review all of these sources for potential areas of cross-examination.
- *Become familiar with the subject matter.* The examining attorney should do whatever possible to gain some understanding of the expert's discipline. The examiner should consult the basic texts in the expert's field and obtain a glossary of the jargon used. If the examiner has employed a consulting expert, that consultant could be very helpful in this process.
- *During the deposition, do not neglect the qualifications.* Many examiners agree to stipulate to the expert's qualifications. This is a mistake. The examiner should budget some time during the deposition for the expert's qualifications. Through careful questioning, the examiner can elicit testimony defining what the expert is—and is not—an expert in. For example, even though an expert may have academic credentials, he may not have practiced in the field or gained real-world experience in it; this may provide a contrast to the examining attorney's own testifying expert. Furthermore, there may be experiences that the expert has not listed on his curriculum vitae that may be relevant to the opinion offered.
- *Explore the nature and terms of the expert's engagement.* Although no expert is ever paid on a contingent basis, in virtually every case, the expert has a financial incentive to offer an opinion favorable to the party that has contacted and sponsored the expert. The extent and nature of the expert's incentive in the particular case is worth exploring.[65]
- *Identify the case-specific information that the expert reviewed in reaching an opinion and preparing for the deposition.* Careful questioning could reveal that the expert was provided with a selected set of documents favorable to one side of the case. Showing the expert other documents that the expert did not review could elicit a response that the document might have changed his opinion had he known of its existence before preparing for the deposition.
- *Identify all communications the expert has had in preparing for the deposition.*

---

65. Bought and paid-for analyses can sometimes be deemed to be unreliable due to the inherent bias created by the paid testimony. *See In re* Apollo Group Inc. Sec. Litig., 527 F. Supp. 2d 957, 961 (D. Ariz. 2007).

- *Crystallize the expert's opinion and exhaust the expert's knowledge of the facts of the case.*

Defending the Expert Deposition

A party calling an expert witness takes a risk. Theoretically, the expert is not a party and cannot make binding admissions. Practically, however, the trier of fact will align the expert with the sponsoring party. Accordingly, if the expert offers nonsupportive opinions or fails to offer promised supporting opinions, the expert can harm a party's case. The following are a few tips for counsel preparing to defend a deposition of an expert:

- *Know the expert's strengths and weaknesses.* A professional expert witness—a witness employed by a litigation consulting firm whose primary job is to offer expert testimony—has the advantage of familiarity with the judicial process and the adversary system. Professional witnesses, however, can be expensive and may have a relative lack of credibility based on their status as professional witnesses. Academic witnesses are usually credible because their testimony grows out of their life's work and research; however, their unfamiliarity with the adversary process could be a liability.
- *Provide experts with all relevant material before they complete their opinions.* Counsel should provide the expert, as early as possible, with a complete file of the materials in the case, including the pleadings and the significant evidence produced during discovery, that has any bearing on the expert's opinion or potential testimony at a deposition or on cross-examination at trial. The file should contain both good and bad evidence; failure to do so could reveal the expert's opinion to be biased based on the selection of evidence reviewed.
- *Make the expert aware of litigation tactics.* The defending attorney should prepare the expert for the examination through meetings, going over the material, and a mock examination.

Conclusion

Complex securities investigations and cases are tailor-made for expert testimony. Understanding the benefits and risks of employing either a consulting or testifying expert in these cases enables counsel to more effectively litigate or defend them.

EXPERTS IN EMPLOYMENT LITIGATION

D. Michael Henthorne[1]

Trials are stages for the telling of human stories.[2] This is especially true in employment cases, where the stories focus on people in their workplaces. According to James McElhaney, "every part of the trial is a story—opening statement, direct examination, cross-examination, final argument—even trial objections and post-trial motions."[3] McElhaney observes, "The secret to a good story is the word picture—the verbal snapshot that lets people see what happened. People believe what they can see. . . . And in a good story, what happens makes the jury want to take your side."[4]

With the premise that each part of the trial is a story, the role of the expert witness in employment litigation is clear—to allow the judge or jury to understand what happened from the perspective of the learned professional. Depending on the word pictures the expert crafts and shows to the jury, the expert's opinion—or story—will ideally reinforce and enhance your client's story or expose the weaknesses and deficiencies in your opponent's story.

Once you have made the strategic decision to use an expert in your employment case, you should then determine how to use the expert to tell your client's story. In particular, you should consider the audience for your expert's testimony, the various types of experts available in employment cases, the selection of the best expert for your case, the preparation of that expert, and the elicitation of your expert's testimony. This subchapter addresses each of these topics in turn, with the goal of helping you to use your expert to tell your story effectively.

---

1. Mr. Henthorne is of counsel with Littler Mendelson, PC, in the firm's Columbia, South Carolina, office.

2. *See* Paul Gewirtz, *Narrative and Rhetoric in the Law, in* LAW'S STORIES: NARRATIVE AND RHETORIC IN THE LAW 2 (Peter Brooks & Paul Gewirtz eds., 1996) ("Both scholars and the public have increasingly been drawn to the law as an arena where vivid human stories are played out—where stories are told and heard in distinctive ways and with distinctive stakes.").

3. JAMES MCELHANEY, MCELHANEY'S TRIAL NOTEBOOK 188 (4th ed. 2005).

4. *Id.* at 189.

Determine Whether an Expert Will Help Tell the Story

In telling the story from the perspective of the learned professional, the expert can serve a variety of distinct functions in the course of providing an opinion. The expert can explain facts, teach applicable methods or procedures, establish baseline standards, process and evaluate data, reinforce theories, and uncover fallacies. Subject to the qualification of the witness and the admissibility of the witness's testimony, both of which are discussed in earlier chapters of this book, attorneys have the opportunity to be creative in telling and retelling their client's stories through the use of experts.

An employment attorney considering whether to use expert testimony to tell a story should ask himself the following preliminary questions:

- Will the expert's testimony help the judge or jury to understand the evidence or to decide a fact in dispute?[5]
- Does the expert possess scientific, technical, or "other specialized knowledge?"[6]
- Does the expert have sufficient facts to make his story reliable?[7]
- Is the expert's story—or the inferences to be gleaned from the story—authentic, reasonable, and consistent with the facts?[8]
- Does the expert's story make it easier for the judge or jury to see what really happened?

If these questions can be answered affirmatively, the use of an expert witness is at least worth exploring. Admittedly, there are times when the client's story is so clear that the use of an expert would be redundant, would run the risk of overexplaining the story (and, in the process, alienating the judge or jury), or would not justify the additional cost or expense to the client. However, those cases are generally the exception rather than the norm.

Remember the Audience for the Story

At the trial level, the judge and jury are the primary audience for any expert testimony because they ultimately decide whether your client's story is worthy of credence. Nevertheless, in the course of litigation, a number of other persons may be influenced by an expert's credentials, methodology, find-

---

5. FED. R. EVID. 702.
6. *Id.*
7. *Id.*
8. *Id.*; *see also* FED. R. EVID. 703.

ings, or opinions. Moreover, these other hearers can influence the outcome of the litigation. Accordingly, these other hearers of your expert's story should not be overlooked or taken for granted. For example, law clerks, mediators, arbitrators, jury consultants, fact witnesses, and even other expert witnesses can just as easily be influenced by an expert's testimony as a judge or jury.

Consider the Various Types of Experts

The type of experts used, as well as the subject matter of the witness's expertise, can be as varied as the facts of the case, the parties and witnesses involved, and the context in which those facts arise. Under Rule 702 of the Federal Rules of Evidence, "[i]f scientific, technical, or other specialized knowledge will assist the trier of fact to understand the evidence or to determine a fact in issue, a witness qualified as an expert by knowledge, skill, experience, training, or education, may testify thereto in the form of an opinion or otherwise, if (1) the testimony is based upon sufficient facts or data, (2) the testimony is the product of reliable principles and methods, and (3) the witness has applied the principles and methods reliably to the facts of the case."[9] Thus, the countless subjects for which expert testimony may be offered are limited only by two considerations: (1) whether the expert's testimony is reliable, and (2) whether the desired testimony is relevant to the facts at issue.

Regardless of the type of expert or the subject matter of the desired testimony, however, it is important for the employment lawyer to remember that expert opinion "must be based on scientific, technical, or other specialized knowledge and not on belief or speculation, and inferences must be derived using scientific or other valid methods."[10] To that end, courts enjoy "broad latitude" in determining whether expert testimony is reliable and admissible, and a trial judge's rulings are generally given considerable deference by appellate courts.[11]

In discrimination, retaliation, and wrongful termination cases, experts are routinely used to establish liability, quantify damages, or both. The *Employment Litigation Handbook*, published by the American Bar Association,

---

9. Fed. R. Evid. 702.

10. Daubert v. Merrell Dow Pharms., Inc., 509 U.S. 579, 592–93 (1993); *see also* Oglesby v. Gen. Motors Corp., 190 F.3d 244, 250 (4th Cir. 1999).

11. Kumho Tire Co. v. Carmichael, 526 U.S. 137, 142 (U.S. 1999) (citing Gen. Elec. Co. v. Joiner, 522 U.S. 136, 143 (1997)).

has suggested that expert witnesses have been traditionally used in employment cases to explain the following:

- Whether discrimination has occurred;
- Disparate impact issues;
- Bona fide occupational qualification issues;
- Disability issues;
- Emotional distress issues;
- Economic damages; and
- The plaintiff's ability to work or maintain employment.[12]

In the liability phase of a trial, for example, an expert in statistics can help a jury understand how the diversity of a company's workforce compares to the pool of applicants from which the company has to draw in a given geographical area. In discrimination cases, whether a single plaintiff case or a class action, this type of evidence can have a profound effect. For instance, the Four-Fifths Rule is routinely used by experts to establish whether a particular employment practice has an adverse impact on a particular race, sex, or ethnic group.[13] Under the Four-Fifths Rule, if members of a protected class are selected at a rate of less than four-fifths (or 80 percent) of the group with the highest selection rate, the selection rate is generally regarded as evidence of a disparate impact.[14] Even then, however, statistical experts will typically be required to verify that the sample size is statistically significant.[15]

In harassment cases, experts can be used to explain or critique antiharassment policies and provide testimony regarding the effectiveness of such policies.[16] These experts are typically employment attorneys or senior-level human resources professionals with practical experience in developing, drafting, and implementing antiharassment policies as well as training employees, supervisors, and managers regarding their contents.

Similarly, in the damages phase of a trial, an economist can help a jury understand the extent to which an employee may have been harmed by an employment action.[17] An economist may even be able to help the jury arrive

---

12. Herbert E. Gerson, Christopher P. Lenzo, Maureen M. Rayborn, & Nancy Erika Smith, *Experts, in* EMPLOYMENT LITIGATION HANDBOOK 94-97 (Jon W. Green & John W. Robinson, IV eds., 1998).

13. *See, e.g.,* Mems v. City of St. Paul, 224 F.3d 735, 740 (8th Cir. 2000); Chisholm v. United States Postal Serv., 665 F.2d 482, 495–96 (4th Cir. 1981).

14. *See* 41 C.F.R. § 60-3.4(D) (1978).

15. *Id.*

16. *See, e.g.,* Valentine v. City of Chicago, 452 F.3d 670, 677 (7th Cir. 2006).

17. *See, e.g.,* Freitag v. Ayers, 468 F.3d 528, 547 (9th Cir. Cal. 2006) (Expert witnesses testified regarding economic damages that plaintiff allegedly suffered as a result of harass-

at an appropriate punitive damages award. In one notable South Carolina case, the plaintiff's expert economist testified at trial regarding the amount of punitive damages that would "get the attention" of the defendant. On appeal, the defendant asserted that the expert's testimony invaded the province of the jury, which had awarded $1.5 million in punitive damages to the plaintiff. The South Carolina Supreme Court held that the trial court did not abuse its discretion in admitting the testimony because the expert, a professor of banking and finance with "extensive practical business experience," was well qualified and "did not tell the jury how much they should award in punitive damages."[18]

Occasionally, an expert may be able to offer information that is useful to the client, even if not directly related to the ultimate issue before the court. In one recent case, a Texas employee sued his employer under the Uniformed Services Employment and Reemployment Rights Act (USERRA), which prohibits employers from discriminating or harassing an employee because of his affiliation with the military. The employee designated an assistant professor at the Southern Illinois University School of Law with "experience with the military legal system" as an expert witness to testify about the employee's legal status and obligations as a member of the Texas Air National Guard, neither of which was disputed by the employer. The employer moved to exclude the expert's testimony on grounds that the expert did not qualify as an expert and that his testimony did not relate to facts at issue. The court disagreed. Relying on the expert's resume and publications, the court determined that the expert demonstrated "specialized knowledge of the military legal system." The court further noted that, although the expert did not classify himself as an expert on USERRA or private employer obligations under the statute, his extensive personal history with the military legal system qualified him as a witness capable of reliably explaining the employee's legal obligations while serving in the Texas Air National Guard and the consequences of noncompliance with military-service obligations. In addition, the court concluded that the expert's testimony was "relevant because it relates to facts that are of consequence."[19]

In another case, a physician-employee of a Kansas medical facility brought a whistleblower retaliation and defamation action against his

---

ment and retaliation inflicted on her by employer; plaintiff's treating psychiatrist testified regarding alleged noneconomic damages. The jury awarded $500,000 in economic damages and $100,000 in noneconomic damages.); Schwary v. Taylor Diving, Inc., Case No. 89-3948, 1991 U.S. Dist. LEXIS 9930 (E.D. La. July 16, 1991).

18. Cock-N-Bull Steak House v. Generali Ins. Co., 321 S.C. 1, 8 (1996).

19. Canamar v. McMillin Tex. Mgmt. Servs., LLC, Case No. SA-08-CV-0516 FB, 2009 U.S. Dist. LEXIS 68312 (W.D. Tex. Aug. 4, 2009).

employer. The employer had issued a report to a state medical board stating that the plaintiff had provided substandard care on several occasions. In opposition to the employer's motion for summary judgment, the plaintiff offered the deposition testimony of medical expert witnesses in an effort to demonstrate that his medical decisions on those occasions were sound. The employee reasoned that, because he had not deviated from the standard of care, the employer must have been motivated by "ill will toward plaintiff" when it declined to renew his contract. Although the court considered the plaintiff's expert testimony, it granted summary judgment to the employer.[20]

Although by no means an exhaustive list, other types of experts in discrimination, retaliation, or wrongful termination cases may include the following:

- Physicians;
- Vocational experts;
- Rehabilitation experts;
- Psychologists;
- Counselors;
- Sociologists;
- Actuaries;
- Demographic experts;
- Business management experts;
- Human resources management experts;
- Organizational development experts;
- Corporate culture experts;
- Education and training experts;
- Industry-specific experts (e.g., construction, trucking, corrections);
- Handwriting experts;
- Forensic computer experts; and
- International law experts.

Select the Best Expert

Homework Required

The criteria for selecting a particular expert in a discrimination, retaliation, or wrongful termination case will vary depending on the type of case, the cast of characters, the facts, the context, and the audience. The most important

---

20. D'Souza-Klamath v. Cloud County Health Ctr., Inc., Case No. 07-4031-KGS, 2009 U.S. Dist. LEXIS 27881 (D. Kan. Mar. 31, 2009).

factor in the selection of any expert witness is determining who is best able to tell or reinforce your client's story to the finder of fact. If the story is indeed only as good as the storyteller, the careful selection of the best person to tell your client's story is critical and will require time, effort, and planning on the part of counsel.

To that end, evaluating a list of qualifications on a curriculum vitae is only part of the process. While education, training, and experience are unquestionably important, gauging the credibility and appeal of an expert witness is equally necessary. Counsel should thoughtfully review the expert's background, experience with the particular type of case at issue, reputation, published works, previous testimony, and standing in the expert's field of expertise. Beyond the routine background information, there is no substitute for spending time talking with the expert—preferably in person—to get a sense of the expert's personality, character, credibility, and, ultimately, the expert's appeal to an arbitrator, judge, or jury.

Pros versus Joes

Invariably, attorneys wrestle with the choice between a professional expert witness and a witness with clear expertise in the desired subject matter, but with far less experience testifying in employment trials. In his book *Employment Trials: A Practical Guide*, Houston employment lawyer Kerry E. Notestine keenly observes as follows:

> Expert witnesses can be classified as either a professional expert who makes his living in whole or in part from testifying, or a nonprofessional expert who the lawyer convinces to testify in a particular case. There are advantages and disadvantages to both of these backgrounds for experts. If there is adequate time, it is usually preferable to locate an expert who is not a professional witness. These individuals tend to be more credible with juries and less subject to effective cross-examination from opposing counsel. However, there are advantages to the professional witness, such as, a track record of testifying in court, familiarity with the legal process, and familiarity with the law regarding the issue on which the expert is retained. Professional experts usually have been cross-examined many times and if there are significant problems in the person's background (such as a felony conviction for tax evasion), that probably would have been discovered previously. That may not be the case with someone who has not been through the process.[21]

---

21. KERRY E. NOTESTINE, EMPLOYMENT TRIALS: A PRACTICAL GUIDE 141–42 (Littler Mendelson, P.C. 2005).

In one race discrimination action in which I was involved, plaintiff's counsel retained an expert witness from a national litigation consulting firm to provide an opinion regarding the statistical significance of the racial composition of employees hired and terminated by the official's department. The expert had earned a doctoral degree (although not in statistics or statistical analysis), had a lengthy and impressive resume, had testified in numerous cases, and also required a significant advance retainer. In response, defense counsel purposefully retained an expert statistician, who, at first glance, appeared to stand in stark contrast to the professional expert hired by the plaintiff's counsel. The defense expert had a terminal degree in statistics, taught statistical methods and analysis to undergraduate and graduate-level students on a full-time basis, and had published a number of research journal articles regarding statistical analysis. As the result of a professional interest in the application of statistics to the law over a 30-year teaching career, the expert had been asked to provide expert testimony in federal court for several state and local governmental entities—specifically regarding the statistical impact of their hiring, discipline, and discharge policies and procedures in Title VII discrimination cases. Because she gave priority to her academic responsibilities, she did not advertise her services as a consultant or expert witness. When contacted to discuss her availability, she exhibited a professional, yet warm and personable, demeanor and was willing to spend the time necessary to understand the case and her role even before she was officially hired. Her advance retainer and hourly rate were a mere fraction of what the plaintiff's expert had charged. More importantly, the defense expert immediately discovered a significant error in the methodology employed by the plaintiff's expert. The case settled shortly after the deposition of the plaintiff's expert, in preparation for which the defense expert had been invaluable.

Each employment case is different, and a uniquely perfect storyteller may not always be available or necessary. Nevertheless, the identification and selection of the right expert is a vital part of telling or reinforcing your client's story.

Prepare the Expert

Preparing an expert witness to tell your client's story from the perspective of the learned professional necessarily involves much more than giving the expert witness the information the witness needs to prepare a report that is favorable to your client and then meeting with the witness months (or years) later to prepare for the expert's testimony at trial the following morning. Authentic preparation of an expert witness requires candor between the witness and the lawyer, full disclosure of any relevant information or documents that may affect, or alter, the expert's testimony, and a continuing dialogue with the expert as additional material facts are discovered during the litigation process. Authentic preparation begins before the expert is retained and, in many cases, continues after the verdict is reached.[22]

At the outset of the relationship between learned professional and counsel, the best expert witness will decline to blindly accept the hiring lawyer's version of the relevant facts. Throughout the case, the expert will challenge the respective inferences, assumptions, and interpretations of not only the employer and the employee, but also their counsel. Likewise, the expert will continue to examine—with counsel—whether his testimony is reasonable in the context and framework of all of the applicable facts and circumstances as well as whether the expert's testimony will withstand the inevitable scrutiny of his research, methodology, and conclusions.

A foundation of mutual trust, candor, and dialogue between the expert witness and counsel over the life of the case serves to enhance not only the actual nuts and bolts preparation for trial, but also the credibility and impact of the story. Authentic preparation helps an expert witness tell a story that rings true with the common experience of the jury and lets them see for themselves what really happened in the workplace.

Tell and Reinforce the Story at Trial

Put On a Show

To allow the judge or jury to see what happened from the perspective of the learned professional, your expert must be an effective teacher and communicator. One common trait of effective teachers and communicators is an ability to help their respective audiences understand and retain information. More often than not, this requires the expert, working in conjunction with counsel, to show as well as tell.

In a recent *National Law Journal* article, Dallas attorney and author Trey Cox discussed how science "supports the common sense conclusion that multimedia evidence makes a presentation more memorable."[23] One study measured the retention of information presented to focus groups during a 72-hour period—roughly the length of a short trial. The study compared the focus groups' ability to recall and understand information

---

22. Issues regarding the preparation of expert witnesses for deposition and trial are explored in greater detail in chapters 2, 3, 5, and 8.

23. Trey Cox, *The Courtroom as Short Attention Span Theater*, 31 Nat'l L.J.S2, Feb. 2, 2009.

presented through three distinct formats: (1) oral, (2) visual, and (3) oral and visual together. The method of presentation had a profound effect on the focus groups' retention:

> The group presented with information solely by oral means retained only 10 percent of the information. The group presented with information solely by visual means retained twice as much information, but still only 20 percent of the total material presented. Those who received the information both orally and visually retained 65 percent of the information presented.
>
> . . .
>
> The results reinforced the idea that individuals presented with both visual and oral information understand better and retain longer the information presented. In addition, showing the jury a diagram, chart or animation lends credibility to what is said by the lawyer or witness. Seeing is believing.
>
> Studies have shown that jurors are overwhelmed by the amount of information presented during a trial and easily become bored, confused and frustrated. . . . Evidence that is not presented in a format that jurors can easily digest is not likely to be remembered.[24]

The author concludes, "[A] trial lawyer's ability to persuade depends first and foremost on the jury's understanding of the evidence. No matter how much bluster occurs in the courtroom, trial attorneys are only heard when they deliver a message that juries can understand."[25]

Experienced courtroom veterans understand the simple concept that people believe what they can see. James W. Alford, a well-known South Carolina defense lawyer for nearly 50 years, loved to tell the story about a case in which an employee claimed that he had been hurt because of a defective ladder provided by his employer. Rather than simply tell the jury that the ladder was not defective, the defense lawyer delivered his entire closing argument from the third rung of the ladder, steadily bouncing up and down on the ladder as a point of emphasis. *People believe what they can see.*

While Cox's article and Alford's story understandably focus on the trial attorney, the same can certainly be said for the expert witness. Again, people believe what they can see. Asking the expert to tell the jury in plain, straightforward language what happened is important, but having the expert *show* the jury what happened is even more important and can be done through a wide variety of methods: photographs, charts, graphics, video,

---

24. *Id.*
25. *Id.*

audio, animation, or a combination of these. Having an experienced mountain climber tell you about scaling Mt. Everest will surely pale in comparison to having the expert show you how to climb the mountain while walking beside you to the summit.

To the extent that counsel is permitted to have the expert come down out of the witness chair, preferably at eye level with the jury, to demonstrate or explain key aspects of his testimony, or the basis for an opinion, so much the better. The best experts are those who are able to engage the jury and involve them in the story—just as if they had been there to witness the story for themselves.

Deal with Rejection

It is worth remembering that, even when the trial court declines to allow expert testimony on a given subject, counsel must proffer the expert's testimony to preserve the issue for appeal. For example, in a frequently cited discrimination case arising under the Fair Housing Act, the U.S. Court of Appeals for the Seventh Circuit reversed the trial court's exclusion of a professor of sociology at the University of Chicago who was offered by the plaintiff to testify regarding the history and patterns of housing discrimination in Chicago. The Seventh Circuit remanded the case for the trial court "to consider a new proffer" of the expert's testimony.[26]

Counsel should keep in mind that, while it is the court's function to ensure that expert witnesses are qualified and possess the requisite background, education, training, and experience, it is counsel's job to ensure that the court has all of the information it needs to properly qualify the expert and then, even if the court declines to do so, to proffer the witness's testimony to preserve the record for appeal.

Conclusion

As Kerry Notestine reminds us, "[e]xperts play important roles in employment trials but typically are not determinative of the merits of the case unless the case is a class action."[27] Nevertheless, an expert witness can be invaluable in telling your client's story. Ultimately, you want the judge or jury to believe your client's story, and an expert witness's testimony might be the deciding factor.

---

26. Tyus v. Urban Search Mgmt., 102 F.3d 256, 263 (7th Cir. 1996) (internal citations omitted).

27. Notestine, *supra* note 21, at 152.

EXPERTS IN BANKRUPTCY LITIGATION

Gary F. Seitz and Henry Flores[1]

The use of expert testimony has always been prevalent in bankruptcy cases and bankruptcy litigation, particularly the use of business valuation and financial experts in connection with a variety of topics, including business or asset valuation, solvency, adequate protection, confirmation, avoidance actions, and recharacterization of debt. In the past, issues of valuation in a bankruptcy case or adversary proceeding were regularly negotiated, compromised, and stipulated to; rarely did the parties actually litigate the issue of valuation. Times have changed. Issues of valuation, among other issues of expert opinion, are now hotly contested. Increasingly, hearings involving expert testimony are spread over weeks or months. Attorneys, financial advisors, turnaround managers, and experts on the valuation of businesses are becoming more sophisticated in the developing subdiscipline of valuing distressed businesses and other related issues that either require or effectively use expert testimony.

With these circumstances in mind, this subchapter (1) sets out a brief discussion of the application of *Daubert*[2] in bankruptcy litigation; (2) discusses cases that demonstrate interesting uses of expert valuation testimony to address substantive bankruptcy issues; (3) discusses special problems that arise under the federal rules when a bankruptcy litigant designates its financial advisor as a testifying expert; (4) provides a sample Q&A for an expert presenting an insolvency opinion for the plaintiff in a lawsuit seeking to avoid a preferential or fraudulent transfer; and (5) provides a sample proffer for a chapter 11 plan proponent presenting an opinion regarding the reorganization value of the post-confirmation debtor.

---

1. Gary F. Seitz is a partner in the Philadelphia office of Rawle & Henderson, LLP, whose practice areas include commercial bankruptcy, commercial litigation, and admiralty and maritime law. Henry Flores is a partner in the Houston office of Haynes and Boone, LLP, whose practice includes commercial bankruptcy and bankruptcy-related commercial litigation.
2. Daubert v. Merrell Dow Pharms., Inc., 509 U.S. 579 (1993).

Application of Daubert *in Bankruptcy Litigation*

As set forth in detail in chapter 6, in *Daubert* and *Kumho*, the U.S. Supreme Court held that expert testimony offered regarding scientific and nonscientific topics must meet rigorous standards of reliability and validity.[3] Bankruptcy courts have applied *Daubert* and *Kumho* to expert testimony presented in bankruptcy cases.[4]

In the bankruptcy setting, an instructive case is *Med Diversified*.[5] In *Med Diversified*, a litigation trust established under a chapter 11 plan sued various defendants to recover $7.5 million paid by the debtor as part of a failed stock purchase. The litigation trust alleged that the payment was a constructive fraudulent transfer or (alternatively) that the payment should be returned because the underlying agreement was unenforceable.[6]

To defend against the fraudulent transfer count, the defendants offered valuation testimony to establish that the debtor received reasonably equivalent value in exchange for the $7.5 million payment.[7] The proposed expert had more than 20 years' experience as an accountant, a liquidating agent, and a bankruptcy trustee, and in prosecuting avoidance actions.[8] The litigation trust filed a motion *in limine* seeking to exclude the expert's testimony on the ground that the proposed expert did not qualify as an expert regarding the valuation of shares of a privately held company in the relevant industry.[9] Notably, the bankruptcy court conducted a *three-day* evidentiary hearing during which the parties and the court conducted a voir dire examination of the defendants' expert.[10]

Citing the guidelines established by *Daubert* and later cases, the bankruptcy court undertook a two-part analysis. The court first considered whether the individual qualified as an expert based on training or experience. The court noted that the individual had no peer-granted certifications, no formal education or training in business valuation, and no real-world

---

3. *Daubert*, 509 U.S. 579; Kumho Tire Co., Ltd v. Carmichael, 526 U.S. 137 (1999).

4. *See, e.g.,* Chartwell Litig. Trust v. Addus Healthcare, Inc. (*In re* Med Diversified, Inc. II), 346 B.R. 621 (Bankr. E.D.N.Y. 2006). Chartwell Litig. Trust v. Addus Healthcare Inc. (*In re* Med Diversified, Inc. I), 334 B.R. 89 (Bankr. E.D.N.Y. 2005); Crisoma v. Parkway Mortgage, Inc. et al., 286 B.R. 604 (Bankr. E.D. Pa. 2002); *In re* Integrated Health Servs., Inc., et al., 289 B.R. 32 (Bankr. D. Del. 2003).

5. *Med Diversified, Inc. I*, 334 B.R. at 94.

6. *Id.*

7. *Id.* at 92.

8. *Id.* at 96–97.

9. *Id.* at 94.

10. *Id.*

experience that could overcome his lack of training.[11] The expert did not issue valuation reports as part of his professional activities, and he admitted that his report could not be considered a "certified business appraisal" because it did not meet uniform appraisal standards.[12] The court also noted that due to a prior engagement involving related parties, the court could infer that the expert either had a bias that would influence his opinion of the $7.5 million transaction, or he intentionally (and inexplicably) ignored relevant facts that he learned in the prior engagement.[13] Based on all of these circumstances, the bankruptcy court concluded that the individual did not qualify as an expert under Federal Rule of Evidence 702.

Notwithstanding the expert's qualifications, the bankruptcy court next considered whether the expert's *opinion* passed muster under Rule 702. Observing that the expert "showed a discernible measure of negligence" in his analysis, the court concluded that the opinion was flawed because the expert failed to consider the most reliable method for business valuation (discounted cash flow), failed to perform independent analysis of the data he used, applied an unexplained (and significant) discount in his analysis, and misused accounting information provided by the debtor.[14]

Based on the expert's lack of qualifications and lack of analytical rigor, the bankruptcy court partially granted the motion *in limine*, striking the report and precluding the expert from offering an opinion other than rebuttal testimony regarding the opposing expert's business valuation methodology.[15] But the *Med Diversified* story did not end there. In a later published opinion, the bankruptcy court considered *the defendant's* motion *in limine*, which sought an order barring the plaintiff's expert from offering testimony in support of the fraudulent transfer count.[16]

Once again applying *Daubert* standards, the court concluded that all three of the expert's valuation methodologies were flawed. In his discounted cash flow approach, the plaintiff's expert selected flawed revenue and expense variables, employed an unexplained high discount rate, and did not adequately explain his selected terminal value, control premium, and discount for marketability.[17] In his guideline company approach, the expert selected improper comparable companies, applied unexplained low multiples to reach value conclusions, and failed to normalize the data he used

---

11. *Id.* at 96.
12. *Id.*
13. *Id.* at 97–98.
14. *Id.* at 98–101.
15. *Id.* at 103–04.
16. *Med Diversified II*, 346 B.R. at 642–43.
17. *Id.* at 632–39.

when comparing comparables to his subject.[18] In his comparable transactions approach, the expert selected improper comparable transactions, excluded transactions that the court concluded were actually comparable, and again applied an unexplained high discount rate.[19] Based on these defects, the bankruptcy court concluded that the expert demonstrated "deliberate, manifest, pervasive and systematic bias" in applying valuation methodologies.[20] The court granted the defendants' motion *in limine* and precluded the expert from testifying.

Med Diversified tells a cautionary tale for litigants seeking to offer expert testimony in bankruptcy court. Bankruptcy litigants should carefully review the sufficiency of their expert testimony in light of *Daubert*. Failure to satisfy the *Daubert* standards may result in exclusion or rejection of the expert's testimony.[21]

Different Facets of Valuation Testimony in Bankruptcy Cases

When most lawyers think about experts in bankruptcy cases, they concentrate on the most common type of bankruptcy expert testimony—appraisal testimony. Although valuation is often a disputed issue in bankruptcy cases, it can arise in different litigation contexts. The following discussion describes three cases in which courts have considered expert valuation testimony to resolve three distinct bankruptcy disputes: (1) whether a plan proponent has met the best interests of creditors test under Bankruptcy Code section 1129(a)(7); (2) how to allocate asset sales proceeds when the bankruptcy court order approving the sale and the underlying transaction documents are silent; and (3) whether a debtor was insolvent at the time it made transfers that are later challenged in an avoidance action.

The Best Interests of Creditors Test

In *Global Ocean Carriers*, the debtors were international ship holding companies that owned 12 commercial vessels.[22] With the support of their secured lender and institutional noteholders, the debtors sought to confirm a

18. *Id.* at 640–41.
19. *Id.* at 641–42.
20. *Id.* at 642.
21. *See, e.g., Med Diversified II*, 346 B.R. at 621; *Med Diversified I*, 334 B.R. at 89; *In re Nellson Nutraceutical, Inc.*, 356 B.R. 364, 374 (Bankr. D. Del. 2006); *In re* Dow Corning Corp., 255 B.R. 445 (Bankr. E.D. Mich. 2000); *In re* Miniscribe Corp., 241 B.R. 729, 739–42 (Bankr. D. Colo. 1999); *In re* Dow Corning Corp, 237 B.R. 364 (Bankr. E.D. Mich. 1999).
22. *In re* Global Ocean Carriers, Ltd., 251 B.R. 31, 35 (Bankr. D. Del. 2000).

chapter 11 plan by cramdown over the objection of several individual note-holders. To demonstrate that the plan met the best interests of creditors test under Bankruptcy Code section 1129(a)(7), the debtors offered testimony from two experts to establish the value of the debtors' assets.[23] These experts testified that the debtors' vessels had a combined value in the range of $96.7 million (without charter agreements in place) and $104.7 million (with charter agreements in place).[24] With asset values in that range, the proposed 50 percent distribution to noteholders under the debtors' plan provided at least as much of a recovery as the noteholders would have received if the debtors were liquidated. In the debtors' view, their plan met the best interests of creditors test.

The primary dissenting noteholder did not offer competing expert testimony. Instead, the noteholder chose to attack certain assumptions and facts used by the debtors' experts:

- The experts did not consider several recent ship sales that reflected higher values for vessels that were similar to those owned by the debtors;
- The comparable sales data that the experts actually considered was stale;
- One comparable sale that the experts used was not a "sale" at all—the transaction did not close because the seller rejected the offer;
- The experts could not adequately explain numerous appraisals that were in the debtors' files that contradicted the experts' value conclusions; and
- The experts relied on information from the debtors that was factually inaccurate. On cross-examination, one of the experts admitted that correct data would have increased the value stated in his opinion.[25]

Based on the noteholder's successful challenge of the expert testimony, the bankruptcy court concluded that the debtors had not met their burden of proof under the best interests of creditors test.[26] After discussing other defects in the debtors' plan, the court denied plan confirmation.[27]

The best interests of creditors test is usually a straightforward point that plan proponents often address through simple proof—namely, by

---

23. Under the best interests of creditors test, each class of claims under a plan must either accept the plan *or* receive value under the plan that is at least as much as the class would receive in a chapter 7 liquidation. *See* 11 U.S.C. § 1129(a)(7).
24. *In re* Global Ocean Carriers, 251 B.R. at 35.
25. *Id.* at 43–45.
26. *Id.* at 46.
27. *Id.* at 50.

presenting evidence that compares a liquidation analysis prepared by the plan proponent (usually, the debtor) and its professionals with the proposed distributions under the plan. Cases like *Global Ocean Carriers* demonstrate that if a plan proponent offers expert testimony in support of plan confirmation under Bankruptcy Code section 1129, the expert should be prepared to present a thorough valuation case, and parties opposing the chapter 11 plan should be prepared to challenge the expert's work.

Allocation of Sales Proceeds after a Court-Approved Asset Sale

In *LTV Steel*, the debtor sold all of its assets (several steel plants, other related facilities, three railroad subsidiaries, and certain current assets) pursuant to bankruptcy court order, resulting in $80 million in sales proceeds.[28] Neither the sale order nor the underlying asset purchase agreement allocated the sales proceeds among the assets sold.[29] After the sale closed, a dispute regarding how to divide the sales proceeds arose among the creditors who asserted liens on the various assets. In essence, each creditor favored an allocation that considered the value of its collateral in a vacuum, without burdening the asset with significant, asset-specific environmental liabilities assumed by the buyer.[30]

In accordance with a provision of the sale order, the debtor submitted its own proposed allocation and asked the bankruptcy court to resolve the dispute. To support its proposed allocation, the debtor offered expert valuation testimony from a senior managing director of the investment banking firm that the debtor retained at the outset of the bankruptcy case.[31] The bankruptcy court first determined that the appropriate valuation standard is set out in Bankruptcy Code section 506(a), which (in pertinent part) provides that the value of a creditor's collateral "shall be determined in light of the purpose of the valuation and the proposed disposition or use of such property."[32] As the assets were sold as a going concern, the court concluded that the assets should be valued as a going concern with all environmental liabilities assumed by the buyer included in the valuation.[33] With this valuation approach in mind, the court described the evidence as follows:

> Many of the objectors' witnesses made appropriate and substantial criticisms of [the expert's] inputs, methodology, and conclusions. Nonetheless,

---

28. *In re* LTV Steel Co., Inc., 285 B.R. 259, 261 (Bankr. N.D. Ohio 2002).
29. *Id.*
30. *Id.* at 267.
31. *Id.*
32. 11 U.S.C. § 506(a).
33. *In re LTV Steel Co., Inc.*, 285 B.R. at 268–69.

[the expert's] testimony remained sufficient to carry the burden of proof and no competent, alternative going concern value was offered. Objectors spent significant time arguing that Debtor's allocation was unreasonable without offering persuasive evidence of going concern values. Most of objectors' witnesses' valuations either lacked analysis or failed to consider environmental liabilities. None made global going concern valuations, and few considered the concept at all. Thus [the expert's] conclusions carry the day in the absence of more persuasive evidence.[34]

The court then considered the expert's valuation opinion on an asset-by-asset basis. The expert relied on third-party appraisals, purchase offers, tax appraisals, income and expense data, past and future environmental costs associated with each site, commodity prices and other accounting information to derive a value for each asset. The court accepted the debtor's proposed value conclusions with two exceptions—with respect to two facilities, the debtor's expert failed to consider third-party purchase offers that reflected asset values that were higher than the values that the expert determined.[35] In those two circumstances, the court sided with the objecting creditors and assigned the higher value reflected in the bids.

LTV demonstrates that expert testimony can assist a bankruptcy court in addressing difficult allocation issues even when the expert does not perform a traditional asset valuation. *LTV* also shows that bankruptcy courts will not simply accept an expert's conclusion if there is credible and contemporaneous proof that contradicts the expert's work.

Insolvency and Reasonably Equivalent Value in Avoidance Actions

In a fraudulent transfer lawsuit, is the behavior of capital markets participants relevant to a determination of whether a debtor was insolvent or whether the debtor received reasonably equivalent value in exchange for a transfer? Some case law suggests that valuation experts should treat such information as relevant—and perhaps highly probative—depending on the facts of the case. Two instructive cases are *VFB* and *Iridium*.[36]

VFB involved a 1998 leveraged spin in which Campbell Soup Co. (Campbell) created a new subsidiary (Vlasic Foods International, Inc. or VFI), sold several underperforming food companies to VFI in exchange for $500 million in borrowed cash, and then issued VFI's stock to Campbell

---

34. *Id.* at 269.
35. *Id.* at 271, 274–75.
36. VFB, LLC v. Campbell Soup Co., 482 F.3d 624 (3d Cir. 2007); Iridium Operating, LLC v. Motorola, Inc., 373 B.R. 283 (Bankr. S.D.N.Y. 2007).

shareholders as an in-kind dividend.[37] After VFI failed and filed chapter 11 in early 2001, VFI assigned all of its claims against Campbell to VFB, LLC (VFB), a Delaware limited liability company whose members were VFI's unsecured creditors.[38] VFB sued Campbell seeking to set aside the leveraged spin transaction as a constructively fraudulent transfer.[39]

At trial, the parties disputed whether VFI received reasonably equivalent value in exchange for the $500 million that it paid for the food companies that it bought from Campbell (the Specialty Foods Division).[40] VFI stock price data during the relevant period reflected significant equity value in VFI, meaning that the investing public perceived that the Specialty Foods Division was worth more than the $500 million in debt that VFI incurred to acquire it.[41] Based on this data, the district court determined that the Specialty Foods Division was worth significantly more than $500 million when VFI bought the businesses.[42] The district court essentially disregarded the expert testimony presented by both VFB and Campbell, in favor of the contemporaneous market information.[43]

On appeal, the Third Circuit affirmed the district court's ruling. Regarding the district court's disposition of expert testimony, the Third Circuit noted the following:

> VFB makes additional arguments concerning its expert witnesses' valuations, urging that it was clear error to dismiss them in favor of the market figures, but we do not think that the district court erred in choosing to rely on the objective evidence from the public equity and debt markets. To the extent that the experts purport to measure actual post-spin performance, as by, for example, discounted cash flow analysis, to reconstruct a reasonable valuation of the company in light of uncertain future performance, they are using inapt tools.[44]

The bankruptcy court in *Iridium* applied the Third Circuit's reasoning in *VFB* to expert testimony offered not as part of a reasonably equivalent analysis, but as part of an *insolvency* analysis in a fraudulent transfer case. Iridium was a Motorola spin-off that developed satellite telephone technology.[45] Despite known limitations in the satellite technology, predictable

37. *VFB*, 482 F.3d at 626–27.
38. *Id.* at 628.
39. *Id.*
40. *Id.* at 629.
41. *Id.*
42. *Id.*
43. *Id.*
44. *Id.* at 633.
45. *Iridium*, 283 B.R. at 305.

service problems, and a limited potential customer base, Motorola successfully sold stock in Iridium through a private placement, and Iridium was
later able to raise substantial amounts of equity and debt in a series of public transactions.[46] After years of research and development, Iridium acti-
vated its phone service in November 1998.[47] By September 1999, Iridium
filed chapter 11 in response to an involuntary bankruptcy petition filed by
Iridium's creditors (Iridium's downfall was a "huge and embarrassing failure," according to the bankruptcy court).[48]

After Iridium filed chapter 11, the creditors committee sued Motorola,
seeking to set aside $3.7 billion in allegedly preferential and fraudulent
transfers.[49] By agreement of the parties, the trial was bifurcated, so that the
court would first consider whether the committee could establish that Iridium was insolvent or had unreasonably small capital during the four-year
window in which the transfers occurred.[50]

To demonstrate that Iridium was insolvent during the relevant period,
the committee presented two experts who considered several generally accepted valuation methodologies but determined that the discounted cash
flow approach was the only appropriate method to value Iridium's business.[51] To perform the discounted cash flow analysis, the committee's
experts developed their own set of financial projections, based on the assumption that Iridium's contemporaneous projections were unreasonable
and that contemporaneous analyses by Iridium, investment bankers, accountants, lenders, and others included "illogical and unreasonable
assumptions."[52] The committee's experts also determined that Iridium had
unreasonably small capital during the relevant period, based on an internal
rate of return that the experts calculated by using the same projections that
they used in the discounted cash flow analysis.[53]

In response, Motorola also presented two experts. The first expert was a
Stanford finance professor who determined that Iridium was solvent at the
time of the transfers by analyzing the behavior of market participants during the relevant period.[54] The second expert was a valuation professional
who determined that Iridium was solvent at the time of the transfers by performing a discounted cash flow analysis that included Iridium's projections

---

46. *Id.* at 305, 320–28.
47. *Id.* at 290.
48. *Id.*
49. *Id.*
50. *Id.*
51. *Id.* at 339.
52. *Id.* at 340.
53. *Id.*
54. *Id.* at 337.

as a starting point and by analyzing contemporaneous private equity invest-ments in Iridium, third-party valuations, extensions of credit to Iridium, Iridium's stock price, and similar information for Iridium's competitors.[55]

The bankruptcy court adopted Motorola's approach. The court deter-mined that the committee's expert analysis was "unreliable" because it failed to consider the following facts and circumstances during the relevant four-year window:

- Iridium's market capitalization;
- Iridium's projections of future cash flows;
- The behavior of analysts, investors, and lenders—sophisticated people believed in Iridium's future and acted accordingly during the relevant time;
- The unqualified opinions issued by Iridium's auditors; and
- Due diligence by several prominent investment banking firms and large accounting firms during Iridium's debt and equity transactions.[56]

The court also made a series of findings regarding the expert's report: the work was "suspect" because it ignored or wrongly discarded Iridium's projections; the expert created his own projections for litigation purposes; the expert's sole reliance on the discounted cash flow method "substantially diminished" the weight of the expert's opinion, as did the expert's "con-scious disregard" of contemporaneous market data; and the expert's opin-ion did not correlate "with the market validation of Iridium's business plan and the value attributed to the business during the relevant period."[57]

Based on its conclusions regarding the committee's expert testimony, the bankruptcy court found that the committee failed to meet its burden of proof on insolvency and the preferential and fraudulent transfer counts of the committee's lawsuit.[58] For valuation experts, one closing thought from the Iridium opinion stands out:

> The fact that Iridium failed in such a spectacular fashion stands out as a disturbing counterpoint to the market's optimistic predictions of present and future value for Iridium, but in the end, the market evidence could not be denied. The capital markets synthesized and distilled what all the smart people of the era knew or believed to be true about Iridium. *Given the overwhelming weight of that market evidence, it may be that the bur-den of proving insolvency and unreasonably small capital simply could not be met under any circumstances, regardless of the evidence adduced, in the*

55. *Id.* at 337–39.
56. *Id.* at 339, 351.
57. *Id.* at 351.
58. *Id.* at 352.

wake of the Third Circuit's VFB decision, an influential case that has helped to illuminate the proper way to resolve the valuation questions presented here.[59]

Whether working for the plaintiff or the defendant in a fraudulent transfer engagement, the lesson for experts from cases like *VFB* and *Iridium* is clear—as part of any valuation analysis, the expert should consider any equity or debt transactions that the debtor engaged in during the relevant time period, the behavior of market participants and analysts with respect to the debtor, any data regarding the perceived equity value of the debtor, and publicly available data regarding competitors. While the expert might ultimately *reject* this information as a basis to determine insolvency or reasonably equivalent value, the failure to *consider* the information might implicate the admissibility or weight of the expert's testimony.

Financial Advisors Designated as Testifying Experts

When a witness will present expert opinion testimony under Federal Rule of Evidence 702, Federal Rule of Civil Procedure 26(a)(2) requires (among other information) the disclosure of all data considered by the witness in forming his opinion(s). With respect to main case bankruptcy litigation, Federal Rule of Bankruptcy Procedure 9014 provides that the initial disclosure requirements of Rule 26 do not apply in bankruptcy *contested matters* unless the court orders otherwise. Accordingly, why should a bankruptcy lawyer be concerned about the requirements of Rule 26(a)(2)? There are at least three practical responses to this question.

First, notwithstanding Federal Rule of Bankruptcy Procedure 9014(c), bankruptcy courts occasionally require expert disclosures in contested matters even in the absence of a local rule that renders Rule 26 applicable.[60] Accordingly, bankruptcy litigants should learn the local practice regarding expert disclosures in contested matters. Second, Rule 26(a)(2) applies in bankruptcy adversary proceedings (subject to possible limitation by local rule). The third reason is the main point of this section—the unique way in which bankruptcy lawyers and litigants often use financial advisors creates special challenges under Rule 26(a)(2).

---

59. *Id.* (emphasis added).

60. *See, e.g., In re* Puig, Inc., 398 B.R. 69 (Bankr. S.D. Fla. 2008) (requiring expert disclosures under Rule 26(a) in the context of a motion to substantively consolidate 13 related debtors).

In bankruptcy cases, debtors, committees, lenders, and trustees often retain financial advisors who take on multiple roles in the bankruptcy case. These financial advisors perform a variety of tasks, including the development or critique of business plans, the review of the debtor's operations and financial performance, and development of bankruptcy exit strategies. When litigation arises during the bankruptcy case, attorneys often call on the financial advisor to present opinion testimony to support a litigation position. In that context, the designation of the financial advisor as a testifying expert might waive any privilege or work product protection that attaches to communications or information that passes between the financial advisor, the attorney, and the client. This problem can arise in bankruptcy contested matters, in adversary proceedings, and in nonbankruptcy litigation involving the bankruptcy estate.

The *Tri-State Outdoor Media Group, Inc.* case shows the potential pitfalls that can arise when a bankruptcy litigant designates its financial advisor as a testifying expert.[61] In *Tri-State*, a group of bondholders formed an ad hoc committee after Tri-State failed to make a semiannual payment on the bonds. The ad hoc committee retained a law firm, and the law firm hired a financial advisor to assist the ad hoc committee. The engagement letter between the parties stated that the financial advisory firm would assist "in connection with the . . . analysis, consideration and possible formulation of potential financial restructuring options" for Tri-State.[62] When the negotiations between the debtor and the ad hoc committee failed, the ad hoc committee filed an involuntary bankruptcy petition against Tri-State. After Tri-State converted the case to a voluntary chapter 11, the U.S. Trustee appointed an official committee of unsecured creditors (the Official Committee) that generally included the members of the ad hoc committee. With bankruptcy court approval, the Official Committee hired the same financial advisory firm that the ad hoc committee retained before bankruptcy, and the parties did not execute a new engagement letter.[63]

Tri-State filed motions seeking an extension of the debtor's exclusive period for filing a chapter 11 plan and the deadline to assume or reject leases. The Official Committee objected to the motions and designated a representative of the financial advisory firm as an expert who would testify at the hearing on the motions. During the expert's deposition, Tri-State's lawyers asked questions about the financial advisory firm's work on prebankruptcy restructuring issues, including the ad hoc committee's decision to file an

---

61. *In re* Tri-State Outdoor Media Group, Inc., 283 B.R. 358 (Bankr. M.D. Ga. 2002).
62. *Id.* at 361.
63. *Id.*

involuntary bankruptcy petition against Tri-State. The lawyer for the Official Committee objected to the questions on attorney-client privilege and work product grounds.[64] During discovery, the Official Committee also produced a privilege log that identified certain documents provided to or by the financial advisory firm. Tri-State filed a motion seeking an order compelling the firm to respond to the deposition questions and compelling production of documents listed on the privilege log that were provided by or to the firm.[65]

In the motion to compel, Tri-State argued that the discovery sought reflected business (as opposed to legal) advice that was not protected by the attorney-client privilege or the work product doctrine.[66] Alternatively, Tri-State argued that even if the discovery sought was subject to a claim of privilege or work product, the Official Committee opened the door to discovery of the information by opposing Tri-State's motions and further waived any protection by designating a representative of the financial advisory firm as a testifying expert. In response, the Official Committee argued that the attorney-client privilege applied because the financial advisory firm was a third-party agent retained by counsel to assist in rendering legal advice; that the discovery sought was subject to work product protection because counsel retained the advisory firm in anticipation of bankruptcy; and that even if the Official Committee waived protection for the information by submitting its expert designation, the waiver only related to the proposed subject of the expert's testimony—valuation.[67]

The bankruptcy court first determined that the firm's advice to the ad hoc committee was subject to the attorney-client privilege and that the documents listed on the privilege log were subject to work product protection.[68] Based on the expert disclosure requirements of Federal Rule of Civil Procedure 26(a)(2) and related case law, however, the court concluded that the Official Committee waived any privilege or work product protection for the information sought. The court analyzed each deposition objection and challenged the privilege log item individually and ordered the firm and the Official Committee to disclose the following information (among other matters):

- Any communications with or information given to or by the testifying expert;

---

64. *Id.*
65. *Id.* at 360.
66. *Id.* at 361–62.
67. *Id.* at 362.
68. *Id.* at 363–64.

- Any recommendation regarding whether to file an involuntary bankruptcy petition against Tri-State. The court reasoned that such a recommendation would be considered an opinion *or* a basis for the expert's opinion regarding valuation;
- Any recommendation regarding the filing of a chapter 11 plan that would include a valuation of Tri-State; and
- Any documents reflecting work performed by other firm personnel working on the case for the testifying expert.[69]

Could the Official Committee in *Tri-Star* have preserved privilege and work product protection for its communications with its financial advisor? Case law suggests that a testifying expert can also serve as a consultant for counsel without creating a waiver of work product protection for material provided to or by the expert in his consulting capacity.[70] However, based on the requirements of Rule 26(a)(2)(B), any ambiguity about the role the consultant was fulfilling when reviewing or creating material will be resolved in favor of the party seeking discovery.[71]

The cases do not set out a laundry list of steps that counsel can take to either (1) preserve a privilege or protect work product when using a testifying expert in a consulting role, or (2) seek additional disclosure when an opponent designates a financial advisor acting in dual roles as a testifying expert. However, the cases suggest a few issues for counsel to consider.

- Does the engagement letter clearly separate the tasks that the professional will undertake in its expert role from the tasks that it will perform in its consulting capacity?[72]

---

69. *Id.* at 365–66.
70. *See, e.g.,* W.R. Grace & Co. v. Zotos Int'l, Inc., No. 98-CV-838S(F), 2000 WL 1843258 (W.D.N.Y. Nov. 2, 2000) (protecting from disclosure materials produced in the expert's separate capacity as a consultant retained to analyze the opponent's expert report and assist counsel with preparations for depositions and trial); B.C.F. Oil Ref., Inc. v. Consol. Edison Co. of New York, Inc., 171 F.R.D. 57, 62 (S.D.N.Y. 1997) (protecting from disclosure materials produced in the expert's separate capacity as a "technical consultant" retained to assist in depositions, formulate discovery requests, and perform other similar tasks); *see also* Detwiler Trust v. Offenbecher, 124 F.R.D. 545, 546 (S.D.N.Y. 1989) (decided before a 1993 amendment that expanded the scope of Rule 26(a)(2); protecting from disclosure materials produced in the expert's separate capacity as a consultant retained to assist in trial preparation and in preparing for depositions of witnesses regarding financial and valuation matters).
71. *See, e.g., B.C.F. Oil,* 171 F.R.D. at 62.
72. *W.R. Grace,* 2000 WL 1843258 at *6–7.

- Do the professional's invoices differentiate between tasks performed in the expert capacity and tasks performed in the consulting capacity?[73]
- Are the same professionals providing services in both expert and consulting capacities?[74]
- Do the consulting services and the expert analysis relate to different subject matters?[75]

None of the factors appear to be controlling under the case law. The careful bankruptcy practitioner should consider all the facts when designating a financial advisor as a testifying expert or when seeking disclosure from such an expert under Rule 26(a)(2).

The scope of required disclosures for financial advisor experts will be limited in the future by an amendment to Rule 26(b)(4) that will extend work product protection to all communications between an attorney and a testifying expert *except* those communications that (1) relate to the expert's compensation, (2) identify facts or data provided by the attorney and considered by the expert in forming an opinion, or (3) identify assumptions provided by the attorney.[76] Even after the amendment is implemented, bankruptcy lawyers should work carefully with financial advisors who will testify as experts. Based on the volume and type of information that often flows between bankruptcy lawyers and financial advisors, a bankruptcy lawyer operating under the amended rule might find himself in the uncomfortable position of having to prove a negative—namely, proving that a particular discussion or document did not convey facts or assumptions that underlie the expert's opinions. For example, if the financial advisor will testify about enterprise value, where do you draw the line establishing what communications conveyed facts and assumptions that are included in the expert's opinion? Even the amended Rule 26 could cast a wide net in that circumstance.

---

73. *Id.*

74. *See, e.g.,* Romala Stone, Inc. v. Home Depot U.S.A., Inc., No 1-04-CV 02307-RWS, 2008 WL 4377445 (N.D. Ga. Sept. 19, 2008).

75. *See Romala,* 2008 WL 4377445 at *4 (noting that the consulting services "directly related to the same issues" for which the plaintiff later designated the consultant as an expert); *see also* S.E.C. v. Reyes, 2007 WL 963442 (N.D. Cal. Mar. 30, 2007).

76. The amended Rule 26 will take effect on December 1, 2010. *See* http://www.us courts.gov/RulesAndPolicies/FederalRulemaking/PendingRules.aspx.; *supra* "Privilege Issues" in chapter 2.

Practical Pointers: Sample Expert Witness Outline and Expert Proffer

The facts of specific cases will affect the content and order of witness examination, and interrogation styles differ. Notwithstanding these circumstances, it can be useful to consult prior outlines of expert witness testimony when developing a direct or cross-examination of an expert witness. Further, given the widespread use of proffers for the presentation of direct testimony in bankruptcy court, it can be useful to consult sample proffers as well. A sample of each follows.

Sample Q&A for Plaintiff's Insolvency Expert

The following sample Q&A demonstrates one possible approach for a direct examination of an expert offering an insolvency opinion for the plaintiff in a lawsuit seeking to avoid a preferential or fraudulent transfer.

Qualifications

- Q. Please state your name.
- Q. Mr. _____, you are here today to provide the benefit of your expertise in the field of accounting and valuation of operating businesses, are you not?
- Q. Mr. _____, would you tell the court what university degrees you have received?
- Q. Did you receive any special honors in your field of study during your university training?
- Q. What is your field of specialty in your professional life?
- Q. You say you are a partner, of what firm or association?
- Q. How long have you held that position?
- Q. Have you authored any articles or books in your field of specialty?
- Q. Could you identify any books you have written?
- Q. You are also the author or coauthor of many articles and annotations on business valuation, are you not?
- Q. Have you written any articles regarding fraud accounting [or other valuation subjects]?
- Q. Have any of those articles been published?
- Q. What publications have published your articles?
- Q. Are you also a lecturer and guest speaker on accounting subjects?
- Q. Do you serve on professional committees in the accounting area?

Valuation Principles

Q. Well, then, could you tell me some of the guiding principles for valuations of retail businesses?

Q. Do you do these three things in every case?

Q. What actual work experience have you had applying those principles?

Professional Resumé

Q. Your Honor, I have marked as Plaintiff's Exhibit _____ a copy of the witness's professional resume, which includes as an attachment the list the witness mentioned, and would offer it into evidence.

Q. Have you testified in court before as an expert?

Q. On more than one occasion?

Q. Does your resume, now in evidence as Plaintiff's Exhibit _____, contain any information regarding your appearances as an expert?

Q. Could you point that out?

Q. I note that most of these relate to valuations of operating a business, is that right?

A. Yes.

Q. Have you also testified regarding solvency issues?

A. Yes, I have. Those occasions are also shown on the attachment. I have testified on _____ prior occasions on issues regarding the solvency or insolvency of a business, and each of those have been in bankruptcy courts.

Materials Reviewed

Q. Have you had an opportunity to review any materials or information relating to the valuation of the business of _____, the debtor in this case?

A. Yes, I have.

Q. Could you generally describe those materials or information that you have reviewed?

A. Well, I looked at all of the financial statements, cash flow statements, consolidated financials, and internal reports that were generated by the debtor for the period of _____ [date] to _____ [date]. I have also reviewed all of the operating reports the debtor has filed subsequent to the petition. I have conducted interviews with three of the debtor's officers—in particular, the president, chief financial officer, and chief of sales. I have also reviewed the

disclosure statement and plan that the debtor has proposed, together with the order approving that plan.

Q. What sort of valuation principles have you applied to these materials?

A. I have not used the factors I mentioned. Since the court has approved the plan and disclosure statement in this case, I took the
information provided in or as attachments to those documents as
true. I also assumed that the information provided in the operating
reports filed with the court was true. However, I did conduct an independent verification of the accuracy of the pre-petition financial
information to the extent possible so far after the fact. I compared
the debtor's financial statements during the year before filing with
the proofs of claim filed in this case, and for purposes of this comparison, I assumed the proofs of claim were true. All of the debtor's
real estate and tangible assets were covered by appraisals that were
included in the disclosure statement. I contacted the appraisers
who did that work and verified with them that their statements regarding the changes in value over the year before the petition were
based on actual sales comparisons or generally accepted databases
and public information. I therefore accepted those estimates of
value changes as true. I then prepared charts extrapolating all of
the debtor's assets and liabilities as they existed on the date of one
year before the petition. I then adjusted those figures, again using
the debtor's own records and the other sources I had verified, to
determine the debtor's financial condition during the period of
_____ *[date]* to _____ *[date]*.

Q. What time periods were covered in the information you reviewed?

A. The information I reviewed covered altogether a period commenc-
ing on _____ *[date]* through and including _____ *[date]*.

Q. Have you had any especially relevant experience or training that
bears on the solvency or insolvency of this debtor?

Q. Your honor, I move that Mr. _____ be permitted to testify as an
expert in the fields of business valuation and the issue of the debt-
or's solvency or insolvency at the time of the transfers complained
of in this case. [Note: The convention of formally asking the court
to recognize the witness as an expert varies from jurisdiction to
jurisdiction.]

Opinion on Insolvency

Q. Mr. _____, do you have an opinion on the solvency or insolvency of the debtor on _____ *[date]* and the periods of time

immediately preceding and following that date for a period of two weeks on either side?

A. Yes, I do.

Q. What is that opinion?

A. Based on the factors I described earlier, my interviews, verifications, and my review of the materials I itemized, my opinion is that, on a test of the fair value of the debtor's assets less the outstanding liabilities, this debtor was insolvent during the entire period.

Q. Okay, let's take this one asset at a time. What assets did you review?

Q. Is the sort of information provided by the _____, on which you relied for your comparison here, the type of information on which valuation and solvency experts generally rely when determining problems of solvency?

Q. Did you reach any conclusion regarding _____?

Q. What was that conclusion?

Q. Could you explain the basis for this conclusion?

[Begin putting figures on a whiteboard.]

Q. You have described the steps you took to verify the debts and obligations of this company. Did you discover any discrepancies between the liabilities shown on the debtor's records and financial statements during the period of _____ *[date]* to _____ *[date]* and the actual liabilities as you were able to verify them?

Q. Could you relate that conclusion to whether the debtor was insolvent in the balance sheet sense?

A. On a balance-sheet basis, with fair valuation of the debtor's assets, it was insolvent during the period of time covered by this exhibit.

Sample Expert Proffer for Debtor's Expert on Reorganization Value

The following sample proffer demonstrates one possible approach for a direct examination of an expert offering an opinion regarding the value of a reorganized debtor after confirmation of a chapter 11 plan.

Introduction

If called to testify, I would state as follows:

1. My name is _____. I am a managing director of the firm ABC Consulting ("ABC Consulting" or the "Firm"), which is a financial advisory and consulting firm that maintains offices at _____.

2. The statements made and conclusions and/or opinions presented in this proffer are based on my personal knowledge and experience.

3. _____ (the "Debtor") retained ABC Consulting pursuant to an order of this court dated _____ as the Debtor's financial advisor and investment banker.

4. This testimony is offered in support of the confirmation of the Debtor's Plan of Reorganization dated _____ (the "Plan"). At the request of the Debtor, I am providing expert testimony through this proffer regarding the reorganization value of the reorganized Debtor on a going-concern basis.

Background and Information regarding ABC Consulting Group, LLC

5. ABC Consulting is an investment banking, restructuring, and management consulting firm. ABC Consulting has extensive experience working with financially troubled companies in complex financial restructurings both out-of-court and during chapter 11 cases. ABC Consulting and/or its professionals have provided advisory services to dozens of debtors, including _____.

Background of [Expert Witness]

6. I received a bachelor's degree in _____ from _____, and a Masters of Business Administration in _____ from _____. I am a Series 7 and 63 qualified registered general securities representative. [*list other degrees, licenses or certifications*]

7. Before my employment with ABC Consulting began in _____, I was employed by _____ [*describe relevant experience*].

8. At ABC Consulting, I have been involved in numerous bankruptcy cases and out-of-court restructuring engagements. In the past, I have led the reorganization efforts as financial advisor in the following chapter 11 cases: _____. I am currently leading the restructuring efforts for _____ in its chapter 11 case.

9. My work at ABC Consulting has focused on bankruptcy and other restructuring situations for various constituencies, including debtors, creditors committees, and lenders. The scope of this work includes the review of debtors' operations, review and development of business plans, review and assistance in the preparation and/or compilation of liquidation analyses, negotiations with creditors, assistance in valuations and determining ranges of debt capacity and potential capital structures, advice on mergers and acquisitions, and review of other bankruptcy-related issues, including assistance to debtors in obtaining

financing necessary for debtors to operate in and emerge from bank-ruptcy.

10. I have been prepared as an expert witness and/or given testimony in the following cases with respect to asset sales, asset values, financing struc-tures, liquidation analyses, and plan confirmation issues: _____. In those cases, my testimony was presented through live testimony, by proffer, or offered through a decla-ration.

Sources of Information

11. With other personnel from ABC Consulting, I have conducted due diligence to develop the valuation estimate (on a going-concern basis) of the reorganized Debtor. I did not rely solely on any single item of information to the exclusion of other information. However, I generally considered the following sources of information: [List information con-sidered. *See* Fed. R. Civ. P. 26(a)(2)].

12. I considered the information described above for the purposes of prepar-ing my valuation analysis, without independent verification of the accu-racy and completeness of this information. With respect to the Debtor's financial projections, I assumed that they have been reasonably prepared by management based on the best currently available estimates and judg-ments of future performance. I also assumed that the Plan will be imple-mented substantially as proposed by management. I have not made any independent valuation or appraisal of the assets or liabilities of the Debtor, and I have relied on management's opinions with respect to those values. My valuation analysis is necessarily based on economic, market, and other conditions in effect on, and the information made available to me as of, the date of the analysis.

Opinion regarding the Debtor's Reorganization Value

13. Based on the summary below and the analysis and data set forth in de-tail in the disclosure statement, I estimate that the reorganized enter-prise value of the Debtor is approximately $_____, based on a range of valuation (using different valuation techniques) of $____ to $____.

14. I used a variety of methods in assessing the reorganization valuation of the Debtor, which methods were dependent on the financial forecasts and the business plan prepared by management.

15. After considering a number of ways to value the Debtor, I concluded, based on the available information, that the best methods of valuing the Debtor were the discounted cash flow (DCF) method and the compa-

rable company method. Both of these methods are generally accepted in the valuation field.

16. [*Describe omitted valuation methods and basis for omission*]

17. In a DCF analysis, the cash to be produced by a company over a period of time and the company's value at the end of that period are forecasted. These amounts are then discounted back to the present using a discount rate that reflects the risk associated with the company. The cash flows used are the net cash flows projected to be produced after taking into account capital expenditures, changes in working capital and non-cash income statement items such as depreciation. The terminal value of the company can be estimated in several different ways, but the most commonly used method is to use a multiple of the company's projected earnings before interest, taxes, depreciation, and amortization ("EBITDA").

18. In performing the DCF analysis, I used inputs that I considered reasonable based on the Debtor's business plan, anticipated capital structure, and the valuations of comparable companies and applied them to the Debtor's projections. Specifically, I used projections prepared from _____ [date range], a discount rate in the range of __ percent to __ percent and an EBITDA multiple range of _____ against projected _____ [*year*] results. This exit multiple was largely based on the market valuations of comparable companies today, including the following entities: _____. The discount rate range employed is based on the Debtor's estimated weighted average cost of capital ("WACC"). This produced an enterprise value range of $___ to $___.

19. Comparable company analysis compares a company's financial statistics to those of other similar companies and values the company by analogy to those companies. This method is especially useful for valuing a publicly traded company, since the valuation is explicitly based on other public companies. However, since the Debtor is not publicly traded, a liquidity discount is applied to the selected multiple. This is a generally accepted approach in the valuation field.

20. Two of the most common techniques of comparable company analysis are price/earnings multiples and enterprise value to EBITDA multiple. Price/earnings multiples value the equity of a company based on reported earnings. This method of valuing public companies is very widely used and easily applied and understood. On the other hand, it can be distorted by the different capital structures or accounting methods used by those companies. For this reason, many financial professionals prefer to analyze companies on the basis of enterprise value (i.e., the sum of market value of equity plus net debt plus preferred stock) to EBITDA, as this largely eliminates those distortions.

21. The public companies most comparable to the Debtor include
_____. While these companies' business plans are not identi-
cal to the Debtor's business plan, they are the most similar. [*Explain
similarities or other characteristics that justify selection*]

22. For the EBITDA valuation, a multiple of EBITDA for the comparable
companies was applied to the Debtor's EBITDA projections from
_____ [*date range*]. Specifically, a multiple range of _____ times
EBITDA was used. After applying a liquidity discount, this produced
an enterprise value range of $_____ to $_____.

23. I based my opinion of the reorganization value of the reorganized
Debtor on a number of assumptions, including (but not limited to) a
successful reorganization of the business and finances in a timely manner, the implementation of the business plan, the achievement of the
forecasts reflected in the business plan, access to adequate exit financing, market conditions as of _____ [*date*], continuing through the
assumed effective date of the Plan, no material adverse change to the
economy, the Debtor's industry or the Debtor, and the Plan becoming
effective in accordance with the estimates and other assumptions discussed in the plan and disclosure statement.

FDA AND REGULATORY EXPERTS

Seth D. Rothman and Jessica S. Studness[1]

As the federal agency that regulates prescription medicines and the companies that develop them, the Food & Drug Administration (FDA) oversees virtually all aspects of drug development and marketing. Pharmaceutical litigation typically features regulatory experts who testify about a drug manufacturer's interactions with the FDA. This subchapter discusses the challenges involved in retaining and using an FDA regulatory expert.

The Role of the FDA Expert

In a typical personal injury case, the FDA regulatory expert fills two important roles. First, the FDA regulatory expert is often the witness who explains to the jury the process for developing a new drug and bringing it to market. Second, the FDA regulatory expert may be asked to opine on key issues in the case such as whether the company tested the drug properly, whether the labeling was adequate, or whether the drug was marketed in a fair and balanced way.

The battle between the opposing regulatory experts often centers on the FDA's decision to approve the drug for marketing. Typically, the plaintiff's expert seeks to downplay or challenge that decision, while the defendant's expert rushes to embrace it. For example, the plaintiff's expert may claim that the defendant withheld information from the agency or that the agency lacked the resources to make a proper decision. The defendant's expert may emphasize the FDA's oversight of the new drug development process and the significance of its finding that the drug is safe and effective when used in accordance with its approved labeling.

---

1. Mr. Rothman is a partner and Ms. Studness is an associate at Hughes Hubbard & Reed LLP in New York. The authors would like to thank William F. Hennessey, 2nd, for his assistance in the preparation of this subchapter.

What FDA Experts Can and Cannot Do

Like all experts, FDA regulatory experts may assist the jury to understand the evidence or to determine a fact in issue.[2] In practice, courts generally permit regulatory experts leeway to describe the FDA, the new drug development process, and the labeling process. Regulatory experts may also give context to company and FDA actions and opine on the propriety of those actions. There are, however, two areas where courts have restricted regulatory expert testimony.

Testifying about the Law

The first issue arises when a regulatory expert is asked to testify about the FDA regulations and whether the defendant has complied with them. Some courts have allowed FDA regulatory experts to testify about the "regulations governing the approval, labeling, advertising and marketing of pharmaceutical and medical products" and whether a pharmaceutical company has complied with them,[3] while others have not.[4] Courts have prohibited testimony that interprets FDA regulations in a way that "runs contrary to

---

2. FED. R. EVID. 702; *In re* Fosamax Prods. Liab. Litig., 645 F. Supp. 2d 164, 191 (S.D.N.Y. 2009) (allowing expert testimony because a "lay jury cannot be expected to understand the complex regulatory framework that informs the standard of care in the pharmaceutical industry"); *see also* Strong v. Am. Cyanamid, 261 S.W.3d 493, 515 (Mo. Ct. App. 2008) (expert allowed "to testify about the meaning of the regulations given their technical and scientific nature").

3. *In re* Guidant Corp. Implantable Defibrillators Prods. Liab. Litig., Nos. 06-25, 05-2596, 2007 WL 1964337 at *7 (D. Minn. June 29, 2007) (allowing expert to testify about "compliance with FDA regulations and guidelines"); American Home Assurance Co. v. Merck & Co., 462 F. Supp. 2d 435, 451 (S.D.N.Y. 2006) (allowing expert testimony that "concerns the proper interpretation of generally applicable biological licensing FDA regulations, as well as drug product salvaging regulations").

4. *See, e.g.,* United States v. Caputo, 517 F.3d 935, 942 (7th Cir. 2008) (expert cannot testify about the meaning of FDA statutes and regulations because this is "a subject for the court, not for testimonial experts"); Steele v. Depuy Orthopaedics, Inc., 295 F. Supp. 2d 439, 446 (D.N.J. 2003) (declining to consider expert's affidavit because it was "replete with recitations and legal interpretations of FDA regulations regarding medical devices" and finding the issue of "whether the FDA's approval of a PMA supplement imposes requirements on a particular device [to be] a question of law to be determined by the Court, not a question of fact for the jury"); Smith v. Wyeth-Ayerst Lab. Co., 278 F. Supp. 2d 684, 702 (W.D.N.C. 2003) (prohibiting expert from providing opinion testimony about defendant's "compliance or alleged lack thereof" with FDA labeling requirements because "such testimony would infringe upon the jury's role in determining an ultimate issue in the case").

controlling law as reflected in [the] regulations,"[5] tells the jury that a defendant acted or did not act illegally,[6] opines on whether a company "violated" the conditions of approval for a drug or medical device,[7] or otherwise usurps the court's role as the sole arbiter of the law.[8]

This area of the law is still developing, and it can be difficult to predict where the lines will be drawn. In practice, a lot may depend on the individual judge. In the Vioxx litigation, for example, one judge ruled that whether the company could have changed its label under the Changes-Being-Effected (CBE) regulation was a question of fact that was properly the subject of expert testimony, while another judge ruled that it was a question of law for the court to decide.[9]

Interpreting Company Documents and Inferring Intent

The second issue arises when the regulatory expert—usually the plaintiff's expert—is asked to comment on the defendant's internal documents and e-mails. An FDA expert may explain the regulatory context of an e-mail and the meaning of certain jargon but may not ascribe an intent or motive to the e-mail's author. Testimony about intent runs afoul of the Federal Rule of Evidence 702 requirement that expert testimony must assist the trier of fact, because intent is a lay matter that the jury can understand on its own.[10] Nor

---

5. *In re* Diet Drugs, No. MDL 1203, 2001 WL 454586 at *18 (E.D. Pa. Feb. 1, 2001). *But see In re* Viagra Prods. Liab. Litig., Nos. 06-1064, 06-1065, 2009 WL 2899881 at *6–7 (D. Minn. Aug. 19, 2009) (allowing an expert to provide a definition of "safety signal" that differs from the *Guidance for Industry* given its non-binding nature).

6. Moses v. Danek Med., Inc., No. CV 95-512, 1998 WL 34024164, at *3 (D. Nev. 1998) (prohibiting witnesses from instructing "the jury as to whether or not Defendant acted 'illegally;' what is 'promotion' under the FDCA; and the interpretation of statutes and regulations" because "[e]xpert testimony is not proper for issues of law").

7. *In re* Guidant Corp. Implantable Defibrillators, 2007 WL 1964337 at *7.

8. *See, e.g., In re* Rezulin Prods. Liab. Litig., 309 F. Supp. 2d 531, 541 (S.D.N.Y. 2004) (Expert witnesses "may not tell the jury what result to reach or communicate 'a legal standard—explicit or implicit—to the jury.' This principle requires the exclusion of testimony that states a legal conclusion, although factual conclusions on an ultimate issue to be decided by the jury are permissible.").

9. *Compare* Plunkett v. Merck & Co., No. 05-4046, slip op. at 55 (E.D. La. Nov. 18, 2005) (permitting expert testimony about the CBE regulation), *with* Mem. and Decision on Mot. at 59, McDarby v. Merck & Co., Inc., Nos. 05-3553, 05-1296 (N.J. Super. Ct. June 8, 2007) (prohibiting expert testimony about the CBE regulation), *aff'd*, 949 A.2d 223, 263 (N.J. Super. Ct. App. Div. 2008).

10. *See, e.g., In re* Rezulin, 309 F. Supp. 2d at 546 ("the intent, motives or states of mind of corporations, regulatory agencies and others have no basis in any relevant body of knowledge or expertise"); *In re* Diet Drugs Prods. Liab. Litig., No. MDL 1203, 2000 WL 876900, at *9 (E.D. Pa. June 20, 2000) (experts are not permitted to make inferences about the intent or motive of parties because "[t]he question of intent is a classic jury question and not one for

may an FDA regulatory expert state his personal views on a pharmaceutical company's ethics and morality.[11]

Courts have also frowned on the practice of some plaintiffs' lawyers who attempt to use an FDA regulatory expert to read company e-mails into the record. In *In re Prempro Product Liability Litigation*,[12] the court struck expert testimony of this nature, finding that the expert had simply read portions of documents into the record. Worse, when the expert did "actually elaborate[] on documents, her testimony did no more than counsel for plaintiff did in argument, *i.e.*, propound a particular interpretation of defendant's conduct."[13] The court concluded that "having an expert witness simply summarize a document (which is just as easily summarized by a jury) with a tilt favoring a litigant, without more, does not amount to expert testimony."[14]

Finding an FDA Regulatory Expert

FDA regulatory experts are hard to find. To qualify as an FDA expert, an individual must have special knowledge and skill regarding FDA operations and regulations. There are a limited number of individuals who possess these qualifications, and relatively few of them have been willing to serve as testifying experts. Some do not like the thought of testifying, while others lack the time or inclination to commit to a protracted litigation.

Current FDA employees are off limits. The FDA generally prohibits them from serving as experts and from testifying in private litigation.[15]

---

experts"); *Smith v. Wyeth-Ayerst Labs. Co.*, 278 F. Supp. 2d at 700 (ruling that a "jury should hear and/or see first-hand any relevant evidence pertaining to the Defendant's intent" after which "the jury, not the witnesses, should consider the facts and make its own determination regarding Defendant's intent"); *In re Fosamax*, 2009 WL 2222910, at *24 (finding that testimony concerning the "knowledge, motivations, intent, state of mind, or purposes" of the company, its employees, the FDA, or FDA official "is not a proper subject for expert or even lay testimony").

11. *See, e.g., In re* Baycol Prods. Liab. Litig., 532 F. Supp. 2d 1029, 1053–54 (D. Minn. 2007) (expert "may be allowed to testify as to the standard of care for pharmaceutical companies, [but] he may not infuse his personal views as to whether [the company] acted ethically, irresponsibly or recklessly"); Apotex Corp. v. Merck & Co., No. 04 C 7312, 2006 WL 1155954, at *8 (N.D. Ill. Apr. 25, 2006) (holding that an expert opining that an individual acted dishonestly or fraudulently is not helpful to a trier of fact).

12. *In re* Prempro Prod. Liab. Litig., 554 F. Supp. 2d 871 (E.D. Ark.), *aff'd in relevant part, vacated in part, and remanded*, 586 F.3d 547 (8th Cir. 2009).

13. *Id.* at 887.

14. *Id.*

15. *See* 21 C.F.R. § 20.1(a) ("No officer or employee of the Food and Drug Administration or of any other office or establishment in the Department of Health and Human Services, except as authorized by the Commissioner of Food and Drugs pursuant to this

Thus, both plaintiffs and defendants look for former FDA employees, professors and other academics with FDA expertise, regulatory lawyers, and pharmaceutical executives. Our preference is for former FDA employees, especially medical reviewers, as their hands-on experience makes them particularly authoritative.

In choosing an FDA expert, practitioners need to keep in mind that the witness must be qualified to serve as an expert. Being a medical doctor is not sufficient to qualify someone as an FDA regulatory expert. In the *In re Diet Drugs Products Liability Litigation*,[16] the plaintiffs offered two experts, neither of whom had worked at the FDA, to opine on FDA regulations, drug warnings, and drug labels. The first witness was a highly qualified medical doctor, pharmacoepidemiologist, and pharmacoeconomist. The second witness was an internationally recognized expert on primary pulmonary hypertension, the alleged injury caused by the drugs. The court held that, although both experts were fully qualified within their specialties, this did not qualify them to "speak as experts in the field of the requirements of the federal regulations regarding labeling and warnings for FDA approved drugs."[17]

CHECKLIST FOR CHOOSING A REGULATORY EXPERT

General Considerations

- Does the expert have experience testifying as well as consulting?
- How many times has the expert been deposed or testified at trial?
- How much money has the expert earned from litigation consulting?
- What percentage of the expert's income comes from litigation consulting?
- Does the expert always work for the same side?
- Does the expert have any preconceptions about the drug or pharmaceutical company at issue?
- Does the expert have sufficient time to commit to the case?
- Will the expert travel to the place of the trial?
- What is the expert's billable rate?
- Has a court or other tribunal ever rejected the expert?

---

section or in the discharge of his official duties under the laws administered by the Food and Drug Administration, shall give any testimony before any tribunal pertaining to any function of the Food and Drug Administration or with respect to any information acquired in the discharge of his official duties.").

16. *In re Diet Drugs*, 2000 WL 876900.
17. *Id.* at *11.

Specific Considerations

- What is the expert's background and experience?
- What is the expert's medical training?
- Does the expert have professional licenses, board certifications?
- Does the expert have any training in epidemiology or statistics?
- Does the expert's specialty relate to the drug?
- Has the expert ever prescribed the drug?
- Has the expert ever studied or researched the drug?
- Has the expert written or spoken on the drug or on issues related to the case?

Special Considerations for Former FDA Employees

- While at the FDA did the expert have responsibility for the drug or for similar drugs?
- In what FDA center or office did the expert work?
- What position did the expert hold at the FDA?
- What experience did the expert gain while at the FDA?
- Did the expert review the type of documents that are at issue in the case?
- How long was the expert at the FDA?
- What is the highest level of seniority that the expert obtained at the FDA?
- What awards or commendations did the expert receive from the FDA?
- Why did the expert leave the FDA?

Working with and Preparing the FDA Regulatory Expert

Once you have retained an FDA regulatory expert, you need to consider how to bring the expert up to speed on the facts of the case. As there is often too much material to dump on the expert at one time, we have found that an incremental approach works best. Shortly after the expert is retained, we like to schedule an initial meeting to provide the expert with an overview of the case. The aim of this meeting is to provide the expert with a framework in which to consider the regulatory issues and a chronology of the key events. During the meeting, you may want to show the expert some of the documents from the company's regulatory file, but the meeting should be for discussion, not for document review.

Following this initial meeting, you should send the expert a small sampling of materials to get him started on document review. These materials may include documents that were mentioned at the initial meeting and may consist of regulatory submissions, medical officer reviews, published studies, and package inserts. You should try to keep this set of material relatively small—two or three loose-leaf binders—since, as before, the aim is only to provide the expert with a framework for the work to come.

Once the expert has reviewed these initial materials, he should get back in touch with you regarding next steps. At this point, if you have not already done so, you should discuss the scope of the expert's engagement and, in particular, whether the expert will need to review all of the regulatory materials in the case or only selected materials. Much depends on the nature of the case, but if you are asking the regulatory expert to opine on the propriety of all of the company's interactions with the FDA, it is prudent to make the entire regulatory file available to him.

For this review, you will want to invite the expert to your office. We typically set up a conference room for the expert's use with hard copies and electronic versions of all the regulatory materials that have been produced in the case. These will include, among other things, (1) the New Drug Application (NDA); (2) the Investigational New Drug Application (IND); (3) all other submissions made to the FDA; (4) all communications with the FDA; (5) all the FDA medical officer reviews; (6) all Advisory Committee materials; (7) all the approved labeling; and, if available, (8) internal FDA documents. This can be a massive amount of material, and the expert should plan for his review to take multiple days.

The review itself should consist of independent reading by the expert, with no lawyers in the room and no lawyer selection of materials. You can simply provide the expert with the documents and let the expert decide what to focus on, what to read, what to skim, and what to ignore. Occasionally, the expert will ask for guidance on how to review the materials. If the expert was an FDA medical officer, you may want to suggest that he review the materials as he did at the FDA. This puts the expert at ease and forestalls later questioning into the adequacy of his review.

In addition to reviewing the documents produced in the litigation, the expert may wish to pursue his own investigations. Most experts will review the FDA website and conduct searches of the published literature on Medline or PubMed.[18] You should encourage these activities, but remind the expert that he must keep track of what he relies on, so that it can be included in his expert report.

Once the expert has reviewed the regulatory materials, you should consider what other case materials the expert should review. You should not, of

---

18. *Available at* http://medline.cos.com/ and http://www.ncbi.nlm.nih.gov/pubmed/.

course, show a testifying expert any document that is privileged or protected from disclosure, and it is a good rule of thumb never to show an expert a document that has not been produced to the other side. But out of the universe of produced documents, now is the time to begin sharing with the expert the internal company e-mails, the marketing materials, and any other materials expected to be used at the expert's deposition. Consider also whether it is necessary or advisable for the expert to review depositions of selected company witnesses, especially those in the regulatory department. These can be helpful to the expert's understanding of the case and provide insight into the issues on which the other side is focusing.

The Expert Report

By the time the expert sits down to write his expert report, he should have completed a full review of the regulatory file. The regulatory expert report is similar to other expert reports. It generally consists of an initial section on qualifications and expertise, followed by a description of each of the expert's opinions.

If the expert is a former FDA employee, he should include a detailed account of his FDA experience, including the positions that he held, promotions, honors, and recognitions. This information is, of course, already contained in the expert's curriculum vitae, but the report gives the expert a chance to describe his experience in a more narrative style. In describing his FDA experience, the expert should describe the types of submissions that he reviewed, highlighting any that are at issue in the case. For example, if the case involves questions about the defendant's clinical trial program, the expert should be sure to indicate that he reviewed, and therefore has experience with, study protocols and clinical study reports. Similarly, in a failure to warn case, the expert should note any relevant experience with labeling, including his review of labeling submissions and participation in labeling discussions with sponsors.

The expert should include a description of the FDA and the new drug development process, from laboratory testing to the IND, through the phases of clinical testing, to the NDA, and into the postmarketing period. This description will differ depending on whether the expert is appearing for the plaintiff or the defendant. For example, the plaintiff's expert might stress that the drug's testing was done by the defendant, not the FDA, and that the FDA was therefore forced to rely on the candor and thoroughness of the defendant's disclosures. The defendant's expert might stress the FDA's involvement throughout the life cycle of the drug and the thoroughness with which it reviews NDAs, including comments on the quality of its scientists and its ability to consult with outside experts when necessary.

The expert must, of course, set forth his opinions and the bases for each of them. In a typical case, both sides' experts may offer opinions about whether the company responsibly investigated the safety profile of the drug and whether it disclosed any potential risks in an appropriate and timely manner. For example, the plaintiff's expert might opine that the company's studies were designed to test efficacy, not safety, or that they were designed to conceal, rather than reveal, safety issues. The plaintiff's expert may opine that the company failed to test the drug in the right kind of patients, in enough patients, or for a long enough time. The defendant's expert might opine that the company responsibly investigated the safety profile of its drug, that it submitted study protocols to the FDA, and that it worked with the FDA to design its clinical study program. The defendant's expert might discuss the number of clinical trials performed by the company, the numbers of patients exposed to the drug, the duration of that exposure, and any special efforts the company took to investigate the type of injury alleged in the case.

CHECKLIST FOR THE EXPERT REPORT—PLAINTIFF

Background and Qualifications
- Profession and education
- FDA experience
- Materials reviewed

FDA Regulations and Role
- Regulates companies and drugs as best that it can
- Lacks resources and expertise
- Does not conduct its own tests
- Relies on the candor of the sponsor to report information accurately and inform it of safety issues

New Drug Development Process
- IND
- Clinical testing
- NDA
- The process represents a minimum standard; sponsors can and should do more.

NDA Review
- Voluminous data
- Safety issues are often missed or hidden.

Postmarketing Oversight and Labeling

- Once the drug is on the market, the FDA's oversight is more limited.
- It is the sponsor's label, and the sponsor must change it when necessary.

Opinions

- Whether defendant responsibly investigated the safety profile of the drug
- Whether defendant properly disclosed any potential risks
- Whether the labeling was adequate
- Whether defendant continued to study the drug and properly disclosed any potential risks
- Whether defendant's interactions with FDA were appropriate

CHECKLIST FOR THE EXPERT REPORT—DEFENDANT

Background and Qualifications

- Profession and education
- FDA experience
- Materials reviewed

FDA Regulations and Role

- Extensively regulates companies and drugs
- Approves drugs under the "safe and effective" standard
- Has or consults with experts in numerous fields
- Communicates with sponsors throughout the life cycle of the drug

New Drug Development Process

- IND
- Clinical testing
- NDA
- The process is rigorous; few drugs make it through.

NDA Review

- Voluminous data
- Thorough and careful review

Postmarketing Oversight and Safety Surveillance Labeling

- FDA continues to monitor drugs after they are approved.
- Companies continue to test drugs after they are approved.
- The FDA must approve changes to the package insert; the FDA has the final say on what the label says, not the drug company.

Opinions

- Whether defendant responsibly investigated the safety profile of the drug
- Whether defendant properly disclosed any potential risks
- Whether the labeling was adequate
- Whether defendant continued to study the drug and properly disclosed any potential risks
- Whether defendant's interactions with the FDA were appropriate

Preparing the Regulatory Expert for Deposition

Each side faces its own particular challenges in preparing its regulatory expert for deposition. But a threshold issue for both sides is how much to educate the regulatory expert about other aspects of the case. There is, for example, generally no need for the regulatory expert to review the plaintiff's medical file, but he should have a general understanding of the nature of plaintiff's injury and be prepared for questions regarding general causation.

As to the particulars, each side will want to review with its regulatory expert any issues or documents that it thinks the other side might show the expert or ask him about. The problem for the expert is that this is not limited to the FDA regulatory file or to the materials on the expert's reliance list. Everything is now fair game, from internal company e-mails to materials pulled off the Internet. The defendant's expert, in particular, needs to be prepared to respond to criticisms not only of the company, but also of the FDA.

The Regulatory Expert at Trial

Preparing and presenting an FDA regulatory expert at trial is no different from preparing and presenting any other expert. The direct examination tends to be relatively straightforward. The regulatory expert will describe his background and qualifications, explain the regulatory context for the issues in the case, and offer his opinions and the bases for them. In planning for this testimony, counsel should select the exhibits that he wants to introduce through the regulatory expert and consider the use of a timeline to illustrate the new drug development process.

The regulatory story will unfold throughout the course of the trial. The plaintiff may be able to tell parts of this story through other experts but generally needs to call his FDA regulatory expert to testify in his case-in-chief.

For the defendant, the decision to call its regulatory expert is dependent on its overall case strategy. By the time the defendant presents its case, the jury will have already heard a good deal of its regulatory story through its opening statement and the cross-examinations of the plaintiff's witnesses. This leads many defense lawyers to place the regulatory expert towards the back of their witness lineup—and some defense lawyers like to have the regulatory expert last, in case there is a need to fill gaps or introduce documents. Because of this, the defendant's regulatory expert may not testify. Certainly, if the defense counsel feels that the plaintiff has failed to carry its burden of proof, he should prefer to rest than to call more witnesses.

Conclusion

An FDA regulatory expert can play an important role in pharmaceutical litigation. In addition to explaining to the jury the complex process of developing and bringing the drug to market, the regulatory expert may opine on key issues such as whether a drug was properly tested and whether its label is adequate. Practitioners should retain a regulatory expert early in the case, as there may be several years of FDA interactions and a correspondingly large number of documents that the expert will need time to review. It takes a good deal of work for the regulatory expert to be ready to write a report or to testify. The final decision on whether to call the expert at trial is often a difficult one, especially for the defendant, who must decide whether to risk exposing another witness to cross-examination.

EXPERTS IN ENVIRONMENTAL LITIGATION

Theodore L. Garrett[1]

Environmental matters are suffused with scientific and technical issues. On a day-to-day basis, companies use engineers and consultants to operate pollution control equipment, undertake sampling and analysis, submit permit applications, and consider the environmental impacts of planned plant modifications. When an adversarial situation develops, whether with an agency or a private party, outside experts are consulted as advisors and potential witnesses. In addition, an expert's analysis may be valuable in settlement negotiations. And, at trial, an expert is usually needed to address critical issues in the litigation that are beyond the normal experience or understanding of jurors. For all these reasons, experts are a crucial part of environmental litigation.

Many if not most environmental issues are resolved without actual litigation. However, that should not result in complacency. A lawyer advising on an environmental matter should be alert to the possible evolution of the matter to an adversarial situation. The possibility that litigation may ensue is relevant to what information is being communicated and to whom, including employees and outside consultants who are potential witnesses. In addition to understanding the substantive legal principles and the scientific issues involved in a particular matter, counsel should be sensitive to potential discovery issues.

Types of Experts in Environmental Litigation

Environmental disputes frequently involve issues that need to be addressed by opinion testimony. This section addresses the types of expert testimony often required in cases involving Superfund liability and apportionment,

1. Mr. Garrett is a Senior Counsel at Covington & Burling LLP, Washington, D.C., whose practice focuses on environmental regulatory and compliance issues and transactions, particularly involving air quality, water quality, climate change, hazardous waste, and natural resource damages. He is a former Chair of the ABA Section of Environment, Energy and Resources.

Superfund remedy selection, natural resource damages, permit issuance and enforcement matters, personal injury or property damage cases, and insurance disputes.

Superfund Liability and Apportionment

Experts play a prominent role in Superfund[2] administrative matters and litigation. At the outset, the issue of liability for contamination often involves technical matters. The allegation may be (1) that your client arranged for disposal of hazardous substances at the site, or (2) that your client is liable as a former owner or operator of a site at a time when hazardous substances were disposed of at the site.[3]

Courts have held that plaintiffs seeking to hold a party liable as one who arranged for disposal must show that the defendant's waste was shipped to a site and that hazardous substances similar to those contained in defendant's waste remained present at the time of the release to the environment.[4] Experts thus may be necessary on the issue of the likely source of contamination. If there is off-site contamination, a "fingerprint" expert may be retained to offer opinions as to whether the contamination at the site in question "matches" the waste produced by a particular company.[5] For example, an expert may be able to present evidence that, although the company handled the general type of product that was found in the soil at a site, sophisticated chemical analysis proves that certain chemicals present in the contamination are absent in the client's product.

If a plaintiff claims that your client is liable as a former owner of contaminated property, experts may be helpful on the issue of when releases of hazardous substances occurred. Courts have held that, unlike present owners, a former owner or operator of property is liable only if hazardous wastes were disposed of during the time the former owner owned or operated the site.[6] An expert may collect aerial photographs showing that the facilities involved or effects of contamination (e.g., distressed vegetation) were not evident until after your client sold the property in question. Where there are gaps in data concerning chemicals used at a facility, an industry

---

2. Superfund is the common name for the Comprehensive Environmental Response, Compensation and Liability Act of 1980, 42 U.S.C. §§ 9601 et seq., as amended (also known by the acronym CERCLA). Superfund is a complex subject and this subchapter will only touch on some of the key issues.

3. 42 U.S.C. § 9607(a).

4. *See, e.g.,* United States v. Monsanto, 858 F.3d 160 (4th Cir. 1988).

5. *See, e.g.,* Turner v. Murphy Oil USA, Inc., No. Civ.A. 05-4206, 2006 WL 91364, at *10 (E.D. La. Jan. 12, 2006).

6. *See, e.g.,* Carlyle Piermont Corp. v. Fed. Paper Bd. Co., Inc., 742 F. Supp. 814 (S.D.N.Y. 1990).

expert might provide opinion testimony concerning production processes used, and wastes generated, during the relevant period of time.

Experts may also testify concerning issues of causation—for example, opining that contamination at a particular site could not have contributed to contamination at another location because groundwater under a client's property does not flow toward the contaminated site. Because CERCLA imposes liability only for a release "which causes the incurrence response costs," the plaintiff must prove a causal link between a defendant's release and the plaintiff's response.[7] Potential witnesses may have expertise in the fields of chemistry, geochemistry, hydrology, and fate and transport.[8] Complex groundwater modeling may be needed.

Finally, in the great majority of cases where there is more than one potentially responsible party, apportionment of liability and contribution raise important issues that likely will involve expert opinion. Superfund liability is generally joint and several, with two important exceptions. The first is that a defendant may be able to establish a basis for equitable apportionment, which will in turn call for experts to assist the defendant to meet its burden of proof that there is a reasonable basis for divisibility, based on factors such as percentage of land ownership, time of ownership, and types of hazardous materials.[9] CERCLA also allows liable parties to seek contribution from other parties who are liable, based on various equitable factors.[10] Courts may allocate cleanup costs based on a number of factors, including the degree of involvement by the parties, the degree of care exercised, and the degree to which cleanup costs were caused by the actions of various parties.[11] Once again, expert testimony will be needed concerning the relevant factors.

Superfund Remedy Selection

Disputes concerning Superfund remedy selection also require expert assistance. Remedy selection usually proceeds in two phases. The first phase of the cleanup process is the remedial investigation, a scientific study to delineate

---

7. *See, e.g.*, Dedham Water Co. v. Cumberland Farms Inc., 770 F. Supp. 41 (D. Mass. 1991), *aff'd*, 972 F.2d 453(1st Cir. 1992).

8. *See, e.g.*, Hatco Corp. v. W.R. Grace & Co.-Conn., 836 F. Supp. 1049, 1060–63 (D.N.J. 1993).

9. *See* Burlington N. & Santa Fe Ry. v. United States, 129 S. Ct. 1870 (2009) (affirming the district court's apportionment of liability based on these factors).

10   10. 42 U.S.C. §§ 9607(a), 9613(f)(1).

11. *See* United States v. A&F Materials Co., Inc., 578 F. Supp. 1249, 1256 (S.D. Ill. 1984); United States v. Davis, 261 F.3d 1 (1st Cir. 2001); *Hatco Corp.*, 836 F. Supp. at 1090. *See also* Barbara J. Graves et al., *Allocating Responsibility for Groundwater Remediation Costs*, 23(4) Trial Law. 159 (Mar.–Apr. 2000).

the extent of contamination. During this phase, there may also be a coordinated effort to identify injury to natural resources. These efforts often involve extensive field investigations and sampling of surface water, groundwater, soil, and biota. The second phase is the feasibility study, which evaluates various alternatives to cleanup, such as removal and disposal or treatment of contaminants in soil and groundwater.[12]

Experts in the fields of hydrology, geology, fate and transport, and treatment technology are typically involved in both phases. The following are a few of the many issues that may be involved in the cleanup process:

- What are appropriate remedial action objectives?
- What are the applicable or relevant and appropriate requirements under federal or state environmental laws? Would compliance result in greater risk to human health and the environment than other alternatives?
- Are the remedial alternatives being considered implementable based on technically feasible and available technology?
- What is the short-term and long-term effectiveness of each remedial alternative?
- What are the costs of construction and operation for each remedial alternative?
- Is there a more cost-effective or less environmentally intrusive way to accomplish the agency's objective?

Litigation concerning the selection of the Superfund remedy is generally based on the administrative record,[13] and it is thus essential that the administrative record contain expert testimony supportive of your client's position. Your trial in effect consists of a court's review of the administrative record assembled by the agency, which will include comments submitted by your client with the assistance of counsel and experts. Involvement by persuasive experts during the administrative process may educate the relevant agency and result in a cost-effective cleanup plan that is acceptable to your client. If you are not successful in persuading the agency to adopt a remedy acceptable to your client, you will have created a solid record for judicial review.

---

12. *See* 40 C.F.R. § 300.430. These regulations are known as the "national contingency plan."

13. There are exceptions with respect to government actions for injunctive relief. United States v. Ottati & Goss, Inc., 900 F.2d 429, 434–35 (1st Cir. 1990) (court considering an injunction is not required to accept Environmental Protection Agency's (EPA's) chosen remedy). There also may be an exception if counsel can show that there were defects in the administrative process. *See, e.g.,* South Carolina Dep't of Health and Envtl. Control v. Atlantic Steel Indus., Inc., 85 F. Supp. 2d 596 (D.S.C. 1999) (court not limited to the record in reviewing a settlement due to procedural irregularities).

If the agency performs the cleanup and seeks to recover the costs it incurs, a trial may be needed to decide whether the agency's claimed cleanup costs are justified. The Superfund statute provides that the government may seek cleanup costs not inconsistent with the national contingency plan (NCP).[14] The question whether cleanup costs are consistent with the NCP is a triable issue of fact.[15] In that situation, your client may wish to retain a forensic accountant as an expert to review the adequacy of the agency's cost documentation. Your client may also wish to retain an environmental remediation expert to review whether the agency's cleanup actions were consistent with the agency's cleanup plan and the EPA's regulations.

Natural Resource Damages

Actions by the government to recover natural resources, because legal in nature, are triable to a jury,[16] and judicial review of the government's decisions is not limited to the administrative record.[17] If natural resource damages are at issue, experts in natural resource damage assessments will be needed, including ecologists and other scientists such as aquatic biologists. There may be issues as to whether a particular environmental use was damaged or, if there is damage, to what degree the environmental uses are impaired.

Natural resource damages can involve elaborate and time-consuming technical studies and analyses under Department of Interior regulations.[18] In more recent years, however, the government has used habitat equivalency analysis as a preferred vehicle to arrive at more focused, timely and

---

14. 42 U.S.C. § 9607(a)(4)(A). The statute allows private parties to seek contribution for costs that are consistent with the NCP. 42 U.S.C. § 9607(a)(4)(B). The NCP regulations are found at 40 C.F.R. § 300.430.

15. *See* Hatco v. W.R. Grace & Co., 849 F. Supp. 931, 961 (D.N.J. 1994); Wickland Oil Terminals v. ASARCO, 792 F.2d 887, 891 (9th Cir. 1986).

16. *See, e.g., In re* Acushnet River & New Bedford Harbor, 712 F. Supp. 994, 999, 1000, 1004 (D. Mass. 1989); United States v. City of Seattle, No. C90-395WD, 1991 WL 208805 (W.D. Wash. Jan. 23, 1991).

17. *See, e.g.,* United States v. ASARCO, Inc., 35 CWLR 971 (D. Idaho 1998) (review of trustees' evaluation of injury to natural resources is not limited to the administrative record); State of Idaho v. Bunker Hill Co., 635 F. Supp. 665 (D. Idaho 1986) (plaintiff must prove a causal link between releases and post-enactment damages).

18. *See* 43 C.F.R. pt. 11. Part A of the regulations provides for simplified assessments with minimal field observation. In contrast, the Part B procedures, for more complex cases, require that the trustees perform field work to identify and quantify injury to resources and determine monetary damages.

streamlined natural resource damage settlements.[19] This approach compensates the public by habitat replacement projects for resources similar to those injured. It will be important for companies to retain experts who are fully versed in this type of analysis.

Most natural resource damage claims are settled, but experts play an essential role in settlement negotiations. The assistance and involvement of a company's experts in negotiations with the relevant natural resource trustees will be valuable and likely will increase the odds of a successful settlement. In one case involving a mine in Idaho, the government's claim focused on reduced salmon populations allegedly resulting from contamination at the site.[20] The defendants disputed the government's claims of injury and argued that dams built by the government were a key reason for the reduced salmon population. A settlement resulted.[21]

Permit Issuance and Enforcement Matters

Permit issuance and enforcement matters frequently raise technical issues requiring the involvement of experts. Air and water permits are typically based, in part, on standards requiring the use of "best available" or "lowest achievable" technology or a similar formulation. In some cases, the standards are specified in regulations.[22] In other instances, case-by-case determinations are made based on expert judgment as to the applicability of control technology to a particular industrial facility or process and the emissions resulting from the application of appropriate technology. Air permits generally are based on monitoring data and modeling of the emissions of particular pollutants. These decisions are suffused with technical issues that are the province of experts.

Enforcement is typically based on monitoring data collected and reported by the company. Where permits are challenged or there is an enforcement action, experts are often needed to present the company's position. For example, a company may be able to defend by showing that an exceedance of permit limits was caused by an upset, by startup, shutdown or

---

19. *See, e.g.,* Habitat Equivalency Analysis: an Overview (NOAA 1995), *available at* http://www.darrp.noaa.gov/library/pdf/heaoverv.pdf.

20. *See* G. Ray, Habitat Equivalency Analysis (U.S. Army Corps 2008), *available at* http://el.erdc.usace.army.mil/elpubs/pdf/ei02.pdf.

21. State of Idaho v. M.A. Hanna, No. 83-4179 (D. Idaho Sept. 1, 1995). The consent decree is available at http://www.gc.noaa.gov/gc-cd/bbm-cd.pdf. *See also* EPA Notice of Lodging of Consent Decree (May 11, 1995), http://www.epa.gov/fedrgstr/EPA-WATER/1995/May/Day-11/pr-114.html.

22. *See, e.g.,* 40 C.F.R. pt. 400 et seq. (effluent guidelines and standards); 40 C.F.R. pt. 63 (national emission standards for hazardous air pollutants).

malfunction, or by force majeure, and that good engineering practice was followed.[23] Expert testimony may be critical to explain the circumstances and persuade the fact finder that the company's conduct should not be the basis for enforcement sanctions.[24]

Personal Injury or Property Damage Cases

In some cases, a Superfund investigation and remediation will trigger a piggyback claim from nearby property owners for personal injury or property damage. A claim for personal injury will typically involve important issues of causation requiring expert opinion. For example, an expert may render an opinion about whether the plaintiff suffered actual injury and, if so, whether the company's actions caused the injury.

Sometimes plaintiffs assert claims for stigma or reduced property value as a result of a Superfund cleanup. The opinions of real estate professionals will be important in such cases. The experts will examine whether the plaintiff's property near the Superfund site is worth less than comparable properties not so located, whether the property value is lower today than it was several years ago, and, if so, whether the lower property value is caused by the Superfund cleanup or a general decline in the economy.

Insurance Disputes

Environmental costs often give rise to claims for insurance coverage that are disputed. The use of experts in insurance cases is a complex subject that will only be touched on here. Insurance carriers often defend by arguing that the damage was not sudden or was expected and intended and thus not covered.[25] The insured company may respond by showing that its environmental practices were consistent with standard practice in the industry and that its operations were not understood at the time to give rise to cleanup issues. Experts often testify about industry practice and about industry understanding of the impacts of contamination. For example, in a case involving hard rock mining at a long abandoned mine, an expert might testify that acid mine drainage was not understood until more recently and that the long-term impacts of mining on groundwater or nearby streams would not have been evident at the time.

---

23. *See* Friends of the Earth v. Facet Enters., 618 F. Supp. 532, 536 (W.D.N.Y. 1984).

24. *See* State of New Jersey v. J.T. Baker Chem. Co., 560 A.2d 739 (N.J. Super. 1989), and letter opinion dated January 3, 1990 (finding, based on expert testimony, that all but one of 22 events were caused by circumstances beyond defendant's reasonable control).

25. *See, e.g.,* Morton Int'l v. Gen. Accident Ins. Co., 134 N.J. 1, 29 (1993).

Retaining Environmental Experts

If it is apparent or likely that one or more experts will be needed, counsel should discuss the matter of expert retention with the client and consider several issues relating to the timing and selection of expert(s).

Timing of Expert Retention

It is usually desirable to retain experts early in the case so that they have adequate time to prepare, become vested in the matter, and help counsel see what theories and approaches are likely to be productive from the outset. Moreover, in a big case involving multiple parties or a field where there are only a small number of recognized experts, the danger of putting off expert selection is that your first choices may have already been retained by other parties by the time you begin to canvass the universe of experts.

Choice between Consulting and Testifying Experts

As discussed more fully in chapter 1, there is a distinction between testifying expert witnesses and nontestifying expert advisors. At an early stage, counsel may not know whether a particular expert will be called at trial. Experts may be held in reserve in the event they are necessary. Experts may also be retained purely to advise counsel. There may be value in retaining one or more spare experts to deal with any unexpected issues or to testify, if you decide for some reason not to use your primary expert. You may also find it useful to have a nontestifying expert available to review the expert reports and to help you prepare for depositions of the opposing experts. Finally, a nontestifying expert might also assist you in selecting your testifying experts and vetting their opinions.

Selection of Expert

Selecting an environmental expert involves careful review of the issues, understanding of the types of experts needed, and identification of particular individuals who are well qualified. For a testifying expert, counsel must be satisfied that the individual is an expert in the particular discipline on which expert testimony is expected. You will likely wish to speak to your client, to other experts, and to litigators who have handled similar issues. Such issues might include, for example, the health impacts of arsenic, the cleanup of polychlorinated biphenyls (PCBs) from river sediments, or the operation of a particular type of manufacturing operation. There are also commercial services that can help to locate experts, and national environmental consulting firms often have experts in various fields with experience as trial witnesses. If all goes well, you will find a few candidates of high quality, who do not have conflicts, and who are interested and appear well qualified to speak to the issues at hand.

In some cases, in-house or outside scientists or engineers will be involved before a matter turns adversarial. In that scenario, a decision needs to be made whether some of them, already familiar with the matter, should be selected as expert witnesses to testify at trial. In other cases, where new experts are needed, the client or outside counsel may suggest certain consultants they have used in other matters.

Unless you are already familiar with an expert, you will want to interview potential candidates. Your client may wish to be present. During the interview, you should assess the expert's strengths and weaknesses as a trial witness. Ask the expert to discuss one or two matters, preferably matters on which expert reports and testimony were provided:

- Does the expert have the ability to communicate in a clear and convincing manner?
- Discuss the specific issues on which you anticipate you will need an expert opinion. Does the expert feel comfortable that he has the requisite expertise?
- This is the time to consider whether the expert's qualifications (e.g., knowledge, training, experience, etc.) might be challenged under Federal Rule of Evidence 702. Has the expert written or testified on the subject?
- Does the expert have comments, suggestions, or reactions that seem helpful to your client?
- Does the expert have the requisite time to devote to the matter, and are there any significant periods when the expert will be unavailable?
- And, important to your client, what fees does the expert charge?

At the end of the interview, assuming all goes well, you should ask the expert to provide you with a budget and with copies of depositions, trial testimony, and expert reports that are available for your review.

Engagement of Expert

Once you have consulted with your client and selected the expert(s), you will want to prepare an engagement letter in which counsel retains the expert. The letter will describe the fee arrangement, recite that the expert is retained to assist counsel in preparing for trial, describe the matters on which the expert is being retained, confirm that there are no conflicts and the expert is available to testify at trial if needed, and explain that no decision has been made at this time whether the expert will be called as a trial witness.

Communicating with Environmental Experts

As with other types of experts, there is a presumption of protection for communications with nontestifying environmental experts under Federal Rule of Civil Procedure 26(b)(4)(B). For testifying experts, Rule 26(b)(2)(B) provides for disclosure of the basis for the expert's opinions. Although counsel's communications with experts may be subject to the work product privilege, it is wise to be conservative and assume that communications with experts may be discoverable and to act accordingly. This means that you may wish to keep written communications, including e-mail, to a minimum. Documents provided to an expert who may be a trial witness should be selected with care on the assumption that they are discoverable, and a list of such documents should be prepared and retained by counsel.[26]

Trial counsel should speak directly with the expert, in person or by telephone, to authorize work and monitor progress. At times when there are a number of issues on the expert's plate, trial counsel will want to stay in touch regularly to make sure that the expert is making good progress on whatever evaluations have been requested. On the other hand, when the case is on hold or matters are otherwise dormant, the client may be best served by trial counsel's asking the expert to stand down, and cease logging billable time, pending further developments.

If more than one expert is expected to testify at trial, counsel may wish to consider the value of arranging meetings or calls, at the appropriate time, in which the experts discuss the areas of their proposed testimony and thereby can understand how the various expert opinions will fit together. However, before arranging any such meeting or call, counsel should think through the possibility that such conversations might serve as a basis for an expert's opinions and thus be discoverable.

Expert Reports and Demonstrative Evidence

Depending on the jurisdiction, an expert report may be required if the case is going to trial. In a federal trial, Rule 26(a)(2) requires that each party make a disclosure for each expert witness, including a statement of all opin-

---

26. *See* Cynthia J. Bishop, *Foraging through the Jungle of Expert Discovery and Testimony*, 22 NAT. RES. & ENV'T 3 (Spring 2008).

ions, the basis and reasons for the opinions, and the data or other information considered by the expert. Before the expert even begins the process of
preparing an expert report, trial counsel may find it useful to ask the expert
how he envisions the report will be organized, namely, the table of contents.
That allows trial counsel at the outset to confirm that the expert is on the
right track and covering issues that need to be addressed. Counsel may also
wish to make suggestions concerning the format for the expert report. In a
federal trial, it is important to make sure that the report satisfies the requirement of Rule 26(a)(2). Finally, if there is more than one expert report,
trial counsel should consider at the outset whether the experts' areas of testimony potentially overlap and should address the potential for cumulative
reports.

Counsel should consider how heavily to be involved in writing the expert report. If the selection process works well and the client and counsel
have confidence in the expert, the client may be best served by having the
expert produce the report without a lot of hovering by trial counsel. Needless to say, it is not helpful, during a deposition or at trial, for an expert to
testify, in response to questions from opposing counsel, that some or all of
the report was written by counsel or that changes were made in the expert's
report at the direction of counsel.[27]

At the end of the day, however, the client and trial counsel need to be
satisfied that the expert report covers the points on which testimony is
needed and is well written. Review by nontestifying experts, if available,
may also be very valuable. Moreover, trial counsel needs to be satisfied that
the expert's testimony will be admissible under the principles for admission
of scientific evidence as set forth in the *Daubert*[28] decision and its progeny.
The admissibility of expert opinions has been discussed at length in Chapter 6
as well as in other publications,[29] but suffice it to say that the expert's testimony must be based on a reliable scientific or technical foundation.[30] Issues
counsel should consider include the following:

- Is the methodology for reaching the expert's opinion sound?
- Does the expert have sampling data or another reliable basis for his
  opinion concerning the cause of contamination?[31]

---

27. *See* Sidney I. Schenkier, *The Limits of Privilege in Communications with Experts*, 33 Litig. 16 (Winter 2007).

28. Daubert v. Merrell Dow Pharms., Inc., 509 U.S. 579 (1993).

29. *See, e.g.*, Cynthia H. Cwik, C., *Guarding the Gate: Expert Evidence Admissibility*, 25 Litig. 6 (Summer 1999).

30. *Daubert*, 509 U.S. at 592–95.

31. *See, e.g.*, Jaasma v. Shell Oil Co., 412 F.3d 501, 514 (3d Cir. 2005).

- Does the expert make incorrect assumptions or depart from traditional scientific approaches?[32]

An expert can also assist counsel by producing trial exhibits that will make the case more understandable to the judge or jury. In an environmental case, site drawings or aerial photographs can be very helpful in depicting the overall site setting and the location of contamination, manufacturing, or treatment facilities. Diagrams or drawings may be useful to depict manufacturing processes, the operation of treatment facilities, or surface or groundwater flow. Computer simulations can show the fate and transport of contaminants over time.

Environmental Experts at Trial

Other chapters in this book discuss in detail the subject of experts at trial. One issue that should be highlighted in the context of environmental experts is the use of court-appointed experts. Under Federal Rule of Evidence 706, experts can be appointed on the court's own motion or the motion of any party. A trial lawyer should consider asking the court to appoint an expert in a case that is technically complex to enhance the court's understanding of the issues.[33] In preparing for trial, if you come to the conclusion that it will be difficult for the court to evaluate the testimony offered by the parties and to exercise the gatekeeping role envisioned by *Daubert*, you should consider asking the court to appoint an expert.[34]

A full treatment of the subject of expert cross-examination is beyond the scope of this chapter. But there are a few useful suggestions that are particularly applicable to cross-examining environmental experts. The following bullet points summarize suggestions made by litigation scholar James W. McElhaney:[35]

- Convert the opposing expert into your witness by using a constructive cross to build up your own case.
- Demonstrate that there are other points of view by asking the expert to identify leading experts, books, and articles in the field and the different approaches taken by these experts.

---

32. *See* Finestone v. Florida Power & Light Co., No. 03-14040-CIV., 2006 WL 267330 (S.D. Fl. Jan. 6, 2006), *aff'd*, 272 Fed. App. 761 (11th Cir. 2008).
33. *See* Gen. Elec. Co. v. Joiner, 522 U.S. 136, 149–50 (1997) (Breyer, S., concurring) (encouraging judges to make greater use of their inherent authority to appoint experts).
34. *See* Jane F. Thorpe, *Court-Appointed Experts and Technical Advisors*, 26 Litig. 31 (Summer 2000).
35. James W. McElhaney, *Expert Cross-Examination*, 30 Litig. 65 (Winter 2004).

- If your client disagrees with the facts relied on by the expert, ask the expert if his conclusion would change if the information relied on turned out to be incorrect.
- Watch out for mousetraps—a perceived omission or weakness for which the witness is primed for a killer response.
- Control the witness by asking follow-up questions to pin down the witness.

Needless to say, trial counsel needs to be well versed in the subject matter and should have specific cross-examination goals in mind.

Conclusion

Experts, including testifying experts, are widely used in the environmental area. If disputes occur, it is prudent to anticipate that they will result in litigation. Thorough development of claims and defenses, using experts as needed for technical opinions, may lead to a settlement and will help focus trial preparation. A court-appointed expert or technical advisor may also be valuable to assist in judicial decision making on complex technical subjects.

EXPERTS IN CONDEMNATION CASES

John C. Murphy and Brad B. Grabske[1]

Eminent domain trials often boil down ultimately to a single issue: the value of the condemned property. In many jurisdictions, the only persons who may testify concerning value, other than the property owner, are expert witnesses.[2] Of course, real estate appraisal experts, like other experts, can be difficult and even unpredictable. Expert witnesses are "a lot like dynamite . . . Handled well, they move mountains. . . . But small mistakes can cause them to blow up in your face."[3]

This subchapter discusses five special challenges lawyers face in dealing with appraisal experts in eminent domain cases. It makes some suggestions for the special handling of the real estate appraisal expert and for effectively challenging your opponent's appraiser during cross-examination.

Real Estate Appraisal Experts: What Makes Them Unique

The valuation phase of eminent domain trials is often referred to as a "battle of the experts."[4] One might assume these appraisal experts would get special respect in light of their key role at trial, but judges and juries often express real skepticism and cynicism about even the most highly qualified appraisal

---

1. John C. Murphy is a partner with Murphy & Evertz in Orange County, California. Mr. Murphy represents a wide variety of public agencies, corporations, and landowners in eminent domain, inverse condemnation, and other complex business disputes. Brad B. Grabske is an associate with Murphy & Evertz. Mr. Grabske's practice also focuses on eminent domain, inverse condemnation, and other complex business disputes.

2. *See, e.g.*, CAL. EVID. CODE § 813; ALA. CODE § 18-1A-192; State Dep't of Highways v. Mahaffey, 697 P.2d 773, 775–77 (Colo. Ct. App. 1984); E-Z Serve Convenience Store v. State, 686 So. 2d 351, 353 (Ala. Civ. App. 1996).

3. STEPHEN D. EASTON, HOW TO WIN JURY TRIALS: BUILDING CREDIBILITY WITH JUDGES AND JURORS 10 (1988).

4. Stempel v. Bucks County, 70 Pa. D. & C.2d 243 (Pa. C.P. 1975); Yamagiwa v. City of Half Moon Bay, 523 F. Supp. 2d 1036, 1091 (N.D. Cal. 2007) ("[T]he issue of compensation was a battle of the experts."); In re McCoy, No. 04-60395 JPK, 2005 Bankr. LEXIS 1796 (Bankr. N.D. Ind. May 12, 2005).

witnesses. This skepticism has spurred several states to enact elaborate rules aimed at just one narrow category of experts: the real estate appraiser. In California, for example, the Evidence Code limits this special category of experts to just three permissible approaches to valuation, identifies the specific type of data and analysis in which such an expert may rely, and excludes any testimony not fully within these strict categories.[5]

Why do real estate appraisers merit such strict regulation? There are at least five reasons why appraisal experts get treated differently, and more restrictively, than other experts.

1. Judges and jurors do not always view real estate appraisers' expertise as particularly remote, arcane, or specialized.[6] Almost everyone has to make a decision about the value of real estate at some point in his life. Most judges and many jurors have bought a house, rented an apartment, or invested in real estate at one time or another. Unlike complicated medical, architectural, or engineering issues, real estate appraisal is not divorced from everyone's common, everyday experience.

2. Real estate appraisers testify about hypothetical, rather than actual, events. Lawyers generally use experts to explain why and how an actual event occurred. Medical experts explain why a patient died. Architects may explain why a building collapsed. Accident reconstruction experts explain why a traffic accident happened. These experts deal with real world events, and after-the-fact issues. Real estate appraisers in eminent domain, by contrast, are charged with predicting the details of a purely hypothetical sales transaction—a transaction between a nonexistent willing seller, and a nonexistent ready, willing, and able buyer. They deal with a transaction that never occurred in the real world and never will occur.

3. The hypothetical standard with which appraisers deal is not only hypothetical, but factually inaccurate. Most jurisdictions require an appraiser to assume a willing seller.[7] But eminent domain does not involve a willing seller. It involves an involuntary transaction—a governmental agency taking private property against the owner's will.

---

5. *See* CAL. EVID. CODE §§ 810–824.

6. *See* Brown & Vaughn Development Co. v. Commonwealth, 393 Pa. 589, 594 (Pa. 1958) (acknowledging that the "Trial Judge at times in his charge placed something less glorious than laurel wreaths on the heads of [appraisal] expert witnesses").

7. *See, e.g.,* Uniform Law Commissioners' Model Eminent Domain Code § 1004 (1984); *see also* ALA. CODE § 18-1A-172; CAL. CIV. PROC. CODE § 1263.320; IOWA CODE § 441.21; MONT. CODE ANN. § 70-30-313; NEV. REV. STAT. § 37.009; N.C. GEN. STAT. § 105-283; 26 PA. CONS. STAT. § 703; WYO. STAT. ANN. § 1-26-704; Cane Tenn., Inc. v. United States, 71 Fed. Cl. 432, 437 (Fed. Cl. 2005) ("An 'early adopted' measure of 'just compensation' as contemplated by the Fifth Amendment of the United States Constitution, 'market value is what a willing buyer would pay in cash to a willing seller.'") (quoting United States v. Miller, 317 U.S. 369, 374 (1942)); State Dep't of Transp. & Dev. v. Hammons, 550 So. 2d 767, 772 (La. Ct. App. 1989).

4. The hypothetical standard appraisers use is also imprecise. It sets forth an objective standard: fair market value. In the real world, however, some owners value their properties more highly than others. Owners of single family homes, for example, often have deep emotional attachments to their property. For the most part, eminent domain laws do not even attempt to compensate for this subjective value.[8]

5. Most importantly, real estate appraisers often differ widely in their conclusions. One appraiser may conclude a property lacks any real value, except for agricultural uses. A different appraiser may conclude the same property has substantial development potential and great value. Bias, whether acknowledged or not, can dictate an outcome. Most appraisers will even admit that appraisal is an art, not a science. In one commentator's words, "at bottom, an appraisal is no more than a subjective opinion of an expert."[9] Many eminent domain proceedings have proven that the "appraisal process involves a series of judgments and decisions, each of which may be questioned, controverted, or shown to be appropriate in particular cases."[10]

Special Issues in Handling Real Estate Appraisal Experts

Selecting Appraisal Experts

Why Use Appraisal Experts

In eminent domain trials, generally only the landowner and appraisal experts may testify to the value of the property.[11] Appraisal experts, however,

---

8. United States v. 50 Acres of Land, 469 U.S. 24, 36 (1984) (rejecting the use of substitute facilities doctrine because it violated the "principle that just compensation must be measured by an objective standard that disregards subjective values which are only of significance to an individual owner."); *Cane Tenn., Inc.*, 71 Fed. Cl. at 437 ("[T]he Supreme Court noted that the measure of just compensation adopted in a particular takings case should not 'conflict with the Court's efforts to develop relatively objective valuation standards.'") (citing United States v. 564.54 Acres of Land, 441 U.S. 506, 516 (1979)). *But see* District of Columbia Redevelopment Land Agency v. Thirteen Parcels of Land, 534 F.2d 337, 340 (D.C. Cir. 1976) ("[T]he right of the owner to testify is based, at least in part, on the recognition of the subjective nature of value. Opinions as to value differ, and the owner has a right to place all evidence pertaining to the value of his condemned property before the trier of fact.").

9. John F. Shampton, *Statistical Evidence of Real Estate Valuation: Establishing Value without Appraisers* 21 S. ILL. U. L.J. 113, 118 (1996).

10. *Id.*

11. *E.g.*, CAL. EVID. CODE § 813; District of Columbia Redevelopment Land Agency v. Thirteen Parcels of Land, 534 F.2d 337, 340 (D.C. Cir. 1976). *But see* Smith v. City of Fort Smith, No. CA03-592, 2004 Ark. App. LEXIS 276 (Ark. Ct. App. Apr. 7, 2004) (noting that

have an appearance of objectivity—at least more so than landowners. Several courts have commented that juries tend to believe appraisal experts more than lay opinions or attorney argument.[12]

Real estate appraisal experts may testify to the ultimate issue—valuation. An articulate, authoritative appraiser can be indispensable at trial in explaining complex valuation evidence and valuation approaches to the jury.

In complex valuation cases, it is not uncommon for the parties to retain two or more appraisers. In these cases, the party may decide to designate only one appraiser as a testifying expert. Alternatively, designating multiple appraisal experts may add critical support for a contested valuation opinion. On the other hand, there is a risk that multiple appraisers may be deemed cumulative and, therefore, excluded.[13]

The case may also call for subsidiary experts to prove foundational facts to support the appraiser's opinion of value. Many experienced counsel seek to assemble a complete team of witnesses with a variety of expertise. For example, impairment of access claims may call for engineering experts to support the appraiser's valuation opinion and opinion as to the highest and best use of a parcel. Other claims may call for land use or planning experts, environmental contamination/remediation experts, architects, economists, construction-cost estimators, and others.

Where to Locate Appraisal Experts

Selection of an appraisal expert is one of the key decisions in a condemnation case. Locating a qualified appraisal expert can be a daunting task, particularly for landowners with no prior experience with eminent domain. Condemning agencies, on the other hand, often have lists of approved, experienced appraisers. Some agencies even have preferred appraisers.

Consider the following sources:

- Talk with and solicit recommendations from members of state eminent domain or real estate litigation bars;
- Check the verdict sheets for eminent domain trials, which often list the parties' respective appraisers;
- Check recent eminent domain appellate opinions;

---

testimony is admissible if there is a reasonable basis for saying that a witness knows more of the subject property than a person of ordinary knowledge).

12. *See, e.g.*, Fla. DOT v. Armadillo Partners, Inc., 849 So. 2d 279, 291 (Fla. 2003) (Appraisal experts' opinion testimony "has heightened—and at times even perhaps undue—influence on the minds of the jurors.").

13. *See, e.g.*, CAL. EVID. CODE § 352; FED. R. EVID. 403.

- Contact the Appraisal Institute (discussed below) and request a list of its local members or check its website;[14] and
- Attend eminent domain seminars for right-of-way professionals and for eminent domain attorneys. National organizations like the International Right of Way Association (IRWA), American Law Institute-American Bar Association (ALI-ABA), and CLE International host seminars across the country.

What to Look for in Appraisal Experts

There are a myriad of general rules and criteria for evaluating and selecting experts. General rules, however, are not applicable to every case and should not trump intuition. Convincing a jury that the appraiser's opinion of value is more accurate than the opinion advanced by the opposition is no easy task. And effectively engaging a jury requires more than objective qualifications.

Some factors to consider in evaluating potential appraisal experts include the following:

Actual Trial Experience. With trial experience, the appraiser's effectiveness can be verified, in part, through verdict sheets and deposition transcripts. The attorney can also investigate how the appraiser fared under the pressures of cross-examination. However, actual trial experience can be overrated and should not be viewed as an absolute criterion. "We learn from experience that men [and women] never learn anything from experience."[15] There can be a real benefit to using an appraiser without trial experience. The appraiser will have no track record, giving the cross-examiner less ammunition. Thorough preparation and simple, disarming candor may also resonate more with a jury than a long list of previous testimony.

Experience Appraising Comparable Properties. Most appraisers try to focus on appraising a broad range of properties. Overemphasis or specialization on specific types of properties can be useful in some situations and present problems in other. For condemning agencies consistently using the same appraiser, public records demands may show inconsistencies in how the appraiser valued comparable properties in different acquisitions or cases. Similarly, previous deposition transcripts may show inconsistencies in valuing comparable properties. This can obviously be a fertile ground for cross-examination.

---

14. Appraisal Institute Home Page, http://appraisalinstitute.org/.
15. George Bernard Shaw.

Bias Due to Extensive Public Agency or Landowner Work. Attorneys keep track of which appraisers are high with their valuation opinions and which are low, and under what circumstances. Appraisers with extensive public agency experience are generally perceived as having a governmental bias, with consistently low valuation opinions. Despite perceptions of bias, there are advantages for condemning agencies in using familiar appraisers. For example, on multiparcel acquisitions, it can be difficult to work with appraisers who lack institutional knowledge about the condemning agency and the agency's project.

Academic Qualifications. Juries generally do not focus on prestige or the rankings of universities and colleges, although a degree from a large institution can be helpful.

Authorship of Appraisal Publications. Publications can be a sign of creativity and are sometimes helpful. For example, it would be helpful if your expert authored a book relied on by the other side. Most experts, however, are reluctant to acknowledge opposing sources.

Accreditations and Professional Associations for Appraisers. Not all jurisdictions require appraisers to be licensed to render eminent domain appraisal services.[16] But any federally related appraisal services must be performed by state-certified appraisers consistent with the Uniform Standards of Professional Appraisal Practice (USPAP).[17]

As a practical matter, many appraisal experts will not only be state certified, but they will also be members of one or more appraisal associations and societies. The Appraisal Institute, for example, is a recognized and regarded appraisal organization. The Appraisal Institute currently grants two designations—MAI (Member Appraisal Institute) and SRA (Senior Residential Appraiser). The Appraisal Institute touts the MAI designation as one of the highest designations an appraiser can attain in commercial real estate. The designation is not an absolute criterion for selecting an appraiser.

Other Practical Tips in Selecting the Appraisal Expert

- *Investigate or inquire whether the appraiser worked for the opposing law firm or public agency in prior cases.* Prior work with the opposing law firm or public agency may bolster the appraiser's appearance of objectivity. Conversely, allegiances to a particular law firm or public agency

---

16. J.D. Eaton, Real Estate Valuation in Litigation 448 (Appraisal Institute 1995); Nichols on Eminent Domain 7 (3d ed. 2009) ("In some jurisdictions, anyone can claim to be an [appraisal] expert in eminent domain proceedings regardless of qualifications.").

17. For a more detailed discussion of professional appraisal societies and credentialing, see Nichols, *supra* note 16.

may, even unfairly, create the opposite appearance—and provide fodder for questioning on cross-examination.

- *Test the appraiser's resilience with contradictions, and see how he reacts.* This exercise can gauge how nimble the appraiser may be on an exacting cross-examination. Intellectually nimble appraisal experts can also evaluate the opposition and anticipate their best arguments.

- *Local experience is helpful.* It may be helpful if an appraiser can discuss experience in the local real estate market and be based in the county where the property is located. Specialists may do well outside their local jurisdictions, however. Regardless, the appraiser should be capable of engaging and communicating with likely jurors.

- *Compatibility with the legal team is an important element that should not be overlooked.* Independence is important, but attorneys should avoid combative, argumentative, or even egomaniacal experts. Also, good experts seldom become defensive or flustered when challenged. Preparing for an eminent domain trial is a team effort, with a common goal. Internal battles may be positive but can also be time consuming and counterproductive.

- *Avoid appraisers with overlapping commitments and deadlines.* The attorney and appraiser should discuss the likely trial date, likely date for exchanging expert information, and likely deposition dates.

The Initial Meeting with the Appraiser

The Preappraisal Meeting

Once the appraiser is selected, the appraiser and the attorney should meet to discuss the assignment. Before beginning the assignment, the appraiser may need the date of value for the appraisal, if one has been established. The appraiser may also need legal instructions that may bear on valuation. For example, appraisers may request such instructions if the condemned property is subject to a dedication requirement, and the dedication has an impact on valuation. The attorney and appraiser should also discuss key dates and scheduling, including the likely trial date, likely date to exchange expert information, and likely deposition dates. The type of appraisal report, if any, should also be clarified.

Avoid Contaminating the Appraisal

Throughout the appraiser's engagement, the attorney should strive to avoid contaminating the appraisal process—or raising the specter of a "directed appraisal." Attorney-appraiser communications may eventually be discoverable under some circumstances, so attorneys should not disclose goals or misgivings to the appraiser. Keep the concept of the file in mind, and avoid unnecessary or overly familiar written communications with the appraiser. Some additional strategies to avoid contamination include the following:

- Initial meetings with an appraiser should normally involve oral, rather than written, reports;
- Appraisal work product should often be stamped as *draft* until exchanged;
- Appraisers often properly prefer to obtain source documents directly from the source rather than relying on representations from counsel. Source documents include, among others, title information, permits, and information regarding the property and construction of the project in the manner proposed.

Report of Results

A narrative appraisal report is often viewed as the final stage in the appraisal—marking an end to the assignment. However, appraisal reports are not necessary in all jurisdictions, or even ideal in all cases. Some jurisdictions require parties to exchange full narrative reports, while others simply require a statement of valuation data.[18] Often, counsel will have appraisers report their conclusions orally and later direct the appraiser to prepare either a report or statement of valuation data before the exchange of expert information.

Reports may provide your opponent a fertile ground for cross-examination of your appraiser, providing another source for possible inconsistencies. The opposition may scrutinize and nitpick, even unfairly, the appraiser's report. This tactic—on which many cases are decided—capitalizes on the old adage, "the only completely consistent people are dead."[19]

Practice Tip: If you instruct your appraiser to prepare a preliminary report, consider instructing him not to number the pages. This will

---

18. For example, California Eminent Domain Law only requires the exchange of a "statement of valuation data." *E.g.*, Cal. Civ. Proc. Code § 1258.260. *But see* Los Angeles Superior Court Local Rules, chapter 16, appendix A (requiring the exchange of a narrative-styled appraisal report), *available at* http://www.lasuperiorcourt.org/.

19. Aldous Huxley.

provide some flexibility for the appraiser to add additional analysis as the case progresses.[20]

Direct Examination of Appraisal Experts

Getting to the Point

Eminent domain trials have been described as sober, (i.e., boring) inquiries into value.[21] But jurors tend to punish overly long, boring presentations.[22] In this context, less may really be more.[23]

In one commentator's words, "trials are stressful, fact-filled, and laced with legal issues. Counsel must not become so obsessed with details as to miss the essential case. The lawyer should be able to write down the main themes of the case in 50 words or fewer, and to hammer those themes home to the jury."[24] Jurors can be fickle. And even the most technically adept, well-prepared appraisal witness may not engage a jury's interest. The jury may not care much about technical competence, cap rates, or comparable sales. It may care instead about the theater, charisma, and deep structure issues. These include the following:

1. Why the land was taken.
2. Evidence regarding how sensitively the government has treated the landowner.
3. Whether fair market value, an objective standard, fully compensates the landowner for a property's subjective value to the landowner. (Note that this issue raises a fundamental irony in real property law. Under a legal fiction, all land is unique.[25] Yet appraisal theory depends on the

---

20. For a more detailed discussion of appraisal reports, see NICHOLS, supra note 16; *see also* NORMAN E. MATTEONI & HENRY VEIT, CONDEMNATION PRACTICE IN CALIFORNIA § 3.12 (3d ed. 2008); Eaton, *supra* note 16, at 444; *see generally* UNIFORM APPRAISAL STANDARDS FOR FEDERAL LAND ACQUISITIONS (1992); UNIFORM STANDARDS OF PROFESSIONAL APPRAISAL PRACTICE (1994).

21. People *ex rel.* Dep't of Transp. v. Clauser/Wells Partnership, 95 Cal. App. 4th 1066, 1072 (2002).

22. *See* MICHAEL E. TIGAR, EXAMINING WITNESSES 35 (2d ed. 2003 [1972]) ("It is the privilege of the rich to waste the time of the poor.") (quoting poet Stevie Smith).

23. *See* SUSAN MACPHERSON, USE OF JURY CONSULTANTS IN A CONDEMNATION CASE 125 (2004).

24. WILLIAM A. BROCKETT & JOHN W. KEKER, EFFECTIVE DIRECT AND CROSS EXAMINATION (2004).

25. *See, e.g.*, Brasurco v. 21st Century Ins. Co., 108 Cal. App. 4th 110, 120 (2003) (stating "the fundamental legal maxim that each parcel of land is unique"); Cottonwood Christian Ctr. v. Cypress Redevelopment Agency, 218 F. Supp. 2d 1203, 1230 (C.D. Cal. 2002)

"principle of substitution": "[p]roperty values tend to be set by the price of acquiring an equally desirable substitute property."[26]).

4. Whether fair market value really is fair. (Note that here is also a fundamental shortcoming in eminent domain law: the Fifth and Fourteenth Amendments require "just compensation" and "due process." Yet the fair market value measure chronically shortchanges owners, who are not compensated for the following: (1) the subjective premium each landowner places on property; (2) transaction costs; or (3) personal stress/disruption, delay, or uncertainty.)

5. Whether the landowner deserves the money, or is overreaching. In other words, is the landowner being greedy? How does the claim compare to the price paid? What private offers has the owner received?

None of these deep structure issues are ones the appraisal expert necessarily addresses. Yet some attorneys believe that these are often the real, key issues—not technical jargon about cap rates and comparable sales. Despite rules, evidence gets in, or inferences are made. Ignore these issues at your own risk.

Choose Your Story Carefully

Most condemnation cases have at least one theme or story. As one practitioner observed: "Every good story, be it a novel, short story, epic, or play has a unifying theme. Exactly the same is true of a trial. The trial must have a theme—a central idea that gives unity to the drama we shall unfold before the jury. Like the literary artist, the trial lawyer must let the theme do its job."[27] "People, including judges and jurors, understand and restate events in terms of stories. They take the relevant evidence and weave it into a coherent whole . . . [a] lawsuit is a contest between two stories."[28] Several overarching themes or stories recur in eminent domain trials. These include the deep structure issues:

- Is the government overreaching or bullying the landowner?
- Is the government sloppy and inattentive?
- Is the government indifferent or arrogant?
- Is the landowner greedy and overreaching?

("Every piece of property is unique and thus damages are an insufficient remedy to the denial of property rights.").

26. Appraisal Institute, The Appraisal of Real Estate 39, 298–99 (13th ed. 2008); *see* Gideon Kanner, *Condemnation Blight: Just How Just Is Just Compensation?* 48 Notre Dame L. Rev. 765, 774 (1973).

27. Irving Younger, The Advocate's Desk Book 42 (1998).

28. Michael E. Tigar, Examining Witnesses 22 (1972) (2d ed. 2003).

- Is there evidence of landowner speculation, the proverbial "castle in the air"?

Consider a Narrative Technique to Cover Standard Bases during Direct Examination

The standard bases to cover include the following:

- The appraisal expert's qualifications;
- The expert's investigation of the condemned property and comparable sale, etc.;
- The expert's analysis of the data; and
- The expert's conclusion.

Understand the Limitations of Appraisers as Witnesses

Appraisers do not think the way many judges—and some jurors—think. Appraisers, like scientists, tend to assume an objective, correct answer always exists. Examples include the following:

- Appraisers generally focus on hard evidence: dates, numbers and the terms, etc.
- Appraisers are bound to be objective, and ignore subjective valuations.
- An appraiser cannot add a premium that the market does not recognize.
- Some appraisers believe that even a sloppy job might yield the correct answer. But even a very technically thorough and complete job could be thrown off by one minor error.

Judges and jurors, by contrast, tend to think like lawyers. The truth is revealed after careful assembly and processing of evidence and the give and take of discussion and argument. Examples include the following:

- The focus is on the expert's qualifications, how the expert spent his time, and the process. Not just the facts.
- This approach acknowledges that any answer is at best an estimate, an approximation.
- This approach can also recognize subjective valuation.

Practical Suggestions for Direct Examination

- Appraisers should avoid technical jargon, theoretical arguments, and cant.
- Appraisers should be prepared to talk about their qualifications regarding real world experience, as well as academic accolades, institutional honors, and previous testimony.

- Appraisers should consider—or at least be aware of—the deep structure issues.
- Appraisers should memorize the address, square footage, and date of value for the valuation of the subject property.
- If the appraiser relied on the comparable sales approach (also known as the market approach) to valuation, the appraiser should have verified the comparable sales and committed to memory the addresses, square footages, and dates of sale for each comparable property.
- Appraisers should also focus on effective communication and process—not just objective, arithmetical facts.

To the extent the appraiser relied on the opinions of subsidiary experts, counsel should consider designating the nonappraisal experts as potential trial witnesses. Counsel should also consider eliciting direct testimony from the subsidiary experts, before the appraiser is called to the stand. This sequence not only lays a foundation for the appraisal expert's opinion, but builds anticipation for his testimony.

Cross-Examination

Effective cross-examinations focus on the four categories of appraiser vulnerability: (1) qualifications, (2) bias, (3) thoroughness of investigation, and (4) overall plausibility. The cross-examination should not necessarily proceed in this order. "It is usually better to start and finish strong, and leave the less interesting material for the middle."[29]

Attacks on the Appraiser's Qualifications

In most jurisdictions, a witness testifying as an expert may be cross-examined to the same extent as any other witness and, in addition, may be fully cross-examined as to (1) his qualifications, (2) the subject to which his expert testimony relates, and (3) the matter on which his opinion is based and the reasons for his opinion.[30] Some tactics and areas of inquiry include the following:

- The appraiser's possible lack of real world experience.
- Whether the appraiser's specialization includes the type of assignment at issue.

---

29. Raoul D. Kennedy & James C. Martin, California Expert Witness Guide § 1.1 (2d ed. 2000).
30. *See, e.g.,* Cal. Evid. Code § 721.

- The limited scope of the appraiser's expertise. For example, is the appraiser an expert on land use, planning, or entitlement issues; construction costs and techniques; architecture; engineering; economics; brokerage; or development?
- Any limitations in education, and other formal training.

Attacks on the Appraiser's Bias

The sum of the compensation and expenses paid to an expert witness may provide a proper subject of inquiry by an adverse party as relevant to the credibility of the expert and the weight of his testimony. Some tactics and other areas of inquiry include the following:

- How frequently does the appraiser represent public agencies, rather than landowners?
- Has the appraiser previously testified for his particular party, lawyer, or law firm? How frequently does the appraiser work with a single attorney?
- Has the appraiser made any inconsistent statements or approaches in other cases?
- Does the appraiser have any financial interests in the case or property— for example, the appraiser's unpaid bills?
- Are there any communications from the client or the lawyer concerning the desired outcome or assumptions?

Attacks on the Appraiser's Thoroughness of Investigation

Exposing an appraiser's lack of thoroughness often hits home with a jury. Jurors may not necessarily understand or care about technical questions or appraisal jargon, but jurors do understand and care about whether the appraiser inspected the property, knows its address, and knows the name of the nearest intersection. The jury is permitted to consider a number of factors in determining the credibility of the appraiser such as the extent of the appraiser's opportunity to observe the property, his ability to recollect, his attitude toward the action, and his demeanor while testifying.[31] If the

---

31. *See, e.g.,* Cal. Evid. Code § 780; Fed R. Evid. 602; State Dep't of Transp. & Dev. v. Hammons, 550 So. 2d 767, 773 (La. Ct. App. 1989) (upholding trial court's discounting an appraiser's testimony because, among other things, he "was apparently not as familiar with the area . . . as were the other two appraisers."); Florence v. Williams, 439 So. 2d 83, 86 (Ala. 1983) (noting the observations of the "demeanor of the witnesses, listen[ing] to the inflections and intonations of their voices during oral testimony, and study[ing] their eyes, facial expressions, and gestures—all of these sensory perceptions which play a critical role in the factfinder's determination of which witnesses are to be afforded credibility when conflicting

appraiser is unfamiliar with the methods or sources that his employees used in arriving at conclusions, and he is unable to demonstrate independent knowledge, courts in many jurisdictions may strike the appraiser's testimony.[32] Some tactics and areas of inquiry include the following:

- Any client-imposed limits or restrictions on time and budget for the appraiser's assignment.
- How the appraiser spent his time and everything he did in investigation of the problem.
- The appraiser's use of assistants to complete the assignment.
- The appraiser's inspection of the property; verification and inspection of comparable sales; interviews with planners, contractors, brokers, developers, and other market participants.
- Legal instructions from the agencies' or landowner's attorney. Common legal instructions include the enforceability of a lease or the validity of a deed restriction.
- The appraiser's ability to recite factual bases.

Plausibility, Reasoning, Data Selection, and Manipulation

Another key area of cross-examination involves the methodology or plausibility of reasoning used by the appraiser in arriving at his property valuation. A common approach used by appraisers is the comparable sales approach. To shed light on the value of the property at issue, comparable sales generally must be near in time, location, character, size, and usability.[33]

---

testimony is given."); City of New Haven v. Tuchmann, 93 Conn. App. 787, 799 (Ct. App. 2006); Raintree Homes, Inc. v. Vill. of Long Grove, 389 Ill. App. 3d 836, 869 (Ill. App. Ct. 2009) (upholding trial court's discounting a witness's testimony because the "trial court, by virtue of its ability to observe the conduct and demeanor of witnesses, is in the best position to assess their credibility").

32. *See, e.g.*, CAL. EVID. CODE § 702; Ark. State Highway Comm'n v. Jensen, 256 Ark. 478, 479 (1974) (reversing denial of motion to strike because "[t]he expert's valuation, upon cross-examination, must demonstrate a foundation in fact or a reasonable and fair basis rather than mere surmise"); State v. Commerce Ctr., Inc., 429 So. 2d 273, 274 (Ala. 1983) ("A witness must be acquainted with the property taken before he can express an opinion as to value.").

33. *See, e.g.*, CAL. EVID. CODE § 816; United States v. 1129.75 Acres of Land, 473 F.2d 996, 998 (8th Cir. 1973) ("Courts have been reluctant to admit evidence of subsequent comparable sales to determine market value when . . . the particular sales involved were not sufficiently comparable to the litigated property in character, locality or time."); United States v. 4.85 Acres of Land, 546 F.3d 613, 619 (9th Cir. 2008); *see also* United States v. 125.07 Acres of Land, 667 F.2d 243, 248 (1st Cir. 1981); Comm'r of Transp. Connecticut v. Chase Crossroads Waterford Square, No. CV010560076S, 2002 Conn. Super. LEXIS 2352 (Super.

Besides attacking an appraiser's comparable sales based on inconsistencies with the property at issue, some cross-examiners may attempt to impeach an appraiser with contradictions with reliable authority in the field. Generally, an expert may be cross-examined concerning the content of any scientific, technical, or professional text, treaties, journal, or similar publication, if (1) he referred to, considered, or relied on it in arriving at or forming his opinion; (2) the publication was admitted in evidence; or (3) the publication has been established as a reliable authority by the testimony or admission of the witness or by other expert testimony or by judicial notice.[34] Some tactics and areas of inquiry include the following:

- The appraiser's adjustments to data—for example, quantitative and qualitative adjustments.
- The appraiser's ability to explain computations or different weight given to seemingly equivalent data.

Sources of Information for the Cross-Examiner

To expose the four vulnerabilities described above, an attorney can look to a number of sources to discover information about an appraiser. These include the following:

- The Internet;
- Other appraisers;
- Other attorneys;
- The appraiser's own curriculum vitae;
- The appraiser's own promotional materials;
- Depositions;
- Texts and articles regarded as authoritative in the field;
- Texts and articles written by the appraiser; and
- Anything else a resourceful attorney can locate.

Conclusion

Real estate appraisers often provide powerful, persuasive, outcome-determinative testimony in eminent domain trials. The usefulness of expert

---

Ct. July 16, 2002) ("In order to be used as a comparable sales approach, a comparable sale must be one that sufficiently resembles the subject property with respect to time, place and circumstances that a reasonable person would consider in evaluating fair market value."); Arkansas Oklahoma Gas Corp. v. Boggs, 86 Ark. App. 66, 77 (Ct. App. 2004); Knabe v. State, 285 Ala. 321, 328 (1970).

34. *See, e.g.*, CAL. EVID. CODE § 721; ALA. R. EVID. 803; FED. R. EVID. 705, 803(18).

appraisal testimony can hinge, however, not only on the appraisal witness's technical skill, but also on the witness's and presenting attorney's presentation skill, level of preparation, and appreciation of the unique and reoccurring themes in eminent domain trials.

EXPERTS IN LEGAL MALPRACTICE CASES

Mike Prince and Kelli Hinson[1]

Legal malpractice cases call for a variety of experts, including both lawyers and nonlawyers. Expert testimony is required when the subject relates to any profession in a way that is beyond a layperson's apprehension—something all too frequently true of the legal profession. In thinking about experts, parties involved in legal malpractice suits should consider such factors as the area of practice in which the alleged misconduct occurred, which jurisdiction's law governs, and whether nonlegal experts will have to testify about an underlying action or damages. This subchapter examines the basic negligence form of the legal malpractice action and some special issues that often arise.

Special Considerations in Choosing a Legal Malpractice Expert

Federal Rule of Evidence 702 (and the corresponding state rules) require that an expert be qualified "by knowledge, skill, experience, training, or education" to testify on the relevant subject matter. This is no different for legal experts. Merely being a licensed lawyer may not be sufficient to qualify someone as an expert in a legal malpractice suit. The prospective expert should have more than academic familiarity with the applicable standard of care in the relevant jurisdiction, ideally having practiced in the jurisdiction

---

1. Mike Prince and Kelli Hinson are both partners at Carrington Coleman Sloman & Blumenthal, LLP in Dallas, Texas. Mr. Prince is the firm's general counsel, and Ms. Hinson is the head of the firm's Professional Liability practice group. Both Mr. Prince and Ms. Hinson practice in the area of professional liability, including defending lawyers and law firms against claims of legal malpractice. Alex More, an associate at Carrington Coleman, also provided invaluable assistance in researching and drafting this subchapter.

and pertinent legal field. Many malpractice claims will be subject to state law (e.g., litigation malpractice, real estate malpractice, and probate malpractice) and will require that the lawyer expert have some experience with that state's standard of care for lawyers or, at a minimum, be able to articulate how experience in another jurisdiction is relevant to the standard at issue. This is not necessarily always true—consider malpractice cases against patent attorneys or other liability deriving from federal statutes. In these cases, no local familiarity is necessary, and instead, the focus should be on whether the lawyer expert has sufficient experience in the particular area of practice.[2]

In general, when choosing an expert witness, a party should ask the following preliminary questions:

• Is the expert familiar with the applicable standard of care (beyond academically)?
• Is the expert licensed to practice law and admitted to the bar of the relevant jurisdiction?
• Does the expert have experience practicing in the area that is the subject of litigation?
• Does the defendant claim to be a specialist? If so, does the expert have that same specialty expertise?

Dangers of Hiring a Legal Scholar, a Specialist, or a Judge

Parties should think carefully before hiring a legal scholar, a specialist, or a judge to testify as an expert witness. Often, an experienced practitioner in the subject area will be more valuable to your client.

First, although it is often tempting to seek out a legal scholar as your expert, parties need to carefully balance experience against academic credentials. A lawyer who has practiced for years in the same kinds of matters as the defendant is likely to be more credible to the jury than a tenured law professor who has never practiced in the real world in a particular area.

Second, just as a lack of experience can undermine a legal expert's credibility, hiring a specialist may also have drawbacks. Such an individual may

---

2. *See, e.g.*, Wright v. Williams, 47 Cal. App. 3d 802, 810–11 (Ct. App. 1975) (in action against maritime specialist, claim depended on ability of expert to testify about standard of care among maritime specialists); Byrne v. Wood, Herron & Evans, LLP, No. 2: 08-102-DCR, 2009 WL 2382415 (E.D. Ky. July 30, 2009) (holding expert with extensive experience in writing and prosecuting patent applications was not qualified to testify in malpractice case because he did not have any experience, training, skill, or education in *legal malpractice* as it relates to the patent application process).

be overqualified and out of touch with the *ordinary* standard of care within the applicable legal community. As a plaintiff's expert particularly, there may be a valid argument that the specialist expert is inappropriately applying a heightened level of scrutiny to the facts at hand. For example, a small town general practice attorney should not be held to the same standard of care in an estate planning representation as an attorney who specializes in complex estate planning and cutting-edge tax shelters.[3] That being said, if a specialist will testify that the defendant followed the appropriate standard of care, then that specialist would undoubtedly be valuable to the defendant as an expert. Likewise, a specialist often will be necessary when the defendant is also a specialist, and the specialist expert should come from the same field of practice.

Finally, although parties, in theory, may use judges as experts in legal malpractice cases, as a practical matter, judges can pose significant problems. In the litigation malpractice context, the original trial judge can easily slip into inappropriate testimony regarding the probable outcome of the original trial had the defendant acted differently. Such testimony should be excluded because resolution of that question is properly in the fact finder's domain. As one California court put it,

> We think it prejudicial to one party for a judge to testify as an expert witness on behalf of the other party with respect to matters that took place before him in his judicial capacity. In such instance the judge appears to be throwing the weight of his position and authority behind one of two opposing litigants.[4]

The Arizona Supreme Court was similarly concerned by the prospect of allowing the prior trial judge to testify in the subsequent legal malpractice suit, writing "[t]he specter of such a scene throws a chill down our judicial spine."[5]

The use of other judges or former judges can present similar prejudice problems. Juries may view an active judge as having as much authority in the courtroom as the sitting judge, not to mention that cross-examining an active judge may prove uncomfortable for the attorney who expects to one day appear in that judge's court. Retired judges may not have practiced recently enough to have knowledge about the appropriate standard of care. The jury also may be easily confused and inappropriately influenced by a judge's

3. *See, e.g.,* Cadle Co. v. Sweet & Brousseau, P.C., No. Civ. A. 3:97-CV-298-L, 2006 WL 435229, at *3–4 (N.D. Tex. Feb. 23, 2006) (former Texas Supreme Court Justice Wallace's expert testimony excluded after successful argument that expertise as a judge did not equate to expertise regarding legal malpractice).

4. Merritt v. Reserve Ins. Co., 34 Cal. App. 3d 858 (1973).

5. Phillips v. Clancy, 733 P.2d 300, 306 (Ariz. 1986).

testimony regarding the law. Some jurisdictions specifically disallow such practice, and even where they do not, the use of a judge as an expert witness may significantly increase the likelihood of reversible error if, for instance, the judge as witness misstates the law on an issue.

Consulting versus Testifying Experts

Using lawyers as experts can also pose unique dangers insofar as parties may be tempted to let the expert participate in discussions of litigation strategy—they are lawyers, after all. Allowing a lawyer expert access to litigation strategy can be harmful if that expert is designated as a testifying expert because any information disclosed to that expert may become discoverable.[6] The attorney-client privilege does not apply to communications with a testifying expert, even if the expert happens to be a lawyer. Moreover, participation in strategizing calls into question the expert's bias. Where a party decides a particular legal expert would be more useful in the war room than the courtroom, it should designate that expert as consulting only to avoid the potentially negative discovery consequences.

Substantive Areas of Testimony

Most legal malpractice claims derive from a negligence theory of liability and, consequently, require proof of duty, breach, causation, and damages. Practitioners should consider the expert testimony that will be needed on each of these essential elements. Both plaintiffs and defendants likely will need expert legal testimony regarding the appropriate standard of care and whether the defendant breached that standard. A lawyer expert also should be prepared to testify regarding causation, although parties will sometimes need nonlawyer experts to testify about causation and damages.

Elements of a Legal Malpractice Claim
1. The defendant attorney owed plaintiff a duty with a professional standard of care;
2. The attorney breached that duty;
3. The breach caused injury; and
4. Damages.

---

6. *See, e.g.,* Fed. R. Civ. P. 26(a)(2).

Although this section focuses on negligence, the analysis applies equally to most other types of claims that could be filed against an attorney, particularly fiduciary duty claims, where expert testimony may also be necessary to establish the proper standard of conduct.[7] Keep in mind, however, that in most jurisdictions a plaintiff may not split or fracture its causes of action against an attorney. In other words, if the gravamen of the complaint is that the lawyer failed to perform his professional duties to the client as a reasonable and prudent lawyer ought to have done, then that is legal malpractice and not also a breach of fiduciary duty or a claim on the attorney-client contract.[8] Generally, to sustain those other types of claims, there has to be a separate injury arising from a claimed breach of fiduciary duty (e.g., misapplication of client trust funds) or a claimed breach of the contract (e.g., failure to render an agreed-upon accounting for amounts in the lawyer's trust account) that is something more, different from, or beyond the lawyer's performance of professional obligations in connection with a particular representation.[9]

Duty

A lawyer's expert testimony generally will be necessary to establish the applicable standard of care in a legal malpractice case, namely, what a reasonably prudent lawyer should have done. This does not mean that the lawyer expert can create a new duty *ex nihilo*—testifying that certain conduct is not what an ordinary lawyer should have done is not the same as testifying that a lawyer has a duty to refrain from that certain conduct. The latter is an issue of law for the court to decide, not the expert.[10]

---

7. *See, e.g.*, Arce v. Burrow, 958 S.W.2d 239, 252 (Tex. Ct. App. 1997), *aff'd in part, rev'd in part on other grounds*, 997 S.W.2d 229 (Tex. 1999).

8. *See* Wong v. Ekberg, 807 A.2d 1266, 1272 (N.H. 2002) ("The modern trend in analyzing legal malpractice causes of action . . . has been to blur the contract-tort distinction and, in most jurisdictions, there is no difference between the remedies for the different theories.").

9. *See, e.g., id.* ("We have held that a plaintiff can maintain a legal malpractice action both in contract, under a third-party beneficiary theory, and in tort, under a negligence theory.") (citing Simpson v. Calivas, 650 A.2d 318 (N.H. 1994); MacMillan v. Scheffy, 787 A.2d 867 (N.H. 2001)); Jarnagin v. Terry, 807 S.W.2d 190, 191 (Mo. Ct. App. 1991) ("The lawyer error . . . was not lawyer negligence, but the failure of the lawyer to follow the instructions of the client. . . . As such, the duty owed by the lawyer to the client is not that as established by the legal profession, but by the law of agency.").

10. *See, e.g.*, Resolution Trust Corp. v. Blasdell, 154 F.R.D. 675, 689 (D. Ariz. 1993) ("The existence of a duty is a matter of law which the court must determine. [] Thus, the legal conclusion by these experts that Jennings Strauss had a duty to advise Sentinel that the

What an ordinary lawyer should do when faced with a particular situation may vary from state to state and between state and federal practice. Therefore, the expert must establish his familiarity with the law and practice of the proper jurisdiction. Out-of-state lawyer experts testifying about the standard of care in a state in which they do not practice may end up having their testimony excluded or, at the very least, their credibility seriously undermined.

Plaintiffs must be particularly cautious about jurisdictional concerns in their initial pleading. Some jurisdictions require the initial pleading to be accompanied by an expert affidavit attesting to the standard of care and the defendant's breach.[11] Significantly, the court in *Fontaine v. Steen* found that a nonspecific statute requiring an expert affidavit when expert testimony would be used to establish a prima facie case applied to legal malpractice cases.[12] Thus, it is important that parties consider not only specific statutory provisions addressing legal malpractice, but also other statutes addressing expert testimony. Moreover, plaintiffs must make sure that when an affidavit is required, that affidavit addresses all of the necessary elements. For example, *Fontaine* requires that the expert affidavit address the duty, breach, *and* causation elements.[13]

The Attorney-Client Relationship

The fundamental question in determining whether the lawyer defendant owed a professional duty to the client is whether an attorney-client relationship existed at the time of the alleged misconduct.[14] Typically this will be undisputed or be a question of fact. But in certain more complex situations where the legal effect of the relationship is in dispute, expert testimony may be admissible on the question of whether an attorney-client relationship was formed. Some jurisdictions treat this question as strictly a legal issue for the court to determine; however, others allow expert testimony to help resolve disputes about facts giving rise to the existence of an attorney-client relationship. Examples of such disputes include the point at which the attorney-client relationship terminated, whether the parties agreed on the

---

Indian School transaction might violate the Loans to One Borrower regulations is not relevant to this court's analysis.") (citation omitted).

    11. *See, e.g.*, Fontaine v. Steen, 759 N.W.2d 672, 676 (Minn. 2009).

    12. *Id.*

    13. *Id.*

    14. There are certain situations when a nonclient can bring claims against an attorney, such as a negligent misrepresentation claim, but this subchapter will largely focus on true legal malpractice claims, which require the plaintiff to prove privity—or an attorney-client relationship.

scope of the engagement, and the reasonableness of the attorney's—or, in some jurisdictions, the client's—belief about the relationship.[15]

Standing

Expert testimony about the plaintiff's standing to assert the malpractice claim is also admissible in certain cases. Standing to assert a malpractice claim is most frequently an issue in bankruptcy proceedings. For example, the parties may contest whether the former client/debtor has standing to bring a malpractice claim outside of the proceeding or whether the trustee owns the claim. Or, the parties may dispute whether the confirmation of the plan of reorganization, or the court's approval of a fee application, extinguished claims at the conclusion of the bankruptcy case. Expert testimony about standing may be admissible in nonbankruptcy contexts as well, however. In *Ott v. Smith*, for example, the plaintiff alleged, among other things, that the defendant attorney was negligent in failing to demonstrate standing for a conversion action.[16] The Alabama Supreme Court in *Ott* permitted expert testimony on plaintiff's standing insofar as the expert testified about facts giving rise to the plaintiff's ownership interest.[17]

The Common Knowledge Exception

Once an attorney-client relationship (and therefore duty) is established, and the plaintiff has standing to bring the claim, evidence of what that duty was is also useful. Generally, an expert must testify about what an ordinary lawyer should have done, but courts typically recognize what is referred to as the common knowledge exception, which applies when the lawyer's error is such that the applicable standard of care is within the common knowledge of laypersons. Practitioners must research the specific applicable jurisdiction to see what conduct falls within it. Situations where expert testimony may not be necessary include missed deadlines, failure to communicate material information to a client, disregarding statutory requirements, administrative errors (e.g., failure to redact sensitive information), failure to file a UCC-1 security interest, and intentional or fraudulent acts.[18]

---

15. *See* RONALD E. MALLEN & JEFFREY M. SMITH, LEGAL MALPRACTICE § 35:21 (2009).

16. Ott v. Smith, 413 So. 2d 1129, 1131 (Ala. 1982).

17. *Id.* at 1134.

18. *See, e.g.,* O'Neil v. Bergan, 452 A.2d 337, 342 (D.C. 1982) (listing examples of lawyer conduct falling within the common knowledge exception to include allowing limitations to run, permitting entry of a default judgment against the client, failing to instruct the client to answer interrogatories, failing to allege affirmative defenses, failing to file tax returns, and failing to follow client instructions). *But see* Se. Hous. Found. v. Smith, 670

Be careful in making this determination, however—jurisdictions vary on what kinds of misconduct require expert testimony. Do not assume that an expert is unnecessary simply because the alleged standard of conduct seems obvious.

Breach

The core of the legal expert's testimony is an opinion about whether the defendant breached the standard of care. Therefore, unless the case involves the kind of negligence that the applicable jurisdiction has recognized as appreciable by laypersons, the parties need to consider whether expert testimony will be needed regarding the breach element.[19] This is not the same thing as testifying that the defendant's conduct caused or did not cause harm to the plaintiff, so parties must be careful to explicitly cover both elements with their expert or risk a finding by the court that the expert's testimony failed to address both breach and causation. Testifying about what would have happened had the defendant done things differently may be off limits,[20] but the lawyer expert can testify about what the defendant should have done to comport with the standard of care. So, for example, when the issue in a legal malpractice case is whether the defendant attorney reasonably interpreted a particular law or legal doctrine, a lawyer expert *may* testify about whether the interpretation was reasonable as compared to how ordinary lawyers interpret the issue.

Parties must be careful, however, that their legal experts do not testify about purely legal issues, which generally is not permitted. It is the job of the trial judge, and not either party's expert witness, to instruct the jury on the law.[21] The court in *Greenberg Traurig of New York, P.C. v. Moody* found not only that the admission of expert testimony regarding legal issues was in error but that it was so prejudicial as to require reversal. It noted as follows:

> The potential prejudicial effect of an attorney testifying as an expert is of greater significance than that of other experts. . . . By permitting attor-

---

S.E.2d 680, 695 (S.C. Ct. App. 2008) (violation of a statute not sufficient evidence of breach of duty without expert testimony).

19. *See* Rose v. Welch, 115 S.W.2d 478, 484 (Tenn. Ct. App. 2003).

20. *See* "Causation" *infra*.

21. *See, e.g.*, Specht v. Jensen, 853 F.2d 805, 807 (10th Cir. 1988) ("There being only one applicable legal rule for each dispute or issue, it requires only one spokesman of the law, who of course is the judge."); Burkhart v. Wash. Metro Area Transit Auth., 112 F.3d 1207, 1212–13 (D.C. Cir. 1997) (stating that "[e]ach courtroom comes equipped with a 'legal expert,' called a judge, and it is his or her province alone to instruct the jury on the relevant legal standards").

neys to state opinions as to what the applicable law is, the trial judge voluntarily allows his role as the legal expert in the courtroom to be usurped or diminished by the testifying attorney. Thus, when attorneys are qualified as experts on certain areas of the law, the jury will be tempted to turn to the expert, rather than the trial judge, for guidance on the law. These concerns are magnified when the expert witnesses are not merely practicing attorneys in a given area of the law, but are cloaked with the authority associated with being a learned legal scholar, a law school professor, or a former supreme court justice.[22]

Causation

Proving causation requires expert testimony when the connection between the defendant's conduct and damages is beyond the jury's common understanding. Here, the expert should testify about the existence or nonexistence of a direct causal link between the defendant's alleged misconduct and the plaintiff's damages.[23]

In the *Alexander* case, for example, a client sued a law firm regarding its handling of a complex bankruptcy case. The client had hired the named partner Alexander personally, but Alexander had passed the case off to a new associate, who ultimately tried the case (to a bad result). The client claimed that causation was obvious, relying on evidence of numerous alleged mistakes made during the trial. The Texas Supreme Court disagreed, noting that "even when negligence is admitted, causation is not presumed."[24] The court in *Alexander* concluded that the court of appeals had erred in holding that the jury was competent to determine causation without expert guidance.[25]

On the other hand, some courts do not allow expert testimony on what would have happened had the defendant acted differently. That speculative scenario can be considered an ultimate issue for the fact finder to resolve, and this boundary makes causation a tricky element for expert testimony. Because some jurisdictions encourage—and indeed require—expert testimony regarding causation, plaintiffs must be prepared to offer it, but both

---

22. Greenberg Traurig of New York, P.C. v. Moody, 161 S.W.3d 56, 99 (Tex. Ct. App. 2004) (internal citations omitted); *see also Specht*, 853 F.2d at 808 (holding such testimony is not only inadmissible, but harmful).

23. *See* Alexander v. Turtur & Assocs., Inc., 146 S.W.3d 113, 119 (Tex. 2002).

24. *Id.* at 119.

25. *Id.* at 122. In a concurring opinion, Justice Hecht expressed doubt as to whether a jury could ever be fairly expected to determine what a judge would have decided in such hypothetical circumstances and questioned what type of expert testimony would be appropriate in such a case but left these and other thorny questions for another day. *Id.*

parties must vigilantly guard against lawyer experts speculating on out-comes under hypothetical scenarios.

   To take a recent example, in *Harrison v. Proctor & Gamble Co.*, plaintiff shareholders of Zooth Inc. sued Taft, Stettinius & Hollister LLP, among others, for allegedly negligently representing them in the sale of Zooth to the Gillette Company.[26] The core of the plaintiffs' claim was that the negoti-ated stock purchasing agreement did not contain a "best efforts" provision or a "change of control" provision that allegedly would have guaranteed Zooth shareholders a higher earn-out.[27] Explaining that these circumstances called for expert testimony as to causation, the court noted as follows: "Ne-gotiations for, and the drafting of, a stock purchasing agreement demands specialized knowledge by an experienced lawyer. . . . The ability to prepare such an agreement and the concomitant evaluation of all factors involved in the context of stock acquisition requires specialized knowledge of the law. This is a skill not ordinarily possessed by lay persons."[28]

   The *Harrison* court concluded that expert opinion was necessary to es-tablish causation because a lay jury cannot ascertain whether the defen-dants obtained a "reasonable agreement."[29] Note that whether the agreement was reasonable appears to concern the duty and breach elements, but here the court insists that it goes to the issue of causation as well, finding that the expert testimony never sufficiently alleged "the direct causal link to Plain-tiffs' alleged damages."[30] The lesson is that courts can muddle breach and causation analysis, and parties would do well to try and keep their own analyses clear. Other states resolve this problem by explicitly not requiring expert testimony on causation.[31]

The Trial-within-a-Trial

In litigation malpractice cases, proving causation may require putting on the so-called trial-within-a-trial, where the plaintiff shows what the outcome of the underlying trial would have been had the defendant acted differently by retrying the case to a different jury. When litigating the trial-within-a-trial in

---

26. Harrison v. Proctor & Gamble Co., No. 7:06-CV-121-O, 2009 WL 304573, at *1 (N.D. Tex. Feb. 9, 2009).
   27. *Id.* at *1–2.
   28. *Id.* at *7.
   29. *Id.*
   30. *Id.* at *8.
   31. *See, e.g.*, McClure Enters., Inc. v. Gen. Ins. Co. of Am., No. 05-3491-PHX-SMM, 2009 WL 73677, at *16 (D. Ariz. Jan. 9, 2009) ("In Arizona, expert testimony may be re-quired to establish the *standard of care* and deviation from that standard, but it is not re-quired to show *causation* of a resulting injury.") (emphasis in original).

a legal malpractice suit, the plaintiff wants to show that, but for the conduct of the defendant lawyer, a different outcome would have occurred. In many jurisdictions, the parties may not use lawyer experts (or juror or trial judge witnesses, for that matter) to testify about the outcome of the trial-within-a-trial because it is considered an ultimate issue for resolution by the second jury or bench trial judge.[32] Some jurisdictions, however, such as New Jersey, allow plaintiffs to present expert testimony regarding the probable outcome of the underlying case to promote more efficient legal malpractice suits.[33]

In any event, parties must use experts to put on their prima facie cases in the trial-within-a-trial to the extent they would have needed those experts in the original underlying suit (e.g., if the underlying suit were a medical malpractice claim, the parties would want to use medical expert testimony just as they would in the original suit). Unless the jurisdiction specifically allows otherwise, the parties should not rely on their lawyer experts to testify about the outcome of the trial-within-a-trial, instead using experts appropriate to the underlying action.

Transactions

Where the alleged malpractice occurred during a transactional representation, as opposed to litigation, a plaintiff must prove causation by showing that the other party to the transaction would have accepted an alternative term or condition if proposed or that the deal ultimately reached would have been more favorable to the plaintiff than the deal actually struck.[34] This may require the use of documents showing the other party's intent, fact testimony by the other party, or a witness with knowledge of the other party's position. If a jurisdiction requires expert testimony on causation as to the direct link between the defendant's alleged misconduct and damages, the parties should prepare the expert to testify as such, while simultaneously remaining cautious of the lawyer expert's competency to speculate on alternative deal outcomes.[35]

Tax and Estate Practice

Tax and estate practice may also call for a case-within-a-case analysis requiring expert testimony. If the estate plan had been better or different,

---

32. *See, e.g.,* Whitley v. Chamouris, 574 S.W.2d 251 (2003) ("No witness can predict the decision of a jury and, therefore . . . could not be the subject of expert testimony").

33. *See* Garcia v. Kozlov, Seaton, Romanini & Brooks, P.C., 845 A.2d 602, 612 (N.J. 2004).

34. *See Harrison*, 2009 WL 304573, at *8.

35. *See, e.g.,* 2175 Lemoine Ave. Corp. v. Finco, Inc., 640 A.2d 346 (N.J. Super. Ct. App. Div. 1994) (finding expert testimony necessary to show causal link between attorney negligence and failure to properly structure a complex commercial transaction).

would the Internal Revenue Service (IRS) have allowed the lower taxes? If the lawyer should have known of some unforeseen tax consequence of, say, a real estate transaction, would the local taxing authorities have allowed it? A probate malpractice claim, like any legal malpractice claim, will likely require lawyer expert testimony about the standard of care and breach.[36] To the extent that some jurisdictions may require proximate cause to be shown by expert witnesses, the experts should be prepared to testify as to the causal link between the defendant's conduct and damages, again with proper sensitivity to the expert's competency to testify to matters such as speculating on the behavior of other parties.

Damages

Without any additional qualifications, a lawyer probably does not have sufficient expertise to testify on the amount of damages. In the litigation malpractice context, parties need to put on the same kinds of damages experts they would have used in the underlying litigation.[37] Depending on the jurisdiction, the parties may also need to put on expert testimony regarding the collectibility of the hypothetical judgment. In the transaction context, the proper damages experts will depend on the type of damages claimed. For example, if the complained-of conduct is the failure to perfect a security interest in personal property, then the expert must be someone with knowledge of the value of such an interest. Such a witness would not of necessity have to be a lawyer since it is a straight time-and-place valuation opinion. However, parties might need additional, separate witnesses with regard to other elements because it is likely that only a lawyer could opine on issues such as the consequence of failure to perfect, the absence of any alternative legal recourse if the Uniform Commercial Code (U.C.C.) filing was defective, and the like.

Breach of the Fee Agreement

A legal malpractice plaintiff may choose to pursue a contract rather than a tort theory of liability. Usually, these cases involve claims for breach of the

---

36. *See, e.g.,* Evans v. McDonald, No. 08-11387, 2009 WL 397472, at *3 (11th Cir. Feb. 19, 2009).

37. *See, e.g.,* Clary v. Little Machs. Corp., 850 N.E.2d 423, 436–38 (Ind. Ct. App. 2006) (CPA's testimony as to lost profit damages in underlying suit showed sufficiently certain damages to support jury award in litigation malpractice claim).

fee agreement. By definition, proof of the reasonableness of the agreement requires, at a minimum, expert testimony by a lawyer familiar with the jurisdiction's standards for fees and familiar with the type of practice to which the fee agreement in dispute applied. For example, if what is being litigated is a contingent fee contract with a plaintiff in a personal injury automobile case, the expert should not be a mergers and acquisitions lawyer who bills by the hour.[38]

Testimony regarding Ethical Violations

Parties often will retain academic ethics experts to testify regarding potential ethical lapses during a representation. But ethical standards such as those found in codes of professional responsibility do not necessarily set the bar for the applicable standard of care.[39] For instance, in *Lazy Seven Coal Sales, Inc. v. Stone & Hinds, P.C.*, the Tennessee Supreme Court held that "in a civil action charging malpractice, the standard of care is the particular duty owed the client under the *circumstances of the representation*, which *may or may not* be the standard contemplated by the code."[40] Therefore, just because an expert testifies to the standard of care set by an ethical rule does not mean that the expert has successfully established the standard of care in a legal malpractice claim.[41]

Still, some courts have permitted parties to cross-apply testimony of ethical standards to the standard of care element when the two converge. In *First National Bank of LaGrange v. Lowrey*, for example, the Illinois Court of Appeals allowed broad-sweeping testimony by a law professor who taught professional responsibility.[42] In *Lowrey*, plaintiff's expert Professor

---

38. *See, e.g.*, D&D Assocs. v. Bd. of Educ. of N. Plainfield, 411 F. Supp. 2d 483, 486–87 (D.N.J. 2006) (finding tendered expert unqualified under *Daubert* and Rule 702 when lawyer expert practiced school law in relevant jurisdiction but had no experience in construction or public bidding law).

39. *See, e.g.*, AMERICAN BAR ASSOCIATION, MODEL RULES OF PROFESSIONAL CONDUCT, Preamble And Scope 20 (2009) ("Violation of a Rule should not itself give rise to a cause of action against a lawyer . . . The Rules . . . are not designed to be a basis for civil liability.").

40. Lazy Seven Coal Sales, Inc. v. Stone & Hinds, P.C., 813 S.W.2d 400, 405 (Tenn. 1991) (emphasis added).

41. *See also* Brown v. Morganstern, No. 2002-T-0164, 2004 WL 1238776, at *7 (Ohio Ct. App. June 4, 2004) ("A violation of a disciplinary rule or ethical consideration is actionable only if it constitutes an independent tort. A plaintiff is not relieved of his burden to establish the standard of care simply because an attorney's actions purportedly constitute ethical violations.").

42. First Nat'l Bank of LaGrange v. Lowrey, 872 N.E.2d 447 (Ill. Ct. App. 2007).

Lubet testified that the Illinois Rules of Professional Conduct created an "absolute duty" to convey settlement offers to the client.[43] Against the defendants' arguments that Professor Lubet was not qualified to testify about the defendants' duty in medical malpractice litigation, the court concluded as follows:

> Lubet's experience handling medical malpractice cases was irrelevant to his testimony and the professional duties which that testimony established. Although Lubet was not an expert in medical malpractice cases, he was an expert advising medical malpractice attorneys of their ethical obligations. As Lubet explained, an attorney's professional responsibilities or ethics is a field that transcends any particular area of practice, and the duties arising out of those professional responsibilities are ones that every attorney owes to his client.[44]

Although this finding flies in the face of recommendations concerning the importance of an expert's experience in the defendant's field of practice and awareness of local standards, it primarily serves to demonstrate the variance in what subjects courts will and will not allow lawyer experts to testify about. Cases like *Lowrey* underscore the importance of familiarity with the local jurisprudence on legal malpractice experts so that parties can make the greatest use of the relevant legal framework.

Conclusion

For the reasons discussed in this subchapter, legal malpractice cases will almost invariably require the use of expert witnesses—sometimes multiple experts. Parties to legal malpractice suits will likely need lawyer experts, if for no other reason than to testify about the applicable standard of care and whether the defendant breached that standard. Lawyer experts may also serve an important role with regard to other elements such as causation, but practitioners should be vigilant in objecting to lawyer experts opining on issues of law and issues outside the scope of their expertise such as what the outcome of an underlying lawsuit may have been if not for the defendant's alleged misconduct. Parties may also need other kinds of experts to testify about underlying litigation or damages, and practitioners should be sensitive to the limits of a lawyer expert's ability to offer opinions on such matters. Practitioners must be wary of local jurisprudence with regard to lawyer

---

43. *Id.* at 464–65.
44. *Id.* at 466.

experts as well as potential statutory requirements such as expert affidavits for legal malpractice complaints. Lawyer experts with little or no practical experience and knowledge of the relevant jurisdiction and area of practice should be avoided.

EXPERTS IN ANTITRUST CASES

Lara Swensen and Cory Sinclair[1]

The U.S. government and the various state governments use the antitrust laws to limit firms' exercise of market power in harmful ways and to control how firms compete with one another. Under the antitrust laws, it is not illegal to be a monopoly, but certain means of achieving and maintaining monopoly power are illegal. As a consequence, antitrust cases often turn into battles of the experts, hinging on how a particular market is defined, what products compete, and whether a firm's behavior is more procompetitive than anticompetitive. This subchapter addresses the use of experts in antitrust cases. Specific topics include the type of expert to retain, the topics the expert can address, and how the expert can assist the lawyer in presenting—and ultimately prevailing in—an antitrust case.

Whom to Use as an Antitrust Expert

Possibly the most important decision to make when litigating an antitrust case is selecting the correct expert or experts. The appropriate use of antitrust experts has become increasingly important as antitrust jurisprudence has evolved towards more frequent application of the fact-intensive,

1. Lara Swensen practices law with Flitton & Swensen in Park City, Utah, focusing, in part, on antitrust matters. In addition, Lara is the managing director of Wasatch Economics, a litigation and damages consulting firm that assists clients with antitrust issues and other matters requiring expert involvement. Cory Sinclair is an attorney at Parsons Behle & Latimer in Salt Lake City, Utah, focusing on antitrust-related issues. Cory also has a Ph.D. in economics and has served as a testifying and consulting expert in antitrust cases.

economics-heavy, rule of reason standard.[2] This section addresses five broad categories of experts, each having a unique skill set. Not every case will require an expert from each category, but selecting the wrong expert for a particular task can lead to disastrous results. In addition, this section provides some useful tips on how to find an antitrust expert for your case.

The Economist

Economists are the most common type of antitrust experts.[3] At its most basic level, economics is the study of choices individuals make when faced with scarcity. This basic principle can be extended to firm behavior and to market conditions. Economists who specialize in antitrust economics have particular training in industrial organization, which is a branch of applied microeconomics. Industrial organization addresses strategic firm behavior, including pricing behavior, market structure, competition (both perfect and imperfect), and antitrust issues. An expert economist is uniquely qualified to address relevant market issues, market structure, competitive forces, barriers to entry, and, in many cases, damages.[4] However, an industrial organization economist will not be as proficient as an accountant or financial economist at reviewing and analyzing financial statements.

The ideal economist to serve as an antitrust expert has a Ph.D. in economics with a particular focus on industrial organization or antitrust.[5] Also, the expert should have a working knowledge of the legal standards at issue in antitrust as well as proficiency in econometrics (or statistics). Knowing the legal standards at issue is critically important, because of the close connection between antitrust law and the economic theories used to analyze particular issues.[6] Indeed, most industrial organization textbooks have entire sections devoted to antitrust laws and the standards courts use

---

2. An unreasonable restraint of trade can be established under the per se test or the rule of reason test. The rule of reason test weighs the procompetitive and anticompetitive effects of the challenged conduct. The per se test is an outright prohibition of conduct (once certain elements have been established) without any attempt by a court to measure any procompetitive benefits that may flow from the challenged conduct.

3. Most cases investigated by the Department of Justice and the Federal Trade Commission have both attorneys and economists assigned to the case.

4. As discussed below, damages may also require assistance from an accountant or financial economist.

5. Similar to lawyers, not all economists know everything about all topics that are tangentially related to economics. There are labor economists, macroeconomists, economic historians, health care economists, econometricians, development economists, and many others.

6. Judge Richard Posner, a famous law and economics scholar and judge on the Seventh Circuit Court of Appeals, has commented that antitrust law has become a branch of

to judge anticompetitive conduct. In addition, a background or knowledge of econometrics can be a great benefit to the client because statistics can be used to verify relevant market definitions or to conduct pricing studies to analyze the level of competition.

The Accountant

In addition to an industrial organization economist, you may also need an accountant to review and analyze financial statements or accounting records.[7] The accountant will be able to translate the more abstract principles opined on by the economist into more factually supported conclusions. The expert accountant should be a Certified Public Accountant (CPA) and Accredited in Business Valuation (ABV). One issue that often arises in antitrust litigation is a firm's capacity to handle the additional demand that it claims it would have serviced but for the alleged illegal acts of the defendant. The expert accountant can review financial records to determine if the firm had sufficient excess capacity to supply any additional demand. The expert accountant also adds value by determining which damages model to employ. There are three basic damages models for antitrust damages: (1) before and after theory, (2) specific business loss theory, and (3) yardstick theory.[8] Each model requires different assumptions and different information to perform. The expert accountant can assess which model will be the most defensible given the information available.

The Financial Economist

In some cases, it may be necessary to retain a financial economist in lieu of or in addition to the accountant. The study of financial economics consists

---

applied economics. RICHARD A. POSNER, THE PROBLEMATICS OF MORAL AND LEGAL THEORY 229 (1999).

7. As with all types of experts in antitrust cases, there are significant advantages to getting the accountant involved early in the case. The accountant can help with discovery (including specific document requests) as well as perform preliminary damage calculations that can be used for settlement or mediation purposes.

8. The before and after theory compares a plaintiff's profits or prices paid during the period of violation with profits or prices paid before the beginning of the violation period. This method may also be used to estimate the market share the plaintiff has lost due to the alleged antitrust violation, which would result in lost profits that could be calculated by the expert accountant. The specific business loss theory is an analysis of specific customers or contracts lost due to the alleged violation. The yardstick method compares the prices paid or profits earned by the plaintiff firm against a similarly situated firm unaffected by the alleged violation. This method requires coordination by the expert economist and accountant to select an appropriate yardstick firm.

of three interrelated areas: (1) money and capital markets; (2) investments, which focuses on the investment decisions of individual firms; and (3) managerial finance, which involves the actual management of the firm. Areas (2) and (3) will be the most relevant to antitrust matters.

Investment decisions can be important to consider if a failed company is alleging the failure was caused by the acts of a competitor or former supplier. A financial economist will be able to review the investment decisions of the plaintiff firm and determine if the firm acted prudently and if the financial condition of the firm can be attributed to the acts of the defendant firm. This can be done with an event study (a statistical analysis evaluating the financial condition of the firm immediately before and immediately following a known event) or with a more factual analysis that reviews a series of investment decisions leading up to the ultimate demise of the plaintiff firm. Managerial finance (along with the overlapping topic of investment finance) also is useful in analyzing capacity constraints, entry decisions, and defenses such as business justification or cost justification.

The Industry Expert

Appropriate usage of an industry expert can be critical to successful presentation of an antitrust case. While the industry expert may not have extensive background in antitrust work, per se, he can be vital to providing the factual context for any economic analysis of markets and antitrust injury. Courts have found industry experts to be helpful even where they discuss the industry as a whole, rather than the specific parties at issue in the case. For example, in *FTC v. Whole Foods Market, Inc.*,[9] the Federal Trade Commission (FTC) sought to enjoin Whole Foods Market, Inc., from acquiring another grocery store, Wild Oats Markets, Inc. The FTC alleged that the acquisition would decrease competition and tend to create a monopoly in the operation of "premium natural and organic supermarkets" nationwide.[10] The FTC challenged the defendants' industry expert for "not analyzing the facts of this case, but rather discussing the food retailing industry more generally."[11] The court rejected this challenge, noting that "the state of the industry itself is an important factor in a case like this."[12] Finding that the industry expert's report was "helpful" and deciding to "rely on

---

9. FTC v. Whole Foods Mkt., Inc., 502 F. Supp. 2d 1 (D.D.C. 2007), *rev'd on other grounds*, 533 F.3d 869 (D.C. Cir. 2008).
10. *Id.* at 3–4.
11. *Id.* at 13.
12. *Id.* (also recognizing that the industry expert was a recognized expert in the field of food marketing).

it as appropriate," the court specifically noted that the FTC could have offered its own industry expert but chose not to do so.[13] In other words, if the other side has proffered an industry expert, attorneys would be well advised to ensure that they have the witnesses to counter that expert.

The industry expert generally will be selected on the basis of having extensive knowledge about the industry predating his retention in the pending matter. However, his testimony and report should support and corroborate information about the industry available from the parties' documents and fact witnesses. In the *Whole Foods* case, the defendants supplemented the industry expert's observations about how grocery stores compete for customers and about the increasing demand for organic food with declarations and internal documents prepared in the ordinary course of business.[14] Although sometimes it is possible to get sufficient industry information from a party's employees, the combination of party information and "neutral" data or observations from an industry expert may present a more compelling story.[15]

In antitrust litigation, an industry expert's report and testimony can be vital to understanding several elements of the case, including the relevant market definition, the impact of alleged anticompetitive conduct, and market power. With respect to market definition, industry experts generally are used in addition to antitrust economists, not as substitutes.[16] Industry experts may assist in defining the relevant market by projecting whether a merger would result in decreased competition from other companies.[17] With respect to the impact of alleged anticompetitive conduct, industry experts can assist economists in examining the potential procompetitive or anticompetitive effects of the challenged practice.[18] Similarly, by explain-

---

13. *Id.*

14. *Id.* at 23–34.

15. *See also In re* Lorazepam & Clorazepate Antitrust Litig., 467 F. Supp. 2d 74, 83 (D.D.C. 2006) (finding that plaintiff's "anecdotal testimony" about the inability to get certain pharmaceuticals after defendants' exclusive agreements was "confirmed" by their pharmaceutical industry expert).

16. *See, e.g.*, United States v. Sungard, 172 F. Supp. 2d 172, 179 (D.D.C. 2001) (utilizing economic expert and industry expert in computer disaster recovery to define the market); *see also* FTC v. Owens-Illinois, Inc., 581 F. Supp. 27, 39 (D.D.C. 1988) (industry expert in packaging evaluated potential alternatives to the glass containers at issue in the challenged merger).

17. *Whole Foods*, 502 F. Supp. 2d at 32 (industry expert evaluated whether Whole Foods grocery chain would face competition from any other stores after acquiring Wild Oats Markets).

18. National Cable Television Ass'n, Inc. v. Broadcast Music, Inc., 772 F. Supp. 614, 645 (D.D.C. 1991) (evaluating the competitive benefits of a blanket license as opposed to alternative types of licenses).

ing the reactions of industry participants to certain conduct or practices, an industry expert may also assist parties in arguing causation as plaintiffs need to show a direct relationship between the claimed injury and alleged anticompetitive conduct.[19]

Finally, industry experts may be used to support economists' evaluation of market power. Industry experts can supply important empirical evidence of market power in an industry, which can corroborate an economist's conclusions.[20]

Consulting Experts

As in other types of cases, consulting experts can be very helpful to an attorney's evaluation and development of an antitrust claim. For an antitrust case, a consulting expert could have any of the above-described areas of specialization and might be hired to help the attorneys assess the merits of the case or to serve as an intermediary between the attorneys and the testifying experts.[21] Federal Rule of Civil Procedure 26(b)(4)(B) makes it very difficult for opposing parties to access the notes, communications, or work of a consulting expert. Where the expert witness is not expected to testify at trial, the party seeking discovery must show "exceptional circumstances under which it is impracticable for the party seeking to obtain facts or opinions on the same subject by other means."[22] Moreover, the Advisory Committee notes provide that experts who were not retained, but merely "informally consulted in preparation for trial" are also beyond the reach of discovery. In addition, a party's employee serving as a consultant on a case also might constitute a consulting expert (e.g., an expert on aspects of the particular industry) who would not need to issue a report, and their materials

19. *See, e.g., In re* Lorazepam & Clorazepate Antitrust Litig., 467 F. Supp. 2d at 85 (industry expert helped establish at trial that the availability of generics influences the average wholesale price, as well as the pharmaceutical reimbursements received by defendants).

20. *See, e.g.,* SCFC ILC, Inc. v. Visa U.S.A., Inc., 819 F. Supp. 956, 986 (D. Utah 1993) (credit card industry expert's testimony supported economist's finding of market power by demonstrating that defendant Visa continued to charge high interest rates even as smaller issuers lowered their rates significantly).

21. *See, e.g.,* Exxon Corp. v. FTC, 476 F. Supp. 713, 717–18 (D.D.C. 1979) (holding that economic report and even the identity of the consulting economists were shielded from discovery by work product doctrine); *In re* Cendant Corp. Sec. Litig., 343 F.3d 658, 660 (3d Cir. 2003) (denying discovery of consulting expert retained to assist counsel in trial preparation).

22. FED. R. CIV. P. 26(b)(4)(B). Discovery from consulting experts who conduct mental or physical examinations of a party are subject to the requirements of Federal Rule of Civil Procedure 35(b), which generally does not arise in antitrust cases.

can fall under protection of the work product doctrine as long as they were prepared in anticipation of litigation.[23]

By employing a consulting expert, attorneys can sort through preliminary theories of the case, examine potential defenses, and even analyze some of the available data without creating a discoverable trail of evidence. Particularly in an antitrust case, it may be helpful to ascertain whether, for example, the available data reflects a price increase over the relevant time period. A consulting economist may be able to talk through some of the potential procompetitive benefits of certain conduct and determine whether any of them will apply to the instant case. This type of preliminary (and ongoing, as additional information becomes available) analysis can be invaluable to the development of a strategy as well as consideration of settlement possibilities. Of course, if the testifying expert uses or relies on some of the work done by a consulting expert, the consultant's papers and work product may become discoverable.[24]

Tips on Finding the Right Expert

Having determined which type of expert would be appropriate to retain, the next issue is locating the right expert. Although this topic is covered in more detail earlier, some general guidelines can help find particular types of experts for antitrust litigation. For an industry expert, often the easiest means of identifying a particular candidate is to ask the client. Because industry experts often work in the particular business at issue, but outside of litigation, their names may be unfamiliar to attorneys or large expert witness firms.

For economists, accountants, or finance experts, there are three primary sources for information: academia, case law, or commercial directories. First, particularly with cases where regional bias (for or against your

---

23. *See* Fed. R. Civ. P. 26(b)(4)(B) (exempting consulting experts from report requirements); Fed. R. Civ. P. 26(b)(3) (exempting from disclosure materials prepared "in anticipation of litigation or for trial"); *see also* United States v. Adlman, 134 F.3d 1194, 1198–1200 (2d Cir. 1998) (finding that even materials prepared for business purposes as well as in anticipation of litigation should be considered work product). *Cf.* United States v. Gulf Oil Corp., 760 F.2d 292, 296–97 (Temp. Emer. Ct. App. 1985) (applying Fifth Circuit's line of reasoning to require that work product protection should apply "only if the *primary motivating purpose* behind the creation of [the materials] was to assist in pending or impending litigation") (emphasis added).

24. *See, e.g.,* cases collected at 6 Moore's Federal Practice § 26.80[2](3d. ed., supp. 2007). *Cf.* Dominguez v. Syntex, 149 F.R.D. 158, 161 (S.D. Ind. 1993) (denying motion to compel production of materials prepared by consulting expert where testifying expert read the materials, but stated he did not consider them in forming his opinion).

client) may be an issue, check the local universities' faculty for potential candidates with relevant areas of specialization. Second, consult published cases with similar facts or industries to identify experts who have testified in similar circumstances or on related issues. With antitrust experts, some of the same names surface repeatedly, particularly for class certification proceedings. Finally, there are firms that specialize in providing expert witnesses and have directories of available witnesses, their experience, and areas of specialization. A simple Internet search will identify many of these firms, and their witnesses.

Substance of Antitrust Expert's Testimony

Antitrust cases, and thus expert testimony in those cases, typically involve a wide range of issues—market definition, market share, justifications for trade practices, entry barriers, competitive effects, efficiencies resulting from trade practices, and damages. However, experts cannot testify on all issues that arise in antitrust cases. The discussion below summarizes those topics on which antitrust experts can—and cannot—offer expert testimony.

Relevant Market

Expert economic testimony is critical to define the relevant product and geographic market. Some courts have gone so far as to say that expert testimony on this issue is essential.[25] The test adopted by courts to measure a relevant product and geographic market comes from the 1992 Horizontal Merger Guidelines put forth jointly by the U.S. Department of Justice and the FTC.[26] Under this test, a relevant market is the smallest set of products (or geographic location) for which a hypothetical monopolist would find it profitable to adopt a small but not insignificant price increase (typically 5 percent).[27] To estimate this, an economist must analyze all competing products, the strength or reach of that competition, and the impact of price

25. See Colsa Corp. v. Martin Marietta Servs., 133 F.3d 853, 855 n.4 (11th Cir. 1998) ("[C]onstruction of a relevant economic market or showing of monopoly power in that market cannot be based upon lay opinion testimony.").

26. On April 20, 2010, the Federal Trade Commission and the Department of Justice jointly issued a proposed revision to the Horizontal Merger Guidelines. The proposed revision included, among other changes, an updated explanation of the hypothetical monopolist test, used to define relevant markets. The proposed revision is available at www.ftc.gov/03/2010/04/100420hmg.pdf/last accessed June 1, 2010).

27. 1992 Horizontal Merger Guidelines § 1.0

changes on competition. While corporate representatives can testify about what products are believed to compete with their own products, the specifics of the relevant market test commonly necessitate expert economic testimony. This testimony requires a rich understanding of the industry, all products that clearly compete as well as those that some consumers may consider to be substitute products, planned and possible entry in the market, how the competing products are priced, and customer information. The market definition adopted by the court can have a dramatic influence on the outcome of the matter and, in some cases, can be dispositive of the antitrust claim.[28]

Market Structure

Economists also can testify about the structure of the newly defined market, including the number of competitors and how the market structure impacts firm performance and behavior. For example, a market with very few large producers is an oligopoly, and economists have long studied the performance of firms operating in oligopolistic markets. The structure of the market is important, for example, in proposed mergers or monopolization cases where a "but-for" world must be constructed by the expert. In a but-for world, the expert is predicting how firms would behave under different assumptions, or, more specifically, how profit-maximizing firms would behave under a different set of incentives.[29] Economic evidence of the market structure also bears on the feasibility of a secret price-fixing agreement, where the defendants have not admitted such an agreement exists.[30]

---

28. For example, in *United States v. Aluminum Co. of America*, 148 F.2d 416 (2d Cir. 1945), the district court had computed Alcoa's market share to be approximately 33 percent. After redefining the relevant market, Judge Hand computed Alcoa's market share to be over 90 percent, and concluded that Alcoa had monopoly power. In *United States v. Microsoft*, 253 F.3d 34 (D.C. Cir. 2001), Microsoft argued that middleware should be included in the relevant market (which the District of Columbia Circuit rejected), which would have greatly reduced Microsoft's market share.

29. One example of how market structure impacts antitrust analysis is through the use of the Herfindahl-Hirschman Index (HHI). HHI is the sum of the squared market shares of all firms that participate in a relevant product and geographic market. If the post-merger HHI (or the change in the HHI as a result of the merger) is too high, the proposed merger will be more closely scrutinized under the assumption that more concentrated markets could more easily generate harmful effects on consumers. Those assumptions are largely based on economists' research and analysis of concentrated markets.

30. *See, e.g., In re* High Fructose Corn Syrup Antitrust Litig., 295 F.3d 651, 655 (7th Cir. 2002) (recognizing economic evidence as to the structure of the market and whether the market behaved in a noncompetitive manner as evidence that defendants were not competing with each other).

In addition, economists can also opine on the barriers to entry that exist in a particular market or industry based, in part, on the structure of the market.

Market Power

Expert testimony is often critical to establish (or dispute) a firm's market power, whether such testimony is based on market shares or some other measure of market power. The most commonly used indication of market power is a firm's market share. It is a fairly straightforward exercise for an expert to calculate market shares after the relevant market has been defined—it is simply determining the market shares of all firms that compete in the newly defined relevant market. The value the expert brings here is the proper measure by which to judge a firm's level of participation in the relevant market. It can be as easy as the number of sales made by the firm divided by the total number of sales made by all market participants. However, in markets where sales or levels of participation are not so easily measured, an expert can determine the best measure of a firm's participation.[31] Courts also now recognize that other factors, including the absence of barriers to entry, may undermine the inference of market power, even if the market participants have very high market shares.[32] Thus, the antitrust expert will carefully study the possibility and likelihood of entry. One court has held that even a firm with 100 percent market share does not imply monopoly power where entry barriers are low.[33]

Collusion or Conspiracy

Economists can testify as to whether conduct is indicative of collusive behavior, including conducting pricing studies to determine if competitors' prices move together. Although insufficient to establish a conspiracy,[34]

---

31. For example, in hospital mergers, one key metric for a hospital's presence in the market is its number of available beds. The number of patients seen by the hospital is another metric, but the FTC and the Department of Justice have both used the number of available beds to measure a firm's level of participation in the market.

32. *See, e.g.*, United States v. Microsoft Corp., 253 F.3d 34, 51 (D.C. Cir. 2000) ("Under the structural approach, monopoly power may be inferred from a firm's possession of a dominant share of a relevant market that is protected by entry barriers."), *cert. denied*, 122 S. Ct. 350 (2001).

33. Fabrication Enters. v. Hygienic Corp., 848 F. Supp. 1156, 1160 (S.D.N.Y 1994), *rev'd on other grounds*, 64 F.3d 53 (2d Cir. 1995).

34. Plaintiffs' allegations of concerted action are frequently based on consistent or uniform acts by their competitors, which courts refer to as conscious parallelism. However, it is insufficient under the antitrust laws for a court to infer a conspiracy among competitors

parallel pricing behavior is circumstantial evidence (or indirect evidence, as it is known in antitrust case law) of a conspiracy to fix prices. However, an expert is commonly prevented from testifying about the ultimate issue of whether an agreement exists, although some courts have allowed that type of testimony.[35] Expert economists are prevented from offering this testimony because the legal definition of collusion and the concept of collusion in economics are different.[36] Thus, to ensure that the expert is not precluded from testifying, the expert should focus on the nature of the practice (collusive behavior) and its likely motivations, rather than speculating about the actual existence of collusion in the case presented. For example, the plaintiff's expert may explain how the alleged conspirators' prices all move together and that the defendants' actions are only consistent with rational, profit-maximizing firm behavior if there is an agreement among competitors.[37] Furthermore, absent such agreement among competitors, the challenged conduct would cause the firm to lose customers, profits, or goodwill.

Standing and Damages

A private plaintiff seeking damages under the antitrust laws must establish standing to sue. Antitrust standing requires more than simply meeting the "injury in fact" and the "case in controversy" requirements of Article III of the U.S. Constitution. To meet the standing requirement under the antitrust laws, the plaintiff must establish that it suffered damages "of the type

---

based solely on the fact that competitors' prices move together or that firms in the same market respond in the same way to competitive threats. After all, rational, profit-maximizing firms *should* respond in similar ways to such threats. Additional facts, or "plus factors," are needed for a court to find that a conspiracy exists among competitors. *See* Theatre Enters. v. Paramount Film Distrib. Corp., 346 U.S. 537 (1954). One commonly cited plus factor that requires expert testimony, typically by an industrial organization economist, is that the observed conduct is only in the parties' best interests if there is an agreement among competitors, because the observed conduct is contrary to a firm's economic interest if it were acting alone.

35. *See, e.g., In re* Citric Acid Litig., 191 F.3d 1090, 1102 (9th Cir. 1999); City of Tuscaloosa v. Harcros Chems. Inc., 158 F.3d 548, 570 (11th Cir. 1998).

36. The law requires a "unity of purpose," a "common design and understanding," or a "meeting of the minds in an unlawful agreement." *See* Am. Tobacco Co. v. United States, 328 U.S. 781, 810 (1946). In contrast, in economics, the requirements are lower—economists consider whether firms are cooperating, which can be shown through sophisticated game theory models.

37. *See* Re/Max Int'l, Inc. v. Realty One, 173 F.3d 995, 1009–10 (6th Cir. 1999) (reversing summary judgment for defendants and holding that plaintiff's expert testimony that defendant realtor's adoption of a commission-splitting scheme would not have been in its economic interest without an agreement was sufficient to permit the case to proceed to trial).

the antitrust laws were designed to protect against."[38] In other words, a competitor does not have standing to sue for antitrust violations when it is the only party to have suffered damages, and there has been no impact on competition itself as a result of the alleged anticompetitive conduct.[39] One way to establish that competition has been injured is to establish that consumers now pay higher prices as a result of the alleged conduct. This analysis typically requires an industrial organization economist to do a market study of the relevant market and isolate the impact of the challenged conduct from normal market forces.

After the plaintiff has established that it is a proper plaintiff (by establishing that it has standing), the antitrust plaintiff must also establish that it has suffered damages that are materially caused by the challenged conduct. As in other types of cases, the antitrust plaintiff must establish both the fact of damage and the amount of damages. In an antitrust case, the fact of damages must be proved with a fair degree of certainty and can be established by inference or circumstantial evidence. However, a defendant may then refute this inference by establishing that the decline in the plaintiff's business was caused by other facts (i.e., changing economic conditions, mismanagement, or government regulation). This analysis, for both the plaintiff and defendant, must involve the use of economic experts, and typically an industrial organization economist.

Proof of the amount of damages is sufficient if it permits the trier of fact to make a reasonable estimate of the amount of damages. This is one area where accountants or financial economists may provide useful testimony because reasonably estimating the amount of damages may require analysis of financial statements and accounting records. Most litigators know damage experts; however, antitrust damages are somewhat unique. In antitrust, the expert must, when possible, construct damages cause by cause, otherwise known as disaggregation.[40] A failure to disaggregate damages by the

---

38. *See* Brunswick Corp. v. Pueblo Bowl-O-Mat, Inc., 429 U.S. 477, 489 (1977).

39. For example, in *Four Corners Nephrology Associates v. Mercy Medical Center*, the Tenth Circuit affirmed the district court's decision to dismiss the plaintiff's antitrust case because it did not have standing to bring the suit. Four Corners Nephrology Assocs. v. Mercy Med. Ctr., 582 F. 3d 1216, 1227 (10th Cir. 2009). The court held that dismissal was warranted because, at most, only the plaintiff had suffered injury as a result of the defendant's conduct but that competition in general (i.e., the consumers) had not suffered any effects of the alleged conduct.

40. *See* MCI Commc'ns Corp. v. AT&T, 708 F.2d 1081 (7th Cir. 1982). In *MCI*, the court held that the plaintiff's damage theory failed because it did not establish any variation on the outcome depending on which acts of AT&T were held to be illegal. At trial, the jury found that some of AT&T's conduct was legitimate business competition, but because the expert failed to disaggregate the damages model by claim, the jury was left without any guidance on how to adjust the claimed damages.

various causes of action in an antitrust case may be fatal to an expert opinion. The key is for the expert to identify, and account for, the effect of legitimate market competition. Ideally, the damage model would isolate the antitrust offense as the single causal factor that accounts for the difference between the but-for world (where competition prevails) and the actual world (where competition was hindered). Without this disaggregation, the expert runs the risk of having his testimony excluded under Federal Rule of Evidence 702, which requires the expert testimony be "helpful to the trier of fact."

Defenses

There are several affirmative defenses available to defendants that require some degree of expert testimony, including business justification, cost justification, failing company (mergers), meeting competition, sophisticated buyer, and changing conditions.[41] For example, accountants or financial economists may be useful for defendants to prove the affirmative defense that the plaintiff business failed or was harmed for reasons independent of the challenged conduct. A failed company may attempt to attribute the failure to a canceled contract or dominant competitor, but an accountant can assess the financial health of the failed firm before the contract was cancelled or before the defendant achieved significant market share.

Winning Your Case with an Antitrust Expert

Using an Antitrust Expert throughout Discovery

Experts can play a vital role in the discovery process of an antitrust case. While experts can be helpful in many types of cases, antitrust cases often present particularly complex issues, detailed data, and economic nuances that may escape the legal eye. Attorneys understand the applicable legal standards but not necessarily the types of proof that may meet those standards. Accordingly, antitrust experts should be active in most phases of discovery. For example, an antitrust expert can review and suggest specific requests for production that will garner the necessary data for their pricing analysis or market definition. Similarly, antitrust experts can be extremely helpful in depositions, both attending and reviewing transcripts of deponents' testimony. At a minimum, the expert should attend the deposition of

---

41. For a general discussion of available affirmative defenses, see ABA Section of Antitrust Law, Law Developments 892 (5th ed. 2002).

the opposing expert to suggest follow-up questions that may be too techni-cal for the attorney to anticipate.

Not only can the experts assist the attorneys, but their involvement may increase their confidence in their opinions. Some experts find it helpful to tour the facilities of the company in question or personally interview some of the key party witnesses. Even if certain data does not exist, being able to indicate that the expert asked for the data and received the ensuing expla-nation as to its absence can strengthen the expert's report. In short, the greater the expert's familiarity with the information being discovered, the greater his credibility will be, and the more likely the attorneys are to gather the necessary information.

Using an Antitrust Expert to Dissect Opposing Expert Opinions

Although the *Daubert*[42] standard is well known to attorneys, an antitrust expert's perspective may reveal certain flaws in the opposing expert's report that can be difficult to evaluate without a background in economics, fi-nance, accounting, or the relevant industry.

Qualifications

Many experts may appear qualified solely by the degrees listed by their names and the titles they give themselves. However, an antitrust expert may assist the attorneys by examining opposing experts' qualifications more closely, including whether their professed expertise is supported by their academic focus, courses taught, published articles, and certifications. For example, not every economist has expertise in examining mergers and calculating market concentration. Further, not all accountants can testify reliably as to proper financial disclosures or their impact on profit mar-gins. Although not unique to antitrust litigation, using an expert to assess the opposing expert's qualifications can be significantly helpful.

Methodology

It can be nearly impossible for most attorneys to personally evaluate whether an antitrust economist has properly used a regression analysis or adequately addressed the problem of multicollinearity in his pricing study. An attorney's primary duty should be reminding the expert, if necessary, to consider whether the opposing expert took the correct approach, rather than merely checking the calculations and conclusions. Similarly, an attor-

---

42. Daubert v. Merrell Dow Pharms., Inc., 509 U.S. 579 (1993).

ney should work with the expert to examine the inherent and explicit assumptions contained in an opposing expert's report. Although not always stated up front, at times the opposing expert may have assumed away hotly contested elements of their analysis such as causation. These assumptions may be contradicted by known facts and can be a focus of a rebuttal expert's report.

Using an Antitrust Expert in Support of Motions

Antitrust experts can be critical to the success of various motions, including summary judgment, preliminary injunctions, and *Daubert* motions challenging the other expert's admissibility. One area that is particularly critical to many antitrust cases is class certification. Accordingly, this section will provide one interesting illustration of antitrust experts at summary judgment and then focus on the role of antitrust experts at the class certification stage of motion practice.

It is important to keep in mind that utilizing expert opinions in support of preliminary motions, whether in the form of reports, affidavits, or declarations, may expose the expert to multiple depositions. In particular, due to the need for expert analysis to support or oppose class certification, some antitrust experts may end up submitting multiple reports—a report or declaration at the class certification stage and then a more extensive report before trial. Parties can successfully claim that if a preliminary expert opinion is to be used in support of such a motion, they should be entitled to depose that expert before completing their response. However, if the litigation continues, and the same expert prepares either a full report making use of newly available evidence or an additional report on slightly different topics, that expert likely will be subject to being deposed again and will be somewhat tied to his earlier opinions. As a result, sometimes litigators may opt to use a different expert for preliminary motions. This does have the unfortunate trade-off of potentially paying for duplicative work from different experts as both individuals come up to speed on the relevant facts of the case. Accordingly, attorneys should be careful not to view their case only from a short-term perspective when seeking expert opinions for upcoming motions.

Summary Judgment

The Seventh Circuit case *In re High Fructose Corn Syrup Antitrust Litigation*[43] illustrates the uses of antitrust experts in summary judgment mo-

---

43. *In re* High Fructose Corn Syrup Antitrust Litig., 295 F.3d 651 (7th Cir. 2002).

tions. First, both parties presented economic experts to opine on the issue of whether defendants had an agreement to fix their prices for high fructose corn syrup. The court noted that this issue can be addressed by different types of evidence, not all based on expert testimony; however, in the absence of an admission as to the underlying agreement, an economic expert generally will address whether the defendants were, in fact, competing with each other. This analysis commonly examines (1) whether the market structure made secret price fixing feasible, and (2) whether the market participants behaved in a non-competitive manner.[44]

In this case, plaintiffs' economic expert opined that the structure of the high fructose corn syrup market was favorable to price fixing (few sellers, a highly standardized product, and excess capacity).[45] This opinion was "pretty much" conceded by defendants.[46] However, the second prong of the analysis, evidence of noncompetitive behavior, was hotly contested. The issue became a complex duel of experts as the plaintiffs' economic expert conducted a regression analysis that found the prices of high fructose corn syrup were higher during the period of alleged conspiracy than they were at other times.[47] Defendants then submitted a competing regression analysis from one of their economic experts that rebutted the plaintiffs' expert's conclusion.[48] Far from giving up, plaintiffs then submitted still another expert report solely on the issue of the statistical methodology used.[49]

Although economic conclusions are frequently evaluated by judges, the Seventh Circuit noted, "Resolving this dispute requires a knowledge of statistical inference that judges do not possess."[50] Instead, the court recommended that the district judge appoint his own expert witness, "rather than leave himself and the jury completely at the mercy of the parties' warring experts."[51] The court noted that, by directing the party-designated experts to agree on a neutral expert for the judge, the primary objections to such a tactic could be avoided.[52] Finally, in a comment that reveals little confidence in the standard expert witness procedure (at least with respect to complex issues), the Seventh Circuit concluded as follows:

---

44. *Id.* at 655.
45. *Id.* at 656–57.
46. *Id.* at 656.
47. *Id.* at 660.
48. *Id.*
49. *Id.*
50. *Id.*
51. *Id.* at 665 (citing Fed. R. Evid. 706 as authority for this solution).
52. *Id.*

The neutral expert will testify (as can, of course, the party-designated experts) and the judge and jury can repose a degree of confidence in his testimony that it could not repose in that of a party's witness. The judge and jurors may not understand the neutral expert perfectly but at least they will know that he has no axe to grind, and so, to a degree anyway, they will be able to take his testimony on faith.[53]

Of course, the Seventh Circuit did not address how accepting expert testimony "on faith" was consistent with the goals of expert testimony or the gatekeeping function of the judiciary under *Daubert*.[54]

Class Certification

As part of the requirements of Federal Rule of Civil Procedure 23, plaintiffs seeking class certification must establish that they can prove the elements of their claim by common proof and that those elements are predominant.[55] This type of analysis frequently requires the testimony of expert witnesses in support of or in opposition to class certification.

One common issue at the class certification stage is whether judges should merely look at the experts' qualifications and the existence of their opinions or whether they should examine the substance of their opinions to resolve disputes between experts. In *Cordes Financial Services v. A.G. Edwards & Sons*,[56] plaintiffs sought to certify a class of individuals harmed by a horizontal price-fixing conspiracy. In support of certification, plaintiffs offered the declaration of an expert who testified that he had derived a common formula for calculating the damages suffered by each class member due to the alleged price-fixing conspiracy.[57] Defendants countered with their own expert, who claimed that calculating the injury to class members would require an individualized, plaintiff-by-plaintiff analysis of 10 factors.[58] The trial court denied class certification, finding that damages were not equivalent with the requisite showing of antitrust injury and declining to determine which expert was correct.[59] In an opinion that clearly looked beyond the simple characterization of the reports, the Second Circuit

---

53. *Id.*

54. Presumably, if this type of expert selection satisfies the standard concerns with qualifications and methodology, then perhaps the entire notion of opposing experts could be done away with and replaced by mutually agreeable, neutral experts, thus saving both sides much time and money.

55. *See* FED. R. CIV. P. 23(a)(2), (b)(3).

56. Cordes Fin. Servs. v. A.G. Edwards & Sons, 502 F.3d 91 (2d Cir. 2007).

57. *Id.* at 97.

58. *Id.*

59. *Id.* at 97–98.

reversed. The Second Circuit found that while the questions asked of the experts were different, both experts ultimately addressed the central question of whether injury-in-fact was susceptible to common proof.[60] Further, the court remanded for the district court to resolve the dispute between the experts as to the appropriate calculation.[61]

There has been a split among the circuits regarding a court's duty to examine and resolve disputes between opposing experts at class certification. Some courts hold that a district court merely must conclude that the expert testimony is "not so flawed that it would be inadmissible as a matter of law" and should not weigh conflicting expert evidence.[62] This line of cases views the court's role at the class certification stage as merely determining "whether plaintiff's expert evidence is sufficient to demonstrate common questions of fact warranting certification of the proposed class, not whether the evidence will ultimately be persuasive."[63]

However, the majority of circuits find that a court's duty to resolve disputes concerning the factual setting of the case "extends to the resolution of expert disputes concerning the import of evidence concerning the factual setting—such as economic evidence as to business operations or market transactions."[64] The courts requiring a more rigorous analysis hold that expert testimony should not be "uncritically accepted as establishing a Rule 23 requirement merely because the court holds the testimony should not be excluded, under *Daubert* or for any other reason."[65] Rather, an expert opinion may be assessed for weight, as well as admissibility, at class certification.[66]

---

60. *Id.* at 107.

61. *Id.*

62. *See, e.g., In re* Visa Check/Mastermoney Antitrust Litig., 280 F.3d 124, 135 (2d Cir. 2001).

63. *Id.; see also* J.B. *ex rel.* Hart v. Valdez, 186 F.3d 1280, 1290 n.7 (10th Cir. 1999) (finding that a district court should accept the complaint's allegations as true when deciding class certification).

64. *See* Blades v. Monsanto Co., 400 F.3d 562, 575 (8th Cir. 2005) (finding that trial court appropriately resolved disputes between the experts to assess class certification on price-fixing claims); *see also* Cooper v. S. Co., 390 F.3d 695, 712 (11th Cir. 2004); Gariety v. Grant Thornton, LLP, 368 F.3d 356, 365 (4th Cir. 2004); West v. Prudential Sec., Inc., 282 F.3d 935, 937 (7th Cir. 2002).

65. *In re* Hydrogen Peroxide Antitrust Litig., 552 F.3d 305, 323 (3d Cir. 2008) (remanding for district court to consider all relevant evidence and arguments, including expert testimony).

66. *See id.* ("Like any evidence, admissible expert opinion may persuade its audience, or it may not."); *see also In re* Polymedica Corp. Sec. Litig., 432 F.3d 1, 5 (1st Cir. 2005) (affirming district court's review that "went well beyond the four corners of the pleadings, considering both parties' expert reports and literally hundreds of pages of exhibits focused on market efficiency").

Still, a court will avoid ruling on expert disputes that go to the merits of the case rather than merely the issues of class certification. In *Herrwagen v. Clear Channel Communications,*[67] the court found that it *could* weigh the expert testimony because class certification's requisite inquiry as to predominance was sufficiently independent of the merits of the plaintiff's monopolization claims.[68] However, the court distinguished the case from one where "statistical dueling" between the experts as to commonality and typicality overlapped with the merits of the purported class's discrimination suit—in that case, assessing the relative weight to accord expert testimony would constitute an erroneous preliminary adjudication of the merits.[69]

Using an Antitrust Expert at Trial

Very few antitrust cases progress all the way to trial, in large part because expert reports often educate parties of the "true" merits of their case before trial. In the rare case where a trial is warranted, expert witness testimony is critical. Below are a few things to remember if your antitrust case is set to go to trial.

1. As described above, while antitrust cases rarely go to trial, it is important to plan as if your case undoubtedly will go to trial. This means retaining an expert with trial testimony experience if possible. Also, professors or experts who have experience teaching frequently will make stronger witnesses because they are accustomed to explaining complex topics in simple, straightforward language. An expert who is not primarily a professional witness may also come across as less polished, and more credible, but may not be as comfortable with litigation tactics such as cross-examination.
2. Instruct your witness to prepare his expert report with the expectation that any chart or table could be used as a demonstrative exhibit at trial.
3. Seek and trust your expert's instincts and judgment on how to present his testimony to the trier of fact. Demonstrative exhibits are very useful for antitrust experts and can effectively summarize (and simplify) several complex points. Using maps to identify the relevant geographic market and simple charts to explain the relevant product market can make these complex topics seem relatively straightforward.
4. Allow your expert to educate the trier of fact. Topics addressed by antitrust experts, at their most basic level, can be intuitive. How products

---

67. Herrwagen v. Clear Channel Commc'ns, 425 F.3d 219 (2d Cir. 2006).
68. *Id.* at 232–33.
69. *Id.* at 231 (citing Caridad v. Metro-N. Commuter R.R., 191 F.3d 283 (2d Cir. 1999)).

compete, how they are priced, why there are no other competitors in the market, etc., all are topics that people with no antitrust or economic background can understand when explained in simple terms.

5. Have your expert attend as much of the trial as he can.[70] Trial testimony that the lawyer may find irrelevant or only related to a separate point potentially can be very useful for topics such as relevant market definition or damages. This requires an ongoing dialogue with your expert about his impression of the trial and testimony that has come out.

6. Instruct your witness to read and reread his deposition before testifying at trial. Even minor or wholly innocuous inconsistencies between deposition and trial testimony can be interpreted by the trier of fact as evidence the witness is evasive or not independent.

Conclusion

There are two key lessons the authors have learned when dealing with, and acting as, antitrust experts. First, where possible, do not compromise quality when selecting an antitrust expert. As discussed above, antitrust law is a fact-intensive, economics driven area of the law, where cases rise and fall based in large part on the expert testimony offered. Selecting an unqualified expert or one whose skill set does not match the needed task can lead to adverse judgments and unhappy clients.

Second, once you find your expert, get the expert involved as early as possible. Antitrust experts likely will have experience in the type of restraint you are dealing with and can offer useful input on discovery requests and responses, topics to notice for a Federal Rule of Civil Procedure 30(b)(6) deposition, and dispositive motions. The most challenging, and often the least successful, expert reports dealing with antitrust issues are those requested on an expedited basis with a fast-approaching deadline and with little time for the expert to become involved in the overall litigation strategy.

---

70. Recall that experts are permitted to attend trial even if opposing counsel exercises the exclusionary rule and closes the courtroom to all fact witnesses. *See* FED. R. EVID. 615.

AFTERWORD

Art Justice[1]

Clearly, the use of expert witnesses in all types of litigation is increasing. The Expert Witnesses Committee believes this book will be a valuable resource to litigators, whether young lawyers or seasoned veterans, as they use expert witness testimony in their cases. No matter your experience, it is always worthwhile to polish advocacy skills, including those required when using expert witness testimony.

When Diane Sumoski, former cochair of the Expert Witnesses Committee, first discussed her proposal of this book with me, I immediately thought of one of the best practical legal guides I have read, Judge Joseph F. Anderson's book, *The Lost Art: An Advocate's Guide to Effective Closing Argument*.[2] Judge Anderson's book contains hundreds of quality pearls of wisdom from experienced litigators, providing wise and practical guidance. We agreed that the readers of our committee's book might also gain insight from distinguished litigators offering their own pearls of wisdom. Thus, the committee solicited contributions from select experienced litigators across the country. No matter where in the country the litigator practiced, or in what area of the law, we found many common themes. The responses, to no surprise, provided the same type of advice you find throughout this book. While we wish we could print all of the responses, we have selected some representative insights.

First, many litigators emphasized the importance of establishing a strong relationship between the expert and counsel well before disclosure. Working with expert witnesses, like all other areas of litigation, requires preparation

---

1. Arthur E. Justice Jr. is a partner with Turner Padget Graham & Laney, PA in its Florence, South Carolina, office. His practice is concentrated in employment law, professional liability defense, and complex business litigation. He served as cochair of the ABA Section of Litigation, Expert Witnesses Committee from 2007 to 2008 and is currently cochair of the Section of Litigation, Health Law Litigation Committee. He wishes to thank Jake Kennedy of Turner Padget in Florence, South Carolina, for his valuable assistance.

2. JOSEPH F. ANDERSON, JR., THE LOST ART: AN ADVOCATE'S GUIDE TO EFFECTIVE CLOSING ARGUMENT (3d ed. 2008).

and attention to minute details. Preparation begins with vetting the expert and does not stop until the case is over:

> Preparation is necessary to assist the expert's understanding of the facts, the law, and judicial/political climate in the venue.
>
> Tom Segalla, Buffalo, NY

> The key to successful expert testimony is preparation. It is the lawyer's responsibility to make that happen. Expert witnesses often need *more* preparation than lay witnesses. It is usually a mistake to trust the expert who tells you he does not need preparation because he has testified many times. The lawyer does not know who prepared the expert in the past or if the expert has developed a lot of bad habits. If the expert resists preparation, find a new expert.
>
> Daniel Small, Boston, MA

> An effective expert begins with an effective lawyer. The lawyer cannot present an effective witness or expose weaknesses in adverse experts without at least an entry-level understanding of the subject matter. Before you retain an expert, spend some time in the library or cyberspace.
>
> James J. Dries, Chicago, IL

> An effective expert witness not only prepares himself but teaches the attorney to ask him the right questions in the right way. This requires rehearsal, early and often, which will not only strengthen direct examination but also reveal potential pitfalls on cross-examination for the attorney to anticipate and avoid through direct examination or with a strong redirect.
>
> Todd Holleman, Detroit, MI

> Expert witness is a two-word concept. Equal attention must be paid to the witness part. The most seasoned expert needs to recognize he or she has never encountered these particular facts built into the examination of this particular opposing counsel. Allowing the expert to "wing it" is a recipe for disaster. Like any witness, the expert witness has a role as both a teacher and a student. The expert must teach the attorney how to master the subject matter while also recognizing there is always more to learn about being a better witness.
>
> Damian Capozzola, Los Angeles, CA

In addition, many litigators warned about the dangers of an overly compliant expert. The agreeable expert may be easier to deal with at the outset but usually causes problems as you go forward:

> Beware the expert who gladly accepts every suggestion and allows counsel near free rein when drafting the report. This usually results in nightmarish testimony because the expert cannot defend his position. It is

better to scrutinize your expert and make sure he can defend every nuance before disclosure.

James A. Reeder Jr., Houston, TX

And the lawyer has to avoid falling into the same trap. The lawyer must develop a good working relationship with the expert, but he must also play the devil's advocate at the right time:

> You should be your expert's harshest critic. Question their assumptions and challenge their conclusions. Develop a relationship with your expert which allows you to play this role. Explain that it is your obligation to critique the expert's thinking and conclusions. Make sure that all points of attack have been fully examined and addressed before the witness heads to a deposition or the witness stand.
>
> Timothy L. Bertschy, Peoria, IL

Others discussed the quandary faced in almost every case: the cost-benefit analysis of retaining an expert. It is often the case that cutting corners to save costs can turn out to be very expensive:

> Considering the effect of expert witness fees on already delicate trial budgets, many attorneys are tempted to severely limit the expert's scope of engagement or delay consultation until the last possible second. This can be a serious mistake. A good expert can be invaluable to educating the lawyer and client during all stages of litigation. This can actually reduce overall costs by allowing your expert to become well-versed in the facts as they develop, refining the claims or defenses, developing a more focused discovery plan, and creating an effective mediation presentation.
>
> James "Marty" Truss, San Antonio, TX

At the same time, it is crucial for the expert to understand the scope of the engagement:

> An effective expert understands his role in the overall strategy. It is not enough for the expert to simply review file materials and arrive at opinions regardless of whether the opinions are relevant or even helpful. The unfocused expert can quickly engage in excessive work which results in over-billing and exceeding the budget.
>
> Stephen C. Pasarow, Glendale, CA

The responses also underscore the importance of presenting a credible expert witness. There is no substitute for doing your homework and making sure your expert does his:

> In my experience, the best experts are "subtle advocates." Too much advocacy and the expert loses credibility. Too little advocacy and the expert

loses impact. As attorneys, we are the advocacy experts and thus our primary role is to help the expert become a better subtle advocate.

H. Douglas Hinson, Atlanta, GA

A truly great expert witness must first be a great witness. This means he or she must be able to explain the opinions in a way that the judge or jury understands. Most importantly, the expert must be credible. Do not equate scholarship with credibility. I have seen experts with multiple degrees who are not credible and others with no degrees who could convince a jury of anything. Before you retain experts, try to see them in action, read a transcript of their prior testimony, or, at the absolute minimum, talk to someone you know who can confirm their quality as a witness.

Steve Weiss, Chicago, IL

Credibility, credibility, credibility. First, the expert has to be a real expert by training and, where possible, also by experience. It is much more effective to present an expert who not only has a degree in the field but one who can also say he or she has actually practiced in the field every day for "x" years. Second, the expert must really understand what he or she is talking about. That means the expert has to read everything relevant to the issue and has conducted the analysis in the past or specifically for the case. Third, the expert should believe what he or she is saying without appearing to push the idea like a salesperson. The expert should admit things that should be admitted and say "I don't know" when that is a correct response to the question.

Loren Kieve, San Francisco, CA

It hurts credibility to be the dog who will hunt for anyone who will feed it. It also hurts credibility to be Dr. Jekyll during direct and Mr. Hyde on cross. The best (and most dangerous) expert witnesses concede the points they should even when it harms the client who hired them. It helps to tell the truth.

Alan Thomas, Birmingham, AL

Finally, many litigators emphasized the importance of good communication skills. Ultimately, how your expert communicates with the finder of fact will determine whether your expert is effective:

The fundamental characteristic of an effective expert witness is the ability to communicate. The attorney must do more than review the expert's *curriculum vitae*. The attorney must take time to know the expert and his or her communication style.

Joseph M. Gagliardo, Chicago, IL

I look for experts who are great communicators who can handle tough cross-examination questions with answers that are not evasive or self-serving. Jurors are smart. They cut through "expert-speak" and quickly reach instinctual feelings about trustworthiness and honesty. If your expert loses the juror on that score, the rest is meaningless.

Barry J. Fleishman, Washington, D.C.

Your expert should have the qualities that made your favorite high school teacher your favorite—the ability to make complex concepts familiar, the sensibility to know when to stop lecturing, and enough sense of humor to recover gracefully if he falters.

Diane M. Sumoski, Dallas, TX

Even the smartest, most technically competent expert is of little to no value if he does not win the jury's trust and/or help them resolve the issue with relevant information presented in understandable language. In my experience, the most effective witnesses are those who are engaging, courteous, and forthcoming on direct and especially cross-examination. The expert should not use the witness stand to dazzle the jury with his brilliance on all topics. Finally, an effective expert respects the courtroom, judge, and protocols. If the judge calls out the expert for violating some protocol, the expert quickly loses credibility.

J. Tracy Walker, IV, Richmond, VA

We appreciate all the hard work by so many. We hope this book will provide practical insight to all and help you become a better litigator or better expert.

Florence, South Carolina
June 2010

INDEX

AAJ Exchange, 11
ABA. *See* American Bar Association
abuse of discretion, 264–66
ABV. *See* Accredited in Business Valuation
accident reconstruction, 212
accountants. *See also* Certified Public
  Accountants; financial advisors;
  financial damages experts
  antitrust experts, 505, 505 n.7
  securities litigation experts, 398–99
accounting
  Daubert challenge, 212
  fraud, 87, 89
  GAAP, 398
Accredited in Business Valuation (ABV),
  384, 505
Accredited Valuation Analyst (AVA),
  385
active data, 360, 360 n.44
actuaries, 386, 420
Adams v. Ameritech Serv., Inc., 211 n.13
Adams v. Gateway, Inc., 147 n.27
admissibility
  challenging expert, in cross-
    examination, 331–32
  challenging expert, in opinions, 331–32
  data, 309–10
  exhibits, 340–41
  facts, 309–10
  issues, in *Daubert v. Merrell Dow
    Pharms., Inc.*, 58
  opinions, in state courts, 266–67
agency opinions, 14
AICPA. *See* American Institute of Certified
  Public Accountants
Aircraft Gear Corp. v. Marsh, 163 n.126
Akeva L.L.C. v. Mizuno Corp., 163 n.127,
  165 n.137
Alabama, 258, 264, 269, 273, 495

Alaska, 258, 264, 269, 273
Alexander v. Turtur & Assocs., Inc., 497
ALI-ABA. *See* American Law Institute–
  American Bar Association
allegations, 403, 408
  addressing, 56
  in class certification, 520 n.63
  of concerted action, 512 n.34
  fraud, 400–401
  responding to, 81
  reviewing, 84
  scienter, 402
Allen v. Pennsylvania Eng'g, Inc., 195 n.5
Allison v. McGhan Med. Corp., 228 n.89
allocation of sales proceeds, 431–32
Am. Fid. Assurance Co. v. Boyer,
  155 n.79
AMA. *See* American Medical Association
American Bar Association (ABA), 121,
  417–18
  Litigation Expert Witness Committee,
    374
  Model Rules of Professional Conduct,
    131, 131 n.9, 135
American Board of Medical Specialties, 8
American Board of Surgery, 8
American Institute of Certified Public
  Accountants (AICPA), 384
American Law Institute–American Bar
  Association (ALI-ABA), 478
American Medical Association (AMA), 8
antitrust
  damages, 381–82, 505
  laws, 381, 503
antitrust experts
  accountants, 505, 505 n.7
  in class certification, 519–21
  on collusion, 512–13
  on conspiracy, 512–13, 512 n.34